VSAM

A COMPREHENSIVE GUIDE

VSAM

A COMPREHENSIVE GUIDE

Constantine Kaniklidis

VNR VAN NOSTRAND REINHOLD
New York

Van Nostrand Reinhold
115 Fifth Avenue
New York, New York 10003

Van Nostrand Reinhold International Company Limited
11 New Fetter Lane
London EC4P 4EE, England

Van Nostrand Reinhold
480 La Trobe Street
Melbourne, Victoria 3000, Australia

Nelson Canada
1120 Birchmount Road
Scarborough, Ontario M1K 5G4, Canada

16   15   14   13   12   11   10   9   8   7   6   5   4   3   2   1

Library of Congress Cataloging-in-Publication Data

Kaniklidis, Constantine.
   VSAM: a comprehensive guide.

   Bibliography: p.
   Includes index.
   1. Virtual computer systems.   I. Title.
QA76.9.V5K36   1989   004.5'4   88-33782
ISBN 0-442-24641-2

This work is dedicated to the memory of my Father,
John Kaniklidis
and to my Mother,
Athanasia Kaniklidis

PREFACE

VSAM is IBM's most extensively used file organization and access method for its large-scale systems in both the batch and online/database environments, and one of the most 'strategic' of the software products in the ever-evolving IBM systems landscape. A solid understanding of VSAM has become imperative for programming professionals working with IBM computer systems. This text is a comprehensive treatment of VSAM, including its design objectives, its structure and operation, and its use and programming. It is intended both for those readers seeking the essentials of practical coding for VSAM, as well as for those who, in addition, want a deeper appreciation of VSAM's internal mechanisms, its optimization, and recent developments in VSAM.

Chapters 1 through 10 present basic concepts, facilities, and principles of VSAM, as well as the necessary IDCAMS coding for basic functions, taking particular care to supply the reader with a strong grasp of VSAM fundamentals. Chapters 11 through 14 then build on this foundation, including an examination of the structure and operation of a VSAM primary index; a detailed discussion of how to read and interpret LISTCAT output; a detailed treatment of Alternate Index (AIX) facilities, including the IDCAMS coding for setting up such facilities; and a presentation of VSAM application programming in COBOL, including the new FILE STATUS '2' facility of VS COBOL II.

Certain specialized areas of VSAM are treated in Chapters 15 through 18: backup and recovery in VSAM, VSAM data security, an in-depth examination of the 'new VSAM' (officially *Data Facility Product/VSAM,* or *DFP/VSAM*), and extensive coverage of the complex area of VSAM performance and optimization. Several technical appendices present reference and specialized information, including an extensive bibliography.

The fundamental objective of the text is to provide the reader, in a single, technically up-to-date guide, with in-depth knowledge and mastery of the major aspects of VSAM facilities and programming, and to provide insight into its internal operation. In addition to, and towards achieving, this fundamental goal, there are a number of secondary objectives.

1. The text covers both standard VSAM (technically known as 'Enhanced VSAM') and the 'new VSAM' (DFP/VSAM, with the Integrated Catalog Facility (ICF) component), along with the latest technical advances and updates introduced by IBM, including the fourth and newest cluster type, the Linear Data Set (LDS). Extensive and integrated full-length coverage of DFP/VSAM can be found in a

chapter dedicated solely to that topic (Chapter 17), but other discussions of DFP/VSAM exist throughout the text where appropriate. The chapter on performance (Chapter 18), in particular, carefully discriminates techniques and considerations for Enhanced VSAM versus DFP/VSAM, where different, and details many performance enhancements associated with recent versions and releases of DFP/VSAM under MVS/XA and ESA.

2. The text also includes extensive coverage of other specialized and critical areas in VSAM: VSAM performance and optimization, including detailed specific recommendations and guidelines (Chapter 18); VSAM backup and recovery (Chapter 15); and VSAM security (Chapter 16), among others.

3. Programmers often have only a cursory knowledge of how to read LISTCAT output: a few fairly straightforward fields may be familiar, but the function and interpretation of many other fields containing valuable information, especially for performance and problem determination, are either unknown or only vaguely understood. This text, therefore, provides unique detailed coverage — a 'guided tour' — of the art of interpreting LISTCAT output, which has the additional benefit of, in many ways, giving the reader a more detailed knowledge of the inner workings of VSAM (see Chapter 12).

4. VSAM has undergone a very significant and sometimes quite dramatic evolution since its inception in 1973, with important and generally quite technically sophisticated, often subtle, extensions and revisions appearing, at first slowly and, more recently, in rapid succession. Many of these changes exploit associated advances in the underlying operating systems (and subsystems), especially those of three major stages of MVS: (1) *MVS/SP Version 1,* the various forms of MVS using 24-bit addressing, all sometimes collectively known as 'MVS/370'; (2) *MVS/SP Version 2,* generally known as *MVS/XA (Extended Architecture)* and using 31-bit addressing; and (3) *MVS/SP Version 3,* widely known as *Enterprise Systems Architecture* (ESA), which retains 31-bit addressing but vastly extends virtual storage capacity by allowing multiple *chained* address spaces per batch or TSO user, rather than only one in pre-ESA systems. This text attempts to provide the most current technical information about VSAM, against the backdrop of these changing and evolving systems. Information about such recent features as *Enhanced ICF Recovery* (including the Catalog Locking Facility and the Catalog Address Space), *Linear Data Sets,* the *Catalog in Data Space Feature, VSAM Hiperspaces,* the *Multilevel Alias Facility,* among others (some just beginning to become available, others awaiting release). Wherever possible, efforts have even been made, for a number of topics, to anticipate modifications which are pending but had not appeared as of the time of this writing, in order to assist the reader's access to the most timely technical information and, in turn, allow for true forward planning in the VSAM environment.

One example of this is the new capability (scheduled for December 1988) under DFP Version 3, supporting the *Storage Management Subsystem,* or *DFSMS,* of defining VSAM data sets strictly through JCL, without using the Access Method Services utility program, IDCAMS. To a generation of programmers taught that VSAM data sets are always uniquely and only defined through IDCAMS and only thereafter referred to in (not created by) the JCL, this will probably come as quite a surprise; indeed, some programmers I've informed about this pending development expressed complete disbelief! This development, among others, is presented in this text in order to maximize the text's usefulness and timeliness, and to assist the reader in achieving state-of-the-art technical mastery of VSAM.

5. Although the text is written primarily with the application programmer in mind, systems and tech support staff, as well as many technical managers, should find the text useful in obtaining insight into the critical functions and operation of VSAM. The chapters on the Structure of a VSAM Index (11), the Art of Interpreting LISTCAT (12), Alternate Index Facilities (13), and especially those on DFP/VSAM (17) and VSAM Performance and Optimization (18), among some others, should be of special interest to systems-oriented technical staff.

6. Everywhere, an effort has been made to provide both rare insight into the 'inner workings' of VSAM, and to avoid the common 'mythology' and misunderstandings about VSAM which regrettably have taken root in much of the IBM technical community using VSAM.

Finally, the above objectives are implemented in a way as to everywhere make the text as practically oriented as possible concerning how VSAM actually works in the real commercial environment and how VSAM facilities can be effectively programmed and managed. In conclusion, true success can be measured by the ultimate objective that subsumes all of the above, that after completing this text there will be, for the reader, few real mysteries remaining about VSAM.

ACKNOWLEDGMENTS

First and foremost, I must thank Sylvia Lowenthal, without whom this work would never have been completed and whose extraordinary perceptions and suggestions for improvements were invaluable to me at every stage of writing, editing, and organizing. She has modestly (and perhaps shrewdly) declined to be made co-author. My thanks also to John Ritter for kind moral support as well as for many astute suggestions for enchancing the value of the text.

On the 'publication end,' my thanks first to Robert Hauserman, formerly Computer Science Editor at Van Nostrand Reinhold, who in that capacity way back in 1985 contacted me with the offer to develop the text and who saw it through the proposal stage. Ms. Dianne Littwin, Senior Editor, had the (mis)fortune to inherit the project thereafter and has been patient and supportive much beyond the call of duty; I cannot fully express the debt of gratitude I owe her. Along with Dianne, I also thank the other VNR staff — especially, but not only — Alberta Gordon (Managing Editor) and Ray Kanarr (Senior Manuscript Editor) who worked (and surely suffered) on the text throughout its long life-cycle, for their intelligence, superb professional capabilities, and exceptional diligence and patience.

Many others, unnamed, have at various times and in various ways given support and encouragement, and to these my sincere gratitude.

CONTENTS

VSAM

A COMPREHENSIVE GUIDE

1

THE PRE-VSAM ENVIRONMENT

1.1 PRE-VSAM ACCESS METHODS

In 1973, IBM released what has since turned out to be one of the most successful software products in history: *Virtual Storage Access Method*, or *VSAM*, as it is most commonly known. At this time, almost all commercial installations configured with IBM mainframe (the discontinued 360 and 370, and the current 303X, 308X, and the new 309X 'Sierra' classes) and midframe (43XX) processors, as well as the recently introduced 9370 super-minicomputer, make critical use of the VSAM product in batch (DOS, VS1, MVS), online (IMS, CICS), conversational (VM/SP CMS, TSO), and in certain database (DL/I, DB2) environments. VSAM is arguably the most ubiquitous non-PC software ever developed; to a programmer, VSAM permeates all aspects of systems operations: programming, backup and recovery, and performance and design, among many other areas.

In order to begin to understand exactly what VSAM is, we can start by examining one part of the fabric of VSAM, namely VSAM as an *access method* (the 'AM' part of VSAM). An access method is a collection of service routines that manages the transfer of records between main storage and external (or auxiliary) storage, thus controlling actual input/output operations over an I/O channel on behalf of the program. The access method routines provide their data management facilities, typically, by being attached to the program itself, as part of the load module (although this has changed for recent releases of VSAM, a point we shall return to in Chapter 18).

It is worthwhile to note here the distinction between an *access method* and a *file organization.* Records stored on some physical medium are organized into certain well-defined formats, and it is such *file organization* that permits the records in the file to be *accessed* (stored, retrieved, updated, deleted) in different ways, depending on the specific access method being used. VSAM is, in this sense, both an access method and a (unique) file organization, as will become increasingly clear over the next several chapters. Let's now briefly review the three basic access methods that dominated the scene before the introduction of VSAM.

1.1.1 Sequential Access Method: QSAM

A *sequential access method*, typified by the *Queued Sequential Access Method* (*QSAM*), accesses the records of a file in their physical order, that is, as they are successively encountered, one after another, on the actual storage medium. Given

1

this, a defining property of QSAM is that, in order to access record *n,* the previous *n-1* records must be read. If access to all, or a large number of records, of the file is required, QSAM is an exceptionally fast access method to use. If, however, a very small percentage of the file's records are to be accessed, QSAM will yield poor performance; in such cases, BDAM (see below) is the more appropriate method. (In the extreme case, to access the last record of a file, all preceding records must be read, needlessly.) A recent enhancement of QSAM is SAM/E, which runs under a collection of IBM programs for the MVS environment known as *Data Facility Product* (*DFP*) (which includes a new version of VSAM, to be examined later in this text). Note, however, that SAM/E operates in essentially the same manner as QSAM.

1.1.2 Direct Access Method: BDAM

With a *Direct Access Method,* typified by the *Basic Direct Access Method* (*BDAM*), any arbitrary record *n* may be accessed independently of the previous *n-1* records, or of any other record whatsoever. The records on a file with direct organization, which makes BDAM access possible, are stored in such fashion that there is some well-defined relationship between the key of a record and the actual physical location of that record on the storage medium. Since the record key determines the physical address of the record, any target record is said to be *directly* or *randomly* accessible.

For access to a relatively small percentage of the total records in the file, BDAM provides exceptionally fast retrieval, but rapidly becomes less than optimal as the retrieval percentage grows larger (QSAM being the appropriate method in such cases). Thus, for limited retrieval, BDAM avoids the extra overhead (performance degradation) of reading all records preceding the (few) target records. However, with larger numbers of target records, the cost of multiple numbers of computations of record addresses is associated with declining performance.

1.1.3 Sequential + Direct Access Method: ISAM

The *Indexed Sequential Access Method* (*ISAM*) provides both sequential and direct access to the records of a file within a single access method. A file that has *indexed sequential organization* (supporting ISAM) contains, in addition to the actual data records, a set of *indices* which serve to locate a data record in its correct *logical* sequence over some key, that is, in ascending key order, whatever its actual physical location is in the file. The indices were structures of pointers and pointer chains which had to be accessed first in order to locate any particular record by direct (random) access. In addition, the index structures also had to be used for sequential access, since the physical order of records and their logical order (ascending key) were not necessarily the same under ISAM. Because ISAM allowed for the flexibility of both sequential and direct access to the same file (within the same program), ISAM quickly became the dominant and most extensively exploited IBM access method. The ISAM market was the primary target of IBM's introduction of VSAM.

1.2 PROBLEMS WITH PRE-VSAM ACCESS METHODS

1.2.1 The Technical Problems

Cumulative experience with ISAM during its dominant period in the commercial landscape began to reveal several serious technical problems having adverse consequences on ISAM file access performance.

Record Addition. ISAM handles *inter*-record insertion—insertion of a record in its correct logical sequence by ascending key between two existing records—by adding the record at the correct point of insertion and then shifting over *all of the records* with higher keys than the inserted record. This *record chain shift* would entail mounting performance degradation as the number of successive records which required physical shifting increases, inevitable with regular file growth.

Overflow. ISAM records are stored and located on the physical tracks of the file. At some point after record insertion activity, the limit of track capacity for any particular physical device on which the file is stored would disallow further record insertion: there are just so many records that can fit on one track of any device. ISAM handles this by providing various *overflow areas* within the file: the last record (and then the next to the last record, etc.) of the track is 'bumped' into some overflow area to make more room for the inserted record.

Such record bumping has two consequences. Firstly, one of the indices—the *track index*—which keeps track of the high key on the track, must be updated to reflect the new high key value. Secondly, another index—the *overflow index*—which keeps track of the low key value of records in the overflow area, must also be updated to reflect the new overflow area low key value. These double operations may be required a large number of times as the file continues to grow and tracks continue to overflow.

Second-Order Overflow. Track overflow areas, being finite in size, may themselves overflow after significant record insertion activity, into another type of overflow area: an *independent overflow area.* (Both the cylinder and independent overflow areas are optional.) This *second-order overflow* adds still more overhead to ISAM file processing under significant record insertion activity. Furthermore, unlike a cylinder overflow area, an independent overflow area requires an additional seek on the device to locate the overflow record(s); this is not the case with cylinder overflow, because the cylinder overflow area resides on the same cylinder as the data records for which it provides overflow.

Retrieval Time. ISAM uses both track indices and cylinder indices for direct access facilities, and there may even be an additional (optional) *master index* which indexes the cylinder index (should this latter index prove to be large). This entails that the retrieval of a single record involve at least three read operations: one to the cylinder index, another to the track index, and another to actually retrieve the target data record. Furthermore, if an independent overflow area was employed, this would involve another read before the final read of the target record. Additionally, ISAM uses a complex and time-consuming method of *chained addressing* to thread through the file by pointers in order to retrieve records from overflow areas, and following long pointer chains adds further overhead to the retrieval process.

Record Deletion.   Records may be deleted by processing activity from an ISAM file. However—and this is another serious technical problem with ISAM, in addition to the above—under *no* circumstance does ISAM actually *physically* delete the target of a deletion request; the 'deleted' record remains, physically, in its original location on the storage medium. ISAM performs only a *logical deletion*: the target records are marked 'doomed,' as it were, by placing a value of hexadecimal (hex) 'FF' (HIGH-VALUES in COBOL) in the record's lead (first) byte. This means that space is not *reclaimed* after record deletion activity: an ISAM file only continues to grow larger and larger, unless it is at some time completely reorganized (such *ISAM reorganization* will reclaim the space that such logically deleted records occupied), but this involves extensive restructuring of the entire ISAM file.

Device Dependence.   ISAM is said to be heavily *device dependent*: its operation as an access method, its capacity limitations, and its tuning are intimately tied to the physical characteristics of the storage medium on which the ISAM file resides, and the programmer must have fairly detailed knowledge of some of these physical characteristics in order to effectively use ISAM. In addition, moving an ISAM file from one storage device of a particular type to a different type of storage device means fairly significant reorganization to accommodate the file to the new device characteristics. *Cross-device portability* is said to be poor with ISAM.

1.3   THE DESIGN LIMITATIONS

Independent of the technical problems discussed above, ISAM's design objective can be seen as insufficiently comprehensive to adequately meet the demands of an increasingly complex computer systems environment, especially in commercial installations. Some of the serious design limitations are listed below.

1.3.1   Complex Reorganization

ISAM file reorganization involves relatively complex procedures to effect reorganization, and reorganization is itself needed frequently for highly active ISAM files to retain acceptable levels of performance.

1.3.2   Absence of Utility Support

An ISAM file cannot be loaded by a general purpose IBM utility program (IEBDG can be used—a not widely known fact—but this is complex and unwieldly):

ISAM files are typically created by a *program load*, output verbs issued against the file, like WRITE and PUT. The IEBISAM utility, often mistakenly thought to create ISAM files, only copies, loads and unloads backup copies of, and prints ISAM files. Changing ISAM files, or converting them into another file organization, or other similar types of 'utility' functions, must be effected by programming. (Although IEBISAM can be used to unload an ISAM file for sequential backup to tape or disk, this sequential backup copy of the file is unusable directly; IEBISAM must be used against this backup copy to reload it back into ISAM form before it can be processed.)

1.3.3   Absence of Security/Integrity/Sharing Facilities

ISAM provides no support whatever for securing ISAM files—password protection, for example, is not available (through ISAM)—and no means for the assurance of read and/or write integrity. Furthermore, lacking any means for implementing an integrity scheme of any sort, ISAM files can not consequently be shared by concurrent tasks. But concurrent access by multiple tasks is a common requirement in many sophisticated environments, especially in mixed batch/online environments, where files may need to be shared among several online transactions, and between these and multiple batch tasks.

1.3.4   Absence of Recovery Facilities

ISAM provides the user with no recovery scheme in the event of system or other serious failure while processing an ISAM file. If such failure leads to data loss or data corruption, as is typically the case, it is the responsibility of the user to—independently of and without assistance from ISAM—implement whatever recovery may be possible (usually very little) under the circumstances.

1.3.5   Absence of Global Performance Parameters

Performance (fine) tuning with ISAM is at best exceptionally 'unfine.' Few parameters exist (primarily DCB subparameters in the JCL for ISAM files) which may be manipulated to influence performance. Furthermore, most performance tuning is *nonglobal*, that is, *program-dependent*, so that the benefits of such tuning are often *local*—accruing only to the individual program providing the coding for performance, and not to all users of the ISAM file itself.

1.3.6   Absence of System Portability

ISAM provides no facilities to *transport* ISAM files from one operating system environment to another, without recreating the file in the second system. This lack of *system portability* is a serious deficiency in large commercial multisystem environments, where the need for such file transportation support arises frequently.

1.3.7   Absence of Centralized Control

An ISAM file (regardless of its importance to an application) is, to the operating system (DOS, VS1, MVS), just another file; a systems catalog knows about the ISAM file only to the same extent as its knowledge stretches for other non-ISAM files: namely, it knows the name of the file, and only the unit(s) and volume(s) on which it resides. Space information must be garnered from the label (DSCB) of the file within the volume's VTOC, where DCB information is also kept. The full facts about the ISAM file (physical and logical properties, processing activity history, etc.) are in no centralized location to facilitate control. Indeed, information such as the processing activity history is not available anywhere at all, as it is not traced by either ISAM or systems routines, and can only be obtained if the programmer explicitly codes to trace it.

1.3.8   Absence of Alternate Pathing

An ISAM file is organized by a single unique field—the *key*—in ascending character sequence. All access is said to be *over* this key, which thus provides the (single) path through the file, whether sequentially or directly in terms of program access mode (a social security number field, SSN, is a common instance of such a key). Using this key field for random retrieval, for example, allows fetching of any arbitrary record (there is only one) containing that key value.

However, in commercial applications, retrieval by other than this single key may be needed on an extensive basis. For example, we may need to access, for update, all 'Smith' records—access in this case is over some *alternate path* (key field), the last name field, rather than the SSN field (we may not know or want to have to know what the SSNs for all 'Smith' records are). Also, for various applications, or combinations of applications, access to the file records may be needed over several such alternate paths (last name, employee number, department, etc.), in addition to access over the single *prime* key.

ISAM, however, provides no support whatever for such alternate pathing: all access is over the single (prime) key. Alternate pathing, therefore, would have to be simulated by creating multiple copies of the ISAM data records in different ISAM files, each of these files being organized over a different prime key (one over SSN, one over last name, etc.). This is clearly inefficient: all files contain exactly the same records, replicated with different prime keys, solely for alternate pathing simulation (this creates high storage overhead, given large ISAM files). In addition, multiple files may have to be opened in a single program to provide for access over different paths for different processing needs within the program, or multiple separate programs would have to be used, and their processing coordinated.

Most critically, however, any change to any one of these files would have to be *synchronized* with parallel changes to all of the others (precisely, simultaneously, and without error), in order to maintain cross-file accuracy and level of *updatedness*, and this must be provided by application programming, as ISAM treats each of these files as independent (unrelated and unconnected) of all of the others. This design limitation of ISAM—the absence of alternate pathing, and consequently, absence of *multifile synchronization* facilities—was arguably what proved to be ISAM's greatest, and ultimately fatal, flaw.

1.4 SUMMARY

The discussion above of both the technical problems of ISAM and its inherent design limitations, should make clear what the software scene was in the years preceding the 1973 introduction of VSAM. The most powerful and extensively used (at that time) IBM access method available, ISAM, proved to be seriously—indeed, fatally—flawed when evaluated against the emerging, increasingly more sophisticated requirements of the commercial computer systems community, both with respect to fundamental design considerations as well as critical performance concerns. A new and completely different approach to access method facilities was needed, was indeed inevitable.

2

THE EVOLUTION OF VSAM

2.1 THE INTRODUCTION OF STANDARD VSAM

The first version of VSAM was introduced by IBM in 1973, and has since come to be known as *Standard VSAM*. Standard VSAM was primarily conceived to address the inadequacies of ISAM as an access method, providing a comprehensive functional replacement hand-in-hand with superior design and performance. This functional replacement was provided essentially through a new type of data set, a *Key-Sequenced Data Set* or *KSDS*. (We will be discussing the functional components of VSAM, and the various types of VSAM data sets in subsequent chapters; we leave the discussion here at a very general level.)

In addition, Standard VSAM also introduced a second VSAM data set type, the *Entry-Sequenced Data Set* or *ESDS*, to serve as a functional replacement of QSAM data sets. IBM clearly intended, by the introduction of KSDSs and ESDSs, to ultimately provide a single master access method to replace non-VSAM counterparts. The KSDS was *organically*, as it were, necessary, given the shortcomings of ISAM.

The ESDS, however, lacked intrinsic motivation of any compelling sort: QSAM is a simple and extremely efficient access method, with no particular technical problems ever having been observed (SAM/E, mentioned earlier, is the most recent enhancement of QSAM). Still, the ESDS has (even to the present) retained low usage within the commercial programming community (more about this later).

Furthermore, Standard VSAM was modest in terms of the total ambitiousness of IBM's long-term objective of making VSAM *the* premier access method: *at that time* (from 1973 to 1975, during which Standard VSAM was active) no attempt was made to provide BDAM-type support outside of the KSDS—direct file organization and access methods were not available under VSAM. (This would be addressed by IBM subsequently in a new version of VSAM; see below.)

In addition, IBM made no effort whatever to provide VSAM support (*within* VSAM) for another critical access method, *Basic Partitioned Access Method* or *BPAM*, which handled the processing of *Partitioned Data Sets* (*PDSs*), or *libraries*. This has remained true to this day, so that it is clear now (by the perfect vision of hindsight) that VSAM should be thought of as the *dominant* access method, but not exclusive: non-VSAM facilities like QSAM or SAM/E, and like PDS (library) support will continue in usage relatively unaffected by VSAM developments.

Nonetheless, Standard VSAM became rapidly successful, and the KSDS in particular began to slowly but surely replace the tremendous number of ISAM files in commercial usage. In conclusion, it is interesting to note that, to this day, IBM has not completely discontinued ISAM support, although it is the case that so many *individual* strategic IBM products have separately dropped ISAM support, that this constitutes a *de facto* discontinuation. It is very safe to assume, at this time, that no *new* applications would hereafter be developed in ISAM.

2.2 ENHANCED VSAM

After only two years on the scene, Standard VSAM was replaced by the IBM 1975 introduction of *Enhanced VSAM*, which continued VSAM's evolution into a still more powerful facility and delivered several critical (and in certain ways, predictable) enhancements and extensions. Let's briefly turn to these now.

As noted earlier, Standard VSAM only implemented part of the range of functions made available by non-VSAM access methods: the functionality of ISAM and QSAM was captured and improved upon (by the KSDS and ESDS data set types, respectively), but strictly direct access corresponding to that available under BDAM was not provided under Standard VSAM. Given that a large number of applications used BDAM for very fast access against directly organized data sets, there was considerable motivation for IBM to revise Standard VSAM to provide BDAM-type support. Enhanced VSAM therefore introduced the third type of VSAM data set, the *Relative Record Data Set* or *RRDS*, which provided BDAM-type support along with some significant performance improvements.

But Enhanced VSAM went further still in extending the previous (Standard) VSAM. The reader will recall from the earlier discussion of ISAM that ISAM (and all other pre-VSAM access methods) lacked any facilities for *alternate pathing* (access to the data records of a single data set by some key other than the (single) prime key of the data set, that is, access *over* some alternate path: last name, department, what have you). Surprisingly, the first version of VSAM—Standard VSAM—also lacked any such support. It was only with Enhanced VSAM in 1975 that a VSAM facility for alternate pathing was introduced. This facility is known in VSAM as the *alternate index (AIX)* facility, one of the most important access methods facilities ever developed. An arbitrary number of alternate indices (AIXs) can be built over a VSAM data set—KSDS and ESDS types only: no AIXs can be built for RRDSs—to allow any degree of multiple pathing. (AIX facilities are treated in detail in Chapter 13.)

In addition to RRDS and AIX facilities, Enhanced VSAM added several other features to VSAM, the most important of which was that of *catalog recovery*. VSAM catalogs are a critical and central part of VSAM (Chapter 4 treats catalogs in detail), but Standard VSAM provided no facility for the *recovery* of VSAM catalogs in the event of system failure or other abnormal system termination events, not uncommon events, all told, in commercial environments.

Enhanced VSAM introduced a comprehensive catalog recovery facility which essentially *duplexed* (replicated) catalog information in areas known as *catalog recovery areas (CRAs)* from which the catalog could be recovered—fully or partially reconstructed—in the event of damage to or corruption of catalog information. (Catalog recovery facilities using these CRAs will be discussed in Chapter 15.) Along with still other specialized facilities, Enhanced VSAM became the de facto standard for access methods in the overwhelming majority of IBM installations, a status it retained for almost a decade.

2.3 DATA FACILITY/EXTENDED FUNCTION (DF/EF): THE NEW VSAM

IBM introduced Data Facility/Extended Function (DF/EF) in 1979 as a functional replacement of Enhanced VSAM. Unlike the previous product (Enhanced VSAM), which extended VSAM in terms of functionality, but retained the basic internal structure and operation—as well as the essential design objectives—of Standard VSAM, DF/EF was a new and substantively different implementation of VSAM. It was designed to address and correct many of the weaknesses of even so sophisticated a product as Enhanced VSAM, as these were slowly discovered by commercial users working with Enhanced VSAM in complex operating environments.

In particular, DF/EF introduced a dramatically different approach to VSAM catalogs and their management, known as the *Integrated Catalog Facility* (or ICF) component of DF/EF. Many users refer to DF/EF informally as the 'New VSAM,' and regard ICF as *the* new VSAM: although ICF is easily the most significant new facility of DF/EF, it is nonetheless only one among several other new facilities of DF/EF. (We will deal with DF/EF in detail in Chapters 17 and 18 of this text.)

There are two points to note in connection with DF/EF before we conclude this brief tracing of the evolution of the VSAM product. First, IBM has *not* announced the discontinuation of Enhanced VSAM support upon the introduction of DF/EF (unlike Enhanced VSAM, which effectively replaced Standard VSAM). Given the advantages and disadvantages of DF/EF (to be explored later), most commercial installations are *mixed* VSAM environments, continuing to support Enhanced VSAM alongside DF/EF. This makes such *mixed* environments—Enhanced VSAM plus DF/EF—complex and subtle to effectively control and tune, a point to which we will return later in the text.

The second point to note is that, technically speaking, the newest version of VSAM is something known as *Data Facility Product/VSAM* or *DFP/VSAM*, introduced by IBM in 1983. However, the key *base* of the DFP/VSAM product is DF/EF itself, and although DFP/VSAM adds some significant enhancements to this base product, nonetheless DFP/VSAM is of a single fabric with DF/EF. The informal term 'new VSAM' will therefore be taken to refer to this base DF/EF product; where we need to distinguish new features under DFP/VSAM, we will explicitly note them at the appropriate time. (Chapter 17, on the new VSAM, treats this issue of DF/EF and DFP/VSAM in a technically precise fashion.)

The dates here are sometimes deceptive. Although IBM announced DF/EF as early as 1979, most commercial installations began to adopt it only in 1981-82. Indeed, conversion in these environments to DF/EF really only has achieved significant proportions in the 1983-85 period; it is not unknown in even quite sophisticated commercial installations for the Enhanced VSAM-to-DF/EF migration to be only

1.   STANDARD VSAM (1973)

2.   ENHANCED VSAM (1975)

3.   VSE/VSAM (1979)

---

4.   DATA FACILITY/EXTENDED FUNCTION: DF/EF (1981–82)

5.   DATA FACILITY PRODUCT: DFP/VSAM (1983)

- DFP/XA: Version 2, Rel. 1.0   (April, 1985)

- DFP/XA: Version 2, Rel. 1.0 Update   (December, 1985)

- DFP/XA: Version 2, Rel. 2.0   (June, 1986)

- DFP/XA: Version 2, Rel. 3.0   (June, 1987)

- DFP: Version 3   (December, 1988)

Note: DFP/XA = DFP running under MVS/XA (MVS/EXTENDED ARCHITECTURE).
DFP is also available under non-xa systems, as DFP/370.

Figure 2-1. VSAM evolution.

'midstream,' as it were, although migration activity at the time of this writing is rapid and intense. Figure 2-1 summarizes the evolution of VSAM in terms of versions and their introduction dates.

Note that in June 1987, IBM introduced DFP/VSAM, version 2, release 3.0 (see Figure 2-1), which—for the new VSAM—adds a *fourth* VSAM cluster type for the first time, the *Linear Data Set* (LDS). This is a highly specialized facility under a new release (release 2) of MVS/Extended Architecture (MVS/XA), so we defer all discussion of this cluster type until Chapter 18. Therefore, before that point, we often make reference to the three VSAM cluster types—KSDS, ESDS, RRDS—although strictly speaking there is now a fourth type, the LDS. This is solely for simplification, and does not affect our earlier treatments of clusters in any significant way. Still more recently, DFP Version 3 (scheduled for December 1988) brings further technical enhancements and changes to DFP/VSAM, and these are taken up in Chapters 17 and 18.

This completes our discussion of the evolution of VSAM, and we turn, without further ado, to the basic structure and operation of VSAM, in the following chapters.

3

FUNCTIONAL COMPONENTS OF VSAM

The VSAM product, here interpreted to mean Enhanced VSAM, consists of several distinct components which collectively provide the spectrum of functionality which identifies VSAM. Below, we briefly describe each of these functional components of VSAM. They are shown in Figure 3-1.

3.1 CATALOG MANAGEMENT

Catalog Management is the technical heart of VSAM: this component manages all aspects of the control and operation of *VSAM catalogs*—their creation, maintainance, update, backup, and recovery. It is the critical and logically primary of all VSAM components. A VSAM data set is considered to exist if and only if it is cataloged in a VSAM catalog (generally, several are used). Through Catalog Management routines, all physical, logical, and statistical (relating to the history of processing activity against the VSAM data set) attributes of all VSAM data sets are traced and recorded in VSAM catalogs functioning as *central reservoirs* of critical VSAM-related information, and thus yielding comprehensive centralized control of all VSAM activity in the

VSAM
1. CATALOG MANAGEMENT
2. RECORD MANAGEMENT
3. INPUT/OUTPUT MANAGEMENT
4. CONTROL BLOCK MANAGEMENT
5. ACCESS METHOD SERVICES (AMS): THE IDCAMS PROCESSOR
6. ISAM INTERFACE PROGRAM (IIP)

Figure 3-1. Functional components of VSAM.

system. VSAM catalogs are discussed fully in Chapters 4 and 5, while DF/EF Catalog Management—known, as we mentioned earlier, as the *Integrated Catalog Facility* (ICF)—is taken up in Chapter 17.

3.2   RECORD MANAGEMENT

The *Record Management* component of VSAM (also sometimes known as *Data Set Management*) handles the control and operation of VSAM objects other than catalogs, such as the KSDS, ESDS, and RRDS VSAM data set types discussed earlier, as well as alternate indices (AIXs), and certain other special-function objects to be considered later. Record Management handles OPEN/CLOSE and End-of-Volume (EOV) processing, virtual storage management, and VSAM space management.

3.3   INPUT/OUTPUT MANAGEMENT

The *Input/Output Management* component of VSAM is responsible for the control of the actual physical input and output operations issued against VSAM data sets. In particular, this component contains the I/O drivers, which help build channel programs to be processed by the I/O Supervisor (IOS) of the operating system (as well as containing various specialized appendage and asynchronous routines, among others, for other needed I/O services).

3.4   CONTROL BLOCK MANAGEMENT

The *Control Block Management* component of VSAM (also sometimes known as *Control Block Manipulation*) provides for the dynamic generation of certain critical VSAM control blocks, as well as for user displaying, modifying, and testing of these control blocks at execution-time, i.e., dynamically.

The two most critical VSAM control blocks are the *Access Method Control Block*, or *ACB*, and the *Request Parameter List*, or *RPL*. The ACB is the direct VSAM counterpart to the DCB (Data Control Block) for non-VSAM data sets. The non-Assembler programmer often encounters reference to the ACB in the early control block portion of a typical systems dump (say, SYSUDUMP) when an abend arises and (at least some) VSAM data sets were being used. Below the formatted dump portion of a DEB (Data Extent Block, which locates the DCB), one will find (for a VSAM data set) the following message:

```
*** FOR THIS DEB THERE IS NO DCB.  THE CONTROL BLOCK POINTED
    TO BY THE DEB IS AN ACB ***
```

signalling that one is dealing with a VSAM file, which has no DCB (we are assuming a local I/O environment; VTAM uses an ACB just like VSAM, but this is not relevant to such an environment).

The RPL control block contains information concerning the actual processing requested against some particular VSAM data set. This includes information such as whether an input (READ, GET) or an output (WRITE, PUT) operation is requested, whether the access mode is to be sequential or random, what is the target key, etc. The RPL, through a special field within it known as the *Feedback* or *FDBK* field, also provides comprehensive error checking information which can be invaluable to the application programmer attempting VSAM debugging.

Until recently, this vital error feedback was only available to the Assembler programmer, or to a programmer knowing enough VSAM internals to be able to trace to this field within a dump. However, under the new IBM programming language, *VS COBOL II*, this information is available for the first time to the COBOL application programmer (if using this 'new COBOL'). Control Block Management handles still other VSAM control blocks, but the ACB and the RPL are the two most critical.

3.5 ACCESS METHOD SERVICES (AMS): THE IDCAMS PROCESSOR

Access Method Services (*AMS*) is a multifunction utility program which provides the user with extensive commonly needed VSAM-related services; these include data set definition, copy and conversion functions, listing of catalog information, space allocation, security and integrity functions, and backup and recovery facilities, among many others. One can think of AMS as providing, through a single set of routines for VSAM data sets, the same range of functionality brought to non-VSAM data sets by IBM data set and system utility programs such as IEBGENER, IEBPTPCH, IEBISAM, IEHLIST, IEHMOVE, and IEHPROGM.

The Access Method Services utility program is made available by invoking, typically through JCL, the *IDCAMS command processor*, which fields requests from VSAM users to the actual AMS routines themselves for execution. Many programmers think—incorrectly—of the IDCAMS processor as being 'VSAM.' As we can see from the above discussion, AMS is just one (very important) functional component of the VSAM product. Utilization of the IDCAMS processor is the subject of Chapter 6, but let us briefly take a look at AMS here to more fully understand its status within the VSAM product.

Figure 3-2 is the basic JCL needed within an MVS system to invoke the services

```
1.    // JOB . . .
2.    // EXEC     PGM=IDCAMS
3.    //STEPCAT   DD DSN=TRUCAT,DISP=SHR
4.    //SYSPRINT  DD SYSOUT=A
5.    //INDD      DD DSN=TRU.TSUSER01.MSTR,DISP=OLD
6.    //OUTDD     DD DSN=TRU.TSUSER01.MSTR.BACKUP,DISP=OLD
7.    //SYSIN     DD *
8.      REPRO -
9.                INFILE(INDD) -
10.               OUTFILE(OUTDD)
11.   /*
12.   //
```

Figure 3-2. Sample IDCAMS job: REPRO.

of AMS, in this case for the purpose of creating a backup copy of a VSAM file. (Line numbers are used solely for reference purposes.) Omitting the JOB statement, let's look at each statement briefly in order to understand a typical AMS invocation.

DISCUSSION
(Numbers refer to line numbers in Figure 3-2.)

2. This statement invokes the IDCAMS command processor by standard IBM name. Like other IBM utility-type routines, the leading three characters, here, IDC, do not stand for anything, but make it unlikely that the IBM program name would ever duplicate a programmer-chosen name.

3. There are two JCL DD statements that are solely used to identify VSAM catalogs: *JOBCAT* and *STEPCAT*. Whenever a VSAM data set is being referenced, the VSAM catalog containing the entry for the data set (the 'owning' catalog) must be explicitly or implicitly identified. This statement (3) is an explicit identification of the VSAM catalog in which the two VSAM data sets involved in this job are cataloged: the catalog name is given as TRUCAT (a VSAM catalog for the 'Trust Area' applications of a bank). This is unlike OS data sets which, once cataloged, need no catalog identification in any job which references them. (There is another way to explicitly identify a VSAM catalog, and another for implicit definition, both of which we will cover later.) Like the non-VSAM JOBLIB and STEPLIB DD statements, JOBCAT is used for multistep jobs, and STEPCAT is used on a step basis. Also note that the DSN with JOBCAT and STEPCAT is that of a VSAM catalog, while with JOBLIB and STEPLIB it is a *private load library*.

4. The SYSPRINT DD statement is required in IDCAMS jobs, and is used by AMS routines to write messages and completion codes concerning the syntax and execution of the job. An IDCAMS job will terminate without running if SYSPRINT is omitted.

5. This statement identifies the VSAM data set we wish to copy. It is a VSAM data set cataloged in the TRUCAT catalog. The DISP parameter is set to OLD to ensure exclusive use of the data set during the copy operation. This is the input data set for the copy operation to be carried out by AMS routines.

6. This statement identifies an *unloaded* (empty) VSAM data set, into which the records of the input data set (TRU.TSUSER01.MSTR) are to be copied. The data set has already been defined to VSAM prior to this job, by a technique which we will be examining in detail in the next several chapters of the text; that definition is also effected by invoking the IDCAMS command processor (with an AMS DEFINE command). Unlike OS data sets, all VSAM data sets are *predefined* to VSAM (appropriate catalog entries are created at this DEFINE time), and hence are considered preexisting at time of first processing/reference. Thus, the DISP for VSAM data sets is *never NEW*: it is either OLD, for exclusive control, or SHR, for shared control. UNIT, VOL, and all other information has already been priorly stored in a VSAM catalog, so the JCL typically specifies only DSN and DISP parameters.

7. The SYSIN DD statement defines the *AMS control data set*, which contains—in this case, in-stream   the AMS commands that the user codes to specify what AMS

services are being requested. These AMS commands follow a particular syntax (to be covered in Chapter 6) and are read by the IDCAMS command processor and are passed by it to the actual AMS routines for execution. The command processor will do syntax checking on this control file and return messages to the SYSPRINT data set.

8. REPRO is the AMS command for requesting copying services; the next two lines represent REPRO command *parameters*, which further define the exact nature of the copy request: input and output files.

9. INFILE is a REPRO subparameter (keyword, in this case) which identifies the data set to be copied, the *input* data set. In parentheses after the REPRO command is the *DD name* of the DD statement in the JCL which defines the input file (INDD).

10. OUTFILE is another REPRO subparameter (keyword, again) which identifies the *empty* VSAM data set into which the records are to be copied; that is, the *output* data set. Again, identification is by DD name (OUTDD).

11. End of file delimiter for the SYSIN control file.

12. End of job (optional).

This example should give the reader an idea of how powerful (and simple, by and large) the AMS component (invoked through IDCAMS) is, and some basic understanding of its operation. Again, although AMS is just one of several components of VSAM, it is the component many programmers are most familiar with. Much of this text deals with AMS as called up through IDCAMS.

3.6   THE ISAM INTERFACE PROGRAM (IIP)

The last component of VSAM that we will be discussing is known as the *ISAM Interface Program*, or just the *IIP*. The IIP allows the programmer to continue to use an unmodified program with ISAM-specific coding and ISAM macros to process a VSAM data set. VSAM provides an ISAM-to-VSAM interface, in the form of the IIP, which thus allows the user to avoid recoding ISAM applications into VSAM-specific code. It is intended by IBM as a transitional migration aid until the user converts the program into pure VSAM coding.

There are several points to note here in connection with the IIP. First, the *data sets* themselves which are being processed must already be *VSAM data sets* (and, more particularly, KSDSs), and hence must have been converted from ISAM to VSAM priorly; the REPRO command is generally used for this purpose, as it includes both copy and conversion functions.

Second, the IIP routines must *capture* (intercept prior to execution) all ISAM-specific requests (ISAM macros) issued by the program, and translate them systematically into their VSAM counterparts, in addition to having to construct the appropriate VSAM control blocks.

Third, the performance overhead of this approach may be quite significant if there are many ISAM macros to translate, and although the IIP has been optimized by IBM, one is well-advised to ultimately convert all ISAM code to VSAM code, which will bypass macro conversion facilities under IIP altogether. Finally, IBM has been effecting a 'forced migration' from ISAM to VSAM, as we have already pointed out, by introducing new products with no ISAM support, as well as issuing new versions and releases of existing products which discontinue ISAM support (CICS/VS 1.7 and VS COBOL II are two very prominent examples). There should be little future use of the IIP, especially since new applications would be invariably developed in VSAM directly.

4

VSAM CATALOGS—STRUCTURE

4.1 THE VSAM CATALOG SYSTEM: AN OVERVIEW

At the heart of a VSAM system are VSAM catalogs: all VSAM facilities critically involve VSAM catalogs in one way or another. Just as we can describe MVS as essentially an interrupt-driven operating system, so we can describe VSAM as a *catalog-driven system*. This will become clear in the following discussion. For now, let's briefly consider the key design objectives of a VSAM catalog system.

4.1.1 Centralized System Control

VSAM catalogs are the basic control mechanism of a VSAM system. All VSAM objects—data sets, alternate indexes, and paths (these latter two the subject of discussion in Chapter 13), among others—must be cataloged in some one VSAM catalog (VSAM supports multiple catalogs in a single system), and these objects are said to be *controlled* by that catalog. All access to these objects is *through* the catalog, which contains all of the information necessary to process the object, including that necessary to create or delete the object, in addition to processing it.

Indeed, *a VSAM object, to exist, must be defined to (cataloged in) a VSAM catalog*. The act of creating a VSAM object is essentially one, minimally, of creating for the object an entry, in a VSAM catalog, the entry comprehensively describing the object. This differs dramatically from OS data sets, which may be created without cataloging them, cataloging an OS data set always being optional. The AMS command DEFINE is the basic mechanism for creating VSAM objects; this command generates a catalog entry for the object being created. Once this catalog entry is successfully created, all activity against the object is reflected in the catalog by constantly updating the object's catalog entry. This is done by the Catalog Management component of AMS, discussed earlier in Chapter 3. The catalog entry for a VSAM object may be listed at any time by the programmer by issuing a LISTCAT command; to better understand catalogs and the entries they contain, we will look at a typical catalog entry later in Section 4.4. Similarly, the act of deleting a VSAM object consists essentially of the removal (deletion) of the object's catalog entry from the catalog. Again, in OS the mere deletion of a catalog entry for a data set (through, for example, the JCL DD statement subparameter UNCATLG of the DISP parameter) has no effect on the existence of the data set itself. (DFP Version 3 is different, however; this is taken up in Section 9.4.)

4.1.2 Comprehensive File Information

A VSAM catalog entry for a VSAM object contains very comprehensive information about the object: the physical and logical attributes of the object, space allocation information, authorization and protection information, statistics concerning all major processing activity against the object, and much additional information. Indeed, virtually any essential information about the object and its usage is contained in the object's catalog entry. Our examination of a typical catalog entry, below, will look more closely at this comprehensive information. It suffices to say for now that, prior to VSAM, no such collection of information was available *in one location* either to the programmer or to the system (information from multiple sources had to be brought together, such as from the application program, from data set labels, from control blocks, etc.). Indeed, certain types of information—such as processing activity history (number of records added, deleted, updated)—were not being tracked by the system at all, it being the (optional) responsibility of the programmer to track such information if it was needed. This generally had to be done in the programming code itself, it being additionally the programmer's responsibility to assure the accuracy of such information. Due to the comprehensive information contained in VSAM catalogs—and tracked by VSAM itself—VSAM offers the programmer extensive system-type support, which can be used for a variety of purposes, such as problem determination, performance tuning, reporting functions, etc. This feature of VSAM is unique to VSAM and constitutes one of its most important and dramatic advantages over other access methods.

4.1.3 Data Integrity/Security

Given that, as noted above, all access to VSAM objects is through a VSAM catalog, the catalog is the made-to-order place at which mechanisms of authorization and protection may be applied, and this is exactly what VSAM does. Authorization and password information for VSAM objects is stored in VSAM catalogs and is used to apply basic VSAM data security; sensibly, the information is itself protected by VSAM from unauthorized access or display, so that the request to display a VSAM object's catalog entry, through LISTCAT, yields a display only of non-security related fields (unless authorization to see such information is demonstrated to VSAM by the user). Catalogs themselves, therefore, require adequate protection, and this may be provided both by VSAM mechanisms and by add-on access-control software products like RACF or ACF2.

4.1.4 Recoverability

VSAM catalogs, when first defined (that is, created, in VSAM), may optionally be made *recoverable* by specifying the *RECOVERABLE* attribute in their definition. A *recoverable catalog* offers some degree of *recoverability* of catalog data—entries—in the event of catalog damage, loss, or corruption due to a variety of adverse circumstances. With a recoverable catalog, well-defined VSAM procedures exist for restoring and/or correcting such affected catalog data. Given that VSAM catalogs are the central mechanism of control in a VSAM system, it is customary practice to define VSAM catalogs as recoverable. Note that this recoverability feature is a VSAM-provided service, and is independent of user-initiated *backup* (copying) of catalogs.

4.1.5 Simplicity of Use

AMS provides a host of relatively easy-to-use AMS catalog-related commands that assist the programmer—application and system—in dealing with all aspects of VSAM catalogs, as well as providing the basic LISTCAT command which allows the listing of both whole catalogs or of selected entries within them. The commands offer a level of flexibility and control unknown with OS catalogs. Again, given the critical status of VSAM catalogs in a VSAM system, simplicity of use is a key design objective of VSAM catalogs.

4.1.6 Cross-System Portability

VSAM catalogs may be *transported* out of one system environment and into another so that they may be used in the new system without having to be reconstructed in that new environment; the systems ('source' and 'target') need not be of the same type (VS1, SVS, MVS, DOS/VS, VSE) since all operating systems have comparable interfaces to VSAM catalogs, and the catalogs themselves are structured essentially identically in all operating systems environments that support VSAM. Using AMS commands (EXPORT and IMPORT), the catalog is disconnected from the source system and then connected to the target system.

4.2 THE VSAM MASTER CATALOG (MCAT)

A VSAM system is generally configured as a *multicatalog system*. VSAM systems allow two types of VSAM catalogs—*Master Catalogs* (*MCATs*) and *user catalogs* (*UCATs*). For any VSAM system, there must be one and only one Master Catalog, and this functions as the highest (logical) level VSAM catalog: all access to VSAM objects must first pass through the VSAM Master Catalog, and all VSAM user catalogs (if any are defined) are considered subordinate to the VSAM Master Catalog, in a sense which will become clearer below. The VSAM Master Catalog must be defined before any VSAM processing can be supported in the system, and hence before any other VSAM object may be defined.

For all systems other than MVS, the VSAM Master Catalog coexists with the system (non-VSAM) catalog: thus, for a VS1 system there is both an OS system catalog, and a VSAM Master Catalog. The MVS operating system, however, is unique: under MVS, the VSAM Master Catalog *is the system catalog*; non-VSAM catalogs may be retained, but only as subordinate objects to the VSAM Master Catalog. This is handled by creating pointers in the Master Catalog to these non-VSAM catalogs, known in this case as CVOLs (control volumes). Figure 4-1 shows the VSAM catalog configuration in MVS. Programmers may continue to process OS

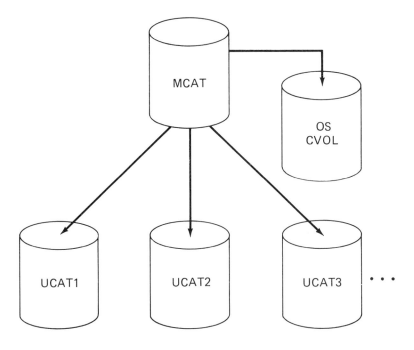

MCAT = VSAM MASTER CATALOG
UCAT = VSAM USER CATALOG
CVOL = CONTROL VOLUME

Figure 4-1. MVS VSAM catalog system.

data sets as they did in pre-VSAM systems (using, say, the old OS catalog for cataloging data sets), but the OS catalog is really being accessed through the VSAM Master Catalog (via a pointer to the OS CVOL), although this is generally transparent to the programmer.

Although it is permissible to catalog user (application) VSAM objects in the VSAM Master Catalog, this is rarely done: rather, only key system data sets are typically cataloged in the Master Catalog (for example, MVS paging data sets), which may contain, in addition, pointers (pointing to OS CVOLs or to other VSAM user catalogs) and other special control objects, leaving user (non-system) data sets to be cataloged in various user catalogs. Given the critical status of the VSAM Master Catalog, it is generally highly protected by both VSAM security mechanisms and access-control software (such as RACF or ACF2), and is additionally backed up regularly to guard against loss or corruption (which would seriously and adversely affect the system). It is invariably made a recoverable catalog, for obvious reasons. By restricting the types of objects that may be cataloged in a Master Catalog, the installation is also minimizing the chance of accidental (or intentional) damage to this most vital resource.

As we will note again in Chapter 6, the VSAM Master Catalog is defined through the issuing of the DEFINE MASTERCATALOG (DEF MCAT) AMS command, generally by a system programmer. The exception to this is under MVS: the Master Catalog is defined—as the system catalog—at system generation (SYSGEN) time through a special SYSGEN macro instruction (DATASET). An attempt to define the Master Catalog under MVS through the AMS DEF MCAT command fails to effect such definition; rather, AMS will convert the request to a DEF UCAT and create only a user catalog.

4.3   VSAM USER CATALOGS

In addition to the required single VSAM Master Catalog, an installation may option-ally define—and typically does—one or more VSAM user catalogs. Each of these user catalogs is subordinate to the VSAM Master Catalog in two senses: (1) the Master Catalog contains a pointer for each defined user catalog, and (2) all objects cataloged in a user catalog are located by first searching the Master Catalog for the appropriate user catalog pointer, in order to locate the user catalog itself, and then by searching the located user catalog for the target VSAM object entry, which finally points to (through volume information) to the object itself.

A VSAM object must be cataloged in *either* the VSAM Master Catalog or in one of the user catalogs (but not in both). Optionally, non-VSAM data sets and OS Generation Data Groups (GDGs) may also be cataloged in a VSAM catalog. Note, however, that VSAM does not retain comprehensive information about OS data sets, even though they are cataloged in a VSAM catalog. There are several reasons for establishing multiple VSAM user catalogs, and examining these reasons will also serve to further clarify the structure and function of user catalogs.

1. VSAM user catalogs allow for the segregation of VSAM objects by *use*. It is widespread practice to dedicate a single user catalog to one particular set of VSAM data sets (and related objects) processed by functionally related applications: one for, say, the Trust Area of a bank or another for the Process Control area of a manufactur-ing installation. A single such project or area may actually have associated with it—generally for its exclusive use, or for limited shared use by related projects/areas—several 'Trust Area' or 'Process Control' user catalogs, depending on the number of VSAM data sets used, although the most common situation is a single user catalog per such project/area. This greatly simplifies processing the appropriate data sets, since all are uniformly accessed through these *private area catalogs*. So, for example, this use of user catalogs as private area catalogs allows a single periodic listing of the catalog entries for all area-specific data sets to be obtained through a simple LISTCAT of the area catalog; unnecessary information about data sets belonging to a different area is thus avoided.

2. Use of VSAM user catalogs allows some decentralization of control in a VSAM system: each area 'owns' one or more user catalogs which that area controls; the area may apply its own distinctive standards, procedures, and controls—including security/protection, backup and recovery, naming conventions, etc.—without detailed

regard for the possibly very different standards, procedures, and controls in effect in other areas of the installation. Generally, under such a scheme of distributed control, the VSAM Master catalog is directly controlled by key systems programming, data center, and/or data security staff as a vital systems-wide resource, while local areas control the various user catalogs.

3. Use of VSAM user catalogs significantly enhance data integrity: the effect of catalog unavailability—due to loss, failure, corruption—is minimized and localized, since VSAM catalogs other than the unavailable catalog are unaffected (unless—and rarely—the problem is with the Master Catalog, and even then the data integrity of the user catalogs is generally not compromised, although connecting pointers may have to be reestablished). VSAM objects cataloged in unaffected user catalogs continue to be available.

4. Use of VSAM user catalogs optimizes catalog search time for a given catalog: the set of all catalog entries for all VSAM objects in the system is distributed across multiple catalogs, and data sets belonging to one area's applications are congregated together so that no extra search overhead is incurred in reading catalog entries for data sets belonging to another area. In addition, search time for systems-related VSAM objects cataloged in the Master Catalog is kept as fast as possible since no user application data sets entries are contained there. This is especially valuable, given that such important systems-related objects are generally accessed a very large number of times for any given time interval, so one wants to minimize access time for the Master Catalog for the sake of system-wide efficiency.

5. Finally, use of VSAM user catalogs facilitates *catalog portability*: the user catalog can be disconnected from one system's Master Catalog and transported into another system, where it is connected to the new system's Master Catalog. Then, once the actual disk volumes are mounted in the new system, no redefinition of the VSAM objects or of the user catalog is required.

4.4   A PEEK AT A CATALOG ENTRY

In order to give the above discussion some concreteness, and further clarify the nature and function of VSAM catalogs, this section looks at a typical catalog entry for a VSAM data set. Figure 4-2 is the output generated by the following LISTCAT command:

```
LISTCAT -
        ENTRIES (STNTESTV.STNKANT.KSDS02) -
        ALL
```

We discuss here only some of the information fields in the LISTCAT output; Chapter 12 provides a fuller treatment, after preceding chapters introduce the VSAM concepts and facilities needed to understand various additional LISTCAT fields. Furthermore, the LISTCAT entry is for a VSAM KSDS, which has both a data component and an index component; we will restrict our attention to data compo-

```
IDCAMS  SYSTEM SERVICES                              TIME: 22:38:22      12/01/83    PAGE   1

   REPRO -
          INFILE(QSAMDD) -
          OUTFILE(VSAMDD)
IDC0005I NUMBER OF RECORDS PROCESSED WAS 40000
IDC0001I FUNCTION COMPLETED, HIGHEST CONDITION CODE WAS 0

   IF MAXCC = 0 -
     THEN -
                LISTCAT -
                       ENTRIES(STNTESTV.STNKANT.KSDS02) -
                       ALL
CLUSTER ------- STNTESTV.STNKANT.KSDS02
     IN-CAT --- MVSYSH.MASTER.CATALOG
     HISTORY
          OWNER-IDENT------STNKANT      CREATION----------83.335
          RELEASE----------------2      EXPIRATION--------00.000
          PROTECTION-PSWD-----(NULL)    RACF---------------(NO)
     ASSOCIATIONS
          DATA-----STNTESTV.STNKANT.KSDS02.DATA
          INDEX----STNTESTV.STNKANT.KSDS02.INDEX
     DATA ------- STNTESTV.STNKANT.KSDS02.DATA
        IN-CAT --- MVSYSH.MASTER.CATALOG
        HISTORY
             OWNER-IDENT-------(NULL)     CREATION----------83.335
             RELEASE----------------2     EXPIRATION--------00.000
             PROTECTION-PSWD-----(NULL)   RACF---------------(NO)
        ASSOCIATIONS
             CLUSTER--STNTESTV.STNKANT.KSDS02
        ATTRIBUTES
             KEYLEN----------------8      AVGLRECL-------------600    BUFSPACE-----------9216    CISIZE-------------4096
             RKP-------------------0      MAXLRECL-------------600    EXCPEXITM--------(NULL)    CI/CA---------------120
             SHROPTNS(1,3)   RECOVERY     UNIQUE        NOERASE       INDEXED     NOWRITECHK     NOIMBED       NOREPLICAT
             UNORDERED       NOREUSE      NONSPANNED
        STATISTICS
             REC-TOTAL----------40000     SPLITS-CI-------------0      EXCPS--------------8396
             REC-DELETED-----------0      SPLITS-CA-------------0      EXTENTS----------------7
             REC-INSERTED----------0      FREESPACE-%CI---------10     SYSTEM-TIMESTAMP:
             REC-UPDATED-----------0      FREESPACE-%CA---------0          X'9687BC388771EC20'
             REC-RETRIEVED---------0      FREESPC-BYTES-----217088
        ALLOCATION
             SPACE-TYPE------CYLINDER     HI-ALLOC-RBA----27525120
             SPACE-PRI-------------50     HI-USED-RBA-----27525120
             SPACE-SEC-------------1
        VOLUME
             VOLSER-----------SYS003      PHYREC-SIZE---------4096    HI-ALLOC-RBA----27525120   EXTENT-NUMBER----------7
             DEVTYPE------X'3050200B'     PHYRECS/TRK------------4    HI-USED-RBA-----27525120   EXTENT-TYPE--------X'00'
             VOLFLAG-----------PRIME      TRACKS/CA-------------30
             EXTENTS:
             LOW-CCHH-----X'01F70000'     LOW-RBA--------------0      TRACKS-------------1500
             HIGH-CCHH----X'022B001D'     HIGH-RBA--------24575999
             LOW-CCHH-----X'00150000'     LOW-RBA--------24576000     TRACKS---------------30
             HIGH-CCHH----X'0015001D'     HIGH-RBA--------25067519
             LOW-CCHH-----X'00160000'     LOW-RBA--------25067520     TRACKS---------------30
             HIGH-CCHH----X'0016001D'     HIGH-RBA--------25559039
             LOW-CCHH-----X'003E0000'     LOW-RBA--------25559040     TRACKS---------------30
             HIGH-CCHH----X'003E001D'     HIGH-RBA--------26050559
             LOW-CCHH-----X'003F0000'     LOW-RBA--------26050560     TRACKS---------------30
             HIGH-CCHH----X'003F001D'     HIGH-RBA--------26542079
             LOW-CCHH-----X'00490000'     LOW-RBA--------26542080     TRACKS---------------30
             HIGH-CCHH----X'0049001D'     HIGH-RBA--------27033599
             LOW-CCHH-----X'00430000'     LOW-RBA--------27033600     TRACKS---------------30
             HIGH-CCHH----X'0043001D'     HIGH-RBA--------27525119
```

Figure 4-2. Sample LISTCAT output.

nent information here, and leave the discussion of index component fields for Chapter 11.

4.4.1   CLUSTER and IN-CAT

The cluster name is given, along with the name of the VSAM catalog containing the entry for this data set; this is actually a system data set and has been cataloged in the Master Catalog for this system (catname = MVSYSH.MASTER.CATALOG).

```
INDEX ------ STNTESTV.STNKANT.KSDS02.INDEX
  IN-CAT --- MVSYSH.MASTER.CATALOG
  HISTORY
     OWNER-IDENT-------(NULL)     CREATION----------83.335
     RELEASE----------------2     EXPIRATION--------00.000
  PROTECTION-PSWD-----(NULL)      RACF---------------(NO)
  ASSOCIATIONS
     CLUSTER--STNTESTV.STNKANT.KSDS02
  ATTRIBUTES
     KEYLEN----------------8       AVGLRECL----------------0     BUFSPACE---------------0     CISIZE------------1024
     RKP-------------------0       MAXLRECL-------------1017     EXCPEXIT---------(NULL)     CI/CA---------------15
     SHROPTNS(1,3)   RECOVERY      UNIQUE           NOERASE      NOWRITECHK      NOIMBED     NOREPLICAT    UNORDERED
     NOREUSE
  STATISTICS
     REC-TOTAL------------57       SPLITS-CI---------------0     EXCPS----------------335     INDEX:
     REC-DELETED-----------0       SPLITS-CA---------------0     EXTENTS----------------1     LEVELS----------------2
     REC-INSERTED----------0       FREESPACE-%CI-----------0     SYSTEM-TIMESTAMP:             ENTRIES/SECT---------10
     REC-UPDATED-----------0       FREESPACE-%CA-----------0        X'9687BC388771EC20'      SEQ-SET-RBA-----------0
     REC-RETRIEVED---------0       FREESPC-BYTES-------3072                                   HI-LEVEL-RBA-------2048
  ALLOCATION
     SPACE-TYPE--------TRACK       HI-ALLOC-RBA-------61440
     SPACE-PRI------------4        HI-USED-RBA--------58368
     SPACE-SEC------------1
  VOLUME
     VOLSER-----------SYS003       PHYREC-SIZE---------1024     HI-ALLOC-RBA-------61440     EXTENT-NUMBER---------1
     DEVTYPE------X'3050200B'      PHYRECS/TRK-----------15     HI-USED-RBA--------58368     EXTENT-TYPE-------X'00'
     VOLFLAG-----------PRIME       TRACKS/CA--------------1
     EXTENTS:
     LOW-CCHH-----X'00070011'      LOW-RBA-----------------0     TRACKS-----------------4
     HIGH-CCHH----X'00070014'      HIGH-RBA-----------61439
          THE NUMBER OF ENTRIES PROCESSED WAS:
                    AIX ------------------0
                    ALIAS ----------------0
                    CLUSTER --------------1
                    DATA -----------------1
                    GDG ------------------0
                    INDEX ----------------1
                    NONVSAM --------------0
                    PAGESPACE ------------0
                    PATH -----------------0
                    SPACE ----------------0
                    USERCATALOG ----------0
                    TOTAL ----------------3
          THE NUMBER OF PROTECTED ENTRIES SUPPRESSED WAS 0
IDC0001I FUNCTION COMPLETED, HIGHEST CONDITION CODE WAS 0
```

Figure 4-2. *(continued)*

4.4.2   CREATION and EXPIRATION

The date the cluster was created is given—rather unfortunately—in julianized form (the 335th day of 1983). The expiration field value of '00.000' indicates that no expiration date (specified in the TO or FOR parameters of the DEFINE CLUSTER command used to create the cluster) was stipulated—this entails that the cluster may be deleted at any time. Had an expiration date been specified, the cluster could not be deleted by a standard DELETE command before that date; rather, a special form of DELETE—namely DELETE with the PURGE option—would have to be issued instructing VSAM to delete the cluster although it is unexpired. For test data sets, it is generally unnecessary to date-protect the data set; however, for non-test data sets the date-protect feature (DEF CLUSTER ... TO/FOR ...) is a valuable precaution against premature and/or inadvertent erasure of a VSAM data set.

4.4.3   PROTECTION-PSWD and RACF

These are two security-related fields. *PROTECTION-PSWD* indicates whether protection provided by VSAM, in the form of multilevel password protection, is in effect. (Details on this are given later in the text.) The value NULL indicates that no password protection has been enabled. A value of SUPP would indicate that password protection is on, but that proper authorization (through the highest level VSAM password, the master password, being provided by the user) has not been established by the user to allow display of password(s). If the user had established such authorization, then the actual password(s) would have been displayed.

The *RACF* field refers to whether or not—its possible values are YES or NO—external protection (not VSAM-provided) is in effect through the IBM security product *Resource Access Control Facility*. This is a widely used product in IBM environments, commonly in effect to either complement or replace native VSAM-provided security. The user should note that if these two security-related fields show no enabled protection against the data set, it does not follow that the file is not (heavily) protected; it simply means that neither VSAM nor RACF are providing any protection facilities. The file may still be protected by some other non-IBM product, for example, by ACF2 (Computer Associates), CA-Top Secret (Computer Associates), or OMNIGUARD (On-line Software International), among many others; being non-IBM, their presence is not indicated in any LISTCAT field.

4.4.4   ASSOCIATIONS

For the entry (STNTESTV.STNKANT.KSDS02) being listed, the names of any related VSAM objects (data and index components for a KSDS, alternate indices, paths, etc.) are given here. Here the entry we are listing is a KSDS which is constituted by a data component and an index component; the names are given here. They are user-generated in this case, but may have been VSAM-generated names if the user failed to explicitly specify these names at cluster definition time.

The following fields are listed under the data component portion of the LISTCAT output.

4.4.5   KEYLEN and RKP

This is a keyed file and *KEYLEN* gives the length of the key as eight bytes (characters), while *RKP* (Relative Key Position) gives the starting position of the key within the record *with respect to a zero start point for the record*; that is, the key is the first (leftmost) field in the record, starting at what the programmer would consider column position 1, but which VSAM considers the zeroth position. Thus, if the key were to have started in column 10, the RKP would be 9 (RKP = column-position−1).

4.4.6   AVGLRECL and MAXLRECL

The average length of the records in the file is given (*AVGLRECL*), along with the length of the longest record (*MAXLRECL*). If the file contained variable-length records, these two field values would be different; this file contains fixed-length records and so the values are, necessarily, identical.

4.4.7 STATISTICS Fields

This group of fields provides statistical (usage) information about the file. *REC-TOTAL* is shown as 40,000: we loaded 40,000 records into this cluster. *REC-DELETED*, *REC-INSERTED*, *REC-UPDATED*, and *REC-RETRIEVED* are all zero: no processing has been done against the file since the records were loaded into it. If we processed the file since that load-time, a LISTCAT output obtained immediately after the processing was done would show through these fields a summary of the activity having just taken place. Thus, it is useful to issue a LISTCAT after each batch of processing activity against the file in order to verify that the activity was completed successfully and is accurately reflected in the catalog entry for the file; this provides a running snapshot summary of the *processing history* of the file over any period of time. If can also alert the programmer early on to any discrepancy between what the programmer expects to be the number of records in the file, and what VSAM takes this to be; such a discrepancy is grounds for closer investigation. Other *STATISTICS* fields are left for later discussion.

4.4.8 ALLOCATION Fields

This group of LISTCAT fields shows that the space allocation for the file was made (at DEFINE CLUSTER time) in units of cylinders (*SPACE-TYPE*), and that the primary allocation (*SPACE-PRI*) was 50, and the secondary allocation (*SPACE-SEC*) was one. (See Chapter 7 for information on VSAM space allocation, and the special interpretation of secondary allocation under VSAM.)

4.4.9 VOLUME Fields

The *VOLSER* gives volume information, but notice that there is no straightforward indication of device type (UNIT in OS) information; this is given only in hexadecimal code in the *DEVTYPE* field; we will show how to interpret such codes in Chapter 12, but a 3350 pack is being used here. Also shown (*EXTENT-NUMBER*) is the total number of space extents the file occupies, here seven. (See below.)

4.4.10 EXTENTS

There are three columns of information under this category; the first two are specialized and will be discussed in Chapter 12. The third column of information has seven lines, one for each of the seven extents of space the file occupies. The first of these seven extents shows a value of 1500 tracks which, on a 3350 pack, is equivalent to 50 cylinders; this is the primary allocation amount requested. Each of the remaining six extents is for 30 tracks, or one cylinder. This is actually allocated secondary extents: what is being indicated by VSAM is that the primary allocation of 50 cylinders was insufficient for holding the 40,000 records loaded into the cluster, given space required by VSAM over and above that for data records, and an additional six cylinders had to be obtained from secondary allocation, so that the actual cluster occupies a total of 56 cylinders on a 3350 pack (which equals 1680 tracks). Looking at such extent information in LISTCAT output is the only reliable way to determine the actual size of the file at any time.

4.5   ADVANTAGES OF VSAM CATALOGS OVER OS CATALOGS

By this point, it should be quite clear to the reader that there are many advantages of VSAM catalogs over their OS counterparts; most of these have been discussed in Section 4.1, in our examination of the design objectives of the VSAM catalog system. As brought out by the discussion in the previous section, which looked briefly at a typical catalog entry, we may also add here the advantages of the ease of monitoring a file, through its catalog entry, for the tracking of processing activity, verification of applied program changes against the file, and — perhaps most importantly — for critical fine-tuning of a file. Against all of this wealth of information and functionality in a VSAM catalog system, compare the OS catalog system containing only data set name, unit, and volume information: not even space allocation information is available (this must be obtained from the VTOC on a volume by volume basis). Later, we will see that the superior VSAM catalog system has even been further improved under the 'New VSAM,' Data Facility/Extended Function.

5

VSAM CATALOGS—OPERATION

5.1   VOLUME OWNERSHIP BY VSAM CATALOGS

In a VSAM catalog system, there are certain principles of volume ownership which apply to a VSAM catalog, whether it be a Master or a user catalog:

1. A VSAM catalog *owns* any volume on which reside VSAM objects defined in that catalog (the objects have entries contained in that catalog).
2. A VSAM catalog owns such a volume *exclusively*: no VSAM object defined in some other catalog, say CATy, may reside on the volume owned by some particular catalog, call it CATx; thus all VSAM objects on a volume owned by CATx must be defined in CATx. We say that volumes *may not be shared by multiple VSAM catalogs* (this applies only, remember, to Enhanced VSAM, not to the 'new VSAM,' DF/EF).
3. A single VSAM catalog may own, exclusively, multiple volumes: indeed, a VSAM catalog owns all volumes on which reside any VSAM object(s) defined in that catalog.

There are several points to note concerning the above principles of VSAM volume ownership. First, the ownership of a volume by VSAM *does not in any way preclude OS (non-VSAM) data sets from residing on that volume* (as long as there is sufficient space other than that occupied by VSAM objects).

Second, it follows from the above that, for any particular VSAM object, it is defined in one and only one VSAM catalog: this is whatever VSAM catalog owns the volume on which the object resides, or is to reside. Thus, for any specific volume, we speak of the (one and only) *owning (VSAM) catalog* for that volume. All VSAM objects co-resident on that volume must therefore be cataloged in one and the same owning VSAM catalog.

Third, a data set name must be unique *within* any one VSAM catalog (no duplicate names), but two or more different VSAM data sets may have the same data set name as long as they are each cataloged in different VSAM catalogs.

In business applications, it is important to note that VSAM volume ownership is exploited heavily to implement what we have called in an earlier discussion (Section 4.3) *private area catalogs*. Separate project/areas of an installation generally have their own user catalog or, occasionally, more than one user catalog; this private area catalog would own one or more DASD volumes exclusively: only VSAM objects belonging to or serving that one project/area would be cataloged in the private area catalog, and only such VSAM objects could be stored on any of the owned volumes. Thus, users within each distinct project/area of an installation learn what user catalog they must use for their project/area data sets and what volumes the catalog owns, which then become the project/area 'private packs.' As we shall see later, this very useful and widely exploited aspect of VSAM volume ownership is not available under the new VSAM.

5.2   HOW CATALOGS ARE SPECIFIED TO VSAM AND OS

There are three techniques for identifying VSAM catalogs in the JCL statements of a job processing VSAM objects, whether this is an IDCAMS job or a user application job. Generally, only one technique is used within any job.

5.2.1   JOBCAT and STEPCAT JCL DD Statements

These two DD statements are used in JCL only for identifying VSAM catalogs. JOBCAT identifies a VSAM catalog for the duration of the job: that is, it refers to the VSAM catalog being used by all steps of a job. It must follow the standard JOB JCL statement and any JOBLIB DD statement, if used.

The STEPCAT DD statement identifies the VSAM catalog being used for a single particular step of a job. STEPCAT must follow the JCL EXEC statement, but need not follow it immediately: it may be placed among, or even after, the DD statements for that step, as long as it precedes the EXEC statement of the next step of the job. However, it is advised that it be coded immediately after the EXEC statement, as this is the most common practice. The form of these statements is straightforward:

```
//JOBCAT    DD DSN=cat-name,DISP=SHR
//STEPCAT   DD DSN=cat-name,DISP=SHR
```

The disposition is generally SHR: VSAM catalogs are typically processed concurrently by multiple users; it is rare and only under highly specialized circumstances that a user will require exclusive access to a VSAM catalog, so DISP=OLD should not be coded.

Both DD statements may be used in the same job, as in Figure 5-1. Here, the JOBCAT DD statement applies to all steps of the job, except if overridden explicitly by a STEPCAT statement in any step: it is so overridden in STEP3, where the coded STEPCAT indicates that *for that step only*, the VSAM catalog FINCAT is to be used, while the catalog TRUCAT is to be used elsewhere (STEP1, STEP2, and STEP4). Thus, VSAM would locate the VSAM data sets KSDS01, KSDS02, and KSDS04 by accessing their catalog entries in TRUCAT, and KSDS03 by accessing its entry in FINCAT; these entries would provide the needed VOLUME information (among much else). Note that the catalogs themselves are assumed to be user catalogs, and they are located by VSAM through their entries in the Master Catalog—there is no need to code a JOBCAT or STEPCAT statement for the Master Catalog, as it

```
// JOB . . .
//JOBCAT DD DSN=TRUCAT,DISP=SHR
//STEP1  EXEC PGM= . . .
//DD1A   DD DSN=KSDS01,DISP=SHR
   .
   .
//STEP2  EXEC PGM= . . .
//DD2A   DD DSN=KSDS03,DISP=SHR
   .
   .
//STEP3   EXEC PGM= . . .
//STEPCAT DD DSN=FINCAT,DISP=SHR
//DD3A    DD DSN=KSDS03,DISP=SHR
   .
   .
//STEP4   EXEC PGM= . . .
//DD4A    DD DSN=KSDS04,DISP=SHR
   .
   .
```

Figure 5-1. JOBCAT and STEPCAT DD statements.

```
// JOB . . .
//STEPX EXEC PGM= . . .
//STEPCAT DD DSN=TRUCAT,DISP=SHR
//          DD DSN=FINCAT,DSIP=SHR
//DD1       DD DSN=ESDS01,DISP=SHR
//DD2       DD DSN=ESDS02,DISP=SHR
```

Figure 5-2. Concatenating user catalogs.

is searched automatically by VSAM. If, for instance, KSDS01, KSDS02, and KSDS04 all resided on volume TRU008, and KSDS03 on FIN005, then these two volumes must be owned by the VSAM catalogs TRUCAT and FINCAT, respectively.

CONCATENATING USER CATALOGS

There are instances in which we may need to identify more than one VSAM catalog, either for a single job step or for the entire job. Consider the coding of Figure 5-2. Note the coding of the DD statement after the STEPCAT statement: the absence of a ddname makes this a *concatenation* of two data sets, namely the VSAM catalogs TRUCAT and FINCAT; this assures that after VSAM searches the TRUCAT catalog for a data set it will, if the entry is not found there, automatically then search FINCAT for the entry. Note that if the entry is not found in either catalog, VSAM will search the Master Catalog by default (as noted in our discussion below), generating an error if the entry is still not found.

The reason for the concatenation in this case is that the VSAM data set ESDS01 referred to in the DD1 statement is cataloged in TRUCAT, while ESDS02 (see DD2) is cataloged in FINCAT; thus we are required to identify *both* catalogs for this step, since not all of the catalog entries needed to locate the data sets of this one step are contained in a single catalog. (We could have also used a JOBCAT concatenation, but this is less appropriate since we are dealing only with a single step job.)

WARNING

It would be *incorrect* to try to accomplish the same objective as that of the JCL coding just examined by using a JOBCAT statement to refer to one catalog (say, TRUCAT) and a STEPCAT statement to refer to the other (FINCAT): the STEPCAT statement *overrides* the JOBCAT statement, so that after VSAM searches for the target entry in the STEPCAT catalog (TRUCAT), it *will not* search the JOBCAT catalog (FINCAT) *at all in the same step as that for which the STEPCAT statement was coded*. It is important to remember that, for any single given step, VSAM searches *either* the STEPCAT or the JOBCAT identified catalog, never both. Thus, if a single step must refer to multiple VSAM objects defined in multiple VSAM catalogs, then a concatenated JOBCAT or STEPCAT DD statement must be coded identifying all of the catalogs involved.

SUGGESTION

When coding a concatenated JOBCAT or STEPCAT DD statement, it is recommended that the DD statements be in an order such that the first catalog identified is the one most frequently searched, and the last catalog identified being the least frequently searched, and any intermediate ones falling off according to this ordering scheme. The reason is simple: VSAM will search the catalogs in the order of the DD statements encountered, so that we can assist VSAM to do the least amount of searching by coding earlier those catalogs which are most heavily used. If the most heavily referred-to catalog were the last of the concatenation, then VSAM would often be searching the previously coded catalogs unnecessarily.

5.2.2   The AMS CATALOG Parameter

The second technique for identifying VSAM catalogs is through the use of the *CATALOG* parameter on certain commands in an IDCAMS job, most notably on the DEFINE, ALTER, DELETE, and LISTCAT commands. This is clearly a technique possible only when an IDCAMS job is involved, but is an alternative to the JOBCAT/STEPCAT technique in such cases. Yet although it is often the case that either can be used, they are not always interchangeable: consider a job that is to list catalog entries from a VSAM catalog that is password-protected, as in Figure 5-3. The first technique of catalog identification — using JOBCAT/STEPCAT — could not handle this case, since there is no DD statement parameter for specifying password information. Here the CATALOG parameter had to be used, providing the name of the catalog and the required password (in this example, an 8-byte character string).

```
// JOB . . .
//STEPX EXEC PGM=IDCAMS
     .
     .
//SYSIN DD *
    LISTCAT -
          ENTRIES (TRUCAT.TSUSER01.MSTRV001) -
               ALL -
                    CATALOG (TRUCAT/password)
/*
```

Figure 5-3. Catalog specification using CATALOG parameter.

WARNING

Note that the omission of JOBCAT/STEPCAT in a job like this requires that the volume on which the TRUCAT catalog resides is physically mounted, that is, that it is either a permanently resident volume or a reserved volume; VSAM will dynamically allocate the volume in this case. If, however, the catalog's volume were not physically mounted at the time, or could not be assured of being so mounted, then in addition to the CATALOG parameter (needed to specify the password), we would also have to add a JOBCAT or STEPCAT DD statement, even though such a statement only adds disposition information over and above the information provided on the CATALOG parameter. This is a VSAM JCL requirement.

SUGGESTION

The rules that govern under what circumstances a JOBCAT/STEPCAT DD statement is required in addition to the CATALOG parameter are complex and command-dependent (different for the DELETE command than for the LISTCAT or DEFINE commands, etc.). Rather than grappling with them and risking the possibility of omitting the JOBCAT or STEPCAT statement in some specialized case when required, coding JOBCAT or STEPCAT whenever using the CATALOG parameter in an IDCAMS job is always recommended: this will never be in error, at worst being redundant, but completely safe and simple.

5.2.3 The High-Level-Qualifier (HLQ) Technique

The third technique for catalog identification applies only to MVS systems, but in those systems is perhaps the most widely used of the three approaches. It is generally known as the HLQ (high-level-qualifier) technique, for reasons which will become obvious in a moment. When used, it is an alternative to supplying catalog identification through JOBCAT/STEPCAT or CATALOG parameter specification. Here's how it works.

The catalog is identified *implicitly* in the entryname (data set name, object name, etc.) of the VSAM object itself, by using a *qualified* (multipart) name whose *high-level-qualifier* (the leftmost part of the name preceding the first period of the name) is either: (1) the name of the user catalog to be identified, which must be the catalog in which the data set is defined, or, (2) a valid *alias* for that catalog. An *alias* is an alternate entryname for a VSAM user catalog (or a non-VSAM data set, but this latter usage is rare and will not be discussed further). It allows for any user catalog to be known by both the name by which it was originally defined (through a DEFINE UCAT command)—its *define-name*—and also by any of several possible aliases explicitly defined for the user catalog. Aliases are defined for a user catalog by issuing a DEFINE ALIAS command for each alias to be used; this is almost invariably done by systems programming or technical support staff, rather than by application programmers, as this is considered a systems administrative function. The form of the command is given by illustration below:

```
DEFINE ALIAS -
     (NAME (TRUCAT) -
     RELATE (PACIFIC.TRUST.UCAT01) -
     CATALOG (AMASTCAT/MASTERPW))
```

Here the define-name of the user catalog is given in the RELATE parameter of the AMS DEFINE ALIAS command: PACIFIC.TRUST.UCAT01, the first (UCAT01) of possibly several user catalogs for use by the TRUST area of PACIFIC National Bank. Rather than having programmers have to explicitly specify this cumbersome define-name, in either a JOBCAT/STEPCAT statement or in a CATALOG parameter (when an IDCAMS job is involved), or possibly in both under certain circumstances, the DEFINE ALIAS command is used to define an alternate name to this catalog, namely the alias TRUCAT. After this command is successfully issued, programmers may implicitly identify this catalog simply by making the high-level-qualifier of the entryname for any VSAM object defined in this catalog the same as the alias TRUCAT. Thus, a cluster name such as

```
TRUCAT.TSUSER01.MSTRV001
```

implicitly (no JOBCAT/STEPCAT or CATALOG parameter) identifies the owning catalog for this cluster as TRUCAT, itself an alias for PACIFIC.TRUST.UCAT01; similarly, the JCL DD statement

```
//DDX DD DSN=TRUCAT.TSUSER01.MSTRV001,DISP=SHR
```

is by itself sufficient to identify both the data set *and simultaneously* the owning catalog in a single reference.

Another use of this facility is to allow multiple areas/projects to use the same user catalog, but maintain at the same time their own individual naming conventions for their data sets. Say that users and programmers in the Custody area of the installation need to share use of the catalog PACIFIC.TRUST.UCAT01 with users and programmers in the Trust area; we can issue another DEFINE ALIAS command

and create CUSTCAT as a second (along with TRUCAT) alias of this same user catalog PACIFIC.TRUST.UCAT01. Then Custody area users can create and process data sets cataloged in PACIFIC.TRUST.UCAT01 by simply using CUSTCAT as the high-level-qualifier when referring to data sets by either entryname in IDCAMS jobs, or dsname in JCL references. Thus, both of these cluster names implicitly identify one and the same user catalog as their owning catalog:

```
TRUCAT.TSUSER01.MSTRV001
CUSTCAT.TSUSER30.PAYV006
```

(these are *two distinct* data sets.)

Furthermore, the HLQ technique can, and often is, used to implement a *synonym* facility for data set names: two different names for one and the same data set, allowing individual naming conventions by different areas/projects to resolve to identical objects. Thus, we can have

```
TRUCAT.TSUSER01.MSTRV001
```

and

```
CUSTCAT.TSUSER01.MSTRV001
```

as alternate names used by Trust area users and Custody area users, respectively, to reference the same VSAM data set: the same, because the data set names differ only in their high-level-qualifiers, and these are both synonyms for the one user catalog whose define-name is PACIFIC.TRUST.UCAT01.

Note also in this connection that TRUCAT and CUSTCAT are now valid forms of reference to the user catalog PACIFIC.TRUST.UCAT01 in all VSAM contexts; so, for example, if we wanted to list the entire contents of this user catalog, we could code any of these commands as shown in Figure 5-4.

```
(1)    LISTCAT -
            CATALOG (PACIFIC.TRUST.UCAT01/CATPSWD) -
               ALL

(2)    LISTCAT -
            CATALOG (TRUCAT/CATPSWD) -
               ALL

(3)    LISTCAT -
            CATALOG (CUSTCAT/CATPSWD) -
               ALL
```

Figure 5-4. Equivalent LISTCAT commands using catalog truename and aliases.

5.3   THE CATALOG ORDER OF SEARCH

For any given job step, VSAM searches the one or more catalogs involved in a fixed sequence, known as the *catalog search order*. The precise rules are quite complex and are dependent on the nature of the AMS service being requested: the rules are somewhat different for the commands ALTER, DEFINE, DELETE, and LISTCAT (among others), but the basic order is generally the following (the programmer rarely needs any more detailed knowledge about catalog search order), given in first to last sequence:

1. the catalog specified on the CATALOG parameter of an AMS command;
2. the catalog specified on the STEPCAT DD statement, or on the JOBCAT DD statement if no STEPCAT statement exists for the job step (including any additional catalog referenced in a concatenated DD statement, if any); if both STEPCAT and JOBCAT DD statements are present, STEPCAT overrides (for that step) the JOBCAT statement, so that only the STEPCAT-identified catalog is searched;
3. the catalog *implicitly* specified by the high-level-qualifier (HLQ) of the entry-name of a VSAM object, if and only if the HLQ is either the name of, or a valid alias for, some user catalog (which must therefore have a user catalog *connector*, or pointer, entry in the VSAM master catalog);
4. the VSAM Master Catalog, which is always implicitly known to VSAM in any VSAM job processing, without requirement of any DD statement or CATALOG parameter referring to it.

If a reference to a VSAM object is made in a job, and the entryname is not located by VSAM after exhausting the above process in the order given, an error statement is returned by VSAM to the user which indicates *entry not found*; no further processing is allowed by VSAM after such an error.

Furthermore, VSAM observes the above catalog search order when a VSAM object is first being created; thus, if we are first defining a cluster (through the DEFINE CLUSTER command), VSAM will catalog the cluster in whatever catalog is encountered first in this search order.

WARNING

Consider the coding in Figure 5-5. We have coded a JOBCAT DD statement here because STEP1 and STEP3 both need to reference the FINCAT user catalog (of the installation's Financial area); however, STEP2 of the job is creating a VSAM cluster, to be cataloged not in FINCAT, but in TRUCAT, which is the HLQ of the cluster's name. Had there been no JOBCAT statement needed, there would be no problem with this coding and VSAM would have, as intended, created the cluster and cataloged it in TRUCAT. But VSAM observes the catalog search order in a case like this (there are multiple catalogs involved), and by the rules of that order (given

```
// JOB . . .
//JOBCAT DD DSN=FINCAT,DISP=SHR
//STEP1  EXEC PGM= . . .
       .
       .
//STEP2  EXEC PGM=IDCAMS
       .
       .
//SYSIN DD *
     DEFINE CLUSTER -
          (NAME (TRUCAT.TSUSER01.MSTRV001) -
       .
       .
/*
//STEP3  EXEC PGM= . . .
       .
       .
```

Figure 5-5. A problem with VSAM JOBCAT DD statement.

above), VSAM, when processing STEP2 of the job, will access the JOBCAT-identified catalog (FINCAT) before the HLQ-identified catalog (TRUCAT) and will therefore catalog the cluster in FINCAT, rather than in TRUCAT as intended.

The solution: do not code any JOBCAT DD statement. Rather, code two separate STEPCAT DD statements, one for STEP1 and the other for STEP3 of the job, both referring to the same FINCAT user catalog. STEP2, left unchanged, will now correctly cause the created cluster to be cataloged in TRUCAT, since for *that* step there is—in the VSAM catalog search order—no JOBCAT/STEPCAT statement to be encountered earlier than the HLQ-identified catalog.

Another solution, better still, would be to not use JOBCAT/STEPCAT statements at all, and have all steps identify the appropriate catalogs to be referenced through use of the HLQ technique: for example, if STEP1 needs to refer to some data set cataloged in FINCAT, then—if FINCAT is a valid alias of the define-name of the requisite user catalog—simply use data set names of the form:

```
FINCAT._____._____...
```

Remember, the HLQ technique is used only in MVS systems.

6

AN INTRODUCTION TO USING IDCAMS

6.1 INVOKING THE IDCAMS PROCESSOR

The reader has already been presented with a brief and basic introduction to IDCAMS (see Section 3.5: *Access Method Services* (*AMS*): *The IDCAMS Processor*). In this chapter, we will extend and complete that earlier treatment. This section in particular will take up the matter of invoking the IDCAMS Command Processor.

6.1.1 Region Size For IDCAMS Execution

VSAM applications, like those of other access methods, execute in the user region (within the Private Area) of the user's Address Space. Storage for the following must be available within this user region when executing an IDCAMS utility job: (1) VSAM buffers, (2) VSAM control blocks, (3) control blocks and buffers owned by non-VSAM system components providing service in the user region. For a standard IDCAMS job, storage sufficient for (1) and (2) is approximately 220K (MVS environment). For (3) above, approximately 100K is generally sufficient, giving:

(1) and (2)	$\rightarrow$	220K
(3)	$\rightarrow$	100K
Min. Region	$=$	320K

Thus, the execute statement for a typical IDCAMS job would be:

```
//  EXEC PGM=IDCAMS,REGION=320K
```

Certain special IDCAMS functions, given the work they perform, require additional storage. These special functions and their storage requirements are given below:

BLDINDEX (External Sort only)	$\rightarrow$	170K
EXPORTRA	$\rightarrow$	445K
RESETCAT	$\rightarrow$	270K

Furthermore, there is relatively fixed storage overhead for both Catalog Management and Record Management control blocks. Catalog Management control

VSAM buffers and control blocks	$\rightarrow$	220K
System Component storage	$\rightarrow$	100K
Catalog Management control blocks	$\rightarrow$	4k
Record Management control bocks	$\rightarrow$	8.5K*
Region Size	=	332.5K
* 7.3 K + ((strno $-$ 1) $\times$ 1.2K)	=	
7.3 K + ((3 $-$ 1) $\times$ 1.2K)	=	
7.3 K + 1.2K	=	8.5K

Figure 6-1. Estimating VSAM region size.

blocks require approximately 4K of storage. Record Management control block requirements are dependent on two factors: cluster type and string number (number of concurrent requests supported against the data set). The following formulas can be used to obtain a good approximation of these storage requirements:

Catalog Management	$\rightarrow$	4K
KSDS	$\rightarrow$	7.3K + ((strno $-$ 2) $\times$ 1.2K)
ESDS or RRDS	$\rightarrow$	3.8K + ((strno $-$ 1) $\times$ 1.2K)

The reader should remember that the strno defaults are 2 for a KSDS and 1 for an ESDS or an RRDS.

Let's take an example, shown in Figure 6-1, using a standard KSDS, assuming a strno of 3 (1 greater than the default). Therefore, we would code for this job:

```
//  EXEC PGM=IDCAMS,REGION=334K
```

(after rounding up to the next integral even K value).

6.1.2 The SYSIN Control Data Set

The control data set for an IDCAMS job is SYSIN. This data set will contain the AMS commands to be passed by the IDCAMS command processor to AMS. It need not be an in-stream (DD *) data set, but may be any file which contains the proper command coding (disk, tape, etc.).

6.2 COMMAND SYNTAX

6.2.1 Basic Form

The basic syntax of an AMS command is:

command separator(s) parm1 separator(s) parm2 . . . terminator

Command: This is the AMS command keyword itself (REPRO, DELETE, etc.).

Separator: One or more separators are required between the command and its parameters, where the separator may be a comma or one or more blanks. For certain commands, the separator may be parentheses (these cases will be shown explicitly wherever they occur in the text). In this case, no blanks are required either before or after either parenthesis.

Terminator: This may be either a semicolon (;), or the absence of any continuation mark; in this latter case, the terminator is simply null. This is the most commonly encountered form of command termination: it is very rare to see an explicit terminator like a semicolon used in IDCAMS coding.

Parameters (parm*n*, where *n* equals sequential parameter number): These may be either *keyword* or *positional*. Both types of parameters are illustrated in the following command:

```
DELETE -
            ‹entryname› -
            PURGE
```

The entryname (a cluster name, etc.) of the object to be deleted is given as the first, positional, parameter after the DELETE command itself. After this positionally defined parameter follow the keyword parameters, if any. In this case there is one keyword parameter, PURGE, used to indicate that the delete operation should be effected regardless of retention period or expiration date protection on the object. There are also *subparameters* which may be associated with a parameter.

```
DELETE -
              ‹entryname› -
              CATALOG(TRUCAT/'&IGG++++')
```

Here CATALOG is a (keyword) parameter, with two subparameters, both positional: the first is the name of the catalog (here, TRUCAT) containing the target of the deletion, the second being the catalog's password; the password is enclosed in quotes because it contains special characters: '&' and '+'. The reader should consult the appropriate AMS reference manual for the fine details of special characters and related issues; use of special characters is generally discouraged.

6.2.2 The Entryname Subparameter

The entryname subparameter, used in most AMS commands, follows these restrictions:

Length: 1 to 44 characters, drawn from the sets given in Table 6-1.

Table 6-1. Allowable characters in entryname.

Alphameric	A-Z, 0-9	
National	@ , $, #	
Special Characters	ampersand	[&]
	asterisk	[*]
	blank	[ ]
	braces*	[( )]
	brackets*	[[ ]]
	comma	[,]
	equal sign	[=]
	hyphen	[-]
	parenthesis*	[( )]
	period	[.]
	plus sign	[+]
	semicolon	[;]
	single quote	[']
	slash	[/]

*Left or right.

Lead character: The first character of the entryname must be either *alphabetic* (A-Z only, *not alphameric* which includes numbers) or *national*.

Format: Two entryname formats are supported. In an *unqualified* format, the entryname is a single-part name (containing no periods) of one to eight characters, for example:

MSTRFILE.

In a *qualified* format, the entryname is a multipart name, with each part—known as a *qualifier*—separated by a period from an adjacent part; each such qualifier may be up to eight characters in length, with the entire entryname a maximum of 44 characters *including the periods*. An example of an qualified entryname, with three qualifiers, is:

TRU.TSUSER01.MSTRFILE.

Here, the first qualifier—the high-level-qualifier or HLQ—may indicate a particular project or area of the commercial installation that the programmer works in; for example, the *TRUST* area of a bank or brokerage house. Similarly, we might use *CUST* as the HLQ for VSAM applications within the bank's CUSTODY area, etc. The second qualifier may identify in some way the programmer owning the file if this is a test file created and controlled primarily by one programmer; here this might be the TSO ID of such a programmer (TSUSER01). The third qualifier may be a descriptor of the file itself (MSTRFILE). VSAM itself imposes no constraints (other than syntactic: characters, length, placement of periods, etc.) on the number or interpretation of the various qualifiers of a qualified entryname. Either each programmer freely chooses whatever conventions s/he sees fit, or—and this is far more likely—the installation adopts general conventions which apply to all VSAM applications at the site (we return to this issue of *naming conventions* again below).

6.2.3   Command Continuation

An entire AMS command, with the appropriate parameters, subparameters, and values coded would typically be longer than a line with its default margins of 2 and 72, especially for complex commands like DEFINE; in AMS syntax, the hyphen [-] is used to indicate command continuation. As we have already seen, it is coded at the end of each line to be continued, with at least one preceding blank:

```
DELETE -
        CUSTODY.TEST.ACTIVITY.MSTRFILE -
            ERASE -
            PURGE
```

A number of points should be noted here. First, the last line—as makes sense—has no continuation character. Second, even though it would have been possible in this case to code the entire command syntax on a single 70 character line, a convention common in VSAM environments is being followed instead. This convention is to code the command keyword(s) and each of the parameters on a separate line for ease-of-readability and to facilitate changes to the coding, since changes would be localized to just those lines that require them, leaving the remainder of the coding unaffected. Third, indentation is used to reflect the 'logical structure' of the command in some natural way: DELETE, the command keyword is at the highest logical level, the entryname CUSTODY.TEST.ACTIVITY.MSTRFILE at the next logical level, being the object of the command (the target of the deletion), and finally the parameters ERASE and PURGE are at the lowest logical level together, specifying, as they do, special options of the command. (These options and the DELETE command are covered in detail in Chapter 9; here they are used solely to illustrate AMS command coding principles.) AMS also has a *value continuation* character: a plus sign [+] can be used to interrupt a value (like the entryname of CUSTODY.TEST. ACTIVITY.MSTRFILE) on one line and continue it onto another, but we feel that this is, in general, inadvisable practice: always code a complete parameter and its value together on a single line to avoid the need for value continuation, which compromises readability of coding.

6.3   FUNCTIONAL COMMANDS: AN INTRODUCTION

There are two classes or types of AMS commands: the more familiar *functional commands* which request basic AMS services and facilities (like REPRO, DELETE,

DEFINE, etc.), and those which control the execution of functional commands in various ways, the *execution-control commands* (these are typified by IF . . . THEN . . . ELSE, and will be discussed in Section 6.4 of this chapter). We now turn to several basic functional commands to illustrate utilizing IDCAMS to request common AMS services and facilities.

6.3.1 The Print Command

The AMS PRINT command is used to print the contents of VSAM, ISAM, or SAM (OS QSAM) data sets. Parameter options allow selective printing of only parts of a data set instead of the entire data set, and allow choice over the format of the output listing. Let's start by looking at a basic example, shown in Figure 6-2.

DISCUSSION
(Numbers refer to line numbers in Figure 6-2.)

3. This statement identifies the owning catalog: the catalog containing the entry for the data set we wish to print (the *target* data set); here it is a catalog within an Investigations Department of a bank, and resides in the Test(ing) Data Center of the installation.

4. This is, as we observed in earlier discussions, the data set to which output from the command processor, IDCAMS, is sent: error messages, completion codes, and actual requested output (here, the print listing of the contents of the target data set). This SYSPRINT data set is required in all IDCAMS jobs.

5. This is the DD statement identifying the data set to be printed; the DDNAME (here, TARGETDS) is programmer-chosen. Generally, only the data set name (here, CUSTODY.TEST.ACTIVITY.MSTRFILE) and the disposition (SHR) need be given. Shared control is generally the disposition coded for VSAM data sets, with some specialized exceptions which we will always note wherever appropriate in the discussion.

6. The SYSIN data set is the control file for any IDCAMS job, and contains the AMS commands requesting AMS services.

7. The PRINT AMS command keyword.

```
1.    // JOB ...
2.    // EXEC PGM=IDCAMS
3.    //STEPCAT  DD DSN=INVEST.TEST.CAT,DISP=SHR
4.    //SYSPRINT DD SYSOUT=A
5.    //TARGETDS DD DSN=CUSTODY.TEST.ACTIVITY.MSTRFILE,
      //          DISP=SHR
6.    //SYSIN    DD *
7.       PRINT -
8.             INFILE (TARGETDS) -
9.                CHAR
10.   /*
```

Figure 6-2. Sample PRINT command.

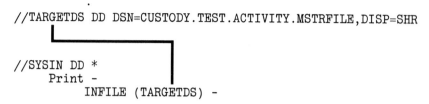

```
//TARGETDS DD DSN=CUSTODY.TEST.ACTIVITY.MSTRFILE,DISP=SHR


//SYSIN DD *
     Print -
          INFILE (TARGETDS) -
```

Figure 6-3. DD statement and PRINT INFILE parameter relationship.

8. The INFILE parameter of the PRINT command identifies to IDCAMS the target data set to be printed, by virtue of specifying as the parameter value the DDNAME—not the data set name—of the JCL DD statement in the IDCAMS JCL job stream (our statement 5) which references the target data set. The connection between the AMS command coding and the JCL is therefore as shown in Figure 6-3.

In an MVS environment, using the INFILE parameter of the PRINT command is one of two different techniques for identifying the target data set to the IDCAMS processor; the second technique will be detailed below.

9. The printed listing of the target data set contents may be elected by the programmer in one of three possible formats/representations. These are:

CHAR: The contents are to be printed only in character form; in this case, if the contents contain any data not having a character representation—packed decimal data, for example—then IDCAMS will print periods [.] in those untranslatable character positions. This choice (CHAR) is fine for data sets which contain wholly, or primarily, character data, but will not display any genuinely numeric data. To capture numeric data in the printed listing, the programmer must use one or the other of the two remaining formats defined below.

HEX: The contents, regardless of data type, are to be printed strictly in hexadecimal representation. The HEX option can be used when one wants to work only in hex, knowing much of the data is numeric and would not be displayed if character representation were used; system dump-level debugging would be a case in point.

DUMP: This gives the best of both worlds simultaneously: both the hex representation is given, along with a character transliteration of nonnumeric data, with periods *within the character portion of the printed listing* again used for character-untranslatable data. The printed listing will be formatted in system dump format: eight columns of four bytes each (equal to eight hex digits) across the page, followed on the right by the character transliteration of those 32 bytes. This format gives maximum information and flexibility

```
1.   // JOB ...
2.   //STEPCAT DD DSN=INVEST.TEST.CAT,DISP=SHR
3.   // EXEC PGM=IDCAMS
4.   //SYSPRINT DD SYSOUT=A
5.   //SYSIN DD *
6.        PRINT -
7.             INDATASET (CUSTODY.TEST.ACTIVITY.MSTRFILE)
8.   /*
```

Figure 6-4. PRINT command using INDATASET parameter.

when significant volumes of numeric data are involved, or again when working in dump-type situations, the character transliteration being a helpful fast guide to the character data of the data set. If the format option is not coded on the PRINT command—it is optional—then the *default is DUMP*; therefore, code CHAR or HEX only if you wish to override the default.

Alternative technique for identifying target of print (MVS only).
In an MVS environment only, the data set to be printed may be identified to IDCAMS by an alternative technique to that of using the INFILE parameter. This technique uses the INDATASET parameter instead. Let's look at the coding, in Figure 6-4, to accomplish the same thing as the IDCAMS job just discussed.

Note that the INDATASET parameter is coded instead of INFILE, with the programmer supplying the value of the parameter in the form of the data set name of the target data set (instead of DDNAME). Notice in particular that, under this technique, *no JCL DD statement* referring to the data set is provided in the IDCAMS job: we say that the target data set is in this case *dynamically allocated*. When using dynamic allocation, the named data set must of course both exist and be cataloged: VSAM requires catalog information to perform the allocation properly. Notice that the term *dynamic allocation* is misleading; VSAM doesn't actually 'allocate' the data set, in the usual OS sense of data set allocation, since the data set already exists (and naturally has been previously allocated space at create-time). In fact, space allocation is not involved at all, but rather a *data set location* process. What actually goes on is the following: VSAM uses the programmer-provided data set name given as the value of the INDATASET parameter and performs a catalog lookup against the specified catalog (here, identified on the STEPCAT DD statement) using this name as the entryname. Once the catalog entry for the target data set is thus obtained, VSAM looks up the volume serial number to ascertain where the data set resides. The data set is now located and the PRINT function can be performed.

Although, clearly, the INDATASET approach is easier to code (requiring no JCL DD statement), our recommendation is to use the INFILE approach: with INFILE, the JCL DD statement referring to the target data set explicitly provides volume serial information, which is absent when using INDATASET; in the latter case, VSAM will learn and know the volser of the data set, but the programmer doesn't. Thus, INFILE is self-documenting. However, if the programmer neither knows nor cares to know at this time volser information, or knows but doesn't care to explicitly provide the volser, then INDATASET may be used.

6.3.2   The LISTCAT Command

The LISTCAT AMS command provides a listing of VSAM catalog entries, as well as of entire VSAM catalogs (except password and security-related information unless proper authorization is established). The command has numerous options which allow highly tailored output in terms of selective listings; these will be covered in detail in later chapters. The only concern here will be the basic format, which will serve in the vast majority of common uses of this command by programmers.

The basic form of the LISTCAT command is used to request the listing of the catalog entry for some one specific VSAM data set. Two parameter keywords are used: ENTRIES, whose value is the name—or names if more than one data set is to be listed—of the target data set, the data set whose catalog entry listing is being requested, and ALL, which indicates that a comprehensive listing is being requested.

Let's look at the coding to request a comprehensive listing for a VSAM data set (see Figure 6-5), and at the resulting output (Figure 6-6, repeated from Figure 4-2).

DISCUSSION
(Numbers refer to line numbers in Figure 6-5.)

7. The ENTRIES parameter identifies the target data set(s); if more than one data set is named, separated by commas, then there will be multiple separate listings generated, but all will be directed to the same SYSPRINT data set. Different listings result depending on the type of entryname used as the value of the ENTRIES parameter. As we will see in Chapter 12, the most useful output is generally that resulting from an entryname which is the *cluster name* of the data set.

8. The ALL parameter requests a comprehensive listing of all catalog information about a data set: its history, statistical information about processing activity against the data set, volume and space allocation information, etc. It is an alternative to a narrower request, effected by coding, say, ALLOCATION instead of ALL to

```
1.    // JOB ...
2.    //STEPCAT DD DSN=INVEST.TEST.CAT,DISP=SHR
3.    // EXEC PGM=IDCAMS
4.    //SYSPRINT DD SYSOUT=A
5.    //SYSIN DD *
6.         LISTCAT -
7.             ENTRIES (STNTESV.STNKANT.KSDS02) -
8.                 ALL
9.    /*
```

Figure 6-5. LISTCAT command with ALL parameter.

obtain only information of that type. Unless, under a special circumstance, one wishes restricted type information, we recommend always coding for a comprehensive listing through the ALL parameter.

Also note that for the IDCAMS job above, no JCL statement is needed referring to the data set whose catalog entry is to be listed. The reason for this is simply that access to the data set is not required for VSAM to obtain LISTCAT information—only access to the catalog. Indeed, the data set need not, in general, even be mounted at the time of the LISTCAT request. We have already given a brief overview of the

```
IDCAMS  SYSTEM SERVICES                              TIME: 22:38:22      12/01/83     PAGE    1

    REPRO -
            INFILE(GSAMDD) -
            OUTFILE(VSAMDD)
IDC0005I NUMBER OF RECORDS PROCESSED WAS 40000
IDC0001I FUNCTION COMPLETED, HIGHEST CONDITION CODE WAS 0

    IF MAXCC = 0 -
       THEN -
                   LISTCAT -
                         ENTRIES(STNTESTV.STNKANT.KSDS02) -
                         ALL
CLUSTER ------- STNTESTV.STNKANT.KSDS02
    IN-CAT --- MVSYSH.MASTER.CATALOG
    HISTORY
        OWNER-IDENT------STNKANT       CREATION----------83.335
        RELEASE----------------2       EXPIRATION--------00.000
      PROTECTION-PSWD-----(NULL)       RACF----------------(NO)
    ASSOCIATIONS
      DATA-----STNTESTV.STNKANT.KSDS02.DATA
      INDEX----STNTESTV.STNKANT.KSDS02.INDEX
      DATA ------- STNTESTV.STNKANT.KSDS02.DATA
        IN-CAT --- MVSYSH.MASTER.CATALOG
      HISTORY
          OWNER-IDENT-------(NULL)       CREATION----------83.335
          RELEASE----------------2       EXPIRATION--------00.000
        PROTECTION-PSWD-----(NULL)       RACF----------------(NO)
      ASSOCIATIONS
        CLUSTER--STNTESTV.STNKANT.KSDS02
      ATTRIBUTES
        KEYLEN-----------------8     AVGLRECL-------------600   BUFSPACE------------9216   CISIZE--------------4096
        RKP--------------------0     MAXLRECL-------------600   EXCPEXITM--------(NULL)     CI/CA----------------120
        SHROPTNS(1,3)   RECOVERY     UNIQUE       NOERASE       INDEXED      NOWRITECHK    NOIMBED      NOREPLICAT
        UNORDERED       NOREUSE      NONSPANNED
      STATISTICS
        REC-TOTAL----------40000     SPLITS-CI-------------0    EXCPS--------------8396
        REC-DELETED-----------0      SPLITS-CA-------------0    EXTENTS---------------7
        REC-INSERTED----------0      FREESPACE-%CI---------10   SYSTEM-TIMESTAMP:
        REC-UPDATED-----------0      FREESPACE-%CA---------0         X'9687BC388771EC20'
        REC-RETRIEVED---------0      FREESPC-BYTES-----217088
      ALLOCATION
        SPACE-TYPE------CYLINDER     HI-ALLOC-RBA----27525120
        SPACE-PRI-------------50     HI-USED-RBA-----27525120
        SPACE-SEC-------------1
      VOLUME
        VOLSER-----------SYS003      PHYREC-SIZE--------4096    HI-ALLOC-RBA----27525120   EXTENT-NUMBER---------7
        DEVTYPE------X'3050200B'     PHYRECS/TRK-----------4    HI-USED-RBA-----27525120   EXTENT-TYPE-------X'00'
        VOLFLAG-----------PRIME      TRACKS/CA------------30
        EXTENTS:
        LOW-CCHH-----X'01F70000'     LOW-RBA---------------0    TRACKS-------------1500
        HIGH-CCHH----X'0228001D'     HIGH-RBA--------24575999
        LOW-CCHH-----X'00150000'     LOW-RBA--------24576000    TRACKS--------------30
        HIGH-CCHH----X'0015001D'     HIGH-RBA--------25067519
        LOW-CCHH-----X'00160000'     LOW-RBA--------25067520    TRACKS--------------30
        HIGH-CCHH----X'0016001D'     HIGH-RBA--------25559039
        LOW-CCHH-----X'003E0000'     LOW-RBA--------25559040    TRACKS--------------30
        HIGH-CCHH----X'003E001D'     HIGH-RBA--------26050559
        LOW-CCHH-----X'003F0000'     LOW-RBA--------26050560    TRACKS--------------30
        HIGH-CCHH----X'003F001D'     HIGH-RBA--------26542079
        LOW-CCHH-----X'00490000'     LOW-RBA--------26542080    TRACKS--------------30
        HIGH-CCHH----X'0049001D'     HIGH-RBA--------27033599
        LOW-CCHH-----X'00430000'     LOW-RBA--------27033600    TRACKS--------------30
        HIGH-CCHH----X'0043001D'     HIGH-RBA--------27525119
```

Figure 6-6. Sample LISTCAT output.

```
INDEX ------ STNTESTV.STNKANT.KSDS02.INDEX
  IN-CAT --- MVSYSH.MASTER.CATALOG
  HISTORY
     OWNER-IDENT-------(NULL)      CREATION----------83.335
     RELEASE---------------2       EXPIRATION--------00.000
  PROTECTION-PSWD-----(NULL)       RACF---------------(NO)
  ASSOCIATIONS
     CLUSTER--STNTESTV.STNKANT.KSDS02
  ATTRIBUTES
     KEYLEN---------------8         AVGLRECL---------------0         BUFSPACE---------------0         CISIZE------------1024
     RKP------------------0         MAXLRECL-----------1017          EXCPEXIT---------(NULL)          CI/CA---------------15
     SHROPTNS(1,3)   RECOVERY       UNIQUE            NOERASE        NOWRITECHK      NOIMBED          NOREPLICAT    UNORDERED
     NOREUSE
  STATISTICS
     REC-TOTAL-----------57         SPLITS-CI--------------0         EXCPS---------------335          INDEX:
     REC-DELETED----------0         SPLITS-CA--------------0         EXTENTS--------------1           LEVELS-----------------2
     REC-INSERTED---------0         FREESPACE-%CI----------0         SYSTEM-TIMESTAMP:                ENTRIES/SECT----------10
     REC-UPDATED----------0         FREESPACE-%CA----------0            X'9687BC388771EC20'          SEQ-SET-RBA------------0
     REC-RETRIEVED--------0         FREESPC-BYTES-------3072                                          HI-LEVEL-RBA--------2048
  ALLOCATION
     SPACE-TYPE--------TRACK        HI-ALLOC-RBA-------61440
     SPACE-PRI-------------4        HI-USED-RBA--------58368
     SPACE-SEC-------------1
  VOLUME
     VOLSER-----------SYS003        PHYREC-SIZE--------1024          HI-ALLOC-RBA-------61440         EXTENT-NUMBER----------1
     DEVTYPE------X'3050200B'       PHYRECS/TRK-----------15         HI-USED-RBA--------58368         EXTENT-TYPE-------X'00'
     VOLFLAG----------PRIME         TRACKS/CA--------------1
     EXTENTS:
     LOW-CCHH-----X'00070011'       LOW-RBA----------------0         TRACKS----------------4
     HIGH-CCHH---X'00070014'        HIGH-RBA-----------61439
        THE NUMBER OF ENTRIES PROCESSED WAS:
                        AIX -----------------0
                        ALIAS ---------------0
                        CLUSTER -------------1
                        DATA ----------------1
                        GDG -----------------0
                        INDEX ---------------1
                        NONVSAM -------------0
                        PAGESPACE -----------0
                        PATH ----------------0
                        SPACE ---------------0
                        USERCATALOG ---------0
                        TOTAL ---------------3
        THE NUMBER OF PROTECTED ENTRIES SUPPRESSED WAS 0
IDC0001I FUNCTION COMPLETED, HIGHEST CONDITION CODE WAS 0
```

Figure 6-6. *(continued)*

LISTCAT output earlier in the text (in Section 4.4: *A Peek at a Catalog Entry*), so we will not need to say anything further at this time; later chapters look at LISTCAT output in greater detail, wherever appropriate.

6.3.3 The REPRO Command

The basic general function of the AMS REPRO command is to copy one data set to another (REPROduce). Hidden within this general function is a world of special-purpose functions; these will be taken up later in the text. There are two key uses of REPRO. The first is a straightforward copy function, copying the contents of a data set into another, the second is a conversion function, converting a data set of a particular type (file organization, like a SAM or ISAM file) into another type (like VSAM). We have already treated and illustrated with a detailed example an IDCAMS job using REPRO for a VSAM-to-VSAM data set copy function (see Section 3.5). Here we will illustrate another IDCAMS job using REPRO, this time for its *file conversion* function, in Figure 6-7.

```
 1.    // JOB ...
 2.    //STEPCAT DD DSN=INVEST.TEST.CAT,DISP=SHR
 3.    // EXEC PGM=IDCAMS
 4.    //SYSPRINT DD SYSOUT=A
 5.    //INDD DD *
       089302165MOORE BUSINESS FORMS            ILLINOISXXXXXX
       760983421MISCO                           NEW JERSEYXXXX
       982307762INMAC                           CALIFORNIAXXXX
       068506388ULTIMATE COMPUTER SUPPLIES      NEW JERSEYXXXX
 6.    /*
 7.    //OUTDD DD DSN=SYSTEM2.TEST.LISTFILE,DISP=OLD
 8.    //SYSIN DD *
 9.        REPRO -
10.            INFILE (INDD) -
11.            OUTFILE (OUTDD)
12.    /*
```

Figure 6-7. REPRO command copying instream data set.

DISCUSSION
(Numbers refer to line numbers in Figure 6-7.)

5. This is the DD statement defining the source data set—the data set that is to be copied, considered to be the input file of the REPRO function. In this case, the source or input file is an instream data set: the records of the file follow immediately the DD * statement. This allows the programmer to load—by copying—a VSAM data set from a small number of records available from the terminal which the programmer may just key in. This is useful for the fast creation of small test VSAM data sets. Clearly, it is not viable for very large numbers of records or for records which are longer than the length permitted as terminal input.

7. This is the DD statement defining the target data set—the data set into which the source records are to be copied. Here, this is a VSAM cluster, which must have been previously created (by the AMS DEFINE command), and hence previously cataloged in a VSAM catalog (referred to in the STEPCAT DD statement). Typically —and this is what is assumed here—the target data set is an empty cluster, with the REPRO being used to first load the cluster with actual records. (It is possible to use REPRO to load records into a nonempty cluster, but this will be discussed in Chapter 9.)

10-11. The INFILE parameter is used to identify the source data set, and the OUTFILE parameter identifies the target data set. Both have as their value the DDNAME of the DD statement in the JCL which refers to the corresponding data set. The reader should note here that the INFILE parameter of the REPRO command is used and coded precisely the same as the INFILE parameter of the PRINT command (see the discussion of that command earlier in this chapter). In addition, like the INFILE parameter, one can choose the alternative INDATASET parameter for MVS systems; the OUTFILE parameter also has an equivalent counterpart: OUTDATASET.

The values of these alternative parameters are the data set names (not DDNAMES) of the corresponding data sets. Using one of these alternative parameters, the coding to accomplish the same result as the IDCAMS job just discussed is given in Figure 6-8.

DISCUSSION
(Numbers refer to line numbers in Figure 6-8.)

9-10. Notice that we again use the INFILE parameter here; this is necessary, since the alternative INDATASET parameter requires a data set name as value and the source file is an instream data set which, by definition, has no data set name. For the target data set, however, we code OUTDATASET instead of OUTFILE, allowing us not to have to provide a JCL DD statement defining the data set to contain the copied records—we simply code the actual data set name of this target file as the value of the parameter. In this case, VSAM will locate the file by obtaining volume serial information from the catalog entry for the file (the catalog itself defined in the STEPCAT DD statement).

Finally, note that, with respect to both IDCAMS jobs above using the REPRO command, we are exploiting the *conversion* facility/function of REPRO: the source data set, being instream, is a sequential data set (I/O performed by a Sequential Access Method: SAM), while the target data set is a VSAM data set. Several other useful conversions are possible using the REPRO command, and these are taken up later in the text.

6.3.4 The DEFINE MCAT/UCAT Commands

Defining the VSAM Master Catalog (MCAT).   As we have already learned, there is one and only one VSAM Master Catalog in a system, while there may be any number of user catalogs. There is both a DEFINE MASTERCATALOG

```
1.    // JOB ...
2.    //STEPCAT DD DSN=INVEST.TEST.CAT,DISP=SHR
3.    // EXEC PGM=IDCAMS
4.    //SYSPRINT DD SYSOUT=A
5.    //INDD DD *
      089302165MOORE BUSINESS FORMS           ILLINOISXXXXXX
      760983421MISCO                          NEW JERSEYXXXX
      982307762INMAC                          CALIFORNIAXXXX
      068506388ULTIMATE COMPUTER SUPPLIES     NEW JERSEYXXXX
6.    /*
7.    //SYSIN DD *
8.      REPRO -
9.        INFILE (INDD) -
10.       OUTDATASET (SYSTEM2.TEST.LISTFILE)
11.   /*
```

Figure 6-8. REPRO using OUTDATASET parameter.

and a DEFINE USERCATALOG (abbreviation: DEF(INE) MCAT/UCAT). The coding and parameters of these two commands are virtually identical, so we will cover only the DEFINE UCAT coding below. In addition, it should be noted here that MVS does not even allow the definition of the VSAM MCAT through the AMS DEFINE MCAT command: if this command is issued, VSAM creates only a user catalog, not a Master Catalog. This is because in MVS the VSAM Master Catalog, which is the MVS *system catalog*, is defined at *system generation (Sysgen)* time. This is done using a sysgen macro instruction known as the DATASET macro; using this macro, the VSAM MCAT is created with a unique name of VSCATLG. The coding would look like this:

```
VSCATLG     DATASET     VSCATLG,SPACE=(CYL,(100,20)),
                        NAME=SYS1.VSCATLG
```

Defining a VSAM USERCATALOG (UCAT).   Although there are many parameters, most optional and specialized, that can be coded to define a UCAT, the basic coding is quite straightforward; see Figure 6-9.

DISCUSSION
(Numbers refer to line numbers in Figure 6-9.)

4. This DD statement defines the volume on which the UCAT is to reside. Note the syntax: only volser, unit, and disposition information is coded; exclusive control should be requested as a disposition (DISP=OLD), not shared control, when defining a VSAM catalog.

8. This parameter works in conjunction with the JCL to inform the IDCAMS processor of location, device type, and disposition information. The value of FILE is the DDNAME of the associated JCL statement (here, VOLX) which refers to where the UCAT is to reside. The volume referred to must not be owned by another VSAM

```
 1.    // JOB ...
 2.    // EXEC PGM=IDCAMS
 3.    //SYSPRINT DD SYSOUT=A
 4.    //VOLX DD VOL=SER=CAT001,UNIT=3380,DISP=OLD
 5.    //SYSIN DD *
 6.         DEFINE UCAT -
 7.              (NAME (INVEST.TEST.CAT) -
 8.              FILE (VOLX) -
 9.              VOL (CAT001) -
10.              CYL (50 10) -
11.              TO (89365) -
12.              RECOVERABLE)
13.    /*
```

Figure 6-9. Defining a user catalog.

catalog; this coding will establish INVEST.TEST.CAT as the exclusive owner of this volume.

9. The value of this VOL(UME) parameter is the explicit volser of the volume on which the UCAT is to reside, and this value must match the volser coded in the JCL DD statement (4, above). This may seem redundant to the reader, and in part it is, but it is the necessary coding nonetheless (we have seen this sort of redundancy before in AMS commands).

10. This is the space allocation requested for the UCAT. (Computations for UCAT space allocation estimates are quite complex, and will not be discussed further; there is a complex worksheet that can be used for estimating a VSAM catalog's space requirements—consult the IBM publications: *Catalog Administration Guide*, Appendix E; and the *VSAM Catalog Administration: Access Method Services Reference*, under the DEFINE USERCATALOG command; exact order numbers and references are given in an appendix therein.)

11. This specifies the retention period for the UCAT: here, it indicates that this UCAT is to be retained until the last day (__365) of the year 1989 (89__); the catalog may be deleted starting in 1990.

12. This parameter is a recovery option, allowing some basic reconstruction of the catalog in the event of damage or loss. VSAM catalogs are commonly defined as *Recoverable*. VSAM backup and recovery are taken up in Chapter 15.

6.4 EXECUTION-CONTROL COMMANDS

The above discussion dealt with AMS functional commands (like PRINT, REPRO, LISTCAT, DEFINE UCAT). As we noted earlier in this chapter, however, there is another class of AMS commands: *execution-control commands*, and we turn to these now in this section. Let's look at a sample IDCAMS job that uses both functional commands and execution-control commands, and brings out most of the major features of this new command type.

Figure 6-10 is a *single-step IDCAMS job*—the IDCAMS command processor is invoked only once through the EXEC statement of step 2—but is additionally a *multistep AMS job*: there are five separate AMS services involved (one REPRO, one PRINT, 2 LISTCATs, and one DELETE). Furthermore, all but the first functional command (REPRO) are conditional on the success or failure of one or more previous commands (AMS steps). The different AMS steps are identified in the job below by AMS comment statements which are coded between the comment delimiters: '/*' on the left and '*/' on the right. The statements of the SYSIN control file (lines 8 through 33 here) are known collectively as the *AMS job stream*.

DISCUSSION
(Numbers refer to line numbers in Figure 6-10.)

9. This is a basic IDCAMS job using the functional command REPRO to create a backup copy of some original VSAM data set (referred to in the INDD DD statement) by copying its records into a previously created (by DEFINE CLUSTER command)

```
 1.    // JOB . . .
 2.    // EXEC    PGM=IDCAMS
 3.    //STEPCAT  DD DSN=TRUCAT,DISP=SHR
 4.    //SYSPRINT DD SYSOUT=A
 5.    //INDD     DD DSN=TRU.TSUSER01.MSTR,DISP=OLD
 6.    //OUTDD    DD DSN=TRU.TSUSER01.MSTR.BACKUP,DISP=OLD
 7.    //SYSIN    DD *
 8.         /***************STEP 1***************/
 9.         REPRO -
10.              INFILE (INDD) -
11.              OUTFILE (OUTDD)
12.         /* PRINT & LISTCAT CONDITIONALLY ON REPRO SUCCESS  */
13.         IF LASTCC EQ 0 THEN -
14.           DO
15.         /****************STEP 2**************/
16.              PRINT -
17.                   INFILE (OUTDD)
18          /****************STEP 3**************/
19.              LISTCAT -
20.                   ENTRIES (TRU.TSUSER01.MSTR.BACKUP) -
21.                        ALL
22.           END
23.         /*** LISTCAT CONDITIONALLY ON REPRO FAILURE ***/
24.         ELSE -
25          /****************STEP 4*************/
26.              LISTCAT -
27.                   ENTRIES (TRU.TSUSER01.MSTR) -
28.                        ALL
29.         /****** DELETE CONDITIONALLY ON SUCCESS ******/
           /****** OF PREVIOUS COMMANDS   ******/
30.         IF MAXCC EQ 0 THEN -
31.         /****************STEP 5*************/
32.              DELETE -
33.                   TRU.TSUSER01.MSTR
34.    /*
```

Figure 6-10. Multistep IDCAMS job.

empty VSAM data set (referred to in the OUTDD DD statement). It uses execution-control commands to perform additional AMS services *conditionally* based on the success or failure of execution of this REPRO operation.

Condition Codes: Every AMS functional command, like REPRO, PRINT, etc., has associated with its execution some one *condition code* which reflects the success or degree of failure encountered by AMS routines when command execution was attempted. These condition codes are assigned by the IDCAMS command processor to each step of an AMS job (which, as we noted above, may have multiple steps) and may be tested directly by the programmer using execution-control commands. The possible condition codes and their meaning are given below.

0—Function executed, no problems encountered.
4—Some problem was encountered in function execution, but execution was continued as far as was possible; however, there is no assurance that the results

of function execution are as intended by the programmer. An example would be if IDCAMS was directed to list a catalog entry (LISTCAT) for some VSAM data set, but no catalog entry for that data set was located. (Generally, a warning message is issued.)

8—Function execution was completed, as far as was possible, but major aspects of the command request as coded by the programmer were bypassed. Results of function execution would not be as intended by the programmer. An example would be if IDCAMS was directed by the programmer coding to delete a data set, but no catalog entry for that data set was located.

12—Function execution was not performed due to serious problems encountered. An example would be if IDCAMS was directed to create a VSAM cluster with a key longer than 255 bytes.

16—A severe error was encountered and the entire AMS job stream (all steps) from the point of error to the end of the job was flushed. Leaving out the SYSPRINT data set for IDCAMS output would be an example of a severe error for which the IDCAMS processor would return a condition code of 16, with no AMS function execution being attempted at all. This is sometimes known as *fatal termination*.

Testing Condition Codes (*LASTCC and MAXCC*): The IDCAMS processor stores the value of the condition code for any AMS functional command and makes the value available for inspection and testing by the programmer through two special variables, LASTCC and MAXCC, which have the following interpretation:

LASTCC Contains the condition code associated with ('returned by') by the immediately preceding (in the AMS job stream) functional command. For the first step of an AMS job stream (the REPRO step 1 in our example), LASTCC (and MAXCC below) is undefined and should not be tested, as there is, by definition, no 'previous' step.

MAXCC Contains the *highest* condition code returned by *any* previous step in the AMS job stream.

We will now see, below, how these two variables are tested in an IDCAMS job (refer, again, to Figure 6-10).

13. This begins the IF-THEN-ELSE execution-control *command sequence*; it explicitly tests LASTCC for a zero condition code, which in effect tests the success of the previous AMS step (step 1), the REPRO command. As only a zero condition code completely assures success of an AMS functional command, this statement indicates that the two AMS functions—the PRINT of step 2 (line 16) and the LISTCAT of step 3 (line 19)—within the scope of the IF clause (between the DO of line 14 and the END of line 22) are to be executed only if the previous REPRO command of step 1 executed completely successfully. If the REPRO function's execution returns a nonzero condition code, indicating at least that some error was encountered, then *both* commands (PRINT and LISTCAT) are to be bypassed. This makes sense. The

PRINT command of line 16 requests a listing of the target file of the REPRO operation, namely the data set TRU.TSUSER01.MSTR.BACKUP (referred to in the OUTDD DD statement of line 6 above) into which AMS was to copy the source records of TRU.TSUSER01.MSTR (referred to in the INDD DD statement of line 5 above); but if the REPRO was in some way not wholly successful, the target file may still be empty. Similarly, if the REPRO failed, then the catalog entry for the target data set may not contain any useful information, or may not have changed since the last time we may have inspected the catalog entry (it is assumed that a LISTCAT would have been done immediately after the data set was created in some previous DEFINE CLUSTER job).

Note the use in lines 14 and 22 of another execution-control facility: the DO-END structure. This serves to *bracket* the intervening code together so that it may be performed or bypassed as a single unit; in this case it is used to indicate that both the PRINT command of line 16 and the LISTCAT command of line 19 are to be performed if the preceding REPRO was successful: we say that both of these commands are *under the scope of* the IF command of line 13. Had we wanted only a single command performed under the scope of the IF, the DO-END brackets would have been unnecessary. Note also that the DO and END are coded without a terminating hyphen: this is the one exception to the rule that continued command lines end with the hyphen; the IDCAMS command processor is prone to misinterpreting the continuation character if coded after DO or END, so it is wise to avoid this.

24. This ELSE clause of the IF-THEN-ELSE indicates that if the condition code of the REPRO step is nonzero (some error encountered), then the catalog entry of the source file is to be listed, as it may provide some clue as to why the REPRO failed. For example, we may have thought that the source file contained data records, but in actual fact—shown possibly by a zero RECTOTAL in the LISTCAT output—it is empty.

30. This IF clause tests the MAXCC variable, and in effect requests that the source file should be deleted if *all* preceding commands that *were to be executed*, were indeed executed successfully, that is, no step returned a condition code higher than zero. (We say *were to be executed*, since with an IF-THEN-ELSE structure, only the commands in the scope of the THEN clause *or* those in the scope of the ELSE clause, but not both, will be executed.) Note that the LASTCC variable could not have been used here, since it would test only the condition code of the immediately preceding step, not of all preceding steps.

SUGGESTION

To simplify the coding of conditionals like the above, the programmer may use MAXCC exclusively: the case of a single step preceding the test point is just a special case of MAXCC, which tests all preceding steps, regardless of how many. We would accordingly change line 13 to read:

```
IF MAXCC EQ 0 THEN -
```

Doing this frees the programmer to deal with only a single type of condition code test, always through MAXCC, rather than two.

TEST OPERATORS

Although we have only used the EQ operator in our code above, any of six possible (comparison) operators may be used, as given in Figure 6-11.

This concludes our discussion of the execution-control commands; although there are actually some other such commands available (SET and PARM), they have limited utility and the interested reader is directed to the *Access Method Services Reference* manual (Chapter 3) for further information.

SUGGESTION

The programmer is advised to always test for the successful execution of an AMS command step in any step (of a multistep AMS job) subsequent to that step: the easiest way to do this is to code

```
IF MAXCC EQ O THEN -
```

before any functional command in every step except the first. It is also advised that an explicit ELSE clause be coded to trap for command failure: minimally, the ELSE clause can request LISTCAT output for the various data sets that were involved in the functional command requests, as this may prove useful in attempting to ascertain what may have gone wrong with the step(s) of the job.

6.5 JCL FOR VSAM DATA SETS

The JCL for referencing VSAM data sets has been presented and discussed above and in previous chapters. Here we discuss the use of only one additional feature: *the AMP parameter*.

```
EQ  or  =
NE  or  =
GT  or  )
LT  or  (
GE  or  )=
LE  or  (=
```

Figure 6-11. Comparison operators.

The AMP parameter is a DD statement parameter used only in conjunction with VSAM data sets. It has three major uses.

1. When using the ISAM Interface Program (IIP), a VSAM file being accessed through the IIP may be defined by a DD statement which contains UNIT and VOL information; to avoid OS mistaking this for an OS file (since VSAM files, apart from a special case like this, don't contain UNIT and VOL parameters), the AMP parameter is coded to signal to OS that this DD statement refers to a VSAM file. In this case, the DD statement is coded as follows, where AMORG is a subparameter of AMP, indicating *A*ccess *M*ethod Services *ORG*anization—in effect a VSAM file.

```
//DDX DD DSN=TRANSFILE,DISP=OLD,UNIT=3380,VOL=SER=FIN001,
//       AMP='AMORG'
```

2. In testing situations, the programmer may require a *dummy* VSAM file—one whose DD statement contains only the DUMMY parameter—to avoid doing any actual I/O against the file. In this case, the file is identified as a VSAM object by this coding:

```
//TRANSDD DD DUMMY,AMP='AMORG'
```

3. Certain parameters whose values are normally left to default, may be overriden explicitly by the programmer through subparameters of the AMP parameter. These are primarily performance-related (buffer allocation: BUFSP, BUFND, BUFNI, and degree of concurrency: STRNO), so we will leave the discussion of AMP coding in this connection to Chapter 18, on performance.

7

VSAM SPACE MANAGEMENT

7.1   THE CONCEPT OF VSAM SPACE

The concept of a *VSAM space* is a relatively novel one to programmers making VSAM's acquaintance for the first time. Unlike OS space, which is seen as a pool of unallocated device space from which allocations are honored, VSAM space is a VSAM *object* like any other (catalogs, data sets, alternate indices, etc.), and so is treated by VSAM much as a file is treated by OS: as an entity with definite boundaries, ownership, and other properties. A VSAM space is cataloged in a VSAM catalog, just as VSAM data sets are (but does not have a programmer-manipulable name).

More strictly, a VSAM space is space on DASD which is owned and managed exclusively by VSAM (with one exception, discussed below). Furthermore, for the most commonly used type of VSAM data set, VSAM space is *pre-allocated*: if one wishes to create a VSAM data set, typically sufficient VSAM space for that, or several, data set(s) must have been priorly reserved for exclusive use by VSAM on whatever volume is to be used; VSAM data sets are thus not stored into OS space, but rather into pre-allocated VSAM space. This will become clearer after we briefly consider VSAM *clusters* and discuss the two different techniques for allocating VSAM space to VSAM objects.

7.2   THE CONCEPT OF A VSAM CLUSTER

A VSAM *cluster* is a VSAM object into which data records *may* be loaded; when a cluster is created it is said to be *unloaded*, that is, initially contains no records. A cluster which, initially empty, is loaded with data records is a (loaded) *VSAM data set*, equivalent to the notion of data set we typically have in OS. Thus, a VSAM cluster represents *reserved* VSAM space for loading records into. Each of the three types of VSAM data sets we have referred to in earlier discussion—KSDS, ESDS, RRDS—is a cluster: a KSDS cluster, an ESDS cluster, etc.

Clusters may be manipulated by AMS commands even if they have never been loaded; thus, it is possible to delete a cluster into which no records were stored at any time (but it is not possible, sensibly enough, to copy an empty cluster). The catalog entry for a cluster may be listed by the programmer at any time subsequent to the initial definition of that cluster, regardless of whether it is loaded or unloaded; if unloaded, the catalog entry will show a zero record count total at that time.

It may be instructive to recall the previous chapter's example of a simple IDCAMS job to copy a VSAM data set. There, the input data set was, necessarily, a loaded cluster, while the output data set was an empty cluster (previously defined to VSAM) into which we wished to copy the input data set's records. Both are VSAM objects priorly cataloged into some VSAM catalog. From this point on we will speak of VSAM data sets and VSAM clusters as equivalent, differentiating the two technically only if necessary.

7.3 HOW VSAM ALLOCATES CLUSTER SPACE

Now let's examine how exactly VSAM space is allocated to a cluster (of whatever type: KSDS, ESDS, RRDS). There are two, and only two allocation techniques in VSAM: *suballocation* and *unique allocation*.

7.3.1 Suballocation

Suballocation is a two-step space allocation process for VSAM clusters. The first step involves a request by VSAM (actually, by the AMS component of VSAM) *to the OS Space Manager—OS DADSM (Direct Access Device Space Manager)*—for OS allocated space to be given to VSAM. This request is made through the AMS command *DEFINE SPACE*, which specifies the unit and volume upon which VSAM space is being requested, and the amount of space (primary and secondary) required. If there is sufficient unallocated OS space on the target volume to satisfy the request, the space is granted to VSAM; thereafter the space ceases to be OS space and is exclusively VSAM's: only VSAM objects may use any part of that VSAM space. The label in the VTOC for this space will have a particular bit set on to indicate (exclusive) VSAM ownership of this space (bit 0 in byte 84 (=X'54') of the Format-4 DSCB).

There are three important points to note here concerning this first stage of the suballocation process. First, OS and VSAM space may co-reside on the same volume, on a strictly separate basis, and the volume is neither exclusively an OS or a VSAM volume (in toto); this is quite common especially with very high storage capacity DASD such as 3380 volumes. Second, more and more space may be requested from OS for VSAM use on any volume, and if available the VSAM space requests would be honored.

Futhermore, the volume may at some point in time become exclusively VSAM's: no OS data sets may be stored on the volume. This could come about in one of two ways. Either the OS space could be eventually consumed through a series of granted VSAM space requests, or at some one time the DEFINE SPACE command which makes the request could explicitly and intentionally ask for *in a single request* a space allocation which represents the entire storage capacity of the volume. An example would be a DEFINE SPACE request for 555 cylinders on a 3350 pack: 555 is the number of usable cylinders of a 3350 DASD. The volume would be a VSAM-only volume if this request were honored, and this is one commonly used technique for effecting just this result.

Finally, any one volume may contain multiple VSAM spaces, but no single VSAM space may span across a volume: that is, the maximum size of a single VSAM space is one DASD volume (of whatever type). These VSAM spaces are, once obtained from OS, thereafter under the control of a VSAM space management facility, and not under OS DADSM control.

Once at least some (minimum, one) VSAM space exists on a volume, it is then possible to carry out the second step of the two-step VSAM suballocation process. This consists of granting to an individual cluster its requested amount of space *from the (aggregate) pool of VSAM-reserved space* within one or more VSAM spaces. The space dedicated solely to the cluster is in this sense *suballocated* from/out of the larger free space within VSAM space. From this it can be seen that a single VSAM space can—and typically does—contain multiple clusters; these multiple clusters within a single such space are said to *co-reside* in that space. Figure 7-1 graphically represents the concept of such suballocation of aggregate space to co-residing clusters.

Let's take an example. At some point in time, a programmer (often a systems programmer) issues a DEFINE SPACE command requesting from OS DADSM 100 cylinders of DASD space on volume VSAM04, a 3380 pack. We can consider this allocation, when granted, as a *VSAM Space Pool* (VSP) residing on volume VSAM04; no OS data sets may be stored within this VSAM space pool: the pool space is reserved exclusively for VSAM use. Furthermore, it is reserved in order to build VSAM clusters within its boundaries: that is, data records *may not* be loaded directly

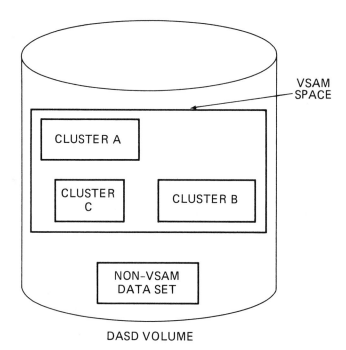

Figure 7-1. VSAM suballocation.

into this VSAM space pool. VSAM clusters must first be created within the VSAM space pool, and then loaded with data records. This VSAM space pool may contain an arbitrary (finite) number of such clusters, each created by a separate DEFINE CLUSTER command. It is possible to create 10 VSAM clusters, each with an allocation of 10 cylinders, or two 50-cylinder clusters, etc. within this VSAM space pool. Each of the VSAM clusters created within the pool is a *suballocated cluster* — one created by the allocation technique known as suballocation. At any time there may exist, therefore, some amount of *unallocated suballocatable VSAM space* within the VSAM space pool.

Now let's assume that this VSAM space pool, which we will hereafter refer to as VSP1, is the only such pool on the VSAM04 volume. If a programmer, immediately after the allocation of VSP1, issues a DEFINE CLUSTER command requesting the creation of a 30-cylinder VSAM cluster on VSAM04, then this cluster will be suballocated from VSP1. A second DEFINE CLUSTER for a 40-cylinder VSAM cluster, also to be allocated on VSAM04, will again be suballocated from VSP1, leaving 30 cylinders of unallocated space within VSP1. A third DEFINE CLUSTER for a 35-cylinder cluster on VSAM04 will fail: there is insufficient remaining space within VSP1 for this suballocation (remember, we are assuming that VSP1 is the only VSAM space pool on this volume). But a subsequent allocation request not exceeding 30 cylinders can be accommodated from within VSP1, and this suballocation process continues until all of the allocated space (100 cylinders) of VSP1 is consumed, or until allocation requests exceed the size of the remaining unallocated space of VSP1. All suballocated clusters of VSP1 therefore co-reside together in VSP1. This process of suballocation is the one most commonly used by the applications programmer.

It should be noted, before we turn to the other VSAM space allocation technique, that there may be several VSAM space pools built on a single volume. Assume there are now two such VSPs on VSAM04: VSP1 and VSP2. Requests for cluster allocations (through DEFINE CLUSTER commands) on VSAM04 may now be satisfied by suballocation within *either* VSP1 or VSP2, assuming both contain sufficient free (unallocated) space for the allocation request(s). Furthermore, for any particular DEFINE CLUSTER request which can be satisfied by either VSAM space pool, VSAM makes the selection through internal rules, and it is not possible for the applications programmer to influence this selection directly.

Finally, let's consider a common misunderstanding concerning the VSAM suballocation process. Assume a programmer runs a two-step job, the first step of which issues a (successful) DEFINE SPACE command for creating a VSAM space pool on some volume VOL00x, and the second of which issues a DEFINE CLUSTER command to suballocate a VSAM cluster on the same volume. There is no assurance whatever that the cluster of step two shall be allocated in the VSAM space pool created in the previous step, if there are other VSAM space pools (as there may very well be) on the target volume. VSAM will satisfy the cluster allocation request from any VSP on the volume, as it sees fit.

7.3.2 Unique Allocation

The second method of VSAM space allocation is known as *unique allocation*. With unique allocation, no DEFINE SPACE command is involved at all, but rather the space allocation for a cluster is done in a single step which both creates the needed space for the cluster and creates the cluster within this space and—and this is a critical point—the cluster is *coextensive* with the space it resides in. What this means is that VSAM allocates only and exactly the space requested for the cluster, and thus no other cluster could possibly coreside within this space. So, if a DEFINE CLUSTER is issued for a 30-cylinder cluster *using unique allocation*, precisely 30 cylinders of VSAM space are acquired from OS, and all 30 are committed to the created cluster, which is said to be a *unique cluster*. Space allocation and cluster definition/creation hence occur concurrently, so that the cluster occupies *exhaustively* and *exclusively* the space within which it resides.

7.3.3 Unique Allocation Versus Suballocation: A Comparison

Now let's compare the two VSAM space allocation techniques. Unique allocation is said to be *restrictive*, while suballocation is *unrestrictive*. These are the major restrictions involved with unique allocation:

1. In order to create a unique cluster on some target volume, that volume *must be mounted* at cluster create-time (DEFINE CLUSTER time) for the create to succeed.' This is how it must be, since the space allocation is concurrent with the creation of the cluster. With a suballocated cluster, however, the volume upon which the cluster is to reside need not be mounted at cluster creation time; VSAM knows, through entries in a VSAM catalog, all about the one or more VSAM space pools on the target volume, including how much unallocated space there is in any one such pool. From this knowledge, VSAM can determine if sufficient space to honor the allocation request exists within any VSP on the volume; if it does, than VSAM selects a single VSP to *host* the created cluster.

The creation of the cluster, through the DEFINE CLUSTER command, is *implemented in VSAM wholly by the act of creating a catalog entry for the cluster*, and this—involving only the catalog volume—can clearly be done whether the target volume is mounted or not. Indeed, there are appropriate catalog entries for any VSAM space pool on the volume, and these catalog entries contain all the allocation information VSAM may require for any space *suballocation* request. Remember, with unique allocation, there is no DEFINE SPACE process involved, and hence no pre-allocated VSAM space pool; since the space is allocated only when the cluster is created (it is not pre-allocated), no catalog information exists for VSAM to use to determine space availability on the target volume—VSAM must read this information directly from the volume's VTOC, which is possible only if the volume is mounted.

2. A unique cluster (that is, a uniquely allocated cluster) may not be *reusable*; no such restriction exists on a suballocated cluster. If it is desirable to reuse a cluster

(reopen and overwrite it without first deleting it), then suballocation must be used to create the reusable cluster.

3. A unique cluster may be allocated only in cylinder allocation units; track or record allocation is not supported. A suballocated cluster may be allocated in any unit whatever.

4. A suballocated cluster may have a total allocation of up to 123 extents (one primary, and 122 secondary extents); this is a feature of allocation true only of VSAM data sets. In contrast, OS data sets are restricted to a maximum of 16 extents (one primary, 15 secondary). A unique cluster, like an OS data set, is similarly restricted to 16 extents. Indeed, it is important at this time to understand why this is so, and *necessarily* so. Although we have spoken of two techniques for the allocation of VSAM clusters, namely suballocation and unique allocation, only suballocation is actually handled by VSAM routines themselves. These routines collectively make up *VSAM space management*. Space allocation for unique VSAM clusters is actually under the control of the OS Direct Access Device Space Manager (OS DADSM), not VSAM space management: the request for uniquely allocated space is made *by* VSAM *to* OS DADSM, which carries out the allocation *on behalf of* VSAM. With respect to space allocation, therefore, a unique VSAM cluster is treated as an OS data set. It is for this reason that such clusters have up to but no more than 16 extents— this is the maximum for any data set whose allocation falls under the control of OS DADSM.

5. As a reflex of the above, a unique VSAM cluster is represented directly in the VTOC for the volume on which it is allocated: that is, there is a Format-1 DSCB entry for the data set; if the data set has both a data and an index component, than each component is considered a unique data set, and hence each has a separate F-1 DSCB of its own. This contrasts with a suballocated cluster which has no direct entry in the VTOC: in this case, only the VSAM data space within which the cluster is suballocated has an entry in the VTOC (a Format-1 DSCB, and also one Format-3 DSCB, if the data set has more than three extents). Thus it is possible to derive all space management information about a unique VSAM cluster simply through inspection of the appropriate VTOC entry, while it is only possible to derive general space information concerning the host VSAM data space from the VTOC, but not any information about how the space internal to the host VSAM data space is being used by any resident suballocated clusters. The latter type of information is only available through VSAM catalog entries (which may be displayed through the LISTCAT command).

7.4 CREATING VSAM SPACES: THE DEFINE SPACE COMMAND

With this understanding of space allocation for VSAM clusters, let us now turn to the coding of the DEFINE SPACE command itself, given in Figure 7-2. Throughout this discussion, keep in mind that this command creates a VSAM space pool for *suballocation* only; unique allocation does not involve any such pre-allocated VSAM

```
1.    // JOB . . .
2.    // EXEC PGM=IDCAMS
3.    //STEPCAT   DD DSN=TRUCAT,DISP=SHR
4.    //SYSPRINT DD SYSOUT=A
5.    //TARGET    DD UNIT=3380,VOL=SER=TRU005,DISP=OLD
6.    //SYSIN     DD *
7.       DEFINE SPACE -
8.            (VOL(TRU005) -
9.             FILE(TARGET) -
10.            {TRK/CYL/REC}(pri sec))
11.   /*
12.   //
```

Figure 7-2. DEFINE SPACE command.

space pool at all. Let's discuss the function of these statements in turn. Statements which require no explanation are not discussed.

DISCUSSION
(Numbers refer to line numbers in figure.)

3. This identifies the VSAM catalog that the created VSAM space pool is to be cataloged within—remember, a VSP is treated as a VSAM object and must be cataloged in one specific VSAM catalog, which controls (and 'owns') the VSP.

5. This defines the target volume—the specific volume on which the space is to be created. Note that only UNIT, VOL, and DISP are coded; this is coded as for an *OS* data set (with UNIT and VOL). The DISP=OLD assures exclusive control during the DEFINE SPACE operation. Note further that there is no data set name (DSN) coded. VSAM space pools created by the DEFINE SPACE command may *not* be named; there will automatically be a VSAM-generated name associated with this VSP in the VTOC DSCB (label) for this space. This name will always have the following form:

```
Z999999x.VSAMDSPC.T_____.T_____
```

Here the underscores stand in for seven characters of timestamp-type information, (which can be safely ignored by the programmer); the x has the following interpretation, based on value:

$$x = 2 \rightarrow \text{Suballocatable data space}$$
$$x = 4 \rightarrow \text{Master or user catalog}$$
$$\text{(also suballocatable data space)}$$

7. This is the AMS command for requesting allocation of a VSAM data space.

8/9. The volume on which the allocation is requested is specified in the VOL-(UMES) parameter. The FILE parameter specifies the ddname of the JCL statement which identifies the UNIT and VOL information for the requested allocation (the VOL information is redundant with the VOL parameter).

10. The allocation amount is given in primary and secondary space requested, just as in any other space allocation request. Sufficient space is requested here to hold the anticipated total capacity of the (to be) suballocated clusters from this VSAM data space.

COMMON OPTIONAL PARAMETERS OF THE DEFINE SPACE COMMAND

CANDIDATE: This parameter is coded *instead* of the space allocation unit (CYL, etc.) to (1) reserve the volume(s) specified (VOL) for VSAM to use for future space allocation requests and (2) to assign the ownership of the volume to a specific catalog; no VSAM data space is allocated at this time. This is mainly for facilitating installation management over what volumes are to be controlled by what catalogs. Note that OS data sets are not by the CANDIDATE parameter prohibited from residence on the *candidate volume*: but no catalog other than the specified catalog may control any data sets allocated on the volume.

CATALOG: (catname/pswd): This parameter identifies the catalog which is to own (control) the VSAM data space being created; it is specified if the catalog is not otherwise identified (JOBCAT/STEPCAT not coded), or if the catalog is password-protected, as it permits specification of the required password.

7.5   HOW VSAM SPACE APPEARS TO OS

Let's now, in conclusion, look more precisely at the process of VSAM space allocation, especially as it is perceived from the vantage point of OS DADSM. The process begins with the request for VSAM data space being presented to OS DADSM. OS DADSM begins a search of the set of Format-5 DSCBs associated with the target volume. A F-5 DSCB lists the unallocated extents on the volume; in general, there will be multiple F-5 DSCBs: one for each set of 26 *noncontiguous* extents of unallocated (available) volume space. OS DADSM will choose, if available, the smallest set of extents on the volume sufficient to satisfy the request. A Format-1 DSCB is generated to honor the request, describing the first three extents of the allocation. In the event that the allocation requires more than three extents to be satisfied, a Format-3 DSCB is generated which describes extents 4 to 16. As a VSAM data space is treated as an OS-allocated data set, it may have no more than 16 extents allocated.

At this point a VSAM-generated name is stored into the F-1 DSCB. In addition, bit 3 of byte 93 (X'5D') in the F-1 DSCB is turned on. This is the *Data Set Security Bit*, which provides read and write protection to the VSAM data space, thereby prohibiting access by any non-VSAM access methods. Furthermore, if this is the first VSAM object being created on the volume, then the *VSAM Volume Ownership Bit* is turned on; this bit is located in the Format-4 DSCB (bit 0 of byte 84 (X'54')), known as the *VTOC DSCB*, which describes the device and volume attributes, and the size and contents of the VTOC itself (hence this F-4 DSCB is often referred to as the *self-describing DSCB*). The same process is followed for the allocation of a unique VSAM data set, as this too is treated as an OS data set and its allocation handled by OS DADSM. If such a data set has multiple components, each component is itself treated as a unique data set, such that the individual component names are associated with separate F-1 DSCB entries.

With suballocated VSAM clusters, after the actual host VSAM data space is created, there is no further involvement of OS DADSM. VSAM space management handles the suballocation of the clusters from within the host VSAM data space, coordinating the process with VSAM Catalog Management: each cluster is given a unique VSAM catalog entry describing all aspects of the cluster, including volume/space allocation information. The programmer may request any or all of this information through the LISTCAT command, and is well-advised to obtain this information regularly—in the current jargon of VSAM, we say the programmer is well-advised *to snap* the LISTCAT information—as it may provide valuable performance-related data (discussed later in the text).

8

VSAM CLUSTERS–BASIC
CONCEPTS AND FACILITIES

8.1 THE BASIC STRUCTURE OF A VSAM CLUSTER

Central to VSAM is the concept of a *cluster*, the closest equivalent under VSAM to an OS data set. A cluster can be considered a *logical file* for storing records: it *can* be treated by VSAM as a single data set whenever appropriate, but it is *not necessarily* a single physical data set in actual fact. The reason for this lies in the fact that a VSAM cluster is comprised of two distinct *components*: a *data component* (DC) and an *index component* (IC), each of which—although structurally and functionally related to the other—is physically an independent data set. Indeed, when a VSAM cluster is created (at DEFINE CLUSTER time, that is, when the AMS DEFINE CLUSTER command is issued), these two components of the cluster need not even be on the same volume. It is in this sense that a VSAM cluster is a logical file: it is the logical grouping of two associated data sets—the data component and the index component—manipulable as one entity under VSAM processing. We will shortly need to qualify and enrich this conception of a VSAM cluster, but let's first briefly look at the two basic components of a cluster.

8.1.1 The Data Component

This component of a cluster, as its name plainly suggests, contains the actual data records of the file, along with certain important control information used by VSAM in its operation on, and processing of, these records. In the terminology of VSAM, these records are generally known as *logical records* (LRs).

8.1.2 The Index Component

This component of a cluster contains the control objects—the *pointers*—which 'index' the logical records of the data component; the pointers are used by VSAM to locate any arbitrary record of the data component, that is, determine its physical location for access and retrieval. Note the difference here in design from that of non-VSAM data sets: the index structure in the latter is typically part of the data set itself, as in ISAM data sets, while with VSAM clusters the index structure is a physically independent and separate data set with respect to the data component.

The structure and content of a VSAM index component will be taken up below and further detailed in Chapter 11.

8.2   TYPES OF VSAM CLUSTERS

The above discussion was intentionally general: clusters were seen as logical files consisting of two physical components related functionally and structurally to each other, the data component and the index component. However, there are actually four different types of VSAM clusters, as we have anticipated briefly earlier in this text, and only the first type—the *KSDS*, see below—is structured with both a data and an index component. The other three types—the *ESDS*, the *RRDS*, and the *LDS*—contain only a data component, but are still considered to be clusters by VSAM, with the qualification that the index component is null. This allows the concept of cluster to retain generality and applicability for all four types of VSAM clusters. Thus, we can express this as follows:

$$CLUSTER = DATA\ COMPONENT + INDEX\ COMPONENT$$
$$= \qquad DC \qquad + \qquad IC$$

where IC is null for non-KSDS clusters. This chapter will discuss the KSDS, ESDS, and RRDS. Linear data sets (LDS), the newest type of VSAM cluster, will be discussed later in Chapter 18, on performance.

8.2.1   The Key-Sequenced Data Set (KSDS)

As discussed briefly earlier in the text, a VSAM *Key-Sequenced Data Set* (KSDS) is just that: a VSAM data set whose logical (data) records are ordered ascendingly in collating sequence over some key field, called the *prime key* of the cluster. An employee file consisting of employee records, each of which contains— among many other fields—an employee social security number (SSN) field, may be organized as a VSAM KSDS by making the SSN field the prime key and ordering the records in ascending order of employee SSN.

VSAM specifies certain requirements for a field to meet in order to function as the prime key of a KSDS. The values of the field must be unique: the key value of any record must be different from that of all other records in the cluster (the 'no-duplicate-key' condition); an SSN prime key clearly meets this condition, but a employee-last-name field typically would not (in the general case), as there may be several employee records, each for a different employee, but with the same last name. When a VSAM KSDS is created, by the DEFINE CLUSTER command, VSAM generates an error and terminates the operation if it encounters any duplicate values over the designated prime key field, or if the records are not presented in strictly ascending order over prime key—that is, are not pre-sorted by prime key. In addition, the prime key field must be a fixed-length, contiguous field (no gaps) found at a constant offset within each logical record, with a maximum length of 255 bytes. For example, as illustrated in Figure 8-1, the SSN prime key field shown is nine bytes in length and found, always, starting at the ninth byte of each record (with other employee-related fields flanking it before and after).

A KSDS cluster's prime key field values may not be modified at all by any processing whatever: the entire record may be deleted from the file, but the value of any record's prime key cannot change over the life cycle of the cluster. Any new records added to a KSDS cluster are always inserted in collating sequence by prime key value—that is, wherever they would be added in 'natural' order of key value, in our example in SSN order. The prime key field is used by VSAM for three fundamental purposes:

1. to create the cluster by sequencing its logical records in a fixed (ascending) order over the prime key;
2. to seqentially access the logical records of the cluster by moving through the file in prime key order, that is, retrieving records by their prime key value in ascending order;
3. to randomly (directly) access the logical records of the cluster by retrieving any arbitrarily specified record according to its prime key value: the programmer specifies some target record to be retrieved by passing to VSAM the particular SSN value, for example, associated with that record.

Thus, we see that a VSAM KSDS cluster supports, by virtue of *keyed access*, both sequential processing and random processing over its prime key field; its closest OS counterpart, which it was intended to replace, is the ISAM data set. Like ISAM, a KSDS supports both fixed-length and variable-length records. A KSDS is easily the most widely used of the four types of VSAM clusters; indeed, many programmers, when speaking simply of a VSAM data set typically mean a VSAM KSDS cluster.

Also note that the index component is involved in implementing purposes 1, 2,

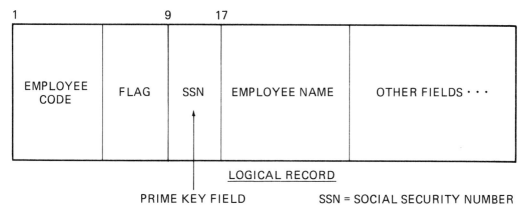

Figure 8-1. Prime key of KSDS.

and 3 above: the index component is constructed by VSAM from the presented prime key values when first creating the cluster, and the index component is accessed for both sequential and random record retrieval, in that the index associates, for any key value, a unique pointer that gives the location of the target record in the data component of the cluster. This is represented schematically in Figure 8-2 (and detailed below). As earlier noted, the index component may be allocated on the same volume as the associated data component, or they may be on two different volumes (this is primarily, as we shall see later, a performance consideration).

In terms of supported processing activity, all record operations are allowed: record addition (insertion), deletion, and update, both in sequential and random access modes. Furthermore, *unlike* ISAM, record addition and deletion are *physical* rather than *logical*: a record to be inserted into a KSDS between two existing records (by virtue of its key value) is physically inserted in its proper place by VSAM by 'shifting over' by one record slot records with higher keys in order to make room for the inserted record, and similarly a record to be deleted from a KSDS is physically removed from its storage location, and the space it occupied is *reclaimed* automatically by VSAM by shifting back by one record slot the subsequent records with higher key values. In both cases, only *some* of the cluster's records are shifted or moved for the addition or deletion operation, not all of the higher-keyed records; how this is actually handled by VSAM will be described later in this chapter. (Strictly speaking, although ISAM never performs a physical deletion, it does perform both physical and logical insertion under various circumstances, but by and large with large highly active files, ISAM primarily performs logical record insertion.)

Now, all of this talk of 'shifting over' records clearly implies that the data component of a VSAM KSDS cluster generally is not filled to allocated capacity wholly with logical records, but rather contains internal empty space to allow for such physical insertion activity, and its associated record shifting operations, and this is precisely the case. The internal empty space in the data component of a KSDS is

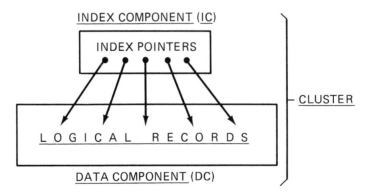

Figure 8-2. Index and data components of VSAM cluster.

known as *distributed freespace*, or just *freespace*; we will be examining how freespace is exploited by VSAM more precisely in a later section of this chapter. Suffice it to say for now, in summary, that a KSDS's freespace allows for physically real record additions and deletions, in contrast to ISAM, which always only logically deletes a record (marks it as 'doomed,' but does not physically remove it and reclaim its space for other use), and only under certain circumstances, physically inserts a record (generally, only logically adding the record by maintaining a pointer to its real whereabouts, rather than actually inserting it in its proper place according to key sequence). Figure 8-3 illustrates record addition, and Figure 8-4 record deletion, in a KSDS cluster. (Later in this chapter we will look at the precise mechanics of these operations in a KSDS.)

Before Record Insertion:

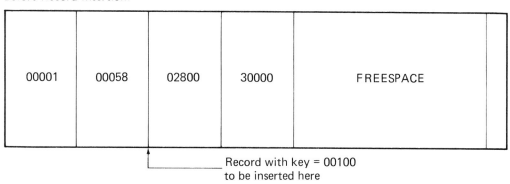

Record with key = 00100
to be inserted here

After Record Insertion

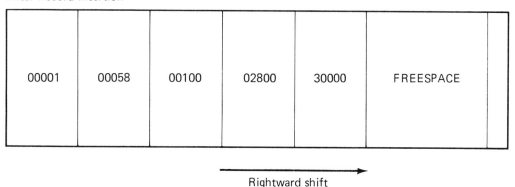

Rightward shift

Figure 8-3. Record addition.

Before Record Deletion

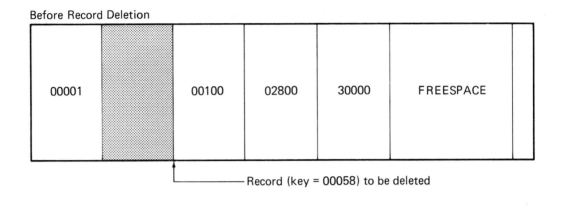

Record (key = 00058) to be deleted

After Record Deletion

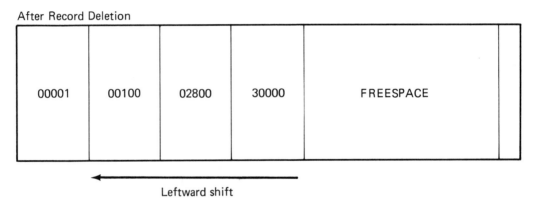

Leftward shift

Figure 8-4. Record deletion.

8.2.2   The Entry-Sequenced Data Set (ESDS)

The second type of VSAM cluster, and the second most widely used, compared to the KSDS (and *not* a close second by any means), is the *Entry-Sequenced Data Set (ESDS)*. It is a VSAM cluster organized by *entry-sequence*: the logical records of an ESDS are stored in physical order of entry at load-time; we say that they are *time-arrival-sequenced*, since they are stored sequentially as they are presented to VSAM when loading the records into the cluster, and new records are added to the end of the ESDS cluster, again, in such time-arrival sequence. It is critical to note that an ESDS *has no prime key*, and in this sense has as its closest equivalent an OS SAM data set (a simple sequential file).

Like a KSDS, an ESDS supports both fixed- and variable-length records. Unlike a KSDS, however, record insertion is supported only as *EOF-addition*: records may be added to an ESDS only at end-of-file (EOF), after the current physically last record; in this sense, this is parallel to specifying DISP=MOD in the JCL for an OS file—the file is opened in *extend mode* (in COBOL processing terminology) at EOF and all records are added to the end of the file in the order presented. No *internal-addition* (insertion between two adjacent existing records) is permitted, nor may any record be changed in length. And, very importantly, records may not be deleted for an ESDS.

Many programmers circumvent the prohibition against deletion in an ESDS by their own internal deletion scheme, generally by using a deletion-marking convention to mark records to be considered by subsequent processing *as if* deleted. A common convention, modelled on ISAM logical deletion, is to use the first byte of each record as a delete-status byte, a hex 'FF' in this byte generally being used to mark a record as logically deleted, and '00' (or any value other than X'FF') signifying an active (non-deleted) record. Two points must be remembered, however, in connection with any such an internal deletion scheme.

First, the record is not *physically* deleted at all, but only marked as such *by the user*. Second, VSAM does not recognize or honor any user-defined internal deletion scheme: as far as VSAM is concerned, the record is present, and is returned by VSAM processing as such; it is the user's responsibility to provide code that reads and recognizes the delete-status byte, and processes accordingly (for example, by bypassing a marked-for-deletion record). The user must weigh the overhead of such additional user-provided processing against the extra flexibility such schemes afford with ESDS files.

An ESDS is used largely for what may be termed *content-independent* applications: the data records are inherently unordered with respect to record content, no field providing any natural sequencing. Various kinds of transaction files used in update processing applications are constituted by records stored in whatever order they arrive (usually from data entry terminals), and so are natural candidates for ESDS organization, assuming that record deletion is not required by the application (as is typically true in such cases). An example of this is CICS's temporary storage facility, generally ESDS-implemented. Another class of applications that form a natural use of ESDS files is that of *event-sequenced* applications: records are generated as certain key recordable/ monitorable events occur in a system, and added in event sequence to a file, commonly referred to as a *journal* or *log*. A database log recording all updates against the database records is often implemented as an ESDS.

8.2.3   Relative Record Data Set (RRDS)

A *Relative Record Data Set* (*RRDS*) is perhaps the type of VSAM cluster least familiar to most programmers (aside from the Linear Data Set, which is so recent and technically complex that few have heard of it as yet or understand it if they have). An RRDS is constructed of a series of fixed-length slots into which records may be stored—one per slot—and each of these slots has associated with it a unique *relative record number* (*RRN*), the slots being numbered consecutively from one up to however many records the file may fit. An RRDS slot may be occupied (contain a data record) or empty (no data record stored within it); typically, in applications using an RRDS, not all slots of the cluster are occupied. An example would be an employee file where the employee number, say a four digit field (up to 9999), would be equivalent to the RRN, so that the record for employee 2000 is found in the 2000th slot of the file. It may be that the employees with employee numbers 800, 3000, and 4000, among others, have left the company, in which case the slots with RRNs of 800, 3000, and 4000, among others, would be empty. Furthermore, if we assume that each employee record is 80 bytes in length, the first record slot, with an RRN of 1, would be located (stored) zero bytes offset from the beginning of the RRDS, the second record slot would be located 80 bytes offset from this beginning, etc., regardless of whether the slot is occupied or not. Figure 8-5 illustrates a simple RRDS with some empty record slots. Several points concerning RRDSs should be noted here.

1. Given the structure of an RRDS, the location of a stored record is fixed: a record's RRN cannot change. If one wanted to effect moving the 50th record from its slot to the 100th record slot (assuming the latter is empty), this cannot be done directly; rather the record would have to first be deleted from slot 50 (RRN=50), and then a new record—actually another copy of the record we wish to move—would have to be written to the 100th slot.

2. RRNs are *not* keys: an RRN is not an embedded field of the data records of an RRDS, but is external to the record. RRNs represent the numbering of the fixed-length slots of the RRDS consecutively from one until the last slot of the RRDS, each slot being associated with a unique RRN, regardless of whether the slot is occupied by a data record or is empty.

3. An RRDS is a non-indexed file, consisting only of a data component, with no freespace (FSPC), unlike a KSDS. An RRDS uses empty slots for record insertion: a record to be added must always be written to an existing empty slot, so that records following the point of insertion are not shifted over in any way (as they are in a KSDS).

4. Given that there is no FSPC in an RRDS, record deletion is—unlike that in a

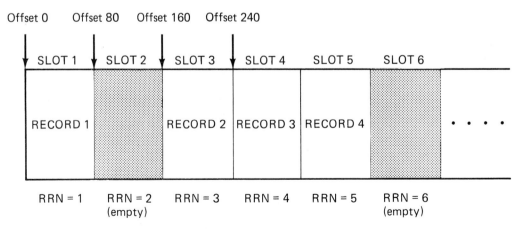

Figure 8-5. Structure of an RRDS.

KSDS—strictly logical, not physical: that record is marked as deleted by turning off a *occupancy* bit in a control field associated with the slot of the record. The slot may then be used to store another record in, but the space the record occupied is *not reclaimed*. VSAM does not return to the program anything but occupied slots; empty slots are bypassed in sequential and random retrieval. A request by the program for a specific record by supplying an RRN which is associated with an empty slot yields a message from VSAM indicating 'record not found.'

5. Access to the records of an RRDS may be either in physical sequence (sequential access) or by RRN (random access), in the latter case the programmer being obliged in the program to provide to VSAM the RRN value of any record to be retrieved or written. VSAM receives all RRNs and converts them to relative byte addresses (RBAs), which are then used to locate the associated record slots.

6. An RRDS is the VSAM counterpart to OS BDAM files, with one major difference: OS BDAM files are typically unblocked, so that, although random access may be very fast, I/O operations transfer only one record at a time across the channel. RRDSs are more efficient than OS BDAM files in that they are intrinsically 'blocked': an entire control interval (CI) containing multiple logical records is transmitted across the channel, and although not necessarily as a single *physical block* in a single I/O operation (we will discuss this point further in Chapter 18, on performance), it is nonetheless generally the case that multiple records are transferred by one I/O operation.

7. Programmers may be familiar with the basic logic of direct access files under the OS BDAM facility. In Assembler, these are simply known as *direct* files. In COBOL, BDAM files are supported as *relative* files. PL/I has three related file organizations for BDAM support: *regional(1)*, *regional(2)*, and *regional(3)* files. An Assembler, COBOL, or PL/I program coded for BDAM processing can be used with little modification to access the VSAM counterpart, RRDS files.

8. RRDS, like their OS counterparts, BDAM files, are primarily used when very fast random access is required, especially in on-line transaction processing (CICS, for example). However, there is often a countervailing burden of increased program complexity associated with RRDS processing. This is because RRDS records have no keys and the RRN—which, remember, is external to the records and not part of them—of a record must somehow be associated with some particular record *by the programmer*: VSAM plays no role in this association at all, and only effects the conversion of an RRN presented to it into a unique RBA for locating some particular record slot. Nor is it always, or even frequently, possible to effect a simple one-to-one correspondence between the RRN value and some field within the record.

In the example with which we began our discussion of RRDSs, we may simply make the RRN identical in value to the employee number field within a record if, for example, the employee numbers range only from 0000 to 9999, being four bytes. Here the RRDS need only have 10,000 record slots which, assuming 80-byte records, would require a space allocation of only 800,000 bytes: on a high-capacity disk like the widely used 3380, just two cylinders of space would hold the entire RRDS. The best case would be if a high percentage of the total number of possible employee numbers (that is, 10,000) represent active employees at any one time, so that there would be relatively few empty slots in the RRDS (avoiding what is often known as the *sparse array* problem: the intrinsic inefficiency of processing a sparsely occupied data structure).

However, consider another case, one in which the employees of the company are tracked by social security number (SSN). We may try to maintain simplicity and have a one-to-one correspondence between the SSN field of an employee record and the RRN associated with that record's slot location (the record with an SSN field of 000050000 would be stored in the 50,000th record slot of the RRN). Given that SSNs are nine bytes in length, then even if there were as many as 10,000 employees of the company, only one thousandth of one percent of the slots of the RRDS would be occupied: if we have one slot for each possible SSN, one billion (1,000,000,000) slots would be required. A file, or an array, with only one-one thousandth of its space actually used for active records, is a *very* sparse data structure indeed, and even on a 3380, would require 80 billion bytes (a 3380 can store as an absolute maximum 3.780 billion bytes), so that the RRDS would have to be stored over twenty two 3380 packs!

Cases like this are generally handled, therefore, not by a one-to-one mapping between RRNs and some field within the records of the RRDS. Rather some *transformation* is generally used: the value of the field to be used in tracking the records of the RRDS—let us call this the *tracking* field, in that it is not an actual *key* field (an RRDS, remember, contains no key)—is associated with some corresponding RRN by application of some *function*, so that given any target tracking field (associated with some desired record), the RRN of the record may be computed from the function, and vice versa: given any RRN, the value of the corresponding tracking field may be derived. It is the programmer's responsibility to design an appropriate, and efficient, function of this sort.

Nor does the transformation always need to be one-to-one: one RRN may be associated with more than one tracking field; in this case we say that we are using a *hashing function* or *algorithm*. This requires even greater ingenuity to program efficiently. (Experienced COBOL programmers may be familiar with this sort of processing from non-VSAM OS files known in COBOL as *relative files*. The processing of such files is sometimes known as *direct file processing*, and a certain class of processing techniques used with direct files is often referred to as *randomizing algorithms*.) Because of these complications, RRDSs are generally used when the values of the tracking field are close together (few, and small, gaps) and/or when the size of the tracking field is modest, so as to not entail an abnormally large file for implementation. In such cases, a simple, usually one-to-one mapping of tracking field to RRN is feasible and the programming is entirely straightfoward, allowing relatively simple programs to obtain very fast random access to a file. The performance of such an RRDS in random mode will typically be much better than that of a randomly accessed KSDS, since such access in a KSDS involves use of an index (and of two distinct files for the data and index components). If the design goals of an application, therefore, permit use of an RRDS, it may provide the best performance for predominantly random access, as may be the case in certain online CICS applications.

8.3   COMPARISON OF VSAM CLUSTER TYPES

The three types of VSAM clusters, KSDS, ESDS, and RRDS (we exclude here the fourth, most recent and highly specialized cluster, the LDS, taken up in Chapter 18, on performance), have been designed to effectively implement different file organizations and access methods covering the full range of processing needs in common practical applications. We have already discussed their features and uses above; Figure 8-6 presents a contrastive summary of that discussion. We leave for a later chapter a treatment of some of the design/performance issues associated with VSAM cluster type.

	KSDS	ESDS	RRDS
Record Sequence	Key order	Time-arrival (entry) order	Slot number (RRN) order
Sequential Access	By key	By entry sequence	By ascending RRN order
Random Access	By key	Not supported unless alternate index built over the ESDS	By RRN
Record Addition	Anywhere in cluster, using distributed freespace	Only at EOF (end-of-file)	Anywhere into empty slots
Record Deletion	Fully supported; space reclaimed by VSAM	No deletion allowed	Fully supported, leaving behind an empty slot for future use
Variable-length Records	Fully supported	Fully supported	Not supported (fixed-length records only)
Spanned Records	Yes	Yes	No
Alternate Indices	Yes	Yes	No
Change of Record Length	Yes	No	No
Reusable	Yes	Yes	Yes

Figure 8-6. Comparison of VSAM cluster types.

8.4   CONTROL INTERVALS (CIs)

The *control interval (CI)* is a basic—indeed, *the* basic—unit of VSAM file structure. We can best understand the nature and function of the CI in VSAM by considering it under four separate but related categories:

8.4.1   The CI as a Unit of Logical Organization

The logical records (LRs) of a VSAM file, regardless of cluster type, are organized or grouped into control intervals, as shown in Figure 8-7, with the entire file

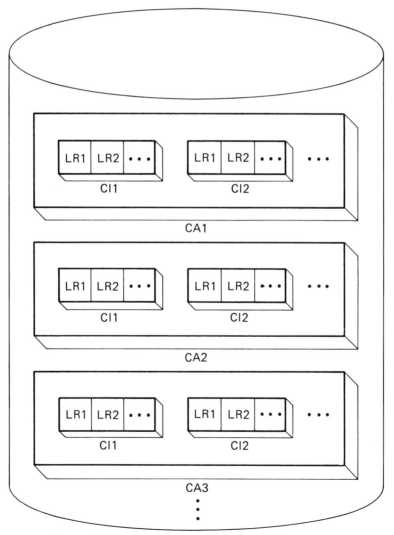

Figure 8-7. Logical records within a control interval.

being viewed as containing some specific number of CIs. The size of a CI is fixed throughout any specific cluster and may either be explicitly determined by the programmer when creating the cluster, or implicitly defined by VSAM default if no specification is made by the programmer. If the VSAM file is an RRDS, or a KSDS or ESDS with fixed length records, then the number of logical records that can be stored within a CI is constant for each CI of the file and is determined at cluster definition time. If the file is a KSDS or ESDS with variable-length records, then the actual determination of the number of logical records per CI is made at load time (when the actual records are first written to the empty cluster), and this number—known as the *LR-density* (number of LRs per CI)—is not the same for each CI of the file.

Consider an example, shown in Figure 8-8. The size of the CI (its *CISZ*) is 512 bytes. Assuming fixed-length records of 100 bytes, then a CI will contain five records (some bytes of the 512 CISZ will contain control information, a topic we will treat later). It may be the case that the last CI containing the last few records of the data set may contain fewer than five records (if there were only a final two records, for example, left to fit at the end of the data set after each preceding CI was filled with the requisite five records). The point is that in the case of fixed-length records, the LR-density (here five) is determined at cluster definition time and represents a limiting factor of the data set's characteristics: at most five records per CI will, at load time, be stored in each CI, and indeed VSAM will load precisely five records to each CI when they are first written to the data set, for all CIs other than the one that contains the last few data records (which may or may not have five records, but cannot have more).

Note that, as we shall see later, it does not follow that, when dealing with a KSDS, the LR-density is fixed *after* load time: post-load time processing may change the actual number of records in any CI, which then need not be the same for each CI of the data set. For an ESDS with fixed-length records, the LR-density remains the same after processing activity against the data set since record insertion is not allowed in an ESDS (records are added only at end-of-file (EOF)). Similarly, the LR-density of an RRDS also remains fixed: the RRDS consists of a fixed number of fixed-length slots organized into CIs such that record addition occurs only as the act of inserting a record into an empty slot position without any change to the configuration or clustering of slots throughout the RRDS.

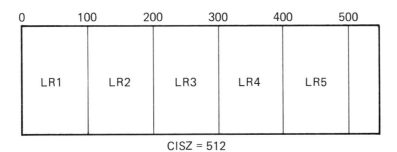

Figure 8-8. LR-density equal to five in a CI.

8.4.2   The CI as a Unit of Access/Retrieval

The clustering of logical records into CIs allows VSAM to handle all of the records of a CI as a single unit with respect to access/retrieval: when a programmer requests a particular record of a VSAM file, an entire CI-full of records—the CI which contains the target record—is actually accessed by VSAM and made available to the application program (or utility). High-level language access to VSAM files is therefore said to be at the CI-level, whether the request is a sequential or a random one. Thus, although a program will typically store only the target record in its own (working) storage, VSAM will have accessed and returned to the program (in its buffers; see Subsection 8.4.3) the entire *target-CI* (the CI containing the target record).

8.4.3   The CI as a Unit of Storage

VSAM will store records onto DASD in units of a CI: we can view the DASD storage as *structured* into CIs, which in turn contain the logical records. (The exact connection between the CI and the primary unit of DASD physical storage, the track, will be examined later in this chapter.)

8.4.4   The CI as a Unit of Buffer Management

The size of a CI (CISZ) is constant throughout a VSAM data set. The connection between a CI as a VSAM unit and an I/O buffer is precisely this: *the CISZ determines exclusively the size of a program's I/O buffer, and each program I/O buffer holds one CI-full of VSAM records*. Thus, if the CISZ for a particular VSAM file is 2048 bytes, or 2K, then the program buffer size is 2K, however many buffers the program uses, and each program access to any record of the file causes VSAM to transfer the target CI, as it is stored on DASD, into a program I/O buffer. The larger the CISZ for any particular VSAM file, therefore, the larger the program's buffer storage overhead will be (it does not follow that this is necessarily bad from a performance point of view, as will shall see in Chapter 18).

Now that we have considered the nature of a CI as a unit of VSAM structure under the listed categories, there are a number of additional points concerning the CI that we wish to discuss at this time.

8.4.5   Data CIs and Index CIs

In the above discussion, we have been deliberately casual about CIs: for a KSDS, in particular, there are two types of CIs, not one. There are *data-CIs* containing the *data records* of the data component (DC), and *index-CIs* containing the *index records* of the index component (IC) of the cluster. Note that both the DC and the IC of a KSDS cluster are organized into CIs, but there are two points to observe concerning data versus index CIs.

One, the CISZ is constant *for the component*, not for the data set in the case of a KSDS: thus, the data-CISZ may (and typically is) different from the index-CISZ; as we shall see, there are different principles and considerations for the two. So, for example, we may have a KSDS with a data-CISZ of 4K and an index-CISZ of ½K (512 bytes).

Two, a data-CI can and typically does contain several logical records (i.e., data records); however, *an index-CI always contains one and only one logical record*, this LR being an index record—thus, there is one index record per index-CI. (The details of index records will be presented in Chapter 11.)

Given the above facts, it can now be appreciated that (for KSDSs only), a program's I/O buffer allocation includes both buffers for data-CIs and buffers for index-CIs, that is for holding data and index records, respectively. *Unless overridden by the programmer, a VSAM default allocates two buffers for containing data-CIs and one buffer for containing index-CIs* (why two data buffers and one index buffer will be clarified later). Again, by way of example, consider a KSDS with a data-CISZ of 4K and an index-CISZ of ½K: the total program buffer requirement under the default just stated would be 8.5K ((2 × 4K) + ½K).

8.4.6 Allowable VSAM CISZs

VSAM has different requirements for a DC versus an IC (if any) of a VSAM cluster.

8.4.7 Data Component CISZ

This may be a minimum of 512 bytes (½K) to a maximum of 32K, with the following range restrictions: for CISZs between ½K and 8K: increments of ½K are allowed; for CISZs from 8K to 32K: increments of 2K are allowed. CISZs are coded in byte form; given the above rules, we may have CISZs of 512, 1024, 1536, etc., up to 8192; thereafter, 10240 (=10K), 12288 (=12K), etc., up to 32768 (=32K).

8.4.8 Index Component CISZ

The CISZ of an IC may only be one of the following four values: 512, 1024, 2048, 4096 bytes (½, 1, 2, 4K). (But see Chapter 18.)

8.5 CONTROL AREAS (CAs)

As we have seen, groups of logical records in VSAM files are organized into control intervals. Control intervals are, in turn, organized into larger units known as *control areas (CAs)*, with the entire data set finally (at the highest level) being made up of CAs. The basic features and use of CAs in VSAM processing are given below.

8.5.1 The CA as a Unit of Storage

A CA is a fixed-length area of *contiguous* DASD storage, with a minimum size of one track and a maximum size of one cylinder. Note, however, that the CA is *not* a unit of retrieval; the CI is the retrieval unit in VSAM processing.

8.5.2   CASZ Determination

There is no IDCAMS parameter for specifying the size of a CA—we shall use the term *CASZ* for convenience—for a VSAM file. Rather, CASZ determination is made indirectly through the space allocation parameter coding. The rule is:

$$CASZ = MIN\ (p, s)$$

where p, s are the primary and secondary allocation quantities coded after CYL, TRK, or RECORDS in the space parameter coding at DEFINE CLUSTER time expressed into whole track units, or cylinder (max = 1). Thus, if we had coded TRK (100, 2), then CASZ is equal to the smaller of primary and secondary allocation quantities, here secondary, so that CASZ is equal to two tracks; if we had coded CYL (20, 4), CASZ would be equal to one 1 cylinder—note that although MIN (p, s) here is equal to four, CASZ is a maximum of one cylinder in any case.

Now, consider the harder case of a coding for space allocation of RECORDS (10000, 200), assuming records with lrecl equal to 80, and the device type equal to 3380. The total byte capacity needed for the *secondary* allocation (remember, VSAM uses the smaller of the two quantities, here—and generally—the secondary allocation) is 16,000 bytes, which fits onto a single 3380 track (about 47,000 byte capacity), so CASZ is equal to one track. Note that if no secondary allocation were coded, or zero were coded, VSAM would determine the CASZ to be one track, since that is the minimum.

8.5.3   The CA as a Unit of Extenting

When VSAM allocates extents for a VSAM data set, each extent is required to be a whole number of CAs; that is, a whole number of tracks or cylinders, thus avoiding excessive space fragmentation. LISTCAT output will show this extent information. Notice that this applies to both primary and secondary extent allocations.

Note also that neither the CA as a unit of extenting, nor the CA as a unit of storage with minimum and maximum values of one track and one cylinder, respectively, implies that the CA is necessarily allocated on a cylinder boundary. If space allocation were made in units of RECORDS or TRACKS, then a CA may span a cylinder boundary. It is only when the allocation is made in cylinder units (CYL) that VSAM assures that each CA begins on a cylinder boundary (and ends on a cylinder boundary also, since the CASZ in this case is guaranteed to be one cylinder). It is for this reason that space allocation in cylinder units is recommended for performance optimization: all of the records of a CA can be accessed with a single arm movement on the DASD device; if a CA spans a cylinder boundary, then multiple arm movements are required, slowing retrieval proportionately.

8.5.4   The CA as a Unit of Preformatting

When first loading records into an empty cluster—that is, at load time—VSAM does the load in what is called *recovery* mode, unless this is overridden by the programmer (the default is RECOVERY, overridden by coding SPEED at DEF CLUSTER time; more about SPEED in Chapter 18, on performance.) This means that VSAM loads the cluster with a CA-full of records at a time. Just before each CA-full of records is loaded, the CA is said to be *preformatted* by VSAM: VSAM writes certain control information for each CI in the CA, and in addition writes an end-of-file (EOF) indicator to keep track of the EOF *up to that point of the load*. This is done to assist in recovery of part of the records loaded should the load operation be interrupted by a fatal error (one terminating the load prematurely). Recovery in such a case is done at the CA level: either an entire CA-full of records (or several) is recoverable, or no part of the CA-full of records is recoverable. Here, recoverable implies that it may be possible to continue the loading of records from the point of the last full CA loaded, without having to restart the load completely from the beginning. (As we shall see later, however, this is more of a theoretical benefit than a practical one in commercial programming environments.)

8.6   THE RELATIVE BYTE ADDRESS (RBA)

A central concept of VSAM file organization and of VSAM as an access method is that of the *relative byte address* (RBA) (and we speak of VSAM using *relative byte addressing*). A VSAM file is considered to have a *logical start-of-data-set*: this is by convention an offset of zero (the start of the file is offset zero bytes from its logical beginning), so that we say that a VSAM file always begins at an *RBA equal to zero*. Then any record of the file is considered to be *x* bytes displaced from the arbitrary zero starting point, where the *x* byte offset is the record's RBA. Assuming a VSAM file with fixed-length records of 80 bytes, the first record is located at an RBA of zero, the second record then has an RBA of 80, the third an RBA of 160, etc. (see Figure 8-9). The RBA as used by VSAM is a fullword binary integer, but is generally given in hexadecimal in VSAM output, such as LISTCAT; so, the first record's RBA is equal to X'0', the second record's RBA is equal to X'50', etc., but we will often use decimal equivalents for convenience.

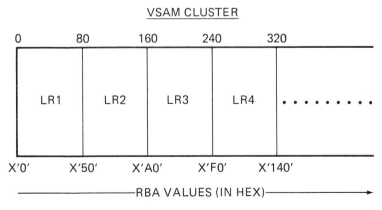

Figure 8-9. Relative byte addressing in VSAM.

VSAM, therefore, considers a cluster to logically be a stream of records stored one after another, with the location of any individual record being determined uniquely by the record's RBA or offset from the zero start point, even though the actual records may not all be physically contiguous on the storage device (they rarely are). This makes record location in VSAM *device-independent*: for non-VSAM access methods, record location is device-dependent, varying from device type to device type—from a 3330, to a 3350, to a 3380 disk, etc.—in terms of track and cylinder addresses. Thus, changes in DASD technology do not essentially affect VSAM as an access method in any way, and by and large a programmer need not be concerned with device-dependent information. We say by and large in that it is still necessary for the programmer to deal with some device-dependent information for purposes of both space allocation—the number of tracks or cylinders needed for a VSAM file is clearly dependent on whether a 3350 or a 3380 is being used, for example—and in certain circumstances for performance tuning of VSAM files, but generally, once these considerations have been made, device-dependent information need not be considered again. We will see more and more of VSAM's usage of RBAs as we go along from this point forward.

8.7 DISTRIBUTED FREESPACE (FSPC)

VSAM can reserve space within each CI of a KSDS as *distributed freespace*, other than for the loaded records of a cluster. This (distributed) freespace (often referred to as FSPC after the IDCAMS parameter which controls it) is kept free by VSAM for the subsequent insertion of new records into the cluster in their proper key sequence within a CI, or for lengthening existing records. FSPC is the facility which allows VSAM to perform *physical addition* (insertion) of records, as opposed to merely *logical addition*: since empty space has been distributed throughout the cluster, new records are inserted wherever they belong by virtue of key value simply by moving the records of the target CI (the CI whose key sequence range contains the records to be inserted) over one position by a *rightward physical shift*, as shown in Figure 8-10, which repeats here Figure 8-3.

This is one of two types of VSAM FSPC, the form known as *CI-internal FSPC*: space *within each CI* kept free by VSAM for insertion activity. In addition, VSAM can reserve *one or more CIs within each CA* for FSPC, in which case this is *CA-internal FSPC* (that is, entire CIs within each CA are kept completely empty for VSAM use related to record insertion activity). CI-internal and CA-internal FSPC (both optionally requested by the programmer) participate in the process of *splitting* (*CI-splits* and *CA-splits*), described fully in Chapter 10. Both types of FSPC are *reclaimable* by VSAM: if records are deleted from a KSDS, the space released goes back into that allocated for FSPC in the relevant CIs and CAs. Thus, FSPC decreases with the growth of record insertion activity, and increases with the growth of record deletion activity. Note that FSPC is used only with KSDSs; there is no FSPC in an ESDS or an RRDS.

Space other than that allocated for logical records—*data space*—and other than

Before Record Insertion:

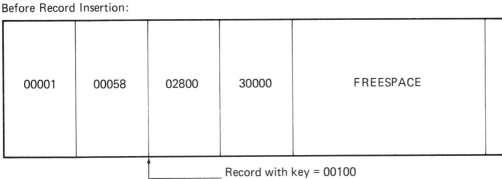

Figure 8-10. Rightward shifting with record insertion.

that explicitly requested for FSPC, is known as *unused space*; thus a KSDS cluster's CIs contain, potentially, three types of 'space': Data space; FSPC; and unused space. The data space, when it contains actual logical records (that is, when it is full) is known as the *logical record area* (*LRA*). Careful definition of the cluster should attempt to minimize the amount of unused space throughout the cluster so as to allow maximal use of the LRA (to contain the records) and FSPC (for anticipated record insertion activity). Some guidelines for accomplishing this are given later in this chapter, and then expanded upon in Chapter 18, on performance.

8.8 CONTROL FIELDS IN A CONTROL INTERVAL

In the above discussion, we indicated three constituents of a control interval; there is also a fourth (and last): *control fields* (CF) used by VSAM routines for control purposes in VSAM file processing. Thus, to summarize, these are the consituents of a control interval, in order of their occurrence from left to right in the CI (see Figure 8-11):

1. Logical Record Area (LRA)
2. Distributed Freespace (FSPC)
3. Unused Space (US)
4. Control Fields (CF)

There are two types of control fields. Each CI of a cluster contains, at the end of the CI (rightmost locations) a four-byte *control interval definition field* (CIDF) as the far rightmost field, and one or more *record definition fields* (RDFs), each of which is three bytes in length, and occurring immediately to the left of the CIDF. The CIDF contains information concerning the CI itself, and the RDFs contain information concerning the records in that CI. As we will discuss below, in the special case of a CI which contains no records, there are no RDF fields at all, just a single CIDF.

8.8.1 The CIDF

There is one CIDF per CI, and this 4-byte field is composed of two 2-byte fields (see Figure 8-12), which are detailed below:

FSPC-Area Offset (FAO). The FAO field gives the offset, in hex, of the beginning of the FSPC area within the CI, which begins (if any) immediately after the LRA. It simultaneously locates for VSAM both the end of the LRA and the beginning of any allocated FSPC.

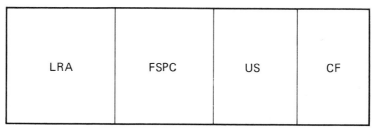

A CONTROL INTERVAL

LRA = LOGICAL RECORD AREA (STORAGE FOR LRs)
FSPC = DISTRIBUTED FREE SPACE (FOR RECORD INSERTION)
US   = UNUSED SPACE
CF   = CONTROL FIELDS (RESERVED BY VSAM)

Figure 8-11. Control interval constituents.

FSPC-Area Length (FAL).   The FAL gives the length, in hex, of the FSPC area within the CI. VSAM uses this field, along with the FAO, to keep track of the changing size—and hence changing location—of the FSPC-area within the CI.

Let's consider an example, as shown in Figure 8-13. Here we have a CI with a CISZ of 1024 bytes. Assume that the CI can contain only nine logical records, each 80 bytes in size, because of an explicit programmer request to have VSAM maintain

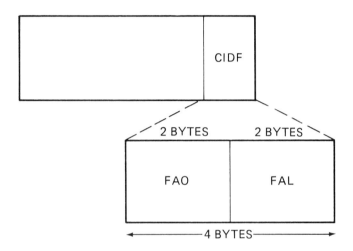

FAL = FSPC-AREA LENGTH
FAO = FSPC-AREA OFFSET

Figure 8-12. The structure of a CIDF.

FAL = X'100' = 256
FAO = X'2D0' = 720

Figure 8-13. Example of CIDF subfields.

25 percent of the CI as distributed freespace, which would set the FSPC-area length (FAL) at 256 bytes. In this case, the LRA is 720 bytes in size (9 LRs × 80 bytes), so that the FSPC-area would begin at the 720th byte of the CI (counting leftwards from an offset of zero), giving, in hex, FAO = X'2D0', with FAL = X'100' (256 bytes in decimal). Once we learn how to determine how many RDFs are needed in this case, we can then determine the number of bytes used by the two other constituents of the CI, namely control fields (CF) and unused space (US), and we turn to this directly below.

Special cases.   1. Empty CI. If the CI is empty, the CIDF has a special structure. In this case, the FAO is set to zero — in effect, FSPC begins at the start of the CI, since there are no logical records in the CI. The FAL value is the CISZ less four bytes, indicating that the amount of available FSPC is the entire CI minus the four bytes reserved for the CIDF field itself. Thus, in our example with CISZ equal to 1024 bytes, the FAL is equal to 1024 minus 4, which equals 1020 bytes (in hex: X'3FC'). Note that we subtract out only the CIDF bytes: there are no RDFs in this case, since RDFs are used only if there are actual records present in the CI.

2. Software-End-of-File (SEOF). VSAM uses a specially formatted CIDF to mark *software-end-of-file* (SEOF) — the end of the content-portion (portion containing actual data records) of the cluster. This is a CI whose CIDF contains zeroes for both the FAO and FAL subfields; note that this is a special convention: the values cannot be interpreted literally, since an FAL equal to zero would normally mean that the CI contains no FSPC, and here the CI actually contains *nothing but* FSPC (except for the CIDF field itself).

For a KSDS, the SEOF is the first CI of the CA immediately following the last CA that contains any data records, that is, the first CI of the first completely unused CA (VSAM always attempts to keep several empty CAs at the end of the cluster for future space needs and file growth). For an ESDS or an RRDS, the SEOF is the first wholly unused CI after the last CI containing any data records at all.

8.8.2   The RDF

For nonempty CIs, there will be one or more RDFs, each three bytes in length, immediately to the left of the CIDF, in right to left order: the first RDF is the rightmost RDF, the second is immediately to the left of the first, etc. (see Figure 8-14). Each RDF consists of two subfields: a one-byte *control field* (*C-subfield*) on the left, and a two-byte *length/count field* (*LC-subfield*). The RDF is complex, and we will not discuss all of its various bit settings, but rather consider it only under the special categories given below, which represent common cases in VSAM processing. This will expose the reader to how to determine the number of RDFs within a CI. Once this determination is mastered, the reader can compute how many bytes out of a given CISZ are reserved for VSAM control fields, and hence not usuable for either data records or FSPC.

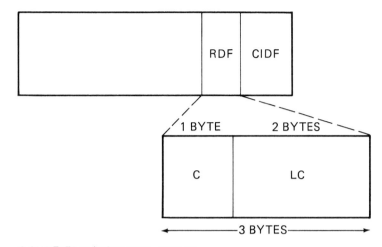

C = C-SUBFIELD (CONTROL FIELD)
LC = LC-SUBFIELD (LENGTH/COUNT FIELD)

Figure 8-14. The structure of an RDF.

	C	LC	C	LC	C I D F
LRA + FSPC	X'08'	X'0009'	X'40'	X'0050'	

←————RDF2————→ ←————RDF1————→

RDF1:   LC = X'0050' ——→ lrecl = 80 bytes
        C = X'40'   ——→ this RDF has following (to left) RDF
RDF2:   LC = X'0009' ——→ run–number = 9 (80-byte records)
        C = X'08'   ——→ this RDF is not continued (last of pair)

Figure 8-15. Example of RDF subfields.

Cluster with only fixed-length records (KSDS and ESDS).   When all of the records of a KSDS or an ESDS are fixed-length records (single common length), VSAM requires two RDFs within each CI. The first RDF (the rightmost one) contains the *common-length* information: in the example of Figure 8-15, the lrecl is 80, so RDF1 contains a X'0050' (which is equal to the decimal number 80) value in its CL-subfield (remember the CL-subfield is two bytes in length, so four hex digits are needed to represent its value). The second RDF (moving leftward) contains the *run-number* information: the run-number is the number of *contiguous equi-length records* being referred to by this RDF: in our example, there are nine logical records, all with the same length, to the CI, so the run-number is 9, and RDF2 will contain a X'0009' as the value of its CL-subfield.

VSAM will use the C-subfield of each RDF to indicate (among other things) that the RDF is or is not immediately followed—and this means to the left—by another RDF that works together to *continue* control information: thus, RDF1 will be marked to show that it is paired together with the following RDF2 field, the two associated RDFs collectively providing the information about records in the CI; the second RDF (RDF2) will not carry any continuation marking (as it is the second and last RDF of the pair). Without going into the bit settings that accomplish this, it can simply be noted that, in such a case as that which we are considering (all fixed-length records), the C-subfield of RDF1 will contain a X'40', while the C-subfield of RDF2 will contain a X'08'. Figure 8-15 shows all of these values in hex. Note that the total overhead per CI for a fixed-length record-type cluster is therefore 10 bytes: four for the CIDF, and six for the two three-byte RDFs needed. Out of a CISZ of, say, 1024, only 1014 are actually usable for records or FSPC.

Cluster with only fixed-length records (RRDS).   VSAM handles RRDSs, which are always fixed-length record files, differently than KSDSs and ESDSs. In an RRDS, there are a fixed number of slots in the entire data set, and a fixed number of slots per each CI throughout the data set. As with all VSAM clusters, there is a single CIDF per CI, but VSAM uses *one RDF per record slot in the CI, regardless of whether the slot is occupied* (contains a data record) *or empty*.

Furthermore, as shown in Figure 8-16, the pairing of RDFs and slots is always that the rightmost RDF (RDF1) is paired with the leftmost slot, the next RDF leftward (RDF2) is paired with the next slot rightward (the slot with an RRN equal to two), etc. Each RDF contains indication (through bit 5 of the C-subfield) of whether the slot is occupied (bit off) or empty (bit on): this translates to a X'00' for occupied slots, and X'04' for empty slots as the values of the C-subfield of the RDF.

The CL-subfield *for all RDFs*—those associated with occupied and empty slots indifferently—contains exactly the same value, namely the length of a slot, which is the same as the lrecl of the fixed-length records. Figure 8-17 gives an example with a CISZ equal to 1024, 80-byte records, and an LR-density (number of LR per CI) of 12. The LRA size is 960 bytes (12×80) and 12 RDFs are needed, one for each slot, so that 40 additional bytes are needed for control fields: four for the CIDF and 36 for the 12 RDFs, leaving 24 bytes of unused space (remember, not FSPC, since an RRDS does not contain distributed freespace, only a KSDS does).

Cluster with variable-length records (KSDS and ESDS only).   There are two cases to consider here:

1. Every record has a different length. This does not happen often—a variable-length record file with all different size records—but it represents the easier case and

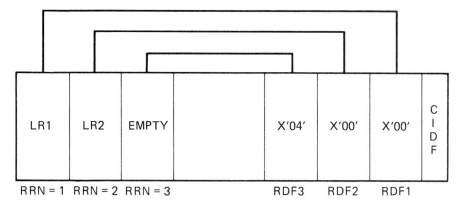

RRN = 1 RRN = 2 RRN = 3   RDF3   RDF2   RDF1

RDF VALUE: X'00' ──────► SLOT OCCUPIED
RDF VALUE: X'04' ──────► SLOT EMPTY

Figure 8-16. RDF-to-RRN pairing.

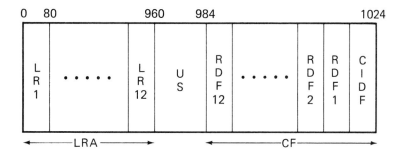

LRA SIZE = 960 BYTES (12 80-BYTE RECORDS)
CF SIZE   = 40 BYTES (1 4-BYTE CIDF + 12 3-BYTE RDFs)
US   = 24 BYTES (OF UNUSED SPACE)

Figure 8-17. The structure of a CI with fixed-length records.

will help establish a general principle which will assist us in the second, and harder, case. For this case, VSAM will use one RDF per record in the CI: this RDF will contain the length of the associated record, given that all such lrecl values are different. To take an example: assume a CI containing seven records of different lengths; this will require seven RDFs in the CI. Hence 25 bytes of the CISZ are reserved for control fields by VSAM (four for the CIDF and 21 for the seven RDFs).

2. Some equi-length contiguous records. A block of equi-length contiguous records within a variable-length record file is called a *run*—as, for instance four

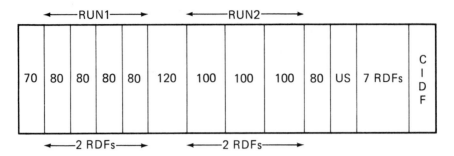

Figure 8-18. RDF determination with variable-length records.

adjacent 80-byte records—and the number of records in such a block is the *run-number* (referred to earlier). Consider the example of Figure 8-18. There we have two runs, a run1 of four 80-byte records, and a run2 of three 100-byte records; the remaining three records (70, 80, and 120 bytes in length) are not part of any such runs: no record adjacent to them has the same length as they do; note that the single 80-byte record is not part of run2, even though sharing a common length (80 bytes), since it is not contiguous with any of the records in this run.

Now let's consider how VSAM will handle the RDFs required for this case. Each one of the three records that are not part of any run of adjacent equi-length records will require one RDF of its own, this RDF giving the lrecl of the associated record. In addition, *each run requires two RDFs*: one RDF, the first, for containing the common length of all records in the run, and another, the second, for containing the run-number. Thus, a total of seven RDFs are required in this case, as seen in Figure 8-18. Two and only two RDFs are required per run, regardless of how many records (more than one) are involved in the run, since we need only encode common length and run-number information to completely describe the run.

Note one important implication of this principle: using variable-length KSDSs or ESDSs may incur larger control field overhead within the CI than the fixed-length record case (which requires only two RDFs), since the number of RDFs increases as the number of records not in runs increases, and this may be quite significant with many KSDSs or ESDSs. More bytes reserved for control fields means fewer bytes are available for storing data records and using for FSPC. This has to be kept in mind in considerations of performance (and we will revisit this point in Chapter 18, on performance).

8.9 PRINCIPLES OF CISZ

Let's now use one of the examples we've been using above to consolidate the discussion of CISZ and the various components of CISZ within the CI. Consider an example where the CISZ is equal to 1024, records are fixed-length (80 bytes), and the requested FSPC is 25 percent of the CI. The FSPC request is honored by VSAM by reserving 256 bytes of the CI for distributed free space. (If there were a fraction of a byte resulting from the computation, VSAM would *round down*.) Then an additional 10 bytes are reserved by VSAM for control fields: one four-byte CIDF, and two three-byte RDFs. This leaves 758 bytes for storing logical records. Given 80-byte records, nine records can be stored per CI (10 would require 800 bytes, more than is available after FSPC is honored and control fields are allocated), so that the LR-density is equal to nine. Now, with an LR-density of nine, the LRA size is equal to 720 bytes. Out of the CISZ of 1024, therefore, 38 bytes are unused space (US).

We can now articulate the first of three principles of CISZ that we will develop in this section:

> *CISZ Principle 1*: The CISZ should be chosen such that, given the requested FSPC (if any) and the known amount of space reserved for control fields (CF), the resulting LR-density gives an LRA size such as to minimize the amount of unused space (US) in the CI.

To both see this principle in action in rejecting some choice of CISZ, as well as to develop the underpinnings of our second principle of CISZ, let's modify one feature of the example just discussed, namely the lrecl, but leave all other features the same. If the records are now 256 bytes in length, the computations would run as follows. First, with the same FSPC request of 25 percent against the same CISZ of 1024, 256 bytes, just as before, will be reserved by VSAM to honor our FSPC request. Second, the same 10 bytes are reserved for CF (CIDFs and RDFs) as before. And once again, this leaves 758 bytes for storing logical records.

Now let's compute the LR-density in this case: this must be two, since two 256-byte LRs would yield 512 bytes for the LRA, but three would require 768 bytes, more than is available. With an LRA size of 512 bytes, 246 bytes *per CI* are unused space (US = 246). This is an extraordinarily large amount of unused, and *unusuable*, space: 24 percent of each CI. To get a sense of how much space may be wasted in this case, consider the features presented as associated with, say, a 50 cylinder data set on a 3380 disk: without going into the actual computations (the reader will learn how to perform these in Chapter 18, on performance), suffice it to say that close to *six million bytes* of space is unused throughout the data set. Performance will certainly and significantly be affected adversely.

This leads us to the second CISZ principle:

> *CISZ Principle 2*: Compute the *theoretical LR-density*:

$$\frac{(\text{CISZ} - \text{FC} - \text{FSPC-bytes})}{\text{lrecl}}$$

This division should either be: (a.) an integer (whole number), or (b.) a number x.yyy…where normal rules of rounding would round down, not up. The closer the value of .yyy to zero, the better (less unused space).

If the theoretical LR-density is a whole number, then essentially no unused space will result (US=0), the best case. Clause b of principle 2 assures that the decimal portion of the resulting division (when not zero, as in the case of an integer) is less than half a decimal point (less than .500...) since that is the rule for rounding down; if the decimal value is such as to cause rounding up, then it is greater than .500... and will yield a significant amount of unused space, since despite normal rounding rules, VSAM *always* rounds down.

Let's look at this principle applied to the example we just traced through:

$$\text{Theoretical LR-density} = \frac{1024 - 10 - 256}{256}$$

$$= \frac{758}{256} = 2.96...$$

This would be a clear warning of trouble with respect to unused space: we would normally round this up to three, but VSAM rounds down to two, so that only 512 bytes (two 256-byte records) of the 758 can be used, leaving 246 bytes unused.

But say we adjust the FSPC request down even just two percentage points, to 23 percent rather than the original 25 percent. This request translates into 235 FSPC-bytes (.23 × 1024 = 235.52..., rounded down), just 21 bytes less than the original amount of 256 FSPC-bytes. Now the computation is:

$$\text{Theoretical LR-density} = \frac{1024 - 10 - 235}{256}$$

$$= \frac{779}{256} = 3.04...$$

with normal rules of rounding dictating our rounding down to three, just as VSAM would (it always rounds down, remember). This should yield a very small amount of unused space, according to principle 2, since the .04... value is very close to zero. Since we will be able to store 3 LRs in the 779 bytes of available space (after control fields and FSPC has been allocated), then 768 bytes (3 × 256) of the 779 available is used for the logical record area (LRA), leaving only 11 bytes per CI unused, slightly more than one percent of the CISZ, obviously a vast improvement.

To take this principle one step further and show just how beneficial the careful application of it may be, let's be even more conservative in adjusting the FSPC request downward: now let's just move down to a 24 percent FSPC request, merely one percent less than the original 25 percent. This 24 percent FSPC translates into 245 bytes of FSPC (.24 × 1024 = 245.76, rounded down), so the computation is now:

$$\text{Theoretical LR-density} = \frac{1024 - 10 - 245}{256}$$

$$= \frac{769}{256} = 3.0003...$$

Of the 769 bytes available (after FSPC and CF are allocated), 768 bytes are used for LRs (that is, the size of the LRA = 3 × 256 = 768), yielding just one byte as unused space! And remember that this result was obtained just by adjusting the FSPC request from 25 percent down to 24 percent! In sum, with 256-byte records against a CISZ of 1024, an FSPC request of 25 percent of each CI to be reserved for record insertion yielded 24 percent of each CI as unused space, while an FSPC request of 24 percent yielded less than one-tenth of one percent of each CI as unused space (unused space = one byte). Although the programmer is involved in carrying out these computations for a few choices of FSPC against a fixed CISZ, the payoff in terms of performance can be very appreciable, so the reward is well worth the labor invested.

We can now articulate our third and last CISZ principle at this time:

> *CISZ Principle 3*: If a large amount of unused space results from the computation used in applying principle 2 above, adjust the FSPC request down a percentage point at a time until a satisfactory result is obtained (small unused space).

Note that this principle cannot be applied directly to a case in which no FSPC was requested. That case entails more radical adjustment—in CISZ chosen, generally—but we defer consideration of this special case to Chapter 18, on performance. In general, however, application of the above three principles to the vast majority of standard cases will allow the programmer to obtain better performance by minimizing the overhead due to large amounts of unused space in the CIs of a VSAM cluster.

8.10   PRINCIPLES OF CA SIZE (CASZ)

There are just two principles of CA size (which we will call *CASZ* although there is no 'CASZ' parameter available to the programmer, as there is with CISZ). Remember that CASZ can only be controlled indirectly through the space allocation request at DEFINE CLUSTER time.

> *CASZ Principle 1*: Larger CASZ will generally be associated with better performance.

> *CASZ Principle 2*: Wherever possible, allocate space to a cluster in cylinder units.

The motivation behind principle 1 can only be appreciated after we have discussed certain VSAM operations, as well as the structure of a VSAM index, so we defer this until the appropriate time.

Principle 2 is more straightfoward. VSAM allows CAs to span across a cylinder boundary (start on one cylinder and end on another) whenever space allocation for the cluster is in units of records or tracks, but prohibits cylinder-spanning by CAs if cylinder units are specified. Performance, however, is appreciably better if an entire CA can be processed with a single arm access on the DASD device: this is assured if the whole CA is on one cylinder, but if cylinder-spanning exists, then it will require two (or more) arm accesses to process an entire CA. Therefore, except for very small data sets, it is good practice from a performance point of view to allocate by cylinder, guaranteeing no cylinder-spanning and yielding the maximum CASZ of one cylinder (which also meets principle 1 above).

9

VSAM CLUSTERS—DEFINING, LOADING, AND OTHER OPERATIONS

9.1 DEFINING VSAM CLUSTERS

In this section we will present the basic IDCAMS coding used to create VSAM clusters—KSDSs, ESDSs, and RRDSs. We will use the KSDS coding as the foundation from which, through relatively low-level and minor changes, we derive the coding for ESDSs and RRDSs. We treat here only the major and most commonly specified parameters: there are close to three dozen DEFINE CLUSTER parameters, many for extremely specialized functions; we will deal with still others than those treated in this section in later sections of this text, as appropriate, by function (performance-oriented parameters are dealt with in Chapter 18, on performance, security-oriented parameters in Chapter 16, on data security and integrity, etc.). For highly specialized parameters, the reader should consult the appropriate reference manual (where, unfortunately, the reader may not be much the wiser for the effort in many cases).

9.1.1 Defining a KSDS

The JCL and IDCAMS commands, in general form, for defining a VSAM cluster (KSDS, ESDS, RRDS) are given in Figure 9-1. We have generally used the common abbreviations for most parameters, except where we felt this might compromise readability; for example, the REUSE/NOREUSE parameter choice allows the abbreviations RUS/NRUS, but this short form is rarely used and would be unfamiliar to many programmers. In addition, where choices are to be made in any parameter, as in SUBAL/UNQ, this is indicated by a slash character separating the possible choices; any VSAM defaults are indicated by underline, as in SUBAL/UNQ. Now let's look at a sample coding of the IDCAMS commands (the JCL remains the same, so we do not repeat it), using the same numbering for reference purposes, given in Figure 9-2.

DISCUSSION

(Numbers refer to line numbers in figure.)

5. *NAME*: The cluster name is given as the value of this parameter. Here, as is customary in many MVS installations, the cluster name is in qualified form, and in

```
1.    // ... JOB ...
2.    // EXEC PGM=IDCAMS
3.    //SYSPRINT DD SYSOUT=A
4.    //SYSIN DD *
5.      DEFINE CLUSTER -
6.         (NAME (cluster-name) -
7.          VOL (volser) -
8.          CYL/TRK/REC (pri sec) -
9.          RECSZ (avg max) -
10.         KEYS (len off) -
11.         FSPC (ci-fspc ca-fspc) -
12.         INDEXED/NONINDEXED/NUMBERED/LINEAR -
13.         SUBAL/UNQ -
14.         REUSE/NOREUSE) -
15.      DATA -
16.         (NAME (data component name) -
17.          CISZ (cisz)) -
18.      INDEX -
19.         (NAME (index component name))
20.    /*
```

Figure 9-1. Defining a VSAM cluster.

```
5.      DEFINE CLUSTER -
6.         (NAME (TRUCAT.TSUSER01.MSTRV001) -
7.          VOL (TRU008) -
8.          CYL (50 3) -
9.          RECSZ (80 80) -
10.         KEYS (9 19) -
11.         FSPC (25 10) -
12.         INDEXED -
13.         SUBAL -
14.         NOREUSE) -
15.      DATA -
16.         (NAME (TRUCAT.TSUSER01.MSTRV001.DATA) -
17.          CISZ (1024)) -
18.      INDEX -
19.         (NAME (TRUCAT.TSUSER01.MSTRV001.INDEX))
```

Figure 9-2. Defining a KSDS cluster.

addition the HLQ technique of identifying the catalog in which this cluster entry is to be made is used: this cluster is being cataloged in a catalog (one of) whose alias is the HLQ, *TRUCAT* (as we discussed earlier in the text, in Section 5.2). Note that here we are providing a *cluster name*, as opposed to a *component name*, which provides a name for the actual component data sets, the data component and, if a KSDS, then also the index component. See the discussion of statements 15 and 17, below.

6. *VOL*: This parameter specifies the volume serial number of the volume on

which the data set is to be created and stored. If the cluster is to be a multivolume data set, then each of the volume serial numbers are given here as a list: for example, VOL (TRU008, TRU009, TRU010). The volumes must be of the same device type (all 3380s, or all 3350, etc.).

Note that the sample coding forces the data and index components of a KSDS cluster to coreside on the same volume (here, TRU008). VSAM allows, however, for the data and index components to reside on two separate volumes, which may even be different device types (one a 3350, say, and the other a 3380). This is sometimes done for performance reasons, but in Chapter 18, on performance, this motivation is discussed and it is concluded that the objective is not often realized in actual circumstances; nonetheless, if the programmer had good reason for separating the two components in this fashion, it is done by *not* coding any VOL parameter on the cluster level (as coded here), but only coding VOL on both the data and index component level and specifying two different volume serial numbers (we have only coded NAME, and on one level, CISZ, at the component level in statements 14 through 18, but VOL could have been added for this purpose). Note that the VOL parameter could not be coded both at the cluster level and at the component level: in terms of actual storage, the cluster does not have an existence independent from its components, which are the physically real data sets.

8. *Space Allocation*: Allocation may be in units of cylinders (CYL), tracks (TRK), or records (REC). If REC is specified, then another parameter, recordsize (RECSZ) must also be coded in the form RECSZ (avg max), giving as subparameters the average record length (avg) and the maximum record length (max); if the records are fixed-length, then avg is equal to max and the same value is coded for both subparameters.

The allocation request must request a primary quantity (pri), which must be satisfiable on the particular volume for which space is being requested in order for the DEFINE CLUSTER to succeed, and optionally a secondary quantity (sec). If the cluster is being defined as a *unique* cluster, then primary and secondary allocation is handled by the OS space manager (OS DADSM) and follows familiar OS rules: the primary must be satisfiable in five or fewer extents, and the secondary may be satisfied in as many as 15 extents, if only one extent was needed for the primary, but in all cases the primary and secondary quantities collectively can involve a maximum of 16 extents.

If the cluster is a *suballocated* cluster, then the space allocation is handled by VSAM space management routines, not by OS DADSM, with the primary quantity following the same procedure as in OS, but the secondary allowing as many as 122 extents in addition to the one primary, or if more than one extent is needed for the primary quantity, the primary and secondary extents together cannot exceed the maximum of 123 extents total. Given this, therefore, it is important for the programmer to be much more conservative about secondary allocation quantities when dealing with VSAM suballocated clusters than when dealing either with OS files or VSAM unique clusters. Many programmers, in dealing with OS data sets, make the secondary quantity between 10 and 20 percent of the primary quantity, but VSAM calls for more modest amounts: 5 percent or fewer will generally suffice. To appreciate this, consider this coding under OS and VSAM:

```
CYL (100 20)
```

When handled by OS (for OS files *and VSAM unique clusters*), then as many as 400 cylinders may be used for the growth of the associated file ($100 + 15 \times 20$). When handled by VSAM, however, then the file may grow to as much as 2,540 cylinders ($100 + 122 \times 20$), almost certainly an unintentionally excessively large allocation! A seconday quantity of two or three cylinders would probably be more reasonable and still provide a sufficient secondary backup amount. Remember also that, if acceptable, allocation in cylinders has performance advantages (see Section 8.10 earlier).

9. *RECORDSIZE*: This parameter is coded in the form RECSZ (avg max), giving as subparameters the average record length and maximum record length; if the records are fixed-length, then avg = max and the same value is coded for both subparameters.

10. *KEYS*: This parameter refers to the prime key field for the KSDS, giving its length and location, the latter through the byte offset of the field within the record *against a zero starting position*: if the field is found starting in the twentieth byte position of the record, by standard counting, then its VSAM offset is 19, counting from zero. A common error is to specify the familiar 'column' position of the field, which will be off by one byte, generally resulting in some 'duplicate key' error condition, since VSAM will be looking at a field consisting of the last byte of the previous field, followed by all but the last byte of the intended key field, and this is unlikely to give a unique set of key values. We have already discussed keys in a KSDS comprehensively in Subsection 8.2.1, and the reader may review that discussion at this time, if necessary.

11. *FSPC*: This parameter, the essentials of which we have already discussed, specifies how much distributed freespace is to be reserved by VSAM throughout the data set for its use in insertion operations. Records will not be loaded into this reserved FSPC at cluster load time. Ci-fspc is CI-internal FSPC: the percentage of the CI to be kept free, and ca-fspc is CA-internal FSPC: the percentage of the CIs within the CA that should be kept wholly free. FSPC (25 10) translates into a request that 25 percent *of each CI* should be reserved for FSPC (rounding down to a whole number of bytes, as we have seen), and 10 percent of the CA (one CI out of every ten CIs) should be kept wholly empty, where this CA-internal request must yield a whole number of CIs (VSAM *rounds down* to the next lower integral number of CIs). Note also that VSAM will assure at least one free CI per CA whenever any nonzero value is specified for ca-fspc, even if the percentage figure, interpreted literally, would yield less than an entire free CI per CA: so, for example, with FSPC (25 10), if there were fewer than 10 CI per CA (that is, CI-density < 10), then 1 CI per CA would still be reserved for FSPC.

12. *INDEXED/NONINDEXED/NUMBERED/LINEAR*: This parameter choice determines cluster type: INDEXED (abbreviation: IDX), the default, yields a KSDS,

NONINDEXED (NIXD) yields an ESDS; NUMBERED (NUMD) yields an RRDS, and LINEAR yields an LDS (whose discussion is deferred to Chapter 18, on performance).

13. *SUBAL/UNQ*: We have already discussed VSAM suballocation versus unique allocation for clusters (see the comprehensive treatment in the chapter on VSAM space management, Chapter 7, Section 3). We have also detailed the restrictions on VSAM unique clusters. One additional point, however, can be made about the tradeoffs involved in suballocated versus unique clusters: unique clusters tend to perform better strictly at DEFINE time than suballocated clusters, especially on a volume relatively congested with VSAM data spaces and clusters. This is due to the fact that the VSAM space manager is designed to be very DASD-conservative and will perform an extensive search to find the smallest possible allocation to satisfy the primary space allocation request, which can be quite time consuming, this in an effort to avoid DASD fragmentation (this is a 'best fit' strategy), but the OS space manager (OS DADSM) avoids this overhead and selects the first suitable allocation. However, keep in mind that this is only for DEFINE time, and does not exist at any later time of processing the data set (from load time on), so this is not a decisive advantage.

14. *Reusable versus Non-Reusable Clusters*: Unless explicitly overridden by the programmer at DEFINE CLUSTER time, VSAM clusters are said to be *non-reusable*: such a cluster may be loaded only once; whenever the cluster's contents need to be replaced *in entirety*, the cluster must be deleted and then recreated by a new DEFINE CLUSTER being issued. A *reusable* cluster, however, supports multiple distinct loads: whenever it is desired to replace the entire cluster by overwriting the existing records with any new records written to the cluster, the programmer need only either:

1. issue a CLOSE for the cluster, followed by an OPEN for OUTPUT, which may be in the same program as the close, or in a separate program;
2. issue an IDCAMS REPRO command with the REUSE option, thus allowing any records written from the input data set to overwrite the existing records of the output data set, the reusable cluster.

Note that in both cases it is necessary for the cluster to have been DEFINEd with the REUSE option (not the default, NOREUSE); there is a minor exception to this rule, but it is rarely of any practical use, so we will leave the generalization stand.

REUSABLE CLUSTERS AND THE HURBA

VSAM enables the reusable cluster facility by manipulating something called the *high used relative byte address* (*HURBA*), a critical concept in VSAM processing. Associated with any VSAM file is the HURBA field, which functions as a VSAM indicator for end-of-file (in terms of the part of the file that contains actual data records). HURBA contains the offset of the last byte of the file, and VSAM works to maintain HURBA to reflect the changing growth of a file under VSAM processing so that, ideally, whenever the offset of the file's last byte changes (records are added or deleted, for example), the value of the HURBA field for that file is updated to be in synchrony with the latest fact of the file's actual end-of-file point. VSAM maintains the HURBA as an internal control field in virtual storage under VSAM's control, *but only writes the value of this field to the catalog at CLOSE time.* After a DEFINE CLUSTER but before any records are loaded into the file, VSAM sets HURBA to zero (X'0'). Then, after the records are loaded and the file is CLOSEd, the HURBA is revised to reflect real end-of-file by pointing to the last byte of the file. Subsequent to this, after any processing against the file *which is followed by a valid CLOSE*, VSAM updates the HURBA again in synchrony with the known EOF point at that time.

With a reusable cluster, VSAM always *resets HURBA to zero* after the sequence:

```
CLOSE macro
OPEN...OUTPUT
```

or its equivalent: REPRO + the REUSE option is considered equivalent to the above sequence. Since a value of HURBA = X'0' denotes that the cluster contains no records (the last byte is at offset zero, namely at the logical-start-of-file), the cluster is thus marked *empty*, and so available for reuse as if no records had ever been loaded or stored in the cluster. The actual resetting is done at OPEN for OUTPUT time, so that thereafter VSAM will treat the cluster as empty, when in actual fact it contains data records, thus allowing it to be used as a work file over and over again without having to delete and redefine it. Each new OPEN for OUTPUT issued is treated as another load of the file, so that all previous contents are overlaid with any new records written; the previous contents can be read and processed at any time prior to another OPEN for OUTPUT. This feature of reusable clusters makes them invaluable as test data sets, the most common use of such clusters.

RESTRICTIONS ON REUSABLE CLUSTERS

- A reusable cluster may not be a unique cluster (only suballocated reusable clusters are supported)
- No alternate index (AIX) may be built over a reusable cluster (that is, the *base cluster* may not be reusable, although any of the AIXs built over the non-reusable base may themselves be reusable).
- A cluster defined as reusable (DEFINE CLUSTER + REUSE option) may not be altered (by the ALTER command) to non-reusable.
- *Keyranges* cannot be defined for a reusable cluster (we discuss the VSAM *keyrange* facility later in the text).

TWO WARNINGS CONCERNING REUSABLE CLUSTERS

1. A reusable cluster is restricted to having a maximum of 16 extents; this may be surprising since a reusable cluster must be a suballocated cluster which generally

allows a max of 123 extents. In this case, although a reusable cluster may not be unique, its space allocation behavior is like that of unique clusters.

2. At any time, just like any other VSAM cluster, a reusable cluster may go into secondary extents (require extents over just the primary extent(s)), with a maximum of 16 extents total, as indicated above. Note, however, that whenever the cluster is reused (at OPEN for OUTPUT time), *all secondary extents are released*, so that the file occupies only its originally specified primary extent(s). This can be unexpected: a reusable cluster with a primary allocation of, say, 30 cylinders, which at some point required five additional secondary extents, each of two cylinders in size, would be seen by the programmer at that time as a 40 cylinder data set, but when reOPENed for OUTPUT, the cluster reverts back to 30 cylinders in size! (Programmer beware!)

16. *Component Naming*: VSAM only requires the programmer, when creating a cluster, to name the cluster; it is optional to, in addition, provide names for the individual components, data and index. It is, however, strongly recommended that the programmer name all three entities—cluster, data, and index component— explicitly. There are two principal motivations for this. First, if the programmer fails to name the data and index components, then they will be assigned VSAM-generated names which are impossibly unwieldly to work with; here are two sample component names actually generated by VSAM, for data and index components, respectively:

```
T19CEAB0.VSAMDSET.DFD81132.T91F26B5.T19CEAB0
T19CFA00.VSAMDSET.DFD81132.T91F26B5.T19CFA00
```

We could rest our case against VSAM-generated component names on just this, but there is a second rationale for user-supplied names: when all three VSAM entities are separately named, then they may be referenced and processed individually. So, we could, for example, issue a PRINT command against just the index, and if we are coding in Assembler we could process either component wholly independently of the other. (Neither COBOL nor PL/I allows program-processing of other than the cluster, in a batch environment.)

RECOMMENDATION

We have followed here a particular naming convention which, although not in any way an official standard, is nonetheless widely used and meets common commercial programming requirements. The convention is to name the data and index components by simply appending a final qualifier of *DATA* and *INDEX*, respectively, to the cluster name. Although other conventions are certainly possible, this is a simple, effective, and consistent convention that assures easily predictable and recognizable names for any cluster and its associated components. We will extend this convention throughout the text to apply to other VSAM objects (AIXs, paths, etc.). Here the convention is simply represented as:

```
cluster-name
cluster-name.DATA
cluster-name.INDEX
```

where cluster-name can, and generally is, a qualified (multipart) name with, in addition, the HLQ (high level qualifier, the leftmost part of the name) usually being the alias (or, more rarely, the one and only truename) of some VSAM catalog, again usually a user catalog. (Remember, however, that the name of any VSAM object cannot exceed a total of 44 characters including the periods used in qualified names.)

17. *CISZ*: Here we have chosen to specify CISZ not at the cluster level, but at the component level, and—at this time for purposes of illustration—only for the data component (the index component CISZ will be determined by VSAM default rules, and depends on cluster characteristics and device type considerations). Had CISZ been specified at the cluster level and not at the component level, then the CISZ selected would have been used for both, not a desirable result, in general. We have already discussed CISZ in Chapter 8, and given some basic principles for CISZ selection (see Sections 8.4 and 8.9). However, selection of CISZ for performance optimization is quite complex, and we defer such discussion until Chapter 18, on performance.

9.1.2 Defining an ESDS

Defining an ESDS is a relatively simple variation on KSDS definition, adjusting for the characteristics of an ESDS type cluster. An ESDS cluster has no index component, so parameters are generally coded only at the cluster level, to be inherited downward to the data component. Furthermore, an ESDS contains no key field and no distributed free space, so the parameters KEYS and FSPC are omitted (they apply only to KSDS clusters). Finally, the NONINDEXED parameter is required (instead of INDEXED) when defining an ESDS. Therefore, the sample coding in Figure 9-3 generally reflects what is required to define an ESDS cluster.

9.1.3 Defining an RRDS

Like an ESDS, an RRDS has no index component, no key field and no distributed free space. The coding is almost identical to that of an ESDS, but instead of coding NONINDEXED, we code NUMBERED for an RRDS cluster definition; sample coding is given in Figure 9-4.

9.2 HOW TO LOAD A VSAM CLUSTER

As we have noted repeatedly, defining a cluster yields an empty data set, ready for subsequent loading. Loading is the operation of writing data records into the empty cluster after the cluster has been defined. VSAM supports two different techniques for such record loading, discussed in the following two subsections.

9.2.1 Program Load

In this technique, a programming language supporting VSAM operations (COBOL, PL/I, Assembler, etc.) is used to code a load program which writes the data records

```
DEFINE CLUSTER -
  (NAME (TRUCAT.TDTKANTT.TRANSIN1) -
  VOL (TRU007) -
  CYL (10 1) -
  RECSZ (80 80) -
  CISZ (8192) -
  NONINDEXED -
  SUBAL -
  NOREUSE)
```

Figure 9-3. Defining an ESDS cluster.

```
DEFINE CLUSTER -
  (NAME (FINCAT.MVS003T.INQR0021) -
  VOL (FIN006) -
  CYL (8 1) -
  RECSZ (80 80) -
  CISZ (1536) -
  NUMBERED -
  UNIQUE -
  REUSE)
```

Figure 9-4. Defining an RRDS cluster.

into the cluster from another file, or from instream data. The cluster is OPENed for OUTPUT and WRITE or PUT macros are issued to load the records into the cluster one at a time, just as might be done to load records into any file, VSAM or otherwise.

VSAM imposes some additional requirements on the load operation.

- The records to be loaded into the cluster must be presented in ascending (sorted) order by value of the prime key field.
- There must be no duplicate key fields: that is, the prime keys must be *unique*.
- The WRITE or PUT operations must be in *sequential* mode for a KSDS or ESDS, and may be in either sequential or random mode only for an RRDS.

VSAM considers a program to be in *load mode*, and therefore subject to the above requirements from the point of a VSAM OPEN macro being issued against a cluster with an HURBA equal to X'0' (empty cluster, or a resettable (reusable) cluster) to the point of a CLOSE macro being issued, with *at least one sequential write operation* being issued between these two points. Input, update, and random mode processing (except for an RRDS) must follow at least one successful write operation and the CLOSE macro, these post-CLOSE operations being considered by VSAM to be post-load time operations. (The program coding for COBOL, which is quite straightforward, is given later in the text.)

A NOTE ON SO-CALLED RANDOM LOAD OF A KSDS (CICS ENVIRONMENT)

As noted above, VSAM does not support random loading of a KSDS cluster—only sequential loading—yet it is sometimes the case that something like a random load is called for under special circumstances. This may arise in an on-line environment like that of CICS, where many VSAM files may be shared by the batch (MVS) and CICS system. Consider the following situation. An online VSAM file is to contain records solely written from online terminal input; the records may arrive from multiple online terminals in random order, and it is not predictable where the first records to be loaded into the cluster (empty before this time) will come from, with all records to be written in random mode.

Here, the customary way in which this is handled is to satisfy, minimally, the VSAM requirement of sequential load by OPENing the cluster for OUTPUT, writing in sequential mode a *single* 'control' or dummy record with a key value that is arbitrarily the lowest or the highest possible value of the prime key field (with the record typically containing no other actual user data), and then issuing a CLOSE macro. Once this single dummy record has been written to the file, the load mode is over, and records may now be written to the file in random as well as sequential order. This may not always assure high performance, but it does solve the problem.

9.2.2   Utility Load: The REPRO Command.

Instead of using a program to load records into an empty cluster, the IDCAMS REPRO command may—and commonly is—used. We have already discussed the basic function and coding of the REPRO command (see Subsection 6.3.3, earlier). Here we will examine the use of the REPRO command for copy/conversion functions, especially in generating VSAM clusters as output.

OS SAM TO VSAM KSDS CONVERSION

One very easy way to load records into an empty cluster is to copy the record contents of an input file into the VSAM cluster (which, of course, must have been priorly defined). In Figure 9-5 we convert a preexisting OS sequential file into a VSAM KSDS cluster. Several points should be noted in this coding.

First, the OS data set which is the input to the REPRO command is assumed to be cataloged, so that UNIT and VOLUME parameters are not needed. This file is referred to indirectly in statement 8: the ddname coded as the INFILE subparameter is that of a preceding JCL statement (4) which references the file by data set name; the output file (a VSAM KSDS cluster) is similarly indirectly referred to. An alternative coding would be to omit the two JCL statements defining the input and output files and use this special form of the REPRO command to make direct file references:

```
REPRO -
     INDATASET  (FINCAT.MVSOO3T.INQROO21) -
     OUTDATASET (TRUCAT.MVSOO3T.INQROO21.VS)
```

```
 1.    // JOB . . .
 2.    // EXEC     PGM=IDCAMS
 3.    //SYSPRINT DD SYSOUT=A
 4.    //INDD      DD DSN=FINCAT.MVS003T.INQR0021,DISP=OLD
 5.    //OUTDD     DD DSN=TRUCAT.MVS003T.INQR0021.VS,
       //          DISP=OLD
 6.    //SYSIN     DD *
 7.       REPRO -
 8.                 INFILE (INDD) -
 9.                 OUTFILE (OUTDD)
10.    /*
```

Figure 9-5. REPRO for converting SAM to VSAM.

As we noted earlier, VSAM is said to *dynamically allocate* the files in such an approach; however, there are several special restrictions that must be met for dynamic allocation to be valid, especially concerning the data set name structure, and we recommend avoiding the niceties of such restrictions and simply coding with the INFILE and OUTFILE parameters and associated JCL.

Second, most programmers are used to seeing the JCL DD statements referring to VSAM files with a DISP=SHR coded; when, however, VSAM clusters are being created (DEFINE CLUSTER time) and—as here—when VSAM clusters are first being loaded, the coding should be DISP=OLD to guarantee that the cluster is held in exclusive control during the load operation, thus disallowing any user concurrent access to the cluster while the create or load is in operation. (At other than define and load time, the cluster can, and generally is, sharable.)

Third, note that the REPRO operation will effect a *conversion* from OS sequential organization to VSAM KSDS organization; VSAM will automatically construct the appropriate data and index components. The index component is constructed by VSAM by using whatever prime key field was specified for the cluster at DEFINE CLUSTER time. Say the relevant parameter was coded as KEYS (9, 19), where the prime key field is a social security number (SSN). VSAM will locate the field starting at the twentieth byte (offset of $19 \rightarrow$ column position of 20), for a length of 9, *of the input file* (FINCAT.MVS003T.INVR0021)—which, remember, is a sequential file and has no key field defined for it while an OS file—and use it as the prime key field on which to order the records when constructing the output VSAM KSDS cluster. Two conditions must be assured for the conversion of an OS SAM file—as above—into a VSAM KSDS cluster to succeed.

One, the records of the input OS SAM file must be in strict ascending order over whatever field will constitute the prime key field in the target (output) cluster; if this is not already the case (and it may not be, since the OS SAM file is intrinsically an unkeyed file), then the records must be sorted into strict ascending sequence before being presented to VSAM. Thus, there may be an original unsorted version of the OS file, and a sorted version, the latter of which will be the input to the REPRO operation.

Two, the values of the field in the input file which shall be used as a prime key field in the output file must contain no duplicates: the field must be *unique*, as VSAM does not allow duplicate keys in a KSDS prime key field (duplicate keys are allowed only in an *alternate index*).

In our example, the records of the input OS SAM file are assumed to be stored in ascending social security number order, and since SSNs are inherently unique, we satisfy both of the requirements given above. (If the records were not already sorted, then a sort program like Whitlow's SYNCSORT or IBM's recent DFSORT is generally used to pre-sort the records.)

9.2.3   How VSAM Builds a Cluster

KSDS Cluster.   We speak of a *cluster build* as the process by which VSAM loads actual data records into a previously defined cluster, and builds whatever structure is necessary for the cluster. VSAM loads records into the cluster CA by CA. The default load process is said to be in *recovery mode* (RECOVERY parameter is specified or defaulted to at DEFINE CLUSTER time). This means that VSAM preformats each CA *prior* to loading any records into the CA. Preformatting consists of two operations:

1. VSAM overwrites ('clears') all data previously left on the DASD space to be now occupied by the new cluster. (This is generally done through overwriting with binary zeroes.)
2. VSAM writes a SEOF (software-end-of-file) indicator, consisting of a CIDF field with all zeroes, into the first CI of the next CA (after the one about to be loaded with records). This assists in recovery of records already loaded if the load operation is prematurely interrupted: records before SEOF need not be reloaded, and the load can resume from the SEOF point on. (This turns out to be of more theoretical than of actual use, as will shall see in Chapter 18, on performance.)

Immediately after preformatting of a CA, VSAM loads records into the CA, CI by CI, writing the appropriate CIDF and RDF fields into each CI. Records are loaded in ascending order of prime key field values. After each entire CA which is successfully loaded, VSAM updates the HURBA field in the catalog entry which was created for this cluster (at DEFINE CLUSTER time) to indicate the SEOF *so-far*, changing this HURBA after each CA is loaded until all records have been loaded and HURBA therefore indicates end of data set.

For a KSDS, VSAM also constructs the index as the records are loaded into each CA, using the prime key field specified at DEF CLUSTER time. Essentially, this consists of extracting the values of the prime key field and associating with each such prime key value a corresponding pointer which points to the data component record with that value in its prime key field. This is a simplification, as we shall see in Chapter 11, on the structure of a VSAM index—the keys extracted are stored in the index component in *compressed* form, not as full key values, and the pointers do not target the exact data component record with that key value, but only the CI which that record must be contained in—but the simplification is satisfactory for our purposes here.

ESDS Cluster.   The process for building an ESDS differs from that of a KSDS in the following ways. Preformatting is still done, but the SEOF indicator is written in every CI in a CA, CA by CA. In the KSDS case, if the load is interrupted abnormally, we do not know in which CI the load terminated, only in which CA (SEOF is written to the next CI of the *next CA*), but with an ESDS preformatting is done such that we know the point of interruption accurate to the particular CI. Records are loaded in the physical order in which they are encountered. As there is no index component, the cluster build terminates when the data component is completely loaded.

RRDS Cluster.   The building of an RRDS cluster follows the same process as that used for a KSDS cluster, with two exceptions. One, the preformatting of a CA prior to the loading of records into that CA also involves marking every RDF (each associated with one record slot of the cluster) as indicating an empty slot; the RDF is changed from empty status to occupied status indication if and only if a record is loaded into the slot associated with that RDF. Two, as with an ESDS, there is no index component in an RRDS cluster, so cluster build terminates when the data component is completely loaded.

9.3   IDCAMS UTILITY FUNCTIONS FOR CLUSTERS

9.3.1   Copy and Conversion Facilities: More on REPRO

We have already seen the use of the REPRO command in two basic functions: (1) copying the contents of an in-stream data set into a cluster, thus loading the cluster, and (2) loading a KSDS cluster by converting an OS SAM data set into a VSAM KSDS cluster. Below we will consider some additional functions of REPRO.

VSAM to VSAM copy.   The REPRO command also allows the user to copy one VSAM cluster into another: in this case we are loading one cluster with the contents of a pre-existing cluster. Note that no essential change to the coding given earlier is required: the JCL does not differentiate a VSAM cluster from a cataloged OS data set.

ISAM to VSAM conversion.   There are two points to observe in using REPRO to effect a conversion from an ISAM data set into a VSAM cluster, generally a KSDS. First, the DD statement referencing the input ISAM file would have the following coding:

```
//INDD DD DSN=isam-dsname,DISP=OLD,
//       DCB=DSORG=IS
```

with the DCB parameter explicitly identifying ISAM data set organization. Second, ISAM dummy records—those considered deleted by virtue of the lead byte containing an X'FF' value—are not copied by the conversion operation, since it is assumed that one wants all and only the active (non-deleted) records of the ISAM file to be loaded into the KSDS cluster. If this is *not* desirable, then the following coding for the input file is required:

```
INFILE (indd) -
    ENVIRONMENT (DUMMY)
```

VSAM will then copy *all* ISAM records, active and deleted, into the target cluster.

File pruning options.   A REPRO operation need not copy all records of the input data set: it may be a *selective copy*; this is called *file pruning*. Let's look at an example, given in Figure 9-6, of pruning a KSDS file in order to create a smaller test data set (also a KSDS) with only selective records copied. Here we use the FROMKEY and TOKEY options on the INFILE parameter to selectively copy only records within the range '000000000' to (and including) '499999999' from the input file into the target cluster. Note that if there is no exact match to the specified FROMKEY value, then VSAM will begin the selective copy with *the next higher key* in the file; similarly, if there is no exact match to the specified TOKEY value, VSAM will terminate the selective copy with whatever is the next *lower* actual key in the input file.

Generic Key Processing.   The programmer can request *generic key processing* with the REPRO command: the key criterion is based on a match against the leftmost x bytes of the key field, where x is less than the full key length; for example, we may want to copy all keys whose first three bytes are '500,' followed by any digit

```
 1.    // JOB . . .
 2.    // EXEC     PGM=IDCAMS
 3.    //SYSPRINT DD SYSOUT=A
 4.    //INDD      DD DSN=TRUCAT.MVS003T.INQR0021.VS,
       //             DISP=OLD
 5.    //OUTDD     DD DSN=TRUCAT.MVS003T.INQR0021.TESTVS,
       //             DISP=OLD
 6.    //SYSIN    DD *
 7.      REPRO -
 8.               INFILE (INDD) -
 9.                   FROMKEY (000000000) -
10.                   TOKEY   (499999999) -
11.               OUTFILE (OUTDD)
10.    /*
```

Figure 9-6. File pruning with the REPRO command.

pattern whatever ('500000000,' '500356198,' and '500999999' are all acceptable). This can be coded as follows:

```
REPRO -
        INFILE (INDD) -
            FROMKEY ('500*') -
        OUTFILE (OUDD)
```

The asterisk is the VSAM notation for a generic key value: in this case, the lead bytes '500' followed by anything in the rest of the key. Note also that no TOKEY option has been specified: when TOKEY is omitted, the rest of the data set is implied; this is useful when the terminus of the copy is either not known or is intended to be end-of-file.

COUNT/SKIP Options.   A file can be pruned in still other ways. VSAM offers two additional pruning options on the REPRO command: SKIP and COUNT. SKIP (*n*) is an instruction to VSAM to begin selective copying of the input records from the *n*+oneth record, thereby skipping the first *n* records. SKIP is mutually exclusive with FROMKEY/TOKEY. COUNT (*n*) specifies the number of records to be (selectively) copied; it is mutually exclusive with TOKEY. Two examples should clarify these options.

```
REPRO -
        INFILE (INDD) -
            SKIP (50) -
            COUNT (100) -
        OUTFILE (OUTDD)
```

This will skip the first 50 records of the input file, then copy (from the fifty-first record) the next 100 records, into the output file.

```
REPRO -
        INFILE (INDD) -
            FROMKEY (200000000) -
            COUNT (1000) -
        OUTFILE (OUTDD)
```

This will begin copying input records from the record with the key of '200000000' (or the first record with a higher key if no record contains this exact key) until a total of 1000 records from this point on are copied into the output file.

FADDR/TADDR and FNUM/TNUM.   The FROMKEY/TOKEY options are used with keyed files: both VSAM KSDS and non-VSAM ISAM files. FADDR/TADDR options (short for FROMADDRESS/TOADDRESS) are for use with ESDS and KSDS files, where the value given must be an RBA value. Assume that an ESDS cluster consists of 80-byte fixed-length records.

```
REPRO -
        INFILE (INDD) -
            FADDR (240) -
            TADDR (400) -
        OUTFILE (INDD)
```

This coding would copy from the fourth record of the file to the sixth record of the file, so that only the fourth, fifth, and sixth records are copied. (The first record is at offset zero, the second at offset 80, the third at offset 160, etc.) Here we have given the value in decimal notation, but hex could have been used: FADDR (X'E0'), TADDR (X'0190'). When FADDR/TADDR are used for a KSDS file, VSAM is forced to copy the records in *physical sequential* rather than in *logical sequential* (ascending key) order; the need to read a KSDS in physical sequential order is a highly specialized one, so it will probably be very rare to encounter FADDR/TADDR coding for a KSDS.

FNUM/TNUM (short for FROMNUMBER/TONUMBER) options are used for file pruning of an RRDS. The options specify the RRNs of the first and last records to be copied selectively; otherwise, these options follow the same principles as those given above for the other file pruning options.

Merge operations with REPRO.   Up to this point we have only considered copy/conversion operations using REPRO when the target data set was empty. REPRO, however, can also be used to perform *merge operations* in cases in which both input and output (target) data sets contain records. The key issue here is what the REPRO operation will do when there are some matching keys in the input and target files, that is, when some records in the input file have the same keys as some of the records in the target file. This is wholly determined by the REP/NREP (short for REPLACE/NOREPLACE) option on the REPRO command.

The default is NREP, and when this option is in effect matching keys across the files are considered in error: for each pair of input/output records with matching keys, VSAM generates a 'duplicate record' error message. VSAM in such cases disallows any replacement of the target record by the source record, and VSAM processing simply continues with the next record. Thus, no merging of records occurs in the default case.

If merging of input and output records is desired, then the REP option must be specified on the REPRO command. In this case, for every match (where the source record key is equal to the target record key), VSAM *replaces* the target record with the source record, thus performing an elementary update-type logic. For all other source records (those whose keys do not match any record keys in the target data set), the source records are simply inserted into the target data set in their proper key order. Thus, the records of the two files are merged, with automatic replacement of target records by source records under key-match conditions. If no records match in the two files, only insertion of source records into the target data set (in key order) is performed. The REP option on the REPRO command is, therefore, a fast and exceptionally simple way to merge the records of two files together into one file, without recourse to program coding.

9.3.2 Deleting and Purging Clusters: The DELETE Command

The DELETE command is one of the simplest commands to use, as can be seen by the example in Figure 9-7. The coding requires the entryname of the VSAM object to be deleted to be given as the primary parameter (statement 6). The keyword parameter CLUSTER simply specifies the type of VSAM object being deleted. Note that no JCL DD statement is needed to refer to the target object.

Other VSAM objects that may be deleted (with the keyword, generally given in abbreviated form, required in the coding in place of CLUSTER) are: an ALIAS, an AIX (alternate index), a GDG (generation data group), a NVSAM (non-VSAM) data set (if cataloged in a VSAM catalog), a PATH, (VSAM) SPACE, and a UCAT (usercatalog), along with a few more specialized objects which we will not discuss here. Note that this form of the command will *not* work if the user is attempting to delete VSAM space or a UCAT that is not *empty*.

Note also in connection with the above coding that when deleting a cluster, the entryname must be the cluster name; it may not be a component name—a data or index component name—as VSAM does not allow data and index components to be separately deleted. There are several special keyword options that may be coded in addition to the shown basic coding and we will discuss these immediately below.

PURGE/NOPURGE. A VSAM object may be *date-protected*: at DEF CLUSTER time, a retention period can optionally be specified for the cluster; the coding is *TO (date)* with the date given in Julian form, or *FOR (days)* giving the number of days. If neither of these options is coded, then the VSAM cluster may be deleted at any time; otherwise, if it is date-protected, it may be deleted only by a DELETE command with the PURGE option (NOPURGE is the default, meaning that if the to-be-deleted cluster is date-protected, the DELETE will fail prior to the end of the

```
1.    // JOB . . .
2.    // EXEC    PGM=IDCAMS
3.    //SYSPRINT DD SYSOUT=A
4.    //SYSIN    DD *
5.      DELETE -
6.              TRUCAT.MVS003T.INQR0021.TESTVS -
7.                 CLUSTER
8.    /*
```

Figure 9-7. Sample DELETE command.

specified retention period. An example is given after discussion of two other special-ized DELETE command options, below.

FORCE/NOFORCE.   It is sometimes necessary to have VSAM do what is called a *forced-deletion*: to delete UCATs or VSAM spaces that are *not empty*, normally disallowed in a standard DELETE command approach. If this is desired, the FORCE option is specified on a DELETE command (the default is NOFORCE— the UCAT or VSAM space must be entirely empty in order to be validly deletable). This sort of decision is generally exercised by systems programmers rather than application programmers, although the latter do occasionally require such a service in certain special circumstances.

ERASE/NOERASE.   The standard operation by VSAM at DELETE time is to delete the *catalog entry* of the cluster, and mark the space the cluster occupied as *reclaimable*. This is a *logical deletion* of the cluster, not a *physical deletion*: the data contents of the cluster are not generally available, but are nonetheless still present in the cluster's allocated space. A logical delete is done primarily for performance reasons: additional execution time is consumed if VSAM must actually physically delete the occupied space by overwriting with some neutral value, generally binary zeroes, to completely obscure the original contents. (Do not confuse the fact that VSAM does a *physical* deletion of a *record* with the fact that VSAM only does a logical deletion of an entire VSAM object.)

However, there is a problem—an *exposure*, as it is called in the language of data security—with such a logical deletion: if the volume on which the cluster resides is accessed at the volume level by special utilities—the class of DUMP/RESTORE utilities often used by Data Center and Operations staff—the original data contents of the logically deleted cluster are retrievable. IBM's DFDSS (Data Facility Data Set Services) product is widely and commonly used for such DUMP/RESTORE functions, as are certain IBM system utilities and non-IBM products. For certain classes of sensitive data, this may be an unacceptable security exposure, to be avoided wher-ever possible for such sensitive data. One excellent precaution in such cases is the specification of the ERASE option on the DELETE command, which instructs VSAM to overwrite the *data component* of the deleted cluster with binary zeroes (the index component contains no data records). Again, the default is NOERASE, so if overwriting as a security feature is required, ERASE must be explicitly coded.

Two points to note concerning this ERASE option. First, the volume on which the target cluster (to be deleted) resides *must be mounted*, since it must be accessed to allow the physical overwrite operation by VSAM. In general, for VSAM clusters it is *not* required that the volume be mounted at DELETE time (since only a logical delete is performed, essentially the deletion of the cluster's catalog entry).

Second, the ERASE/NOERASE options are also available at DEF CLUSTER time. If at DEF CLUSTER time the ERASE option is specified, VSAM is instructed to physically delete the cluster whenever its catalog entry is deleted (at DELETE time). If these options are specified at both DEF CLUSTER and DELETE time, the

```
1.   // JOB . . .
2.   // EXEC     PGM=IDCAMS
3.   //SYSPRINT DD SYSOUT=A
4.   //TARGET    DD DSN=TRUCAT.MVS003T.INQR0021.TESTVS,
     //          DISP=OLD
5.   //SYSIN     DD *
6.      DELETE -
7.                 TRUCAT.MVS003T.INQR0021.TESTVS -
8.                     FILE (TARGET) -
9.                     PURGE -
10.                    ERASE -
11.                    CLUSTER
12.  /*
```

Figure 9-8. DELETE command with special options.

specification at DELETE time overrides whatever was specified at DEF CLUSTER time.

Now let's look at an example, in Figure 9-8, of the use of some of these options we've discussed, which will bring out some additional points. This IDCAMS job deletes a date-protected cluster whose retention period has not yet expired (PURGE option), and overwrites the data component with binary zeroes (ERASE option). Note especially statement 8, the FILE parameter whose value is the ddname of the DD statement referencing the data set to be deleted. This parameter and its associated DD statement is required to ensure that the target cluster is mounted at DELETE time, and this is necessary whenever ERASE is specified, since no overwrite is possible otherwise. Thus the DD statement (4) is required.

WARNING: THE SPACE PARAMETER OF THE DELETE COMMAND

Great care must be taken in using the SPACE parameter on the DELETE command: a common misapplication of it, with unintended consequences, is to attempt to delete some VSAM space on some specific volume. It does *not* delete some one particular space—indeed, it is not possible to refer uniquely to some particular VSAM space, as a VSAM space has no manipulable name—but rather deletes *all empty VSAM spaces on the volume*. This is usually not what was intended. Furthermore, DELETE with the FORCE option, along with the SPACE parameter (no entryname is given anywhere) will delete all VSAM data spaces of the volume, whether empty or not! This sort of operation (deletion of all of a volume's VSAM spaces) is best left to authorized systems programmers or technical support staff.

9.3.3   The PRINT Command, Again

We have already discussed the basic form and function of the PRINT command earlier in the text (Subsection 6.3.1). Here we will draw out some additional facilities of the PRINT command.

```
1.    // JOB . . .
2.    // EXEC    PGM=IDCAMS
3.    //SYSPRINT DD SYSOUT=A
5.    //INDD     DD DSN=TRUCAT.MVS003T.INQR0021.TESTVS,
      //         DISP=OLD
6.    //SYSIN    DD *
7.       PRINT -
8.                 INFILE (INDD) -
                      FROMKEY (200000000) -
                      COUNT (1000) -
                      CHAR
10.   /*
```

Figure 9-9. Sample PRINT with file pruning.

First, the PRINT command allows printing at the cluster or at the individual component level. Thus, one can print the index component of a KSDS separately from the data component, useful in certain difficult debugging situations dealing with what appear to be malfunctioning VSAM KSDS clusters.

Second, in addition to printing VSAM clusters, catalogs and other VSAM objects, the PRINT command can also be used to print OS SAM and ISAM data sets. Be sure to provide the appropriate DD statements for all OS files: DSN and DISP for cataloged data sets, and DSN, DISP, UNIT, and VOL parameters for an uncataloged OS file.

Finally, the PRINT command supports all of the special file pruning options associated with the REPRO command: FROMKEY/TOKEY for KSDS and ISAM files, FADDR/TADDR for ESDS and KSDS files, FNUM/TNUM for RRDS files, and the special options SKIP, and COUNT. Figure 9-9 illustrates this. Selected records of the VSAM KSDS cluster referred to in the INDD DD statement are to be printed, starting with the record containing a key of '200000000' (or the next higher key if this key does not appear in the data set) for a total of 1000 records following this point, with the output to be in character representation.

9.3.4 Altering Cluster Attributes: The ALTER Command

VSAM allows a user to change many of the attributes of a cluster, as defined at DEF CLUSTER time, to other values at any time after the original definition. As most VSAM parameters are ALTERable, the simplest way to get at the power of the ALTER command is to enumerate what major attributes *cannot* be altered.

NON-ALTERable ATTRIBUTES

1. Space allocation parameters
2. CISZ
3. Cluster type

```
 1.    // JOB . . .
 2.    // EXEC    PGM=IDCAMS
 3.    //SYSPRINT DD SYSOUT=A
 4.    //SYSIN    DD *
 5.      ALTER -
 6.              TRUCAT.MVS003T.INQR0021.TESTVS -
 7.                  FSPC (35 20) -
 8.                  FOR (120)
 9.                  ERASE
10.    /*
```

Figure 9-10. Using ALTER command.

4. REUSE
5. The index options: IMBED and REPLICATE
6. The AIX features: UNIQUEKEY/NONUNIQUEKEY

An example of the use of the ALTER command follows. The above list suggests how useful the ALTER command may be. We may, for example, make an initial specification of FSPC at DEF CLUSTER time which, after some processing experience with the cluster, may prove insufficient to support the large volume of insertion operations we may find necessary against the cluster. In addition, we may have date-protected the cluster for 30 days (by coding FOR (30) at DEF CLUSTER time), and may now want to extend the protection for an additional three months. Finally, we have learned after the creation of the cluster that it is to contain some sensitive records which should not be exposed to any user after the cluster is deleted. The coding of Figure 9-10 will effect these changes. As we will see later in the text, the ALTER command is particularly useful for gradually changing the values of certain performance-related parameters (like FSPC, and numbers of buffers) in order to see the changing performance behavior of the cluster for VSAM optimization study and tuning. Note, however, that one very important performance-related parameter, CISZ, is not ALTERable, and therefore has to be very carefully chosen at DEF CLUSTER, in that the user doesn't get a second chance, short of completely deleting the cluster and recreating it from scratch, to 'correct' a poor choice of CISZ.

10

VSAM IN OPERATION

10.1 BASIC OPERATIONS ON VSAM DATA SETS

10.1.1 Record Insertion

Record insertion (addition) is a relatively straightforward process in VSAM clusters; only with a KSDS which has, for the CI in which the record belongs, insufficient freespace to allow the insertion, is the VSAM processing more complex (see below). (Remember, from our earlier discussions, that record insertion in VSAM is *physical insertion*, not *logical insertion*, as is often the case with OS ISAM files.)

A KSDS is generally accessed by key, so record insertion is in key sequence, using available FSPC (if any). As described earlier in the text, if the target (to-be-inserted) record belongs between two existing records, by virtue of its key value, then records with higher keys (to the right of the insert point) are shifted over one position (so-called 'right-shifting') to make room for the new record. If at some point insufficient FSPC exists within some CI for record insertion within that CI, then the operation known as a *CI-split* is performed by VSAM; this is discussed fully in the following Section (10.2) of this chapter.

With an ESDS, records may only be added to the file *at EOF* (that is, after the current last record of the file), and all record insertion is in physical order of time-arrival (see the earlier discussion of ESDSs in Subsection 8.2.2) since an ESDS (without an alternate index associated with it) is essentially a sequential (non-keyed) file.

With an RRDS, records are inserted only into *existing empty slots*, by RRN, unless the record belongs after the last slot of the cluster, in which case it is assigned the next available RRN.

10.1.2 Record Deletion

With a KSDS, record deletion is—like record insertion—a physical operation, not just a logical one: the record is actually removed from the file, and the space it occupied is immediately reclaimed by VSAM for further file growth (it goes back into the pool of available distributed freespace (FSPC)).

An ESDS does not support record deletion, as we noted earlier in the text. The programmer may invent some scheme for *logically* deleting a record, but VSAM ignores this and it is the programmer's responsibility to provide program coding logic to bypass such 'logically' deleted records in actually processing. Deletion may also be simulated by the one-to-one exchange of the target record by a replacement record which may be a dummy record but may not be wholly empty (must contain at least one byte of 'data'). Of course, this is not a real deletion operation, but simply a special case of an update operation.

10.1.3   Record Update

All three types of VSAM clusters support standard record update operations: an existing record is changed and then written back to the same record position, or an existing record is replaced in toto by another record. In addition, *for KSDS clusters only*, a record's length may be changed. Finally, a critical restriction exists on record update in a KSDS: the prime key field may not be changed in any way.

10.2   CONTROL INTERVAL SPLITS (CI-SPLITS)

The *control interval split* (*CI-split*) is one of the most central processes of VSAM. First, we will describe CI-splitting at a general level, and then proceed to refine our understanding. Bear in mind throughout the discussion that CI-splitting occurs only in a KSDS.

At any point in VSAM processing, there may be insufficient FSPC (or no FSPC at all) for inserting a record into, or lengthening an existing record within, the target CI (the CI within which the record belongs or resides by virtue of its key value) of a KSDS cluster. In this event, VSAM causes a CI-split: some of the records of the target CI are moved out of that CI into a new *free-CI*—one kept empty for just such an event—in order to reclaim the vacated FSPC in the original (old) CI and thus permit the process of record lengthening or new record insertion to successfully complete.

Let's look at an example. Figure 10-1 represents the sole two CAs of a KSDS cluster whose original definition included:

```
CISZ (1024)
FSPC (25 10)
```

and into which we have loaded 250-byte records. In order to simplify the discussion, assume that there are only four CIs per CA (CI-density equal to four).

CI-internal FSPC (hereafter *CI-FSPC*) is specified as 25 percent, which means that 256 bytes out of each CI in the cluster will be kept empty as FSPC (25 percent of the CISZ of 1024, rounded down if there were a decimal fraction, which there isn't in this case). Since we are using fixed-length records, ten bytes of control fields are required at the extreme right of each CI: four bytes for the CIDF, and six bytes for two three-byte long RDFs (only two RDFs are ever needed by VSAM when using fixed-length records in a KSDS). This leaves 758 bytes for loading logical records. Given 250-byte records, three records can be stored per CI, so that the LR-density is equal to three. Now, with an LR-density of three, the LRA size equals 750 bytes. Out of the CISZ of 1024, therefore, eight bytes are unused space (US). All this is represented in Figure 10-2. (We have already described fully how these computations

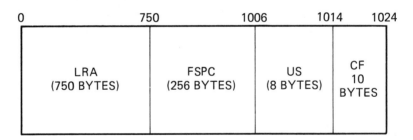

00100	00200	00300	FSPC	CF	CI1
00400	00500	00600	FSPC	CF	CI2
00700	00800	00900	FSPC	CF	CI3
				CF	CI4

CA1

01000	01100	01200	FSPC	CF	CI1
01300	01400	01500	FSPC	CF	CI2
01600	01700	01800	FSPC	CF	CI3
				CF	CI4

CA2

Figure 10-1. Sample KSDS cluster.

0	750	1006	1014	1024

LRA (750 BYTES)	FSPC (256 BYTES)	US (8 BYTES)	CF 10 BYTES

Figure 10-2. Sample CI structure.

are performed earlier in the text, in Sections 8.7 and 8.9 especially; the reader may wish to briefly review these sections at this time before proceeding.)

Furthermore, the CA-internal FSPC (hereafter CA-FSPC) is specified as 10 percent, meaning that VSAM will assure that at least one CI of every 10 CIs within a CA will be kept completely empty, with a minimum of one CI kept empty per CA in the event that (1) a nonzero amount was specified for CA-internal FSPC, and (2) the amount specified when used as a percentage would yield a fraction of a CI; here, since we are assuming four CIs per CA, 10 percent CA-FSPC would yield 40 percent of a CI, so VSAM honors this as one whole empty CI per CA.

Note that the LR-density is determined at DEF CLUSTER time, in this case with

00100	00200	00250	00300	CF	CI1
00400	00500	00550	00600	CF	CI2
00700	00800	00900	FSPC	CF	CI3
				CF	CI4

CA1 BEFORE CI-SPLIT

Figure 10-3a. Control area before CI-split.

00100	00200	00250	00300	CF	CI1
00400	00500	FSPC	FSPC	CF	CI2
00700	00800	00900	FSPC	CF	CI3
00550	00580	00600	FSPC	CF	CI4

CA1 AFTER CI-SPLIT

Figure 10-3b. Control area after CI-split.

a value of three: when VSAM loads the cluster with actual data records, it will only load (a maximum of) three records in each CI (the last partially filled CI may contain fewer records), so that the *load-time* LRA (logical record area) size is 750 bytes of the 1024 total bytes of CISZ, 256 additional bytes out of this CISZ being reserved for CI-FSPC. These 256 bytes are kept free by VSAM for the insertion of additional records for post-load time processing, and with the 250-byte records of our example, each CI can accommodate one additional record due to insert activity.

Now, let's assume some post-load processing against the cluster has occurred, and that Figure 10-3a represents the state of CA1 of the cluster after this processing. Notice that two records have been added within CA1, the first with a key of '00250,' the second with a key of '00550,' inserted into their proper positions in CI1 and CI2, respectively. There was sufficient freespace (256 bytes) to add the records, simply by moving rightward the last record of CI1 and CI2, and then inserting in key sequence using 250 out of the 256 bytes of freespace. No records were added to CI3, and CI4 is reserved as an empty CI.

Suppose, now, that we wish to add one more record to the cluster, one with a key of '000580,' which by key sequence belongs between the current third and fourth records of CI2.

Thus, as shown in Figure 10-3a, we are assuming that the target record (to-be-inserted record) belongs in a target CI (the CI in which the record belongs by virtue of its key) that has insufficient FSPC for the insertion; in the figure, that CI already contains four records (we have added one in processing activity after load-time), for a total LRA (logical record area) size of 1000 bytes. As there are only six bytes of FSPC left (the original 256 bytes minus 250 bytes for the one record previously inserted), VSAM must perform a CI-split to insert the record in its proper key sequence. The basic goal of a CI-split is to partially empty the contents of the 'congested' CI (CI2) into another wholly empty CI (CI4), and thus gain additional FSPC in both CIs to allow for the current and future record insertion.

Let's now examine how VSAM performs a CI-split in the case under consideration. We are going to assume that the target record is to be inserted as a *direct insert* (not a sequential mode insert, which we will consider later); that is, we are accessing the KSDS in random mode. Figure 10-3b illustrates the CI-split process. The steps VSAM performs for this operation are as follows:

1. VSAM determines the *midpoint* of the CI, to the nearest logical record (no fractions of records), and this midpoint defines a *low-keyrange* (the lower half of the CI's records with lower keys values) and a *high-keyrange* (the higher half of the CI's records with higher key values, relative to the midpoint). Thus, the low-keyrange consists of the two records with keys '00400' and '00500,' while the high-keyrange consists of the '00550' and '00600' records.

2. VSAM obtains an empty CI (CI4) within the same CA as the target CI (we can call this the target CA). In the case we are examining, a whole CI has been left empty per CA of the cluster, by virtue of the CA-FSPC (later, we will consider what VSAM does to obtain an empty CI if no empty CI exists or has been reserved in the target CA). We call this empty CI fetched for purposes of split activity *the control-CI*. The original target CI (CI2) which must be split is called *the split-CI*.

3. VSAM moves the high-keyrange records of the split-CI into the (wholly empty) control-CI, leaving the low-keyrange records behind in the original split-CI; thus, about half of the split-CI's records have been stored into the reserved control-CI, with each of these CIs now having approximately 50 percent FSPC for record insertion activity. Records '00550' and '00600' are moved from CI2 to CI4.

4. VSAM inserts the target record into whichever of the two CIs it belongs by virtue of key sequence (in our example, CI4). The CI-split is complete and the target record has been added to the cluster.

Several points should be noted about this CI-split process. First note that after records have been loaded into the cluster, but before any CI-split has occurred, the *logical CI order* is the same as the *physical CI order*: if we look at the order of CIs as they must occur to assure strictly ascending key values, this is the same as the order in which the CIs are actually physically stored within the DASD space the cluster occupies. If we were to fetch the CIs in strictly physical order, one after another, the records would be fetched in strict key sequence.

However, after a CI-split occurs, the logical and physical CI order is *not necessarily the same*, as can be seen in Figure 10-3b. This is because the wholly empty CI—the control-CI—used in the split process is fetched from the end of the target CA, and half of the records belonging to an earlier (in physical sequence) CI are moved into this control-CI; these records, as can be seen from the figure, will have key values which are lower than some of those present in CIs physically after the split-CI. The keys as encountered in reading the cluster in strict physical sequence of CI occurrence are no longer strictly ascending; however, VSAM will return sequentially fetched records in logical CI order—in ascending key sequence—even though the CIs are out of order and must be fetched by key sequence and not their physical order of storage.

As we will see later in Chapter 18, on performance, this affect of CI-split activity can compromise execution-time efficiency in processing the cluster. In addition, the split operation itself takes an appreciable amount of execution-time to perform. Wherever possible, therefore, FSPC should be made sufficiently ample to avoid large numbers of CI-split operations. (We will return to some strategies for this later.) LISTCAT output reports CI-split activity, and this should be monitored on a regular basis for earlier detection of a rising number of CI-splits; this generally is due to insufficient freespace, and may require FSPC adjustment by the ALTER command.

Second, we may ask at this point how VSAM assures a ready supply of empty CIs to use for CI-splits. Two cases are of concern here. The first is the more extreme: assume that there are no empty CIs in the target CA. This may happen with this sort of FSPC coding at DEF CLUSTER time:

```
FSPC (x 0)
```

where x is any value. It is the second subparameter of FSPC that controls how many, if any, CIs per CA should be kept wholly empty by VSAM. Thus, CA-FSPC is primarily used to provide some control-CIs for use in CI-split activity, by reserving—through a nonzero value—at least one CI per CA wholly empty.

So what happens when zero percent CA-FSPC has been specified and yet a record must be inserted into a congested (insufficient FSPC for record insertion) target CI? Will the insert operation fail? The answer is that a CI-split still must occur, but since there is no control-CI in the CA, then prior to a CI-split VSAM must obtain some empty CIs from outside of the target CA, using an operation known as a *control area split (CA-split)*. Similarly, a second case may yield no empty CIs within a target CA although a CI-split needs to be performed: when after considerable processing activity—even though we specified a nonzero value for CA-FSPC—any free CIs we had within the target CA have been used for previous CI-splits. No matter what value of CA-FSPC we specify, it is still possible that the one or more empty CIs are ultimately expended on split activity, leaving no wholly empty CI to be used as the control-CI for a CI-split. Again, VSAM must perform a CA-split before the required CI-split. We now, appropriately, turn to a discussion of the nature and operation of a CA-split.

10.3   CONTROL AREA SPLITS (CA-SPLITS)

In the event that a CI-split is required for record insert activity, but no empty CIs exist within the target CA, VSAM performs a higher-order operation, the *control area split (CA-split)*. The basic operation of a CA-split involves the following steps (see Figure

00100	00200	00250	00300	CF	CI1
00400	00500	FSPC	FSPC	CF	CI2
00700	00800	00900	FSPC	CF	CI3
00550	00580	00600	FSPC	CF	CI4

TARGET CA BEFORE CA-SPLIT OPERATION

FSPC	FSPC	FSPC	FSPC	CF	CI1
FSPC	FSPC	FSPC	FSPC	CF	CI2
FSPC	FSPC	FSPC	FSPC	CF	CI3
FSPC	FSPC	FSPC	FSPC	CF	CI4

CONTROL-CA FETCHED FROM END OF FILE

Figure 10-4. Control areas before CA-split operation.

10-4). Here we assume that we wish to insert a record with a key of '00280,' which belongs between the third and fourth records of CI1 (of CA1), the problem being that there is neither sufficient freespace in CI1 for this addition, nor is there a wholly empty CI in CA1 to use for a CI-split.

1. VSAM obtains a wholly empty CA—called a *control-CA* in this connection— from the end of the cluster's data component.

2. VSAM moves half of the CIs (CI3 and CI4) in the target CA (the one that contains the congested CI requiring a split, here CA1) into the newly obtained control-CA, leaving the other half behind in the (old) target CA. This is a midpoint break or split, like a CI-split, but at the CA level. The CIs that are moved are the *high-keyrange CIs*: those with the higher key values represented in the target CA, and those left behind are the *low-keyrange CIs* (containing the records with the lower key values of the CA), assuming a midpoint break. This is shown in Figure 10-5, where CI3 and CI4 of the (old) CA, CA1, have been moved into the wholly empty control-CA.

3. Now the original target CA contains one or more empty CIs (CI3 and CI4) that can be used as a control-CI for honoring CI-splits, since about half of the CIs in the target CA have been vacated through the CA-split just performed. At this point, VSAM simply performs a regular CI-split in this target CA, following exactly the steps for a CI-split which we detailed in the previous section. In our example, CI1 of the old CA1 is the object of a CI-split operation, allowing the '00280' record to be inserted (the high-keyrange records are moved to CI3). See Figure 10-6. Thus, after first a CA-split (to obtain some empty CIs for a CI-split), followed by a CI-split, VSAM has effected the insertion of the target record in its proper location (whatever CI contains the appropriate key range).

00100	00200	00250	00300	CF	CI1
00400	00500	FSPC	FSPC	CF	CI2
FSPC	FSPC	FSPC	FSPC	CF	CI3
FSPC	FSPC	FSPC	FSPC	CF	CI4

CA1 AFTER START OF CA-SPLIT OPERATION

FSPC	FSPC	FSPC	FSPC	CF	CI1
FSPC	FSPC	FSPC	FSPC	CF	CI2
00700	00800	00900	FSPC	CF	CI3
00550	00580	00600	FSPC	CF	CI4

CONTROL-CA AFTER START OF CA-SPLIT
OPERATION

Figure 10-5. Control areas after start of CA-split operation.

00100	00200	FSPC	FSPC	CF	CI1
00400	00500	FSPC	FSPC	CF	CI2
00250	00280	00300	FSPC	CF	CI3
FSPC	FSPC	FSPC	FSPC	CF	CI4

CA1 AFTER COMPLETION OF CA-SPLIT
OPERATION

FSPC	FSPC	FSPC	FSPC	CF	CI1
FSPC	FSPC	FSPC	FSPC	CF	CI2
00700	00800	00900	FSPC	CF	CI3
00550	00580	00600	FSPC	CF	CI4

CONTROL-CA AFTER COMPLETION OF
CA-SPLIT OPERATION

Figure 10-6. Control areas after completion of CA-split operation.

Now, we may ask how VSAM assures a ready supply of empty CAs at the end of the cluster, to be control-CAs for CA-split activity. Are there always some empty CAs at the end of the cluster, and if not, where does VSAM fetch an empty CA from to perform CA-splits?

There are two sources of control-CAs. One source is from allocated but unused space at the end of the cluster, due simply to the fact that not all of the allocated *primary* space has records loaded into it. The primary allocation is often larger than what is actually required to store the records of the cluster. If there exists at the end of the cluster (after the last actual record) at least one CA which is wholly free of any records, then VSAM will preempt that CA for its use as a control-CA when needed for CA-split activity.

But in some cases all CAs of the primary allocation of the cluster may contain at least one record, and hence cannot function as a control-CA. Moreover, it may come to pass after sufficient VSAM processing activity, including record insertions, that any wholly empty CAs that there may once have been have been expended by either (1) actual records loaded into them in the course of cluster growth, or (2) consumption by being used for previous CA-splits.

At that point, the primary allocation cannot provide any empty CAs, so VSAM turns to its second source of empty CAs: secondary allocation extents. VSAM will automatically go into secondary extenting, and use the acquired secondary extent(s) for fetching wholly empty CAs, one at a time as needed, to be used for CA-split activity. It is only, therefore, after both primary and secondary allocations have been completely expended—there is at least one record in every CA at the end of the cluster—that VSAM cannot perform any further CA-splits. At that time, the programmer would have to reorganize the cluster completely to provide for greater space allocation. This can be done either by using the REPRO command to copy the original cluster into a new cluster with larger space allocation and/or FSPC specification, or even more radically, by deleting and then redefining the cluster anew. This suggests a good reason for always (1) providing for some CA-FSPC and (2) some secondary allocation, for clusters which are anticipated to sustain a high amount of record insert activity.

Finally, it is important to note that although VSAM can always—as long as some secondary allocation was defined for the cluster—fetch empty CAs from secondary extents, this is not recommended, as going into secondary extenting compromises performance appreciably. Therefore, it is better to avoid this by providing for at least some CA-FSPC when coding the FSPC parameter at DEF CLUSTER time: thus, code a nonzero amount for both the CI-FSPC and CA-FSPC subparameters of FSPC, unless little or no record insert activity is anticipated for the cluster.

10.4 REVISITING CI AND CA SPLIT ACTIVITY: SEQUENTIAL INSERT MODE

Our discussions of CI-splits and CA-splits thus far in this chapter have been only under what is called the *direct insert strategy* (*DIS*): the mode of handling split activity

INSERT POINT FOR
RECORD '00280'
(SEQUENTIAL INSERTION)

00100	00200	00250	00300	CF	CI1
00400	00500	00550	00600	CF	CI2
00700	00800	00900	FSPC	CF	CI3
				CF	CI4

CA1 BEFORE CI-SPLIT

00100	00200	00250	00280	CF	CI1
00400	00500	FSPC	FSPC	CF	CI2
00700	00800	00900	FSPC	CF	CI3
00300	FSPC	FSPC	FSPC	CF	CI4

CA1 AFTER CI-SPLIT

Figure 10-7. CI-split with sequential insertion.

when such activity was triggered by records to be inserted in random (direct) mode. But records may also be inserted into a cluster in sequential mode; in this case VSAM handles split activity using the *sequential insert strategy* (*SIS*), and we therefore need to examine this process as opposed to DIS.

An essential feature of DIS, described above, is that it honors splits by using *midpoint break* logic: splitting either the CI in half (CI-split) or the CA in half (CA-split). When performing record insertion in sequential mode VSAM, in contrast, uses an *insert-point break* logic. The insert-point is at whatever point in the target CI the record-to-be-inserted belongs by virtue of its key value. Insert-point break logic requires that the split be performed at the insert-point: all records with key values higher than the key value of the target record are now the high-keyrange records and are moved into the empty CI, the control-CI when a CI-split is taking place; all records with lower key values than the target record remain in the original CI, the split-CI. The final piece of SIS-type insertion is the insertion of the target record itself, and this is always inserted *at the end of the* (*old*) *split-CI*, at the insert-point. A representation of SIS applied to a CI-split for sequential insertion activity is given in Figure 10-7. Here again, the intent is to insert a record with key '00280' into CI1, which has insufficient freespace, but the insertion is to be done in sequential mode. The insert point is after the third record of CI1, so only the '00300' record is moved to a new empty CI (CI4), the first three records remaining behind in CI1. The target record is then inserted at the insert point immediately after the third record, becoming the last record of CI1.

There is a special case that VSAM recognizes, when the insert-point is at what is called the *logical-end-of-CI* (*LECI*), that is, the record is to be inserted, by virtue of its key value, after the current highest-key record of the target CI. In this case, since there is insufficient space within the target CI to perform the insert (by definition, since we are dealing with only situations which require a split to be performed), VSAM obtains a control-CI (a wholly empty CI for split activity)—either from within the target CA, or from the end of the cluster after a CA-split is performed—and inserts the target record into the (new) control-CI, where it will be the first and lowest key record of that CI.

Note that the original split-CI therefore remains congested and unchanged; in fact no real "splitting" has occurred: just the insertion of a target record into a control-CI. This is always the operation VSAM goes through when the insert-point is at LECI, and is called (for obvious reasons) a *pseudo CI-split*. A CA-split under SIS is parallel to the logic for a SIS-type CI-split: half of the CIs of the target CA are not vacated, but only whatever CIs occur *after* the CI containing the insert-point are moved into a control-CA. After this CA-split is effected, VSAM performs a SIS-type CI-split, and the target record is finally inserted into its proper place in the cluster.

Finally, note that most discussions of CI-splits and CA-splits are extremely misleading, in that the split operation is described solely as a midpoint break-type logic; as we have seen, that is only half of the truth: such midpoint logic (DIS) is used for direct insertions causing a split, but insert-point logic (SIS) is used for sequential insertions.

WARNING

We have already noted that a significant amount of CI-split activity can compromise VSAM performance. CA-splits have even more dramatic effects in terms of VSAM performance degradation, being much more complex than CI-splits, and involving the movement of much larger numbers of records. The reader is therefore especially warned against significant CA-split activity. Like CI-split activity, CA-splits are also reported in LISTCAT output, which should be closely and regularly monitored for split activity levels; we strongly recommend that CI-splits be kept as low as possible (possibly through ALTERing the FSPC specification upwards), but that *CA-splits be kept as close to zero as possible*, given their highly adverse impact on VSAM performance.

10.5   GENERAL TYPES OF VSAM PROCESSING

VSAM supports three primary types of processing against VSAM clusters, although not all are supported for each cluster type. This section describes these processing types.

10.5.1 Keyed Processing

The most common type of processing of a cluster is *keyed processing*: accessing the records by using some key field defined with—and sometimes within—each record. For KSDSs this is straightforward: the prime key field, which is a record-internal field, is used. Keyed processing is not supported for an ESDS without—as is typically the case—an alternate index, since there is no key field, the records being in arrival-time sequence.

Keyed processing of an RRDS operates by treating the externally maintained RRN as the 'argument' for access requests, so that the RRN functions as an *external* pseudo-key; it is a pseudo-key, in that the RRN is not directly used by VSAM for access, but rather, behind the scenes, VSAM converts each presented RRN into the equivalent RBA offset, and then uses this derived value for access purposes. However, this transformation is generally transparent to the programmer, so that most programmers regard RRN access as keyed processing, although this is not strictly true (but true enough for programmers!).

10.5.2 Addressed Processing

Since each record of a VSAM cluster has a unique RBA value associated with it—thus 'locating' the record—it is possible to access records by using this RBA as the argument for access requests, sometimes referred to as the *search argument*: the value—key, offset, or otherwise—associated with the record to be accessed. Addressed (RBA) processing is supported for a KSDS in addition to the more usual keyed processing. However, it would be somewhat reckless—without a great deal of very complex and sophisticated programming being added by the programmer—to process a KSDS in this mode. The reason for this is that, although it is possible to record or compute the RBA values of all records as they are being first loaded into a KSDS cluster, these are not constant over the processing life of a cluster: after any CI- or CA-split activity, RBA values for all records moved out of the old CI or CA change to reflect their new positions in the new control-CIs or control-CAs involved in split activity. Thus, the original RBAs of load-time are no longer valid after any split activity within the cluster, and hence cannot be reliably used for record access purposes by RBA search arguments.

Obtaining the new, changed RBAs after split activity is extraordinarily intricate and requires exceptional care, with comparable difficulties for any attempt to *compute* the new values from knowledge of the complex internals of VSAM split processing; by and large, the only feasible approach involves a special Assembler VSAM program monitoring and logging all RBAs that are modified by VSAM (through special *journal exits*), and the processing overhead of such a 'service' program—to say nothing of assuring its robustness under all cases of changed RBAs—would be discouraging unless authored by a very high-level VSAM systems programmer intimately acquainted with VSAM internals and with VSAM performance and optimization methodologies. Again, this is not impossible, but over the course of almost 14 years experience with VSAM, I have only rarely encountered anyone who wholly succeeded in this venture. High-level programming language users can therefore safely dismiss the possibility of addressed processing against a KSDS.

Addressed processing is the standard mode of processing an ESDS, which lacks a key. VSAM uses RBAs to access the records of an ESDS in sequential mode; this is generally completely transparent to the programmer. Note that since insertion is only allowed at EOF for an ESDS and never between two existing records, the RBAs of records already in such a cluster do not change (and no CI-/CA-splits occur within an ESDS cluster), so that there is no problem of reliability of RBA values for an ESDS. Addressed processing is not supported for RRDSs. (Some of the performance implications of keyed versus addressed processing are taken up in Chapter 18, on performance.)

10.5.3   Control Interval Processing

Control interval processing (or *CNV*, after the Assembler option required to use it) is the most powerful, efficient, but complicated type of VSAM processing of a cluster: the programmer, not the VSAM access method routines, is responsible for processing the individual records of a CI by accessing them in the VSAM I/O buffers, rather than in any program work areas. This aspect of CNV processing is comparable to what is termed *locate mode I/O* in standard OS processing; in addition, CNV processing allows full programmer control over control fields of the CI (the CIDF and RDFs), record RBAs, the index component records, and any alternate indices associated with the cluster.

CNV processing is generally encountered only in advanced Assembler system-type programs, where the complexity of program logic necessitated by this type of access is traded off against the benefits of extremely high performance (CNV processing is typically the fastest way to process a cluster), user-controlled tailoring of special advanced VSAM facilities—such as *Improved Control Interval Access* (the 'ICI' facility), the *User Buffering Facility* (UBF), and the *Control Blocks in Common* (CBIC) *option*, among several others—and user-controlled repair and restoration of damaged clusters. These facilities, and the details of CNV processing, are beyond the scope of this text, but they are sometimes encountered in advanced applications and it is invaluable to have at least one high-level VSAM system specialist acquainted with them and able to exploit them under special circumstances. The interested reader should consult the relevant technical publications for further information (see the bibliography).

10.6   SPECIALIZED VSAM PROCESSING

In addition to the primary types of processing discussed above, VSAM supports two special types of cluster processing in certain well-defined circumstances.

10.6.1   Mass Sequential Insertion (MSI)

VSAM uses a special strategy when, for a KSDS, it detects that two or more records *in ascending key sequence* are to be inserted *in sequential mode* between two adjacent records currently in the cluster; such a group of records is a *mass-group*, and the insert strategy used by VSAM in such cases is termed *mass sequential insertion* (*MSI*). For example, the cluster may contain two adjacent records with the keys of 200 and 210, and we wish to insert four records with keys 203, 206, 207, and 209.

Under MSI VSAM uses, in effect, special buffering for the entire mass-group to allow for the insertions to be done 'en masse' as a single insertion operation rather than as multiple separate insertions; this is possible because there is a single insert-point and the entire group of target records (the mass-group) is (1) in ascending order, and (2) buffered as a single unit available for a group insertion operation. Considerable performance benefit is gleaned by virtue of the dramatically reduced number of I/O operations needed to effect the mass insertions. VSAM also handles the mass insertions in such a fashion as to minimize the number of CI/CA-splits that may be needed, if any split activity is required; in general, VSAM is able to avoid any subsequent splits after the first split at the insert-point (VSAM uses SIS when processing MSI), and this too is a performance benefit. We have deliberately simplified the conditions for a MSI operation, which are somewhat broader than stated at the beginning of this section. The full conditions that must obtain for VSAM to perform MSI are as follows.

1. Sequential access mode only (no MSI when doing direct inserts);
2. There is a mass-group (a set of records all of which are to be inserted between two adjacent records of the cluster), and the records of the mass-groups are in strictly ascending key sequence;
3. The mass-group is either:
   a. to be inserted at EOF, or
   b. to be inserted into an empty cluster, and hence is participating in a load operation, or
   c. to be inserted between two adjacent records currently in the cluster

Case c above is the one of direct interest to the programmer, as a and b are provided automatically and transparently by VSAM; case c is one that the programmer can influence to occur in order to obtain the performance benefits of MSI.

What is required to be done is that whenever a group of records is to be inserted into a cluster between two adjacent records, the programmer should (1) order the group of records in strictly ascending key sequence (rather than presenting them unordered), and (2) perform the insertion operations in sequential mode, not direct mode, even if there are only a small number of records to be inserted (compared to the number of records in the cluster), despite the fact that normally under such circumstances direct mode would be called for. Direct mode must be avoided, otherwise VSAM will use DIS to govern how the insertions are performed, which will split the CI at midpoint, rather than at insert-point. The best strategy, using MSI, is for VSAM to perform a split at insert-point, since all the records are known to belong here in a string, one after the other.

It is worthwhile, wherever possible, therefore, to collect groups of records to be inserted between two adjacent records so as to apply the insertions in a batch, forcing MSI by pre-sorting the records, if necessary, and always performing the inserts in sequential mode under such circumstances. The performance benefits of MSI are also obtainable in the online environment: in CICS (command level) the write command can be coded in this form:

```
EXEC CICS WRITE . . . MASSINSERT
```

the special MASSINSERT option forcing VSAM to use MSI processing.

10.6.2 Skip-Sequential Processing (SKP)

If certain records of a KSDS are to be accessed and form a *scattered-group*—belong in scattered (non-adjacent) locations throughout the cluster—then the programmer can avoid the overhead of a series of direct insertions, each having to perform a complete top-down search of the index component of the cluster (more on this in the Chapter 11), by presenting the records to VSAM in strictly ascending key sequence (with gaps). When VSAM encounters such an ordered (sorted) scattered-group in *sequential* mode, VSAM will retrieve the target records by moving through the index sequentially in a forward manner ('horizontally'), not top-down, since the records—although scattered—are known to be strictly ascending. Once VSAM locates the first record of such an ordered scattered group, it can 'skip' forwardly along through the index records for retrieval of the remainder of the records. (We describe top-down, versus horizontal, index searches in Chapter 11, on the index component.)

The performance benefit derives from the fact that only a single sequential pass through the index need be performed, given that the search for successive records can always be resumed from whatever point the previous search left off, since the records are presented in strictly ascending order. Like MSI, skip-sequential processing (SKP) can be influenced by the programmer by doing the retrievals in sequential mode and presenting the records strictly ascendingly, which may involve pre-sorting the scattered-group of records before presenting them to VSAM.

Finally, note that although we have discussed SKP only with respect to a KSDS cluster, VSAM supports the SKP for RRDSs as well (but not ESDSs). However, this is a very restricted sense of skip-sequential processing, since an RRDS lacks an index, and given its limited currency of use, this will not be discussed further in the text.

11

THE STRUCTURE OF A VSAM INDEX

11.1 VSAM INDEXING AND CHAINS OF POINTERS

Prior to the introduction of VSAM, the dominant technique of indexing a file to provide random access by key was that used in OS ISAM files. Avoiding unnecessary detail, we may generalize and say that ISAM index processing has the following major features: (1) a multilevel index structure (cylinder and track indices, and, optionally, a master index); (2) access/retrieval of records by *physical address* of the track on which the record resides: the *CCHH* form—a two-byte cylinder number, and two-byte number of the read/write head that accesses that track; (3) access/retrieval by threading through a *chain of pointers*: through the multilevel index, and into records on a track, or for inserted records that 'overflowed' (could not fit onto an already full track), following a record into an overflow area where each record is stored with a *link* field used as a forward pointer chaining all of the overflow records together.

A fundamental part of the access method, therefore, involved constant threading through these chains of pointers for record access/retrieval; a high overhead was incurred due to both the threading operation, and the storage needed for each overflow record to have appended to it a link or forward pointer field. In contrast, VSAM has a much reduced level of threading over pointer chains (as we will see shortly), a simpler structure to its multilevel index, and no overhead on the logical records themselves which do not have link or forward pointer fields grafted onto them. Furthermore, VSAM does not locate records by physical address—which is intrinsically device-dependent—but by device-independent offsets from a logical-start-of-data-set, namely by RBAs, treating all the logical records of the cluster as a stream of contiguous records, strung logically one after another, and yielding an exceptionally simple conceptual organization and primitive operation. We turn now to detailing the structure and organization of a VSAM index.

11.2 THE ORGANIZATION OF INDEX RECORDS

A VSAM index component (remember: KSDS only), or simply an index, is comprised, like the data component, of a set of records, the *index records* stored in the CIs of the index. However, unlike a data component, where each CI typically contains multiple logical records, only a single index record is ever stored in any index CI, in addition to the control fields needed by VSAM (CIDF and RDF). Furthermore, unlike data-CIs which generally have more than one RDF, an index-CI contains only the index record itself plus one CIDF and *only one RDF*. Thus, the size of an index record is just the

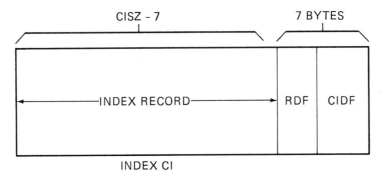

Figure 11-1. An index CI.

CISZ minus seven bytes for control fields; this is illustrated in Figure 11-1. Remember in this connection that there are only four possible CISZs supported for the index component: ½K (512 bytes), 1K, 2K, and 4K. Index records themselves are organized into two (sub)sets, which can be considered two subdivisions of the index component. These are the *sequence set* (*SS*) and the *index set* (*IS*), which we will discuss immediately below.

11.2.1 The Sequence Set (SS)

The *sequence set* (SS) is the lowest level of the multilevel index component: lowest, in the sense that the index records of the sequence set—called *sequence set records* (SSRs) contain pointers pointing directly to the CIs of the data component. Each such sequence set record indexes—contains pointers to—all of the CIs of a single particular CA of the data component. Thus, there is one sequence set record for each CA in the cluster's data component, and we say that a sequence set record *governs* the associated data component CA that it indexes. Given that each CA of the data component has a governing sequence set record, then it follows that the number of sequence set records is precisely the number of CAs in the cluster's data component. See Figure 11-2 for a general representation of this.

To take a simple example, assume a 50 cylinder cluster, and further assume that the CASZ is the maximum of one cylinder, then there are 50 CAs in the data component and consequently 50 sequence set records in the index component; furthermore, since each CI of the index contains only a single index record (here a sequence set record), then the sequence set of the index component contains precisely 50 (index) CIs. How sequence set records are structured to point to data-CIs is taken up in a later section of this chapter.

11.2.2 The Index Set

VSAM indexes the sequence set itself by using a hierarchy of index levels: the lowest level—the sequence set—indexes the CIs of the data component, the second

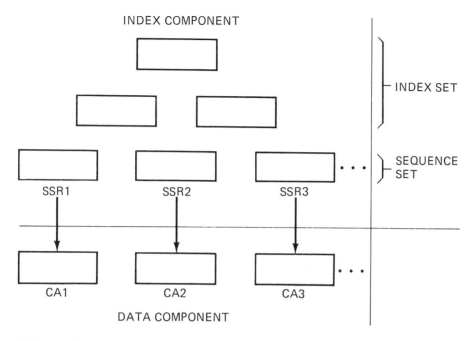

Figure 11-2. The structure of the index component.

level (one just above the sequence set) indexes the sequence set, the third level indexes the second level, etc., if any higher levels need be used at all. As we shall see later, the number of index levels is a function of several attributes of the cluster itself, both data and index component attributes. It is possible for an index to have a single level, although this is rare and generally occurs only for very small clusters; two, three, and four level indices are most common. The levels are such that they must satisfy the requirement that there be only a single index record at the highest index level. All levels above the sequence set together constitute the *index set* (IS). The index set (higher levels) of a KSDS are used by VSAM when performing direct processing of the KSDS (that is, the program accessing the KSDS is in random mode); for sequential processing, only the sequence set of the index is used.

Now let's take a look at an example of a VSAM index and how it indexes the data component, and how the index set in turn indexes lower levels of the index. Figure 11-3 gives a simple illustration of a KSDS cluster which—to avoid complicating the discussion unnecessarily—consists of a data component with two CAs, each containing four CIs (CI-density equal to four). We are assuming a CISZ of 512 bytes, and a FSPC (20 0) so that only four records, maximum, are loaded into each CI at cluster load time (LR-density equal to four), and 102 bytes of each CI are reserved for FSPC (20 percent of 512, rounded down), allowing for subsequent (post-load) record insertion of one additional record without a CI-split. (Note: lrecl = 100 bytes.)

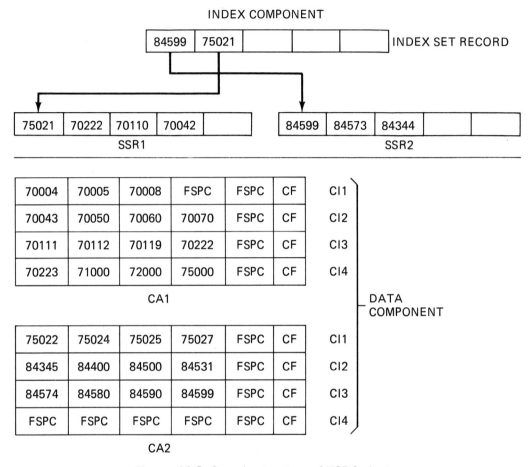

Figure 11-3. Sample structure of KSDS cluster.

Now, to understand how a VSAM index works, we must address the question of the kind of pointer VSAM uses. There are three possible types of index pointers VSAM could use in a KSDS index component; we will consider only the first two possible approaches here, and will leave the third approach—the most complex and actually the one VSAM employs internally—for discussion in the last section of this chapter (Section 11.5).

1. *CI-High-Key (HK)*: for each CI being indexed, VSAM could maintain the value of the highest actual key in that CI.
2. *CI-Highest-Possible-Key (HPK)*: for each CI being indexed, VSAM could maintain the value of the highest possible key that may be inserted in that CI. This would be one less than the lowest key in the next logical CI (the CI that follows the CI under consideration in ascending key order; this is not neces-

sarily the physically next encountered CI, since CIs may be stored sequentially out of order if any split activity has occurred).

Virtually all discussions of VSAM (including many found in IBM VSAM technical publications) present index operation in VSAM as essentially using the first approach above, that is, that VSAM stores and uses for indexing purposes, the CI-high-key, for each CI of the data component of a KSDS cluster. This is entirely in error. What this approach would predict for the example of Figure 11-3 would be that the index entry for, say, the second CI of the first CA shown would contain the key value '70070,' which is the highest actually occurring key of the last record in that CI.

But VSAM doesn't use this HK approach for performance reasons: on this approach, a record with a key of '70071' could not be stored in CI2 of CA1, because its exceeds the highest key value of '70070' for that CI; yet there is room for that record to be inserted in that CI, right after the last record (using reserved FSPC). Indeed, this approach would disallow any records to be stored in a CI after the last actual record, even if the last actual record is the first and only record in that CI and the rest of the CI consisted of reserved FSPC. Furthermore, if VSAM used the actual high key of the CI to index that CI, then if the last actual record were deleted, VSAM would have to update the index immediately with the new high key value (of what was the next to the last record before the deletion).

The second approach above is better and is very close to—but not exactly—how VSAM actually handles the index operation. Under this approach, VSAM uses the highest-possible-key (*HPK*) of the CI to index that CI, and there may not be an actual record in that CI with precisely this HPK value. So, for example, for CI2 of CA1, VSAM would store in the index entry for that CI the value '70110': VSAM looks at the lowest actual key of the logically next CI, in this case CI3 of CA1 (since this continues the ascending key sequence), and subtracts one from this value. In our example, this yields $70111 - 1 = 70110$.

This would predict that if we had a record with a key of '70071' to be added to this cluster, it would be inserted by VSAM in CI2 of CA1, after the last current record (with a key of '70070'), given sufficient FSPC, which there is in our example (the record is 100 bytes in length, and the CI has 102 bytes of reserved FSPC, by virtue of the FSPC coding cited earlier); and that is in fact what VSAM would do in actual practice (and can be confirmed by the programmer, although doing this is surprisingly complicated without systems programmer-type knowledge of the structure of a VSAM index).

With this understanding, we draw the reader's attention to the index entries shown stored in the first sequence set record, SSR1. This index record indexes, or governs, the first CA, CA1, of the data component. Furthermore, the entries are stored, and therefore read, from *right to left*:

    70042 is the HPK of data CI1 (of CA1)
    70110 is the HPK of data CI2 (of CA1)
    70222 is the HPK of data CI3 (of CA1)
    75021 is the HPK of data CI4 (of CA1)

where each value is derived by the rule:

$$(\text{lowest key of next logical CI}) - 1.$$

The second sequence set record is structured comparably. This SSR2 indexes (governs) the second (and last) CA of the cluster and provides the HPK values for all of the CIs in this CA. Two points may be noted here. First, the HPK value for CI3 of CA1 is '70222,' which is also precisely the highest *actual* key of the CI. This was due to the fact that the lowest key of the next CI, namely CI4, was '70223', and this all makes sense, given that lowest key of the next CI, '70223' minus one, is really the highest key value that can be possibly stored in CI3.

Second, notice the HPK for CI3 of CA2: it is also the highest *actual* key of that CI, but for a different reason: in this case, CI3 of CA2 is the last non-empty CI of the cluster containing data records. The CI after that, the last CI of the data set, is empty (not by virtue of FSPC coding, but simply by virtue of the fact that no records were loaded into that CI, so that there is no lowest key of this CI from which to subtract one to obtain the HPK of the previous CI. When this occurs, as it has here, then the HPK is equal to the highest actual key for the last non-empty CI of the cluster.

Now that we have a sense of the very general structure of an SSR—consisting of index entries which give the HPK for each CI in the data-CA that SSR governs—let's look at the index set, which here consists of one level above the sequence set level (so we have a two-level index) and, moreover, consists of a single index set record, ISR1. The second level of an index, we have observed earlier, indexes the first, sequence set level. Here, therefore, ISR1 indexes the two sequence set records, SSR1 and SSR2: the first (remember: rightmost) entry is '75021,' and represents the high key of the first sequence set record (SSR1), and the second entry, '84599,' represents the HK of SSR2.

Note here that these are *high key* values, because the value itself is already a highest possible key at the sequence set level; thus an HK within the index set records is equivalent to an HPK within sequence set records. Furthermore, we only needed a two-level index, since a single 512-byte index CI (with an index record size of 512 minus 7, equal to 505) is large enough to hold the two entries needed to provide the HK values of each of the two SSRs we have at level one, at the same time satisfying the VSAM requirement that the highest level of an index contain only a single index record.

Notice also that an entry in an ISR can be seen in two perspectives. In our example the first ISR entry of '75021' is, from one perspective, the HK of the lower SSR1 which this ISR indexes. From a second perspective, however, this value is also the *highest possible key of the entire first CA of the cluster's data component*; in this sense it can be referred to as a CA-HPK. Similarly, the second entry of ISR1 is the CA-HPK for CA2 of the cluster's data component. This completes the discussion of the organization of index records, and we now turn to an examination of *how* VSAM actually uses the index records, both sequence set and index set, in performing sequential and direct access/retrieval of the records of a KSDS cluster.

11.3   HOW VSAM SEARCHES AN INDEX

VSAM uses the records of the index component of a KSDS cluster to locate the whereabouts of specific records to be accessed in or retrieved from the cluster's data component, where the 'whereabouts' means which data-CI contains the target record. Once VSAM ascertains the correct data-CI containing a target record, it then simply retrieves that *entire CI* and reads all of the records in that CI, from left to right, until it finds the record whose key matches the key of the so-called *search argument*: the key value we are searching in the data component. Notice that once an index search is completed and VSAM knows which data-CI to fetch, VSAM then moves out of the index component (which is a data set distinct from the data component data set) and enters the data component to actually fetch the target CI and then search it strictly sequentially until a key match is encountered (the search argument key and the key of the target record). VSAM employs two different types of index search, depending on whether sequential or direct (random) access is requested: a *horizontal search* for sequential access, and a *vertical search* for direct access.

Before we turn to a discussion of these two index search techniques, there is one additional concept we must examine briefly, and that is that of a *CI-pointer*. An *index entry* in an index record must contain at least two fields (it actually contains more, but this is not of concern at this time) for each CI of the data component being indexed: the first field is known as the *K-field*, and contains the HPK value for that CI; the second is the *P-field*, and contains the *CI-pointer* which is a binary integer identifying the CI with which this entry is associated. For index entries within index set records, the P-field CI-pointer points to a CI at the next lower level of the index; more pertinently for applications programmers, for an index entry within a sequence set record, the P-field will point to the CI within the data component whose HPK is the K-field value associated with this entry. Let's demystify this by looking at the K-field and P-field of the index entries for the first CA of our example (Figure 11-3); see Table 11-1.

Note that the P-field refers to the data-CI associated with the K-field by number, but the convention for P-fields is to start the CI numbering at zero, whereas in discussing the data-CIs conceptually within some particular CA (here CA1) we follow ordinary custom and begin at one; so a P-field equal to zero refers to data CI1, a P-field equal to one refers to CI2, etc. A pair of K-field plus P-fields constitutes (part of) an index entry; there are four such pairs in the first sequence set record, since that

Table 11-1. Sample K- and P- fields.

K-FIELD	P-FIELD	DATA-CI
70042	0	CI1
70110	1	CI2
70222	2	CI3
75021	3	CI4

record must contain an index entry for every data-CI in the CA that that record governs (here CA1). (We are simplifying matters here for the time being, but the discussion nevertheless presents a sufficiently accurate representation of index structure for our immediate purposes.) Now, finally, we can turn to the two types of index searches VSAM employs in processing a KSDS.

11.3.1 Horizontal Search

This type of index search is used for sequential and skip-sequential processing; VSAM accesses only the sequence set of the index component, not the index set (higher levels). Most programmers express surprise that VSAM needs to use the index of a KSDS cluster at all for sequential type processing. Surely, the reasoning often goes, VSAM need only open the data component and read records in physically successive order. However, it is a fact that VSAM *always* uses the index in even strict sequential processing of a KSDS. The reason for this is the following: sequential retrieval requires that the logical records of the KSDS be returned in strictly ascending key order; however, the records of a KSDS cluster are not necessarily in such sequence when read physically one after the other as encountered for any time after load time. At any post-load time, record insertion activity could cause splitting activity (CI or CA type), and once even a single split has occurred, the records of the cluster are out of order in terms of key sequence: the physical sequence (how the records are actually stored) is no longer the same as the logical sequence (the sequence of records when fetched in ascending key order).

VSAM deals with this difficulty—of the logical and physical sequence of records differing—by reading the sequence set records which have been structured by VSAM to point to the data-CIs of the cluster in *logical sequence*, regardless of how the data-CIs are actually physically stored, thereby assuring that the records are returned in key sequence for all sequential processing requests. The retrieval of the index records of the sequence set themselves (as opposed to the records of the data-CIs) is effected by following what are called *horizontal pointers* stored in each SSR: each SSR contains a forward pointer field which points to the next SSR record to be retrieved within the sequence set.

Here again, one may well ask what the need for such forward pointers is: aren't the index records of the sequence set in the proper order for retrieval? The answer is, very simply, no they aren't. The records of the entire index component—both sequence set records and index set records—as CIs, are not organized into larger CAs; there are no CAs for an index component. The records are stored as they are constructed by VSAM, and no attempt is made to segregate index set records from sequence set records: all are mixed together as a stream of undifferentiated records, with internal flag settings alerting VSAM to what level of index any particular record belongs to. Thus, VSAM uses the horizontal pointers located in each SSR to thread through all and only the index records of the sequence set in their proper order for sequential processing, since the index set records are not needed at all in this case, and hence must be skipped over by VSAM.

11.3.2 Vertical Search

This type of search, used in direct processing (also known as *random access*), is a top-down search in which VSAM enters the index component at the highest level of the index, which points down ('vertically') to the next highest level, and so on for all levels of an index until the sequence set is reached; at that point, the particular sequence set record at the end of this trail of vertical pointers then points directly to the target CI of the data component. Here VSAM uses the search argument to perform a compare operation against the K-field of the index entries it is searching, and upon a match being found, the P-field associated with the matching K-field provides VSAM with a pointer to the target data-CI.

Let's look at an example of this in operation, using our sample KSDS cluster of Figure 11-3. Assume we are to randomly retrieve the record with a key of '84400,' this therefore being our search argument. Since this is a direct processing request, VSAM will perform a top-down vertical search of the index component in order to thereby locate the data-CI containing a record with a matching key value.

Step 1: VSAM first accesses the single highest index record, the index set record ISR1 and reads the index entries stored there (there are only two in our example) to find the first entry greater than or equal to the value of our search argument: the first entry found—'75021'—is too small, and since this entry is the highest possible key of the entire first data-CA of the data component, this tells VSAM that the target record could not possibly be located in this CA1 (given that the search argument '84400' is larger than this HPK, '75021'). The second entry—'84599'—however satisfies the search criterion: it is a value greater than or equal to our search argument. Therefore, we know that the target record must be located in the second CA of the data component, although from just this level of index we don't know in exactly which CI of CA2 to search.

Step 2: When VSAM encounters the '84599' value of the K-field of ISR1, it will then extract the associated P-field value, which points vertically down to which CI at the next level of index VSAM should retrieve to home in on the target record. Now, remember that this second entry of ISR1 is also the high key of the second CI of the next lower index level, that is, it is the high key of SSR2 (as can easily be seen in the figure), which governs ("indexes") the second data-CA (CA2). The P-field associated with the K-field value of '84599' therefore contains a pointer to this sequence set record, SSR2. (It is not important to know the actual representation VSAM uses for this pointer, so we omit such discussion here.) In terms of the vertical index search VSAM is performing, we say that at this point VSAM is *positioned* at SSR2.

Step 3: VSAM now reads the entries of SSR2 one at a time until it finds the first K-field value greater than or equal to the search argument; in our case, VSAM stops the search when it encounters the second K-field value, that of '84573.' Being the *second* entry, this K-field will have associated with it a P-field value pointing to the second data-CI of the second data-CA, that is, to CI2 in CA2: this is because this SSR entry represents the highest possible key (HPK) of CI2 (in CA2), and our target record must therefore be located in this CI (if it is stored in the cluster at all).

Step 4: There is nothing subtle about what VSAM does now to locate the target record within this target CI: VSAM starts at the beginning of the CI (the left) and reads record after record, comparing its prime key field to the search argument for a match; if a match is found—and in our example it is when VSAM reads the second record in CI2 of CA2—then the search is completed and the target record is returned to the requesting program. If, on the other hand, there is no record with the same key field as the search argument—as there wouldn't be if the search argument were '84401'—then VSAM returns a 'record not found' condition indication; for our example, VSAM would know to stop searching for '84400' once it encountered the third record of the CI with a key of '84500,' which is already too large, so VSAM can safely conclude a "not found" condition. A record insertion operation would follow comparable logic, but in this case VSAM does not expect to find a matching key; VSAM will simply locate the first record with a key exceeding the value of the search argument, and then insert some user-provided record just before this record, using available FSPC if sufficient, or causing a CI-split otherwise. Deletion simply uses the same logic as a retrieval but the target record is deleted upon retrieval.

11.4   THE STRUCTURE OF AN INDEX RECORD

As we have already noted, an index CI consists of a single index record, besides two required control fields, the CIDF and RDF. The index record itself has the basic internal structure shown in Figure 11-4. The two control fields are at the rightmost side of the CI. On the leftmost side, the index CI begins with a 24-byte header, which contains a number of control subfields that VSAM requires for the complex work of index record processing; for example, the level number is stored here (one if this is a sequence set record), as well as the horizontal pointers referred to earlier (pointing to whichever is the next logical index record at the same level as this index record). Also included here is the RBA of the data-CA that this index record governs, among several other specialized subfields that need not concern us further here, and which are generally traced only by high-level system programmers with VSAM internals knowledge.

Immediately after the header, VSAM stores a set of *free data-CI-pointers*—only for sequence set index records—which point to any and all free data-CIs in the data-CA governed by this index record; these allow VSAM to keep track of the wholly empty CIs (if any) reserved in data-CAs for use in split activity. Following these free data-CI-pointers there may be some *unused space* before the actual *index entries* are encountered, because VSAM stores the index entries from right to left and the length of the set of index entries required in any record may leave some intervening space between the last index entry (the leftmost) and the end of the free data-CI-pointers on the left side of the CI; note that this is unused space, not FSPC: an index record contains no FSPC (and CI-splits are wholly a data component phenomemon; no CA-splits can occur for the excellent reason that the index component contains no CAs at all).

Now let us turn to the structure of the index entries of a sequence set record.

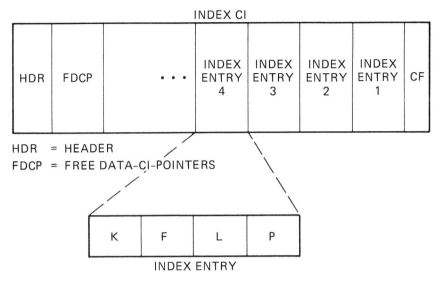

HDR = HEADER
FDCP = FREE DATA-CI-POINTERS

K = COMPRESSED KEY FIELD
F = FRONT-COMPRESS FIELD
L = COMPRESSED KEY LENGTH FIELD
P = CI-POINTER FIELD

Figure 11-4. The structure of an index entry.

Remember that a particular sequence set record governs—"indexes"—one data-CA, with SSR1 governing data-CA1, SSR2 governing data-CA2, etc. Given this, a sequence set record must contain one index entry for each data-CI within the governed data-CA, as we have already seen in Section 11.2. Figure 11-4 also shows the internal structure of an index entry. Such an entry contains, potentially, four fields, two of which we have already disussed: the K-field containing the highest possible key (HPK) value for the data-CI associated with this index entry, and the P-field containing the CI-pointer that identifies this data-CI uniquely. Now let's revisit briefly the K-field.

The reader may recall that in Section 11.2.2 we indicated that there were three possible approaches to a key field representation in a KSDS cluster's index component, but we discussed only the first two and deferred discussion of the third approach, which we will do now. The first approach, that of the K-field representing the highest *actual* key of a CI we rejected; we accepted temporarily the second approach, that of a K-field representing the highest *possible* key of the CI through assigning it a value of one less than the lowest key of the next logical CI. This is very close to the truth, but not exactly right: it assumes that the interpretation of a key (in the K-field) in the index is the HPK of a data-CI, along with the assumption that the key is necessarily a *full key*, one having the same length as the prime key field embedded in the records of the cluster's data component. Thus, if our prime key field is a social security number (SSN) field in the data records, then the index K-field will be precisely the length of this field, namely nine bytes in this case. But the truth of the matter is more complex than this. VSAM uses full keys in the data component of a KSDS cluster, but uses *compressed keys* in the index component, for the value of the K-field of an index entry, and a compressed key is rarely the same length as a data component prime key which is a full key. Let's see what's going on here in a bit more detail.

VSAM exploits the fact that key values often have a large degree of *key redundancy*: the pattern of key values stored in an index is often such that many groups of key values have lead characters, and possibly also trailing characters, that are redundant in the sense that they can be suppressed by VSAM for storage in the index and yet be reliably reconstructed by VSAM to an extent that is satisfactory for the purposes of index searching. By very complex algorithms, VSAM determines for each HPK value in the index (which gives the HPK of an associated data-CI) what lead and/or trailing characters of the full key are redundant with respect to the pattern of other HPK values elsewhere in the index. Having made that determination, VSAM then *compresses* the key by removing those redundant (to VSAM) characters and storing in the index only a compressed key value for the contents of the K-field. (We return to the topic of key compression in the next section of this chapter, Section 11.5).

In sum, therefore, the third and only really correct approach to key field representation in a VSAM index is that of a K-field that contains the highest possible key of a data-CI *in compressed key form*. The stored compressed key is reconstructed— partially—by VSAM in such a way that it still has a highest *possible* key interpretation, rather than highest *actual* key, but the *possible* part of the interpretation is *not* arrived at by any subtracting of one from the lowest key of the next logical CI; this was a useful *fiction*—and will continue to be a *proximate* and easy way to understand VSAM index key fields for the sake of discussion throughout much of this text—but a fiction nonetheless. Just how a compressed key can be interpreted as a highest possible key of anything will be revealed in the last section of this chapter.

Given that compressed, not full, keys are used in the index component, VSAM requires two additional fields—besides the K-field and the P-field—in each index entry to assist it in the partial reconstruction of the original full prime key. The third field shown in Figure 11-4 is the *L-field* which gives the length of the K-field, that is, the number of bytes remaining in the compressed key. A full prime key may be anywhere from one to 255 bytes in size, so a compressed key—and therefore the value of the L-field—can be *at most* 255 bytes if VSAM was not able to compress the key at all due to insufficient redundancy in the patterns of the original prime keys; but, rather amazingly, the compressed key can be a minumum of *zero bytes*—implying, correctly, that in certain cases of high redundancy in key patterns, VSAM may compress the prime key out of existence altogether, resulting in an L-field equal to zero. It is a VSAM convention to, when this occurs, refer to the resulting zero-byte compressed key as a *fully compressed key* (and one has to admit that a key that compresses to nothing is about as fully compressed as it gets!). It is a remarkable fact that in such cases VSAM can reconstruct enough of the original prime key *from nothing* to allow completely reliable index operation. Indeed, in terms of performance, a fully compressed key is the optimal situation, as it consumes no storage in the index at all, yet supports full indexing in any form of VSAM processing that uses an index. (More on key compression in the next section.)

Finally, the fourth and last field of an index entry is the *F-field*, which records the number of *leading characters* that were deleted from the full key by VSAM's key compression operation, the *F* designating *front-compression*. This field too is exploited by VSAM to assist in partial reconstruction of the original full key, since it indicates how many lead characters need to be prefixed to the compressed key to recreate all but the trailing portion of the full key. At this point, the reader might wonder why another field isn't necessary as part of a index entry, namely a field that records the number of characters VSAM truncated off of the righthand side of the original full key (this operation is known as *rear-compression*), if any, for how could VSAM otherwise know how many bytes to suffix to the compressed key for reconstruction purposes. The answer is that VSAM already knows the length of the *full* prime key stored in the data component: this is recorded in the *len* subparameter of the KEYS parameter, specified at DEF CLUSTER time and also recorded by VSAM in the catalog entry for this KSDS file. Then, armed with knowledge of the values of len, of the L-field (compressed key length), and of the F-field (number of front-compressed characters), VSAM can determine the number of rear-compressed characters by this computation:

$$R = len - (L + F)$$

where R = number of rear-compressed characters
F = number of front-compressed characters
L = length of compressed key
len = length of (original) full prime key

Finally, two further points to observe about an index entry. First, it is variable in length due to the fact that the K-field is itself variable in length: a full key may compress to any length from zero to 255. (The P-field, for technical reasons, is also variable in length, from one to three bytes). Indeed, in the special case of a fully compressed key, an index entry actually contains only three fields, not four: the F-field, the L-field, and the P-field, since the K-field is really null (zero characters). Second, VSAM marks software-end-of-file (SEOF) of the sequence set by a specially structured index entry. This SEOF index entry contains no K-field, and in addition has hex zeroes (X'00') loaded into both the F-field and the L-field. By scanning for this special index entry, VSAM knows when it has read the last index record of the sequence set.

11.5   VSAM KEY COMPRESSION

There are two key objectives in effecting key compression in the index component of a KSDS cluster. The first is storage conservation: compressed keys occupy less storage and hence allow the index to be more compact, which in turn assists in reducing index processing time. The second is search optimization: the efficiency of VSAM's search routines is increased, as they need only process a smaller field. This process of key compression is a central and unique feature of VSAM: no other access method works with other than a full key in providing any index support at all. Furthermore, as a performance feature it is *not* defeated, as some might think it would be, by the reverse process of key reconstruction. The reconstruction algorithms are highly optimized to retain the original performance benefits of compression; moreover, VSAM does not incur the appreciable overhead of attempting to reconstruct the entire full key, but rather only partially reconstructs the key *to the point of restoring only the characters suppressed in a front-compression operation; rear-compressed characters are deliberately not reconstructed.* To understand this better, let's now look at an example of key compression and partial reconstruction. The exact details of these processes are extremely complex and beyond the scope of this text to describe completely; however, we can still appreciate the general nature of the processes without undue rigor, and this will also assist us later in understanding some of the performance implications of key compression in VSAM (in Chapter 18, table 11-2 on performance).

Let's examine key compression and reconstruction in its application to the original example of VSAM index operation (Figure 11-3). Table 11-2 gives the original uncompressed high (actual) key of each of the seven CIs of the data component associated with that index, and then in the next column the compressed key which VSAM's key compression mechanism would generate from that full key, and finally in the last column the key as reconstructed by VSAM's partial reconstruction algorithms.

For CI1, the five-byte full key compresses to the four lead bytes. The reconstructed key consists of the compressed key plus X'F' in the final position. Notice that VSAM does not attempt to reconstruct the character that was deleted by rear-compression (the '8'), but simply substitutes the highest possible hex value of 'F' in its

Table 11-2. Key compression in VSAM.

CI	FULL KEY	COMPRESSED KEY	RECONSTRUCTED KEY[a]
CI1	70008	7000	7000F
CI2	70070		700FF
CI3	70222	222	70222
CI4	75000	500	7500F
CI5	75027		750FF
CI6	84531	8453	8453F
CI7	84599	99	84599

[a] The hex 'F' character shown in the last column is actually a hex 'FF' since two hex digits substitute for one character, but no material difference in operation is at issue, so we leave the more simple representation, which has the virtue of showing the reconstructed value visually as having the same number of characters as the original.

place. It's this substitution of X'F' digits for the original rear-compressed characters which yields the 'possible' interpretation of the index key: any key with the lead four characters of '7000' followed by any value in the fifth position will be treated by VSAM as belonging in CI1. Similarly, for CI2 the reconstructed value is interpreted as meaning that any key greater than '7000F,' and whose first three characters are '700' followed by any two digit values whatever, shall belong in this CI2. Notice also that this is not the same as the highest possible key interpretation settled on earlier for reasons of simplicity, since that interpretation made the reconstructed key always one less than the value of the lowest key in the next CI. Now we see that a 'highest possible' interpretation is too strong a statement of what VSAM actually does. The reconstructed key is less misleadingly called the *effective high key* (*EHK*) in more exact VSAM terminology. Still, it will continue to be useful to use the HPK (highest possible key) interpretation for the sake of simplified discussion, remembering that it is only an approximation to the strictly correct EHK (effective high key) interpretation.

In addition, the table also shows that two original full keys—the key of '70070' in CI2, and the key of '75027' of CI5—yielded the most optimal compressed key, namely a fully compressed key of zero bytes. In both cases, VSAM was able to delete the first three characters of each key through a front-compression operation, and the last and remaining two characters were deleted through rear-compression, leaving no characters in the resulting compressed key. VSAM simply reconstructs, when needed, the front-compressed characters—and it knows how many by examining the value of the F-field in an index entry—by looking at the corresponding characters in the previous entry's K-field. Thus, for CI2, VSAM uses the first three characters of the previous CI's EHK, namely '700' as the reconstructed values of the front-compressed characters of this (CI2) EHK value, simply appending X'FF' to complete the reconstructed value.

Another point to observe here is that the index contains the *compressed key*, not the reconstructed *EHK*. The EHK is not stored anywhere by VSAM, but is dynamically reconstructed by VSAM control routines as needed in any index search operation. Of course, given that VSAM stores the compressed key in the index, then, in cases of a fully compressed key, there is no K-field at all, so that anyone inspecting the index could not, without very sophisticated knowledge of VSAM internals and specifically of VSAM key compression and reconstruction algorithms, deduce anything directly about the structure of the index entries. Indeed, since even if a key is not fully compressed it is nonetheless typically compressed to some degree, the print of the index component through, say an IDCAMS PRINT command, by the applications programmer generally leads to what appears to be an incoherent output of relatively random characters (in hex) and is therefore rarely a worthwhile thing to do.

We leave the discussion of key compression at this point, and will return to the issue of some performance implications of key compression later in the text, in Chapter 18, on performance. The reader should now have a fairly solid understanding of the structure and operation of a VSAM index.

THE ART OF INTERPRETING LISTCAT OUTPUT

12.1 USING IDCAMS TO TAILOR LISTCAT OUTPUT

The IDCAMS LISTCAT command makes available to the user extensive information about any VSAM object, as reflected in the comprehensive catalog entries VSAM maintains for such objects in master and user catalogs. (A brief introduction to LISTCAT was given in Subsection 6.3.2.) The command itself provides a set of parameters which can be used for very fine tailoring of the resulting output. Although the command is relatively frequently issued by programmers on almost a casual basis, much of the information is not utilized, due (in part) to the difficulty of interpreting many of the entries in the output. This section details how to code the LISTCAT command in order to tailor output to specific purposes.

We have already seen the basic and perhaps most useful form of the LISTCAT command, namely that using the ENTRIES parameter with the ALL option. The basic syntax for LISTCAT is:

```
LISTCAT -
   ENTRIES (entry name/generic name) / LEVEL (level) -
      CREATION (days) / EXPIRATION (days) -
      ‹entry type› -
      ‹field group name›
```

where '/' indicates a mutually exclusive choice: either ENTRIES or LEVEL is coded, not both; similarly, the value of ENTRIES is either an entry name or a generic name, not both. We will now discuss each of the options shown above in turn, beginning with a joint discussion of the two related parameters, ENTRIES and LEVEL.

12.1.1 ENTRIES/LEVEL

To see how these two parameters tailor the output from LISTCAT, consider the clusters as shown in Table 12-1 as the only objects in a small test user catalog. The easiest way to illustrate the operation of these parameters is to see how various codings of the ENTRIES and LEVEL parameters below yield different results:

```
ENTRIES (TRUCAT.MVS003T.INQR0021.*)
```

Table 12-1. Some sample entry names.

CL1	TRUCAT.MVS003T.INQR0021.VS
CL2	TRUCAT.MVS003T.INQR0021.TESTVS
CL3	FINCAT.MVS003T.INQR0021.VS
CL4	FINCAT.MVS003T.INQR0021.TESTVS
CL5	CUSTODY.TEST.INVENTR.TRANS0001
CL6	CUSTODY.PROD.INVENTR.TRANS0001
CL7	TRUCAT.MVSSYSH.MSTRFILE
CL8	TRUCAT.LOGREC
CL9	TRUCAT.MVS003T.INQR0021
CL10	AUDIT.MVS003T.TRAN0021.MSTR

This shows the use of a generic name: the '*' is a so-called 'wildcard' placeholder; here it refers to all objects whose first three qualifiers are as specified, and whose fourth—*and only other*—qualifier may be anything at all. Thus, CL1 and CL2 will be listed. Note that CL9 is *not* listed: the ENTRIES coding given above requires that all objects to be listed have a four-part qualified name; the '*' in the fourth position allows the fourth qualifier to be anything, *but not nothing*.

```
ENTRIES (*.*.INQR0021.*)
```

This would list all *four-part* qualified object names whose third qualifier is that specified: CL1, CL2, CL3, and CL4. Again, the three-part CL9 name would not be listed.

```
ENTRIES (*.MVS003T.*.*)
```

Here the clusters CL1, CL2, CL3, CL4, and CL10 would be listed.

```
ENTRIES (TRUCAT.*)
```

Now only CL8 would be picked out (it alone has a two-part name).

```
ENTRIES (*.*.INQR0021)
```

Only CL9 is listed by the above coding (there are other clusters whose third qualifier is INQR0021, but they also have a fourth qualifier, and that is ruled out by the above coding).

Now let's turn to the other parameter, mutually exclusive with ENTRIES, namely LEVEL. Again, a few examples will quickly illustrate the basic operation of the LEVEL parameter.

```
LEVEL (TRUCAT.MVS003T)
```

This is interpreted as a reference to *all* object names whose first and second qualifiers are TRUCAT and MVS003T, respectively, followed by any number of qualifiers. Thus, the four-part names of CL1 and CL2 are picked out, as well as the three part name of CL9. It should be noted that the above coding accepts only names with more than two parts: at least one qualifier must follow the sequence TRUCAT.MVS003T. This can be seen more clearly in interpreting the following coding:

```
LEVEL (TRUCAT.LOGREC)
```

WARNING

This coding would result in *no* clusters at all being listed, not even CL8, since the coding refers to clusters whose names begin with TRUCAT.LOGREC followed by something, not nothing. If we had wanted to pick out CL8, we should have coded ENTRIES (TRUCAT.LOGREC) and not used the LEVEL parameter at all.

Now let's look at coding that uses both the LEVEL parameter and a wildcard option.

```
LEVEL (TRUCAT.*.INQROO21)
```

This would pick out CL1, CL2, *and CL9*: when using a wildcard option with LEVEL, it is *not* necessary that there be any qualifiers after the last one specified in the coding (as witness CL9). Only if no wildcard options are used in the LEVEL coding is it required that the names picked out must have at least one additional qualifier after the last one specified in LEVEL.

```
LEVEL (TRUCAT)
```

CL1, CL2, CL7, CL8, and CL9 are referenced by the above coding.

WARNING

Consider the following coding:

```
LEVEL (*.*.INQROO21.*)
```

This might have been coded by a programmer with the intention of picking out CL1, CL2, CL3, and CL4, and at face appears to be a reasonable coding to effect this. However, no cluster will be listed, and an *error* is returned by VSAM: VSAM disallows the wildcard option in the *last position of a LEVEL coding*, regardless of what is coded in front of it. Given the same intention as just specified, the proper coding would use ENTRIES, not LEVEL:

```
ENTRIES (*.*.INQROO21.*).
```

12.1.2 CREATION (Days) / EXPIRATION (Days)

These two parameters allow the programmer to exercise *date control* over what entries are to be listed. Thus, the following coding requests the listing of all cluster entries which were created at least 365 days ago (one year or older clusters):

```
LISTCAT -
     CREATION (365) -
     CLUSTER -
     ALL
```

(Remember that ALL indicates that the entire catalog entry for any object specified is to be listed, rather than only specialized subparts of the entry.) One can also control what entries are to be listed by when the associated objects are due to expire (are eligible for deletion without date protection); EXPIRATION (30) restricts the LISTCAT output only to objects due to expire in 30 days or under.

12.1.3 Entry Type

LISTCAT output can be restricted to listing entries only of a particular type, for example, only cluster entries, or only data component entries, or only non-VSAM data set entries. Entry type is therefore most useful when ENTRIES is *not* coded, in order to obtain the listing of all catalog entries for a *class of VSAM objects*. The possible entry types and their abbreviations, if any, are given in Table 12-2.

Table 12-2. Entry type and abbreviations.

ENTRY TYPE	ABBREVIATION
ALIAS	none
ALTERNATEINDEX	AIX
CLUSTER	CL
DATA	none
GENERATIONDATAGROUP	GDG
INDEX	IX
NONVSAM	NVSAM
PAGESPACE	PGSPC
PATH	none
USERCATALOG	UCAT

WARNINGS

1. If you are requesting the listing of only a single object, say a cluster, *do not* code the entry type in addition to the entry name:

```
AVOID: LISTCAT -
          ENT (AUDIT.JOURNAL.OCT87) -
             CLUSTER
```

This will list only cluster-level information about the file named in the ENT(RIES) parameter; the data and index component entries for this file are *not* listed. Since it is rarely useful to have only cluster-level information, and not also component-level information, the proper coding is simply:

```
LISTCAT -
     ENT (AUDIT.JOURNAL.OCT87)
```

which will list cluster and component-level catalog data.

2. If both ENTRIES and an entry type are coded, the programmer must be absolutely certain that the named entry is indeed of that particular entry type, for otherwise the catalog entry for the named entry will *not* be listed. Consider the following coding:

```
LISTCAT -
     ENT (AUDIT.JOURNAL.OCT87) -
          DATA
```

If it turns out that AUDIT.JOURNAL.OCT87 is not the name of the data component but rather the name of the cluster, nothing will be listed, since the entry type specified does not match the actual entry type of the object named, as VSAM knows it through its catalog information. Thus, it is recommended that in requesting LISTCAT output for a single VSAM object, the programmer should only code ENTRIES with the appropriate entry name of the object, and no entry type be specified.

12.1.4 Field Group Name

For any given VSAM object, or class of objects, the user may request LISTCAT output only of a certain type, called a *field group*. These are organized into a *hierarchy*, shown in Figure 12-1, with NAME providing the most restrictive information,

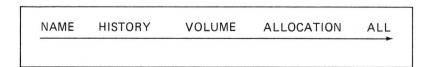

Figure 12-1. Hierarchy of LISTCAT groups.

Table 12-3. LISTCAT field group names and functions.

GROUP NAME	FUNCTION
NAME	Name of object and entry type information only.
HISTORY	NAME information, plus ownerid, and creation and expiration date.
VOLUME	HISTORY information, plus volume serial number and device type information.
ALLOCATION	VOLUME information, plus comprehensive space allocation information, including primary and secondary extents and their associated low and high RBAs, along with track and physical record information, and HARBA and HURBA fields (which we will discuss later).
ALL	ALL NAME, HISTORY, VOLUME, and ALLOCATION information together; essentially this is the entire catalog entry except for fields that may have security/ authorization restrictions (e.g., passwords).

and ALL the least restrictive, namely all fields of a catalog entry (everything VSAM stores about the object except security or restricted authorization information), and with each field group name providing all of the information of the preceding group field name, plus additional fields. Thus, HISTORY gives all the information provided by NAME as well as some additional fields, VOLUME gives all the information provided by HISTORY (which includes that of NAME) along with additional fields, etc. Table 12-3 presents this hierarchy of field group names and what information each generates in LISTCAT output.

SUGGESTION

Unless you have only a very restricted special need which is satisfied by the specialized field group options NAME, HISTORY, VOLUME, or ALLOCATION, it is strongly recommended that the field group option ALL be specified to obtain the entire catalog entry for any particular VSAM object. The reasons for this are, firstly, that the full information needed for performance monitoring and tuning is available only through this option, and secondly, the full listing is only a few pages long (three or four pages, on an average).

12.2   A GUIDE TO LISTCAT FIELDS

This section discusses how to interpret the various fields of LISTCAT output within the most important (field) groups, listed below. A firm understanding of what LISTCAT

```
IDCAMS  SYSTEM SERVICES                              TIME: 22:38:22    12/01/83    PAGE   1

   REPRO -
         INFILE(QSAMDD) -
         OUTFILE(VSAMDD)
IDC0005I NUMBER OF RECORDS PROCESSED WAS 40000
IDC0001I FUNCTION COMPLETED, HIGHEST CONDITION CODE WAS 0

   IF MAXCC = 0 -
      THEN -
            LISTCAT -
                  ENTRIES(STNTESTV.STNKANT.KSDS02) -
                  ALL
CLUSTER ------- STNTESTV.STNKANT.KSDS02
      IN-CAT --- MVSYSH.MASTER.CATALOG
      HISTORY
         OWNER-IDENT------STNKANT     CREATION---------83.335
         RELEASE----------------2     EXPIRATION--------00.000
      PROTECTION-PSWD-----(NULL)      RACF---------------(NO)
      ASSOCIATIONS
         DATA-----STNTESTV.STNKANT.KSDS02.DATA
         INDEX----STNTESTV.STNKANT.KSDS02.INDEX
      DATA ------- STNTESTV.STNKANT.KSDS02.DATA
         IN-CAT --- MVSYSH.MASTER.CATALOG
         HISTORY
            OWNER-IDENT-------(NULL)     CREATION---------83.335
            RELEASE----------------2     EXPIRATION--------00.000
         PROTECTION-PSWD-----(NULL)      RACF---------------(NO)
         ASSOCIATIONS
            CLUSTER--STNTESTV.STNKANT.KSDS02
         ATTRIBUTES
            KEYLEN----------------8   AVGLRECL------------600   BUFSPACE-----------9216   CISIZE-------------4096
            RKP-------------------0   MAXLRECL------------600   EXCPEXITM--------(NULL)   CI/CA--------------120
            SHROPTNS(1,3)  RECOVERY   UNIQUE       NOERASE   INDEXED   NOWRITECHK   NOIMBED   NOREPLICAT
            UNORDERED    NOREUSE      NONSPANNED
         STATISTICS
            REC-TOTAL----------40000   SPLITS-CI-------------0   EXCPS--------------8396
            REC-DELETED------------0   SPLITS-CA-------------0   EXTENTS----------------7
            REC-INSERTED-----------0   FREESPACE-%CI---------10   SYSTEM-TIMESTAMP:
            REC-UPDATED------------0   FREESPACE-%CA----------0       X'9687BC388771EC20'
            REC-RETRIEVED----------0   FREESPC-BYTES-----217088
         ALLOCATION
            SPACE-TYPE------CYLINDER   HI-ALLOC-RBA----27525120
            SPACE-PRI-------------50   HI-USED-RBA-----27525120
            SPACE-SEC--------------1
         VOLUME
            VOLSER-----------SYS003   PHYREC-SIZE---------4096   HI-ALLOC-RBA----27525120   EXTENT-NUMBER----------7
            DEVTYPE------X'30502008'   PHYRECS/TRK------------4   HI-USED-RBA-----27525120   EXTENT-TYPE-------X'00'
            VOLFLAG-----------PRIME   TRACKS/CA------------30
            EXTENTS:
            LOW-CCHH-----X'01F70000'   LOW-RBA---------------0   TRACKS-------------1500
            HIGH-CCHH-----X'0228001D'   HIGH-RBA------24575999
            LOW-CCHH-----X'00150000'   LOW-RBA--------24576000   TRACKS--------------30
            HIGH-CCHH-----X'0015001D'   HIGH-RBA------25067519
            LOW-CCHH-----X'00160000'   LOW-RBA--------25067520   TRACKS--------------30
            HIGH-CCHH-----X'0016001D'   HIGH-RBA------25559039
            LOW-CCHH-----X'003E0000'   LOW-RBA--------25559040   TRACKS--------------30
            HIGH-CCHH-----X'003E001D'   HIGH-RBA------26050559
            LOW-CCHH-----X'003F0000'   LOW-RBA--------26050560   TRACKS--------------30
            HIGH-CCHH-----X'003F001D'   HIGH-RBA------26542079
            LOW-CCHH-----X'00490000'   LOW-RBA--------26542080   TRACKS--------------30
            HIGH-CCHH-----X'0049001D'   HIGH-RBA------27033599
            LOW-CCHH-----X'00430000'   LOW-RBA--------27033600   TRACKS--------------30
            HIGH-CCHH-----X'0043001D'   HIGH-RBA------27525119
```

Figure 12-2. Sample LISTCAT output.

fields mean can give the programmer better control over the VSAM environment, and can provide invaluable information for performance tuning, problem determination, and recovery. Although many programmers routinely generate—we say 'snap'—LISTCAT output, only a handful of fields are inspected, since the meaning and use of most other fields are either unknown to the programmer, or only vaguely understood. Furthermore, as we shall see below, not all of the major fields are reliable, and (in addition) many are labelled in such a fashion as may mislead the programmer into an invalid interpretation and/or use of the field's information.

```
INDEX ------ STNTESTV.STNKANT.KSDS02.INDEX
  IN-CAT --- MVSYSH.MASTER.CATALOG
  HISTORY
       OWNER-IDENT-------(NULL)       CREATION---------83.335
         RELEASE---------------2      EXPIRATION--------00.000
    PROTECTION-PSWD-----(NULL)        RACF---------------(NO)
  ASSOCIATIONS
     CLUSTER--STNTESTV.STNKANT.KSDS02
  ATTRIBUTES
       KEYLEN---------------8         AVGLRECL--------------0      BUFSPACE--------------0      CISIZE-------------1024
          RKP---------------0         MAXLRECL-----------1017      EXCPEXIT---------(NULL)      CI/CA---------------15
       SHROPTNS(1,3)   RECOVERY       UNIQUE            NOERASE    NOWRITECHK      NOIMBED      NOREPLICAT    UNORDERED
       NOREUSE
  STATISTICS
       REC-TOTAL-----------57         SPLITS-CI-------------0      EXCPS--------------335      INDEX:
     REC-DELETED------------0         SPLITS-CA-------------0      EXTENTS---------------1      LEVELS---------------2
    REC-INSERTED------------0         FREESPACE-%CI---------0      SYSTEM-TIMESTAMP:            ENTRIES/SECT---------10
     REC-UPDATED------------0         FREESPACE-%CA---------0         X'9687BC388771EC20'      SEQ-SET-RBA-----------0
   REC-RETRIEVED-----------0          FREESPC-BYTES------3072                                  HI-LEVEL-RBA-------2048
  ALLOCATION
     SPACE-TYPE--------TRACK          HI-ALLOC-RBA-------61440
      SPACE-PRI-------------4         HI-USED-RBA--------58368
      SPACE-SEC-------------1
  VOLUME
       VOLSER-----------SYS003        PHYREC-SIZE--------1024      HI-ALLOC-RBA-------61440     EXTENT-NUMBER----------1
      DEVTYPE------X'3050200B'        PHYRECS/TRK----------15      HI-USED-RBA--------58368     EXTENT-TYPE-------X'00'
      VOLFLAG-----------PRIME         TRACKS/CA-------------1
      EXTENTS:
      LOW-CCHH-----X'00070011'        LOW-RBA---------------0      TRACKS----------------4
     HIGH-CCHH----X'00070014'         HIGH-RBA----------61439
        THE NUMBER OF ENTRIES PROCESSED WAS:
                       AIX -------------------0
                       ALIAS -----------------0
                       CLUSTER --------------1
                       DATA -----------------1
                       GDG -------------------0
                       INDEX ----------------1
                       NONVSAM ---------------0
                       PAGESPACE -------------0
                       PATH ------------------0
                       SPACE -----------------0
                       USERCATALOG -----------0
                       TOTAL ----------------3
        THE NUMBER OF PROTECTED ENTRIES SUPPRESSED WAS 0
IDC0001I FUNCTION COMPLETED, HIGHEST CONDITION CODE WAS 0
```

Figure 12-2. Continued.

Our discussion of LISTCAT fields will be against the sample LISTCAT output of Figure 12-2 (which we also considered earlier in the text, in Section 4.4: *A Peek at a Catalog Entry*); the reader may want to briefly review that discussion at this point. So, without further ado, let's begin our guided tour of LISTCAT output fields. (Note: an '(I)' next to a field indicates a field associated with the index component of a cluster.)

12.2.1 The ATTRIBUTES Group

This group of fields within LISTCAT output presents comprehensive information about the physical and logical properties of the VSAM object whose catalog entry is being listed. The key fields of the ATTRIBUTES group are presented immediately below.

KEYLEN. The key length of the primary (full) key for a KSDS, or of the alternate key ('alt-key') for an alternate index (AIX) file. For both KSDSs and AIXs, keylen ranges from one to 255.

RKP. This field, the *relative key position*, gives the offset (byte displacement) of the key from the logical start-of-file, which is by convention always the zeroth byte.

Thus, in our example, the RKP equal to zero value shown indicates that the key begins in the *first* position of the actual data records. A common programmer error is to define the key offset in the KEYS parameter of the DEF CLUSTER command, on which the RKP field value is based, the same as the column position of the key in the data record; this generally results in a VSAM error indicating that the prime key contains duplicate values (which is disallowed). The relationship can be expressed:

$$\text{Column Position of Key} = \text{RKP} + 1$$
or
$$\text{RKP} = (\text{Column Position of Key}) - 1.$$

SHROPTNS. This is the SHAREOPTIONS parameter (abbreviated to SHROPTNS when reported in LISTCAT output), specified at DEF CLUSTER time. It determines the degree of concurrency for the VSAM data set, that is, the degree of multiple concurrent access against a single file, thereby 'shared' by several users. There are two positional subparameter values coded on this option which essentially determine the exact type of data integrity—read, write, read and write, or none—that may be assured for such a shared data set. Other than these few general remarks, we will otherwise defer complete discussion of SHROPTIONS until later in the text where it will more appropriately be integrated with our performance and design considerations for VSAM data sets.

ORDERED/UNORDERED. These are parameters used in connection with the special facility for KSDSs known as the *keyrange facility*; we will defer discussion until Chapter 18, on performance, where the keyrange facility is presented as a performance and design option in VSAM processing.

RECOVERY/SPEED. These two parameters, SPEED and RECOVERY, determine whether a certain VSAM recovery facility is to be used, or supressed, at program-load time; although the determination is for load time, the parameter choice is specified at DEF CLUSTER time. The issue of SPEED versus RECOVERY is largely decided on the basis of performance considerations, and so these parameters are taken up later in the text. Note that at any *post-load time* there is no choice allowed, and RECOVERY is always on after records have been loaded into the cluster. Our example of Figure 12-2 represents LISTCAT output snapped after we have loaded 40,000 records into the KSDS cluster, so RECOVERY is indeed on automatically.

REUSE/NOREUSE. This parameter choice determines whether a cluster is reusable or not, that is, whether it can be reused by simply reopening it (a *reusable* cluster), rather than otherwise having to delete and recreate the cluster for reuse. (See our original discussion in Subsection 8.11.1.)

AVGLRECL/MAXLRECL. The average and maximum record lengths, respectively; these are different only for a file containing variable length records (KSDS and

ESDS support this, but not an RRDS); thus, for a file containing only fixed length records, AVGLRECL is equal to MAXLRECL. These record lengths must be less than the CISZ by at least the number of bytes reserved for the VSAM control fields, the CIDF and one or more RDFs.

UNIQUE/SUBALLOC.   This specifies whether the cluster is a unique cluster or a suballocated cluster, as per our discussion earlier in the text (Section 7.3). Note that this parameter choice is not valid for other than Enhanced VSAM—the new VSAM (Data Facility/Extended Function: DF/EF) does not support a distinction between unique and suballocated clusters.

SPANNED/UNSPANNED.   VSAM has a provision for large records which may exceed the size of the CI that they are to be stored in; in this case VSAM allows such a record to *span* (cross) a CI boundary, that is, to start on one CI (filling it completely) and complete on one or more others, the record being known as a *spanned record*. It is sometimes useful to define a cluster with the SPANNED parameter at DEF CLUSTER time, if it is known that one or more records of a file with variable length records have a MAXLRECL larger than the cluster's defined CISZ, but there are only a few such 'spanning' records so that it is not worthwhile to increase the CISZ just for a handful of records. However, as we will see in Chapter 18, on performance, spanned records have certain adverse performance effects and should therefore be avoided unless no other means of handling this special case is feasible.

ERASE/NOERASE.   As we discussed earlier (Section 8.13.2) in connection with the DELETE command, by default VSAM performs only a logical deletion of a cluster when a DELETE command is issued against the cluster: the cluster's catalog entry is deleted, and the space occupied by the cluster is marked reclaimable, but the data contents of the file physically remain in the occupied space until such time as the space is reclaimed and then overwritten with new data. As a security precaution—to avoid possible exposure of sensitive data—the programmer may insist that VSAM perform a physical deletion of the cluster by overwriting the data component with binary zeroes immediately upon the issuing of the DELETE command. There are three different ways in which to force a VSAM physical delete of a cluster (there are actually even more ways, but they are used for very specialized circumstances):

1. Specify the ERASE option on the DEF CLUSTER command, or on the DEF AIX (alternate index) command if an AIX is to be deleted.
2. Specify the ERASE option on the DELETE command.
3. Specify the ERASE option on the ALTER command, thereby overriding whatever was specified at DEF CLUSTER time.

BUFSPACE.   This field is derived either directly from the program, from the JCL, or from the BUFFERSPACE parameter on the DEF CLUSTER command, and specifies the minimum space available for VSAM program buffers. If no buffer allocation is specified by the programmer, than VSAM will use its default minimum buffer allocation:

VSAM MINIMUM BUFFER ALLOCATION
Two Data (Component) Buffers
One Index (Component) Buffer (for KSDS)

The two data buffers are allocated as follows: one to hold the data CI containing the target record of any access request, the other as a *control-CI* to hold a wholly empty CI reserved for possible split activity. If the cluster is a KSDS, than VSAM also reserves one CI to hold an index CI for potential use in index processing of the KSDS. Under the data component part of our sample LISTCAT output, BUFSPACE is shown with a value of 9216. Let's see how VSAM derived this number (buffer allocation was allowed to default). The data CISZ is equal to 4096 and the index CISZ is equal to 1024, so the default yields two times 4096, which is equal to 8192 bytes for data buffers and an additional (one times) 1024 bytes for an index buffer, giving BUFSPACE equal to 9216 (which equals 8192 plus 1024) as a total. It is very important to check this field in LISTCAT output, as buffer allocation is a major determinant of VSAM processing performance, as we shall see later in the text. Rarely is the VSAM-provided minimum default satisfactory for environments requiring high optimization.

INDEXED/NONINDEXED/NUMBERED/LINEAR. This parameter specifies the cluster type:

INDEXED   KSDS(KEY-SEQUENCED DATA SET)
NONINDEXED   ESDS(ENTRY-SEQUENCED DATA SET)
NUMBERED   RRDS(RELATIVE RECORD DATA SET)
LINEAR   LDS(LINEAR DATA SET)

Note that the fourth type of VSAM cluster, a *Linear Data Set* (LDS) is new to VSAM: only the new VSAM supports this type, and the new VSAM must be at least the level of DFP/VSAM (Data Facility Product/VSAM), Version 2, Release 3.0 and this in turn is supported only if the operating system is the newest release of MVS/XA (Extended Architecture), which means it must be at least at the level of MVS/SP Version 2, Release 2.0 or higher. The LDS implements the new MVS/XA advanced facility known as *Data-in-Virtual* (*DIV*). We will defer discussion of LDSs and the Data-in-Virtual facility until Chapter 18 on performance.

WRITECHECK/NOWRITECHK. If a cluster is defined at DEF CLUSTER time with the WRITECHECK option on, then VSAM attempts to assure the validity of *every* write operation by doing in addition to the actual write output opertion an extra read checking that the write operation was correctly executed: this is called *testing for a data check condition*. It should be understood that this is a

VSAM check for *hardware* reliability, felt to be sometimes needed as a precaution with certain early DASD devices (largely pre-3330), and the data check operation consumes a significant amount of execution time. With high-reliability DASD like the 3350 and 3380 disks, it is really no longer advisable to have VSAM perform such checking: validity checking of data transfer operations is more effectively, and transparently, performed by DASD hardware, generally either by the DASD control unit for some models, or by the HOS (*head of string*) for other models. (Sophisticated error correction codes (ECCs) are typically used in conjunction with DASD hardware.) Therefore, this parameter should always be set off (NOWRITECHK).

CISIZE.   The CISZ, in bytes, for the data and index components is given separately and should be checked by the programmer to assure that these are indeed the intended values: VSAM rounds to the next higher multiple if the specified CISZ is not an integral multiple of either ½K or 2K. Furthermore, many programmers allow the index CISZ to default, so the programmer should check what value VSAM indeed chose (later we shall see that there are important performance consequences to VSAM's choice, which is not always the best one possible). In our sample LISTCAT, VSAM chose 4096 as the data CISZ default and 1024 as the index CISZ default.

CI/CA.   This field gives what we have been calling the *CI-density* of the cluster. Here, the data component has a CI-density of 120 CIs (each 4K in size) per CA, where the CASZ is the maximum one cylinder by virtue of the fact that we allocated cluster space in cylinder units.

IMBED/NOIMBED AND REPLICATE/NOREPLICAT.   These are performance options for the index component of a KSDS cluster; discussion is more appropriately deferred to Chapter 18, on performance.

12.2.2   The ALLOCATION Group

The fields in this group describe the space allocation characteristics of the VSAM object. There are five fields in the group, and the first three we will discuss together, the other two being given separate focus.

SPACE-TYPE/SPACE-PRI/SPACE-SEC.   These are relatively straightforward to understand: SPACE-TYPE shows the allocation unit used at DEF CLUSTER time (TRACK, CYLINDER, RECORD), and SPACE-PRI and SPACE-SEC the primary and secondary space amounts requested, respectively.

WARNING

The space allocation amounts shown here do *not* represent the actual size of the cluster if the primary allocation proved insufficient to hold all records; in such a case, the actual size is not reported directly by VSAM in LISTCAT output. The space actually occupied by the cluster must be derived from the EXTENTS field of the VOLUMES group. In our sample LISTCAT output, the cluster should not be assumed to be 50 cylinders in size, since we may have needed to go into secondary extenting — and indeed, we did in this case. As we shall see in our discussion of the EXTENTS field, our cluster is actually 56 cylinders in size, not 50.

Understanding the HI-ALLOC-RBA field.   This field, known more simply as *HARBA*, gives the highest RBA, plus one, available within the space allocated to the cluster that can be used to store data records. (The plus one is for adjusting the byte displacement for the fact that VSAM begins counting at zero rather than at one; otherwise it can be safely ignored by the programmer.) This translates to the RBA of the last byte of the last CA allocated to the cluster. Notice that there is no implication that any data is actually stored at this location: HARBA deals strictly with *potential*: how far from the logical start-of-data-set — considered to be offset X'0' — could we store data, if we had any data to store. Our data set may be ten tracks in size — through a primary allocation request for this amount — and we can store to the end of this data set, whether or not we actually have enough records at any time to fill the ten tracks entirely. We may, in fact, at any time have no more than eight tracks, say, of data records stored in the file.

Thus, we can speak of HARBA as representing the *maximal end-of-file* (*MAX-EOF*), as opposed to the *data end-of-file* (*DATA-EOF*), which is where the actual data records end, which may be considerably less than the MAX-EOF. VSAM will translate all of this (MAX-EOFs and DATA-EOFs) into RBA values, but the concepts are independent of any mode of representation. Figure 12-3 portrays these two concepts graphically.

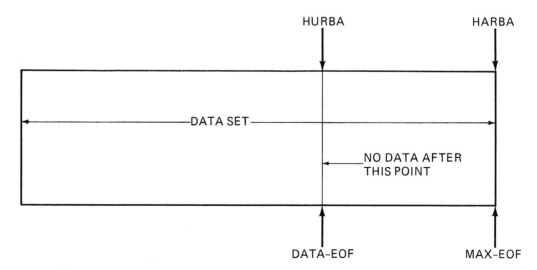

Figure 12-3. The HURBA and the HARBA.

Our sample LISTCAT represents a special case: we loaded 40,000 records into the cluster, and it turns out (how, we will study in Chapter 18, on performance) that the primary allocation amount requested — 50 cylinders — was insufficient to contain the necessary VSAM control fields, distributed free space, and unused space *in addition* to the storage needed strictly for the data records themselves. Indeed, as noted earlier, we went into secondary extenting to the tune of an additional six cylinders (the cluster immediately after load is 56 cylinders in size). Thus, we used more than our primary allocation amount, and in this case the MAX-EOF and the DATA-EOF are equivalent — some data records had to be loaded as far into the cluster as the last CA of the cluster's data component, which is also the last cylinder of the data component (we allocated in cylinders so each CA was equal to one cylinder, with the cluster containing 56 CAs equivalent to 56 cylinders of space).

To anticipate briefly the discussion of a related field HURBA (HI-USED-RBA), it's the case that VSAM uses HARBA to represent the maximal end-of-file, MAX-EOF, and uses HURBA to represent the data end-of-file, DATA-EOF. Our LISTCAT shows both fields to be the same due to the use of secondary extents.

What about the actual value of HARBA? Where does the value, here '27,525,120', come from? Here are the facts of this cluster's data component:

    CA-DS   = 56
    CI-density   = 120
                   (from the LISTCAT CI/CA field)
    CISZ   = 4096

where CA-DS means number of CAs in the data set, which we will derive below under the EXTENTS field of the VOLUMES group. Since there are 56 CAs in the data set, each CA containing 120 CIs, each 4096 bytes in size, then:

$$\text{HARBA} = 56 \times 120 \times 4096 = 27,525,120$$

exactly! What VSAM is telling us is that if we were to use all of the space in the cluster's data component — 56 cylinders — then the RBA of the last byte of the last CA would be the HARBA value shown. If we needed more secondary extents, then the HARBA value would increase to represent the new potential end-of-file (our MAX-EOF) as the file grows. Now let's turn to the closely related field HURBA, and then draw the connection between them.

A final technical note on HARBA.   In the strictest terms of VSAM internals, HARBA is computed by VSAM *on a CA boundary*: whether we allocate by tracks, cylinders, or records, HARBA points to the last byte of the last CA. If, for instance, we had allocated 60 cylinders for our primary allocation instead of 50 plus the six secondary extents it turned out we needed, then HARBA would point to the last byte of the sixtieth CA — the sixtieth cylinder — even though the last four CAs (CA57, CA58, CA59, and CA60) would, in this case, be entirely empty (since we know from our sample LISTCAT that precisely 56 cylinders were necessary to store our

40,000 loaded records, given otherwise identical conditions). HARBA will always represent the potential we have for expansion within primary allocated space, or up to the end of any secondary space that was actually allocated to the cluster. Thus, in sum, we could say that HARBA represents the maximal end-of-file, MAX-EOF, in the strict sense of pointing to the last byte—used or unused for data—of the *last current extent of the cluster*, whether that is a primary or an actually allocated secondary extent.

Understanding the HI-USED-RBA field. The HI-USED-RBA field, more simply known as HURBA, gives the highest RBA, plus one, within the space allocated to the cluster's data component that contains actual data. (Again, the plus one is for adjusting the byte displacement for the fact that VSAM begins counting at zero rather than at one; otherwise it can be safely ignored by the programmer.) This is the *data end-of-file* (*DATA-EOF*) referred to above: the real end of file in the sense that no data records are stored in any location that is physically after this RBA value.

The HURBA field is one of the most vital fields in VSAM processing, as it determines where VSAM considers the cluster to have ended in terms of feeling assured that after the point in the cluster pointed to by HURBA there is no subsequent data. However, it can occur that the HURBA value stored as a LISTCAT field may not represent the *true end-of-data* (*true-EOD*), due to a failure of a VSAM update against this HURBA to reflect some set of processing activity; if the VSAM file is being shared by both a batch system and an online system like CICS, for example, a crash of the CICS system—a regrettably not uncommon event—while a file update against the file, including record additions, was in progress, would leave the HURBA in a non-updated state if the program did not succeed in issuing a valid CLOSE against the file before the crash. This is because HURBA is updated to reflect actual processing activity against the file only at CLOSE time—we say that HURBA *is 'snapped' upon CLOSE*—so that if a system event such as an online crash were to prevent the HURBA update, then HURBA would have whatever value it retained before any of this last processing activity started.

Yet we may have completed adding, say, 5,000 records to the file just pre-CICS system crash and before we were able to normally terminate with a CLOSE macro issued. VSAM, through this out-of-date (really, non-updated) HURBA will assume the file ends much earlier than it actually does (since the 5,000 records were successfully written to the file before the crash). After whatever point the old HURBA pointed to in the file, VSAM assumes there to be no data records, counterfactually in this case, in that there may be hundreds or thousands of records added by the prematurely terminated last processing activity. If VSAM were to act on this wholly erroneous perception of where the data ends, by using some of the succeeding space for split activity, for instance, then data records added after the old HURBA point may be partially or wholly overwritten (a CA split is the most likely phenomenon to generate this case), a potentially disastrous and very likely unrecoverable event.

Even if this worst scenario were not to come to pass—no VSAM split activity occurs needing this post-EOD space—and no fatality to the added data records transpire, nonetheless no access could be made to these records since VSAM, by definition, considers space after the HURBA point (which is the data end-of-file as far as VSAM is concerned) to be wholly free of records, and so does not search it for record retrieval. A *record not found* condition would be returned to the program for any attempted access to such records, even though the records are indeed physically present in the file. Defensive VSAM procedures are commonly implemented—not always wholly successfully or without quite serious degradation of VSAM performance—in an attempt either to avoid this situation or to gracefully recover from it as soon as possible, before any adverse consequences result. A fundamental goal of scrupulous monitoring of VSAM activity is to assure, to the greatest extent practical, that HURBA reflect true-EOD as closely as possible at all times. We will take this issue up again later in the text, but the reader should by now have a good understanding of HURBA and its vital importance in VSAM processing.

The actual HURBA value given in our sample LISTCAT can be derived by the following computation:

$$HURBA = (CA\text{-}DS) \times (CI\text{-}DENSITY) \times (CISZ)$$

For our sample LISTCAT, this yields the same computation and result (27,525,120) as HARBA. This is so because secondary extents over and above the primary extents had to be allocated to the cluster by VSAM during program load to even fit the loaded records, so the MAX-EOF and the DATA-EOF are equivalent: VSAM allocates just enough secondary extents to store the required records, in whatever units were used to allocate cluster space (here, cylinders).

To see how the HARBA and HURBA values might be different, consider the same cluster as represented in our sample LISTCAT, but with one critical change: assume that our primary allocation request at DEF CLUSTER time is 60 cylinders, instead of the 50 cylinders shown in the sample LISTCAT. HURBA will not change, since it will still require the same 56 cylinders to store the same 40,000 records under identical circumstances. However, HARBA will be different, since the cluster will be allocated all 60 cylinders of the primary allocation amount, which is more than sufficient to store all data records without any secondary extents being needed at all. The HARBA computation will now be:

$$HARBA = 60 \times 120 \times 4096 = 29,491,200$$

Thus, the MAX-EOF represented by HARBA is higher than the DATA-EOF represented by HURBA, and this makes sense: quite roughly, the MAX-EOF of the sample cluster is the allocated 60 primary cylinders, while the DATA-EOF is the 56 cylinders within this primary allocation that actually contain stored data records. A HARBA value that is very much larger than HURBA should be an EWS (early warning sign) that the cluster has been overallocated and that considerable space is being wasted.

A final technical note on HURBA.   In the strictest terms of VSAM internals, HURBA is computed by VSAM, for KSDSs (data component only) and

RRDSs, *on a CA boundary*: whether we allocate by tracks, cylinders, or records, HURBA points to the last byte of what is termed the *last-ever-used-CA*: the last CA of the data component which contained data *at any time*, whether it now contains data or not. For an ESDS and for the index component of a KSDS, the strict interpretation of HURBA is somewhat different: it points to the last byte of the *last-ever-used-CI* (not CA).

Finally, let us note that there are *two* HURBA fields, not one: the first is the *catalog HURBA* field that is part of the catalog entry for a cluster (shown in LISTCAT output). The second, and more fundamental, is the *control block HURBA* field: this field is part of a VSAM control block known as *ARDF*—the *Address Range Definition Block*—which is stored in virtual storage owned by VSAM (called the *control block structure*), the field itself being known as the *ARDHRBA*. It is from this ARDHRBA field that VSAM obtains the value that it snaps to the associated catalog HURBA field. Although, as we have noted, the catalog HURBA field is only updated at CLOSE time (when a CLOSE macro is explicitly or implicitly issued), the ARDHRBA is maintained by VSAM continuously, being updated anytime the value changes by any processing activity whatsoever against the cluster.

ARDHRBA is the most accurate representation of the true-EOD (true end-of-data) maintained by VSAM, while the catalog HURBA is accurate only *after a batch (by a single program, for example) of processing activity has normally terminated and a CLOSE macro issued.* Any system failure event that interrupts processing activity before the CLOSE macro could be issued, or—less likely—while the CLOSE event was still in progress, will leave the catalog HURBA unreliable as a true-EOD indicator, while ARDHRBA will generally be wholly reliable. Of course, unfortunately, VSAM does not report ARDHRBA in LISTCAT output, even if it is not the same as the catalog HURBA field. Programmers typically issue the VERIFY command (discussed fully later in the text) after known system failure events, which corrects an unreliable HURBA by VSAM reading the cluster itself to determine true-EOD and updating the catalog HURBA appropriately.

12.2.3 The VOLUMES Group

The fields of this group give comprehensive information about the device and volumes on which the object resides, including precise extents information.

VOLSER (self-explanatory).

DEVTYPE.   Amazingly enough, LISTCAT does not give in plain English the device type upon which the object resides, but rather gives a hexadecimal code for each major category of device, and this hex value—the DEVTYPE—must be translated into the equivalent common form of device name through a Device Type Translate Table. (The hex values themselves are translations of bit pattern flags stored as fields in the Unit Control Block (UCB), a key I/O control block.) The Device Type Translate Table for commonly used device types is given in Table 12-4.

Table 12-4. Device type translate table.

DEVTYPE		DEVICE TYPE
3050	2006	2305-1 DASD
3050	2007	2305-2 DASD
3050	2009	3330 DASD
3050	200D	3330-1 DASD
3058	2009	3330V (MASS STORAGE)
3040	200A	3340 DASD
3010	200C	3375 DASD (FIXED BLOCK ARCHITECTURE)
3010	200E	3380 DASD
3000	8001	9 TRACK TAPE
3400	8003	9 TRACK 1600 BPI TAPE
3200	8003	9 TRACK 6250 BPI TAPE

The LISTCAT DEVTYPE code always appears as a hex character string of eight (hex) digits, such as that shown in our sample: X'3050200B,' but it is actually a two part field, each part consisting of four hex digits (X'3050' and X'200B') and this is how we show it in the table. The astute reader may have noticed that the first two hex digits of the second part of DEVTYPE distinguish DASD from tape devices: an X'20' indicates DASD, and an X'80' indicates tape. Other, more specialized device types, and the associated hex DEVTYPE value, are possible but are more rarely encountered. The IBM *Debugging Handbook* (several volumes) for the appropriate operating system gives all the possible values and interpretations in the UCB (Unit Control Block) Data Area section of that reference.

VOLFLAG.   There are three possible values for this field:

PRIME   First volume of a Keyrange cluster
OVERFLOW   Overflow volume of a Keyrange cluster
CANDIDATE   Candidate volume

The topic of Keyrange clusters is taken up in our chapter on performance. We have already discussed *candidate volumes* (Section 7.4): volumes marked (by the CANDIDATE parameter on the DEF SPACE command) as reserved for future use by VSAM.

EXTENTS.   We have already discussed part of this field, the third and last column of information, earlier in the text (Section 4.4). To review briefly, the third column—always appearing in the form: 'TRACKS----------,' with the number of tracks given on the right—specifies the *allocated* extents of space the cluster occupies, both primary and, if any, secondary space. The first entry is the primary allocation, in our sample LISTCAT 1500 tracks, which on a 3350 disk (DEVTYPE = X'3050200B') is equivalent to the 50 cylinders of requested primary allocation space. As we noted earlier, we loaded 40,000 records, each 600 bytes in size, into the cluster and, given the VSAM characteristics of the cluster (CISZ, FSPC, CI-density, key size and key compression, among others), the 50 primary cylinders proved insufficient, causing VSAM to go into secondary extenting, obtaining sufficient space only after six additional (secondary) allocations of one cylinder each, for a total of 56 cylinders. This is shown in the EXTENTS field by the six entries after the first primary entry, each of the form TRACKS-------------30, equivalent to one cylinder on a 3350, giving a total (primary and secondary) of 1680 tracks, which is equal to 56 cylinders.

The first column of information under the EXTENTS field in LISTCAT gives the physical addresses associated with each extent allocation, whether primary or secondary, in the form of a pair of entries: LOW-CCHH and HIGH-CCHH, representing the starting and ending physical address, respectively, of the extent. The physical address consists of a two-byte cylinder number ('CC') and two-byte 'head' (device read-write head) address ('HH'), which identifies the track within the cylinder. This is rarely of any interest or consequence to the application programmer, although it can be used by systems programmers interested in controlling the physical placement of the file on the DASD device for certain possible optimization benefits.

The second column of information gives the LOW-RBA and HIGH-RBA pairs, representing the RBA of the start and end of the extent, respectively. The LOW-RBA of the first (primary) extent will always be '0' since VSAM considers all files to begin at an arbitrary zero offset. Notice also that the HIGH-RBA of the last extent of the cluster is one less than the value of HURBA (we said that HURBA is this HIGH-RBA + 1).

WARNING

Our sample LISTCAT shows that 56 cylinders on a 3350 were needed to store the 40,000 600-byte records loaded. Do not attempt to determine this allocation solely from a byte-capacity point of view, as it will typically underestimate the needed capacity. To illustrate, consider that 40,000 600-byte records have a total byte requirement *for records alone* of 24 million bytes (40,000 times 600 is equal to 24,000,000). Now, the track capacity on a 3350 is 19,069 bytes and there are 30 tracks per cylinder, so that we have a cylinder capacity of 572,070 bytes. Given 24 million bytes of data alone, about 42 cylinders on a 3350 would be required to store the data (24,000,000/572,070). Allocating, however, just 42 cylinders for this file would be a serious mistake, for we would underallocate by 14 cylinders, and hence end up with 14 secondary extents. As it is, we underallocated by six extents (50 rather than 56 cylinders).

The underallocation is due to the fact that we failed to take into account considerations such as how many CIs could actually be fit onto a track, how many records would be loaded into each CI, how much space would be reserved for distributed freespace, how much unused space would be scattered throughout the cluster, and how many bytes would be required just for VSAM control fields (CIDFs and RDFs), among many other factors. Clearly all of these considerations add up to a surprising amount of additional storage needed (six cylinders, approximately 3 million bytes!) for the file, over and above what is strictly needed for the records alone. Going into secondary extenting has considerable adverse performance consequences (we will discuss this fully in Chapter 18) and should be avoided wherever possible. It certainly should not happen that secondary extents be needed at load time before any processing against the file has even begun. When discussing VSAM performance issues, we will provide guidance on how to compute needed space allocation for a cluster without undue over- or underallocation.

PHYREC-SIZE.   This field gives the size of a *physical record*—what in OS is called a *block*—which is the true unit of I/O transmittal, that is, the amount of data transmitted across an I/O channel with a single I/O operation. This may surprise many programmers, who are led to believe that the CI is the unit of transmittal, even from official sources; this view of the CI is misleading. Access and retrieval in VSAM processing is always at the CI-level as a *minimal transmittal unit*, in the sense that an entire CI-full of records is fetched by VSAM for any processing request and stored into a VSAM program buffer, with the target record from that CI then being returned to the program; thus, *no less* than a CI is ever accessed/retrieved by VSAM in honoring any processing request.

Nonetheless, the CI as a minimal transmittal unit is still not the true transmittal unit, which is a block in VSAM, as it is in OS (non-VSAM) access methods, also. This can be demonstrated quite easily by a simple experiment: define a cluster with a data component CISZ of 1536, for example, and check this PHYREC-SIZE field in a requested LISTCAT taken after the DEF CLUSTER command (it is not necessary to actually load any records into this empty cluster; the outcome is unaffected in either case). If the CI were the true transmittal unit—the size of a physical record—then we would expect the value 1536 in this field. What would actually be found, however, would be a value of 512 bytes, not 1536 bytes. This entails that VSAM performs three I/O operations each time a CI of 1536 bytes is transmitted across a channel, and that is indeed precisely the fact of the matter. It just happens that, in our sample LISTCAT, the data CISZ is 4096 bytes, and in this case the physical record size will also be 4096 bytes. The PHYREC-SIZE is dependent on the choice of CISZ, and understanding this will be quite important for performance considerations affecting VSAM processing.

PHYRECS/TRK.   This field specifies the number of physical records—not CIs, for which, see above—that can be stored on a track of the device on which the VSAM object resides. In our sample LISTCAT, this field indicates that four CIs, each 4096 bytes, can be fitted onto a single 3350 track (which has a byte capacity of 19,069).

WARNING

Although the above fact—that four 4096-byte CIs can fit on a 19,069-byte track—makes sense and appears to be derived from the fact that four is the largest integer quotient obtained by dividing 19,069 by 4096 (rounding down), this is *not* how to derive any equivalent result for other choices of CISZ and track capacity. For example, consider a cluster with a data CISZ of 4096 stored on a 3380 device, which has a track capacity of 47,476 bytes. Here some quick—and wholly misleading—arithmetic gives the computation 47,476 divided by 4096, with the result being 11.59. . ., rounded down to 11 CIs to the track. And this too appears to make sense: 11 whole CIs, each 4K in size, would take up exactly 45,056 bytes, well under the known track capacity.

However, this is all completely wrong: only ten 4K-CIs would ever be stored by VSAM onto a 3380 track, despite the above arithmetic. And note that the ten CIs would consume only 40,960 bytes of the 47,476 bytes of the track, leaving 6,516 bytes unused, which certainly look enough to have squeezed in another CI of 4096 bytes. DASD control information, address markers, count areas, interrecord gaps (IRGs), and interblock gaps (IBGs), among others, represent device overhead from what is often termed *hardware data*, needed by the DASD hardware for critical control operations, and all of these consume sufficient bytes out of the remaining 6,516 bytes derived above to leave less than 4K for an additional CI. The computations for hardware data device overhead for various devices and organizations are too technical to compute on even an isolated basis; typically, a device characteristics chart is consulted, and one such chart is provided for the reader's technical reference as Appendix A. There, the number of physical records per track for each of the most commonly used DASD is given; note that VSAM only allows physical record sizes of 512, 1024, 2048, and 4096 bytes. (This changes with the new VSAM, but Enhanced VSAM, which we are discussing, has this restriction.)

TRACKS/CA. The number of tracks to the CA can be computed by using other known attributes of the cluster, but it can simply be read off of this LISTCAT field. However, for the two most common cases of space allocation, namely by cylinder and by track, the derivation of TRACKS/CA is straightforward:

> *Cylinder Allocation*: Here the TRACKS/CA is simply equal to the number of tracks per cylinder—*TRK/CYL*—for the device type being used, and this in turn is most easily read directly off of a device characteristics chart (see Appendix A). In our sample LISTCAT, TRK/CYL is equal to 30, since.we are using a 3350 device.

> *Track Allocation*: When allocating by tracks, the TRACKS/CA is simply the smaller of the primary and secondary allocation values: min (p s). If we had coded, for example, TRK (30 5), then TRACKS/CA would be equal to five. Note that the value derived must be no more than the equivalent of one cylinder on the device being used, since the maximum CASZ is one cylinder.

HI-ALLOC-RBA and HIGH-USED-RBA.   These two fields of the VOL-UMES group are the same as in the ALLOCATION group whenever the object resides on just a single volume; if the object is a multivolume file, then EXTENTS information and VOLUMES information will be shown for each volume of the file. In such a case, the ALLOCATION HARBA and HURBA values would be different than the VOLUMES HARBA and HURBA values for each volume except the last: the ALLOCATION HARBA and HURBA are the values for the entire file, while the VOLUMES fields are specific to each volume. The HARBA and HURBA values of the last volume of a multivolume file are necessarily the same as the HARBA and HURBA values for the entire file.

EXTENT-NUMBER.   This gives the total number of extents, primary and secondary, if any, actually allocated to the object. In our example, seven extents are occupied by the file, one primary and six secondary (see EXTENTS earlier).

EXTENT-TYPE.   The possible values and their meanings:

X'00' --------------- Extents represented are contiguous.
X'40' -------------- Extents represented are not preformatted.
X'80' -------------- Sequence set is imbedded (discussed later).
                      (This value occurs only for the index
                      component of a KSDS entry.)

12.2.4   The STATISTICS Group

These fields detail the activity that has occurred in the processing of the object; a processing history profile of the object is thus determinable.

REC-TOTAL.   The total number of records in whatever component is being listed. There is a REC-TOTAL field in the DATA and in the INDEX portion of LISTCAT for a KSDS cluster. This field should be checked regularly against the user's expectation of what the value should be, given known processing activity. An unaccountable discrepancy is an EWS (Early Warning Sign) that should be investigated thoroughly and resolved before any further processing is permitted against the cluster.

REC-DELETED (self-explanatory).

REC-INSERTED.   This field is misleading. The field reports for KSDSs and ESDSs the number of *post-load time* records inserted *pre-EOF* (before the last record) only. Records used to create the first data records of the cluster, at load time, are not included; thus, in our example, this field is zero. Records added at EOF are also not included. For an ESDS, this means that REC-INSERTED is equal to zero always, since all records added to an ESDS are at EOF. For an RRDS, however, all inserted records, including those used for originally loading the RRDS, are counted in this field.

REC-UPDATED. This returns the number of records that have been fetched for update that have either been rewritten or have been deleted after such a fetch.

REC-RETRIEVED. This returns the number of records fetched, whether or not for update.

SPLITS-CI. This field should be carefully monitored for performance considerations; a high amount of CI-split activity is associated with degraded performance, and may suggest that FSPC amounts for the cluster are insufficient for the volume of record insertion activity actually occurring against the cluster. (More on this in Chapter 18, on performance.)

SPLITS-CA. Monitor this field even more scrupulously than SPLITS-CI, as the performance degradation from significant CA-split activity is many orders larger than that from CI-split activity. Again, FSPC amounts may be insufficient for the volume of record insertion against this cluster. FSPC adjustment (upwards) may have to be tried, and possibly even complete cluster reorganization. See Chapter 18, on performance, for further details.

FREESPACE-%CI and FREESPACE-%CA. These fields return the CI-FSPC and CA-FSPC amounts either specified for the cluster at define time or subsequently specified on an ALTER command.

WARNING

These fields do not reflect current *actual* FSPC amounts, only amounts that were in effect at define time. Processing activity against the cluster since that time typically changes the FSPC amounts, but the changes are nowhere directly reflected in any LISTCAT output. The only way to ascertain the current space distributions for a cluster is to write an Assembler systems routine using VSAM control interval processing (CNV) to examine each of the CIs of the cluster.

FREESPC-BYTES. This is the total number of bytes in all (wholly) empty CIs within total allocated space; any CI with even a single data byte is not included in this total. In our sample LISTCAT, we have FREESPC-BYTES equal to 217,088. To determine how many *FREE-CIs* (equal to the total number of empty CIs in the data set) this represents, divide this number by the CISZ:

$$\text{FREE-CI} = (\text{FREESPC-BYTES})/\text{CISZ}$$
$$= 217{,}088/4096$$
$$= 53$$

so that we know there are precisely 53 CIs containing no data in our data set (in this case, in the data component of the cluster).

EXCPS. This gives the number of EXCP (EXECUTE CHANNEL PRO-GRAM) macro instructions issued against the data set (here, data component) *since the data set was allocated*. An EXCP macro instruction causes an SVC interrupt (SVC 0), which will start the complex process of I/O against the data set (lead to the issuing of a START I/O—SIO—or equivalent instruction), so this field represents I/O activity. The volume of EXCPs for a component indicates, in part, its *volatility*: the degree of processing activity against it. We will return to some performance considerations of this in Chapter 18, on performance.

EXTENTS. (see discussion of the EXTENTS field under VOLUMES group, page 000).

SYSTEM-TIMESTAMP. This gives what is called the *system TOD* (time-of-day) *clock* value, representing the time of last closure of the data set, but only, however, under certain circumstances of processing activity. It is not important to understand the specific details, or even to be able to read this value (it's in the hex representation of binary values), but a comparison of the SYSTEM-TIMESTAMP values for the data and the index component of a cluster (here they are identical) *may* indicate a *synchronization problem*: one of the components may have been opened and processed without opening the other. However, there are valid instances of opening a single component, so the point is that a compare failure does not necessarily mean a real problem situation. The programmer should consider the recent processing history of the data set in trying to determine whether such a compare failure requires any corrective action, or further investigation. In any case, the timestamps can be resynchronized by issuing a VERIFY command against the cluster.

12.2.5 Some Index Fields

Below, we will discuss some of the more important LISTCAT fields associated with the index component; these are listed separately from the data component fields in the LISTCAT output. (Many whose interpretations have already been discussed in connection with the corresponding data component fields are not repeated; several that are special-purpose fields are referred to, but discussed more fully later in the text in the appropriate chapters.)

AVGLRECL and MAXLRECL (I). The values of these fields for an index component are interpreted differently than for a data component. AVGLRECL always equals zero for the index, and MAXLRECL is equal to the index CISZ less seven bytes for control fields (always a single four-byte CIDF and a single three-byte RDF). Thus, MAXLRECL is equal to the Index-CISZ minus seven. With an index

CISZ equal to 1024 in our sample LISTCAT, this gives 1017 for the MAXLRECL value.

BUFSPACE (I).   This field is misleading. It appears to say, for our sample LISTCAT, that no space was allocated for index buffers. However, whenever an index component exists, and it always does in a KSDS, *some* buffer space must be available for the index. The 'zero' value here means only that the programmer did not explicitly allocate buffer space at DEF CLUSTER time for index buffers, so that VSAM had to apply its default allocations; as we have seen when discussing the BUFSPACE field for the data component, this default is two data buffers (here each 4K in size), and one index buffer (here, 1K). The value of '9216' found in that earlier field represents the total buffer allocation (9K) for both the data and index component, despite the fact that it is listed only under the data component. Had we allocated index buffer space explicitly, a nonzero value would appear in this index field.

CISIZE (I).   The index CISZ is shown here to be 1K. Note that we did not explicitly code an index CISZ in the original DEF CLUSTER, so that in this case this field informs us of what VSAM chose this value to be as a default (it will vary under different characteristics of the cluster). Performance considerations concerning index CISZ are taken up in our performance discussion later in the text; index CISZ determination is extremely complex, and often the programmer allows VSAM to choose a size by default, although as we shall see, the programmer can, and in certain cases should, avoid a VSAM default, which, surprisingly, is not always optimal.

CI/CA (I).   This entry appears to imply that the index CIs are organized into larger CAs, just as in the data component. This is incorrect: no CA organization is used by VSAM for the index component. This entry is, therefore, misleading, and has a different interpretation which we will explain later in the text; the programmer can, by and large, safely ignore this field altogether.

IMBED/NOIMBED and REPLICATE/NOREPLICAT (I).   These are the same as the corresponding fields referred to above for the data component (see earlier, under the ATTRIBUTES group), and are index performance options to be discussed more fully later in the text. Oddly enough, they are listed for both the data and the index component in LISTCAT output, although one listing under the index component would have been less confusing.

REC-TOTAL (I).   This gives the number of index records in the index component. Since there is one index record per index CI, then this equivalently gives the number of index CIs, shown here to be 57. Our data component, we have already determined, has 56 CAs, and there is one sequence set record for each of these data CAs, so 56 of the 57 index CIs are sequence set CIs. This implies, correctly, that there is one additional index CI in the index set ('above' the sequence set) of the index, so that the index is a two-level index (and this is actually verified explicitly in the LEVELS field, discussed below).

SPLITS-CI and SPLITS-CA and FREESPACE (I).   The index contains no distributed freespace (FSPC) in the sense used for the data component, and therefore no split activity occurs against it.

FREESPC-BYTES (I).   This is interpreted like its data component counterpart (see FREESPC-BYTES above). Here the value is '3072,' which when divided by the index CISZ (1024), gives 3 free CIs (wholly empty) within the index, to be used by VSAM for index growth.

EXCPS (I).   This, like its data component counterpart (see earlier), represents the volume of I/O activity against the data set, in this case, the index component. The value of this field should be relatively small compared to its data component counterpart. (We shall be looking at the *relative ratio* of these two EXCPS fields for performance considerations later in the text.)

EXTENTS under STATISTICS and VOLUMES groups (I).   These fields indicate the total number of extents actually allocated to the index component data set, here shown to be just one extent in size. Typically, the programmer does not explicitly code for space allocation of the index component at DEF CLUSTER time (only, generally, for the entire cluster); in this case, VSAM splits the cluster space allocation between the data and index components by its own internal (and complex) rules. The EXTENTS field of the VOLUMES group for the index component shows that the single extent for the index is four tracks in size (out of the total 56 cylinder allocation for the entire cluster). We will return to index size considerations more appropriately in Chapter 18, on performance.

LEVELS (I).   This gives the number of levels in the index (see our previous discussion of index levels in Chapter 11), shown here to be two. By and large, the smaller the number of index levels (minimum one, usually achievable only for very small test data sets), the better VSAM random access performance. See our discussion of REC-TOTAL for the index component earlier, which shows how the programmer may, in at least this case, verify this level number; more—much more—on LEVELS as a key performance parameter later.

SPACE-TYPE, SPACE-PRI, and SPACE-SEC (I).   These fields give space allocation information for the index component data set, provided by VSAM defaults since we did not explicitly code for such index allocation at DEF CLUSTER time. Our primary allocation is four tracks, with one track secondary backup (total possible extents equals 123, primary plus secondary).

HARBA and HURBA (I).   These are the counterparts for the index component of HARBA and HURBA for the data component, except that they relate to 'index data,' namely index records, rather than data records. HARBA is shown to have a value of '61440' in our sample LISTCAT. If we divide this by the index CISZ (1024), we see that the MAX-EOF of the data component is 60 CIs: the index may grow to as much as 60 CIs (which represents four tracks, each containing 15 CIs) before requiring secondary extent allocation. HURBA is shown to be '58368,' and if we divide this by the 1K index CISZ, we obtain 57 CIs as the DATA-EOF, namely as actually containing index records (the 'data' of the index component), which is cross-verified by the REC-TOTAL field for the index discussed above—the number of index records and the number of index CIs being equivalent. Notice also that if we subtract the HURBA value from the HARBA value shown, we obtain a difference of 3072 bytes, which is exactly the value of the FREESPC-BYTES shown. And this too makes sense: 3072 bytes equals 3 CIs, precisely the difference between the 60 CIs represented by the HARBA value, and the 57 CIs represented by the HURBA value; these three CIs allow for future growth of the index, within primary allocated space, with secondary extents possible for growth beyond even this.

12.2.6 Some Final Words on Interpreting LISTCAT Output

At this point, the reader should have a good grasp of how to interpret some of the most important of the dozens of LISTCAT output fields. Some of those discussed above will be expanded upon as appropriate in later chapters of the text, which will thus add to and sharpen the reader's skill at LISTCAT interpretation. This is an absolutely vital skill in the working VSAM environment, yet unfortunately most programmers look at or understand only a few selected fields, missing the amazing wealth of information provided by VSAM through such output, which can be invaluable for many purposes, including performance tuning, backup and recovery, and problem determination, among many others. LISTCAT output should be 'snapped' and studied after each batch of processing activity against the cluster (or other VSAM object).

Particularly important is analyzing, in the fashion we have described above, the HARBA and HURBA fields: discrepancies in what these fields predict about the MAX-EOF and DATA-EOF of the cluster, and the known or ascertainable facts of the cluster, or failure of the computations (given above) to yield consistent and coherent information, should be EWSs (early warning signs) that some serious problem might exist with respect to the cluster; problems with HURBA interpretation are particularly grave for future processing of the cluster, with the possible compromise of data integrity, or even inaccessible data, resulting. In the worst case, disastrous consequences can result if critical data is permanently overwritten and lost. Thus, a fundamental goal of this text is to leave the reader with a very high level of skill in the art of LISTCAT interpretation.

13

ALTERNATE INDEX (AIX) FACILITIES

13.1   THE CONCEPT OF AN ALTERNATE INDEX (AIX)

VSAM supports two types of access by index to a VSAM cluster, one of which we have examined extensively, namely access through what may now be called the *primary index* of a KSDS cluster: that is, over the primary key field of the cluster upon which the records of the data component are sequenced in ascending order. As we have seen, the index component of the KSDS cluster contains a compressed version of the primary key field values of the data component, and VSAM uses this index for access to the data component records by key. The obvious limitation of such access by primary index is that all keyed access is only by the single primary key field; for example, in a typical employee file using a VSAM KSDS, the employee's social security number (SSN) may be used as the primary key field, in which case all random access by key to any employee record would be only by this SSN.

But, say we wished to access the file by employee number (EMPNO), a unique numeric code assigned by the company to each employee, in order to retrieve the three employee records for the employees with EMPNOs '02000,' '03000,' and '04000.' We could not do so directly, but rather we would first have to find out the SSNs of each of the three employees and then use the SSNs as search arguments in three separate random retrievals. This may be unacceptable in many common business applications. The matter is even worse if we require access over several different fields, say on some occasions by employee number, on others by last name, or account balance, etc. In all of these cases, we would have to always determine the SSN of the records we wish to retrieve and this may simply not be practical, if the information is even known at all in this form.

There are two distinct alternatives here. One is to create another complete copy of the cluster, duplicating all records but ordering them by say, EMPNO, as opposed to SSN, as they are ordered in the original file. There are three very formidable problems with this first alternative. Firstly, there is the overhead of storage duplication: two (or more) files now contain exactly the same information, but are organized differently by different primary key fields (SSN in one case, EMPNO in the other). Secondly, the two files must now be kept exactly synchronized: whenever any changes are applied to one, they must be applied by the user to the other file (and virtually concurrently to avoid inconsistencies). Note that such synchronization is solely the user's responsibility and must be explicitly provided through user-generated programs; VSAM takes no part in any of this at all. Furthermore, the more different fields over which we may want access to the records of the cluster, the more separate

175

and duplicate data sets we must provide, requiring more storage overhead and more programming to assure synchrony across all data sets, occasioning execution-time degradation.

Thirdly, this approach only works for fields like EMPNO which are typically unique (no two employee records for different employees have the same EMPNO field). But, what if access were required by last name? The last name field is typically nonunique: there may be several 'Smith,' 'Jones,' or 'Katz' records. In this case, we could not create another cluster duplicating the original file, but ordered by last name: VSAM requires the primary key field to be unique (and so does ISAM, which would not be a good alternative, independently). We would have to use some sequential file organization and access method (QSAM or SAM/E, for example), but then the file is non-keyed and we lose the ability to access records randomly by key.

Fortunately, there is another alternative. VSAM provides direct support for multiple nonprimary indices, called *alternate indices* (*AIXs*), that can be used for access to the cluster records over any fields of the records other than the primary key field, these fields then being known as *alternate key* fields, and the values they contain being known as *alt keys*. So, for example, we may have VSAM construct several alternate indices over our original employee file—known as the *base cluster*—which will provide us with random access by EMPNO, last name, balance, or indeed by any field other than the primary key field (SSN), without our needing to know or determine what the associated SSNs are for any of the target records of the retrieval. Thus, we can set up an EMPNO AIX, a last name AIX, and a balance AIX over our base cluster through VSAM AIX facilities, and let VSAM deal with the technical details and coordination of synchronizing the AIXs with each other and with the base cluster itself. There are several advantages to using this second alternative of VSAM AIX support.

1. Although each of the AIXs is set up by VSAM as a separate data set, so that if we build three AIXs over a base cluster, we have four distinct data sets—three for the AIXs, one for the base cluster (at least: if the base cluster is a KSDS, then it is actually two separate data sets itself, the data and index components)—this is still not comparable to the vast overhead of the first solution which was to create multiple duplicate copies of the base cluster, each sequenced on a different field. Why is this, since both approaches involve the same number of separate data sets?

The answer rests more on the nature of the data sets involved, and less on the number of data sets (the same in the two approaches). In the first approach, each additional data set used to provide alternate access to the base cluster is a complete duplication of *all* of the information in the base cluster, but simply sequenced on a field other than the primary key field; all fields are replicated, without exception. Assuming that the base cluster occupied 100 cylinders on a 3380 pack, then each of the copies would also (on the same DASD) require 100 cylinders of space.

But a VSAM AIX facility is very different, and much more efficient. The AIX data set does *not* contain a copy of *all* of the fields of the base cluster, but *only* of the alternate key field, plus space for a set of pointers that associate each alt key with the set of records in the base cluster containing that alt key. We will examine this in more precise detail later in this chapter, but suffice to say here that a VSAM AIX is a *control* data set providing alternate access to the base cluster's records, and not a full replication of these records: nowhere in (for example) the AIX constructed over the EMPNO field is there, for instance, any employee name or employee balance information. Each AIX therefore has a fraction of the storage overhead of the base cluster and thus avoids the high storage expense associated with the entire replication of the base cluster's records.

The AIX data set functions, in part, as a conduit or *path* into the base cluster, allowing the user to retrieve all fields of the cluster's records through the specification of alt key fields. To clarify this more concretely, say that we have established — how, we will see later on — an AIX over the last name field, and want to retrieve all 'Ritter' records, in order to see the date-of-hire field information for the associated employees, and to see if any have been hired within the last three years. The alt key 'Ritter' would be used as the search argument and all base cluster 'Ritter' records would be returned to the program making the retrieval request. Within these returned base cluster records would be contained the date-of-hire field for the information we want. Notice that date-of-hire information is not in any way contained in the records of the last name AIX data set, but is available only in the base cluster records, so that to obtain this information we must retrieve the target 'Ritter' records and inspect the date-of-hire field in each. This is quite 'DASD-conservative,' we might say, in that we do not redundantly have more than one copy of the date-of-hire field, and yet can access this information without having to know the primary key values, namely the SSNs, of the target records (the 'Ritter' records).

2. A second point to note about the VSAM AIX facility is that the AIX is itself a data set, and more specifically it is always a KSDS, therefore containing both a data and an index component. Under certain circumstances, the AIX data set may be opened and processed independently of the associated base cluster, although great care must be taken not to leave the base cluster and AIX in an unsynchronized state. Such separate processing of an AIX is supported for Assembler VSAM programs, but not for COBOL or PL/I. (We will look at the structure of the AIX data set in more detail later.)

3. An AIX, unlike a primary key, may either be unique (no duplicate alt keys) or nonunique; the choice is made at define time for the AIX, through the DEFINE AIX command. This is a very useful facility, since no comparable non-VSAM facility exists, as keyed files generally require unique keys. When the alt key is specified as nonunique, VSAM returns all the base cluster records containing any particular alt key value.

4. As noted above, multiple AIXs may be built over a base cluster. The various alt keys are allowed to partially overlap both each other, and the primary key (but may not overlap the entire primary key).

5. An AIX may be built over both a KSDS *and* an ESDS, in the latter case providing random access, *in addition* to the ESDS's typical sequential access mode of

processing. (We will explore some performance issues concerning AIXs over KSDSs versus over ESDSs in Chapter 18, on performance.) An AIX may not be built over an RRDS, nor over any cluster type that is reusable.

13.2 THE CONCEPT OF A PATH

A base cluster may be accessed through an AIX only after the user defines to VSAM a *logical association* between the base cluster and some specific AIX, this logical association being known as a *path*. Thus, a path can be thought of as defining a pair of VSAM objects, namely the base cluster and a particular AIX, and access to base cluster records *over* the AIX is said to be established by access *through* the associated path. Typically, in a high-level language such as COBOL or PL/I, alternate index processing is effected by OPENing the path associated with the appropriate AIX, *not* by opening the AIX directly. Unless otherwise instructed, VSAM will automatically open the appropriate AIX *and* base cluster whenever the associated path is opened; as pointed out earlier, high-level language programming does not open or access the AIX directly.

A path is another VSAM object, along with clusters, components, AIXs, and catalogs, among others. Like a cluster, and unlike components, AIXs, and catalogs, a path is a *control object, not an actual data set*. As such, it exists as an entry in a catalog containing the control information VSAM needs to establish the logical association of AIX and related base cluster pairs. It is necessary to define a path (as well as define the AIX itself) before VSAM will build an AIX over a base cluster. Later in this chapter we will discuss and detail the coding for defining both AIXs and paths, as well as the coding for actually instructing VSAM to build the AIX over the base cluster (BLDINDEX command); we will also see how both an AIX and a path may be printed, and the latter demonstration should help demystify what, to many, is the rather vague concept of a path. For now, suffice it to say that the VSAM AIX facility requires that there be (at least) one path associated with each different AIX defined over a base cluster; thus, if we wanted to access our employee file not only by SSN (the primary key), but also by EMPNO, employee last name, and date-of-hire, for example, we would have to define three AIXs—one for each intended alt key field—and three related paths through which we would gain access to the base cluster records by the three different alt keys. In summary, therefore, we can regard a path as the facility for accessing a base cluster via an AIX. (There is another side to a VSAM path—much less widely known—that has nothing to do with AIXs and is quite useful for certain special purposes; this is discussed in Section 13.7.)

13.3 THE CONCEPT OF AN UPGRADE SET

In dealing with the VSAM AIX facility, a critical aspect that must be understood very clearly is that of the *AIX-upgrade*. This refers to synchronization of the base cluster and its AIX(s): VSAM assumes, unless explicitly instructed otherwise, that whenever changes are made to the base cluster that may change any associated AIX(s) over that cluster, it should perform an AIX-upgrade on those AIXs, that is, update the AIXs to reflect those changes made to the base cluster.

Let's look at an example in order to appreciate this notion of AIX-upgrade better, using the same employee file that we discussed above. Let's assume that three AIXs are associated with this base cluster (EMPFILE): employee number (EMPNO), last name (LAST), and date-of-hire (HIREDATE). At any time, we may need to update the base cluster EMPFILE: a new employee may be hired (an insertion/addition operation), an existing employee may be terminated (a deletion), or some of the information kept in the employee record for some particular employee may need to be modified (an update). Any of these operations—record insertion, deletion, and update—may entail a change to one or more of the three AIXs associated with EMPFILE: record insertion and deletion certainly will, and record update may, depending on what fields need to be updated. Consider the hiring of a new employee named 'Ritter,' that is, of adding a new employee record. All three AIXs must be updated in order to maintain synchrony with the base cluster and with each other. A new record must be added to EMPNO (since there is a new employee number assigned to the new hire). With respect to the LAST AIX, no new record need be added, assuming there was already at least one employee named 'Ritter,' but the record in LAST with the alt key 'Ritter' (there is one record for each different alt key value) must be updated to contain an additional pointer entry for this new 'Ritter' so that any request to retrieve all 'Ritter' records returns the new hire as well as the existing 'Ritter' records. In addition, a new record must be added to the HIREDATE AIX to reflect the new date-of-hire for this employee (assuming no other hires were made on the same day).

Similarly, if an employee is terminated, then the removal of that employee's record (say, a 'Katz' record) from the base cluster requires updates to all AIXs in order to keep the information in all objects 'in sync.' A record must be deleted from the EMPNO AIX, the 'Katz' record in the LAST AIX must be updated to show one fewer 'Katz' record (and if this were the last or only Katz, then the entire 'Katz' record would have to be deleted), and finally, the record in HIREDATE whose alt key is the date-of-hire of the just terminated employee must be updated to remove the entry for this 'Katz' (there are now one fewer employees with the same date-of-hire as the terminated employee, if there are any left at all).

Finally, say we need to update one or more fields in some of the base cluster records. The key question here is: does this mean that (one or more of) the AIXs need to be updated also? The answer depends on what fields are to be modified. Only changes to one or more of the alt key fields (employee number, last name, date-of-hire) require AIX-upgrading; a change to, say, the balance field of the base cluster records has no consequence on any AIX and VSAM routines will detect this fact at update time. Indeed, as one would think, VSAM performs an AIX-upgrade only when needed by the nature of the changes to the base cluster.

Founded directly on this notion of AIX-upgrade is the VSAM concept of the *upgrade set* associated with a base cluster which has at least one AIX built (defined) over it. The upgrade set is the collection of all AIXs for which VSAM is to automatically perform an AIX-upgrade, that is, the set of all AIXs to be automatically opened and updated by VSAM whenever required by a change to the 'underlying' base cluster. When the base cluster is opened for any form of output (write) processing—which includes both output and update mode—then VSAM will open all of the AIXs in the upgrade set (we speak loosely of VSAM 'opening the upgrade set') for that base cluster and perform the necessary changes to leave the base cluster and all of these *upgradable* AIXs in complete synchrony with each other. The VSAM AIX facility gives the user complete control over whether or not VSAM should perform an AIX-upgrade for any particular AIX: this control is exercised through the UPGRADE/NOUPGRADE parameter on the DEF AIX command, the default being UPGRADE unless overridden explicitly. (We look at the actual coding below in Section 13.6.) In our example, if we did not indicate otherwise, VSAM would make the three AIXs EMPNO, LAST, and HIREDATE all members of the upgrade set for the EMPFILE base cluster, so that synchronizing them would be wholly the responsibility of VSAM, to be done automatically and transparently to the user.

There are several points to note here. First, if the base cluster is opened only for input processing (read-only), then VSAM routines, detecting this, will avoid the overhead of opening the upgrade set since no AIX-upgrade is called for in this case. Second, if the base cluster is opened for output/update processing, VSAM will open the upgrade set whether or not it subsequently turns out that one or more AIXs in the set need to be updated due to changes to the base cluster; VSAM routines cannot tell before the actual update processing of the base cluster is in effect whether any AIX in the set has to be updated, so VSAM opens the upgrade set along with the base cluster in any case except strict read-only mode.

Thus, once an AIX is part of the upgrade set for some particular cluster, any opening of the base cluster in output/update mode incurs the overhead of VSAM's opening of all members of the upgrade set *whether or not this is necessary*. As we have seen above, it is certainly necessary when entire records are added or deleted from the base cluster, but it may or may not be necessary if records are changed, depending on whether any of the alt key fields are changed. It is for this reason that a large number of AIXs cannot *casually* be built over a base cluster and included in the associated upgrade set, since the overhead of multiple files being opened—and possibly updated—whenever the base cluster is processed in non-read-only mode can be very high and can easily adversely affect performance, especially for VSAM files used heavily by online systems like CICS and IMS. We are well advised to build and make upgradable (part of the upgrade set) only as many AIXs as are absolutely necessary for critical processing needs in order to avoid excessive performance overhead; we will explore this issue further in our treatment of VSAM performance and see that there are certain things we can do to minimize the performance consequences of an AIX-upgrade, but the basic caution we have given should, nonetheless, be taken very seriously.

A third point to note about the concept of an upgrade set is that if the user chooses *not* to include some AIX in the upgrade set—by coding NOUPGRADE on the DEF AIX command—then it is wholly the user's responsibility to maintain the

AIX in synchrony with the base cluster. VSAM in this case will not automatically perform AIX-upgrade when changes are made to the base cluster. This means that a user-provided program must open the AIX and apply whatever updates are needed, under all cases in which changes to the base cluster require associated changes to the AIX. This is both quite complex in terms of coding and quite risky, in that failure to be absolutely vigilant and accurate about the updating will result in an AIX that is not in sync with the base cluster, a circumstance bound to cause trouble at some point.

To take an example, say that there are at some point 20 employees named 'Ritter' represented in our sample EMPFILE base cluster; that is, there are 20 records in the file with a LAST alt key of 'Ritter.' If the LAST AIX is not made part of the upgrade set, and another 'Ritter' is hired at some later point, the base cluster will contain 21 'Ritter' records, but the LAST AIX will not reflect this fact. A retrieval through the LAST AIX of all 'Ritter' records will return, incorrectly, only 20 'Ritter' records. To obtain the correct results, the user would have to open the LAST AIX and add another pointer to the record with the alt key of 'Ritter,' this last pointer locating the new (twenty-first) 'Ritter' record in the base cluster, and, moreover, this would have to be done almost instantly after the addition is made to the base cluster to assure timely up-to-date information returned by AIX processing. This is far from trivial to assure, and requires some sophisticated programming—and generally in Assembler, since neither COBOL nor PL/I allow direct processing of an AIX. Furthermore, this requires knowledge of the precise internal structure of an AIX data set and knowledge of the internals of how VSAM performs AIX updating. Typically, therefore, the user allows VSAM to perform the necessary AIX-upgrade by making key AIXs part of the upgrade set.

A fourth and final point to note about the upgrade set is that the automatic AIX-upgrade of all AIXs that are members of the upgrade set applies when the base cluster is opened and processed directly. But a base cluster can be updated indirectly through any AIX built over it; in this case, we are not opening the base cluster explicitly, but rather we open a path associated with some AIX, and this permits us to add, delete, or update base cluster records by an alt key field. So, for example, we may delete an employee record either by accessing it directly by its primary key (social security number), or by (for instance) specifying the associated employee number alt key of that record in a delete operation using the EMPNO AIX. The latter constitutes an *indirect update* of the base cluster, but otherwise has consequences for one or more of the other AIXs associated with the base cluster—for example, both LAST and HIREDATE AIXs must be updated to reflect the deleted record—just like a direct update of the base cluster.

However, the point to note here is that making any particular AIX a member of the upgrade set does *not automatically* assure that VSAM will perform an AIX-upgrade when the changes to the base cluster are made *indirectly through an AIX* over the cluster, rather than by direct processing of the base cluster. Whether or not VSAM performs an AIX-upgrade under conditions of indirect update to the base cluster over some AIX is determined wholly by a different parameter (namely UPDATE/NOUPDATE) which, unlike UPGRADE/NOUPGRADE, is not specified on the DEF AIX command, but rather on the DEF PATH command. We will look further at the subtle but extremely important difference in interpretation of UPGRADE/NOUPGRADE versus UPDATE/NOUPDATE later in this chapter (see Subsection 13.7.1 below); for now it suffices to understand that the UPGRADE attribute for an AIX assures only that changes made directly to the base cluster (by opening and processing that cluster) will be reflected in that and any other AIX in the upgrade set.

13.4   THE STRUCTURE OF AN ALTERNATE INDEX (AIX)

In this section, we will look at the internal structure of an AIX in more detail, which will give us further insight into, and understanding of, the way VSAM handles AIX processing.

13.4.1   AIX Pointers (AIX-PTRs)

An AIX is an actual data set separate from the base cluster over which it is built, and more specifically is a special type of KSDS cluster, complete with both data and index components. The index component serves the same function and has the same internal structure as the index component of any KSDS cluster, with one important exception: the key field—which is now the alt key field—is maintained in full key form, not in compressed key form as in the index of a non-AIX KSDS. In this case, then, the number of AIX index records is the same as the number of data records in the base cluster, since for every employee record identified by a unique SSN primary key, that record also contains a unique employee number alt key.

The data component consists of a set of AIX records, one for each different alt key value in the AIX. Thus, for our EMPNO AIX, there are as many AIX records as there are distinct employee numbers (and there is one employee number for each employee, since EMPNO is a unique AIX (no duplicate alt keys permitted)). However, for our LAST AIX there will be only as many AIX records as there are *distinct* last name alt keys, that is, as there are *different* last names: although there may be 21 'Ritter' records in the base cluster, there will only be one associated AIX data record with an alt key value of 'Ritter' in the AIX's data component; this one 'Ritter' data AIX record will contain, in addition to the alt key of 'Ritter' itself, 21 distinct pointers locating the 21 'Ritter' records in the base cluster's data component. In the two sections below, we will look at the nature of these AIX pointers (AIX-PTRs). Note that an AIX may be built over a KSDS—which is very common—and, much less commonly, over an ESDS, and the types of AIX-PTRs used in these two cases are different, and it is for this reason that we treat the two cases separately below.

13.4.2   The Structure of an AIX over a KSDS

As we have already noted above, the index component of any AIX, whether built over a KSDS or an ESDS, functions and is structured like the index component of a non-AIX KSDS, except in that the alt key is stored in full, not compressed, form.

Each alt key stored in an index entry (in the K-field) points, by virtue of its related P-field, to the associated AIX data record in the data component (this being done by a CI-pointer which uses a binary number to identify the data CI that this alt key indexes).

The data component of an AIX is where the distinctive nature of an AIX KSDS versus a non-AIX KSDS becomes clear. Figure 13-1 shows the basic internal structure of an AIX data record, which at this level is the same for both underlying KSDS and ESDS base clusters (the difference arises in the content of the third constituent—the AIX *pointer set*—as we will see later). Let's look at each of these constituents in turn.

Each AIX data record begins with a five-byte long *system header*, which contains four subfields providing vital control information to VSAM; Figure 13-1 gives the subfield names, and we will here briefly discuss their basic functions:

AIXFG. This one-byte subfield is an AIX *flag* which indicates the type of pointers used in the AIX data records. There are two types possible, and the last (eighth) bit of this field specifies the type: if the last bit is '1,' then the pointers are *prime-key pointers* (*PRIME-PTRs*) which are used by VSAM whenever the underlying base cluster is a KSDS, and if it is '0,' then the pointers are *RBA pointers* (*RBA-PTRs*) used by VSAM when the underlying base cluster is an ESDS. (We will discuss these two types of pointers fully later in this chapter.) The front seven bits are reserved and are not presently used for anything. Thus, just by looking at this eighth bit setting, VSAM (and if desired, the user) can determine what kind of base cluster this AIX is built over, KSDS or ESDS.

AIXPL. This is a one-byte *pointer length* subfield: it gives the length of each pointer used in the AIX data record (in the *AIX pointer set* part of the record; see

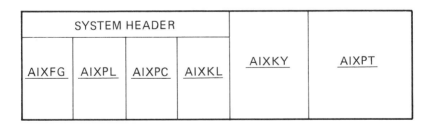

```
AIXFG = AIX Flag
AIXPL = AIX Pointer Length
AIXPC = AIX Pointer Count
AIXKL = AIX Key Length

AIXKY = AIX Alt Key
AIXPT = AIX Pointer Set
```

Figure 13-1. Internal structure of an AIX data record.

under AIXPT). For prime-key pointers, this is whatever is the (full) length of the primary key of the base cluster; for RBA pointers, which are fullword addresses, this is always a four-byte length.

AIXPC.   This is a two-byte *pointer count* subfield which gives the number of pointers this AIX data record contains (in the AIX pointer set part at the end of the record). If the AIX is unique, then there is—by definition—one pointer per AIX data record (the alt key picks out one and only one base cluster record), so the AIXPC is equal to one; if the AIX is nonunique, then there are a variable number of pointers per different alt key, and hence per AIX data record. Thus, with respect to our LAST AIX, there may be 50 'Smith' base cluster records, so that, for the AIX data record with the alt key of 'Smith,' the AIXPC subfield is equal to 50. Different alt keys may, of course, have different AIXPC values.

AIXKL.   This is a one-byte (alt) *key length* subfield that gives the length of the alt key field. Note that the length of the alt key field as stored in the AIX index component records, the length of the alt key field as stored in the AIX data component records, and the length of the alt key field as stored in the base cluster's data component records are all equivalent. Note that this AIXKL subfield gives the length of the alt key *field*, not the length of any particular alt key; the alt key field length is constant throughout the cluster.

AIXKY.   Following the above four subfields of the system header is the *AIXKY* subfield, which contains the actual alt key in full (uncompressed) form. The length of this subfield is given in the AIXKL subfield (see above) found in the preceding five-byte system header.

AIXPT.   The final constituent of an AIX data record is the AIXPT, which is the *(AIX) pointer set*: the collection of all pointers to base cluster records which have the same alt key value. For the case we are considering here, that is, an AIX built over a KSDS, the pointer set contains prime key pointers, which are simply the values of the prime key field for all base cluster records with some particular alt key. Using the EMPNO AIX, we would have one AIX data record with the alt key of, say, '00200,' and since EMPNO is a unique AIX (each employee is assigned a different employee number from all other employees), there would be only one pointer in the pointer set of this data record, and that pointer would be whatever nine-byte social security number—say '080402161'—is stored as the primary key field value for the employee with an employee number of '00200.' This is represented graphically in Figure 13-2.

The reader should note that, for a unique AIX (one whose alt key field never contains duplicate values) such as the EMPNO AIX, the LRECL of the AIX's data component records is a fixed value. In our example, for each AIX data record there is a five-byte system header, followed by the five-byte employee number alt key field, followed by a single nine-byte social security number field, giving an LRECL of 19 bytes.

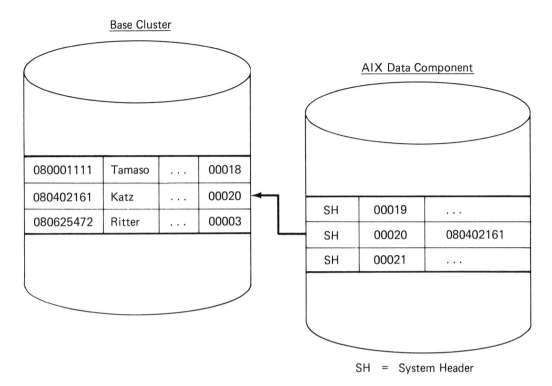

Figure 13-2. Unique AIX.

Now let's consider the situation when the AIX is nonunique, as with the LAST AIX. For a particular alt key, say, 'Barnes,' the number of pointers in the pointer set would be the number of 'Barnes' records in the underlying base cluster (the EMPFILE KSDS); if there are three such 'Barnes' records, then the pointer set would consist of the three different social security number values (the primary key field) stored as primary key field values in these base cluster data records. Each of these three pointers are nine bytes in length (the length of the SSN primary key field), so that the total length of the 'Barnes' AIX data record would be (assuming that the last name alt key field in the base cluster is 20-bytes in length):

5 bytes	for system header
+ 20 bytes	for the last name alt key (AIXKL equal to 20)
+ 27 bytes	for 3 primary key pointers (each 9 bytes in length)
52 bytes	= LRECL of this AIX data record (with AIXKY equal to 'Barnes')

and this is shown graphically in Figure 13-3. For an alt key of 'Kaniklidis,' however, the situation is likely to be quite different: there is probably only a single employee named 'Kaniklidis,' so that the pointer set in this case would consist of a single nine-byte primary key for the SSN of that employee, yielding:

5 bytes	for system header
+ 20 bytes	for the last name alt key (AIXKL equal to 20)
+ 9 bytes	for 1 primary key pointer (9 bytes long)
34 bytes	= LRECL of this AIX data record

These two calculations of the size of two different AIX data records for our sample LAST AIX—one with an LRECL equal to 52, the other with an LRECL equal to 34—demonstrate a basic principle concerning AIXs: unique AIXs have fixed-length records (since, by definition, there is always exactly one primary key pointer for each distinct alt key value), while nonunique AIXs have variable-length records. The size of the pointer set is the factor that determines what any one AIX data record's LRECL will be, and this in turn is a function of the number of *synonyms* associated with any particular choice of alt key, where we say that some alt key has x synonyms, just in case there are x base cluster records with that particular alt key. Thus, in our example, when AIXKY is equal to 'Barnes,' the number of synonyms equals three, and when AIXKY is equal to 'Kaniklidis,' the number of synonyms equals one.

13.4.3 The Structure of an AIX over an ESDS

An AIX may be built over an ESDS, allowing random access to the ESDS, in addition to its standard sequential access mode. At present, this AIX plus ESDS

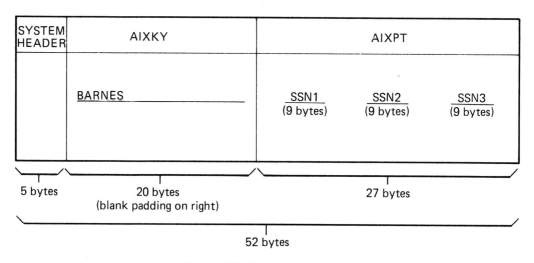

Figure 13-3. Nonunique AIX.

facility is not available in batch COBOL environments, but it is supported in online environments such as CICS. It is still the case that the AIX so built is a KSDS, but the structure and operation of the AIX is simpler than that of an AIX built over a KSDS. One obvious difference is that the base cluster involved is simpler: there being no indexed access to an ESDS, the ESDS contains only a data component. Furthermore, bear in mind that an ESDS is not a keyed file, so that the pointer set of an AIX data record cannot contain primary key pointers (there being no primary key in an ESDS), as it did when the AIX was built over a KSDS. VSAM must, therefore, use a different means of picking out the set of records in the base cluster that share a common alt key value, and we will see what that means very shortly.

To clarify this, let's consider a client listing file which contains the client name, client number, local (street) address, city, state, phone number, and other client information of relevance to the company owning this file, which has been set up as an ESDS whose cluster name is CLIENTLIST. Assume that this file is a comprehensive listing of any client, however long that client remained a client to the company. Some clients are very 'transient': a client may be taken on for a single transaction alone, and the client status may be dissolved a few minutes after the transaction is complete (one sale is made, for instance, on a one-time basis only), so more accurately this is a file listing any entity that has ever been a client, whether that entity is currently a client or not. The client records are assumed to be added sequentially, as the occasion arises, from various in-the-field terminal workstations. As such, this sort of file is often referred to as an *archive* file, used mainly for reference purposes, such as for internal or external auditing of the company's activity over a long period (five or ten years, say), other online files being used for the extensive day-to-day business of the company (whatever that might be). The records are ordered simply in entry-sequence ('time-arrival') whenever the client relation is first established. Given the archive nature of this file, no records are deleted from the file, as we are maintaining a comprehensive listing of all clients, current and past, so the ESDS is a reasonable choice for this file's organization.

Now assume further that, although the vast predominance of activity against this file is in sequential mode, occasionally we also wish to access the CLIENTLIST randomly, sometimes by a 40-byte client name field (NAME), sometimes by a four-byte client number field (NUMBER), and sometimes by a 19-byte state (geographical) field (STATE). This can easily be accomplished by building three AIXs—CLNAME, CLNUMBER, and CLSTATE—over the three fields, NAME, NUMBER, and STATE, respectively. Note that the CLNUMBER AIX is unique (each different client is assigned a distinct client number), while CLNAME and CLSTATE are obviously nonunique.

Again, the index component of each AIX, which is a KSDS, is just like the index component of any KSDS, except that full alt keys are used instead of compressed keys. It is the data component of an AIX which is distinctive. With respect to the CLNUMBER AIX, for example, each AIX data record consists of the five-byte system header, followed by the four-byte NUMBER field, followed finally by the pointer set.

The question is, what's in the pointer set? Well, we certainly know there is only one pointer in the set: the CLNUMBER AIX is unique, so for any particular alt key value there is only one associated synonym (one base cluster record with that alt key value). The critical point here is the *type* of pointer contained in the pointer set: as we briefly noted earlier, VSAM uses an *RBA pointer* whenever, as here, the AIX is over an ESDS, rather than a primary key pointer as is used with underlying KSDS base clusters. Remember, the primary mode of access for a KSDS is by key, for an ESDS, by RBA, and for an RRDS, by RRN. Thus, VSAM accesses the base record(s) associated with any specific alt key by means of relative byte addressing (when the base cluster is an ESDS), which gives the record location directly, all records in the base cluster being considered to be some exact number of bytes offset from an arbitrary zero start point of the cluster's data component, the byte displacement dependent on record length (which may be variable in an ESDS). So for our unique CLNUMBER AIX, each AIX data record is 13 bytes long (LRECL equal to 13): five bytes (for the system header) plus four bytes (for the alt key field itself) plus four bytes (for the single RBA pointer in each record's pointer set).

If we now consider the case of the CLSTATE AIX, which is nonunique, the situation is different. The system header of each AIX data record is always five bytes (and will have the eighth bit of the first byte set to '0' to indicate that RBA pointers are being used in the pointer set), the next field being the 19-byte STATE alt key value, and this is followed by a variable-length pointer set field. If AIXKY equals 'South Dakota,' for example, there may be only one associated base cluster record (one client, ever, from South Dakota), so that the pointer set consists of one RBA pointer (equal to four bytes), yielding a total LRECL of 28 bytes (5 plus 19 plus 4). But, if the alt key were 'Wisconsin' (AIXKY equal to 'Wisconsin'), and if there were four clients located there, we would have a pointer set consisting of four RBA pointers, for a total LRECL of 40 bytes (5 plus 19 plus 16). So, again, the nonunique AIX—whether it is over a KSDS or an ESDS, as here—is seen to have variable-length data records.

Finally, note that the ESDS can now be accessed sequentially by simply opening the CLIENTLIST ESDS file itself, or randomly by any of the AIXs built over it (CLNAME, CLNUMBER, or CLSTATE). Furthermore, the process of building an AIX over an ESDS, rather than a KSDS, still consists of the same three steps (whose coding we examine in detail below): (1) defining the AIX (DEF AIX command), (2) defining an associated path (DEF PATH) which allows access to the base cluster over the defined AIX, and (3) constructing the AIX itself (the previous two steps only *define* VSAM objects, but create no actual data set) through the BLDINDEX command.

13.5   ADVANTAGES OF AIXs OVER ESDSs

Although we will take up this issue in full detail in Chapter 18, on performance, it is worthwhile to note here briefly that the implementation of an AIX over an ESDS has two major advantages over the implementation over a KSDS, assuming that the constraints of ESDS processing are acceptable in certain well-defined circumstances. First, in terms of storage considerations, the AIX plus ESDS implementation is generally more compact than that of the AIX plus KSDS. This is largely due to the nature of the pointer set within the AIX data records: under the ESDS implementation, the pointer set contains RBA pointers, always only each four bytes long, while with KSDSs as the underlying base cluster, the pointers are always primary key pointers which, although varying in length, typically tend to be longer than just four bytes. With a nonunique AIX over a KSDS, the space overhead of a large number of primary key pointers in the pointer set—due to a large number of synonyms associated with many alt keys—can be considerable compared to the more modest overhead of multiple four-byte pointers involved in the ESDS implementation.

Furthermore, execution-time performance can be appreciably better for AIX access over an ESDS rather than a KSDS, for two basic reasons: (1) RBA pointers are more efficient to 'follow' than primary key pointers, in that VSAM treats the latter as character strings, and AIX processing with them involves time-consuming string search and compare operations, while RBA pointers involve only byte displacement calculations that VSAM was designed to handle optimally; and (2) once an RBA pointer is extracted by VSAM from the pointer set in an AIX data record, VSAM can make a 'dead hit' to the base cluster data record, without having to go through index processing first, and then locating the record. Contrast this with the AIX plus KSDS using primary key pointers (in the AIX data records) which *do not* point directly to the target record in the base cluster's data component, but rather point to the base cluster's *index component* from which index pointers are extracted (by VSAM index processing) which then, finally, point to the base cluster's data component. We gain considerable performance advantage, therefore, from the simpler structure of an ESDS which only contains a data component, without also an index component, unlike a KSDS.

However, as hinted at earlier in the discussion, one must be able to accept the processing constraints associated with an ESDS implementation, which are, primarily: (1) records cannot be deleted from an ESDS; and (2) records may be added to an ESDS only at end-of-file. The first constraint can be partially dealt with by substituting dummy records (marked 'doomed') for those to be considered deleted, but the user-provided coding must assure skipping, or not returning, these logically deleted records; furthermore, the file can never grow smaller, only larger and larger, since the logically deleted records are not physically deleted at any time. The second constraint can be acceptable if the file is primarily *archival* in nature: queried/browsed, and sometimes extended, but not requiring significant internal restructuring. Certain online event-sequenced inquiry files are good candidates for such implementation. Note again that we are not restricted to strictly sequential processing—as we would be if the file were solely an ESDS without any AIX built over it—but can perform random access/retrieval and update through any AIX we care to build over the file. Finally, there are certain cases in which a KSDS may prove to be impractical: the key field on which we sequence the cluster's records may simply not be unique (without duplicates), a requirement of a primary key field in a KSDS. In such cases we can simulate a keyed-access facility to the file by using a nonunique AIX built over an ESDS and simply using this as a 'pseudo-primary key.' If circumstances permit, therefore, the ESDS plus AIX implementation can be realistic in certain well-defined cases where narrower facilities than those of a KSDS can meet our processing requirements and we can thereby gain some excellent performance advantages.

13.6   DEFINING AN ALTERNATE INDEX: THE DEFINE AIX COMMAND

The first step in creating an AIX over some base cluster is to identify to VSAM the AIX data set itself as a VSAM object to be defined in a VSAM catalog. This is done by the DEF(INE) ALTERNATEINDEX command, generally abbreviated to DEF AIX. The basic coding of the IDCAMS job is given in Figure 13-4, and Figure 13-5 gives a sample coding; for equivalent statements, we use the same line numbers in the two figures, and the discussion below is indexed to the line numbers in either or both of these figures.

DISCUSSION

6. The value of the NAME parameter is the name of the AIX being defined. There are many conventions used for AIXs, but one of the most widely used and sensible expands on the naming convention we recommended earlier in the text for

```
1.    // ... JOB ...
2.    // EXEC PGM=IDCAMS
3.    //SYSPRINT DD SYSOUT=A
4.    //SYSIN DD *
5.      DEFINE AIX -
6.        (NAME (aix-name) -                        [required]
7.        RELATE (base cluster-name) -              [required]
8.        VOL (volser) -                            [required]
9.        KEYS (len off) -            [required: see 9 below]
10.       CISZ (cisz) -
11.       CYL/TRK/REC (pri sec) -                   [required]
12.       RECSZ (avg max) -
13.       FSPC (ci-fspc ca-fspc) -
14.       SUBAL/UNQ -
15.       UNIQUEKEY/NONUNIQUEKEY -
16.       UPGRADE/NOUPGRADE -
17.       REUSE/NOREUSE) -
18.     DATA -
19.       (NAME (data component name)) -
20.     INDEX -
21.       (NAME (index component name))
22.   /*
```

Figure 13-4. Basic coding of the DEFINE AIX command.

VSAM clusters in general (Subsection 9.1.1). In our sample coding we used the following name for our AIX:

```
FINCAT.K.EMPLOYEE.LAST.N.AIX
```

The high-level-qualifier, 'FINCAT,' is being used—we are assuming an MVS system—as an alias of a valid user catalog. The next qualifier position is being used to identify the cluster type of the underlying base cluster: 'K,' as here, indicating a KSDS and 'E,' an ESDS, important information for a user of an AIX to know in many cases; being part of the name saves the user from having to determine this from other sources. The third qualifier position gives the cluster name of the base cluster itself, with any high-level-qualifier used for catalog identification being omitted: the base cluster name is shown to be (Figure 13-5, statement 7) 'FINCAT.EMPLOYEE,' so we strip this down to 'EMPLOYEE.' The fourth qualifier position gives the name of the alt key field associated with this AIX, which is here the employee last name field 'LAST.' The fifth qualifier position is used to specify whether the AIX is unique (defined with the UNIQUEKEY parameter), in which case a 'U' would be coded, or nonunique (as here), in which case an 'N' would be coded. And in the sixth and final qualifier position, 'AIX' is coded to identify this cluster as an AIX.

Notice also that, in statements 18 through 21, we also provide data and index component names (we are assuming a KSDS) distinct from the cluster name to facilitate ease of identification of these objects and to allow, if needed, access to one

```
 1.    // ... JOB ...
 2.    // EXEC PGM=IDCAMS
 3.    //SYSPRINT DD SYSOUT=A
 4.    //SYSIN DD *
 5.      DEFINE AIX -
 6.         (NAME (FINCAT.K.EMPLOYEE.LAST.N.AIX) -
 7.         RELATE (FINCAT.EMPLOYEE) -
 8.         VOL (FIN007) -
 9.         KEYS (20 15) -
11.         CYL (1 1) -
12.         RECSZ (115 160) -
13.         FSPC (10 5) -
14.         SUBAL -
15.         NONUNIQUEKEY -
16.         UPGRADE -
17.         NOREUSE) -
18.      DATA -
19.         (NAME (FINCAT.K.EMPLOYEE.LAST.N.AIX.DATA)) -
20.      INDEX -
21.         (NAME (FINCAT.K.EMPLOYEE.LAST.N.AIX.INDEX))
22.    /*
```

Figure 13-5. Sample IDCAMS job: DEFINE AIX.

or the other of the components, separately from cluster-level access (if the programming language being used allows this). The data and index component names are simply the cluster name of the AIX followed by the qualifier 'DATA' and 'INDEX,' respectively. All in all, using the naming convention illustrated here provides any user with valuable detailed information about the AIX file and its associated base cluster, just from inspecting the name, avoiding the need to find this information either by running one or more LISTCAT jobs, or by the usual, not-always-reliable, 'asking around' approach.

7. The RELATE parameter identifies to VSAM the name of the base cluster over which this AIX is being built, and we say that VSAM can now establish an *association* between the two VSAM objects, the base cluster and the AIX. *Association* is a technical term in VSAM and there is an *associations group* as part of LISTCAT output which lists all—at that time—known associations which one VSAM object has to other related VSAM objects; this group appears under the heading ASSOCIATIONS. If the IDCAMS DEF AIX job shown in Figure 13-5 is run, and then, immediately after successful execution, we were to run a LISTCAT job against FINCAT.K.EMPLOYEE.LAST.N.AIX, the ASSOCIATIONS group would appear as this:

```
ASSOCIATIONS
    DATA-----FINCAT.K.EMPLOYEE.LAST.N.AIX.DATA
    INDEX----FINCAT.K.EMPLOYEE.LAST.N.AIX.INDEX
    CLUSTER--FINCAT.EMPLOYEE
```

Note that the CLUSTER entry refers to the base cluster over which this AIX has been built, not to the name of the AIX cluster itself (which we already know to be named FINCAT.K.EMPLOYEE.LAST.N.AIX). (As we will see in the following section, if we had defined a path after defining the AIX (which we haven't at this point) and then ran the LISTCAT job, another line of output would be included for the PATH entry.)

8. The VOL(umes) parameter identifies the volser of the volume on which the AIX is to reside. Remember, given that an AIX is itself a KSDS, it may be either a suballocated cluster or a unique cluster (see statement 14); if the default (which is suballocation) is accepted, then there must already be at least one VSAM space on the volume specified with sufficient space to meet the storage needs of the AIX. Furthermore, although it is possible to allocate the data and index components of the AIX on different volumes (by not coding VOL at the cluster level, as here, but coding a separate VOL parameter at the data and index component levels), typically they are co-resident.

9. The KEYS parameter identifies the alt key being used in this AIX, by length and by offset (remember this latter is from a zero starting point, and therefore is one less than the absolute column starting position of the alt key field). As noted earlier, the alt key may be a substring of any other field, or it may overlap other fields, or be wholly distinct from any other field, but may not be the entire prime key field. Also note that, contrary to the treatment of this parameter as optional in IBM's *Access*

Method Services Reference manual, this parameter is shown in Figure 13-4 as required: clearly, when defining an AIX, the alt key must be defined. The IBM manual is, strictly speaking, correct in stating that the parameter is optional, but only in the sense that, if omitted, a VSAM default will apply, but the default is that the alt key will be assumed to be 64 bytes in length and starting at offset zero (beginning of record), and it would clearly be nothing short of a miracle if this default were to match the actual fact of the matter. Thus, it is much more sensible to treat the KEYS parameter as required altogether.

10. Although the programmer may choose a CISZ for an AIX at the cluster level, or at either or both the data and index levels, the parameter is typically allowed to default, in which case VSAM would select the CISZ as a function of the maximum LRECL (recordsize) of the AIX data component and of buffer space allocation (we deliberately omitted coding any CISZ parameter in Figure 13-5, but show it as an optionally codable parameter in statement 10 of Figure 13-4). However, given that an AIX is itself a KSDS cluster, the programmer may specify the CISZ for performance reasons, making this selection as for any KSDS (see our earlier discussion of principles of CISZ in Section 8.9, and especially our later discussion of CISZ selection in Chapter 18, on VSAM optimization).

11-12. These two parameters provide VSAM with space allocation information concerning the AIX being created, and are equivalent in form and interpretation to the same parameters for any KSDS. (The *Access Method Services Reference* discusses how to determine space allocation requirements for AIXs.) In the example of Figure 13-5, we have requested a modest single cylinder of primary space allocation, with one cylinder as secondary backup. The average recordsize (RECSZ) is given as 115 bytes (the reader may consult the reference cited for information on computing such estimates), with the maximum recordsize estimated as 169 bytes. Note that the AIX is defined (statement 15) as having a nonunique key (last name) and so, as we learned above, the records are variable in length, not fixed.

13. Since an AIX is a KSDS cluster, it (its data component, more precisely) may contain distributed freespace for the purpose of cluster growth. The considerations for FSPC selection are the same as those for any KSDS (we take these up explicitly in Chapter 18, on VSAM optimization).

14. The choice of making the AIX a suballocated, versus a unique, cluster is no different than for any AIX.

15. The AIX is identified as having a nonunique alt key (last name).

16. This parameter specifies whether or not the AIX is to be a member of the upgrade set, as was discussed in detail earlier in this chapter (see Section 13.3).

17. As with any KSDS, the AIX may be optionally made reusable. This is sometimes done with *nonupgradable* AIXs which are rebuilt (BLDINDEX is reissued against them) at regular intervals by the user, rather than allowing VSAM to perform automatic AIX-upgrade against them. An upgradable AIX, as here, is typically non-reusable. (We take up this issue again briefly in Chapter 18, on performance.) Note that VSAM allows any AIX over some base cluster to be reusable, but the base cluster itself cannot ever be reusable.

18-21. See our discussion of the NAME parameter (statement 6), above.

13.7 DEFINING A PATH: THE DEFINE PATH COMMAND

Having defined the AIX object, the next step is to define a path which will establish an association between the AIX and the base cluster. The basic form of this coding is given in Figure 13-6, and sample coding presented in Figure 13-7; here we discuss the coding by statement number.

DISCUSSION

6. The NAME parameter gives the user-selected name that the path is to have. We continue to follow the naming convention discussed and adopted earlier in this chapter (see Section 13.6); here, we simply change the last qualifier of the AIX name from 'AIX' to 'PATH.' Notice that we do *not* provide separate component names, as we did for the base cluster and the AIX: as noted earlier, a path is the first VSAM object that we have encountered which is *not* a data set, and hence has no data or index components. It is a *control object* and exists solely as a specialized connector catalog entry reflecting the formal association of base cluster and AIX VSAM objects. The concept of a path is quite confusing and even a bit mysterious to many programmers dealing with VSAM for the first time, and indeed it tends to remain that way even after long years of experience. At the very end of this chapter, in a special 'technical appendix,' we try to demystify the concept of a path a bit further, but at this

```
1.    // ... JOB ...
2.    // EXEC PGM=IDCAMS
3.    //SYSPRINT DD SYSOUT=A
4.    //SYSIN DD *
5.       DEFINE PATH -
6.          (NAME (path-name) -                    [required]
7.          PATHENTRY (aix-name) -                 [required]
8.          UPDATE/NOUPDATE)
9.    /*
```

Figure 13-6. Basic coding of the DEFINE PATH command.

```
1.    // ... JOB ...
2.    // EXEC PGM=IDCAMS
3.    //SYSPRINT DD SYSOUT=A
4.    //SYSIN DD *
5.       DEFINE PATH -
6.          (NAME (FINCAT.K.EMPLOYEE.LAST.N.PATH) -
7.          PATHENTRY (FINCAT.K.EMPLOYEE.LAST.N.AIX) -
8.          UPDATE)
9.    /*
```

Figure 13-7. Sample IDCAMS job: DEFINE PATH.

point our treatment should suffice and the reader need only view the path as the logical relationship that connects a particular AIX with its underlying base cluster.

7. The PATHENTRY parameter identifies the AIX associated with this path; note that the base cluster is not, and need not be, directly identified, since the catalog entry for the AIX already contains this information: the AIX entry identifies the underlying base cluster in its RELATE parameter, as we saw in Section 13.6. (The acute reader may refer to the last section of this chapter for another use of the PATHENTRY parameter—other than to identify an associated AIX—namely, that of establishing an *alias* for a base cluster, but this is a very specialized use and we therefore leave it for the technical appendix (Section 13.10) to the chapter.)

Now let's look at the ASSOCIATIONS group within two different types of LISTCAT output, assuming we have successfully created the path as coded in Figure 13-7. The first case is a LISTCAT issued against the AIX (whose cluster name is FINCAT.K.EMPLOYEE.LAST.N.AIX) associated with this path; remember that, in Section 13.6, we looked at the ASSOCIATIONS group *after* we defined the AIX but *before* we had done the DEF PATH. Below is shown the ASSOCIATIONS group and the immediately following ATTRIBUTES group for a LISTCAT against the AIX after the path has been defined:

```
ASSOCIATIONS
   DATA-----FINCAT.K.EMPLOYEE.LAST.N.AIX.DATA
   INDEX----FINCAT.K.EMPLOYEE.LAST.N.AIX.INDEX
   CLUSTER--FINCAT.EMPLOYEE
   PATH-----FINCAT.K.EMPLOYEE.LAST.N.PATH
ATTRIBUTES
   UPGRADE
```

DATA and INDEX give the component names of the AIX (not of the base cluster), CLUSTER gives the cluster name of the base cluster, and PATH gives the path name of the associated path. The ATTRIBUTES group for the cluster entry of this AIX shows the AIX to be upgradable (we issued the DEF AIX with the UPGRADE parameter).

The second case involves a LISTCAT against the *path* (FINCAT.K.EMPLOYEE. LAST.N.PATH) rather than the AIX; the ASSOCIATIONS and the immediately following ATTRIBUTES group would be:

```
ASSOCIATIONS
   AIX------FINCAT.K.EMPLOYEE.LAST.N.AIX
   DATA-----FINCAT.K.EMPLOYEE.LAST.N.AIX.DATA
   INDEX----FINCAT.K.EMPLOYEE.LAST.N.AIX.INDEX
   DATA-----FINCAT.EMPLOYEE.DATA
   INDEX----FINCAT.EMPLOYEE.INDEX
ATTRIBUTES
   UPDATE
```

Here (reading top-down), AIX gives the *cluster name* of the AIX that this path is associated with, and the following DATA and INDEX give the data and index component names of the AIX, followed by the data and index component names of the base cluster (which is a KSDS). The base cluster's cluster name is not given directly, but we know it to be FINCAT.EMPLOYEE. Finally, the ATTRIBUTES group shows that we have specified UPDATE for the path (we will discuss this parameter's meaning and use immediately below).

8. The UPDATE/NOUPDATE parameter choice *of the DEF PATH command* determines what is known as *path-updatability*, which is related to, but different from *AIX-upgradability*, the latter determined by the parameter choice of UPGRADE/ NOUPGRADE *on the DEF AIX command*. As we learned earlier, the upgrade set associated with some particular base cluster is the set of AIXs built over that cluster, against which VSAM is to perform automatic AIX-upgrade: any changes to the base cluster that affect any of the AIXs will be (by VSAM) automatically reflected in the AIXs of the upgrade set. VSAM will simply update all appropriate AIXs (if in the upgrade set) to reflect base cluster changes. We also learned that, in order for the AIX-upgrade facility to be active, VSAM opens all members of the upgrade set whenever the base cluster is opened for output/update (where the update mode is just a special case of output mode, which also includes deletion operations). Furthermore, we know that an AIX is a member of the upgrade set if and only if the UPGRADE parameter was either explicitly enabled or allowed to default (UPGRADE is the VSAM default) when the AIX was defined through the DEF AIX command; VSAM performs no AIX-upgrade for any AIX marked NOUPGRADE at DEF AIX time.

Finally, the reader might remember an additional point which we made in our earlier discussion of the upgrade set (Section 13.3), which will now tie into the new concept of path-updatability: AIX-upgrade is solely performed when changes are made to the base cluster *directly*, that is by explicitly opening the base cluster itself, sometimes known as *base processing*. However, a base cluster may be processed *indirectly*, that is, via some AIX built over the base cluster, in which case we open (explicitly) the path alone, sometimes referred to as *path processing*. Path processing still gains us access to the base cluster, indirectly, and allows indirect changing of the base cluster. We may delete a base cluster record, for example, through a path simply by opening the path and fetching the record for deletion by an appropriate alt key, not by the primary key. Now, whether we delete a base cluster record directly using base processing or indirectly using path processing (we say, *through* the path and *over* the associated AIX), the base cluster record gets deleted, period (it's hard to argue with a deletion: there is something so very final about it). Note that such a deletion may require one or more AIXs of the upgrade set to be updated to reflect this fact, as we saw in Section 13.3 (which the reader may wish to briefly review at this time). But AIX-upgradability only concerns automatic AIX-upgrades under base processing, not under path processing: the second kind of deletion, for example, done through the path and over some AIX, does not automatically cause VSAM to perform an AIX-upgrade to assure synchrony of all AIXs with the base cluster.

The critical point here is that whether or not AIXs in the upgrade set are automatically synchronized by VSAM to reflect changes to the base cluster, as needed, *is wholly determined by the UPDATE/NOUPDATE parameter of the DEF*

PATH command—that is, it is a matter of path-updatability, not AIX-upgradability. If the path is made updatable by coding (or allowing VSAM to default to) UPDATE on the DEF PATH command, then, in addition to allocating the upgrade set when the base cluster is accessed and changed directly, VSAM will also allocate the upgrade set when the base cluster is processed indirectly through a path (over an AIX). In both cases, VSAM will, having opened all members of the upgrade set ('allocated' them), automatically perform whatever updates are necessary to the appropriate AIXs to reflect any base cluster changes that affect any AIXs of the upgrade set.

We can understand this better still if we consider what happens when a particular AIX is upgradable (UPGRADE parameter specified at DEF AIX time) but the path is nonupdatable (NOUPDATE parameter specified at DEF PATH time). When we open the base cluster itself for output/update processing, all members of the upgrade set are allocated and maintained automatically by VSAM in synchrony with changes to the base cluster. However, if we open a path associated with one of these AIXs, then—despite the fact that the AIX is in the upgrade set—only the base cluster is opened, but the upgrade set remains unallocated (all members besides the one we are using are not opened and hence not accessed at all). If we make any changes through the path (and over the particular AIX associated with the path), these will *not* be reflected in the AIXs of the upgrade set, and indeed could not be, since the upgrade set is not allocated by VSAM under these circumstances (and remember that any AIXs that are not in the upgrade set are never candidates for VSAM AIX-upgrade). Thus, if we want to assure absolutely complete synchrony of the base cluster and all members of the upgrade set, then UPDATE must be specified (on the DEF PATH command) for the path associated with each AIX in the set. Then all changes to the base cluster, directly or via a path, are guaranteed by VSAM to be reflected in all upgrade set members. But there are circumstances in which we may be satisfied with a lesser level of synchrony assurance. For example, it may be the case that output/update processing against the base cluster is allowed only in base processing mode—opening and changing the cluster itself—but only queries (read/browse mode) are allowed when performing path processing; in this case, since no base cluster changes are possible via a path, then we could define all paths as NOUPDATE without any loss in synchrony. Furthermore, if this condition were to hold (query mode only for path processing), then performance is enhanced by specifying NOUPDATE since this instructs VSAM to avoid the (unnecessary) overhead of allocating the upgrade set when no updates to the set during path processing are required. In Chapter 18, on performance, we will explore some further performance issues associated with paths, and demonstrate a special trick that allows the user to often avoid the overhead associated with updating a large number of members of the upgrade set.

13.8   BUILDING AN ALTERNATE INDEX: THE BLDINDEX COMMAND

In this section, we turn to the third and last step in establishing a functioning AIX over some base cluster, namely the actual building of the AIX data set itself, which is effected through the BLDINDEX command.

13.8.1   How VSAM Builds an Alternate Index

VSAM builds the actual AIX data set over some base cluster in four distinct steps.

1. Alt key plus pointer extraction: VSAM first reads the data component sequentially and extracts all alt key values from the alt key field (located at some predefined fixed offset) in such a fashion that, when it locates and extracts one alt key value from one data record, it immediately locates and extracts the associated pointer, which is either the prime key field value within that same record (if the underlying cluster is a KSDS) or the RBA of the record (if the underlying cluster is an ESDS and hence has no prime key field). The alt key plus pointer pair is stored as a single record. VSAM repeats this process for each data record of the base cluster, yielding as many temporary 'constructed' AIX records as there are data records in the base cluster.

2. Alt key sort: VSAM next reads through the constructed records and sorts them ascendingly in alt key character sequence.

3. Merge record operation: If the AIX is marked NONUNIQUEKEY, then there are duplicate alt key values, that is, there will be among the constructed records of the previous operations more than one record with the same alt key value. VSAM will merge all such 'duplicate alt key' records, yielding a temporary data set containing only one record for each distinct alt key value, and the single record associated with any particular alt key will contain the pointer set for that alt key value (the set of all pointers, prime key or RBA, identifying all of the base cluster records with that alt key value in their alt key field).

4. KSDS construction: The above three steps collectively only create the content of the data component of the AIX which, remember, is always a KSDS. In this fourth and last step, VSAM, from the AIX data records, constructs the index component by the same means as it does for the index component of any KSDS, with the one exception that the alt keys stored in the index are stored in full form, not compressed form as for non-AIX index components. All temporary work data sets are deleted and the final form of the AIX data set is implemented. At this point we will say that the AIX has been built.

VSAM may perform steps 2 and 3 above (sort and merge) in one of two ways, by an *external sort* or by an *internal sort*, and these are discussed in the next two subsections below.

13.8.2   External Sort

As with any sort, VSAM may be instructed to perform an *external sort*—a sort using DASD storage, a 'disk sort,' in which case VSAM will use two auxiliary storage files as sort work files on which to perform the sort and store nonfinal results. The programmer is responsible for providing JCL DD statements for these two sort work files, while VSAM will actually build the files as special-purpose ESDSs. Although the programmer may change this, it is preferable to use the special ddnames IDCUT1 and IDCUT2, as these are the ddnames VSAM chooses as a default. There are two different acceptable ways to code these DD statements, 'minimal' coding, and 'full' coding:

```
Minimal Coding:
    //IDCUT1 DD DISP=SHR,UNIT=unit,VOL=SER=volser
    //IDCUT2 DD DISP=SHR,UNIT=unit,VOL=SER=volser

Full Coding:
    //IDCUT1 DD DSN=dsname1,DISP=OLD,UNIT=unit,
    //         VOL=SER=volser,AMP='AMORG'
    //IDCUT2 DD DSN=dsname2,DISP=OLD,UNIT=unit,
    //         VOL=SER=volser,AMP='AMORG'
```

The second, full, coding is sometimes used in order to be very cautious in avoiding any possibility that OS job management, in 'reading' the JCL, does not mistake IDCUT1 and IDCUT2 as OS files, rather than VSAM files; the AMP parameter unambiguously—through the AMORG (Access Method (services) Organization) keyword—identifies the files as VSAM files, for otherwise there may be confusion in that, generally, VSAM file DD statements only contain DSN and DISP parameters, while here UNIT and VOL are also coded.

Two final points to note. First, the UNIT and VOL parameters should identify a volume that contains sufficient suballocatable VSAM space for the defined sort work files; the space requirement, which is *not* coded in the JCL, is generally modest and need not be computed, but the specified volume should, defensively, have a generous amount of unallocated VSAM space (preferably on a high-capacity pack such as a 3380).

Second, the DSN parameter could be viewed as just a frill, as these are temporary sort work files and will be automatically deleted by VSAM upon *successful* completion of the BLDINDEX operation; note the emphasis on 'successful': VSAM does not necessarily delete either or both of the files if the BLDINDEX operation terminates unsuccessfully. That is why it is a good defensive measure to name both files distinctly so that in the event of a BLDINDEX failure, the volume can be inspected to see if the work data sets have been unnecessarily left behind; simply scan for the user-provided data set names. One convention I commonly follow is to name the two files as follows: the high level qualifier would be the truename or, more commonly, the alias of a user catalog 'owning' the volume on which the temporary data sets are allocated, the second qualifier is 'BLDINDEX,' the third is 'IDCUT1' and 'IDCUT2' for the two different files, and the fourth and last qualifier is the jobname of the BLDINDEX IDCAMS job using the data sets, this last qualifier allowing the user to differentiate particular sort work data sets from any others (from other jobs) that may also appear on the same pack (unlikely, but possible). Assuming a user catalog alias of 'FINCAT,' then the DD statements would be as follows:

```
//IDCUT1 DD DSN=FINCAT.BLDINDEX.IDCUT1.BLDJOB01,
//         DISP=OLD,UNIT=unit,
//         VOL=SER=volser,AMP='AMORG'
//IDCUT2 DD DSN=FINCAT.BLDINDEX.IDCUT2.BLDJOB01,
//         DISP=OLD,UNIT=unit,
//         VOL=SER=volser,AMP='AMORG'
```

13.8.3   Internal Sort

Although VSAM sometimes has to perform an external sort such as described above, generally an internal sort is far more efficient: an internal sort is one that uses virtual storage ('internal,' as opposed to 'external' auxiliary storage) to perform the sort operation; it is sometimes loosely referred to as an 'in-core' sort. This is so because VSAM thereby avoids having to perform real I/O operations across a channel to DASD, as with external sorting; however, there must be sufficient virtual storage available to the job/task for VSAM to use for internal work areas holding intermediate results of the sort process. How to compute how much virtual storage may be required by VSAM to successfully perform an internal sort is detailed in the *VSAM Administration Guide*, but suffice it here to note two points about this.

First, VSAM (by default) always attempts to perform an internal sort first, it being more efficient than an external sort, and will only resort to an external sort if either the programmer has explicitly overridden the default INTERNALSORT parameter of the BLDINDEX command with the EXTERNALSORT parameter, or if VSAM finds that there is insufficient virtual storage available to successfully perform a strictly internal sort. In this connection, note that *if* VSAM attempts an internal sort and fails, then an external sort can be performed only if the sort work files have been allocated, and it is for this reason that we recommend that the IDCUT1 and IDCUT2 DD statements be provided in all BLDINDEX jobs just in case an external sort is resorted to; if VSAM must resort to an external sort after the failure of an internal one, then the entire job will fail if the sort work data sets have not been allocated through the appropriate DD statements, and this is obviously not a desirable situation.

Second, an increasing number of installations are running an *XA* (Extended Architecture) operating system, such as MVS/XA, VM/XA, or MVS/ESA, and here there is considerably less likelihood that virtual storage would prove insufficient for a BLDINDEX job: the address space that the job runs within is 2Gb (giga, or billion, bytes) in size, as opposed to non-XA systems (like MVS/SP Version 1) with only 16Mb (mega, or million, bytes) of virtual storage to the running job. Although certainly not all of the 2Gb of virtual storage would be available to the BLDINDEX job under MVS/XA, nonetheless typically something of the order of 32Mb or higher may be available, and this is usually sufficient for most BLDINDEX operations to execute as internal sorts (but the programmer should determine that (1) the system is indeed an XA system, and (2) that the BLDINDEX job is running while the system is actually in what is termed *XA-mode*, not *370-compatibility mode* where virtual storage is still restricted to a maximum of 16Mb).

13.8.4   BLDINDEX Coding

Figure 13-8 gives the basic form of a BLDINDEX job, while Figure 13-9 shows a sample coding; the discussion below is keyed to the line number in these figures.

DISCUSSION

4. This statement identifies the base cluster, which must be preexisting and nonempty. Note that, although most JCL referencing VSAM files have DISP=SHR,

```
 1.    // ... JOB ...
 2.    // EXEC PGM=IDCAMS
 3.    //SYSPRINT DD SYSOUT=A
 4.    //BASEDD DD DSN=base cluster name,DISP=OLD
 5.    //AIXDD  DD DSN=aix name,DISP=OLD
 6.    //IDCUT1 DD . . .              [see section 16.8.2]
 7.    //IDCUT2 DD . . .              [see section 16.8.2]
 8.    //SYSIN DD *
 9.      BLDINDEX -
10.        INFILE (basedd) -                    [required]
11.        OUTFILE (aixdd) -                    [required]
12.        EXTERNALSORT/INTERNALSORT -
13.        WORKFILES (ddname1 ddname2) -
14.        CATALOG (cat-name/pswd)
15.    /*
```

Figure 13-8. Basic coding of the BLDINDEX command.

```
 1.    //BLDJOB01 JOB ...
 2.    // EXEC PGM=IDCAMS
 3.    //SYSPRINT DD SYSOUT=A
 4.    //BASEDD DD DSN=FINCAT.EMPLOYEE,DISP=OLD
 5.    //AIXDD  DD DSN=FINCAT.K.EMPLOYEE.LAST.N.AIX,DISP=OLD
 6.    //IDCUT1 DD DSN=FINCAT.BLDINDEX.IDCUT1.BLDJOB01,
        //         DISP=OLD,UNIT=3380,
        //         VOL=SER=FIN001,AMP='AMORG'
 7.    //IDCUT2 DD DSN=FINCAT.BLDINDEX.IDCUT2.BLDJOB01,
        //         DISP=OLD,UNIT=3380,
        //         VOL=SER=FIN002,AMP='AMORG'
 8.    //SYSIN DD *
 9.      BLDINDEX -
10.        INFILE (BASEDD) -
11.        OUTFILE (AIXDD) -
12.        INTERNALSORT
15.    /*
```

Figure 13-9. Sample IDCAMS job: BLDINDEX.

in a BLDINDEX job the base cluster should be held in exclusive control (not shareable) for the duration of the BLDINDEX job by coding DISP=OLD.

5. This statement identifies the AIX that is to be built by this BLDINDEX job; remember that the previous DEF AIX job only *defines* the AIX, but does not *build* it in terms of (loading) its actual contents. IBM VSAM manuals indicate that the programmer may in this statement alternately identify the path, rather than the AIX: both are acceptable, but regardless of the coding, the BLDINDEX operation is creating the AIX data set itself, not the path (which has been predefined and, as we have noted, is not an actual data set object), so it is more accurate, and less confusing, if the AIX is specified here. In addition, the specification of the AIX, rather than the path, is somewhat more efficient: if the path is identified, then the AIX is not directly

known to VSAM, and VSAM therefore first must either look up the path entry in the appropriate VSAM catalog to see what AIX is associated with the path, or look up the base cluster catalog entry to ascertain the same information (through the ASSOCIATIONS group), and using this information VSAM can then construct the AIX specified. Preferable, therefore, to specify the AIX directly.

10. The INFILE parameter specifies the ddname of the DD statement referencing the base cluster over which the AIX is being built. (Any acceptable ddname could have been used, but 'BASEDD' is an obvious (good) choice.) Instead of INFILE plus the ddname, the programmer could have coded in MVS the INDATASET parameter along with the actual data set name of the base cluster (so, for example: INDATASET (FINCAT.EMPLOYEE)), in which case VSAM will attempt to dynamically allocate the volume the base cluster resides on.

11. This statement identifies the 'output' file (by ddname), and the output file of a BLDINDEX operation is necessarily the AIX being built; again, any valid ddname would do, but AIXDD is an obvious choice. (Note again that VSAM allows a path to be identified, instead of an AIX, but as suggested above, the temptation should be resisted.) Like the base cluster, the AIX data set should also be held in exclusive control (DISP=OLD rather than DISP=SHR) for the duration of the BLDINDEX operation. (OUTDATASET and the AIX data set name using VSAM dynamic allocation is an alternative in MVS systems.)

12. VSAM is instructed to attempt to perform the sort operation entirely in virtual storage, given sufficient virtual storage (generally available in an XA environment). We could have omitted this parameter, as INTERNALSORT is the default, but (as coded) it is self-documenting. Note that we have explicitly coded DD statements for the two sort work files IDCUT1 and IDCUT2 (statements 6 and 7, respectively), just in case the internal sort cannot be performed and an external sort is put in operation.

13. This parameter can be used to select ddnames other than the default names IDCUT1 and IDCUT2 for the sort work files, but as noted above, it is preferable to retain the VSAM names (see Subsection 13.8.2, earlier).

14. This parameter identifies the catalog owning the volume on which the sort work files are to be allocated (*not* necessarily the same catalog owning the volumes on which the base cluster and AIX reside). An alternative would have been to make this identification through a JOBCAT or STEPCAT DD statement. Note that in the sample coding of Figure 13-9, we have not coded the CATALOG parameter, *nor* have we provided a JOBCAT or STEPCAT statement; this is valid: VSAM will use the catalog identified via the high level qualifier of the data set names of the work data sets (here, 'FINCAT'), when running on an MVS system.

The reader might justifiably wonder what would happen if no data set name had been provided for these files (the names are wholly optional). The answer is that, in the absence of the other catalog identification means we cited earlier, VSAM would use the Master Catalog; this should generally be avoided. Our recommendation is to use the same catalog for all four data sets involved in a BLDINDEX operation: the base cluster, the AIX, and the two external sort work data sets, and in our sample coding we used the MVS HLQ-technique to identify the owning catalog (FINCAT).

For a password-protected catalog, the update password, or a higher password, must be provided (we will discuss VSAM password protection facilities in Chapter 16 of the text).

In addition, note that although all of these files need not be defined in the same catalog, it *is* required that the base cluster and the AIX be defined in one and the same catalog. Finally, the observant reader may have noted that we have failed to explicitly code a REGION parameter on the EXEC statement; generally, the region size should be coded, but we are simply assuming here sufficient virtual storage.

13.9 RESTRICTIONS WITH ALTERNATE INDICES (AIXs)

There are several restrictions that programming languages and the system environment (batch versus online) impose on the use of AIXs. AIX support for batch and on-line environments exists for PL/I, COBOL (including the 'new COBOL,' VS COBOL II), and Assembler when the AIX is built over a KSDS base cluster. However, only Assembler supports, in batch, AIX facilities over an ESDS. AIX plus ESDS support does, however, exist in an online CICS environment for all three programming languages. In addition, only Assembler allows the ESDS to be opened directly and processed as a KSDS file, independently of the base cluster and associated path. COBOL and PL/I gain access to AIX facilities by opening the path associated with the appropriate AIX, not by opening the AIX itself.

To illustrate this and to also note an additional restriction concerning COBOL support for AIX processing, let's look at the basic coding and COBOL-to-JCL connections, given in Figure 13-10. First, note that the ASSIGN clause (statement 4) gives the ddname of the base cluster, here BASEDD in the matching DD statement 9, and since the base cluster in such processing is generally shareable, DISP is given as

```
1.    // ... JOB ...
2.    // EXEC COB2UCLG
3.    //COB.SYSIN DD *
             .
             .
             .
4.            SELECT <vsam filename> ASSIGN TO BASEDD
5.            ACCESS IS DYNAMIC
6.            RECORD KEY IS <prime key field>
7.            ALTERNATE RECORD KEY IS <alt key field>
             .
             .
8.    /*
9.    //GO.BASEDD DD DSN=FINCAT.EMPLOYEE,DISP=SHR
10.   //GO.BASEDD1 DD
      //          DSN=FINCAT.K.EMPLOYEE.LAST.N.PATH,
      //          DISP=SHR
11.   //
```

Figure 13-10. JCL for COBOL AIX processing.

SHR. The RECORD KEY clause of statement 6 names the prime key field, while the ALTERNATE RECORD KEY clause is used to name the alt key field. Although in the Environment Division only a SELECT. . . ASSIGN need be coded for the *base cluster*, nonetheless in performing AIX processing in COBOL the JCL requires a DD statement referencing the *path*, as seen in statement 10. There are two points to note here about this path DD statement, the first of which we have already observed: there is no SELECT. . . ASSIGN corresponding to this DD statement.

The second point concerns the naming convention for the path DD statement's ddname. COBOL forms the ddname of the path associated with some base cluster by appending a numeral to the base cluster's ddname, starting at 1 for the first path, 2 for the next path, etc. Here, since the base cluster's ddname is BASEDD, then the first path would be referenced in a DD statement whose ddname is BASEDD1; if there were another AIX, and therefore another path, being accessed by the program, then the DD statement for this second path would be BASEDD2. Now, remember that a ddname in OS is a maximum of eight characters long, so that if we chose BASEFILE as the ddname in the base cluster's DD statement, then there would be no room at the end of the ddname to append a numeral according to the COBOL convention. In this case, the rightmost (eighth) character of the base ddname would be truncated, and then the numeral appended, giving BASEFIL1; if there were 10 or more AIXs built over the base cluster, then the tenth path's ddname would be formed by truncating the rightmost two characters of the base ddname, and then appending the numeral, giving BASEFI10, and so on for the others in ascending numeral order (BASEFI11, BASEFI12, . . .).

To accommodate to this COBOL convention, therefore, the programmer should select a ddname for the base cluster that is no longer than six characters—BASEDD, for example—to allow for as many as 99 AIXs over this one cluster. (It is unlikely that there would be over 99 AIXs built over one base cluster, so six characters should suffice; although 10 or more AIXs over one base cluster occurs relatively infrequently, it nonetheless does occur, and so, defensively, we have avoided a seven character base cluster ddname.)

Finally, note that the JCL requires a DD statement referencing the *path* associated with whatever AIX we are accessing, *not* the *AIX* itself, which in the JCL is nowhere directly referenced. VSAM uses the DD statement for the path to locate the path entry in the appropriate catalog (here FINCAT, the high level qualifier), and this entry names the AIX associated with the defined path.

13.10   A 'TECHNICAL APPENDIX' ON THE PATH IN VSAM

From our earlier discussions of the path (Sections 13.2 and 13.7), we have learned that the path establishes the association between a particular AIX and the particular base cluster over which that AIX is defined. We further learned that a path is *not* a VSAM data set (like a cluster or an AIX or a catalog), but rather a *control object*, which exists as a catalog connector entry, defining the logical relationship of the AIX to an associated base cluster. From this, one would not think that a path could be the object of, say, an IDCAMS PRINT command, given its contol (non-data set) status. However, we *can* issue a PRINT command against a path; this will not, strictly speaking, print the contents of the path itself, which consists of (directly) unprintable specialized control information ('connector' objects), but rather *prints the base cluster records in alt key sequence*, over the alt key field used by whatever AIX is associated with the path referred to. To unpack this conceptually: (1) the pseudo-printing of a path returns base cluster records only (not, for example, the data records of the associated AIX), and (2) not in primary key sequence, which is how the records would be returned if we printed the base cluster itself, but sequenced in ascending order over the alt key field used by the AIX associated with the path. For example, if we use our earlier example, the base cluster was FINCAT.EMPLOYEE, a KSDS employee record file, and one of several AIXs built over it was FINCAT.K.EMPLOYEE.LAST.N.AIX, a nonunique key AIX over the employee last name alt key field, with FINCAT.K.EMPLOYEE.LAST.N.PATH being the associated path. Then this command:

```
PRINT -
     INFILE (FINCAT.K.EMPLOYEE.LAST.N.PATH)
```

would return all base cluster records from the employee file, but in ascending alphabetic order by employee last name: the 'Aaron' record(s), followed by the 'Aaronson' record(s), followed by the 'Abbott' record(s), etc. Notice, we said 'record(s)': if there were several 'Abbott' records, for example, they would all be returned, each as a separate record, but *not necessarily* in primary key order (technically, we say that VSAM does not preserve primary key order when applying AIX-upgrades to the members of an upgrade set). If, as occasionally happens, the programmer needs a print of the base cluster in this alt key order, rather than in primary key order, then issuing a PRINT command against the path would provide this.

Note, furthermore, in this connection that a PRINT command issued against the AIX (FINACT.K.EMPLOYEE.LAST.N.AIX) would *not* accomplish this. The output of that command would give the contents of the AIX data set itself and hence not return base cluster records at all; for example, if we printed the data component of the AIX, we would simply get AIX data records consisting of five bytes of system header, followed by the alt key value, followed by the pointer set (primary key values, or RBAs if the AIX is built over an ESDS), and no other fields or information from the base cluster records would be returned at all.

A final technical note on paths, which earlier we hinted at darkly in Section 13.7, concerns using paths solely as an *aliasing facility*, completely divorced from any connection with AIXs. Here is how that works. Suppose again that our base cluster is the KSDS employee file FINCAT.EMPLOYEE. Then, whether or not we define any AIX over this cluster, we may still define a path to be associated with this base cluster, though related not to an AIX (if any), but to the base cluster itself. The coding below will clarify this:

```
1. DEFINE PATH -
2.     (NAME (FINCAT.EMPFILE) -
3.     PATHENTRY (FINCAT.EMPLOYEE)
```

Here, no AIX is involved at all; we have simply created a path named FINCAT.
EMPFILE, associated by the PATHENTRY parameter—not to an AIX (as in Figure
13-7, earlier in the text)—but rather directly to the base cluster FINCAT.EMPLOYEE.
The effect of this DEF PATH is to make the path name FINCAT.EMPFILE another
name—an alias—for the base cluster FINCAT.EMPLOYEE. A useful feature of this
'aliasing' path facility is that the path object can be given certain attributes different
from the base cluster: different protection or password characteristics and different
updatability, for instance, and this feature can be exploited for security purposes as
well as performance purposes. Although a facility as powerful as the path in VSAM
can be exploited for still other advanced purposes, we will end our technical appendix on the path at this point, which should be more than sufficient to demystify the
path concept and to suggest its various roles in VSAM processing.

14

VSAM PROGRAMMING IN COBOL

This chapter will examine the elements of coding for VSAM processing in COBOL, both for OS/VS COBOL ('old' COBOL) and VS COBOL II ('new' COBOL). It will assume OS/VS COBOL, Release 2.4, as the default, and note the differences for VS COBOL II, Releases 2.0 and 3.0, wherever relevant.

14.1 ENVIRONMENT DIVISION: SELECT STATEMENT

14.1.1 The ASSIGN Clause

There are currently four VSAM cluster types (DFP/VSAM)—KSDS, ESDS, RRDS, and the recently added LDS (Linear Data Set). As of this writing, high-level-language support ('HLL support') for LDSs will debut with the *data window services* of ESA (Enterprise Systems Architecture)—more formally, MVS/SP 3.1—which will appear in staged delivery beginning in August, 1988, although the data window services facility itself will not appear until the last quarter of 1988. For the remaining three cluster types, there are just two formats for the ASSIGN clause:

```
(1) . . . ASSIGN TO <ddname>          (KSDS, RRDS)
(2) . . . ASSIGN TO AS-<ddname>       (ESDS)
```

In format (1) nothing is coded before the ddname (corresponding to //GO.ddname in the associated JCL), and this informs the compiler and the system that a randomly (directly) accessible VSAM file is being specified. Format (2) is used exclusively for an ESDS: the 'AS' standing for *addressed-sequential*, referring to the fact that the standard mode of access to an ESDS is by RBA. Although an ESDS can also be accessed randomly if one or more AIXs are built over it, this is not supported in batch COBOL, but is in CICS.

14.1.2 The PASSWORD Clause

If the AMS Password Facility is used without an add-on external security program (like RACF), then the appropriate password *could* be supplied in the PASS-WORD clause of the SELECT statement; the details of this coding will be fully discussed later in the text, in Subsection 16.2.2, along with a caution concerning the inherent potential security exposure of this approach, and the interested reader may scan that discussion at this point.

14.1.3 The ORGANIZATION Clause

COBOL uses three distinct ORGANIZATION clauses to discriminate the three types of VSAM clusters:

```
. . . ORGANIZATION IS INDEXED        (KSDS)
. . . ORGANIZATION IS SEQUENTIAL     (ESDS)
. . . ORGANIZATION IS RELATIVE       (RRDS)
```

The reader might ask how the compiler distinguishes these VSAM organizations from the comparable OS organizations, namely ISAM, QSAM, and BDAM. In point of fact, the organization clauses don't make any discrimination: INDEXED is used for both KSDSs and ISAM files, SEQUENTIAL is used for both ESDSs and QSAM files, and RELATIVE is used for both RRDSs and BDAM files. It is the ASSIGN clause that differentiates VSAM clusters from their OS counterparts; the OS codings are as follows:

```
. . . ASSIGN TO DA-I-‹ddname›        (ISAM)
. . . ASSIGN TO S-‹ddname›           (QSAM)
. . . ASSIGN TO R-‹ddname›           (BDAM)
```

Although many programmers also code SYSnnn and UT or DA class and device names in the ASSIGN clause, these are treated as comments by the compiler. (Note finally that, for VS COBOL II, only VSAM and QSAM files are supported: ISAM and BDAM file support has been discontinued under the new compiler.)

14.1.4 ACCESS MODE Clause

COBOL supports the following three access modes for the different types of VSAM clusters:

```
. . . ACCESS MODE IS SEQUENTIAL      (KSDS,ESDS,RRDS)
. . . ACCESS MODE IS RANDOM          (KSDS,RRDS)
. . . ACCESS MODE IS DYNAMIC         (KSDS,RRDS)
```

Dynamic Access. Dynamic access is new with VSAM (ISAM supported sequential and random access only), and its use allows for *nonconcurrent* sequential and random access within one program: nonconcurrent in that at any one time, the program is strictly in one or the other mode (although it is not always possible to determine which from one's program coding; more on this later), so that the program is said to be *serially mode-switching*. To appreciate the operation of dynamic access, let's briefly consider the concept of the *Current Record Pointer* (*CRP*) or the *File Position Indicator* (*FPI*)in COBOL; note that OS/VS COBOL and VS COBOL II (only Release 3.0 of which conforms to the COBOL '85 ANSI standard) makes reference to the CRP, while the ANSI COBOL '85 standard uses the newer FPI for the same concept. IBM's *SAA COBOL Language*, the standardized successor (not yet implemented in any IBM product) to VS COBOL II, which is designed to conform to SAA, uses the newer FPI terminology; here the two terms will be used interchangeably.

First it should be noted that the CRP or FPI is a *logical pointer* only: it is not an actual field, either within a record or within a control block. As a conceptual object, it specifies the next record to be processed in the file by sequential access operations. For the concept of a CRP/FPI to apply, the file must be one that has been OPENed for INPUT or OPENed for I-O, not for OUTPUT or EXTEND, and (in addition) the ACCESS MODE is either SEQUENTIAL or DYNAMIC, not RANDOM; furthermore, even in dynamic mode, the CRP/FPI is relevant only to sequential retrieval and positioning operations. The CRP/FPI setting is affected only by the successful operation of the I/O verbs OPEN, START, READ, and READ. . .NEXT; the setting is wholly unaffected by the WRITE, REWRITE, and DELETE verbs. The START verb is not a *retrieval* operation (no record is fetched), but only a *positioning* operation, setting the CRP/FPI to some specific record position within the file; a subsequent READ or READ. . .NEXT operation then retrieves the record pointed to by the CRP/FPI and resets the CRP/FPI to the immediately succeeding record position.

Typically, in dynamic mode, the program may be coded for what we have earlier termed start-sequential processing: either a START verb is issued to position at a particular record (through setting the CRP/FPI), or a random READ is issued which will both fetch the record and set the CRP/FPI to the immediately succeeding record; thereafter one or more READ. . .NEXT statements sequentially retrieve successive records either to EOF or to whatever terminus the program logic requires.

Dynamic access mode processing is quite complex for two reasons, which also serve to bring out other features of VSAM processing in COBOL. First, a special library subroutine (ILBOVIO0 for OS/VS COBOL, and IGZEVIO for VS COBOL II) handles the determination of which mode, sequential or random, the program is to be in at any time, by highly intricate internal rules, and without intimate knowledge of these internals, it is generally not possible for the programmer to determine which mode is being used in honoring some program I/O statement. The form of the I/O statement is not necessarily an accurate reflection of the *true-program mode*. This is so because the compiler subroutine acts on a principle of *miniminization of mode-switching*: wherever and whenever possible, if the program is already in one mode (sequential or random) by virtue of some I/O statement, it will attempt to stay in that mode until forced to switch to the other mode by virtue of complex internal logic. If, for example, a program at some point in the logic was in sequential mode, then an immediately subsequent successful random READ will *not* be honored as a random I/O operation, but rather as a sequential retrieval operation. The program will remain in sequential mode thereafter until forced into direct mode: this may occur by virtue of an unsuccessful START, READ, or READ. . .NEXT; such a failure associated with any I/O operation which would normally (if successful) set the CRP/FPI, causes the program to 'lose' the CRP/FPI (it is undefined in such a case), and this loss prohibits further sequential retrieval. The program therefore switches to random mode. The internal logic used by ILBOVIO0/IGZEVIO is too complex to unpack in any readily understandable form without forbidding VSAM internals, so that the programmer has to accept that the *logic mode* of a program (the mode suggested by the program's coding) is not necessarily reflective of true-program mode (the actual mode the program is in based on ILBOVIO0/IGZEVIO internals). This may certainly complicate program debugging and maintenance by obscuring program operation.

Second, the CRP/FPI logical pointer, not itself real, must be set from a control block maintained by VSAM that tracks the current record position *for all I/O operations* (not solely sequential ones); this control block is known as the *PLace Holder (PLH)*, and it is from this PLH that the CRP/FPI logical pointer is derived. But given that the PLH is posted for all I/O requests, while the CRP/FPI is only selectively derived, there may be significant performance overhead consequent to dynamic mode processing in COBOL, as an asynchronous POINT macro (which establishes positioning in native (Assembler) VSAM, equivalent to START) may have to be repeatedly issued by VSAM in order to maintain the CRP/FPI logical pointer correctly. The technical details are intricate, but the programmer should at least bear in mind that dynamic mode processing in COBOL is not without both its complications and its potential performance disadvantages compared to strictly sequential or strictly random mode processing. (Later we will consider one more issue related to dynamic access, that of *Mass Sequential Insertion (MSI)*, when we discuss record insertion.)

14.1.5   RECORD/RELATIVE KEY Clause

The KEY clause is used only for files that allow keyed-access: KSDSs and RRDSs (strictly speaking, an RRDS does not use a key, but rather an RRN, but the RRN functions like a key); the form is:

```
. . . RECORD KEY IS ‹prime-key field›      (KSDS)
. . . RELATIVE KEY IS ‹RRN field›          (RRDS)
```

There are several points to note about these KEY clauses. First, the RECORD KEY clause is *required* for all access modes: even if a KSDS is accessed sequentially, the RECORD KEY clause must be coded. For an RRDS, the RELATIVE KEY field is optional for strictly sequential access; the use of the START verb is *not* strictly sequential access (it is termed *start-sequential access*), so the RELATIVE KEY must be then coded. Under such circumstances, both KSDSs and RRDSs are being accessed *keyed-sequentially*, and records are retrieved in ascending prime-key or RRN order, respectively. For a KSDS, all records are returned, while for an RRDS, empty slots are not returned.

Second, the program location requirements for the two types of keys (RECORD and RELATIVE) are quite different. The RECORD KEY field must be defined as a record-internal field in the FILE SECTION (unlike the ISAM nominal key, which is not defined in an FD, but in WORKING STORAGE); it is treated as alphanumeric, although through an 'IBM extension' (not recognized by any ANSI (American National Standards Institute) standard) it may be any unsigned numeric type field.

However, the RELATIVE KEY field used with RRDSs is *not* record-internal, but rather is defined as an unsigned integer data item in WORKING STORAGE.

14.1.6 ALTERNATE RECORD KEY Clause

If a KSDS is to be processed with one or more AIXs built over it, an ALTERNATE KEY clause must be coded to specify the alt-key field for each such AIX; there are two forms of the clause:

```
(1) . . . ALTERNATE KEY IS ⟨alt-key field⟩
(2) . . . ALTERNATE KEY IS ⟨alt-key field⟩
          WITH DUPLICATES
```

Format (1) is used for unique AIXs, that is, those defined through the DEF AIX command with the UNIQUEKEY parameter, while format (2) is used for nonunique AIXs (DEF AIX...NONUNIQUEKEY). There are some niceties to note when performing AIX processing in COBOL, which are discussed immediately below.

AIX processing and the concept of Key of Reference (KOR).   COBOL processing with AIXs involves an understanding of the concept of the *Key of Reference (KOR)*. The KOR is the key used to honor any *input* requests when processing a KSDS with one or more AIXs built over it; it may be either the prime-key, or any one of the alt-keys established (each specified with its own ALTERNATE RECORD KEY clause in the SELECT statement). KOR is affected solely by retrieval and positioning requests (by READ, READ...NEXT, START, but not by any output statements (WRITE, REWRITE, DELETE). Assume that we are processing a KSDS whose prime-key is a social security number (SSN), and that we have defined and built two AIXs over this KSDS, one a unique-key AIX using employee number (EMPNO), the other a nonunique-key AIX using employee last name (LAST); the following SELECT statement coding would be used:

```
SELECT . . .
      ORGANIZATION IS INDEXED
      ACCESS MODE IS DYNAMIC
      RECORD KEY IS SSN
      ALTERNATE RECORD KEY IS EMPNO
      ALTERNATE RECORD KEY IS LAST
            WITH DUPLICATES
      FILE STATUS IS . . .
```

The prime-key (specified in RECORD KEY clause) is the default Key of Reference at OPEN time. Subsequent I/O statements will be assumed to use the prime-key as the KOR, unless explicit indication to the contrary is made. Such explicit indication to the contrary is effected by coding the KEY clause on a START or a random READ. Consider the following:

```
(1) START ... KEY IS EQUAL TO EMPNO
(2) READ  ... KEY IS LAST
```

Statement (1) establishes the EMPNO alt-key as the KOR, while (2) establishes the LAST alt-key as the KOR. After this, however, the question is, what will then be used as the KOR? The rule is that all subsequent sequential requests (both retrieval requests, and purely positioning requests using START) will use the *last-established KOR* (in this case either EMPNO or LAST, depending on which statement, (1) or (2), was issued last), but subsequent *random retrieval requests without explicit indication to the contrary* revert to the *(default) prime-key* as the KOR, even though an alt-key may have been the last-established KOR (as here). However, if a subsequent request (retrieval or positioning)—sequential or random—does have explicit indication to the contrary, in the form of a KEY clause, then whatever key is referred to (prime or some alt-key) becomes established as the (new) KOR.

To further appreciate how this works, consider the following four statements:

```
(3a) START ... KEY IS EQUAL TO SSN
(3b) READ  ... NEXT
(3c) READ  ... NEXT
(3d) READ  ... KEY IS LAST
```

Assume that the program has issued, in that sequence, the statements (3a), (3b), and (3c). The SSN prime-key is made the KOR by (3a); SSN would be the KOR by default in any case. The sequential READ of (3b) uses the SSN as the KOR and sets the CRP/FPI to whatever record matches the key currently stored in the SSN field; no record is retrieved, as the START statement simply establishes positioning. The target record is then retrieved by the sequential READ of (3b). Then (3c), using the same KOR—SSN (since sequential retrieval preserves the last established KOR)—retrieves the next record in ascending SSN key order. Two records have been retrieved by prime-key. However, statement (3d) retrieves, randomly, the record that matches the alt-key currently stored in the EMPNO field, because it carries an explicit indication of switching to AIX processing.

Now assume that statement (3d) was the last I/O statement issued, establishing the LAST alt-key field as the KOR. Let's consider the effects of the following statements.

```
(4a) READ  ... NEXT ...
(4b) READ  ...
(4c) START ...
(4d) START ... KEY IS EQUAL TO SSN
(4e) READ  ... KEY IS LAST
(4e) START ... KEY IS EQUAL TO EMPNO
(4f) READ  ... NEXT
```

Statement (4a) retrieves the next record in ascending order of the LAST alt-key field. However, (4b) is a random retrieval request—under dynamic access, READ..., and READ... NEXT, are random and sequential verbs, respectively (in sequential access mode, both are strictly sequential requests)—and will fetch a record *by prime-key*

(SSN), despite the fact that the last established KOR (established by statement (3d)) was the LAST alt-key field. This is so because *KOR is binding only on subsequent sequential retrieval requests, not on random retrievals*. Since the READ of (4b) does not carry an explicit indication to the contrary, it defaults to the prime-key, and hence fetches the next record in ascending SSN order. Furthermore, this random retrieval *does not* reset the KOR to the prime-key field; it merely uses the prime-key field, but leaves the KOR wholly unaffected; KOR was established as, and still is (after (4b) is executed), the LAST alt-key field. Statement (4c), a START without a KEY clause, also defaults to the prime-key field as the field of retrieval (the absent KEY clause defaults to the prime-key field). However, as a sequential positioning statement, this statement *does* reset the KOR to the prime-key field. Statement (4d) would have precisely the same effect as (4c), since it carries an explicit indication to that effect. Statement (4e) explicitly *uses* the LAST alt-key field as the field of retrieval (fetching the next record in ascending LAST field order), but again *does not reset the KOR* to LAST: random retrievals do not affect the KOR, so the prime-key field is still the KOR (last established by (4d)). However, statement (4e) both switches to the EMPNO alt-key field as the key of retrieval (it carries this explicit indication in its KEY clause), *and resets the KOR to the EMPNO alt-key field*: the START is a sequential positioning statement that affects KOR, although it does not retrieve any record whatever. Finally, since KOR is binding on subsequent sequential requests, statement (4f) uses the previously established EMPNO alt-key field as the KOR, and hence retrieves the next record in ascending EMPNO order.

Processing an AIX WITH DUPLICATES.   IN COBOL, processing by prime-key (using a KSDS base cluster) is simply accomplished by using the RECORD KEY clause which defines the prime-key field. I/O statements are then used to make implicit reference (no KEY clause on the verb), or explicit reference (by virtue of a KEY clause specifying the prime-key field), to the prime-key. AIX processing of an AIX marked UNIQUEKEY (on the DEF AIX command) is accomplished by using the ALTERNATE RECORD KEY clause (*without* the WITH DUPLICATES option), and then using I/O statements making reference (implicit or explicit) to the alt-key field; remember that the KOR can be manipulated by sequential input requests to switch to an alt-key as the KOR, so that subsequent sequential requests may, *implicitly*, process by an established AIX.

The question is, what of processing a nonunique-key AIX (one established by a DEF AIX command with the NONUNIQUEKEY option; in COBOL: ALTERNATE RECORD KEY. . . WITH DUPLICATES)? A program may need to retrieve all records with a particular alt-key value (all the 'Lee' records, for example, when using LAST, a nonunique-key AIX). There are two related problems here: (1) how to determine if there is more than one base cluster record with the target alt-key; and (2) how to determine when all of the records with that target alt-key have been retrieved.

The most reliable way to make both of these determinations is to use the file status code, loaded into the two byte alphanumeric field named in the FILE STATUS IS. . . clause of the SELECT statement; we will refer to this code as the FS1 for, as we will see below, the new COBOL language (VS COBOL II) makes available a second file status code field, to be known as FS2. (As with non-VSAM I/O, it is generally recommended that the file status be tested after each I/O statement, including OPEN and CLOSE). The solution for problem (1) lies in the fact that for both retrieval (sequential or random READ) and positioning requests (START) issued against a NONUNIQUEKEY AIX, an FS1 code of '02' is returned if and only if there is, *in addition to the record fetched by the READ or pointed by the START*, at least one more record with the same target alt-key value. This is a nonerror (but nonzero) FS1 condition, in that it is expected that at least some of the alt-keys in such an AIX are nonunique (this is sometimes referred to as a nonerror duplicate key condition). Regardless of how the record was fetched, or the position established, the entire batch of records sharing the same alt-key value can subsequently only be retrieved by issuing additional *sequential* READs.

The solution for the second problem identified above (how to determine when all records sharing the same alt-key have been retrieved) hinges on the fact that for any retrieval request, an FS1 code of '00' is returned if and only if there are no remaining records with the target alt-key value; that is, when the final record with that alt-key value has been retrieved. Thus, to retrieve the set of all records (from the base cluster, but through an AIX built over the base) with some particular target alt-key value, successive sequential READs are issued as long as '02' is returned in FS1, until an '00' FS1 value is returned, indicating that the last record with the target alt-key has been retrieved.

Note that a READ (sequential or random) against some target alt-key value which returns an FS1 of '00' immediately indicates that there was one and only one record with that target value (and it is obviously the last such record). The most common program coding is to issue a positioning START against the target alt-key value and then issue a cycle of sequential READs while FS1 evaluates to '02' until an '00' FS1 value is encountered, but an initial sequential or random READ will do as well. Observe, however, that the START will, if successful, return '00' as the FS1 value, and this does *not* indicate whether there is more than one record with the target alt-key value: it simply indicates (if successful) that there is at least one record with that alt-key value, and establishes positioning to that record (without retrieving it); for retrieval, only the READ itself returns the '02' FS1 value when a nonerror duplicate key condition is encountered.

Finally, note that for output requests WRITE and REWRITE against a NONUNIQUEKEY AIX, a '02' FS1 value is also returned whenever a record has been added with an alt-key value for which there is already at least one record with that same alt-key value in the file (a KSDS). Clearly, this is also a nonerror (but nonzero) FS1 duplicate key condition. An *error duplicate key condition* is signified by an FS1 '22' value; this will occur whenever duplicate keys, whether prime or alternate, are disallowed for the file. Two situations may raise this error condition: (1) if a WRITE/REWRITE for a KSDS attempts to add a record with a duplicate prime-key (the prime-key field of a KSDS must be unique), and (2) if a WRITE/ REWRITE for a KSDS, but issued against some UNIQUEKEY AIX, attempts to add a record with a duplicate alt-key field.

14.1.7   FILE STATUS Clause

We will defer further discussion of this clause until later in this chapter, when the topic of VSAM error detection is taken up.

14.2   DATA DIVISION: FD ENTRY

The FD entry for a VSAM file follows three simple requirements:

1. there is one and only one required clause: LABEL RECORD(S)...; it is irrelevant what is coded here—STANDARD or OMITTED—as the clause, although required, is treated as comment for VSAM files.
2. the RECORDING MODE clause (an IBM 'extension') is invalid for VSAM files (it may be coded only for QSAM files).
3. all other clauses (BLOCK CONTAINS, RECORD CONTAINS, etc.) are optional and, if coded, are treated as comment.

14.3   PROCEDURE DIVISION

In this section, we will examine the VSAM aspects of the I/O verbs used in the PROCEDURE DIVISION.

14.3.1   OPEN, CLOSE, WRITE, REWRITE Statements

These are essentially the same as for non-VSAM files, with the following minor differences:

OPEN/CLOSE.

1. OPEN EXTEND is supported for KSDS and ESDS, but not RRDS files.
2. For both OPEN and CLOSE against VSAM files, no tape options are permissible, since VSAM files are solely DASD (thus UNIT, REEL, REVERSED, and NO REWIND options are invalid).
3. *For VS COBOL II only*:
   For OPEN, the DISP, LEAVE, and REREAD options are invalid; for CLOSE, the following options may be coded *as comments* for *sequential* I/O only: DISP, FOR REMOVAL, POSITIONAL (it is recommended that these *not* be coded, even as comments, to avoid confusion).

WRITE.

1. For ESDS files, *no* options (BEFORE/AFTER ADVANCING, AT END-OF-PAGE, INVALID-KEY) whatever are permitted on the WRITE statement (the form is simply WRITE...FROM...).
2. For KSDS and RRDS files, the only allowable option on the WRITE statement is INVALID KEY.

14.3.2 READ Statement

Two major features exist for the READ statement when issued against VSAM files.

1. The NEXT option is supported, and takes the form:

   ```
   READ file-name NEXT RECORD. . .
   ```

   effecting a sequential retrieval of the immediately subsequent record. For a KSDS, NEXT is optional in sequential access mode, invalid in random access mode, and *required* in dynamic access mode (on a sequential READ). For an ESDS, NEXT is always *invalid*. For an RRDS in sequential mode, NEXT is required (unlike the sequential mode of a KSDS where NEXT is optional).
2. For random processing in random access mode, and for random retrieval in dynamic access mode, the READ supports the KEY option, which takes the following form:

   ```
   READ file-name RECORD. . .
       KEY IS ‹KOR›
   ```

   where the clause identifies the Key of Reference for that request, which may be either the prime-key field of a KSDS (RECORD KEY), the RRN field of an RRDS (RELATIVE KEY), or any alt-key field (ALTERNATE RECORD KEY) for a KSDS with one or more AIXs built over it. (The use of the KEY clause on a READ has been discussed earlier in this chapter, particularly in our treatment of the Key of Reference in Subsection 14.1.6.)

14.3.3 START Statement

There are two points to note about the START statement when issued against VSAM files.

1. In addition to INVALID KEY, the START supports a KEY clause, of the form:

   ```
   START ... KEY IS ‹relational operator› ...
   ```

   where the relational operator may be: EQUAL (TO) or '=,' GREATER (THAN) or '>,' or NOT LESS (THAN) or 'not <.' (For non-VSAM files, the implied operator was restricted to equality; no KEY clause (except INVALID KEY) was supported.) The effect of the KEY clause is to position the CRK/FPI to whatever record contains the key (prime-key, alt-key, or relative (RRN) key) that satisfies the comparison. The use of START. . . KEY has already been discussed above (see especially Subsections 14.1.4 and 14.1.6).

2. The USING option of the START statement, which was supported for generic key processing against ISAM files, is not supported for VSAM files. (Generic key processing can be, and typically is, handled without the USING option. Under VS COBOL II, the USING option on the START verb is wholly discontinued.)

14.3.4   DELETE Statement

The DELETE statement is new to VSAM files, and effects a physical (rather than merely logical) deletion, with the space freed and reclaimed for use by other records. It is supported for both KSDS and RRDS files; no record deletion is allowed for an ESDS. There are two critical requirements for using the DELETE statement:

1. The file must be OPENed for I-O (not INPUT, OUTPUT, or EXTEND).
2. In sequential access mode, a prior READ must be issued to retrieve the record to be deleted. In random or dynamic access mode, no prior read is required (the record to be deleted is identified by loading its key into the RECORD/ RELATIVE KEY field).

Remember, finally, that neither the CRP/FPI nor the KOR is affected by the DELETE statement.

14.3.5   VS COBOL II Explicit Scope Terminators

Under the new VS COBOL II, the I/O verbs READ, START, WRITE, REWRITE, and DELETE support associated *explicit scope terminators*: END-READ, END-START, END-WRITE, END-REWRITE, and END-DELETE, respectively. Explicit scope terminators delimit statement scope (the range of application of a statement), functionally replacing the use of the period for that purpose. As they are not a VSAM-only feature, we simply note them here and will not treat them further. (Certain non-I/O statements also have explicit scope terminators associated with them in VS COBOL II; explicit scope terminators are not supported for OS/VS COBOL.)

14.4   VSAM ERROR DETECTION IN COBOL

14.4.1   FILE STATUS Testing for OS/VS COBOL: FS 1

OS/VS COBOL supports the FILE STATUS clause of the SELECT statement for both QSAM and VSAM files, in the form:

```
FILE STATUS IS . . .
```

where a two-byte alphanumeric field is named to contain an error code indicator returned by the system (more precisely, the COBOL/VSAM Interface when VSAM files are involved) to the program after the execution of any I/O statement. Although the programmer may code AT END and INVALID KEY clauses to capture certain (so-called) exceptional conditions, these clauses do not capture all exceptional conditions that may be raised upon execution of an I/O verb. Testing the file status field, which we will call the *FS1* field for OS/VS COBOL, can capture a much larger range of error conditions than the AT END/INVALID KEY clause approach, although FS1, too, does not trap for *all* such conditions. (This defect is essentially remedied for VSAM files in VS COBOL II; see below.) Therefore, it is generally recommended that FS1 be tested, defensively, after every I/O statement (including OPEN and CLOSE). The *IBM VS COBOL for OS/VS* manual gives the FS1 error code values (we have discussed some already, earlier in this chapter; for example, the '02' FS1 code used in NONUNIQUEKEY AIX processing). Testing FS1 after each I/O state- ment is especially critical in that the COBOL/VSAM interface routines (ILBOVOC and ILBOVIO for OS/VS COBOL, and certain IGZEVxx routines for VS COBOL II)) typically intercept most system abend conditions, suppressing what would other- wise yield a clear SCC (system completion code (abend code)) and a program abnormal termination, passing back to the program a VSAM error code, and gener- ally allowing program continuation; the error code is always returned, but it must be explicitly coded for through the FILE STATUS clause. There are only a handful of abends that 'peek through' (U100, U200 and U201, and U303 and U304 for OS/VS COBOL) so the programmer cannot trust that serious, indeed fatal, normally-abending, error conditions will cause any program failure whatever.

The action to be taken is both application-specific and also depends critically on the nature of the error as indicated by the value of the FS1 code. Minimally, a descriptive error message would be written out for any *true error* condition and the program terminated (EOF is an exceptional condition which returns a nonzero FS1, namely '10' on a sequential READ, but is clearly not a true error condition in the general case). In certain cases of severe error indication, the program may be abended in order to produce a dump which could subsequently be analyzed for additional problem determination aid. As many programmers probably already know, one can abend a COBOL program by calling the COBOL library routine 'ILBABN' (its 'primary' or true name), using its alias name 'ILBOABN0' (zero at end), thereby 'snapping' a user abend. The basic form of this CALL would be:

```
CALL 'ILBOABN0' USING USER-ABCODE
```

where USER-ABCODE (or any other suggestive name, in that this is an arbitrary name) is a user-defined WORKING STORAGE halfword binary field (PIC S9(4) Comp) containing an arbitrary user error code; for this to work in both OS/VS COBOL and VS COBOL II without a coding change, '9(4)' should be used: OS/VS COBOL allows a three digit user abend code, while VS COBOL II supports four-digit codes. The user-chosen code ('9999,' or whatever) will then appear as the identifier of the user abend code generated and reported in the system messages ('U9999' if '9999' is chosen) accompanying the 'snapped' systems dump (naturally, the programmer must load the value into the field prior to the CALL, either by a VALUE clause, or by a MOVE (or an INITIALIZE in VS COBOL II) statement. In the XA (extended architecture) environment using VS COBOL II, the CALL should be made dynamic by enabling the compiler option 'DYNAM' (or by coding the CALL not with a literal, but with an identifier containing the eight character library subroutine name), as the ILBOABN0 module has an RMODE(24) program attribute (loaded and run below the 16MB boundary) which would cause loss of XA support for the *calling* program if a static linkage (static CALL) were used. The ILBOABN0 routine is included in both OS/VS COBOL and VS COBOL II subroutine libraries. (Alternately, one may call, in the VS COBOL II environment, the new VS COBOL II library subroutine IGZEABN (true name) which has RMODE(ANY) support and can run above the 16MB boundary, whether statically or dynamically called, but this procedure is undocumented at this time.)

14.4.2   FILE STATUS Testing Under VS COBOL II: FS2

The FS1 testing approach to VSAM problem determination under OS/VS COBOL, although more sophisticated and precise than using AT END and INVALID KEY clauses for exceptional condition testing of I/O statement execution, nonetheless has certain unfortunate weaknesses. First, the FS1 codes do not, as we noted earlier, capture *all* VSAM exceptional conditions. Second, some of the codes lack 'fineness,' to put it mildly: an FS1 value of '90' indicates broadly a 'logic error,' a distinctly unsubtle, and often uselessly vague, condition which may mask a very wide range of distinct, and generally unrelated, VSAM I/O error conditions. For instance, a '90' may be returned when a program attempts to use, for AIX processing, an invalid pointer (one pointing to no base cluster record, due to failure of synchrony between the base cluster and the AIX); however, in another instance a '90' may be returned upon a program attempt to DELETE a record from an ESDS (no record deletion allowed). As most such 'logic errors' are due to serious programming errors, the programmer is given no way to discriminate the very different possible causes of such errors.

Ideally, it would be invaluable if, in such cases, there were available another testable field that would differentiate between these two, and more generally between any distinct, possible causes. There *is* such a field, previously available only to Assembler VSAM programmers or programmers with internals-level knowledge of VSAM control block structure and chaining, as for example reported in an dump. It is known as the *FDBK* (feedback) field, found in the VSAM RPL (Request Parameter List) control block. If, when FS1 is '90,' the FDBK field contains a hex '90' (X'90'), or decimal 144, then the cause was an invalid AIX pointer, but if, instead, the FDBK field were to contain an X'50' (decimal 80), then the cause is an invalid attempt to erase a record from an ESDS. FS1 makes no discrimination, but FDBK resolves the ambiguities with almost 'surgical' precision. In addition, there are even other error code fields in other VSAM control blocks (like the ACB), as well as register contents (register 15), which may provide additional problem determination assistance.

VS COBOL II remedies these defects of FS1 by providing a *second* and richer file status field, known generally as FS2, which captures an extraordinarily large range of VSAM I/O-related errors (virtually all detectable ones possible, 265 distinct conditions at last count). In VS COBOL II one codes:

```
FILE STATUS IS fs1 fs2
```

Where fs1 is the name of the FS1 error code field (user-defined) and fs2 is the (user-defined) name of the new FS2 error code field available with the new compiler. There are several points that must be noted about this new FS2 field.

First, it is a six-byte field (FS1 is two bytes in length), made up of three subfields, each a binary halfword field (two bytes), and may be defined as follows:

```
01 FS2-CODE.
    05  VSAM-RETCODE     PIC 99  COMP.
    05  VSAM-AIXCODE     PIC  9  COMP.
    05  VSAM-FDBK        PIC 999 COMP.
```

Second, it is codable only if FS1 has also been coded. Third, FS2 is *unreliable* for VSAM error detection if FS1 is '00' (successful execution of an I/O statement). Fourth, the last two subfields of FS2 (we have named then VSAM-AIXCODE and VSAM-FDBK) are also *unreliable* if the first subfield (VSAM-RETCODE) is '00.' Therefore, the values of FS2 should never be tested unconditionally, but only conditionally to reflect these facts.

Now let us consider the interpretation of these three subfields of the new FS2 (remember, available only under VS COBOL II). The first subfield, VSAM-RETCODE above, contains the contents of register 15, which broadly indicates success ('0') or failure of the I/O request ('8' equals a logic error, '12' equals a physical error; a '4' may occur only under the rare circumstance of asynchronous processing in COBOL). The second subfield, VSAM-AIXCODE above, contains the value of field within the VSAM RPL control block known as the *component code field* (*RPLCMPON*) which contains indication of the success or failure of KSDS processing when at least one AIX is involved. There are six possible values, '0' through '5,' with the even ones signifying success ('0,' '2,' or '4'), the odd ones ('1,' '3,' or '5') signifying a possible error. (Consult *VSAM Administration: Macro Instruction Reference* for more precise interpretations).

Finally, the last subfield, VSAM-FDBK above, is the richest and, as our name suggests, reflects the contents of the FDBK field (discussed earlier in this section) of the RPL; this field may assume 256 possible values ('0' through '255') indicating very precisely the cause of the I/O error detected. We have already illustrated its use in connection with refining the '90' logic error code of FS1. This is invaluable feedback (pun intentional) on VSAM processing errors, and can pinpoint a problem and its specific cause very rapidly and neatly. However, there is some sobering bad news concerning FS2, especially the feedback code subfield: IBM has chosen not to document the values and interpretation of FS2 codes anywhere in the VS COBOL II literature, and the reader is referred instead to the technical publication *VSAM Administration: Macro Instruction Reference* (Chapter 2). This is unfortunate, and doubly so in that the interpretations are Assembler-oriented, not COBOL-oriented (the publication is for VSAM Assembler programmers). There are two possible remedies to this: (1) a (systems) programmer with both Assembler and VS COBOL II knowledge may translate the most useful of these codes (this will vary from installation to installation) and provide documentation as to their interpretation *in COBOL terms* (or two programmers, with Assembler and VS COBOL II knowledge, respectively, may cooperate on this task jointly); and/or (2) a general VSAM error routine may be coded in VS COBOL II which may be passed either the whole of FS2, or any one or more of its subfields individually, with this routine providing, as a general service, the correct interpretation of the most useful of the code values (in VS COBOL II, such a routine would be implemented as a *reentrant* subprogram, preferably loaded into the Extended Link Pack Area (ELPA) of the MVS/XA address space, callable by any system user, and would consist of one massive EVALUATE case structure with WHEN clauses for each of the distinct codes to be captured, with appropriate explanatory messages written out). The interested reader can consult the publication referred to above, which gives the interpretations of the many code values of the FS2 binary subfields. The availability of FS2 is an invaluable aspect of VS COBOL II, but obviously entails some considerable work for exploiting the facility fully; one will find, however, the effort richly rewarding for VS COBOL II VSAM error testing and debugging. (IBM's sample programs of VS COBOL II, in its *VS COBOL II Application Programming: Sample Programs*, merely display the values of the three FS2 subfields, without interpretation, neatly but unfortunately sidestepping the problem.)

14.5 A NOTE ON MASS SEQUENTIAL (RECORD) INSERTION (MSI)

Whenever one is confronted with the need for *Mass Sequential Insertion* (*MSI*) of records into a VSAM file, with all of the records belonging, by virtue of key values, between two existing adjacent records (records with keys of 5, 7, and 9 to be inserted between two existing adjacent records with keys of 3 and 12, say, to take a simple artificial case), then the best performance may be obtained by meeting the following processing requirements:

1. the keys should be presented (possibly by presorting) in an ascending order of keys;
2. ACCESS MODE IS DYNAMIC;
3. all insertion is performed by WRITE statements *without prior READS* (after the program has been put into sequential submode of dynamic access);

VSAM will perform the insertions while remaining in sequential mode, effecting an insert-point CI-split (rather than a midpoint CI-split, as done in random mode) and this will yield performance benefits for reasons we have already detailed in an earlier discussion of MSI (the reader may wish to briefly review Subsection 10.5.1). Wherever possible, MSI should be handled in this fashion for optimal performance. (We take up the performance aspect of this issue again briefly in Chapter 18, on performance.)

14.6   JCL FOR COBOL VSAM PROCESSING

The JCL for VSAM files processed by COBOL programs is handled precisely the same as for any VSAM JCL coding (already detailed earlier in the text), with the one exception of the ddname for paths OPENed in a COBOL program for AIX processing which is documented fully in Section 13.9 of the text (the reader may wish to briefly review that discussion at this point).

15

BACKUP AND RECOVERY

15.1 ISSUES OF BACKUP AND RECOVERY IN VSAM

Many, if not all, of the VSAM resources of an installation are often of vital importance to both that installation's technical community, as well as its end-user community; so very much of the critical activity an installation is involved in depends on the availability and integrity of its VSAM resources: data sets, catalogs, AIXs, and other VSAM objects. Therefore, it is especially important for the installation to design a carefully thought-out and comprehensive *backup and recovery scheme*, as it's often called, which has been tested and found to be both effective and reliable in both testing and production environments. This is an extraordinarily complex undertaking and, typically, each installation designs a scheme that is highly customized to its own unique systems environment. A detailed treatment of such a comprehensive scheme is far beyond the scope of this text, but this chapter will more modestly give the reader an understanding of what's involved, and what the appropriate (range of) tools are for assuring a fairly high degree of effective mechanisms for backup and recovery.

A backup and recovery scheme attempts to address two general classes of problems affecting VSAM resources, which will be addressed in the following two subsections.

15.1.1 Failure-of-Synchronization

Information concerning a VSAM data set is stored in several distinct locations: in a VSAM catalog (in the form of catalog entries for each component), on the physical volume (in the form of VTOC DSCB entries), in the data set components themselves (for example, in the form of CIDF and RDF fields of the CIs of the data set), and in transient VSAM control blocks in virtual storage (the ACB and the RPL, among many others). The data set information stored in these various locations may not, however, always be identical, for a variety of reasons: system or subsystem (CICS, for example) failure, DASD damage, program defects, etc.; this condition is known as *failure-of-synchronization*, or less formally as simply an 'out-of-sync' condition. It is often not possible to easily remedy severe out-of-sync conditions completely, or even partially in certain cases, without highly sophisticated technical tools (assuming that one is even aware of the out-of-sync condition), but for a certain limited and well-defined synchronization problems, VSAM makes available an easy-to-use solution in the form of the AMS VERIFY command (which is covered later in this chapter); the limited and particular *resynchronization* effected by the VERIFY command can be viewed as a form of specialized recovery, in which only certain accurate information about a data set is regained, rather than the entire data set itself.

A final point to observe here is that, as we will see later in this chapter, the act of backup may itself, unintentionally, introduce an out-of-sync condition, although the proper choice of recovery tools may avoid or minimize this possibility.

15.1.2   Data Corruption/Loss

A VSAM resource, like any other operating system resource, whether it be a catalog or a data set (cluster, AIX, etc.), is subject to corruption, damage, or data loss from an alarmingly wide range of adverse circumstances. Indeed, VSAM resources—as opposed to strictly batch OS files—are especially susceptible to corruption/loss, as they are typically shared by a large number of concurrent users in both batch and online environments: so, for example, a 'CICS' VSAM file is actually a batch (say, MVS) VSAM data set which is being shared across the batch (including interactive, such as TSO/E) and online domains, and hence adverse events in either of these domains may lead to data corruption/loss of the shared resource. Thus, it is imperative to implement scheduled backup procedures and—in the event of partial (or whole, more rarely but not impossibly) data corruption or loss—recovery schemes, as well as special disaster contingency schemes for unscheduled backup and recovery. Now let's turn to some of the tools available for VSAM backup and recovery.

15.2   DATA SET BACKUP AND RECOVERY

There are many facilities available in a system that provide some degree of backup and recovery; VSAM itself provides some facilities, and others are non-VSAM, but can be used to assist in the backup and recovery of any data sets, including VSAM ones. Below, we will discuss some of these facilities, starting with a particularly important VSAM facility which addresses the problem of the failure-of-synchronization (out-of-sync) condition.

15.2.1   Failure-of-Synchronization: The VERIFY Command

The reader might recall that we discussed earlier in the text (Chapter 12) the problem of data integrity as it related to the determination of *true end-of-data* (*true-EOD*) for a VSAM file. This determination depended on the *HURBA* (*HIGH-USED-RBA*) field (see especially the discussion in subsection 12.2.2: "Understanding the HI-USED-RBA Field"). VSAM considers the data component HURBA value to point to end of the file's data records, after which all space up to the physical end-of-file (if any) is considered 'recordless,' and thus usable by VSAM as allocated but unoccupied space (VSAM may, and often does, use this space for CA-split activity). As noted in that earlier treatment, there are actually two HURBA fields: one is the *catalog HURBA* field which is part of the catalog entry for the file and is shown in LISTCAT output, the second is part of the ARDB (Address Range Definition Block) VSAM control block and is known as *ARDHRBA*. VSAM routines, during any VSAM processing, track the changing value of the component's HURBA—signifying end-of-data—continuously, updating ARDHRBA anytime that the value changes by any processing activity (record additions, or split activity consequent to such additions) whatsoever against the component.

However, the catalog HURBA field is *not* updated continuously but rather its update is said to be 'event-driven,' in this case the event being the issuance of a CLOSE macro (either explicitly or implicitly) against the file (actually, component, but nothing critical hinges on this, and we will more casually say 'file'). Since the catalog HURBA is only updated at CLOSE time, then if a program performing an update of the file were not to reach CLOSE time successfuly—the VSAM file was being shared by a batch system and CICS concurrently, and the CICS crashes, for example—the catalog HURBA field would not reflect true-EOD: it would, rather, contain EOD information as of the last successful CLOSE, which would be before the update processing began, and hence from this outdated HURBA value VSAM would conclude that the file's data record portion ends earlier than it actually does. This is so even though the other HURBA field—ARDHRBA—would contain a wholly accurate representation of true-EOD. Indeed, VSAM writes the catalog HURBA field value from the ARDHRBA field value, but only at CLOSE time: it is said that VSAM 'snaps HURBA upon CLOSE,' so that if a fatal system event such as an online crash were to prevent a catalog HURBA update, VSAM will know only of a premature EOD since EOD is concluded from the catalog HURBA, not the volatile ARDHRBA. This is an extremely serious misunderstanding which makes the added records unaccessible and, furthermore, subject to possible loss by overwrite whenever VSAM uses the space after the catalog HURBA value pointer: this space is, after all (as far as VSAM is concerned), empty of any data records.

Now, there are several solutions to this out-of-sync condition between the catalog HURBA value and the true-EOD of the file itself, most technically very sophisticated, but one being straightforward, that one being the AMS VERIFY command. This command is typically issued after a VSAM processing program's premature demise before CLOSE time due to an adverse system event, in order to resynchronize the catalog HURBA with true-EOD. VSAM accomplishes this, when instructed to do so by the issuance of the VERIFY command against the file, by exhaustively reading the entire file itself to determine true-EOD and updating the catalog HURBA appropriately.

Before we look at the resynchronization brought about by VERIFY in more detail, let's first look at its basic coding, given immediately below:

```
VERIFY -
    FILE (ddname) ¦ DATASET (entry name)
```

The '¦' indicates a coding parameter choice: either FILE is coded or DATASET is coded, but not both. If FILE is used, then its value is the ddname of the JCL DD statement which points to the file (just DSN and DISP parameters are coded) to be verified. If DATASET is coded, its value is simply the data set name (VSAM entry name) of the file to be verified, and in this case the file is dynamically allocated; since the file must be mounted at the time of VERIFY being issued, it is customary to code DATASET, not FILE, and thus also avoid the need for any DD statement referring to the file. Thus, we might have:

```
VERIFY -
     DATASET (STNTESTV.STNKANT.KSDS02)
```

to verify the STNTESTV.STNKANT.KSDS02 cluster. The VERIFY command can be issued whenever *improper closure* is suspected for a VSAM file, where improper closure results from the failure of a processing program to have successfully CLOSEd the file by virtue of program termination—due to an ABEND in the program itself, or a system failure during program processing—prior to the issuance of the CLOSE macro (explicitly or implicitly), or from (more rarely) failure during CLOSE time itself. A common 'defensive programming' practice in the online domain is to run a series of VERIFYs against all VSAM data sets which may subsequently be accessed by CICS to force (limited) resynchronization prior to any OPEN against the data sets.

We have repeatedly said that VERIFY forces *limited* resynchronization between the data set and its catalog entry values, so let us now see exactly what is resynchronized by VERIFY. First, it is important to distinguish the AMS VERIFY *command* from the VSAM VERIFY *macro instruction*. The AMS VERIFY command causes VSAM to issue three macros against the data set being verified: (1) the OPEN macro, (2) the VERIFY macro, and (3) the CLOSE macro.

The OPEN macro provides access to the data set and it is at this time that VSAM will detect any *output-busy condition*. An output-busy condition occurs when a VSAM component is opened for processing, but VSAM finds that a control bit setting in that component's catalog entry known as the *open-for-output indicator* is already on, indicating that previous processing may have opened the component for output but failed to assure normal closure and hence left the indicator set 'on'; proper closure would normally turn the indicator off before program termination, and hence subsequent programs should find the indicator off at OPEN time. A program that attempts to open a component whose open-for-output indicator is already on will receive an OPEN error, or warning, depending on circumstances of processing, reflecting the output-busy condition. A VERIFY command will, by virtue of its issuance of a CLOSE macro, turn the indicator off so that the output-busy condition is not raised for subsequent programs.

Bear in mind, however, that the output-busy condition is not always reflective of improper closure: in a multisystem environment a VSAM data set that is shared cross-system may raise this condition to users of the data set on one system whenever the data set is actually opened for output at that time by one or more users of the data set on the other system(s). This must be planned for by careful implementation of data integrity facilities. The precise techniques for doing this are far beyond the scope of this text, but suffice it to say here that the most comprehensive solution to problems of cross-system data integrity involves implementation of an advanced

MVS facility known as *Global Resource Serialization (GRS)*; although available now as a standard facility of MVS systems, it is not automatically enabled, but must be implemented by installation systems staff. It is strongly recommended that GRS always be implemented on an MVS system for the highest degree of cross-system data integrity of VSAM data sets (including those shared by online systems).

In addition to removing the output-busy condition, the CLOSE macro part of the AMS VERIFY command also resynchronizes the system-timestamp values of the data and index components of a KSDS if these fail to match due to previous processing activity against one component without concurrent processing of the other component. Now let's turn to the VERIFY macro part of the VERIFY command.

The VERIFY macro's primary function is to verify the validity (accuracy) of certain critical VSAM control block fields and, in the event of invalid values being detected, to update the fields accordingly. The single most important field that the VERIFY macro addresses in this way is the HURBA field, which is supposed to reflect true-EOD for a component. Here is how the VERIFY macro operates (with some simplification to avoid excessive technical detail). VSAM first retrieves the value of the *catalog HURBA* field and begins a sequential read of the component from the point determined by this RBA value (the RBA offset of some CI considered by the catalog to be EOD) until it detects SEOF (software-end-of-file), a special setting of the CIDF with all binary zeroes (see our previous discussion of SEOF in Section 8.8 of the text). This is done to determine the true-EOD by physical inspection of all records in the component. Note that VSAM executes the VERIFY macro in an optimal fashion by starting, not at the beginning of the component, but from where the catalog indicates EOD to be at last recording of this value. One might argue that this value is exactly what we are trying to verify, and hence may be incorrect, so why trust it as a starting point. But, as we noted in an earlier discussion (see "A Final Technical Note on HURBA" in Subsection 12.2.2), HURBA points to the last byte of the *last-ever-used-CI*, and so the true-EOD of the component cannot be *less than* the last recorded HURBA; if the catalog HURBA is in error at all, it can only be that the true-EOD is *greater than* the last recorded catalog HURBA value.

VSAM then sets the value of the ARDHRBA control block field—*not* the catalog HURBA field—to correspond to this determined true-EOD value. If and only if this ARDHRBA value reflecting the true-EOD is higher than the catalog HURBA value (it cannot be less, as we just explained)—meaning that the catalog HURBA is not an accurate representation of true-EOD—then VSAM will, *at CLOSE time* of the VERIFY *command*, not as part of the VERIFY *macro*, update the catalog HURBA to the value of ARDHRBA. Note that the VERIFY macro part of the AMS VERIFY command only determines the true-EOD value and sets ARDHRBA to it; the CLOSE macro part of the command actually effects the 'snapping' of this value—if necessary—to the catalog HURBA field; this is so because the catalog HURBA field is updatable only at CLOSE time, regardless of whether it is a program CLOSE or a CLOSE issued by VSAM as part of the AMS VERIFY command. Therefore, at completion of the entire AMS VERIFY command, the catalog is assured to reflect the true-EOD in its value of the catalog HURBA field.

A final technical note on VERIFY. The VERIFY macro of the AMS VERIFY command also updates certain other control block field information if the catalog fields corresponding to this information are found to be incorrect when the to-be-verified data set is a KSDS: (1) the *high-key-RBA (HKRBA)*, (2) the *high-level-RBA (HLRBA)*, and (3) the *number-of-index-levels (NIL)*; HKRBA is relevant to the data component of a KSDS, while HLRBA and NIL pertain to the index component only. The high-key-RBA (HKRBA) value is the first byte of the CI containing the record with the highest key of all data records of the data set. This value is maintained continuously in the ARDB, in the field *ARDHKRBA*, from which the *catalog HKRBA* is snapped at CLOSE time; only if the KSDS was defined as a *keyrange* data set, however, would the catalog HKRBA value be available in LISTCAT output, as the *HIGH-KEY-RBA* field of the VOLUMES group.

The high-level-RBA (HLRBA) value is the first byte of the single CI *in the index component* which is the CI at the highest level of the index, always read first by VSAM in any vertical index search. This value is maintained continuously by VSAM in the control block known as the *AMDSB (Access Method Data Statistics Block)*, in the field *AMDHLRBA*, from which a part of the catalog field known as *AMDSBCAT* is snapped—*not* just at CLOSE time—but whenever the value changes; it is available as the *HI-LEVEL-RBA* field of the STATISTICS group.

The number-of-index-levels (NIL) value specifies the total number of index levels, including the sequence set level, of the index component of a KSDS. This value is maintained continuously by VSAM in the AMDSB control block, in the field *AMDNIL*, from which a part of the catalog AMDSBCAT is snapped—not just at CLOSE time—but whenever the value changes; it is available as the *LEVELS* field of STATISTICS group in LISTCAT output.

Thus the data and index component HURBA catalog values, the HKRBA value, the HLRBA value, and the NIL value, are all updated by the AMS VERIFY command, which also turns off the open-for-output indicator if an output-busy condition is detected, and resynchronizes the data and index component system-timestamp values. This is a substantial amount of resynchronization between the facts of the data set and its catalog information, but—it is very important to note—it is not *complete resynchronization*: all other catalog entry fields (dozens and dozens of them) are wholly unaffected by the VERIFY command, a not-widely-appreciated fact; so, for instance, the catalog entry for a data component also maintains a REC-TOTAL field (total number of records in the component), but if this field value is incorrect—as it would be after improper closure for any reason—this is *not* updated to a correct value by VERIFY and one could not rely on this value thereafter. It is for this reason that we indicated that VERIFY provides *limited resynchronization* facilities.

15.2.2 Creating Backup Copies: The REPRO Command

An appealingly simple way to backup, and later restore, a VSAM data set—also available for a catalog—is to use the AMS command REPRO. As we have already seen earlier in the text (see Subsections 6.3.3, 9.2.2, and especially 9.3.1), REPRO can be used to copy any VSAM (and certain non-VSAM) data sets into a sequentially organized output or 'target' data set, usually in the form of a sequential tape data set. This achieves the first goal of a backup scheme—simply having a backup copy—and allows for the second goal to be achieved if needed, namely the recovery of the original 'source' data set in the event of corruption or damage, or indeed for any purpose that seeks the assurance of an additional copy of a data set. Such recovery can be effected by (1) deleting the source data set, (2) redefining the (new) data set through the AMS DEFINE command, generally with the same name and attributes, and finally (3) loading the newly defined data set—it is empty up to this point—with the records of the backup copy that was previously created. After these three steps, we say that we have *rebuilt* or *restored* the original data set from its backup copy. There are, however, several points to note concerning REPRO used for backup and recovery in this fashion.

First, in reference to the third step outlined above, the loading—sometimes loosely referred to as 'reloading'—of the newly defined data set from the backup copy created by a still earlier issuance of the REPRO command against the original source data set, it is important to appreciate that the REPRO command triggers *automatic data set reorganization*, something inherent in the REPRO operation itself. What this automatic reorganization entails was first discussed in our earlier treatment of the CI-split process (Section 10.2) where we pointed out that any split activity against a data set can leave the *physical CI order*, their actual physically successive sequence in the data set, different than their *logical CI sequence*, their sequence when arranged in ascending key, as they are when the records of the data component are first loaded. As noted, this can compromise processing performance against the data set. Since the keys, as encountered in reading the cluster in strict physical sequence of CI occurrence, are no longer strictly ascending, VSAM must do extra out-of-sequence fetching of the CIs, by following chains of pointers, in order to return the records by ascending key as required for sequential read operations against the data set; the greater the split activity against a VSAM data set, the more and more such 'disorder' of CI key sequence will result, with processing time increasing reflexively. The automatic reorganization of the REPRO operation consists of VSAM's rearranging of the physical CI order to precisely match the logical CI order, a condition the data set is assured to have only immediately post-load time, or (as here) after a REPRO reorganization. This may be an attractive feature of REPRO when used for backup and recovery purposes, in that subsequent performance of processing of the data set in sequential mode would improve. Freespace percentages are also 'reset' back to their original distributions at load time. Therefore, with REPRO VSAM really effects a data set *rebuild*.

A second point to note is that, regardless of the cluster type of the original source data set being backed up, the target (output) data set is generally a sequential file, *when using REPRO for backup and recovery purposes*. In particular, the index of a KSDS is in this case not copied or processed in any way by the REPRO operation, so that the backup copy is not processable as a KSDS in its 'unloaded' form; it must be reloaded into a predefined empty cluster by another REPRO operation, which will at that time build the index anew.

A third point to be aware of when using REPRO for backup and recovery purposes is that data set/catalog synchronization is *not* assured through REPRO. This is so because only the data records are copied to the backup data set, not the catalog entries associated with that data set. Changes to the original source file will be reflected in *that* file's catalog entry, but neither are reflected in any way in the *backup copy of the file* created by REPRO. Furthermore, future processing changes against the original file, but not the backup, causes further failure-of-synchronization. However, if care is taken by the user to reflect all changes to the original and backup, either at the same time, or to *journal* (capture and write to some control file) all changes to the original made after the backup was created, and then apply those changes to the backup copy at regular intervals, out-of-sync conditions can often be avoided between source and backup data sets. Note also that if a tape backup of a KSDS is made using REPRO, then it is *not* possible to apply changes made to the original file also to the backup: the original is a KSDS with an index component, but the 'unloaded' backup copy on tape is a sequential data set with no index structure at all. The problem of data set/catalog out-of-sync conditions still remains, however, since the files are distinct objects, but the user can always follow the earlier outlined procedure to rebuild the original data set from the backup copy after assuring that all post-backup-time changes to the source are applied to the backup. Once this is done, however, there is one data set only (and no problem of data set/catalog synchronization), since we have done a *data set restoration*, or more simply a *restore*, and we would have to again at some point back up *this* newly restored data set, and so on.

15.2.3 The EXPORT and IMPORT Commands

VSAM provides two AMS commands particularly designed for backup and recovery purposes, EXPORT and IMPORT. The original design objective of the AMS EXPORT/IMPORT facility was to provide *cross-system portability* of VSAM files (including catalogs): a file is first copied—*exported*—to a demountable volume, often tape (the demountable 3330 disk is not encountered frequently these days), and then transported to and installed on—*imported into*—another system (on another processor). A program, for instance, may at some point have to be 'moved into production': the program must be 'shipped' or moved from a test system into a production system, often along with one or more files that it requires for proper execution; the files can be exported out of the test system and into the production system to be available to the program which is to be run in production. The AMS EXPORT/IMPORT commands are often used for this purpose.

EXPORT/IMPORT can also be used for backup and recovery by simply exporting a file onto some volume, which for this purpose need not be demountable, and then importing the exported copy back into the same system, without 'transporting' the file anywhere. An important advantage of this facility over the use of REPRO for backup and recovery is that when a file is exported, the EXPORT operation copies both the file and its critical catalog information onto the exported copy, which is organized in a special format with key catalog information preceding the data set's contents. This makes the exported file unprocessable, but allows the IMPORT command to provide *automatic redefinition and reload*: the IMPORT operation involves both the reloading of the file's contents and the automatic definition of the new (imported) file through the replacement of the original catalog entries with those stored on the exported copy. Note that, unlike a REPRO backup scenario, the user need not issue AMS commands to delete the original file, then DEFINE a new file into which the contents of the backup copy are reloaded; this delete-redefinition sequence is unnecessary, as the import operation incorporates these operations. In addition, another real advantage of this type of backup and recovery is assured data set/catalog synchronization, as the file and its catalog information—strictly, most critical entries, not all—are copied and processed together as a unit. Although a REPRO operation is often faster than the use of EXPORT/IMPORT, these advantages— and the ease of use of the commands themselves—makes EXPORT/IMPORT a superior backup and recovery facility. Furthermore, EXPORT/IMPORT causes automatic reorganization of a data set, just as does REPRO. (Note also that IMPORT of the exported copy, which is the backup copy, is needed only for data set restoration/recovery; EXPORT on its own is sufficient for backup copy creation.)

Now let us look at the basic coding of these commands, through two sample codings and our comments on them. Figure 15-1 shows the EXPORT command being used to create an exported copy of the data set FINCAT.MVS003T.INQR0021.

DISCUSSION

4. This DD statement (referenced in the OUTFILE parameter, line 7, by the DDNAME of TPINQR) specifies the file to be created by EXPORT, the exported copy, here a tape data set with standard labels.

```
 1.    // ... JOB ...
 2.    // EXEC PGM=IDCAMS
 3.    //SYSPRINT DD SYSOUT=A
 4.    //TPINQR   DD DSN=FINCAT.MVS003T.INQR0021.TPBACK,
       //              DISP=(NEW,CATLG,DELETE),
       //              UNIT=TAPE,VOL=SER=TPHD01
       //SYSIN DD *
 5.      EXPORT -
 6.        FINCAT.MVS003T.INQR0021 -
 7.             OUTFILE (TPINQR) -
 8.             TEMPORARY -
 9.             INHIBITSOURCE -
10.             NOINHIBITTARGET
11.    /*
```

Figure 15-1. Sample IDCAMS job: EXPORT.

6. This names the source, to-be-exported, file.

7. See the discussion of 4, above.

8. *TEMPORARY/PERMANENT*: This parameter choice determines whether or not the original source file is to be retained or deleted; PERMANENT, which is the default, instructs VSAM to *delete*—oddly enough, it might seem—the source file upon completion of the EXPORT operation, while TEMPORARY instructs VSAM to retain the source file. The catalog entry for the original source file is marked to signify that another copy exists, making the original replaceable. Since we are creating a backup copy, we want the original file to be retained, so typically TEMPO-RARY is coded, as here.

9. *INHIBITSOURCE/NOINHIBITSOURCE*: It is often desirable to disallow changes of any sort, writes and updates, against the original source file at least until the completion of the EXPORT/IMPORT process, otherwise the source may be rendered nonidentical with its exported copy. The specification of the INHIBIT-SOURCE option makes the source file read/only. This restriction can be lifted at any time through the ALTER command, but it is customary to leave the source inhibited until the following IMPORT process succeeds. If, however, the user does not intend to follow the EXPORT command with its IMPORT counterpart, because backup is the only present objective, then NOINHIBITSOURCE would be specified, allowing normal processing to proceed against the original source file. If the source later becomes damaged or corrupted, then the specification would be changed back to INHIBITSOURCE through the ALTER command just before application of the IMPORT command for file restoration, to prevent further corruption of the source until the restore operation replaces it with the backup copy.

10. *INHIBITTARGET/NOINHIBITTARGET*: This parameter choice deter-mines the accessibility of the target file (the exported copy) *after* it has been imported to another, or the same, system. (Remember, the exported copy as such, before being imported, is not processable in any case.) INHIBITTARGET renders that target file read-only, NOINHIBITTARGET, which is the default, allows normal updating of the target file. Which is chosen depends on the user's objective for the EXPORT/IMPORT process: strict backup only, or the restoration, that is, replacement, of the original source file by its exported copy.

Figure 15-2 gives a sample IMPORT command coding, where the file to be imported is the exported copy created in the previous job of Figure 15-1. The example assumes that our objective is to restore the original source file from its exported copy.

DISCUSSION

4. This refers to the exported copy from which we wish to restore the original source file; it was stored as a tape data set.

7. See the discussion of 4, above.

8. This refers to the original source file which the exported copy is to replace. Whenever, as here, the named file already exists and has been marked TEMPORARY,

```
1.    // ... JOB ...
2.    // EXEC PGM=IDCAMS
3.    //SYSPRINT DD SYSOUT=A
4.    //TPINQR   DD DSN=FINCAT.MVS003T.INQR0021.TPBACK,
      //            DISP=(OLD,KEEP,KEEP)
5.    //SYSIN DD *
6.      IMPORT -
7.         INFILE (TPINQR) -
8.         OUTDATASET (FINCAT.MVS003T.INQR0021)
9.    /*
```

Figure 15-2. Sample IDCAMS job: IMPORT.

VSAM will automatically delete the file and then rebuild it, here under the same name, from the exported copy which, the reader will remember, contains all of the catalog information necessary for such redefinition.

The IMPORT command has another useful option not shown in the coding: INTOEMPTY. The INTOEMPTY option is employed when a new existing file, which must be empty, is to be loaded with the contents of the exported copy. This allows some of the attributes of the original source file to be changed so that the restored file may have different attributes from the original source. If this is desirable, then the EXPORT command should specify the PERMANENT option so that VSAM will delete the original source file; this should be followed by a new DEFINE for the empty cluster before the IMPORT is done. (The IMPORT command has an additional option used in this connection, namely OBJECTS which has several subparameters which represent the attributes of the file that are to be changed; only certain attributes are changeable.) The reader interested in effecting this specialized type of processing using EXPORT/IMPORT should consult the appropriate technical publications (*Access Method Services Reference* and the *Catalog Administration Guide*).

One last note before leaving the topic of the EXPORT/IMPORT facility. These commands both have a special form that is used when a user catalog, not a data set, in one system needs to be transported into a different system. The EXPORT DISCONNECT coding is used to delete the user catalog's connector entry from the Master Catalog of the first system; the user catalog can then be physically transported to the second system on which an IMPORT CONNECT command is issued to build a connector entry for the imported catalog in the second system's Master catalog. Note that no copy operation of the catalog is involved at all when using these special commands; aside from naming the catalog involved, no other parameters are coded for these commands.

15.2.4   Volume-Level Backup: DUMP/RESTORE Utilities

Operating systems invariably provide facilities for backing up ('dumping') and, if needed, restoring entire DASD volumes. These facilities are generically referred to as *volume-level DUMP/RESTORE*, as they provide backup and recovery of all of a volume's data sets and its VTOC together in one operation. A DUMP/RESTORE program or product (many non-IBM) can, therefore, be used to take a full-volume copy of any DASD volume containing VSAM data sets or catalogs. Until recently, such a program's main disadvantage for backup and recovery was that it was *un-selective* ('crude,' to some): all data sets on a volume had to be backed up together, with no provision for limiting the operation only to certain data sets. A secondary disadvantage was, again until recently, that necessarily the dumping of an entire volume's contents was relatively time-consuming compared to any *data set-level* backup. Still, periodic volume-level backup is a fundamental fact of life in any installation's data center operations and can provide comprehensive and reliable—and even, as we will see in a moment, 'fine'—backup and recovery on both a scheduled and unscheduled basis.

Three generations of DUMP/RESTORE programs can be differentiated. First-generation products were typified by the IBM special utility programs IBCDMPRS and IEHDASDR, with their DUMP and RESTORE statements in familiar JCL/utility control statement format and invokable as jobs in a batch environment (in the form: // EXEC PGM=IBCDMPRS or // EXEC PGM=IEHDASDR). The disadvantages mentioned above apply mainly to these first-generation programs.

A second generation of DUMP/RESTORE software technology was ushered in by IBM's *DFDSS* (*Data Facility Data Set Services*) and *DFHSM* (*Data Facility Hierarchical Storage Manager*), often known just as *HSM*, both of which provide data set-level, as well as volume-level, backup and recovery facilities, among many other space/storage management facilities. DFDSS is a batch (typically JCL-invoked) product with powerful DUMP and RESTORE commands, while DFHSM is essentially a command-driven special console, or optionally a TSO console facility with many automated operations, including an automatic 'changed-data set' backup (backup of a data set only if changed since last backup was taken) and command-invoked recovery (typical HSM commands for backup and recovery are HBACKDS and HRECOVER).

The third generation premiered with the advent of IBM's *ISMF* (*Interactive Storage Management Facility*). ISMF runs as an interactive menu-driven ISPF (which now stands for Interactive System Productivity Facility, after some previous name changes) TSO application with what IBM calls 'human-engineered' features that maximize storage manager productivity. ISMF is a single, centralized, comprehensive and easy-to-use interactive data/storage management facility which can invoke the functions of DFDSS, DFHSM, and DFP (Data Facility Product, which, as noted earlier in the text, includes the 'new VSAM,' among other products and features) using a common and completely consistent panel-driven interface. Through interactive panels, ISMF automatically builds any DFDSS JCL and control statements, or DFHSM commands, needed for virtually any storage management task or activity in an MVS environment, for VSAM as well as non-VSAM data sets. The disadvantages referred to at the beginning of this section, therefore, do not apply to ISMF, which also is a high-performance product with special optimization under MVS/XA (there is no use, for instance, of the common area storage, and loading in extended storage above the 16M boundary if used with the XA feature of TSO/E). Many discussions of DUMP/RESTORE utilities cite the limitations of these utilities for VSAM backup and recovery, but now with ISMF, optimal, powerful, and very flexible state-of-the-art facilities can be exploited for implementing almost any comprehensive backup and recovery scheme, complementing native VSAM facilities.

15.2.5   SMF Record Reconstruction

IBM's *System Management Facility* (*SMF*), the primary system-auditing (and accounting) part of the MVS (and MVS/XA, and ESA), as part of its normal collection of MVS processing activity information, can be exploited to assist in the task of VSAM backup and recovery. This entails inspection of the various records SMF uses to record classes of system and user events, including VSAM I/O activity. SMF records are classified by record type, and SMF record types are numbered for identification; 10 record types, SMF records numbered 60 through 69, are devoted exclusively to various VSAM data set and catalog activity events, and are an especially rich source of VSAM-related information that may be critical in the detection of synchronization problems related to backup and recovery issues. However, this use of SMF requires a high degree of technical sophistication, and the delicate and painstaking advanced analysis involved is generally, and best, left to specially skilled system programmers and other technical support personnel.

15.2.6   User Journaling

Another tool that may assist in VSAM backup and recovery is that of *user journaling*: maintaining, through user-provided code, a record or 'audit trail' of critical processing activity,—'transactions,' in online parlance—but most especially updates, against any selected data set. The generated *transaction journal* then holds a history of changes to the data set over any selected period of processing activity, and can be used, for example, to apply the journaled changes to a backup copy in order to resynchronize it with the original for any changes posted after the last backup was taken, and to recover lost update information due to an abnormal system event, and/or to restore a corrupted or out-of-date catalog to current level. Such journals can, and often are used, to even recreate a lost or damaged data set. One way to implement this sort of user journaling for VSAM backup and recovery purposes is to code a user exit routine, the VSAM *JRNAD exit*, coded in Assembler, to post a copy of the to-be-updated (including deleted) record to another data set, the *journal*, *before* the update is applied, after which VSAM will attempt to apply the actual update; if successful, fine, but if not, a backup copy of the record prior to the failed operation is available for subsequent recovery. The JRNAD exit is automatically taken by VSAM under a wide variety of processing circumstances, not just record update (for example, for I/O errors and completions) but it is relatively straightforward to customize the exit to specific recovery objectives.

Online and database systems also often provide their own journaling facilities, which can be used for VSAM data sets: CICS, for example, has very powerful journaling support under its Journal Control Program, through the command-level EXEC CICS JOURNAL... and EXEC CICS WAIT JOURNAL... commands, as well as extensive recovery facilities, both of which may, in turn, be further integrated with associated database recovery facilities, as for instance brought by the relational DB2 database family of products.

Although, unfortunately, COBOL in the batch environment provides no user journaling support—unless the user traces in user-provided code key update activity, and this will not capture VSAM-generated operations consequent to update activity, like CI/CA-splits—the provision by a systems programmer or high-level Assembler programmer with strong VSAM skills of a journal exit such as described above, along with the exploitation and implementation of any online and database recovery facilities as may be available, can be an invaluable adjunct to any comprehensive recovery scheme, although these facilities are too often overlooked or poorly understood, and therefore rarely implemented to best advantage.

15.3 RECOVERABLE CATALOGS AND RECOVERABLE DATA SETS

VSAM provides a very powerful recovery mechanism that facilitates the backup and recovery/restoration of VSAM data sets through special AMS commands. The mechanism is exceptionally simple conceptually, and may be referred to as *duplex-recovery*: for maximal assurance of recovery from any adverse systems events, duplex—duplicate—critical VSAM catalog information in two places rather than one, so that the second copy of the information can be used to restore a damaged, lost, or corrupted catalog, by either partially or wholly rebuilding the catalog. This duplex-recovery strategy simply takes the concept of backup of data sets one step further to the concept of the backup of catalog information. In the sections below, we describe the major features and operation of this recovery mechanism; since the commands used are generally restricted to VSAM systems programmers, technical support, and/or data center staff, and are not available routinely to the application programmer, we do not detail the syntax coding (but the interested reader may consult either the publication *Access Method Services Reference*, or, especially, the *Catalog Administration Guide*).

15.3.1 The Concept of Recoverable Catalogs and Data Sets

A *recoverable catalog* is a VSAM catalog for which VSAM automatically duplexes each of the catalog entries it contains into a separate area known as the catalog recovery area (*CRA*), thus maintaining a duplicate copy of all catalog information in one or more such areas outside of the catalog space itself. Any data sets defined in a recoverable catalog are said to be *recoverable data sets*. The skeleton coding below shows how a catalog is marked *recoverable*:

```
DEFINE UCAT -
       .
       .
       .
       RECOVERABLE
```

Note that this is *not* the default, which is NOTRECOVERABLE, and so must be explicitly enabled for any catalog to be made recoverable. The replicated catalog entry for any one data set is stored in the CRA, which is itself stored on the catalog's *owned* volume(s); for a catalog that owns multiple volumes, there is a CRA on each of these volumes, including one on the volume on which the catalog itself resides. The CRA on any particular volume is acquired when VSAM space is first allocated or reserved on that volume, and is typically one cylinder in size, although this is automatically (if necessary) expandable by the OS Direct Access Device Storage Manager (OS DADSM) by an additional 15 cylinders, to a total maximum of 16 cylinders of space.

The basic design objective of recoverable catalogs and their associated CRAs is partial or whole *catalog restoration*: in the event that there is damage, loss, or corruption of either an entire recoverable catalog or some of the catalog entries it contains, the catalog can be partially or wholly rebuilt from the appropriate duplicated catalog entries from the CRAs, thus restoring the catalog to *integral*—current, most accurate, and uncorrupted—condition. Notice that this is a departure from the traditional method of restoring a catalog, which consists of maintaining a backup copy of the catalog and performing recovery from this backup copy whenever needed. The problem with this traditional method is that the original catalog and its backup copy easily become unsynchronized: changes to data sets defined in the catalog after the last backup was taken are not automatically reflected in the backup copy, and when this occurs we say that the backup copy is *back-level*. Thus, user-provided coding must either constantly update the backup copy whenever the catalog is updated, or the back-level copy must periodically be updated from some journal of all updates posted to the catalog since the last backup was taken. VSAM provides no automatic facilities for catalog/backup copy synchronization when the catalog is nonrecoverable, and synchronization becomes solely a user responsibility, a generally unhappy state of affairs given the fast rate of change associated with a VSAM catalog, a *highly volatile* object. The VSAM-provided automatic backup of catalog entries in a recoverable catalog, therefore offers the user an attractive and simple alternative to the traditional approach of catalog recovery. It is very important to observe here, however, that the CRA is structurally different than an actual VSAM catalog, and cannot itself be used as a catalog.

There are several additional points to note here concerning recoverable catalogs and data sets. First, whenever any data set defined in a recoverable catalog—a recoverable data set—is modified in any way that must be reflected in the catalog, the catalog information reflecting these changes is written by VSAM to the proper CRA *before* the information is posted to the catalog itself. Thus, at any time, the CRA represents the most accurate and current catalog information about recoverable data sets. Indeed, if the duplexing operation itself were to be fatally terminated midstream after CRA updating but before catalog updating, leaving the catalog back-level, the catalog could subsequently be updated from the CRA in a separate operation.

Second, there is a trade-off of performance against duplex-recovery: catalog update time is virtually doubled, since an additional I/O operation to a CRA may have to be performed for every I/O to the catalog itself. This must be weighed against the ease and elegance of an automated approach to VSAM recovery. As we will see in Chapter 17, IBM has, in the new VSAM product (not its strict name, but this will do here) discontinued the mechanism of duplex-recovery: there are no recoverable catalogs and data sets, no duplicate I/O, no CRAs; however, although catalog performance is indeed significantly improved, backup and recovery is complicated considerably. This is part of the reason why many installations still retain Enhanced VSAM with its duplex-recovery feature alongside the new VSAM: both have their advantages and disadvantages, and difficult trade-offs.

Third, there is a complexity added when we deal with multivolume data sets, or even with multicomponent data sets whose components reside on separate volumes (as the data and index components of a KSDS may do). Since the recoverable data set itself is not confined to a single volume, the question arises on which of the several volumes is the CRA to be allocated. The answer is twofold: (1) *all* volumes of a multivolume or multicomponent recoverable data set have CRAs allocated on them, but (2) only *one* of these CRAs contains the duplicate *data set catalog entries*, as well as space allocation/extent information, while the others contain only space allocation/extent information in the form of a duplicate *volume record*. The distinguished volume that contains the duplicate data set catalog information *and* volume record information is known as the *recovery volume*. No data set information will be found in the CRAs of the other (nonrecovery) volumes, but only information about space usage by both VSAM space(s) and VSAM data sets on that particular volume; thus the volume record for a multivolume/component data set is duplicated on each volume in each CRA for that volume.

The recovery volume is so important for the following reason: it is a minimal requirement that whenever a recoverable data set is being processed, the recovery volume for that data set *must be mounted*. Hence, one must know which volume will function as the recovery volume for a recoverable data set. The rules are involved, differing for different types of data sets. So, for instance, for a recoverable KSDS whose data and index components reside on different volumes, surprisingly perhaps, it is the volume containing the *index*, not the data component volume, that is the recovery volume for that data set. Again, perhaps surprisingly, for a recoverable AIX data set, the volume on which the base cluster resides is the recovery volume, and if the base cluster is a KSDS with its components on separate volumes, then again the base cluster's index volume will function as the recovery volume for the recoverable

AIX. Still again, a user catalog's recovery volume is the volume on which the Master Catalog resides.

SUGGESTION

Rather than, however, learning the various not-particularly-intuitive rules of determining the recovery volume for any particular type of data set, there is a simpler, less-error-prone approach. For any recoverable data set, a LISTCAT of that data set's catalog entries that includes the *HISTORY* group (and the usual LISTCAT ALL will always include this) will actually show recovery volume information. In the HISTORY group output, there are three fields that are important in this connection: (1) RCVY-VOL, which gives the volume serial number of the recovery volume for that data set, (2) RCVY-DEVT, which gives the recovery volume's device type (in hexadecimal code; see our discussion of 'DEVTYPE' in Subsection 12.2.3 for how to interpret these codes), and (3) RCVY-CI, which gives the CI number of the CI within the recovery volume's CRA, where the duplex catalog information for the data set is stored. By and large, just RCVY-VOL is inspected and this tells the user the recovery volume without using complex rules.

15.3.2   The EXPORTRA and IMPORTRA Commands

We have already discussed in detail the AMS EXPORT and IMPORT commands and their critical use in VSAM backup and recovery. There are two additional AMS commands that are the functional equivalents of EXPORT and IMPORT, but apply to *only* recoverable data sets—data sets defined in recoverable catalogs—namely *EXPORTRA* and *IMPORTRA*, the 'RA' referring to (catalog) recovery area. Like EXPORT, the EXPORTRA command performs backup copy creation of a VSAM data set, and like IMPORT, the IMPORTRA command performs data set restoration from the created exported copy. Furthermore, like EXPORT, the EXPORTRA command copies not only the data set contents, but also copies the catalog information associated with the data set, storing both on the exported backup copy, and, like IMPORT, the IMPORTRA command restores the original source data set from the exported backup copy, using the catalog information to redefine the data set.

However, the critical difference here is that EXPORTRA/IMPORTRA use the catalog information *stored in the CRA* for such backup and recovery purposes, not the information taken from the catalog entries in the catalog itself. We say that EXPORT/IMPORT, therefore, are *catalog-based* backup and recovery facilities, while EXPORTRA/IMPORTRA are *CRA-based* backup and recovery facilities. We further say that CRA-based backup and recovery assures a higher degree of data integrity in that the CRA, being updated *before* the catalog, contains the most up-to-date information about a VSAM data set, more up-to-date than the catalog itself. Note that EXPORT/IMPORT commands can be used against both recoverable and nonrecoverable data sets and catalogs—in the latter case the CRA is not involved in any way—while EXPORTRA/IMPORTRA, and related commands which we will discuss shortly, can only be used with recoverable data sets and catalogs. Another difference between these two pairs of commands is that EXPORTRA/ IMPORTRA can, unlike EXPORT/IMPORT, be used for concurrent backup and recovery of *multiple* data sets.

The CRAs provided with recoverable catalogs can be used for three distinct but related purposes: (1) backup, using the EXPORTRA command, (2) VSAM problem determination involving catalog and data set synchronization, and (3) restoration/ recovery, one type of which is made available through the IMPORTRA command. We have not discussed the second purpose at all in this connection, and have only discussed IMPORTRA command-based restoration, and this is not the only type available when dealing with recoverable catalogs and data sets. We will now complete the discussion, therefore, by looking at two additional CRA-based backup and recovery commands, *LISTCRA* and *RESETCAT*.

15.3.3   The LISTCRA Command

Let's first turn to the second purpose referred to above, namely that of problem determination. Once we use recoverable catalogs, we have two areas in which critical VSAM catalog information for a data set is stored: one, in the catalog itself, and two, in the CRA for that data set. To facilitate early detection of synchronization problems, we can periodically either list and inspect the various CRAs associated with any particular catalog, and this will give us the most current available information about the VSAM data sets defined in that catalog, or we can have VSAM compare the catalog entry for a data set with its CRA entry, searching for mismatches which will signify failure-of-synchronization of some sort. Both these objectives are met by use of the AMS *LISTCRA* command, which is functionally parallel to the AMS LISTCAT command, but rather than listing catalog information taken from the catalog itself, LISTCRA lists catalog information *taken from the CRA*. LISTCRA can list an image of the CRA allocated on any volume associated with (owned by) a recoverable catalog. If we do a LISTCAT for a particular recoverable data set, and also do a LISTCRA for the same data set, then the entries generated should be identical, a mismatch indicating a failure-of-synchronization which we should attempt to repair immediately (how, we will see in a moment).

Of course, such 'visual' inspection is tedious and highly error-prone. Fortunately, we can instruct VSAM to itself perform the comparison of catalog and CRA entries: this is done through the *COMPARE* option on the LISTCRA command (sometimes referred to as the '*LISTCRA COMPARE*' command). LISTCRA COMPARE will cause VSAM to effect the comparison *and* in addition print a listing of any and all mismatches, obviously an invaluable aid to synchronization problem determination, but available only, obviously, with recoverable catalogs (nonrecoverable catalogs, by definition, have no associated CRAs). It is strongly recommended, therefore, that LISTCRA COMPARE operations be regularly scheduled in a recoverable catalog environment as part of any comprehensive backup and recovery scheme.

15.3.4   The RESETCAT Command

But how do we address any mismatches detected by LISTCRA COMPARE? The answer is through the use of another AMS CRA-based backup and recovery command, namely *RESETCAT*. This command instructs VSAM to use the information from a specific volume's CRA to rebuild catalog entries in the recoverable catalog from their more up-to-update CRA entries. It is critical to note in this connection, that we now know *two* distinct ways to restore a recoverable catalog: (1) we can use IMPORTRA to restore the catalog entries from associated CRA entries (having previously used EXPORTRA), or (2) we can use RESETCAT which performs a restoration of catalog entries from CRA entries, *but without any data set copy operation*. That is, EXPORTRA/IMPORTRA, when used for catalog restoration, have an intrinsic data transfer feature to them: the data set(s) involved are copied, along with associated CRA entries, with subsequent recovery being performed from the exported backup copy which includes the CRA entries. But RESETCAT simply replaces catalog entries with their CRA counterparts, when mismatches occur or when it is known or suspected that the catalog entries are damaged or corrupted (or, in the worst case, lost altogether). In sum, therefore, we say that EXPORTRA/IMPORTRA are backup *and* recovery facilities, while RESETCAT is solely a *recovery* facility. If only a relatively few catalog entries require restoration, then RESETCAT might be used, while if a large number of—or all—catalog entries need to be recovered for some reason from the CRAs, then EXPORTRA/IMPORTRA are better suited to the task.

In conclusion, use of EXPORTRA, IMPORTRA, LISTCRA, and RESETCAT commands by skilled VSAM users—but *not* for new VSAM catalogs and data sets, which do not support duplex-recovery mechanisms—with recoverable catalogs and data sets can be an invaluable part of any installation's backup and recovery scheme, and can be complemented by use of any of the other VSAM and non-VSAM facilities discussed earlier in this chapter. Indeed, the most effective backup and recovery schemes would probably exploit all of the facilities covered in a carefully designed and integrated fashion; although complex, this provides extremely comprehensive backup and recovery assurance.

16

DATA SECURITY

16.1 ISSUES OF DATA SECURITY IN VSAM SYSTEMS

VSAM files and catalogs are often vital facilities to a computer system, holding data critical to the operation of an installation: they are the most heavily used batch files, they are extensively used in online systems such as CICS (CICS actually shares VSAM files with the MVS batch system), and they are widely exploited in certain DBMSs, such as IBM's relational DB2 product. Therefore, given the fundamental role VSAM files and catalogs play, it is especially important to protect these objects from unauthorized use or abuse.

There are a number of facilities available in VSAM which provide different types and degrees of data security and integrity; these are described below under the two general categories of facilities provided by VSAM itself—('native' (VSAM) facilities) and facilities external to VSAM but implementable for VSAM resources. Of the native facilities, the most common and most straightforward is the AMS Password Facility, which is a form of security known as *access control*: the VSAM resource is assigned one or more passwords which must be provided correctly by any authorized user attempting to access the resource.

The true nature of the security protection provided by such a password facility hinges critically on two things: (1) the proper technical implementation of the facility itself (as will be seen shortly below); and (2) the degree to which the passwords are kept secret/undisclosed, each exposure compromising the effectiveness of the security protection. The first issue can be dealt with only through a solid understanding of the nature and principles of the AMS Password Facility. This facility is quite tricky and without considerable care may leave the installation with a false sense of security; we will guide the reader through the necessary tasks that must be correctly performed in order to assure a true sense of security concerning VSAM resources.

Data Security Administrators (DSAs) and related staff (DSA staff) must deal with the second point through a well-designed security-awareness program, possibly supplemented by the mandatory change of passwords on a periodic basis, and upon demand when exposure is suspected, to minimize the risk of exposure to some finite relatively small period, and to discourage casual password 'guessing' by potential violators. (The best general guidelines on passwords for computer security are, to my mind, those issued by the National Computer Security Center of the National Security Agency (NSA), in their publication *DoD Password Management Guidelines*, often just known as the 'Green Book,' part of NSA's excellent (multicolored) "Rainbow Series" of security publications.)

242

An additional, and much stronger, native VSAM security facility is provided, optionally, in the form of *cryptographic access control*: whether direct access to the VSAM resource being protected is allowed or not, the resource itself can be *enciphered statically*, that is, converted by a 'provably secure' means into a meaningless stream of unintelligible characters. Thus, even if an unauthorized user were to succeed in accessing the resource, no security violation is possible as the original information (known as *cleartext* or *plaintext*) is wholly unreadable (it has been converted to *ciphertext*). When an authorized user requires access to the data, provision is made, in a secure manner, for the information to be converted from ciphertext back to cleartext; when access is complete, the data would once again be converted into and stored as ciphertext. Both the operations of enciphering and deciphering require use of a special *key*, known only or made available only to authorized users. Encryption (cryptographic access control) is an extremely effective form of data security if properly implemented by DSA staff, but again much depends on secure *key management*. Encryption facilities for VSAM are a relatively recent, often overlooked, data security feature, and we will take up their discussion more fully below.

Finally, external security facilities may be employed for additional security, sometimes supplementing native VSAM security facilities, and sometimes replacing them, and these are discussed in the final section of this chapter.

16.2   VSAM-INTERNAL ('NATIVE') SECURITY FACILITIES

We begin by examining security facilities for VSAM resource protection inherent in the VSAM product, beginning with the AMS Password Facility that most VSAM users are familiar with.

16.2.1   AMS Password Facility: Introduction

A VSAM resource may be provided with password protection when that resource is first created at DEFINE time. The key resources for which such protection may be provided are of two classes: (1) data set resources (VSAM objects implemented as physically real data sets), which include clusters, cluster components (data and index), AIXs, user catalogs, and page spaces (the latter being a system data set used to hold virtual storage pages, which we will not discuss further, as it rarely concerns an application programmer); and (2) control objects, the only one presently permitted to be password protected being the path. The basic form of password assignment to any of these objects is:

```
DEF...
    (NAME (...) -
        .
        .
        .
    READPW    (rdpw)  -
    UPDATEPW  (updpw) -
    CONTROLPW (ctlpw) -
    MASTERPW  (mrpw)  -
        .
        .
        .
```

VSAM's password protection is *hierarchical*: four levels of passwords are supported, each level including all of the functions permitted at any lower level; for any VSAM resource to be protected, any one or more—including all—of these levels of password protection may be implemented. Let's see how this works by examining the four levels individually.

READPW.   This parameter is coded to assign a *read password* (rdpw) to a VSAM resource, and we say that such a resource is *read-protected*. What this means in terms of security is that the logical records of a read-protected resource may be read by a user only if the user provides the correct (assigned) read password: if we had coded, for example:

```
READPW ('&&++IBEX')
```

then any read operations against the resource's (logical) records is permitted only if the user attempting such a read operation supplies the eight-character read password '&&++IBEX' (how and where exactly such a password is supplied will be detailed below). If we assure that all and only the authorized 'read users' of the resource know the password, then we have implemented a basic level of read-protection.

The password value may be a string of from one to eight bytes consisting of alphameric (A-Z, 0-9) or special characters (see Appendix B for allowable characters). If, as here, the password contains any special characters (we used '&' and '+'), then it must be enclosed in single quote marks, which are optional if only alphameric characters are used (it is a good idea to always use the single quote marks, as this is never in error and avoids syntax errors).

UPDATEPW.   This assigns an *update password* (updpw) to the VSAM resource, assuring it *update-protection*. An update-protected VSAM resource allows the authorized user—one providing the correct (assigned) update password—to perform all update operations against the logical records of the resource: reading (retrieval), adding (insertion), deleting, and changing (update) records. As noted earlier in this chapter, the AMS Password facility is hierarchical, as can be seen here: update-protection includes read-protection, in that authorized update users can, among other things, do at least what read users can, namely read the resource's records, just by supplying the update password. So, for example, if we had assigned both read and update passwords to the resource through the following coding:

```
UPDATEPW ('LINK999X')
READPW   ('&&++IBEX')
```

then any user attempting to access the resource, who provides the update password 'LINK999X,' may perform any read operation—just as if the user had supplied the read password '&&++IBEX'—as well as any update operation whatever against the resource's records. If certain valid users of this resource are to be restricted only to 'passive' access—no alteration of the resource—then we simply make known to them only the read password, not the update password, which would be reserved for just those users who should legitimately have change privileges against the resource.

CONTROLPW.   This parameter assigns a *control password* (ctlpw) to the VSAM resource, assuring it *control-protection*. In addition to allowing authorized users read and update privileges against the resource—by virtue of the hierarchical nature of the AMS Password Facility—it also allows these same privileges when the user is performing what is known as *control interval processing* (often referred to as just *control processing*, or sometimes *CNV processing*, the latter based on an Assembler parameter that enables such processing). We have described control processing in VSAM briefly earlier in the text (see Subsection 10.4.3), but to remind the reader, we may note here that such processing involves directly accessing individual control intervals, including both the logical records stored in the CIs of a file and the special VSAM control fields—the CIDF and the RDFs—which normally (excepting the use of control interval processing) are not processable except by VSAM routines themselves. Control interval processing is an advanced and quite specialized facility of VSAM and is available only to Assembler VSAM programs, and is typically used for high-performance processing of VSAM objects by systems programmers or other high-level technical staff. Given its very specialized nature, we will not discuss control interval processing and its associated password protection any further.

MASTERPW.   This parameter assigns a *master password* to the VSAM resource, assuring it *master-protection*. A master-protected resource allows the authorized user—supplying the correct (assigned) password—all operations against the resource, access thus being essentially unrestricted. Given the hierarchical nature of the AMS Password Facility, the master password—being the highest level password—allows all of the operations that are permissible at all lower levels.

The master password, however, permits even more than just all operations against the resource's logical records: it also permits any operation against index records and catalog records associated with the resource; what this entails is that—unlike the lower-level passwords—the master password allows the authorized user unrestricted access to the index component (if any) of the resource, and also—by virtue of access to catalog records—ALTER and DELETE capabilities against the resource (at the cluster or component levels). Thus, we can consider read, update, and control passwords to be essentially *(logical) record-level* protection facilities, while the master password is an *object-level* protection facility, authorizing access to the object as a whole for ALTER and DELETE purposes, in addition to access merely to the object's records. (Strictly speaking, the read password allows some limited object-level operations, most notably PRINTing the object, issuing a LISTCAT against it, and copying the object (input file function of REPRO), but most IDCAMS functions require more than the passive access that the read password provides.)

16.2.2   How and Where VSAM Passwords are Specified

The correct password at the appropriate level must be supplied by the user in order to gain authorized access to a VSAM password protected resource, and there are many different ways in which this is accomplished, depending on the nature of the attempted access, and these are discussed immediately below.

Batch program access. If a processing program running in a batch environment needs to access a password protected VSAM resource, the password is supplied within the program itself. With a batch COBOL program, this is done in the PASSWORD clause of the SELECT statement:

```
SELECT... ASSIGN TO...
          ORGANIZATION IS...
          ACCESS MODE IS...
          RECORD KEY IS...
          PASSWORD IS...
             .
             .
```

where the name of a COBOL *password data item* is specified after the PASSWORD IS expression; a password data item is simply an alphanumeric WORKING STORAGE field containing the character value of the appropriate VSAM password. For example, we might code the PASSWORD clause of the SELECT statement as follows:

```
PASSWORD IS TRANS-VSAMPW
```

In this case, we are specifying a read password (the name is arbitrary and user-chosen), and we must assure that the correct value is either specified statically in the DATA DIVISION with a VALUE clause, or loaded dynamically in the PROCEDURE DIVISION (typically, through a MOVE statement); the password data item itself is generally defined as a PIC X(8) field (if shorter, COBOL will pad the value with blanks to force it to be eight-bytes in length). If the field is loaded dynamically, this must precede the OPEN statement for the file: if the read password is '&&++IBEX,' then the field TRANS-VSAMPW must be made to contain this precise value prior to OPEN time. Note that correct specification of the read password in this fashion solely authorizes read access: if changes need to be made to the file, then the update or higher password needs to be specified. Otherwise the OPEN will fail, and in certain cases when the AMS Password Facility is supplemented by other external security facilities, the OPEN failure consequent to an incorrect or not-appropriate-level password specification might lead to a security violation being generated and recorded against the user.

The reader might note that this approach to password specification in COBOL is definitely not a very secure procedure: if the value of the password is, as it were, 'hard-coded' into the program, then the password can be read by anyone who sees the program listing output. It is wise to avoid such an obvious exposure risk. A more secure procedure, therefore, would be to supply the password value externally (outside the program): the value of TRANS-VSAMPW, for example, may be ACCEPTed from terminal input keyed by the user, and hence would not appear in a program listing. The weakness of COBOL password specification is often part of the motivation to secure sensitive VSAM files with external add-on security products (discussed later in this chapter) either in addition to, or as a replacement of, the AMS Password Facility. (Assembler batch programs supply the password value in the PASSWD parameter of the ACB macro coding, which otherwise functions similarly to the COBOL approach.)

The CODE and ATTEMPTS security parameters. There is still another alternative. The user may deliberately fail to specify a password for a password protected VSAM resource, in which case the (master) console operator will typically be prompted at that console for the password to be supplied on behalf of the actual user. VSAM will prompt the operator with the actual VSAM resource name. This is sometimes viewed as undesirable from a security point of view in that the operator would then have password access to the resource, in addition to the user's access. It is preferable to avoid this, and this can be done by forcing VSAM to prompt the operator, not with the resource name, but with a *code name*, implemented by the user specifying the *CODE* parameter in the AMS DEFINE command when the resource is created. To see how this works, assume we have coded the following at DEFINE time:

```
DEF...
    (NAME (FINCAT.EMPLOYEE) -
            .
            .
    READPW ('&&++IBEX') -
    CODE ('ZZZZVSAM') -
            .
            .
```

Then if the user fails to specify a password for this resource, the operator will receive a prompt message to supply a read password for the resource with the code name of 'ZZZZVSAM' (we would have had to inform the operator that '&&++IBEX' is the read password for the 'ZZZZVSAM' resource). Notice that at no time does the operator become aware of what the actual name (FINCAT.EMPLOYEE) of the real resource is, and so cannot access the resource since access by the operator, not the user, would require the truename of the resource; the operator is in effect restricted to supplying the password for an unknown resource in order to allow some other user to access the resource, so only the user knows both the truename and the password (but chooses not to supply it so that no visual exposure of the password occurs in the program itself).

Finally, some very security-conscious installations do not allow operators to supply passwords even by code names, so that if a batch program were to fail to specify the password for a password protected VSAM resource, then the operator may still receive a password prompt, but will have been instructed to never supply one—indeed, the operator would in such a case not know any passwords in the first place, so could not supply one even if desired. Often the operator is prompted with a query that asks whether the user (identified by userid to the operator) has valid access to the resource (also identified to the operator) *without* a password, and the operator is instructed to always answer in the negative; this will typically then cause a security

violation to be logged against the user. This can also be rigged by the following coding
when creating the VSAM resource:

```
DEF...
    (NAME (FINCAT.EMPLOYEE) -
        .
        .
    READPW ('&&++IBEX') -
    ATTEMPTS (0) -
        .
        .
```

The ATTEMPTS parameter, if coded, specifies how many times an operator—if
prompted for a password on behalf of a user—may attempt to supply the correct
password (whether the prompt uses the truename of the resource, or a code name).
The values of the parameter may be any number from zero to seven. If, as we have
done above, ATTEMPTS (0) is coded, then that indicates that the operator is not
permitted to supply the password on the user's behalf at all: then either the user
would have had to explicitly provide the password, otherwise a security violation
would be raised against the user.

Each installation will make its own unique decisions concerning how passwords
are to be provided by the user, in various environments, whether operator password
prompting shall occur, and what the consequences—including security issues—shall
be of either failure to provide a password for access to a password protected VSAM
resource, or failure to provide the *correct* password; users should always check with
their installation's data security and/or technical support staff to ascertain the
installation-specific rules and requirements of access for protected VSAM resources.

AMS Commands. When running an IDCAMS job that issues AMS
commands, certain commands require a password specification of a particular level
or higher in order for the operation requested by the command to be honored by
VSAM when the object involved is password protected; the password is generally
specified after the entryname of the object, or after the catalog name of the catalog
containing the object's entry. An example is the DELETE command being issued
against a password-protected resource, which may take one of these two possible
forms:

```
(A) DELETE -
        FINCAT.MVSSYSG.INVMASTR/'$$$+PASS' -
            .
            .
(B) DELETE -
        FINCAT.MVSSYSG.INVMASTR -
            .
            .
        CATALOG (FINCAT/'---+PASS')
```

The DELETE command requires that deletion of a password-protected cluster (as
here) is authorized only if either the master password of the cluster is provided (as in

A, above), or the master password of the catalog owning the cluster is provided (the same rule applies also if the object to be deleted is an AIX or a path). No lower-level password is sufficient for a DELETE operation. If we were attempting to delete a user catalog, the master password of the catalog itself is similarly required. Other AMS commands follow distinct rules of their own, and the reader must consult the appropriate Access Method Services Reference manual for the precise coding and password-level requirements for the operations to be performed.

Interactive environment (TSO and TSO/E). When using VSAM facilities from an interactive environment, such as TSO or TSO/E under MVS (or MVS/XA), attempted access to password-protected VSAM typically occasions the terminal user to be prompted by TSO for the appropriate password (at the appropriate level) at the terminal if the password is not supplied on the AMS command itself. Many AMS commands can be issued in the TSO environment interactively (without JCL), or may be issued through the menu-driven ISPF/PDF (Interactive System Productivity Facility/Program Development Facility) running under TSO. Depending on the installation's particular interactive environment, failure to provide the correct password may result in the logging of a security violation against the user.

16.2.3 Principles of the AMS Password Facility

The AMS Password Facility operates effectively only if several critical principles are followed, and these are detailed immediately below.

Maximal upward inheritance. We have already noted the hierarchical nature of the AMS Password Facility, with its four levels of passwords: read, update, control, and master passwords. We have also noted that, if any password protection is implemented at all, then one may assign any one or more levels of passwords, including (of course) all four. Assume for the purposes of this discussion that, first, all four levels of password protection are assigned for a particular VSAM resource, and that the selected password values are all different, as given (for example) below:

```
MASTERPW    (' $$$+PASS' )
CONTROLPW   (' CNVOOOOO' )
UPDATEPW    (' LINK999X' )
READPW      (' &&++IBEX' )
```

This case is straightforward and implements maximum protection through the AMS Password Facility, allowing us to select what categories of users (or individual users) are to be assigned different sets of privilege, by making the appropriate password(s) known only to the various separate user categories.

Now, however, let us suppose that we, at DEFINE CLUSTER time, assigned to the resource only a single level of password protection, the READPW of '&&++IBEX'; that is, we coded explicitly:

```
READPW      (' &&++IBEX' )
```

VSAM in this case would follow a principle of *maximal upward inheritance*, whereby the password at the highest ('maximal') level assigned is said to be *propagated* or *inherited* upwards, to become the password for *all higher levels*, despite the fact that the higher levels were not actually assigned passwords explicitly at all. Thus, if we started with only: READPW ('&&++IBEX'), then VSAM would actually treat the resource as having the password protection *as if* we had coded:

```
MASTERPW    (' &&++IBEX' )
CONTROLPW   (' &&++IBEX' )
UPDATEPW    (' &&++IBEX' )
READPW      (' &&++IBEX' )
```

Since the read level was the highest or maximal level of password protection explicitly defined for the resource, then the read password value of '&&++IBEX' is inherited (upward) by all higher levels. Note that without this understanding by the user of the principle of maximal upward inheritance, this may be an unexpected, and undesirable, effect: any user who knows the read password and supplies it correctly to VSAM has unrestricted access to the resource, not just read access. It may have been that it was intended that all access to the resource, of whatever kind, was to hinge solely on the single password value of '&&++IBEX,' but this is unlikely and, furthermore, is a poor security procedure for other than test data sets needing no hierarchical protection; it is better than no protection (any access to the resource at least requires a password), but is a distinctly primitive way to implement password protection.

To see the principle of maximal upward inheritance in operation in a more complex situation, let's now assume that we have explicitly assigned the following password protection to a VSAM resource:

```
UPDATEPW    (' LINK999X' )
READPW      (' &&++IBEX' )
```

As can be seen, we have not assigned a CONTROLPW or a MASTERPW. However, probably unexpectedly, VSAM will—through application of the principle—expand our protection to the following:

```
MASTERPW    (' LINK999X' )
CONTROLPW   (' LINK999X' )
UPDATEPW    (' LINK999X' )
READPW      (' &&++IBEX' )
```

What happened is that VSAM first determined the highest level for which password protection was explicitly defined, and this was the update level; then VSAM caused the update password to be inherited by both of the higher levels, namely the control and master levels.

Now let's consider a somewhat more complex final case, where we have coded the following password protection explicitly:

```
MASTERPW    ('$$$+PASS')
READPW      ('&&++IBEX')
```

In applying the principle of maximal upward inheritance, we must note that the MASTERPW is the highest level of password protection explicitly defined, so no passwords are propagated upwards; VSAM does not cause the READPW to be upward inherited since it is not the maximal level defined explicitly. VSAM would therefore interpret our coding to entail the following configuration:

```
MASTERPW    ('$$$+PASS')
CONTROLPW
UPDATEPW
READPW      ('&&++IBEX')
```

The lack of any entry next to UPDATEPW and CONTROLPW indicates that the VSAM resource being protected has *no* password protection at either of these two levels. What does this entail? It entails a rather unfortunate—and almost certainly unintended—consequence, namely, that any user attempting update or control access to the resource (that is, opening the resource in either of these modes) will be assured such access without any password challenge whatever, even though a lower level (read level) and a higher level (master) of access against this same resource are both password protected! This is sometimes referred to as 'gappy' password protection and should, in general, be avoided.

SUGGESTION

Given the above quirks of the AMS Password Facility due to the principle of maximal upward inheritance, the safest strategy is to password protect a VSAM resource at *all* levels *if the resource is password protected at any level*. This assures both consistency and a high level of selective protection.

Separation of component-protection. This principle says, in essence, that protection at any component level does not entail (a) that any other component is automatically protected, or (b) that the VSAM object containing the protected component is itself protected. Given (a), if a data component is password protected, the associated index component is not also protected thereby, and vice versa; all components requiring protection must be individually protected.

Given (b) above, if either or both the data and index component of a cluster are protected, absolutely nothing follows concerning the protection status of the associated cluster; if the cluster had not been separately protected *at the cluster level* with its own set of (cluster-level) passwords, the protection of its components would not disallow access to the entire object as a cluster without any password challenge whatever, again clearly an unintended consequence of the principle of *separation of component-protection*. Thus, no real protection is afforded to a VSAM cluster, unless the cluster itself is password protected, regardless of how comprehensive password protection of the components might be.

Furthermore, this principle entails still another (unintended) consequence: (c) if a cluster is protected at the cluster-level only, this does not disallow accessing the contents of either or both the associated data and index components separately without any password challenge; the cluster is protected, so that any access at the cluster level is password protected, but if either component is accessed directly (for example, by opening either as a separate data set), no protection is in effect. Finally, the separation of component-protection principle entails one last, perhaps not-so-obvious, fact (a positive one, for a change): (d) if a VSAM cluster resource is unprotected at any component-level, but protected at the cluster-level, then access at the cluster-level will be challenged despite the fact that no component of the cluster has any protection at all; this might seem strange, given that the data and index components of a cluster are real data sets, while the cluster object is not, but nonetheless VSAM treats the cluster as a real object for the purpose of password protection.

SUGGESTION

A VSAM cluster resource, if it is to be protected at all, should be protected individually at *all* levels: data component, index component (if any), and cluster-level; only this assures the protection of the cluster object at all levels. Remember that, although COBOL in the batch environment may only access a VSAM cluster at the cluster-level, not at the component-level, this does not prohibit an Assembler program from accessing a cluster-level protected VSAM object through either its (unprotected) data or index component. Note that if the suggestion given is followed (if any part of an object is to be protected, all should be), then VSAM would allow access to a protected component of the object either (1) by the customary means of specifying the appropriate component password, or (2) by the special means of specifying the master password of the cluster; in this second case where no component password is presented by the user, the master password of the cluster is required even if only the lowest level of access (read access) to a component was being requested. Note further, however, that the master password of the cluster, if presented, would authorize any access at any level to any part of the cluster (data and/or index component). It is for this reason that the cluster's master password should not be used casually for authorization that can otherwise be accomplished by either lower level cluster passwords, or by component passwords at the appropriate level (read, up-date, etc.).

Catalog protection prerequisite.   All VSAM resources are cataloged in some *owning* catalog, that is, there is an entry for that resource in whatever catalog the resource was first defined in. The *catalog protection prerequisite* essentially says that no password protection of any VSAM resource is in effect unless the owning catalog is password protected; thus, a cluster that is password protected at all levels is actually wholly unprotected if the catalog in which the resource was defined is itself not password protected. Indeed, despite passwords having been specified everywhere for, say a cluster, any user attempting access to the cluster will not even be challenged by VSAM when the owning catalog is unprotected! The resource's comprehensive password protection is in such a case wholly illusory and misleading: this is a true case of 'false security.'

SUGGESTION

All VSAM catalogs should be password protected. Failure to follow this renders the AMS Password Facility completely useless.

AMS commands and the AMS Password Facility.   The following gives the major rules of what AMS commands require what level of password specification for authorization of that operation; rules for very specialized cases are not included and the reader should consult the *Catalog Administration Guide* for further details. It is assumed that all catalogs are password protected.

1. The DEFINE command, which creates a catalog entry for a VSAM object, requires the user to specify the update, or a higher-level (that is, control or master) password of the catalog involved.
2. The DELETE and ALTER command (deleting and modifying a catalog entry, respectively), require the user to specify the master password of either the entry, or the catalog containing the entry.
3. The LISTCAT command requires, for listing a read-level protected catalog entry, the user to specify either the read password of the object associated with the entry, or the read password of the catalog containing the entry. A catalog entry without any password protection, however, may be listed without any password challenge even though the catalog containing the entry is password protected.
4. The DEFINE, ALTER, and DELETE commands, when issued against a non-VSAM data set, a GDG (generation data group), or a VSAM ALIAS, require the user to specify the update or a higher-level password of the catalog containing the entry.

16.2.4   User-Security-Verification Routines

DSA (Data Security Administration) staff may choose to enhance native VSAM security by providing for customized authorization-checking that is supplemental to the AMS Password Facility. This may be provided in the form of an installation-coded user-security-verification routine (USVR), which is an Assembler program that functions as a special security-related user exit, taking effect immediately after a valid password is supplied by a user in response to the VSAM password challenge normally associated with a password-protected VSAM resource.

Let's clarify how this works. First, the USVR is typically defined at object-definition time through the specification of the AUTHORIZATION parameter of the DEFINE command, which has the following form:

```
DEFINE...
    (NAME (...) -
     .
     .
     .
    AUTHORIZATION (usvr-name usar)
```

The first positional parameter is *usvr-name*, the entry name of the USVR program, which must be precoded as a user-written Assembler exit routine and stored in the special authorized library SYS1.LINKLIB. The second parameter is *usar* (*user security authorization record*) which is a string (up to 256 bytes long) used by VSAM when control is transferred to the USVR, and which is used by VSAM to verify the authority of the user attempting access to the protected VSAM resource. The USAR may contain any data that may be used to further verify (in addition to valid password) accessor authority: social security number, full name, special personal data known only to a valid accessor, a secret code word, etc. What should be in the USAR is decided by whoever is designing the USVR itself; generally DSA staff specify the general design, and a systems programmer does the actual coding to meet the design requirements.

Once the USVR and the USAR are designed and coded (and specified as parameters of AUTHORIZATION at DEFINE time), the scenario runs as follows. The accessor first provides a password at the appropriate level—remember, the USVR facility can be used only if the resource is password protected—and the AMS Password Facility routines check the validity of the password. If the accessor has provided a valid read, update, or control password, then VSAM transfers control to the USVR that was priorly identified to VSAM in the AUTHORIZATION parameter. The USVR will then be used by VSAM to further challenge the accessor to provide the information specified in the USAR, and VSAM will permit access to the protected resource only if the accessor provides the requisite information at this time. Thus the USVR provides another layer of security over the AMS Password Facility, and can be highly customized to individual circumstances. Note, however, that if an accessor specifies at the very onset (technically, OPEN time) the *master* password for the resource—regardless of whether or not this level of password is actually needed for the type of access being requested—then the USVR is not invoked and no further authorization checking occurs; VSAM assumes that a provider of the resources's master password is wholly authorized thereby and not subject to further verification. The reader interested in the technical details of implementing a USVR should consult the *VSAM Administration Guide*.

16.2.5   ERASE-On-DELETE Facility

As we observed earlier in the text (much earlier, so we review the essentials here again briefly), a user deleting a VSAM object may elect what is often termed the *erase-on-delete facility*, which is implemented either at DEFINE time through the coding of the ERASE option on the DEFINE command, or later at ALTER or DELETE time, again by coding the ERASE option on those commands. If this is done, thus invoking the erase-on-delete facility, VSAM is instructed to not just logically delete the object by removing its entry from its owning catalog (which is all that VSAM does normally on a DELETE), but to (in addition) physically delete the object by overwriting all its data component records with binary zeroes, thus completely obliterating the contents of the object. This is an added measure of protection from undesirable exposure of sensitive information stored in a VSAM object, since the default—a logical DELETE—leaves the actual data records unaffected: the object may not be accessed by name, but a dump of the volume on which the logically deleted object resides will expose the unerased records, and there are unfortunately too many special utilities and add-on products at most installations which can take a volume dump in this way (and a sophisticated Assembler program accessing the volume by absolute physical addresses, rather than by file names, can also do the equivalent of such utilities).

SUGGESTION

For any VSAM object containing sensitive information whose risk of exposure should be minimized, the object should be deleted only by an erase-on-delete operation (ERASE option in effect). Furthermore, it is best to implement this right from the beginning by coding the ERASE option at DEFINE time, so that any subsequent deletion operation is assured to be an erase-on-delete; although this can still be implemented later (if it was not done at DEFINE time) through the ERASE option of the DELETE and ALTER commands, this adds the risk that whoever is issuing, say, the DELETE command, may forget to specify ERASE, and since ERASE is never the default, only a logical deletion will occur. (The DEFINE time specification of ERASE causes *any* delete operation against the object to be an erase-on-delete, regardless of whether or not the ERASE option was specified on the DELETE command.)

16.2.6   The AMS Cryptographic Option

The IBM *AMS Cryptographic Option* (sometimes referred to as 'CRYPTO') is a recently implemented facility, available in VSAM as an option of the REPRO command, that provides an extremely high level of security for *offline* data sets through the use of *data encryption*. A *data encryption algorithm* is used to transform the (readable) contents—the *plaintext* (or sometimes, *cleartext*) of a data set to be protected—into an unintelligible stream of characters, the *ciphertext*; the reverse process, *data decryption*, transforms the ciphertext back into the original plaintext. Both processes require the use of an *encryption/decryption key*. The AMS Cryptographic Option is an IBM implementation of a national standard, passed in 1977 by the NBS (National Bureau of Standards), for data encryption known as the *Data Encryption Standard*, or *DES*, and under this implementation the same key is used for enciphering the data as for deciphering it (this may seem odd, but it is a standard, wholly secure, feature of 'symmetric' data encryption algorithms like DES; nonsymmetric algorithms do exist which use distinct keys). Indeed, DES was 'developed' under the auspices of the NBS, but was designed and programmed by IBM under an exclusive arrangement with the NBS, with NSA (National Security Agency) of DoD (Department of Defense) supervision and validation.

Data encryption is effected by the new ENCIPHER option on the REPRO command, which can operate on not only VSAM files, but also on SAM and ISAM files as well; the enciphered data set (the output of REPRO ENCIPHER) is always a sequential file, regardless of the file organization of the plaintext file, and is either a non-VSAM SAM file or a VSAM ESDS. The generated ciphertext file can, at any later time, be deciphered by application of the REPRO DICIPHER option in conjunction with the correct key, an eight-byte string which is the same key that was used to originally encipher the file. REPRO ENCIPHER/DECIPHER, part of the AMS Cryptographic Option, requires (as a prerequisite) installation of either one of two IBM program products: the *Programmed Cryptographic Facility* (*PCF*) or the *Cryptographic Unit Support Facility* (*CUSF*); both of these are themselves part of a larger family of data encryption products (hardware and software) offered by IBM, now referred to as the *Cryptographic Subsystem*, and which includes facilities—the *ACF/VTAM Encrypt/Decrypt Feature*, most notably—for encryption of 'in-flight' data (data being transmitted over network links). Whereas the AMS Cryptographic Option offers what is called *static* encryption security (for off-line data sets), several products within the parent family Cryptographic Subsystem complement this with *dynamic* (network) encryption for on-line data sets and in-flight data. Encryption technology of either form is deadly serious data security and control, and if correctly implemented and managed—and part of a comprehensive data security policy—can offer maximal security in complex computer systems and networks. It is unfortunate that few installations are acquainted with, or implement, these powerful data encryption technologies; the REPRO ENCIPHER/DECIPHER is a particularly elegant and powerful way to ensure the integrity of sensitive information in a VSAM system.

The AMS Cryptographic Option also provides for two different approaches to the management of keys: *private-key management*, which allows the installation to generate and control the keys to be used and their secure distribution and storage, and *system-key management*, where the same functions are carried out by the PCF or CUSF data encryption product. In addition, the data-encrypting key can, in order to further minimize risk of exposure, be itself encrypted; this second order of encryption yields what is called a *secondary file key*.

SUGGESTIONS

1. Install the AMS Cryptographic Option (and the prerequiste PCF or CUSF product) and use the REPRO ENCIPHER/DECIPHER options to secure all sensitive data sets. (*Note:* catalog data sets are not subject to data encryption through these facilities.)
2. Always enable system-key management instead of private-key management; it is known that the risk of exposing the critical data-encrypting key is much higher with private rather than system-key management. It is also known, although the technical details are beyond the scope of this discussion, that user-generated data-encrypting keys may, on a significant number of occasions, yield what are termed *weak keys*, which may be broken by an experienced cryptanalyst in shorter, and often realistic, time than it would otherwise take to break DES under systematic attack. Indeed, data security specialists (this one included) generally feel that DES is fatally compromised as a strong cipher in any case in which a well-designed system-generation of the key is not used. The system-generated keys provided by the prerequisite IBM products referred to above are known to be provably strong and offer the highest level of security available using a DES implementation.
3. For added security, use secondary file keys rather than unencrypted data-encrypting keys; this can be done by the system automatically upon request, rather than by the installation.

16.3   VSAM-EXTERNAL SECURITY FACILITIES

All of the above security facilities are provided by VSAM; however, many installations supplement these security facilities with external ones that function more or less independently of VSAM, but provide some protection for VSAM resources. We will now look at two commonly used external facilities.

16.3.1   The Authorized Program Facility (APF)

The *Authorized Program Facility* (*APF*) is an MVS facility—whether MVS/System Product Ver.1 (MVS/SP), MVS/Extended Architecture (MVS/XA), or the recently introduced MVS/Enterprise Systems Architecture (MVS/ESA)—that restricts access to critical systems resources to only certain authorized users. System resources that may be APF-controlled are not restricted to VSAM, but may be almost any sensitive MVS system program or service. Certain types of advanced VSAM programming facilities require for their use that the user be APF-authorized, that is, identified to APF as an authorized user of the facilities. (This is generally done by systems programmers, often working with DSA staff; the technical details, beyond the scope of this discussion, may be consulted in the IBM two-volume publication *System Macros and Facilities*).

Certain AMS commands require APF-authorization to be issued, the most important being:

CNVTCAT	converting OS CVOL entries into VSAM catalog entries
EXPORT/IMPORT	of a VSAM catalog
PRINT	of a(n) (entire) VSAM catalog
REPRO	of a VSAM catalog
VERIFY	of a VSAM catalog

SUGGESTION

For greater control, the installation may also identify additional AMS commands to be inaccessible without APF-authorization, largely because these commands are intended for systems programmers and special technical support staff, and should not be available to the general programming population; good candidates for requiring APF-athorization are the following AMS commands:

DEFINE ALIAS	creates an alternate name for a VSAM catalog
DEFINE PAGESPACE	creates a 'paging' data set
DEFINE UCAT	(defining a Master Catalog in MVS is not effected through an AMS Command; the DEF MCAT, if issued, causes VSAM to create a user catalog only)
EXAMINE*	analyzes/detects problems of structural consistency associated with a KSDS data and/or index component
EXPORTRA/IMPORTRA*	uses Catalog Recovery Areas for certain recovery functions
LISTCRA*	lists/compares CRA(s)
RESETCAT*	restores catalog entries from CRA entries

16.3.2 The Resource Access Control Facility (RACF)

IBM's RACF product is a widely used general security facility that provides flexible access control within MVS, VM, CICS, and IMS environments; the resources that may be protected by RACF include disk and tape data sets and volumes, programs, transactions, and terminals, among others. RACF is frequently employed to either supplement or replace VSAM-provided security facilities. If a VSAM resource is password protected (under the AMS Password Facility) and the associated catalog is RACF protected, then AMS password checking is wholly bypassed, as

---

*In certain cases with the VSAM product, these commands may already be restricted by APF.

is any USVR associated with the resource. The AMS Password Facility is *not* bypassed, however, if the resource is *not* RACF protected, but the associated catalog is either RACF or password protected. RACF authorization checking for VSAM resources parallels VSAM password checking: RACF authorization levels are *read*, *update*, *control* (exactly like the AMS Password Facility), and *alter*, this latter being the RACF equivalent of the master password level. (For further details of the RACF product, consult *Resource Access Control Facility (RACF): General Information Manual*. There are also many other non-IBM resource access control products (ACF2, OMNIGUARD, TOP-SECRET, etc.) which all invariably provide similar mechanisms for VSAM resource protection. IBM's ACF (Access Control Function) provides security that supplements (not bypasses) AMS password checking, but for the DOS/VSE environment.)

SUGGESTION

An installation's DSA staff may want to implement both the AMS Password Facility and RACF, even under circumstances where RACF bypasses the AMS password checking; this is because VSAM resources may be transported to another system that either lacks RACF protection, or in which RACF protection does not take effect immediately on such imported resources, and in such cases the AMS Password Facility which is transportable and effective across systems would then automatically provide at least some level of protection and avoid possible security exposure.

17

DATA FACILITY PRODUCT/VSAM (DFP/VSAM): THE NEW VSAM

We have already briefly discussed, in Chapter 2, IBM's Data Facility/Extended Function (DF/EF), which was introduced in 1979 as a functional replacement for the then most current version of VSAM, namely Enhanced VSAM. The VSAM we have been covering up to this point has been Enhanced VSAM, which is almost always referred to simply as 'VSAM,' while DF/EF, along with the various extensions and enhancements to it captured under the rubric of DFP/VSAM (Data Facility Product/VSAM), is informally but widely referred to as the 'new VSAM.' Figure 17-1 summarizes early VSAM evolution up to Enhanced VSAM, while Figure 17-2 (repeated from Chapter 2, Figure 2-1) presents a broader view of VSAM evolution which includes DF/EF and the various releases of DFP/VSAM.

At present, the 'new VSAM' is extensively implemented, but Enhanced VSAM has not been by any means wholly replaced by it, with many installations typically running a 'mixed' environment in which both products coexist in the same system. (IBM refers to the Enhanced VSAM product as 'stabilized,' generally meaning that no future new enhancements will be made to the product, although it may not be strictly discontinued at any time.)

In this chapter, we discuss the basic nature, operation, and major features of the 'new VSAM' (backup and recovery facilities, however, a very specialized and complex area in DFP/VSAM, and one rarely involving the application programmer, are not discussed further), and as we do so we will bring out, at the appropriate points, what the key design objectives of the 'new VSAM' are as it continues to evolve over the years, and how the new features address various technical problems inherent in the previous product, Enhanced VSAM. We will begin by discussing briefly just what were the technical shortcomings of Enhanced VSAM. (From here on in, a reference to just 'VSAM' will be understood to be short for 'Enhanced VSAM.' Furthermore, the terms 'new VSAM' and 'DFP/VSAM' will be used interchangeably).

17.1 TECHNICAL SHORTCOMINGS OF ENHANCED VSAM

We can discuss the limitations of Enhanced VSAM under five general categories, as listed below.

<u>STANDARD VSAM (1973)</u>

KSDS Support

ESDS Support

VSAM Catalogs: Master & User

<u>ENHANCED VSAM</u>

RRDS Support

Alternate Index (AIX) Support

Catalog Recovery: using Catalog Recovery Areas (CRAs)

- EXPORTRA

- IMPORTRA

- LISTCRA

- RESETCAT

INDEX Component of KSDS: Separately Processable

Spanned Records

Reusable Clusters

Checkpoint/Restart Processing

Shared Resource Facility

- Local Shared Resources (LSRs)

- Global Shared Resources (GSRs)

Figure 17-1. 'Early' VSAM evolution.

17.1.1   Catalog Management Problems

Volume ownership by VSAM catalogs.   As we have already described in Section 5.1, VSAM adheres to a principle of *volume ownership* whereby each VSAM catalog *owns* and maintains exclusive control over all volumes on which reside VSAM data sets defined in that catalog, so that such 'owned' volumes may not be shared by multiple catalogs. We say that VSAM enforces a *one volume, one owning catalog* restriction. The problem with this is that if VOLx is owned by CATx, then no other catalog may have data sets which are defined in that other catalog and reside on VOLx. This may be a satisfactory arrangement if CATx can effectively use virtually all

1.   STANDARD VSAM (1973)

2.   ENHANCED VSAM (1975)

3.   VSE/VSAM (1979)

---

4.   DATA FACILITY/EXTENDED FUNCTION: DF/EF (1981–82)

5.   DATA FACILITY PRODUCT: DFP/VSAM (1983)

- DFP/XA: Version 2, Rel. 1.0   (April, 1985)
- DFP/XA: Version 2, Rel. 1.0 Update   (December, 1985)
- DFP/XA: Version 2, Rel. 2.0   (June, 1986)
- DFP/XA: Version 2, Rel. 3.0   (June, 1987)
- DFP: Version 3   (December, 1988)

Note: DFP/XA = DFP running under MVS/XA (MVS/EXTENDED ARCHITECTURE).
DFP is also available under non-xa systems, as DFP/370.

Figure 17-2. VSAM evolution.

of the space on that volume. With the low-capacity 3330 disks, and even with the medium-capacity 3350 disks, this condition may often be met; however, with the high-capacity 3380s now in common use, it may turn out that not all of the volume's vast amount of storage may be used by whatever single application or project owns the volume through its catalog. The 3380 is available in single, double, and triple capacity models. The single capacity model alone stores a total of 2.52G ('giga' or billion) bytes, while the double capacity model stores 5.04G bytes! The volume ownership restriction may cause a 3380 pack to be underutilized if the owning catalog simply does not have defined in it sufficient data sets stored on the pack to use all available space, since exclusive ownership prohibits another catalog from using the remaining space for storage of data sets defined in it. DASD conservation and utilization demands are simply different now than they were when Enhanced VSAM was designed, and VSAM must change to reflect the new realities of high capacity DASD units.

Volatile/stable catalog information co-residence.   Upon some consideration, we can see that the catalog entry for a VSAM data set contains information of two distinct classes. The first is relatively stable, like ownership, associations, security, and volume information, which rarely changes over the life cycle of a data set. The second class is highly volatile, changing frequently over the data set's life cycle; this includes most VSAM statistics, such as REC-TOTAL, SPLITS-CI and SPLITS-CA, HURBA, EXCPS, EXTENTS, among many others. The first class of information undergoes little update, while the second must be updated numerous times over even short periods of processing activity, yet VSAM catalogs fail to discriminate between these two classes at all, both being lumped together into a single catalog entry.

Catalog I/O overhead. A VSAM catalog contains *discrete* catalog entries for an object and its associations: there is, for example, a catalog entry for a base cluster, and a wholly separate entry for any AIXs built over that base cluster. If there are three AIXs—AIX1, AIX2, AIX3—associated with base cluster BC, then the catalog information for these four related objects are contained in distinct catalog records. The problem with this approach, however, is that the three AIXs may commonly be members of the upgrade set for that BC, entailing that they must be maintained by VSAM in synchrony with the BC, updates to the BC being reflected in the AIXs as needed. This, in turn, means that the catalog record updating associated with these four objects must generally be performed in unison; we say that the catalog records must be *co-updated*. But an update to BC will be posted to the catalog at CLOSE time of the processing program, *as will the corresponding updates to each of the AIXs of the upgrade set*, yet this will require separate I/O operations for retrieval of the independent catalog records for each of these four objects. This clearly involves considerable overhead for the catalog I/O involved, which could have been avoided, or minimized, by in some way storing the catalog entries for the object and its associations collectively, so that the records may be fetched and updated together without requiring separate I/O operations.

Catalog integrity problems. A VSAM catalog, as we have already seen, may at any time and under a variety of conditions suffer a failure-of-synchronization with the actual VSAM objects defined in that catalog. A major contributing factor to compromise of catalog integrity is the fact that, typically, the catalog resides on a different volume from the volume or volumes on which reside the objects defined in that catalog, so that updates to the catalog and updates to the objects themselves are necessarily separated in both time and space (location), opening the possibility of various out-of-sync conditions. If, however, there were a way to make the catalog and its objects coreside, synchronization problems would be dramatically reduced. With Enhanced VSAM this is not viable, as it would require, given the volume ownership restriction, that each volume would have to be owned by a distinct user catalog, one for each volume in the system, and no one catalog could own any volume except one, the one it resides on. In a real business environment this is simply untractable.

Non-tunable catalogs. Catalogs in Enhanced VSAM are essentially non-tunable in that virtually no control can be exercised by the user to improve catalog performance. The physical blocksize and CISZ are set at a fixed 512 bytes. Separate buffer allocations for the data and index components (a catalog is always a KSDS) are not permitted, but only the total bufferspace—that is, BUFSP, not BUFND (number of data buffers) and BUFNI (number of index buffers)—can be elected by the user, and even here only within the range of 3K to 8K, in units of 1K. Freespace may not be specified at all, despite the fact that the catalog, like all KSDSs, is subject to split activity. STRNO is not specifiable, and has a built-in maximum of seven. IMBED and REPLICATE options are not permitted. Finally, despite the fact that a VSAM catalog is a KSDS, the secondary allocation quantity is fixed at a maximum of 13 extents (not 122 as in a standard KSDS). Clearly, the impact of non-tunable catalogs is compromised catalog performance.

Catalog management security compromise. VSAM catalog management routines are stored in the PLPA (Pageable Link Pack Area), and the control blocks they use are stored in the CSA (Common Service Area), of the Common Area of an MVS address space. As such, they are subject to certain highly sophisticated security compromises which exploit the fact that the common area is mapped to every MVS user's address space. But the trend in MVS has been, in recent years (both for performance and security considerations), to isolate important MVS components into their own address space, a process sometimes referred to as 'address space promotion.' Clearly, the security and integrity of VSAM catalog management routines would be greatly enhanced if they were promoted into their own MVS address space, as has been done for VTAM, JES, and GRS (Global Resource Serialization), among many others.

17.1.2   Record Management Problems

VERIFY problems. VSAM does not always warn or in any way alert a user when failure-of-synchronization conditions occur; certain cases are detected by VSAM and reflected to the user, usually in the form of OPEN time errors or warnings, but this is not performed wholly systematically, so that a user has no absolutely assured way of anticipating when a VERIFY command should be issued.

Inefficient GDG handling. VSAM catalogs have a deficiency that may lead to considerable wasted catalog space (in the high key range records) when *ascending data set names* are used. Two examples of ascending data set names are: (1) FIN.TRANS.KSDS01, FIN.TRANS.KSDS02, FIN.TRANS.KSDS03, etc., and (2) FIN.INVENTORY.G0001V00, FIN.INVENTORY.G0002V00, . . ., FIN.INVENTORY.G0012V00, the latter being Generation Data Set (GDS) names for a Generation Data Group which includes archives of inventory files for a 12 month calendar period. Without entering into the specific technical details, we should point out that use of such names for data sets cataloged in a VSAM catalog can cause an excessive amount of catalog record storage to become unutilizable after the data sets are deleted. But such naming conventions (especially for data sets in GDGs) are the norm, not the exception, and premature 'catalog full' conditions may thereby arise. One partial solution is to not catalog such GDGs in VSAM catalogs, but this simply avoids the problem without solving it, and in addition leads to an unintegrated approach to data set cataloging in VSAM environments.

Erase-CI processing limitation.   A CI that was once (partially) filled with records may be subsequently emptied of all its records through deletion activity; such a CI is known as an *erase-CI* and the range of keys it had when first used is known as its *original CI-range*. With Enhanced VSAM catalogs, only new records with keys which are within this original CI-range may be stored subsequently in the erase-CI. This may be considerably wasteful of valuable CI space, and in the worst case in which no records inserted into the data set fall into the original CI-range of the erase-CI, the CI may go wholly unused. This limitation is too narrow, and less space would be wasted if the to-be-inserted records need only fall within the *CA-range* of keys of the CA within which the erase-CI is stored, rather than just the original CI-range.

17.1.3   Space Management Problems

Dual space management.   As the reader might recall from our earlier discussion of VSAM space in Chapter 7, VSAM clusters are not managed by a single space manager, but rather by two distinct space managers depending on whether the clusters are suballocatable or unique. Suballocatable clusters are managed by a VSAM Space Manager (actually a set of VSAM Space Management routines), while unique clusters are wholly and exclusively managed outside of VSAM altogether, by OS DADSM (Direct Access Device Space Manager). This leads to an unintegrated approach to VSAM space management. Unique clusters, like OS data sets, may only have a maximum of 16 extents, while suballocatable clusters are allowed up to 123 extents; and while unique clusters have direct entries in the VTOC of the volume on which they are allocated, suballocatable clusters do not (only the VSAM space within which they reside shows up in the VTOC), among many other differences. Integrated space management of all clusters of whatever type by a single space manager would avoid such arbitrary differences and limitations.

Use of common area.   VSAM routines, especially catalog management routines, make heavy use of MVS Common Area storage, both in the PLPA and in the CSA. This impacts adversely on the virtual storage left for the user's Private Area, degrading performance, and contributes to the problem of the 'parasitic growth of the Common Area' which MVS/XA (Extended Architecture) and the new ESA (Enterprise Systems Architecture) were designed to address (pardon the pun) by providing what IBM calls Virtual Storage Constraint Relief (VSCR). Although VSAM catalog management routines are only one of several 'offenders' in causing installations to require VSCR, overall performance and usability would be enhanced by their removal from the Common Area of the MVS address space.

Limited XA support.   Enhanced VSAM has few features that exploit the many advantages of extended architecture operating systems like MVS/XA and

ESA. Most VSAM control blocks remain below the 16Mb (megabyte) boundary. Again, improvement in virtual storage utilization and, reflexively, system performance can be achieved if VSAM is provided with significant XA facilities.

17.1.4 Weak Problem Determination

As we have already observed, there are numerous opportunities for consistency and synchronization-related problems in Enhanced VSAM: out-of-sync conditions between a VSAM catalog and any object defined in it, and between either of these and, for example, extent information maintained in the VTOC of any volume(s) owned by the catalog. Furthermore, failure-of-synchronization may occur between a base cluster and any of the AIXs built over it, especially if any of the AIXs are *not* in the upgrade set (so that automatic AIX-upgrade processing would not be performed by VSAM), or if any AIX is opened and processed as a stand-alone data set (not through the associated path). Finally, the index and data components of a KSDS may, after certain events, contain structural inconsistencies, either *within* the component itself, or *between* the two components. In addition, still other more subtle integrity problems may arise in special circumstances. But, despite all this potential for problems, Enhanced VSAM is virtually devoid of any problem determination tools. There are, for example—and somewhat remarkably, in retrospect—no general-purpose AMS commands for detection of the various problems just enumerated. LISTCRA with the COMPARE option is something of an exception, but is restricted only to the specialized environment of recoverable catalogs and data sets, and only to a certain class of synchronization problems. (Note also that VERIFY does not detect problems, but only repairs in a limited way otherwise detected or suspected problems.) In sum, given the scope and (unfortunate) richness of problems in a complex VSAM system, there is critical need for strong and comprehensive problem determination facilities.

17.1.5 Performance Overhead of Duplex-Recovery Mechanism

Enhanced VSAM's primary (but optional) backup and recovery mechanism (that of duplex-recovery, see Section 15.3) imposes, as we have noted in our earlier discussion, a high penalty in the form of virtually doubling catalog I/O: for recoverable data sets an additional I/O operation to the CRA (catalog recovery area) of the volume on which the data set resides may have to be performed for each I/O operation to the catalog itself, degrading catalog update performance. This is a trade-off against the excellent backup and recovery assurance provided by this mechansim, but it is a hard bargain to accept and leaves the user with the thirst for a backup and recovery mechanism without so high a performance price to pay.

17.2 CATALOG MANAGEMENT UNDER THE NEW VSAM: THE INTEGRATED CATALOG FACILITY (ICF)

The single most radical change from Enhanced VSAM to DFP/VSAM, and in many ways the most salient defining feature of DFP/VSAM, is the extensive revision of the Catalog Management functional component. In DFP/VSAM, the Catalog Management component is implemented as the new *Integrated Catalog Facility (ICF)*. Although to many, ICF *is* the 'new VSAM'—so that, for instance, programmers ask when the installation is converting or migrating to ICF—ICF is just one of many important new facilities available under DFP/VSAM: DFP/VSAM is the product that contains ICF and the other critical new features to be discussed in the course of this chapter. We will now turn to examining exactly what ICF is. (Note that the terms 'DFP/VSAM cluster' and 'ICF cluster' will be used interchangeably.)

17.2.1   The General Structure of an ICF Catalog

One very novel feature of catalogs under DFP/VSAM is that they are no longer simple single entities, but rather are always in two parts or components. The entire catalog is known simply as an *ICF catalog*. The first component of an ICF catalog is something called the *Basic Catalog Structure (BCS)*, and the second component is known as the *VSAM Volume Data Set (VVDS)*. Furthermore, every ICF catalog consists of one and only one BCS plus *one or more* VVDSs (at least one). In many ways, as the reader might observe, the name *Integrated* Catalog Facility is the worst possible name: the last thing an ICF catalog is, in many ways, is *integrated*, since it always has two components, the BCS and the VVDS. In this respect, it might have been more aptly, but less sonorously, named the 'Bifurcated' Catalog Facility. (We will see later what is 'integrated' about the new ICF catalogs, and what IBM had in mind with this terminology). Figure 17-3 represents the new two-part ICF catalog

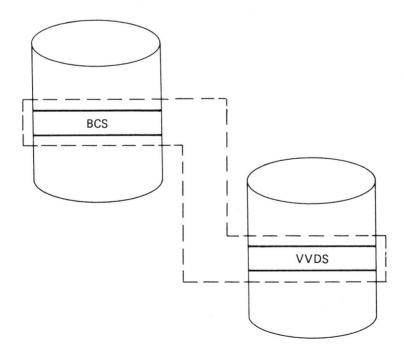

Figure 17-3. Basic concept of the Integrated Catalog Facility (ICF).

```
              - Catalogs:

                      - VSAM Catalogs

                      - ICF  Catalogs

                      - CVOL Catalogs


          - Master & User Catalogs:

                      - either:  VSAM or ICF,
                                 in any combination
```

Figure 17-4. The 'mixed' catalog environment.

schematically, while Figure 17-4 represents the new 'mixed' catalog environment where VSAM catalogs, ICF catalogs and OS CVOL catalogs may coexist. Note that the Master Catalog and any user catalog may be either Enhanced VSAM catalogs, or ICF catalogs, in any combination the installation may care to implement. But although the Master Catalog could optionally be left as a VSAM catalog, in actual practice the VSAM Master Catalog is typically converted very early on (sometimes it is the very first catalog converted) to an ICF catalog, in order to capture the superior performance characteristics of ICF catalogs in general. Now let's turn to exactly what these two parts of an ICF catalog are, both their function and content.

17.2.2   Basic Catalog Structure (BCS)

For each ICF catalog, there is one and only one BCS component, which will contain the relatively stable information concerning the data sets defined in that catalog. This is information such as the owner of the data set, the security applied (e.g., password or RACF protection), the associations of the data set with other VSAM objects (as, for example, the base cluster associations with related AIXs and Paths), and the volume on which the data set resides. Although not absolutely permanent, this sort of data is subject to few changes during the life cycle of the data set. By segregating this stable information into a separate component (the BCS), little in the way of updates need be applied against the BCS, and I/O performance should be, and is, quite good (more on performance later).

A BCS is treated by the 'new VSAM' as a standard KSDS, containing variable-length records which may be spanned, that is, a single logical record may cross a CI boundary, beginning on one CI and ending on another. And like any KSDS, BCS records contain a primary key field, which in the case of a BCS is always 45 bytes long, and is simply the MVS name of the object for which this is a catalog record, followed by a one-byte *pad* character used to indicate that this record has one or more *extension records* associated with it. Let's take an example. Suppose we have defined a VSAM KSDS named VSAM.CK.MVS.VSTEST01 in some BCS. It may be the case that there are a very large number of AIXs built over this base cluster. DFP/VSAM will always store the catalog entries for a base cluster and its associated objects together into a single BCS record, wherever possible. Note that Enhanced VSAM does no such thing: the catalog records for an object and its associations are stored wholly separately in a VSAM catalog, not contiguously. (We will discuss this point, and the benefits of the DFP/VSAM approach, shortly.) Now, given a very large number of AIXs built over our base cluster, it may be the case that not all of the associated catalog entries can be contained in a single BCS record. For although a BCS record is a spanned, variable-length record, nonetheless the creator of the BCS may have specified a maximum record length which proves insufficient to hold the volume of information involved, in which case DFP/VSAM will create one or more *extension records* to hold the remaining information not storable in the first BCS record. If needed, as many as 240 extension records may be created, with the first extension signalled by a pad character of hexadecimal '01' (X'01') appended to the 44-byte MVS name, the second extension having a X'02' pad, the third X'03', etc. for as many extensions as needed, up to the 240 maximum. The pad is empty if no extension records were needed for the BCS record (all information about the object and its associations fit into a single BCS record). Thus, DFP/VSAM can hold related catalog information about an object and its associations in one or more BCS records which, by their extensions, are linked to each other.

17.2.3   VSAM Volume Data Set (VVDS)

The second component of an ICF catalog is the *VSAM Volume Data Set* (*VVDS*). The basic principle of a VVDS is that there is one (and only one) VVDS for each volume *controlled* by an ICF catalog. Although we discuss the concept of a catalog *controlling* a volume—as contrasted, under Enhanced VSAM, with a catalog *owning* a volume—more fully later in this chapter, suffice it to say here that what we mean by a volume being controlled by an ICF catalog is simply that it is a volume on which resides at least one data set defined in that catalog. Thus, an ICF catalog controls all volumes on which are found its cataloged data sets. If cataloged/defined in BCSx are VSAM data sets stored on volumes VOLX01, VOLX02, and VOLX03, then BCSx controls those volumes under DFP/VSAM. In this case, the ICF catalog would consist of one BCS and four VVDSs: four, because there are three on controlled volumes, and there is another on whatever volume BCSx itself resides (assuming it is not on one of the controlled volumes), since the BCS is itself a VSAM KSDS and every volume which contains at least one VSAM data set has a VVDS associated with, and stored on, the volume.

The VVDS on any particular volume contains catalog information solely about the VSAM data sets residing on that volume. Having said this, there are several points to note in this connection. First, the VVDS contains no catalog information concerning any non-VSAM data sets which may reside on the volume, even if the user has elected to define them in an ICF catalog (as opposed to a VSAM catalog or an OS CVOL); in this case, all of their catalog information is stored wholly in the BCS component of the catalog, not in the VVDS.

Second, the VVDS contains catalog entries solely for what we may term *ICF objects*, namely for VSAM objects defined in an ICF catalog. If we consider a VVDSx on volume VOLX00, then there may very well be *strictly VSAM objects*— defined in an Enhanced VSAM catalog—residing on the volume in addition to ICF-objects. A data set, for example, that is cataloged in a VSAM (non-ICF) catalog would not have any entry in any VVDS located on the volume on which the data set resides, nor indeed would it further have any entry in any associated BCS component of an ICF catalog. Such a data set has a catalog entry only in the (Enhanced) VSAM catalog in which it was defined. It is important to realize that in any environment that supports both Enhanced VSAM and DFP/VSAM, a VSAM data set may be defined in either one of these types of catalogs, *but always only in one or the other, not both.* Either it is an ICF object, or it is a VSAM non-ICF object, which we have referred to as a *strictly VSAM object*.

Third, the VVDS contains catalog information that is typically highly volatile, changing frequently over the data set's life cycle; as we have seen earlier in this chapter, this includes most VSAM statistics, such as REC-TOTAL, SPLITS-CI and SPLITS-CA, HURBA, EXCPS, EXTENTS, among many others, and is the sort of information that generally must be updated numerous times over even short periods of processing activity. Thus, part of the design strategy of DFP/VSAM is to segregate the stable catalog information about VSAM objects into the BCS component of an ICF catalog, and the volatile information into a separate VVDS component. Critical to this strategy is that the volatile catalog information about a VSAM data set *coresides* on the same volume with the data set itself, done in part to facilitate a higher degree of synchronization between a catalog entry and the object for which it is an entry: making them coresident, which they were not under Enhanced VSAM, allows catalog management routines to update the catalog entry for a data set by accessing the same volume as that accessed by VSAM routines when processing against that data set, allowing for a reduction of out-of-sync conditions. Figure 17-5 summarizes the basic features of the two components of an ICF catalog, while Figure 17-6 summarizes their status as VSAM data sets.

17.3 ICF CATALOG OPERATION

Now that we have looked at the basic general structure of ICF catalogs, and their two components, let us turn to their basic operation.

17.3.1 Relationship of ICF Catalog Components

The general relationship of a BCS and its associated VVDS(s) is illustrated in Figure 17-7. There the BCS component of an ICF catalog is shown to reside on a volume CATVOL, while its—in this case, one—associated VVDS resides on VOL1 (not a volume serial number, just a convenient means of referring to the volumes in the figures). The BCS contains a pointer to the VVDS on VOL1, and the VVDS in

- Two-Part Catalog: <u>BCS</u> + <u>VVDS</u>

- Each ICF Catalog:

    1. <u>Basic Catalog Structure</u> (<u>BCS</u>)

      - One only

      - Stable Information

        - Name
        - Volume
        - Associations
        - Ownership
        - Security

      - Multiple BCSs per Volume

    2. <u>VSAM Volume Data Set</u> (<u>VVDS</u>)

      - One per Volume Controlled by Catalog

      - Volatile Information

      - VVDS Shared by Multiple BCSs
        (max = 36)

Figure 17-5. The structure of an ICF catalog.

<u>BCS</u> = <u>Variable-length Spanned Record KSDS</u>

    - Treated as standard KSDS

    - Key = 45 characters

      - 44 character data set name

      - 1 character extension identifier

<u>VVDS</u> = <u>Fixed-Length Record ESDS</u>

    - Treated as a special-purpose ESDS

    - <u>Not</u> processable as cluster/data set

Figure 17-6. ICF catalog components.

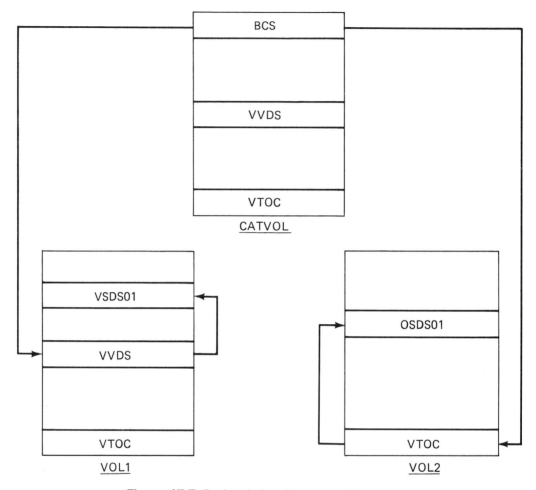

Figure 17-7. Basic relationships in an ICF catalog.

turn contains a pointer to an ICF data set—one cataloged in this ICF catalog—named VSDS01. More strictly speaking, the data set VSDS01 has part of its catalog entry—the stable information—stored in the BCS and part—the volatile information—stored in the VVDS. An ICF data set is located by DFP/VSAM by first performing a name lookup against the BCS, then retrieving from the BCS entry for the data set a *forward RBA pointer* which points to the associated VVDS, which points to the data set through extent information held in the VVDS entry for the data set.

Notice also in Figure 17-7 that the BCS also has a forward pointer to VOL2, which, for the sake of this discussion, we will assume contains only OS (non-VSAM) and/or GDG data sets, a single OS data set (OSDS01) being shown there. Information about such data sets is contained wholly in the BCS and, indeed, for a volume like VOL2 with no VSAM data sets on it, no VVDS catalog component is allocated, or needed, on the volume itself. An OS data set, cataloged in an ICF catalog, is located as shown in the figure: the BCS entry for OSDS01 will contain a forward pointer (not an RBA) to the VTOC of the appropriate volume (volume information is stored in the BCS), and the data set is located through the VTOC like any OS data set (there will be a Format-1 DSCB containing extent information about the data set).

Consider now just VOL1. If the simplified configuration shown in Figure 17-7 existed on VOL1, then the VTOC would contain two entries, as given below, where the arrow indicates a forward pointer in whatever form.

> *VOL1 VTOC*:
>> VVDS $\rightarrow$
>> VSDS01 $\rightarrow$

That is, there would be an entry for the one and only VVDS on the volume (we show it for convenience as 'VVDS,' but it will have a precisely structured VSAM name which we will consider later), and an entry for the one ICF data set on the volume, VSDS01. As we will see later, DFP/VSAM data set allocation is handled in such fashion that every ICF data set on a volume has a direct entry in that volume's VTOC, and this includes the VVDS which is also an ICF data set (a special form of ESDS). This was not the case for Enhanced VSAM, which had direct VTOC entries only for unique data sets, and for VSAM spaces, but not for any suballocated data set. The VVDS of VOL1 would have two entries, given below.

> *VOL1 VVDS*:
>> VSDS01 $\rightarrow$
>> BCS $\leftarrow$

The first entry is a forward pointer to the one ICF data set on the volume, VSDS01. The second entry is a *backward pointer* from this VVDS to the BCS (on CATVOL) associated with this VVDS. Thus, DFP/VSAM chains together the BCS and VVDS with each having a pointer to the other. Note finally that the VTOC on the CATVOL of Figure 17-7 would contain (at least) two pointers, one to the BCS, treated as a KSDS, and one to the VVDS, treated as an ESDS. There would have to be a VVDS on the CATVOL, because one is required as long as even a single ICF data set exists on the volume, and this is certainly the case for a volume holding the BCS, since the BCS is itself an ICF data set.

Now consider Figure 17-8, which shows four ICF catalogs, one of which, MCAT, is functioning as the VSAM Master Catalog of the system. Like any Master Catalog, MCAT contains pointers to all user catalogs in the system, whether the user catalogs are ICF catalogs or Enhanced VSAM catalogs (there will also be pointers to any OS CVOLs being used). The three user catalogs shown are defined as follows. UCAT1 is the easiest, consisting of BCS1 and VVDS1; VVDS1 is shown to reside on VOL1, and BCS1 may be on this or any other volume (BCSs and their VVDSs need not coreside).

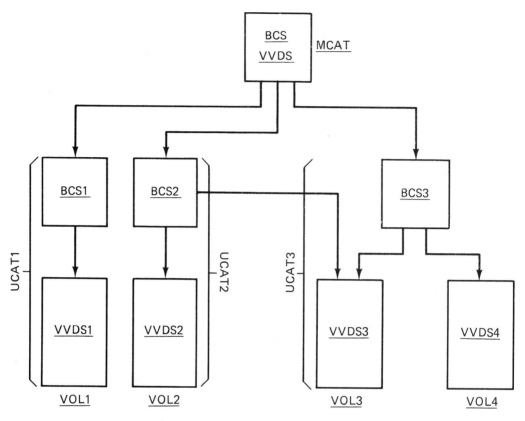

Figure 17-8. More detailed view of ICF catalog relationships.

Leaving aside UCAT2 for a moment, UCAT3 consists of BCS3 (one and only one BCS per ICF catalog), and the two VVDSs, VVDS3 and VVDS4, which are stored on VOL3 and VOL4, respectively. Remember that an ICF catalog must contain at least one VVDS, but may, and often does, contain more than one VVDS, as UCAT3 in Figure 17-8 illustrates. What this means for UCAT3 is that it controls both VOL3 and VOL4, in that it maintains data sets defined in it and stored, variously, on those two volumes; that is, there is at least one data set on each of the two volumes, VOL3 and VOL4, cataloged in UCAT3 (the name of the user catalog is always whatever name is selected for the BCS component, here 'UCAT3'). BCS3 may be located on either of these volumes, or it may be located on another entirely different volume, and in the latter case the ICF catalog UCAT3 can be seen to contain three catalog components, one BCS and two VVDSs. There is no limit on the number of VVDSs that may be associated with any particular BCS (this is discussed further in the next section).

UCAT2 consists, like UCAT3, of a BCS and two VVDSs, namely BCS2, VVDS2 on VOL2, and VVDS3 on VOL3, but the important point to observe here is that UCAT2 shares a VVDS, VVDS3, with UCAT3. A VVDS on any volume, unlike a

BCS, may be a shared catalog *component*, with catalog entries for various data sets residing on that volume and defined in multiple different ICF catalogs. In Figure 17-8, given the configuration shown, we know that VOL3, with its shared VVDS3, has at least one ICF data set cataloged in BCS2 ('UCAT2'), and at least another data set cataloged in BCS3 ('UCAT3'). As a VVDS, VVDS3 contains catalog entries for all ICF data sets residing on VOL3, regardless of what ICF catalog they were defined in. Thus, BCS2 will contain forward pointers to both VVDS2 and VVDS3 and—going the other way—VVDS3 will contain at least the following entries:

> *VVDS3*:
> > BCS2 ←
> > BCS3 ←

That is, two backward pointers to the two BCSs that share this VVDS. As a consequence of this, we say that VOL3 is controlled by both BCS2 (UCAT2) and BCS3 (UCAT3); this was not possible with Enhanced VSAM catalogs: a volume was owned by one and only one catalog, and all of the VSAM data sets residing on that volume must have been defined in that single owning catalog. The ICF data sets residing on VOL3 in our Figure 17-8 may have been defined in either of the two (but only in one for any particular data set) 'controlling' catalogs, BCS2 and BCS3. In DFP/VSAM, this phenomenon is sometimes referred to as shared volume *control*, in that volumes are not owned or controlled by single catalogs, as was the case in Enhanced VSAM. The restrictions on ICF catalogs for shared volume control will be described in detail below.

Finally, just a note on a certain 'naming' awkwardness involved in dealing with ICF catalogs. With respect to Figure 17-8, for example, UCAT1 is, strictly speaking, 'constituted' as it were, by BCS1 and VVDS1 jointly. However, as is customary in discussions of DFP/VSAM, there are references on some occasions to data sets defined/cataloged in UCAT1, and on other occasions to data sets cataloged in BCS1, as if that were the user catalog. The references can be used interchangeably even though, strictly speaking, the user catalog, UCAT1, is not just its single BCS, BCS1, but also VVDS1. The reason for this relaxed way of speaking is that, as we will see later in this chapter, when an ICF catalog is created (through a DEFINE UCAT command with the special parameter ICFCATALOG), the name provided by the user for the user catalog is taken by DFP/VSAM as the name *only of the BCS component of the ICF catalog*. The asssociated VVDS component is not ever provided with a user-chosen name, but is assigned a special name following a strict naming convention for VVDSs (explained later in this chapter), and rarely does the user ever explicitly specify to ICF routines the VVDS name. Since the name specified on the DEF UCAT command is therefore the name assigned solely to the BCS, a reference such as 'UCAT1' is ambiguous between just the BCS component, or the entire ICF catalog with its BCS and VVDS components. Indeed, DFP/VSAM has no name for the ICF catalog as a whole, but strictly for the components individually. However, because of this, the BCS name is conventionally taken to serve as the name of the ICF catalog as a whole, so that it is common to speak of a data set's being defined in a particular BCS. For IBM, the BCS is the *major* component of an ICF catalog so that the latter takes its name from the BCS component name. We will use either mode of reference at various points, but where we need to make a finer distinction, we shall do so explicitly as needed.

17.3.2   ICF Catalog Control of Volumes

As we have noted, Enhanced VSAM implemented a *principle of volume ownership*, whereby a catalog owned all volumes on which resided any VSAM objects defined in that catalog, and no data sets defined in other catalogs could reside on any of these *owned* volumes: one and only one VSAM catalog *exclusively* and *exhaustively* owned a particular volume (as long as the volume contained at least one VSAM object), as volume sharing by catalogs was strictly prohibited. In contrast, ICF catalogs *control* but do not *own* volumes. To appreciate what precisely this involves, we can consider ICF *volume control* as constituted by the following three principles.

Universal scope of volume control.   An ICF catalog controls any unlimited number of volumes: data sets defined in the catalog may be stored on any volume in the system, without constraint (but see below). Thus, a user may catalog an ICF data set in any available ICF catalog, regardless of what volume the user chooses to allocate the data set on. An installation may choose to *administratively* restrict, through installation-specific standards and procedures, a user to certain catalogs and/or volumes, but DFP/VSAM itself imposes no such restriction (and will not police any).

Volume sharing by ICF catalogs.   Any particular volume may have resident ICF data sets defined in up to 36 different ICF catalogs. Thus, in DFP/VSAM, catalog volume control, which replaces Enhanced VSAM's principle of volume ownership, permits a single VVDS to contain catalog entries for data sets that have been cataloged in as many as 36 distinct BCS catalog components (naturally, any *one* data set is cataloged in one and only one ICF catalog). We might, therefore, think of a VVDS as a shared catalog component, whose 'share limit' is 36. Consider Figure 17-8 again in this connection. As we noted, and as can be seen in the figure, VVDS3 is shared by two BCS components, BCS2 and BCS3. Thus, a partial view of VVDS3, schematically, would show this state of affairs:

VVDS3:

BCS2	$\leftarrow$	
BCS3	$\leftarrow$	
VSDS2A	$\rightarrow$	{+BCS2}
VSDS3A	$\rightarrow$	{+BCS3}

There are two backward pointers to the two BCS components that share this VVDS. In addition, there is a catalog entry for a VSAM data set, VSDS2A, that is stored on this volume, but which has been cataloged in BCS2; this catalog entry has both a forward pointer ('→') which through extent information points to the location on the volume of the VSDS2A data set itself, and a field which shows which BCS contains the remaining, stable part of the catalog information for this data set (this is shown symbolically in the figure as '+BCS2'). Similarly, the catalog entry for VSDS3A has a forward pointer to its whereabouts on the volume, and a field indicating which BCS this data set was defined in ('+BCS3').

ICF/Enhanced VSAM catalog independence.   It is important to note that any volume in the system that contains VSAM data sets is not restricted to being exclusively either a volume owned by an Enhanced VSAM catalog, or a volume controlled by one or more ICF catalogs. The principles of the two types of catalogs (in a mixed Enhanced VSAM and DFP/VSAM environment) are independent of each other. Thus, considering Figure 17-8 again, in addition to VSDS2A and VSDS3A on VOL2, two ICF data sets stored on the volume, there may be any number of strictly non-ICF VSAM data sets (defined in an Enhanced VSAM catalog). Say that there are three such data sets, VSAM01, VSAM02, VSAM03. Being non-ICF data sets, they may *not* be defined in BCS2 or BCS3, the two BCSs controlling this volume, and may not appear in any way in VVDS3, which consists of catalog entries solely for ICF data sets. Now assume further that VSAM01 is cataloged in the Enhanced VSAM catalog FINCAT. Then it must be the case that VSAM02 and VSAM03 are also cataloged in FINCAT. Why? Because the principle of volume ownership, an Enhanced VSAM principle, still applies to all Enhanced VSAM data sets—that is, to any VSAM data sets defined in Enhanced VSAM catalogs—and that principle requires that one and only one Enhanced VSAM catalog can own, exclusively and exhaustively, any particular volume with VSAM data sets on it. Thus, since VSAM01 is cataloged in FINCAT, FINCAT must own this volume (VOL2) so that VSAM02 and VSAM03 have to have been also defined in FINCAT.

Note also another critical point, frequently misunderstood about DFP/VSAM, namely the fact that ICF data sets may be stored on any volume of the system, even if that volume is *owned* by an Enhanced VSAM catalog. Ownership of a volume by an Enhanced VSAM catalog prohibits only *other Enhanced VSAM* catalogs from having any of their data sets stored on the owned volume—thus VSAM02 and VSAM03 may not be cataloged in other than FINCAT in which VSAM01 is cataloged and which owns VOL2—but implies no restriction whatever concerning ICF catalogs. Thus, a particular volume that contains both ICF and non-ICF VSAM data sets may be *owned* by one Enhanced VSAM catalog *and* in addition *controlled* by up to 36 ICF catalogs (as many as 37 catalogs involved, in all). Indeed, unless all of the volume's space was deliberately allocated to VSAM, the volume may also contain OS (non-VSAM) data sets, which may be cataloged in *any* catalog (ICF, Enhanced VSAM, or an OS CVOL) whatever.

17.3.3   How ICF Locates a Data Set

For data sets defined in ICF catalogs (ICF data sets), ICF first searches the BCS for the target data set entry, from which it retrieves a forward RBA pointer to the appropriate VVDS (the one for the volume on which the target data set resides). The VVDS catalog entry for the target data set will contain extent information that locates the data set on the volume. For OS (non-VSAM) data sets, the BCS is again first searched. The BCS entry for the target data set in this case contains a pointer to the VTOC, not the VVDS, of the volume on which the data set resides—remember that all catalog information about a non-VSAM data set defined in an ICF catalog is contained in the BCS alone—and the VTOC entry (a DSCB) gives the extent information by which the data set itself is located on the volume. GDG data sets are treated by ICF precisely like non-VSAM data sets (all information is in the BCS, which points to the appropriate VTOC).

17.3.4 Naming Conventions for ICF Catalogs

As we have already noted (Subsection 17.3.1), DFP/VSAM does not strictly provide a name for the entire object of an ICF catalog as a collection of a single BCS and one or more VVDSs. Rather, the BCS name is, by convention, used to refer to the whole ICF catalog, although it is actually the name solely of the *data component* of the BCS, itself a KSDS cluster. When we create an ICF catalog through the DEFINE UCAT command with the ICFCATALOG parameter (we will take up the actual coding later in this chapter), the NAME parameter is exclusively for the data component; DFP/VSAM does not permit a user-provided name for either the cluster level of the BCS, or the index component. The BCS cluster name is always VSAM-generated as 44 bytes of binary zeroes, assuring that it is the first entry returned in a LISTCAT of an ICF catalog. The index component name is also VSAM-generated, always in the form shown in Figure 17-9, where the high-level-qualifier is constant as 'CATINDEX,' the second and fourth qualifiers jointly forming a complex (and

1. BCS

Cluster Name	0000 . . . 000 44 binary zeroes
Data Name	User-assigned name
Index Name	CATINDEX.Tbbbbbbb.VIDyyddd.Taaaaaaa

2. VVDS

Cluster & Data Name: SYS1.VVDS.Vvolser

Figure 17-9. ICF catalog names.

generally useless) time-of-day timestamp (at create time), and the third qualifier being the constant 'VID' followed by the date ('julianized').

The name of the VVDS on any particular volume has a constant form for the first two qualifiers of 'SYS1.VVDS,' with the third and last qualifier always in the form 'V_____,' where a six-character volume serial number identifying the volume on which the VVDS resides follows the lead 'V' character. Thus, we know that the VVDS on volume DSK001 is named 'SYS1.VVDS.VDSK001' by this convention. This is an excellent convention, in that we can, from the name of a VVDS catalog component, immediately know the volume on which it resides. Note that this is both the cluster name *and* the data component name; the VVDS is an ESDS, so there is no index component. Figure 17-10 is a partial listing of an ICF catalog known to DFP/VSAM as 'TESTCAT,' although we can see from the listing's first entry that this is actually the BCS's data component name. Note the cluster name of 44 zeroes, and the index component name in the form we discussed. Note that this ICF catalog is

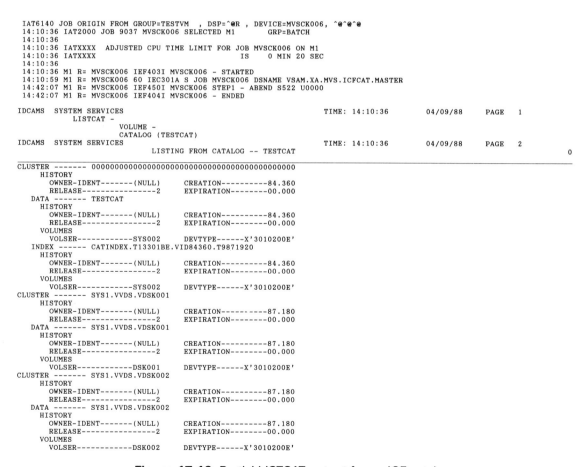

```
IAT6140 JOB ORIGIN FROM GROUP=TESTVM  , DSP=^@R , DEVICE=MVSCK006, ^@^@^@
14:10:36 IAT2000 JOB 9037 MVSCK006 SELECTED M1       GRP=BATCH
14:10:36
14:10:36 IATXXXX  ADJUSTED CPU TIME LIMIT FOR JOB MVSCK006 ON M1
14:10:36 IATXXXX                        IS    0 MIN 20 SEC
14:10:36
14:10:36 M1 R= MVSCK006 IEF403I MVSCK006 - STARTED
14:10:59 M1 R= MVSCK006 60 IEC301A S JOB MVSCK006 DSNAME VSAM.XA.MVS.ICFCAT.MASTER
14:42:07 M1 R= MVSCK006 IEF450I MVSCK006 STEP1 - ABEND S522 U0000
14:42:07 M1 R= MVSCK006 IEF404I MVSCK006 - ENDED

IDCAMS  SYSTEM SERVICES                                    TIME: 14:10:36      04/09/88    PAGE   1
            LISTCAT -
                        VOLUME -
                        CATALOG (TESTCAT)
IDCAMS  SYSTEM SERVICES                                    TIME: 14:10:36      04/09/88    PAGE   2
                              LISTING FROM CATALOG -- TESTCAT                                        0
─────────────────────────────────────────────────────────────────────────────────────────────────
CLUSTER ------- 0000000000000000000000000000000000000000000
    HISTORY
        OWNER-IDENT-------(NULL)         CREATION----------84.360
        RELEASE----------------2         EXPIRATION--------00.000
    DATA ------- TESTCAT
        HISTORY
        OWNER-IDENT-------(NULL)         CREATION----------84.360
        RELEASE----------------2         EXPIRATION--------00.000
        VOLUMES
        VOLSER------------SYS002         DEVTYPE------X'3010200E'
    INDEX ------ CATINDEX.T13301BE.VID84360.T9871920
        HISTORY
        OWNER-IDENT-------(NULL)         CREATION----------84.360
        RELEASE----------------2         EXPIRATION--------00.000
        VOLUMES
        VOLSER------------SYS002         DEVTYPE------X'3010200E'
CLUSTER ------- SYS1.VVDS.VDSK001
    HISTORY
        OWNER-IDENT-------(NULL)         CREATION----------87.180
        RELEASE----------------2         EXPIRATION--------00.000
    DATA ------- SYS1.VVDS.VDSK001
        HISTORY
        OWNER-IDENT-------(NULL)         CREATION----------87.180
        RELEASE----------------2         EXPIRATION--------00.000
        VOLUMES
        VOLSER------------DSK001         DEVTYPE------X'3010200E'
CLUSTER ------- SYS1.VVDS.VDSK002
    HISTORY
        OWNER-IDENT-------(NULL)         CREATION----------87.180
        RELEASE----------------2         EXPIRATION--------00.000
    DATA ------- SYS1.VVDS.VDSK002
        HISTORY
        OWNER-IDENT-------(NULL)         CREATION----------87.180
        RELEASE----------------2         EXPIRATION--------00.000
        VOLUMES
        VOLSER------------DSK002         DEVTYPE------X'3010200E'
```

Figure 17-10. Partial LISTCAT output for an ICF catalog.

associated with (at least—this is a partial listing) two VVDS, namely SYS1.VVDS. VDSK001 on volume DSK001, and SYS1.VVDS.VDSK002 on volume DSK002. In addition, note the IEC message in the job messages portion of the figure (see the eighth line down), where a data set named VSAM.XA.MVS.ICFCAT.MASTER is identified. This is the MVS systems catalog, which is also (necessarily, in MVS) the VSAM Master Catalog, and (by its name) is obviously an ICF catalog. Finally, note that the CREATION field is '84.360'—the three-hundred-sixtieth day of 1984—for the cluster and for both its data and index components, and this agrees with the third qualifier of the index component name ('VID84360').

17.4 ICF CATALOG RECORD STRUCTURE

17.4.1 BCS Record Structure

The BCS component of an ICF catalog consists of two types of catalog records, *sphere records* and *nonsphere records*. Sphere records are used to hold the catalog information only for VSAM objects that are actual data sets, and for VSAM these are either clusters—which include AIXs, themselves KSDS clusters—or Generation Data Groups (GDGs), when these are defined to VSAM (not when they are solely OS GDGs defined only in an OS, not a VSAM, catalog). Nonsphere records are used when either (1) the data set is non-VSAM (an OS data set defined in a VSAM catalog), or (2) when the object is not implemented as a physically real data set; these nondata set objects are: paths, aliases, (catalog) connectors, and truenames (the component names of VSAM objects that VSAM uses to either locate or describe the objects by). Besides this distinction in sphere versus nonsphere records, they are also distinguished by degree of internal structure. Nonsphere records are used for objects treated by VSAM as single objects without any constituent components: non-VSAM data sets, paths, aliases, connectors, and truenames have no component structure. Sphere records are used for objects with component structure, like clusters (with data and index components) and GDGs (made up of individual Generation Data Sets (GDSs)). Figure 17-11 summarizes these distinctions between sphere and nonsphere records.

Both sphere records and nonsphere records are taken to be comprised of *cells*, collections of functionally-related catalog information. For example, a volume cell is used to contain both volume serial number and device type information, along with certain other volume-related status information (such as whether the volume information is for a VSAM or a non-VSAM data set). A connector cell contains the name of the catalog being pointed to and an indicator of whether it is an Enhanced VSAM or ICF catalog. An ownership cell contains the owner-id, creation and expiration date, and an indicator of whether the object is protected by the RACF security product or not (among other status indicators). For sphere records only, DFP/VSAM organizes the cells into a larger unit, the *component*; thus there are volume and owner cells, in addition to many others, for the so-called 'cluster component' (really, the cluster level), the data component, and the index component of a VSAM KSDS. Again, only for sphere records, VSAM in turn organizes the component units into a

Sphere	One or more components, comprised of cells
Non-Sphere	Single component, comprised of cells

Sphere Records	Non-Sphere Records
Cluster GDG	Non-VSAM Alias Connector Path Truename

Figure 17-11. Catalog records: sphere versus nonsphere.

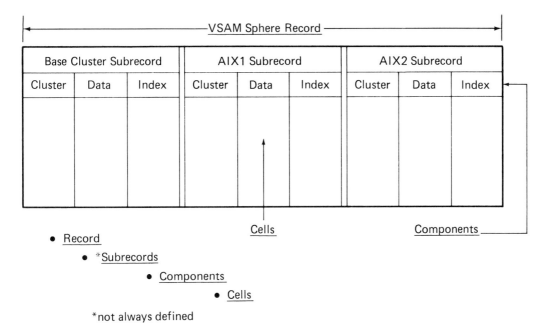

- Record
  - *Subrecords
    - Components
      - Cells

*not always defined

Figure 17-12. General structure of a sphere record.

still larger unit, the *subrecord*, which in turn are further organized into the largest, highest-level unit, the sphere record itself.

This internal structure of a sphere record is clarified in two figures, Figure 17-12 and Figure 17-13. Figure 17-12 shows the basic structure of a cluster-type sphere record (the only other type being a GDG sphere record). The cluster for which this is a BCS record is a KSDS with two AIXs defined over it. Notice a critical difference

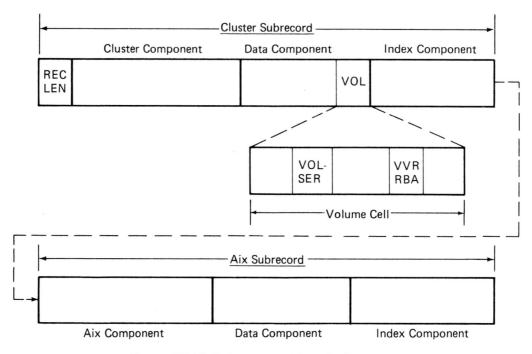

Figure 17-13. Sphere record for KSDS plus AIX.

between Enhanced VSAM and DFP/VSAM catalog organization. Enhanced VSAM would have a separate and distinct record for each of the base cluster KSDS, the first AIX (AIX1), and the second AIX (AIX2); these three records for the three related objects (base cluster plus two associated AIXs) are *not* stored together in a VSAM catalog, and must be separately retrieved by distinct I/O operations. However, all of this catalog information is typically stored together in a single sphere record in an ICF catalog; Figure 17-12 shows the sphere record to contain three subrecords, one for the base cluster, and one for each of the AIXs built over this KSDS base cluster, AIX1 and AIX2. This solves the problem with Enhanced VSAM Catalog Management, namely high catalog I/O overhead, which we discussed in Subsection 17.1.1. Since it is often the case that when processing a base cluster or any one of its associated AIXs, processing activity must be reflected in the catalog entries for all of the objects, namely the base cluster and all upgrade set members, concurrently and in synchrony—we say the objects' catalog entries must be *co-updated*—then it is clearly more efficient to have the catalog records for all of the associated objects stored together, rather than separately, as this avoids multiple I/O operations to fetch the separate records from the catalog. Under DFP/VSAM, a single I/O operation will typically be all that is required to fetch the catalog information for all of the associated objects, as it is all stored together in a single sphere record, as illustrated in Figure 17-12.

Figure 17-13 shows, schematically, the internal structure of a sphere record for a cluster with one AIX defined over it, but adding a representation of cell structure; also represented is a record-length field at the very beginning of the sphere record, needed because a BCS contains *variable*-length records. Note that the sphere record consists of two subrecords, one cluster and the other AIX, with each of these subrecords in turn containing three component units (cluster, data, and index components), which finally consist of a collection of cells. We show just the volume cell of the data component of the cluster subrecord (there will be a volume cell for each component), which itself is a collection of volume-related catalog information: it contains a vol-ser field (shown), a device-type field (not shown), and a special RBA pointer field (which we will discuss later) known as the *VVR-RBA* (shown), among other fields.

It should be noted that DFP/VSAM does not invariably use a component level of unit in BCS catalog records. It does use component units for cluster-type sphere records, but not for the (only) other type of sphere record, that for a GDG; the GDG sphere record is decomposed into subrecords, one for the GDG level itself (the GDG 'base record'), and one for each of the GDSs making up the GDG, with the subrecords consisting directly of cells, rather than component units. (In the latest documentation —the *MVS/XA Catalog Administration Guide* for Data Facility Product (DFP) Version 2, Release 3.0 or higher—IBM dispenses with the component level for GDGs, but IBM's treatment of the issue of the internal structure of sphere records is not wholly consistent. The latest DFP/VSAM publications indicate that a record is decomposed into components, themselves decomposed into cells, so that cells, components, and records are said to be the 'building blocks' of the BCS; the level of subrecord is not even mentioned as one of the 'building blocks' of BCS records, yet in the illustrations of BCS sphere records for both clusters and GDGs (the only two kinds), a subrecord level is explicitly shown for both. Worse still, although the component level is recognized explicitly in the publications, it is not shown or used for GDG sphere records which, as we have seen, move from the record to the subrecord to the cell level without stopping off at a component level. It is less confusing to consider that records, subrecords, components, and cells are all building blocks of the BCS, but not all are used as organizational units for each type of sphere record. In any case, nothing critical hinges on this.)

Now consider Figure 17-14, which shows a representative nonsphere record, one for a non-VSAM data set. Note that the record is immediately organized into cells, without any intervening subrecord or component level units. The 'LL' field contains the record length, followed by a name cell, and owner cell, an optional associations cell, and at least one volume cell (two are shown and the second is optional). Given that nonsphere records—in the earlier publications relating to DFP/VSAM, these records were at one time known as *standard records*—are used for simpler objects than the objects represented by sphere records, the structure of nonsphere records is considerably simpler than that of sphere records, as can be seen by comparing Figure 17-14 with the earlier Figure 17-13. Finally, note that a BCS, like any KSDS, is organized into CIs, and a single CI may contain mutiple BCS records, both sphere and nonsphere, depending on the CISZ chosen or defaulted to.

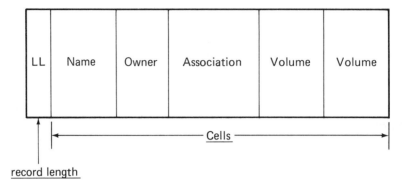

Figure 17-14. Sample nonsphere record: for non-VSAM data set.

17.4.2 Internal Structure of a VVDS

As we have already learned, the VVDS catalog component is a fixed-length record ESDS. Also recall that it is a special-purpose ESDS organized in such a fashion that it is *not* processable as a data set (unlike the BCS which, under certain circumstances, can be processed as a standard KSDS). Like an ESDS, the VVDS is organized into CIs, but—again, unlike a BCS, which allows multiple records to a CI—each CI may hold only a single VVDS record. The CISZ is fixed at 4096 bytes (4K), with a record size of 4086 bytes, allowing 10 bytes of control information for a CIDF (four bytes) and two RDFs (three bytes each). BCS records are spanned, but VVDS records are unspanned (may not cross a CI boundary). The VVDS contains the detailed volatile catalog information about all ICF data sets (not Enhanced VSAM data sets) residing on the same volume as the VVDS itself.

The internal structure of the VVDS is represented in Figure 17-15. The VVDS must always contain at least two records, the first record of the VVDS catalog component being known as the *VSAM Volume Control Record* (*VVCR*), and following this there may be one or more records known as *VSAM Volume Records* (*VVRs*). We will look at both of these types of VVDS records in more detail shortly, but we will note now that each ICF data set on the volume is described by one or more VVRs, that is, the VVRs contain the detailed volatile catalog information about the coresident data sets on the volume that have been defined in ICF catalogs. Each VVDS begins with the VVCR followed by a special VVR known as the *Self-Describing VVR* (*SD-VVR*), in that this is the VVR that contains the catalog information for the VVDS itself: remember that the VVDS is itself an ICF data set, so that even if there were no *other* ICF data sets on the volume, the VVDS would still contain two records, the VVCR and the SD-VVR, the latter needed to describe the one ICF data set that is always on a volume that contains a VVDS, namely the VVDS itself. Apart from its describing the VVDS, the SD-VVR is otherwise no different in structure and function from any other VVRs that the VVDS might contain.

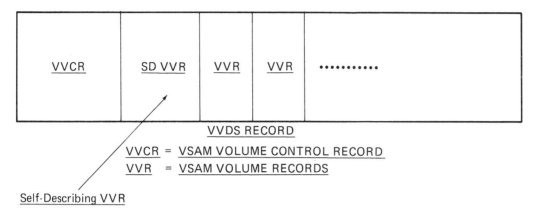

Figure 17-15. The structure of a VVDS.

There will be at least one VVR for each VSAM data set on the volume. More precisely, there will typically be one VVR for each *component* on the volume: thus an ESDS is described by a single VVR associated with its data component, while a KSDS will generally require two VVRs to hold its VVDS catalog information, one VVR apiece for the data and index components. Indeed, even for one component, there may be more than one VVR, in which the first is the *primary VVR*, said to have a VVRTYPE of *Z*, while the remaining VVRs are the *secondary VVRs*, with a VVRTYPE of *Q*. (Actually, the situation is more complex than this latter case, which is true for a KSDS with the NOIMBED index option; if the KSDS was defined with the IMBED index option, then three VVRs in the VVDS would be used to describe the KSDS, one VVR for the data component, another for the index component, and the third for the separately stored index sequence set generated by the IMBED option (this option is described fully in Chapter 18, on VSAM performance). Furthermore, when dealing with potentially multivolume key range clusters (also described in Chapter 18), there will always be one VVR needed for the index component (assuming a KSDS), and either one VVR *per* key range *per* volume, or two VVRs per key range per volume, just in the event that the cluster has been defined with the IMBED option. The exact details of all of this are given in the *Catalog Administration Guide*, but applications programmers generally need not concern themselves with the precise number of VVRs describing any data set, as LISTCAT output displays the total catalog information about that data set held jointly in the BCS and in the VVDS, without discriminating individual VVRs in any way.

Let's consider first the VVCR. This is made up of two fields, each 2K in size (the VVCR being 4K in size). The first 2K field of the VVCR is what may be termed the *controlling-BCS* field: it contains backward pointers to all BCS catalog components that share this VVDS, that is, that control data sets on the volume. As the reader may recall, there may be as many as 36 BCSs jointly controlling the various ICF data sets on a single volume, so that this controlling-BCS field may contain up to 36 backward pointers. The second 2K of the VVCR contains a *CI bit map*, used for DASD space management of each of the CIs making up the VVDS.

The VVRs, where the detailed volatile catalog information for ICF data sets is stored, are simply constructed of collections of cells, in much the same way that nonsphere BCS records were comprised of cells. Following a length field giving the size of the VVR, a header cell identifies the component that this VVR is associated with, as well as the name of the BCS that the component was cataloged in. Then follow the various VVR cells (it is not necessary to detail these individually) which contain the remaining volatile catalog information concerning the component: extent information, HURBA, HARBA and HKRBA, component attributes (like SPEED, UNIQUE, SPANNED, etc.), component statistics (which includes FSPC, CISZ, STRNO, REC-TOTAL, etc.), and essentially all other catalog information besides name, associations, ownership and security, which are held in the BCS, not the VVDS. Generally, as we will discuss in more detail later, a VVDS is allowed to be *implicitly* defined by VSAM; this means that VSAM will automatically define the VVDS, with default attributes, on the volume whenever the first ICF data set (including a BCS component) is defined on the volume. The user may choose, alternatively, to *explicitly* define the VVDS, although this is generally done only when the user wishes to override the space allocation defaults.

17.5 THE DEFINITION OF ICF CATALOGS

In this section, we will briefly look at the *basics* of defining ICF catalogs: we will look only at the minimal coding required to accomplish the definition, which will therefore not necessarily, or even frequently, be an *optimal* one. We will discuss more optimal, that is, performance-oriented, definitions in our chapter on performance.

Figure 17-16 gives the basic coding for defining the BCS component of an ICF

```
DEF  UCAT
      (ICFCATALOG -
      NAME (TESTCAT) -                     ⎫
      CYL (100  5) -                        ⎬ required
      VOL (SYS002))                         ⎭


Disallowed:

            INDEXED
            KEYS
            SPEED    (RECOVERY required)
            NOREUSE
            RECOVERABLE
```

Figure 17-16. The definition of a BCS.

catalog. Only the four parameters shown are required, all others are optional. Since this is the DEF(INE) UCAT command also supported in Enhanced VSAM, a parameter is required to distinguish whether the definition is for an Enhanced VSAM catalog, or for an ICF catalog, and this is done by the parameter choice of VSAMCATALOG or ICFCATALOG. Given that the default is VSAMCATALOG, the creation of an ICF catalog requires the explicit specification of the ICFCATALOG parameter on the DEF UCAT command.

The NAME paramater assigns a user-provided name to the data component of the BCS (which is a KSDS), and by convention this name is used as the name of the ICF catalog object as a whole, which is then treated as a single user catalog, despite containing distinct components, one BCS and one or more VVDSs. (A reference to 'TESTCAT', therefore, is both a specific reference to the BCS component of an ICF catalog, and also a reference to the entire ICF catalog itself.)

Finally, DASD space must be allocated to the BCS, and the volume on which it is to be allocated is specified (VOL parameter). For purposes of space allocation, the BCS should be treated as a standard KSDS with a relatively high amount of activity against it: this is so because, although the BCS catalog information about any particular data set is (by definition) relatively stable, the BCS itself is nonetheless a relatively high activity data set due to the fact that it must be updated whenever new data sets are defined in it, or existing data sets are deleted from it, fairly common and frequent events for any user catalog. Consult the *Catalog Administration Guide* for more specific recommendations concerning the 'sizing' and related space allocation issues of BCSs.

Figure 17-16 also shows which parameters may *not* be specified when defining a BCS. Note several points here. One, although the BCS is a KSDS, the INDEXED parameter normally used for KSDSs may not be specified: DFP/VSAM knows the KSDS structure of this data set from the specification of the attribute ICFCATALOG on the DEF UCAT command. Two, and similarly, although the BCS is a keyed file, like any KSDS, the KEYS parameter may not be specified: the user is disallowed from defining a key field, because the keys of a BCS are always the 45 character strings made up of the data set name followed by a one byte (possibly blank) extension pad character (see Subsection 17.2.3). Three, RECOVERY (rather than SPEED) is always on for a BCS: DFP/VSAM preformats a BCS when for loading, and handles the load in such a fashion that it is resumable (by DFP/VSAM) without redefinition if the load is abnormally terminated midstream. Four, a BCS is considered a reusable data set, allowing it to be reloaded without first having to be deleted and then redefined. Five, and last, the BCS may not be marked RECOVERABLE: as already noted, recoverable catalog support has been discontinued in DFP/VSAM, that is, the duplex method of catalog recovery through CRAs (Catalog Recovery Areas) of Enhanced VSAM is not used for ICF catalogs. Figure 17-17 shows the other major parameters (all optional) that may be coded for a DEF UCAT against an ICF catalog, along with the defaults supplied by DFP/VSAM. We will not discuss these parameters explicitly here (see Chapter 18, on performance), but suffice it to note two points here. First, these are essentially the parameters codable for any KSDS, as the BCS is

Optimization	Defaults
BUFFERSPACE	2 Data CI + 1 Index CI
BUFND BUFNI	min = 1 + STRNO; if STRNO ⠀⠀⠀⠀omitted, default = 2
CISZ	computed by VSAM
FSPC	FSPC (0 0)
IMBED/NOIMBED	
RECSZ	
REPLICATE/NOREPLICATE	
Integrity/Security	
LOCK/UNLOCK	
SHR (cr cs)	SHR (3 4)
STRNO	2
MRPW/CTLPW/UPDPW/RDPW	
ATTEMPTS	2
AUTHORIZATION	
CODE	

Figure 17-17. Other parameters for BCS definition.

indeed considered a standard KSDS. This is a superior feature of ICF catalogs over Enhanced VSAM catalogs. A BCS, being a standard KSDS, is tunable in much the same way as any KSDS, as opposed to an Enhanced VSAM catalog which is essentially 'untunable' (see Subsection 17.1.1 above): for example, an Enhanced VSAM catalog's CISZ is fixed at 512 bytes, and FSPC is not specifiable, despite the fact that in Enhanced VSAM, too, a catalog is a KSDS and as in need of tuning as any KSDS. Second, note that the defaults provided by DFP/VSAM are not necessarily optimal ones: an obvious example is the default of FSPC (0 0); a BCS, like any KSDS, undergoes record addition and deletion activity, which may in turn cause CI- and CA-splits, but a default of no FSPC disallows normal growth and change without split activity overhead.

Now let's turn to the definition of a VVDS, the basic facts of whose definition are summarized in Figure 17-18. As noted there, and already noted earlier in this chapter, the VVDS for a volume is typically defined *implicitly* by DFP/VSAM whenever an

1. <u>Implicit</u>

2. <u>Explicit</u>

```
DEF CLUSTER
    (NAME (SYS1.VVDS.VDSK001) -                ⎤
     VOL  (DSK001) -                           ⎬ ─ required
     CYL  (1  1) -                             ⎭
     NONINDEXED)
```


<u>Assumed</u>:

```
        TRK   (3, 2)
        CISZ  (4096)
        RECSZ (4086  4086)
        SHR   (3 4)
        RECOVERY
        NOREUSE
        NOERASE
        NONSPANNED
```


<u>Disallowed</u>:

```
        KEYS
```

Figure 17-18. The definition of a VVDS.

ICF data set or catalog component is first defined on the volume, in which case it is given default attributes (those labelled 'assumed' in Figure 17-18). The name of a VVDS is always in the form 'SYS1.VVDS.Vvolser' where volser is the volume serial number of the volume on which the VVDS is to reside. Alternately, the user may explicitly define a VVDS; Figure 17-18 shows a sample definition for a VVDS to be allocated on DSK001. It is named, as required, in the form just discussed, marked as an ESDS by the NONINDEXED parameter, and the default space allocation of two primary tracks and three secondary is overridden to one cylinder primary and secondary. Notice that the VVDS, although an (ICF) catalog component, is *not* defined by a DEF UCAT command—only the BCS is so defined—but by a standard DEF CLUSTER command. One might, therefore, ask how DFP/VSAM distinguishes this cluster definition of a VVDS from the cluster definition of an ordinary, noncatalog, ESDS. This is solely through the fixed form required for the name of a VVDS (SYS1.VVDS.Vvolser); if a cluster is named following this naming form, then it is considered by DFP/VSAM to be a special catalog component ESDS, and not a standard ESDS.

As with all ICF data sets, as we will see later, the total primary and secondary extents may be 123 total extents (if one extent is used for the primary, this means that up to 122 allocations of the secondary amount will be available for expansion). It is primarily for this feature alone—the ability to override the default VVDS space allocation—that a user may wish to explicitly define a VVDS, rather than allowing the typical implicit definition, and one would do so if it was felt that the default allocation may be too conservative for the anticipated growth activity of the VVDS.

Note that, in addition, apart from the space allocation parameter, no other attribute of a VVDS, as shown in Figure 17-18, may be overridden by the user: CISZ, RECSZ, etc. are all not only *assumed* to have the values shown, but *must* have these and only these values and settings. Furthermore, unlike a BCS, none of the attributes of a VVDS are alterable by the ALTER command. Having been defined, therefore, the attributes of a VVDS are 'frozen.' (Again, see the *Catalog Administration Guide* for more information.)

Finally, it is important to note that, if chosen, the explicit definition of a VVDS yields what may be referred to as a *null-VVDS* if done before any ICF data set has been defined on the volume. Such a null-VVDS is perfectly acceptable to DFP/VSAM and will contain only two records, the VVCR and the SD-VVR, but no VVRs for ICF data sets on the volume, since we are assuming that the definition is done prior to any such data sets being defined. Furthermore, the VVCR will contain no backward pointers to any BCS components, since at this time the null-VVDS, although it has been allocated space and is a real data set on the volume, is unconnected (not associated with) any BCS whatsoever, and no existing BCS contains any forward pointer to this VVDS at such time. Whenever the first ICF data set is defined on the volume that this VVDS resides on, DFP/VSAM will automatically create the necessary backward pointer to whatever BCS the data set is defined in, create the appropriate VVR(s) for the data set, and create a forward pointer from the associated BCS to this VVDS, thus 'connecting' the BCS and VVDS together. Clearly, a VVDS may not be created for some volume *after* any ICF data set has been defined and allocated on the volume, since DFP/VSAM would automatically have implicitly defined the VVDS, and each volume may contain one and only one VVDS. Again, it is primarily for control over space allocation, and possibly also over the physical location of the VVDS on the volume, that a user may choose to explicitly create such a null-VVDS.

17.6 RECORD/DATA SET MANAGEMENT UNDER DFP/VSAM

In addition to the new facilities brought about by ICF Catalog Management, DFP/VSAM has several other new features, and we will begin by examining those associated with Record/Data Set Managament.

17.6.1 Extended-Unique Attribute for Data Sets

In Enhanced VSAM, as we have already noted, there are two types of space allocation for VSAM clusters, namely suballocation and unique allocation, for suballocated and unique clusters, respectively. In addition, Enhanced VSAM featured *dual space management*, as suballocation was handled by a VSAM Space Manager, while unique allocation was handled by OS DADSM (Direct Access Device Space Manager), unique clusters being treated like OS data sets for the purpose of space allocation and management. This dual space management was perceived by many—correctly, we believe—including IBM, as a major shortcoming of Enhanced VSAM, and DFP/VSAM was designed (in part) to remedy this. Under DFP/VSAM, there is a single uniform space management technique which is neither suballocation nor unique allocation, but rather what may be termed *extended-unique* space management. It is 'extended-unique' in the sense that it is handled, as unique data sets were under Enhanced VSAM, wholly by OS DADSM, the VSAM Space Manager being discontinued altogether under DFP/VSAM, but 'extended' in that extended-unique clusters do *not* take on the attributes of the former unique clusters, but rather have a combination of features from *both* the former suballocatable and the former unique clusters.

There is now only an extended-unique space allocation and management technique, and ICF data sets are of one type only, extended-unique clusters (the concepts of suballocatable and unique clusters no longer being relevant under DFP/VSAM). The fact that ICF clusters are *not* strictly unique, but rather extended-unique, is often misunderstood by users new to DFP/VSAM, but part of the blame rests on a misleading feature of the DFP/VSAM product itself. Consider Figure 17-19, which shows a LISTCAT done immediately after defining an ICF cluster (part (a) shows a portion of the MVS JCL spill for the IDCAMS job run). Part (b) of that figure gives the DEFINE CLUSTER and conditional LISTCAT request that generated the LISTCAT output of parts (c) and (d). Part (c) gives the cluster and data component attributes, and part (d) the index component attributes. We draw the reader's attention to the ATTRIBUTES group shown in Figure 17-19 (c) where, in the second column of attributes for this cluster, is seen *UNIQUE*. This is misleading on two counts. First, no matter how we define an ICF cluster, UNIQUE is shown as the attribute: SUBALLOC never appears. Second, and more importantly, one might expect this cluster to exhibit the standard characteristics of unique clusters, but a really careful look at the LISTCAT ouput itself would show this to be mistaken. Let's see how. The reader might remember (see Subsection 7.3.3) that unique clusters must be allocated in units of cylinders, never tracks or records. But a look at Figure 17-19 (c), under the ALLOCATION group, shows a SPACE-TYPE of TRACK, and this is confirmed in the DEFINE CLUSTER command of part (b) of Figure 17-19. This would not be possible if this cluster were, as suggested misleadingly by the UNIQUE attribute in LISTCAT output, really a standard unique cluster. Under DFP/VSAM, extended-unique clusters may be allocated space in any unit, thus making them more like the former suballocatable clusters, which also had no restrictions on the unit of space allocation.

Now let's consider the distinguishing features of these new ICF clusters, unique-extended clusters. These are presented and discussed below.

```
IAT6140 JOB ORIGIN FROM GROUP=TESTVM , DSP=^@R , DEVICE=MVSCK006, ^@^@^@
13:30:55 IAT2000 JOB 8622 MVSCK006 SELECTED M1        GRP=BATCH
13:30:56
13:30:56 IATXXXX  ADJUSTED CPU TIME LIMIT FOR JOB MVSCK006 ON M1
13:30:56 IATXXXX                        IS    0 MIN 20 SEC
13:30:56
13:30:56 M1 R= MVSCK006 IEF403I MVSCK006 - STARTED
13:30:57 IAT5110 JOB 8622 (MVSCK006) USES D DSK001 SYS88100.T133057.RA000.MVSCK006.R0000002
13:30:57 IAT5110 JOB 8622 (MVSCK006) USES D DSK001 SYS88100.T133057.RA000.MVSCK006.R0000004
13:30:59 IAT5110 JOB 8622 (MVSCK006) USES D DSK001 SYS1.VVDS.VDSK001
13:30:59 M1 R= MVSCK006 IEF404I MVSCK006 - ENDED
     1    //MVSCK006 JOB (ACCTZ2354,'03/25/88'),'C. KANIKLIDIS',        *
          //              CLASS=A,MSGCLASS=A,MSGLEVEL=(1,1)
     2    //STEP1 EXEC PGM=IDCAMS,REGION=330K
     3    //SYSPRINT DD SYSOUT=A
     4    //SYSIN DD *,DCB=BLKSIZE=80
          //
IEF236I ALLOC. FOR MVSCK006 STEP1
IEF237I JES3 ALLOCATED TO SYSPRINT
IEF237I JES3 ALLOCATED TO SYSIN
IEF237I 227  ALLOCATED TO SYS00001
IEF237I 9A4  ALLOCATED TO SYS00002
IEF237I 9A4  ALLOCATED TO SYS00004
IEF285I    SYS88100.T133057.RA000.MVSCK006.R0000002     KEPT
IEF285I    VOL SER NOS= DSK001.
IEF285I    SYS88100.T133057.RA000.MVSCK006.R0000004     KEPT
IEF285I    VOL SER NOS= DSK001.
IEF237I 9A4  ALLOCATED TO SYS00006
IEF142I MVSCK006 STEP1 - STEP WAS EXECUTED - COND CODE 0000
IEF285I    STEP1.SYSPRINT                SYSOUT
IEF285I    JESIO001                      SYSIN
IEF285I    TESTCAT                       KEPT
IEF285I    VOL SER NOS= SYS002.
IEF285I    SYS1.VVDS.VDSK001             KEPT
IEF285I    VOL SER NOS= DSK001.

** START - STEP=STEP1     JOB=MVSCK006    DATE= 4/09/88    CLOCK=13.30.56    PGM=IDCAMS    REGION USED=  352K OF  330K **
** END -                                 DATE= 4/09/88    CLOCK=13.30.59    CPU TIME =  0 MIN  0.32 SEC    CC=     0 **
** I/O COUNTS - DISK=        0,   SPOOL/OTHER=        50,   TAPE=       0,   VIO=        0; TOTAL=          50 **

    DDNAME      I/O COUNT
 SYSPRINT:    SPOOL/DMY
 SYSIN   :    SPOOL/DMY
 SYS00001:          0
 SYS00006:          0
 SYS00002:          0
 SYS00004:          0


** START - JOB=MVSCK006   DATE= 4/09/88   CLOCK=13.30.56
** END -                  DATE= 4/09/88   CLOCK=13.30.59   CPU TIME =    0 MIN   0.32 SEC **
```

Figure 17-19(a). Partial JCL spill from DEF CLUSTER job.

```
IDCAMS  SYSTEM SERVICES                              TIME: 13:30:56    04/09/88    PAGE   1

        DEFINE CLUSTER -
              (NAME (VSAM.CK.MVS.VSTEST01) -
               VOLUMES (DSK001) -
               TRACKS (1,1) -
               KEYS (9 0) -
               RECORDSIZE (80 80) -
               FSPC (25 10) -
               OWNER (STNKANT) -
               INDEXED) -
          DATA -
              (NAME (VSAM.CK.MVS.VSTEST01.DATA) -
               CISZ (4096)) -
          INDEX -
              (NAME (VSAM.CK.MVS.VSTEST01.INDEX))

IDC0508I DATA ALLOCATION STATUS FOR VOLUME DSK001 IS 0
IDC0509I INDEX ALLOCATION STATUS FOR VOLUME DSK001 IS 0
IDC0001I FUNCTION COMPLETED, HIGHEST CONDITION CODE WAS 0

      IF LASTCC = 0 -
          THEN -
               LISTCAT -
                        ENTRIES (VSAM.CK.MVS.VSTEST01) -
                        ALL
```

Figure 17-19(b). IDCAMS job coding to define an ICF cluster.

```
CLUSTER ------- VSAM.CK.MVS.VSTEST01
     IN-CAT --- TESTCAT
     HISTORY
        OWNER-IDENT------STNKANT      CREATION----------88.100
        RELEASE---------------2       EXPIRATION--------00.000
     PROTECTION-PSWD-----(NULL)       RACF---------------(NO)
     ASSOCIATIONS
        DATA-----VSAM.CK.MVS.VSTEST01.DATA
        INDEX----VSAM.CK.MVS.VSTEST01.INDEX
  DATA ------- VSAM.CK.MVS.VSTEST01.DATA
     IN-CAT --- TESTCAT
     HISTORY
        OWNER-IDENT-------(NULL)      CREATION----------88.100
        RELEASE---------------2       EXPIRATION--------00.000
     PROTECTION-PSWD-----(NULL)       RACF---------------(NO)
     ASSOCIATIONS
        CLUSTER--VSAM.CK.MVS.VSTEST01
     ATTRIBUTES
        KEYLEN---------------9     AVGLRECL-------------80    BUFSPACE------------8704    CISIZE-------------4096
        RKP------------------0     MAXLRECL-------------80    EXCPEXIT----------(NULL)    CI/CA----------------10
        SHROPTNS(1,3)  RECOVERY    UNIQUE          NOERASE    INDEXED     NOWRITECHK     NOIMBED      NOREPLICAT
        UNORDERED     NOREUSE      NONSPANNED
     STATISTICS
        REC-TOTAL------------0     SPLITS-CI-------------0    EXCPS------------------0
        REC-DELETED----------0     SPLITS-CA-------------0    EXTENTS----------------1
        REC-INSERTED---------0     FREESPACE-%CI--------25    SYSTEM-TIMESTAMP:
        REC-UPDATED----------0     FREESPACE-%CA--------10        X'0000000000000000'
        REC-RETRIEVED--------0     FREESPC-BYTES-----40960
     ALLOCATION
        SPACE-TYPE--------TRACK    HI-ALLOC-RBA------40960
        SPACE-PRI------------1     HI-USED-RBA-----------0
        SPACE-SEC------------1
     VOLUME
        VOLSER-----------DSK001    PHYREC-SIZE--------4096    HI-ALLOC-RBA-------40960   EXTENT-NUMBER----------1
        DEVTYPE------X'3010200E'   PHYRECS/TRK----------10    HI-USED-RBA------------0   EXTENT-TYPE--------X'40'
        VOLFLAG-----------PRIME    TRACKS/CA-------------1
        EXTENTS:
        LOW-CCHH-----X'04B8000C'   LOW-RBA---------------0    TRACKS-----------------1
        HIGH-CCHH----X'04B8000C'   HIGH-RBA----------40959
```

Figure 17-19(c). LISTCAT output for ICF cluster and data component.

No suballocation.   As already noted above, all space management in DFP/VSAM is now handled by OS DADSM, so that there is no suballocation support whatever, a technique which was always idiosyncratic to VSAM in any case. Space for a cluster under DFP/VSAM is now allocated like any OS data set, in terms of there being no preallocation of an aggregate pool of VSAM-owned data space (what we have called, in subsection 7.3.1 earlier in the text, *VSAM Space Pools*), from which clusters would be allocated. Four immediate and direct consequences of this are:

(a) the concept of VSAM Space Pools ('data spaces') has been abandoned, and no preallocation of VSAM data sets is possible under DFP/VSAM;

(b) as a consequence of (a) above, the AMS DEFINE SPACE command has been discontinued (there being no data spaces to define);

(c) there is no longer any *assured* VSAM allocation: under Enhanced VSAM, the preallocation of data spaces to some extent assured the programmer of a certain amount of dedicated DASD space for VSAM's exclusive use, for all volumes owned by VSAM; now no volumes are owned by VSAM and no space is in any way dedicated to VSAM—it is all 'up for grabs' on a first come, first served basis, and any allocation request for an extended-unique cluster may fail by virtue of there being insufficient *OS* space on the volume required;

(d) under DFP/VSAM *all* DASD space is owned by OS exclusively (but if

```
INDEX ------ VSAM.CK.MVS.VSTEST01.INDEX
   IN-CAT --- TESTCAT
   HISTORY
      OWNER-IDENT-------(NULL)     CREATION----------88.100
      RELEASE----------------2     EXPIRATION--------00.000
   PROTECTION-PSWD-----(NULL)     RACF---------------(NO)
   ASSOCIATIONS
      CLUSTER--VSAM.CK.MVS.VSTEST01
   ATTRIBUTES
      KEYLEN----------------9     AVGLRECL---------------0     BUFSPACE---------------0     CISIZE---------------512
      RKP-------------------0     MAXLRECL-------------505     EXCPEXIT----------(NULL)     CI/CA-----------------46
      SHROPTNS(1,3)   RECOVERY    UNIQUE           NOERASE     NOWRITECHK    NOIMBED        NOREPLICAT    UNORDERED
      NOREUSE
   STATISTICS
      REC-TOTAL-------------0     SPLITS-CI--------------0     EXCPS-----------------0     INDEX:
      REC-DELETED-----------0     SPLITS-CA--------------0     EXTENTS---------------1     LEVELS----------------0
      REC-INSERTED----------0     FREESPACE-%CI----------0     SYSTEM-TIMESTAMP:            ENTRIES/SECT----------3
      REC-UPDATED-----------0     FREESPACE-%CA----------0        X'0000000000000000'      SEQ-SET-RBA-----------0
      REC-RETRIEVED---------0     FREESPC-BYTES------23552                                 HI-LEVEL-RBA----------0
   ALLOCATION
      SPACE-TYPE--------TRACK     HI-ALLOC-RBA-------23552
      SPACE-PRI-------------1     HI-USED-RBA------------0
      SPACE-SEC-------------1
   VOLUME
      VOLSER-----------DSK001     PHYREC-SIZE----------512     HI-ALLOC-RBA-------23552     EXTENT-NUMBER---------1
      DEVTYPE------X'3010200E'    PHYRECS/TRK-----------46     HI-USED-RBA------------0     EXTENT-TYPE-------X'40'
      VOLFLAG-----------PRIME     TRACKS/CA--------------1
      EXTENTS:
      LOW-CCHH-----X'04C4000B'    LOW-RBA----------------0     TRACKS----------------1
      HIGH-CCHH----X'04C4000B'    HIGH-RBA-----------23551
IDCAMS   SYSTEM SERVICES                                               TIME: 13:30:56    04/09/88    PAGE   3
         THE NUMBER OF ENTRIES PROCESSED WAS:
                        AIX  -------------------0
                        ALIAS  -----------------0
                        CLUSTER  ---------------1
                        DATA  ------------------1
                        GDG  -------------------0
                        INDEX  -----------------1
                        NONVSAM  ---------------0
                        PAGESPACE  -------------0
                        PATH  ------------------0
                        SPACE  -----------------0
                        USERCATALOG  -----------0
                        TOTAL  -----------------3
         THE NUMBER OF PROTECTED ENTRIES SUPPRESSED WAS 0
IDC0001I FUNCTION COMPLETED, HIGHEST CONDITION CODE WAS 0

IDC0002I IDCAMS PROCESSING COMPLETE. MAXIMUM CONDITION CODE WAS 0
```

Figure 17-19(d). LISTCAT output for ICF index component.

Enhanced VSAM is supported along with DFP/VSAM in a 'mixed' environment, space is still managed jointly by OS and VSAM space managers *for any remaining (Enhanced) VSAM data sets only).*

Now, a programmer defines a cluster—always extended-unique—under DFP/VSAM directly through the DEFINE CLUSTER command (no preceding DEFINE SPACE command).

Maximum extents allocated is now 123 for all clusters. As the reader may remember, under Enhanced VSAM suballocated clusters had a maximum of 123 allowable extents (being handled by the VSAM Space Manager), but unique clusters were restricted to 16 only (being handled by OS DADSM and treated on this matter like OS data sets, similarly restricted). The sole type of cluster supported by DFP/VSAM, the extended-unique cluster, although unrelated to the former suballocatable clusters of Enhanced VSAM, nonetheless may, like those clusters, have up to 123 total extents of allocated space. This is a valuable flexibility, given that VSAM data sets are frequently highly active and subject to considerable growth, often even over relatively small periods of time. (But we will consider some of the adverse consequences of excessive secondary allocation later in Chapter 18, on performance.)

The astute reader may find this feature of DFP/VSAM extended-unique clusters somewhat puzzling: on the one hand, all space allocation for such data sets is handled by a single space manager, OS DADSM (which handled unique clusters under Enhanced VSAM), yet on the other hand extended-unique clusters have a maximum of 123 allowable extents, whereas OS data sets (and the former Enhanced VSAM unique clusters), always handled by the same manager (OS DADSM), are never permitted more than a total of 16 extents. It is for this reason, among many others that will unfold in the following discussions, that data sets under DFP/VSAM should never be confused with Enhanced VSAM unique clusters (despite LISTCAT output to the contrary). What has happened is that OS DADSM has been extended (no pun intended) to allow the new maximum of 123 total extents for DFP/VSAM VSAM data sets only, making them in this sense *unlike* OS data sets (max equal to 16 extents), even though the latter are also managed by OS DADSM. Here we can see the true 'hybridness' of the new extended-unique clusters under DFP/VSAM: they are nonsuballocated, but have the same total extent maximum which only the former suballocated clusters had, thus making them share the best (arguably) features of both previous cluster types. There will be other such instances of hybrid features of the new extended-unique clusters, as we will see shortly.

No allocation unit restriction.   As the reader might recall, under Enhanced VSAM unique clusters must be allocated in units of cylinders, never tracks or records. But under DFP/VSAM, extended-unique clusters may be allocated space in any unit of allocation, so that they are more like the former suballocatable clusters, which also had no restrictions on the unit of space allocation. (We have already confirmed this property in Figure 17-19.)

All DFP/VSAM clusters are reusable.   Under Enhanced VSAM, only suballocated clusters could be reusable (Subsection 7.3.3); unique clusters could never be reused. But extended-unique clusters under DFP/VSAM, the sole cluster type supported, can be made reusable (the REUSE parameter on the DEF CLUS-TER command).

No secondary extents release under reuse.   When a DFP/VSAM cluster is OPENed for REUSE, secondary extents are *not* released. Contrast this with Enhanced VSAM reusable suballocated clusters, where under the same circumstances these multiple extents are released.

Volume needs to be mounted for dynamic AMS requests.   Due to the fact that OS DADSM handles all space allocation and management for DFP/VSAM clusters, with no support for suballocation, DFP/VSAM clusters must be mounted at the time a *dynamic AMS request* is made: these are AMS requests requiring active access to the volume on which the cluster resides for the request to be executed. The AMS DEFINE, DELETE, and ALTER commands all represent dynamic AMS requests. Thus, under DFP/VSAM, the creation, deletion, and changing of a cluster's attributes all require the volume involved to be mounted, or the request will fail. This will generally not present a problem, as the newer media—the 3380s, and the previous 3350s—are both *nondemountable* and hence always found in a mounted state (unless a hardware drive problem exists); only the much older—and infrequently encountered these days—3330s (and the even more fossilized 2314s) are demountable, and these are rarely used for active VSAM files in current installations.

There are three negative considerations to be noted in this connection. First, this mount requirement may cause some performance degradation when using DFP/VSAM clusters stored on MSS (Mass Storage Systems). Second, whenever allocation information is required, the volume must be mounted, since this information is retrieved from the VVDS on the volume. This entails a volume mount requirement if a LISTCAT ALLOCATION or a LISTCAT ALL is requested (both spill out allocation information from the VVDS); LISTCAT requests that are more restrictive, however—namely, LISTCAT NAME, LISTCAT HISTORY, and LISTCAT VOLUME—do not require the volume to be mounted at the time of the request. Third, some of the allocation information for OPEN processing of a multivolume data set is contained in the VVDSs on each of the volumes involved: no one VVDS contains all of this information. This entails that open processing for multivolume DFP/VSAM data sets requires all volumes involved to be concurrently mounted for successful completion of the OPEN request (Enhanced VSAM has a *subset-mount* facility for multivolume data sets that does not have this requirement, and only the needed volume or volumes—a subset of the total volumes involved—need be mounted at OPEN time).

17.6.2   Direct VTOC Entries

Since all DFP/VSAM data sets are allocated and managed by OS DADSM—they are all extended-unique—there is an entry in the VTOC for each DFP/VSAM *component* stored on any particular volume: thus the data and index components of a KSDS, for example, each have a separate VTOC entry. These entries are in the form of *F-1 DSCBs* (Format-1 Data Set Control Blocks, that is, informally, DASD data set 'labels'). There will be one F-1 DSCB entry in the VTOC per DFP/VSAM component and, depending on the number of extents occupied by the component, there may also be up to 10 addditional F-3 (Format-3) DSCBs. A single F-1 DSCB describes the first three extents the component occupies, while the first additional F-3 DSCB describes extents four through 16, with a total of 10 such F-3 DSCBs and one F-1 DSCB sufficing to describe the total extents possible for an extended-unique data set, namely the 123 maximum. All of these DSCBs contain space allocation/management information, in addition to naming the component itself; the extent information in a component's VTOC DSCB entry contains the critical information for locating the component—all of its extents—on the volume, and this extent information is also held in the VVR entry for that component in the VVDS.

If the reader reexamines Figure 17-19, part (c), we can see from the cluster entry and the ASSOCIATIONS group of the LISTCAT output for this DFP/VSAM cluster that the following names are used because all were explicitly user-provided at DEF CLUSTER time (as seen in part (b) of that figure):

```
CLUSTER--VSAM.CK.MVS.VSTEST01
DATA-----VSAM.CK.MVS.VSTEST01.DATA
INDEX----VSAM.CK.MVS.VSTEST01.INDEX
```

The cluster name does not appear in the VTOC, only component names. If only the cluster name were user-provided, then the data and index component names under DFP/VSAM would be VSAM-generated by default, and these VSAM-generated names are different from those that would be generated under Enhanced VSAM. It is recommended that the programmer always explicitly provide both data and index component names (if there is any index component), as well as the cluster name, as we have done in Figure 17-19. If the programmer, however, allows VSAM to provide default names, then the form of those names, for DFP/VSAM components, would be:

```
hlq.Tbbbbbbb.VDDyyddd.Taaaaaaa
```

and

```
hlq.Tbbbbbbb.VIDyyddd.Taaaaaaa
```

for the data and index components, respectively (a cluster name is always user-provided, not VSAM-generated), where 'hlq' is the high level qualifier, taken from the HLQ of the cluster name provided by the user at DEF CLUSTER time, and 'bbbbbbb' and 'aaaaaaa' are system-generated alphanumeric characters (numbers and alphabetic characters) used to make the names unique throughout the system (a 'scramble' of characters), while the 'T' is used as the first letter of the second and fourth qualifiers of the name. Furthermore, 'VDD' and 'VID' are used to distinguish the data and index component names, respectively, and 'yyddd' is simply a date field. These VSAM-generated names are obviously not in keeping with explicit, sensible, installation-specific standard naming conventions, and should be avoided. Note that whether user-provided or VSAM-generated, only the data and index components (if any) of a cluster have entries in the VTOC DSCBs: cluster names do not appear, as the cluster is not a physically real data set distinct from its data and index component data sets, which are real. Finally, note that the 'bbbbbbb' and 'aaaaaaa' are used by DFP/VSAM to jointly form a timestamp value, but these values will not be the same for the data and index components, because these are created at different times by DFP/VSAM (and can generally be ignored altogether by the programmer).

Now that all clusters are extended-unique under DFP/VSAM, all components have separate DSCB entries in the VTOC identifying them and giving extent information. Under Enhanced VSAM only VSAM unique clusters appeared in this fashion in the VTOC (being handled by OS DADSM), but from a VTOC it was not possible to determine what, if any, suballocated clusters were allocated on the volume, because only the VSAM data space containing suballocatable space for clusters had an entry in the VTOC, but not any of the clusters suballocated within that space, an undesirable situation from the point of view of ease and integration of space management for both OS (non-VSAM) and VSAM data sets. (Remember that VSAM data spaces are no longer used in DFP/VSAM.) Whenever an extended unique cluster is created, VTOC DSCBs for its components are automatically set up by OS DADSM, while ICF sets up the appropriate BCS entry and VVR(s) in the VVDS. Similarly, the VTOC entries, and the BCS and VVDS entries, are all erased when the components are deleted. If a component's extents change, both the VTOC DSCB(s) and the VVDS, which both contain extent information, are updated to reflect the changes.

17.6.3 The Implicit VERIFY

We have already discussed the AMS VERIFY command in detail (Subsection 15.2.1). DFP/VSAM supports a new facility known as the *implicit VERIFY*. In the event that DFP/VSAM detects improper closure of a cluster (the open-for-output indicator is on at OPEN time), then DFP/VSAM will issue at this time an implicit VERIFY *macro* against the data set. The VERIFY macro is said to be implicit in that VSAM issues it automatically and transparently to the programmer (as opposed to the programmer explicitly issuing the AMS VERIFY command). Furthermore, DFP/VSAM issues the VERIFY *macro*, not the VERIFY *command*. Upon issuance of the VERIFY macro, DFP/VSAM determines from the data set itself the true-EOD (end-of-data), and updates accordingly ARDHRBA, a field in the ARDB (Address Range Definition Block) control block in virtual storage, this field containing the HURBA (High-Used-RBA) value for the data set (essentially, end-of-data). In addition, the HKRBA (high-key-rba) value in ARDB, and the HLRBA (high-level-rba) and NIL (number-of-index-levels), both in AMDSB (Access Method Data Statistics Block), are also updated with the correct information as determined from the data set (the reader may wish to briefly review Subsection 15.2.1 at this point for a full discussion of all of these concepts).

The VERIFY command, not the macro, also issues the OPEN macro before the VERIFY macro, and also the CLOSE macro after the VERIFY macro. The CLOSE macro, in particular, performs two vital actions: (1) the open-for-output indicator is turned off, and (2) the HURBA, HKRBA, HLRBA, and NIL values from the DFP/VSAM control blocks in virtual storage—which were set correctly by the previous VERIFY macro—are used to update the corresponding *catalog fields*, thus resynchronizing the data set and its catalog entry.

There are two problems consequent to the fact that DFP/VSAM issues an implicit VERIFY macro, not a VERIFY command, which would also include the actions of OPEN and CLOSE. Since DFP/VSAM does not issue the CLOSE, which would 'snap' the values from the control blocks to the catalog, if issued, the catalog is not resynchronized until a subsequent successful CLOSE is issued against the data set, and if an intervening adverse system event prevents this, the catalog information remains out-of-sync with the true facts of the data set (the control blocks themselves are volatile and held in 'transient' virtual storage and do not survive the adverse system event to 'live' to tell their tale, as it were).

A second, and perhaps more serious problem (from the point of view of perform-ance overhead) is that, if after the implicit issuance of the VERIFY macro by DFP/VSAM the data set is OPENed, not for output/update, but only for input, the open-for-output indicator is *not* turned off. Then, if this is immediately followed by still another OPEN for input, DFP/VSAM will *redetect* the open-for-output indicator, assume this to signal improper closure, and issue *another* implicit VERIFY macro, and this will be repeated automatically and indefinitely until an OPEN for output/update is issued explicitly by the programmer. This is so because DFP/VSAM issues an implicit VERIFY macro on OPEN for input as well as OPEN for output (including for update). But if the data set is repeatedly OPENed for input, say under CICS through browse operations, the overhead of multiple successive implicit VERIFY macros can become quite significant and affect data set performance adversely.

With both of these problems, the best—not the ideal—solution is for the programmer to explicitly issue the VERIFY command against the data set as soon as s/he is informed by DFP/VSAM messages of the state of improper closure. This will update the catalog from the virtual storage control blocks, effecting resynchronization of the catalog and data set, as well as turn off the open-for-output indicator, thus avoiding iterated implicit VERIFYs unnecessarily. However, this is not an ideal situation, since the VERIFY macro may be 'over-issued,' implicitly by DFP/VSAM and explicitly by the programmer for one and the same problem concerning one and the same data set, and given the frequency of the problem and the number of VSAM data sets that may be involved in usual commercial settings, the total systems impact can be quite high and clearly adversely affect performance. At the time of this writing, it is possible to obtain from IBM a 'fix' to DFP/VSAM which would allow the installation to disable the implicit VERIFY facility. If this is elected, then DFP/VSAM would function like Enhanced VSAM in terms of this problem, and it would be the installation's responsibility to have programmers issue the explicit VERIFY com-mand in the appropriate circumstances (which, if done carefully may, in some cases, provide better overall VSAM processing performance).

17.6.4 Improved Erase-CI Processing

As we have already noted (in Subsection 17.1.2), a fully erased CI (technically known as an *erase-CI*)—one that contained records at some time but has been emptied of all of its records through subsequent deletion activity—is subject, under Enhanced VSAM, to an *erase-CI restriction*. This restriction always allows records to be inserted into this erase-CI only if the records contain keys that fall within the range of keys originally established with that CI when it was first created and loaded with records. Records with keys falling out of this original, first-use, range of key values associated with the erase-CI may not be added, therefore, even if the CI remains wholly empty, and clearly this is an inefficient use of DASD space. Under DFP/VSAM, the restriction is weakened: the to-be-inserted-records must have keys within the range of keys established for *the CA containing the CI*, not the CI-range. This is almost invariably a much broader range of keys, increasing the likelihood that the erase-CI will be used, increasing DASD utilization effectively. (Note that the special *high-key CI*—the one containing the highest key value within a CA—is not reclaimed under any circumstances: if it becomes an erase-CI, it remains empty and is not subject to erase-CI processing of any sort, by CI-range or CA-range. Once such a CI is emptied of all records, it will disallow insertion of any records into it until, and if, the data set is reorganized.)

17.6.5   VTOC/Volume-TIMESTAMP Compare Removal

There are two timestamp fields that Enhanced VSAM maintains. One is recorded in the VSAM catalog itself, as a *catalog volume timestamp*, *CV-timestamp*, and this is a field in the catalog's volume record(s). The CV-timestamp is exposed to the programmer in the STATISTICS group of LISTCAT output, as an entry named SYSTEM-TIMESTAMP. The second timestamp field is the *VTOC-timestamp* recorded in the VTOC of any volume owned by a VSAM catalog (it's in the Format-4 DSCB, which describes the VTOC itself) and for any particular catalog provides a check of synchronization between that catalog and its owned volumes. Enhanced VSAM would compare the CV-timestamp and the VTOC-timestamp, which had to be maintained in precise synchrony, and a mismatch—indicating an out-of-sync condition—could render the VSAM data sets on the volume inaccessible. Often the failure of this timestamp compare operation was 'fixed' by ad hoc means to effect resynchronization. This often involved use of the special IBM service aid program named *AMASPZAP*, sometimes known as *SPZAP*, but far more frequently and informally as 'SUPERZAP,' to 'zap' the F-4 DSCB containing the VTOC-timestamp to force it to be the same (by overwriting it) as the CV-timestamp. This generally violates basic canons of system integrity protection and common data security principles; although AMASPZAP has legitimate uses in specialized circumstances, this use of it is probably inadvisable.

Under DFP/VSAM, in part for these reasons, the timestamp compare operation has been discontinued: DFP/VSAM no longer even records a CV-timestamp in ICF catalogs, so there is nothing to compare to a VTOC-timestamp. This may seem inadvisable, since the user is not alerted to an out-of-sync condition between the catalog and its associated volumes, and whether the CV-timestamp is recorded or not, nonetheless out-of-sync conditions can still arise in a variety of circumstances. However, it is intended under DFP/VSAM that the user use a new AMS diagnostic command *DIAGNOSE* for more subtle problem determination of out-of-sync conditions of many different forms, so no real loss of functionality has occurred. (This is taken up in greater detail in this chapter's section on problem determination under DFP/VSAM.)

17.7   PROBLEM DETERMINATION UNDER DFP/VSAM: DIAGNOSE

DFP/VSAM includes two new problem determination facilities, both invoked through new AMS commands: *DIAGNOSE* and *EXAMINE*; DIAGNOSE is supported only for DFP/VSAM objects, while EXAMINE is supported for Enhanced VSAM and DFP/VSAM objects alike. In this section we take up the DIAGNOSE command, while EXAMINE is discussed in a technical appendix (Appendix C), as it is not a strictly DFP/VSAM facility.

DIAGNOSE is a new AMS command providing very powerful problem determination facilities in a DFP/VSAM environment (DIAGNOSE may only be applied against ICF catalogs and DFP/VSAM data sets defined in ICF catalogs). DIAGNOSE will allow verification of the validity of ICF catalogs, both in terms of their internal structure, and in terms of ICF catalog component interrelationships, including consistency with OS VTOCs, and by enhancing early problem detection may alert an installation's technical staff to needed repairs and adjustments before the problems become grave and/or uncontrollable. A very high degree of systems integrity assurance can be had by the systematic use of the DIAGNOSE facility (enhanced still further by additional use of the more recent EXAMINE facility, discussed in a separate technical appendix, Appendix C). Let's see more precisely what DIAGNOSE does and how it is used in VSAM problem determination.

17.7.1   Internal DIAGNOSE Facility

There are two types of DIAGNOSE facilities: *internal DIAGNOSE* and *consistency DIAGNOSE* (the latter sometimes referred to as 'dependency checking'). An internal DIAGNOSE verifies the internal structure—that is, the format and content—of ICF catalog components (BCS and VVDS) and reports any structural errors detected by the DIAGNOSE command. For example, an internal DIAGNOSE will check that cells, components, and records in the BCS and VVDS are of the correct size (the lengths of these constituents of an ICF catalog are rigorously described). Component names are also checked for valid length: a name cannot exceed 45 characters, the last of which is an extension pad character. Furthermore, certain cells must be present in the catalog record(s) for a component; if a data component ICF record is missing a volume cell, for example, the internal DIAGNOSE facility would write out an error message of this form (only the part of the complete message that concerns us here is shown):

```
IDC21364I ERROR DETECTED BY DIAGNOSE:
                   .
                   .
                   .
REASON: 24 - REQUIRED CELL MISSING, CELL TYPE '04'
```

and if this reason code were looked up in the documentation on DIAGNOSE (*Catalog Administration Guide* under 'Checking Catalogs for Errors and Synchronization'), we would be given both the text of the message, as shown above, along with a fuller explanation of the cause of the error, under the heading 'Explanation,' and wherever possible also given a brief indication of how a repair may be effected, under the heading 'Recovery Procedure.' DFP/VSAM's DIAGNOSE facility refers to different types of cells by hexadecimal numbers; in the message above, a X'04' refers to the volume cell. (The *Catalog Administration Guide* contains a full list of the cell types and their type numbers.)

Using an internal DIAGNOSE, either a BCS or a VVDS may be checked for such structural errors; A complete DIAGNOSE error message would generally have the form:

```
IDC21364I ERROR DETECTED BY DIAGNOSE:
 ICFCAT/VVDS ENTRY: ‹name›
 RECORD: ‹record-identification›
 OFFSET: X'        '
 REASON: ‹nn› - ‹explanation›
```

where the second line will always identify the ICF component containing the structural error (either 'ICFCAT' for a BCS, or 'VVDS'). (We will look at both the coding of the command and actual DIAGNOSE output, in the following subsection.)

17.7.2 Consistency DIAGNOSE Facility

The second type of DIAGNOSE facility is the *consistency DIAGNOSE*, which checks the validity of the *interrelationships* between elements of ICF catalogs: a BCS may be compared to its associated VVDS(s), or alternatively, a VVDS may be compared against its associated BCS(s). Since the BCS and the VVDS collectively constitute an ICF catalog, there are certain fixed 'dependencies' that must exist between these catalog components, and a consistency DIAGNOSE checks the components against each other to detect discrepancies in their mutual relationships. To be more precise, a DIAGNOSE, whether internal or consistency, may involve *three* objects, not just two: the BCS, the VVDS, *and the VTOC*. This is so because the VTOC and the VVDS are treated as a unit by DFP/VSAM. But the VTOC is not *always* checked. How do we know when a DIAGNOSE command will effect any checking of the VTOC? The three rules below determine this exactly:

1. If an internal DIAGNOSE is issued against the VVDS (the VVDS is named in the command), then the VTOC is also checked automatically.
2. If a consistency DIAGNOSE is issued (the DIAGNOSE command will have some form of a COMPARE parameter on it) against the VVDS, then the VVDS is checked for consistency with *both* the BCS and the VTOC.
3. In all other types of DIAGNOSE, the VTOC is not checked.

If we therefore only perform an internal DIAGNOSE on the BCS, the VTOC will not be inspected, and if we perform a consistency DIAGNOSE using the BCS as what is termed the *DIAGNOSE object* (the component named in the DIAGNOSE command as the object against which the comparison will be done, or the component being checked if only an internal DIAGNOSE is involved), then only the VVDS will be checked against this for consistency, again with no VTOC checking being involved.

Let's look at an example of the consistency DIAGNOSE facility to clarify this, and to see the form of DIAGNOSE output and its interpretation. Consider Figure 17-20. Part (a) is a portion of the JCL spill for an IDCAMS DIAGNOSE job, and part (b) shows both the actual coding of the command, along with the output generated. We know that some nontrivial error was caught from the condition code of 8 shown for the IDCAMS job in part (a). Note in JCL statement 4 of Figure 17-20(a) that the VVDS is defined in a DD statement that includes UNIT and VOL parameters, along with the AMP parameter explicitly informing JES (in this case JES3) that this should not be mistaken for an OS data set (AMORG meaning a VSAM data set). One might wonder why we code UNIT and VOL for a VSAM data set (typically omitted), since

```
IAT6140 JOB ORIGIN FROM GROUP=TESTVM , DSP=^@R , DEVICE=MVSCK006, ^@^@^@
20:12:57 IAT5200 JOB 7858 (MVSCK006) IN SETUP ON MAIN=M2
20:12:57 IAT5210 VVDS1     USING D DSK001 ON 9A4   SYS1.VVDS.VDSK001
20:12:57 IAT5210 BCS1      USING D SYS002 ON 227   TESTCAT
20:12:57 IAT2000 JOB 7858 MVSCK006 SELECTED M4      GRP=BATCH
20:12:58
20:12:58 IATXXXX  ADJUSTED CPU TIME LIMIT FOR JOB MVSCK006 ON M4
20:12:58 IATXXXX               IS       0 MIN 50 SEC
20:12:58
20:12:58 M4 R= MVSCK006 IEF403I MVSCK006 - STARTED
20:13:00 M4 R= MVSCK006 IEF404I MVSCK006 - ENDED

   1    //MVSCK006 JOB (ACCTZ2354,'03/25/88'),'C. KANIKLIDIS',
        //             CLASS=A,MSGCLASS=A,MSGLEVEL=(1,1)
   2    //STEP1 EXEC PGM=IDCAMS,REGION=330K
   3    //SYSPRINT DD SYSOUT=A
   4    //VVDS1    DD DSN=SYS1.VVDS.VDSK001,DISP=SHR,
        //            UNIT=3380,VOL=SER=DSK001,
        //            AMP='AMORG'
   5    //BCS1     DD DSN=TESTCAT,DISP=SHR
   6    //SYSIN DD *,DCB=BLKSIZE=80
        //
IEF236I ALLOC. FOR MVSCK006 STEP1
IEF237I JES3 ALLOCATED TO SYSPRINT
IEF237I 7A4  ALLOCATED TO VVDS1
IEF237I 227  ALLOCATED TO BCS1
IEF237I JES3 ALLOCATED TO SYSIN
IEF142I MVSCK006 STEP1 - STEP WAS EXECUTED - COND CODE 0008
IEF285I    STEP1.SYSPRINT                       SYSOUT
IEF285I    SYS1.VVDS.VDSK001                     KEPT
IEF285I    VOL SER NOS= DSK001.
IEF285I    TESTCAT                               KEPT
IEF285I    VOL SER NOS= SYS002.
IEF285I    JESI0001                             SYSIN

** START - STEP=STEP1    JOB=MVSCK006   DATE: 4/13/88   CLOCK=20.12.55   PGM=IDCAMS    REGION USED=  332K OF  330K **
** END -                                DATE: 4/13/88   CLOCK=20.12.58   CPU TIME =  0 MIN  0.45 SEC     CC=     8 **
** I/O COUNTS - DISK=        56,  SPOOL/OTHER=        26,   TAPE=       0,   VIO=      0; TOTAL=        82 **

     DDNAME      I/O COUNT
   SYSPRINT:    SPOOL/DMY
   VVDS1   :           50
   BCS1    :            6
   SYSIN   :    SPOOL/DMY


** START - JOB=MVSCK006   DATE: 4/13/88   CLOCK=20.12.55
** END -                  DATE: 4/13/88   CLOCK=20.12.58   CPU TIME =       0 MIN   0.45 SEC  **
```

Figure 17-20(a). Partial JCL spill from DIAGNOSE job.

```
IDCAMS  SYSTEM SERVICES                              TIME: 20:12:56     04/13/88    PAGE    1
    DIAGNOSE VVDS -
            INFILE (VVDS1) -
            COMPAREDD (BCS1) -
            INCLUDE (ENTRIES (VSAM.CK.MVS.VSTEST01)) -
            LIST

IDC3302I   ACTION ERROR ON TESTCAT
IDC3351I ** VSAM I/O RETURN CODE IS 16  - RPLFDBWD = X'93080010'   ←① 
IDC21364I ERROR DETECTED BY DIAGNOSE:
  VVDS ENTRY: VSAM.CK.MVS.VSTEST01.DATA (Z)   ←②
  RECORD: X'00005757'   ←────────────────────────③
  OFFSET: X'0002'   ←───────────────────────────────④
  REASON: 19 - CATLG ENTRY NOT FOUND ←───────────────────⑤
IDC21365I VVDS RECORD DISPLAY:
  RECORD: X'00005757'
000000  012E0057 E9000000 00001AE5 E2C1D44B   C3D24BD4 E5E24BE5 E2E3C5E2 E3F0F14B   *....Z......VSAM.CK.MVS.VSTEST01.*
000020  C4C1E3C1 0015E5E2 C1D44BC7 C34BC4E3   D34BE5E2 E3C5E2E3 F0F10007 E3C5E2E3   *DATA..VSAM.CK.MVS.VSTEST01..TEST*
000040  C3C1E315 E5E2C1D4 4BC7C34B C4E3D34B   E5E2E3C5 E2E3F0F1 00003521 40200000   *CAT.VSAM.CK.MVS.VSTEST01.... ...*
000060  00220000 00010000 01800000 00000000   A0000000 00500000 FFFFFFFF FFFFFFFF   *................ .........&.....*
000080  00000000 00000000 00000000 00000062   60800060 00000000 00090A19 000A0001   *................-..-.............*
0000A0  00000400 00001000 00000050 00000000   00000000 00000000 00000000 00000000   *.................&..............*
0000C0  00000000 00000000 00000001 00000000   00000000 00000000 00000000 00000000   *................................*
0000E0  0000A000 00000000 00000000 00000000   003E2380 01000000 00000000 000000A0   *................................*
000100  00000010 00000A00 0140000F 00000000   00000000 00000000 00140001 04B8000C   *................................*
000120  04B8000C 00010000 00000000 9FFF       00000000 00000000 00000000 00000000   *..............                  *

────────────────────────────────────────────────────────────────────────────────────────────────

IDC3302I   ACTION ERROR ON TESTCAT
IDC3351I ** VSAM I/O RETURN CODE IS 16  - RPLFDBWD = X'93080010'
IDC21364I ERROR DETECTED BY DIAGNOSE:
  VVDS ENTRY: VSAM.CK.MVS.VSTEST01.INDEX (Z)
  RECORD: X'00005885'
  OFFSET: X'0002'
  REASON: 19 - CATLG ENTRY NOT FOUND
IDC21365I VVDS RECORD DISPLAY:
  RECORD: X'00005885'
000000  012F0058 E9080000 00001BE5 E2C1D44B   C3D24BD4 E5E24BE5 E2E3C5E2 E3F0F14B   *....Z......VSAM.CK.MVS.VSTEST01.*
000020  C9D5C4C5 E70015E5 E2C1D44B C7C34BC4   E3D34BE5 E2E3C5E2 E3F0F100 07E3C5E2   *INDEX..VSAM.CK.MVS.VSTEST01..TES*
000040  E3C3C1E3 15E5E2C1 D44BC7C3 4BC4E3D3   4BE5E2E3 C5E2E3F0 F1000035 21402000   *TCAT.VSAM.CK.MVS.VSTEST01.... ..*
000060  00000000 00000100 00018000 00000000   005C0000 00000000 00FFFFFF FFFFFFFF   *................*...............*
000080  FF000000 00000000 00000000 00000000   62600000 60000300 00000900 00002E00   *................-..-.............*
0000A0  00000000 00000002 00000001 F9000000   00000000 00000000 00000000 00000000   *.........9......................*
0000C0  00000000 00000000 00000000 01000000   00000000 00000000 00000000 00000000   *................................*
0000E0  0000005C 00000000 00000000 00000000   00003E23 80010000 00000000 00000000   *...*............................*
000100  5C000000 0200002E 00014000 0F000000   00000000 00000000 00001400 0104C400   **........ ...................D.*
000120  00B4C400 0B000100 00000000 005BFF      00000000 00000000 00001400 0104C400   *..D..........$.                 *
IDC11367I THE FOLLOWING VVDS REFERENCED CATALOGS WERE NOT ENCOUNTERED:
  VSM
IDC21363I THE FOLLOWING ENTRIES HAD ERRORS:
  VSAM.CK.MVS.VSTEST01.DATA (Z) - REASON CODE: 19
  VSAM.CK.MVS.VSTEST01.INDEX (Z) - REASON CODE: 19
IDC0001I FUNCTION COMPLETED, HIGHEST CONDITION CODE WAS 8
IDC0002I IDCAMS PROCESSING COMPLETE. MAXIMUM CONDITION CODE WAS 8
```

Figure 17-20(b). DIAGNOSE output.

this information is retrievable from the catalog. The reason is that such information is indeed retrievable from the ICF catalog involved (named 'TESTCAT,' the BCS name), but we are attempting to validate the very connections and interrelationships between the VVDS and an associated BCS, and so should not assume correct catalog information before this is confirmed by DIAGNOSE. (The DD statement for the BCS named TESTCAT, in JCL statement 5, does not, however, carry UNIT and VOL information: this is an ICF user catalog, and its UNIT and VOL information is retrieved from the Master Catalog, which we are not checking and which is assumed to be without structural or consistency errors (this should be confirmed by systems or tech support staff regularly).

Now examine Figure 17-20(b). At the top is the IDCAMS output that shows the coding of the DIAGNOSE command as actually issued, requesting a consistency

DIAGNOSE. The command shows that the DIAGNOSE object is a VVDS. The INFILE parameter refers by ddname to the VVDS1 JCL DD statement, which identifies the VVDS explicitly (see JCL statement 4 in Figure 17-20(a)). In this example, the VVDS is named SYS1.VVDS.VDSK001, residing on volume DSK001. The COMPAREDD parameter signifies that a consistency DIAGNOSE, rather than an internal DIAGNOSE, is being requested. The VVDS (the DIAGNOSE object) is to be compared to an associated BCS. The BCS is identified by ddname, and the DD statement (of part (a) of this figure) shows this to be named TESTCAT.

There are two additional parameters shown coded on the DIAGNOSE command. The first is INCLUDE, which requests *selective checking*: we are informing DFP/VSAM that only the named entry (or entries) is to be checked; that is, the consistency check is to be restricted solely to the DFP/VSAM data set entry for VSAM.CK.MVS. VSTEST01 in the VVDS, on the one hand, compared to any associated entry in the named BCS, but again solely for this data set. Any number of data sets can be specified on INCLUDE, and only their catalog entries will be explicitly tested and, not surprisingly, there is an EXCLUDE parameter codable on the DIAGNOSE (internal or consistency) which does the complement of INCLUDE, restricting the testing to all but the entry or entries for the data set(s) specified. Selective checking is generally performed when a problem has either been already localized by some other means (an error encountered when opening a data set, for example) or there is the suspicion of, say, possible damage or corruption or integrity compromise to a specific data set or group of objects. Unless there is a special circumstance warranting it, a full or nonselective DIAGNOSE of ICF catalogs should be performed regularly for early problem determination. An important point to note about selective checking is that DFP/VSAM may return error messages concerning entries that were *not* requested to be checked; this may seem odd, but occurs due to the internal operation of the DIAGNOSE facility against complex catalog record structures with intricate interdependencies between records (catalog 'record architecture'), these dependencies sometimes necessitating that the checking scan over and process records for entries in the 'logical path' of other records. (This is sort of an unexpected 'diagnostic bonus' of selective checking with DIAGNOSE facilities.)

The LIST parameter controls whether messages from the DIAGNOSE facility should be restricted only to those about entries with errors (NOLIST), or are to include all entries, whether errors are detected or not. Here, we have chosen LIST to have either explicit confirmation from DIAGNOSE that errors have been encountered, or if no errors are encountered, a statement to that effect.

Item (1) in Figure 17-20(b) is a four-byte *feedback word* carrying error indicator codes, as written to the VSAM RPL (Request Parameter List) control block. Other than here in the DIAGNOSE facility output, this information has been until recently only available to Assembler programmers who issue the RPL macro directly and capture its error feedback indicators, or to programmers performing dump-level analysis of VSAM control block chains. However, since the introduction of IBM's VS COBOL II product (in the last quarter of 1984, although achieving widespread currency only more recently), the most useful form of this information is now available to high-level lanaguage programmers using this product. The last three bytes of the four-byte feedback word seen here are accessible through a second 'FILE STATUS' field (this coding will not be detailed here, as it is covered fully in Chapter 14, on COBOL coding for VSAM). Without entering into all of the technical details, we can interpret this feedback word fairly readily from the documentation on it found in the IBM publication *VSAM Administration: Macro Instruction Reference*, Chapter 2—"Macro Instruction Return Codes and Reason Codes." The first byte (X'93', since one byte is represented by two hexadecimal digits) is generally not very useful for standard problem determination and can be ignored. The next byte (X'08') is the *RPL return code* and gives the contents of Register 15: it is shown as 8, and confirmed by the condition code of 8 which we already saw in Figure 17-20(a). The third byte is the *component code*, identifying which component contains an error when performing AIX processing (the base cluster if a 0 or 1 is found, the AIX itself if a 2 or 3 is found, and a member of the Upgrade Set if a 4 or 5 is found, even numbers indicating success and odd numbers a possible error). When no AIX processing is involved, as here, the code is X'00'. The fourth and final byte is the *reason code*, which (to be interpreted) is paired with the RPL return code of the second byte. We will spare the reader the deciphering of this at this time, and state that a X'10' reason code, when coupled with a X'08' RPL return code, indicates a 'record not found' condition, and we will shortly be able to confirm the correctness of this diagnosis of the problem in this sample DIAGNOSE.

Item (2) of Figure 17-20(b) indicates that an error was detected by the consistency DIAGNOSE facility, and that the VVDS entry involved is VSAM.CK.MVS. VSTEST01.DATA, and a comparable message in the second, lower half of this output indicates that VSAM.CK.MVS.VSTEST01.INDEX was also involved. These two data sets are the data and index components of the cluster VSAM.CK.MVS.VSTEST01, which we are checking. The 'Z' after each component name indicates a *primary VVR*: if a VVDS catalog entry for a component has more than one VVR associated with it (as we discussed earlier in this chapter), then the first is the primary VVR for that component, and any other VVRs are *secondary*, in which case they are considered by DFP/VSAM to be record type 'Q' (not 'Z'). Here, the primary VVRs for both the data and index components are identified.

Item (3) identifies the record involved: for a BCS, this would be the key of the record (which is always a 45-byte name field, naming the component), and, for a VVDS (as here), it is the RBA of the record involved (here X'5757'). Item (4) gives the offset to the beginning of the cell (within the record) involved. The first two bytes (the xeroth and first) contain a *VVR-len* field (here X'012E' or 302 (decimal) bytes long). Immediately after this, at offset '0002' begins the *VVR-header cell*, which contains the record type indicator (either 'Z' or 'Q' for a primary or secondary VVR, respectively), and the component name (VSAM.CK.MVS.VSTEST01.DATA and the equivalent index component name in the lower portion of the figure). Also included in this header is the cluster name (VSAM.CK.MVS.VSTEST01), as well as the actual name of the cluster given the HLQ-technique in MVS for catalog reference: the HLQ of 'VSAM' is an alias for the catalog 'TESTCAT.' (The rest of the record need not concern us here.)

Item (5) gives the reason code (this is the DIAGNOSE facility reason code, not the same as the reason code of the feedback word we discussed earlier (item (1) in the figure). We are told that the problem diagnosed is that of a 'CATLG ENTRY NOT FOUND' and we should then consult the explanation associated with reason code 19, as given in the *Catalog Administration Guide*. If this is done, we learn that the BCS associated with this VVDS (the BCS named 'TESTCAT') was scanned for the presence of a BCS catalog record corresponding to the VVDS entry checked, namely VSAM.CK.MVS.VSTEST01, and that such a record—which should have been present—was not encountered. What this means is that the DFP/VSAM data set VSAM.CK.MVS.VSTEST01 has an entry in the VVDS (SYS1.VVDS.VDSK001) component (and the VVDS record is displayed as part of the DIAGNOSE output, shown in Figure 17-20(b)), but there is no corresponding BCS record entry for this data set; this is certainly an error, in that any DFP/VSAM data set defined in an ICF catalog must have an entry in both the BCS and the appropriate VVDS (the VVDS for the volume on which the data set resides). Thus, the BCS should contain no entry for a DFP/VSAM data set which does not have a corresponding VVDS entry (*non-VSAM* data sets have BCS entries and no corresponding VVDS entries, as they are wholly defined in the BCS component only of an ICF catalog, but that is non-VSAM, not DFP/VSAM, data sets), and similarly, the VVDS should contain no entry which does not have a corresponding BCS entry in whatever BCS the data set was defined, but it is precisely this latter problem that the consistency DIAGNOSE facility has uncovered, and this is certainly a serious problem of catalog inconsistency. When this latter problem occurs—a VVDS entry without an associated BCS entry—we refer to the VVDS entry as an *unrelated VVR*.

Now, what of the cause of this problem. There are many possible, but the most likely ones is that the programmer inadvertently deleted the data set involved, but caused DFP/VSAM to only remove the BCS entry for the data set, and not also—as is the correct procedure—the associated VVDS entry. This would occur if the programmer issued the following AMS command in the DFP/VSAM environment:

```
DELETE -
        VSAM.CK.MVS.VSTEST01 -
        NOSCRATCH
```

This DELETE...NOSCRATCH command requests DFP/VSAM to delete the object named and its BCS catalog entry, but to leave intact the corresponding entry in both the VVDS *and the VTOC* (the VVDS and the VTOC being treated as a unit). This is precisely the cause of the problem detected here by the DIAGNOSE facility. The DELETE...NOSCRATCH command has a valid application in certain types of catalog error recovery and repair situations, but outside of this should not be issued by the general programmer, as it will cause ICF catalog component out-of-sync conditions, as it did here. (Another *valid* use of it is to delete non-VSAM data sets defined in an ICF catalog, since these only require the removal of the BCS catalog entry, there being no VVDS entry for non-VSAM data sets: the VVDS contains entries only for DFP/VSAM data sets).

Finally, one might inquire after the repair to this problem. Again, much depends on individual circumstances, but the most likely scenario here is as follows. We would first verify whether the data set itself (not its catalog entries) has really been deleted, as we suspect. (An attempt to OPEN the data set would, if it failed, confirm deletion, or a utility program can be used to inspect the volume itself.) If it has, as is the case in this example, then we would almost certainly want to remove the VVDS and VTOC entries for it, since the data set no longer exists and should not have any 'false pointers' to it. The proper procedure for removing an unrelated VVR like this, along with the VTOC entry for it, is to issue in the DFP/VSAM environment, the following commands:

```
DELETE -
        VSAM.CK.MVS.VSTEST01.DATA -
        VVR
```

and

```
DELETE -
        VSAM.CK.MVS.VSTEST01.INDEX -
        VVR
```

The DELETE...VVR command is available only in the DFP/VSAM environment, and it removes the VVDS and VTOC entries for the components named whenever the components have no associated BCS entries. It is therefore a 'recovery/repair' command in function and, if issued, would repair the problem detected by the consistency DIAGNOSE facility, as given in Figure 17-20. Note that even though the parameter VVR is specified, both the VVR entry in the VVDS and the VTOC entry for the component(s) named are removed. Note further that of the two commands referred to here, namely DELETE...NOSCRATCH and DELETE...VVR, the latter is strictly a DFP/VSAM command, as there are no VVRs (or VVDSs, or BCSs) in an Enhanced VSAM environment; DELETE...NOSCRATCH, although supported in the Enhanced VSAM environment as well as the DFP/VSAM environment, has distinct uses in each, and furthermore (in Enhanced VSAM), DELETE...NOSCRATCH may *not* be issued against a VSAM object defined in a recoverable catalog (the norm in that environment).

The reader, after this extended examination of the DFP/VSAM DIAGNOSE facility (Figure 17-21 summarizes briefly the major features of the DIAGNOSE facility), can now appreciate the extraordinary power of DFP/VSAM's problem determination facilities through the internal and the consistency DIAGNOSE facilities. Although not capable of detecting every conceivable error or inconsistency in an ICF catalog environment, it nonetheless captures an extremely large range of problems accounting for the vast majority of catalog structural or integrity 'faults.' Ideally, and this is strongly recommended, the installation should schedule DIAGNOSE facilities, both internal and consistency, against all ICF catalogs on a regular, systematic basis as part of (early) problem determination, as well as making judicious use of

Function:

        Validate/Verify: Catalog Structure
                             Consistency

Types:

      Internal DIAGNOSE

          Format/content check of:
                  BCS
                  VVDS (with its VTOC)

      Consistency DIAGNOSE

        - BCS with VVDS
        - VVDS with BCS and VTOC

        - Uses COMPAREDS/COMPAREDD parameter

Special Options

- INCLUDE/EXCLUDE/LEVEL	Selective Verification
- ERRORLIMIT	
- DUMP/NODUMP	
- LIST/NOLIST	List/Suppress entries with no errors

Figure 17-21. Summary of the DIAGNOSE facility.

DIAGNOSE on an unscheduled basis as the need arises, or suspicion of problems warrants. (Although the DIAGNOSE command is unrestricted in DFP/VSAM, many installations limit its use to VSAM system programmers and technical support staff to avoid the overhead that may be associated with its casual use). Although the syntax of the DIAGNOSE command is presented in the *Integrated Catalog Administration: Access Method Services Reference*, the most technically detailed and rigorous discussion is to be found in the *Catalog Administration Guide* (Chapter 6: "Checking Catalogs for Errors and Synchronization"), which also contains the full text of the messages generated by DIAGNOSE, along with an explanation of the error itself and sometimes its (probable) cause, along with what may be attempted as a 'Recovery Procedure' to repair or recover from the error.

    To conclude, the reader can see that there is much that is new, and subtle, about the 'new VSAM' and a firm technical appreciation of DFP/VSAM is now no longer a 'deferrable' skill. At the time of this text's publication release, DFP/VSAM will be — even is now, we believe — a vital skill for all programmers in any way involved in the IBM systems and software landscape. (We treat still other specialized facilities of DFP/VSAM later in this text at the appropriate points, especially in Chapter 18, on performance, including MVS/XA and ESA support facilities.) In many ways, shortly after this text appears, the 'new VSAM' will be something of a 'mid-life' product, mature and well-stablized within the IBM still-developing Systems Application Architecture (SAA) environment of advanced and integrated IBM products and technologies.

17.8   TECHNICAL APPENDIX: A NEW JCL TECHNIQUE FOR DEFINING VSAM CLUSTERS

For over a decade and a half, a generation of programmers has learned and internalized as incontrovertible fact that VSAM data sets, uniquely, are never defined through JCL (or the equivalent, for example, the TSO ALLOCATE command), but only through the DEFINE command of the AMS utility program IDCAMS. Only after creation by IDCAMS may a VSAM data set be referred to in the JCL. Furthermore, given this unique status of VSAM data sets, the DISP parameter of the DD statement could only have the value OLD or SHR, either one implying, correctly, a preexisting data set. Finally, VSAM data sets had to be deleted by the AMS DELETE command in an IDCAMS job, and could not be deleted by JCL, say by coding DISP= (OLD,DELETE) or DISP=(SHR,DELETE).

17.8.1   DFP V.3 and SMS

This has all been changed, however, with the introduction of *Data Facility Product Version 3* (DFP V.3) which, along with the newest operating system, MVS/SP Version 3, collectively make up IBM's largest-scale system, *Enterprise Systems Architecture* (*ESA*), introduced in mid-1988 (DFP V.3 itself being scheduled for December 1988). Under DFP V.3, there is a new storage management facility known as *Storage Management Subsystem*, officially *DFSMS* but often known simply as *SMS*, and data sets managed by SMS are referred to as *SMS-managed data sets*. These relationships are illustrated in Figure 17-22. Table 17-1 lists the types of data sets which are, and those which are not, SMS-managed. To understand the changes affecting VSAM data sets, it is necessary to look a bit more closely at SMS and some of its central constructs.

The SMS component of DFP V.3 functions to automate and centralize storage management and to simplify the complex storage management task of implementing and balancing user objectives concerning data set performance, availability, backup, migration, and optimal space retention and release. Pivotal to the effective use of SMS is the *Storage Administration Group*, headed by a *Storage Administrator*, who is responsible for the definition, implementation, and regular maintenance of largely automated centralized policies for effective system-wide storage management. This is accomplished by the Storage Administrator's use of DFP's ISMF (Interactive

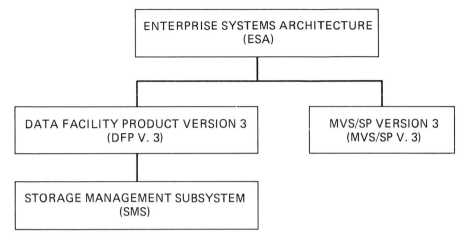

Figure 17-22. The new DFP V.3.

Table 17-1. SMS and non-SMS data set support.

SMS-MANAGED DATA SETS	NON-SMS-MANAGED DATA SETS
Sequential data sets	Tape data sets
Partitioned data sets	ISAM data sets
Direct access data sets	
DFP/VSAM data sets	Enhanced VSAM data sets
ICF catalogs	Enhanced VSAM catalogs
	Enhanced VSAM data spaces
	CVOLs
	Uncataloged data sets
	Data sets defined in two or more distinct catalogs
GDG data sets	TSO terminal-oriented data sets
Temporary data sets	In-stream data sets
VIO data sets	SYSOUT data sets
	MSS data sets (mass storage)
	TCAM message data sets
	Absolute-track allocated data sets
	Unmovable data sets

Storage Management Facility), an interactive interface to SMS, through which the Storage Administrator performs all storage management and analysis tasks. ISMF uses the panel-driven edit and browse functions of ISPF (Interactive System Productivity Facility) that most programmers are familiar with in order to centrally manage data and storage. Functions such as data set and/or volume backup and recovery, data set migration, and unused space recovery, among many other storage management tasks, can be centrally controlled, and to a high degree automated, through the ISMF interactive interface to the new SMS component of DFP V.3.

SMS uses four *constructs—data class*, *storage class*, *management class*, and *storage group*—as they are called in the language of SMS, these constructs being *named collections* of data set and storage group attributes. SMS constructs, and the attributes and values they represent, are defined by the Storage Administrator and are used by SMS to manage data and storage on a centralized system-wide basis. The first three constructs pertain to data sets and may be referred to by the programmer in JCL statements using the new keywords DATACLAS, STORCLAS, and MGMTCLAS. The fourth construct, STORGRP, pertains to storage volumes and is not programmer accessible; only the Storage Administrator accesses the STORGRP construct.

The three data set constructs and their functions are: 1) *Data class* (DATACLAS) —Data set allocation and space attributes; 2) *Storage class* (STORCLAS)—Data set performance, availability, and special volume allocation attributes; 3) *Management class* (MGMTCLAS)—Data set backup, recovery, migration, and retention attributes; while the fourth construct, pertaining to storage volumes, is: 4) *Storage group* (STORGRP)—Attributes of pools of storage volumes with similar backup, migration and dump requirements.

Two points should be noted here. First, as can be seen in Table 17-1, not *all* VSAM data sets are SMS-managed: Enhanced VSAM data sets (that is, those not cataloged in an ICF catalog) are *not* SMS-managed. Second, *all* SMS-managed data sets (VSAM and non-VSAM alike) *must* be cataloged in an ICF catalog. To be SMS-managed, therefore, a data set must be known to DFP/VSAM by being defined in an ICF catalog.

If a VSAM data set is SMS-managed, and this is true of all DFP/VSAM data sets, then it may be wholly defined through JCL. JCL definition of data sets is not especially surprising with certain types of SMS-managed data sets, such as sequential and partitioned (library) data sets, which have always been defined using JCL. But it is rather startling with respect to VSAM (DFP/VSAM only) data sets, which previously always required the use of the AMS utility program IDCAMS for their creation, specifically through the DEFINE command (although they could be *referred* to in the JCL.)

Now, as this section will show, DFP/VSAM data sets *can* be defined solely through JCL. On the other hand, a non-SMS VSAM data set, namely an Enhanced VSAM data set cataloged in a standard non-ICF VSAM catalog, may *not* be defined through JCL, but must continue to be defined through the IDCAMS utility program. In addition, DFP/VSAM data sets may be *deleted* solely by JCL (the IDCAMS DELETE command can still be used as an alternative).

17.8.2   Example: Defining VSAM Clusters Using JCL

Now let's take a look at this new technique for defining VSAM clusters. The example in Figure 17-23 defines a VSAM KSDS cluster under DFP V.3, with SMS active. The discussion below is indexed to the line numbers of that figure. Parts of the coding that require no comment are not referred to in the discussion below.

2. *DISP*. Here for the first time DISP=NEW can be used for a VSAM data set, indicating that it is being created in this statement. The second subparameter, CATLG, used for normal disposition processing, indicates that the data set is to be cataloged in an ICF catalog (again, a requirement for using the JCL definition technique under DFP V.3), while the third subparameter, DELETE (abnormal disposition processing) requests deletion of the data set on abnormal termination of the step this DD statement is part of. Similarly, if the data set had already been defined and we wished to delete it, a DD statement with a DISP=(OLD,DELETE) would suffice, and this is much simpler than an IDCAMS job with a fully coded DELETE command. (There are, unfortunately, dangers here as well, and the relevant pitfalls and precautions will be discussed later in this section.)

3. *RECORG*. This is a new JCL DD statement parameter used exclusively for defining the *cluster type* of VSAM data sets. The possible values are:

KS   Key-Sequenced Data Set (KSDS)
ES   Entry-Sequenced Data Set (ESDS)
RR   Relative Record Data Set (RRDS)
LS   Linear (Space) Data Set (LDS/LSDS)

(As noted elsewhere in the text, the Linear Data Set (LDS), sometimes also referred to as a Linear Space Data Set (LSDS), is the fourth and newest VSAM cluster; it is discussed in Chapter 18, on performance.) RECORG may be omitted if it is supplied, as it can be, through the DATACLAS parameter (see discussion later in the text), although its coding in the JCL provides valuable self-documentation. This new JCL parameter accomplishes two things: first, it signals the operating system (say, MVS/XA

```
 1.    //KSDSDD DD  DSN=FIN.ICF.INQUIRY.MSTR,
 2.    //              DISP=(NEW,CATLG,DELETE),
 3.    //              RECORG=KS,
 4.    //              SPACE=(CYL,(79,8)),
 5.    //              KEYLEN=9,
 6.    //              KEYOFF=0,
 7.    //              LRECL=460,
 8.    //              DATACLAS=KS6144AA,
 9.    //              STORCLAS=VSFASTWR,
10.    //              MGMTCLAS=STANDARD
```

Figure 17-23. An example of the new JCL technique for defining a VSAM cluster.

or ESA) that a DFP/VSAM data set, not an MVS (or ESA) data set, is being defined by this DD statement, and second, it specifies the particular type of cluster being defined (KSDS, ESDS , RRDS, or an LDS).

4. *SPACE*. This parameter may be coded just as in standard JCL for non-VSAM data sets. The SMS facility of DFP V.3 will correctly interpret the secondary allocation request to allow a maximum of 123 total extents to the data set, not the OS limit of 16. SPACE may also be omitted if it is supplied by default through another new parameter, *DATACLAS* (see below), but it is more likely to be explicitly provided for each DFP/VSAM data set, as here.

5. *KEYLEN*. *KEYLEN* is another new parameter which supplies the length of the primary key. Since none of the other cluster types (ESDS, RRDS, LDS) have a primary key, KEYLEN is coded only for KSDSs.

6. *KEYOFF*. This new parameter supplies the offset of the primary key from the beginning of the record, taken (just as in DEF CLUSTER IDCAMS coding) as the zeroth byte. KEYOFF=0 thus indicates that the key begins in the first byte of the record. Note that the KEYLEN and KEYOFF parameters in the JCL DD statement handle the equivalent functions of the KEYS paramater of the DEF CLUSTER command: for the example in Figure 17-23, the equivalent IDCAMS parameter would be KEYS (9 0).

7. *LRECL*. This new parameter—new in the sense of a stand-alone DD statement parameter rather than as a subparameter of the DCB parameter—supplies the record length for fixed-length records (or the maximum length for variable-length records). Note that this is equivalent to the LRECL subparameter of the DCB parameter, but cannot be coded in that manner, as VSAM data sets have no DCBs (an ACB is used, and there is no JCL paramater for an ACB). LRECL may be omitted from the JCL if it is defined with the appropriate value in a named *data class* (see below), but given the extreme variability of record sizes for VSAM data sets, it will most likely be coded, as here, in the JCL.

8. *DATACLAS*. As noted above, a data class is a named list of allocation and space attributes (and, for VSAM data sets, of certain performance attributes) and their values, defined by the Storage Administrator. Many of these may be overridden in the JCL (but not all).

A programmer may code the DATACLAS parameter in the JCL and name an available data class whose attributes and values will be used in the definition of the data set. The DATACLAS parameter may be used to supply predefined values for attributes such as RECORG, RECFM, LRECL, KEYLEN, KEYOFF, RETPD, EXPDT, and certain VSAM-specific attributes such as IMBED, REPLICATE, (data) CISZ, and SHAREOPTIONS, among others.

For example, here (Figure 17-23) an installation-defined data class named KS6144AA is used which has been predefined to supply, among other things, certain acceptable default parameter values, in this case an RECFM of F, a data CISZ of 6144, an FSPC of (32 25), a SHR of (1 3), and NOIMBED and NOREPLICATE. Another data class called, for example, KS6144BB, may have been predefined to also give a data CISZ of 6144 bytes, but with other values of FSPC, SHR, and other attributes.

9. *STORCLAS*. This parameter specifies, by installation-defined (that is, Storage

Administrator defined) names, the storage class construct. As already briefly noted above, a storage class is a list of performance and availability attributes, and their respective values, used by SMS to control data set placement in accordance with user performance and availability objectives.

A storage class may specify, among other things, target values for a data set's response time requirements to be used by SMS to select a device from the installation's available I/O configuration which will meet the requisite level of performance, if at all possible, or the device that otherwise comes closest to yielding that level. The required level of performance is expressed through the *MILLISECOND RESPONSE* storage class attribute. This attribute allows the specification of both a direct access response time value (DIR RESP) and a sequential access response time value (SEQ RESP). A DIR RESP of 22 milliseconds would, for example, request SMS to select, if possible, a DASD device and controller that may yield that target response time or better in terms of direct access operations. (The unit of work is always taken to be the transfer—if any is needed—of one 4K block of data into or from virtual storage.) This is a relatively modest performance level request given current DASD capabilities. For certain critical data sets we might request a (DIR or SEQ) RESP of five milliseconds or better (this will generally be satisfiable only from cached DASD—the 3880 Model 23 or 3990 Model 3 Storage Control—as we will discuss later in Chapter 18, the chapter on performance.)

In addition, a *DIR BIAS* and/or *SEQ BIAS* can be predefined as part of the named storage class. Either type of bias can be 'R' or 'W', to indicate that the data set is processed predominantly in either read or write mode, and this information can be used by SMS to choose the most appropriate I/O facility accordingly.

The storage class can also specify another attribute, *AVAILABILITY*, whose value may be either STANDARD or CONTINUOUS. If CONTINUOUS is specified, a special facility supported only on a 3990, known as *dual copy*, will be used. Dual copy duplexes information (much like Enhanced VSAM's use of Catalog Recovery Areas) to assure high availability for critical data sets (if there is a problem with what is considered the primary copy, the backup copy can be used instead).

The STORCLAS parameter need not be coded in the JCL, but if it is omitted, SMS will use an installation-defined default storage class, which may not provide the performance and/or availability desired. For key applications, it is best to specifically control these requirements through appropriately defined storage classes (and storage classes used for very high optimization can even be protected by RACF and thus restricted in use).

In the example under discussion, the storage class name 'VSFASTWR' was used, and this might have been predefined to require (1) a special highly optimal type of write operation known as *Fast Write*, available only on a 3990 (this will be discussed further in Chapter 18), and (2) both a DIR RESP and SEQ RESP of five milliseconds or better, for certain critical online (CICS) and/or database applications. This would force SMS to allocate the data set (named 'FIN.ICF.INQUIRY.MSTR' in statement 1 of Figure 17-23) on a 3380 device under the control of the 3990 Model 3 Storage Control in order to obtain the requested level of performance.

10. *MGMTCLAS*. A management class is a list of, primarily, backup and

recovery attributes and their values. The management class specification determines backup process facilities, such as the frequency of (automatic) backup, and how many backup versions should be retained and on what retention schedule. SMS will *arrange* the requested facilities, but it will have DFHSM (Data Facility Hierarchical Storage Manager, discussed earlier in the text in Subsection 15.2.4) actually *perform* the operations requested. DFHSM may itself implement certain operations in conjunction with DFDSS (Data Facility Data Set Services, also discussed in Section 15.2.4) which handles certain volume-level DUMP/RESTORE facilities. (Under DFP V.3, the products DFHSM and DFDSS are coordinated through the SMS component of DFP.) In our example in Figure 17-23, we have simply coded for a standard MGMTCLAS (named STANDARD) which will supply acceptable default backup and recovery (and other related) attributes. We could have omitted this specification of MGMTCLAS parameter in the JCL altogether, in which case it would have defaulted to STANDARD.

Note in Figure 17-23 that UNIT and VOL are not coded. Under DFP V.3 with SMS, UNIT and VOL need not, and typically are not, coded, but rather are supplied through an SMS mechanism using *storage groups* (collections of candidate volumes for data set allocation), although UNIT and VOL may, through a special technique, be coded and honored as requested in the JCL. The details are complex, but the basic concept is that of allowing the system to centrally manage known types of data sets through installation-defined names of storage groups for various general and special functions. There may be groups like STGRDB2 (for DB2 databases, STGRCICS (for critical CICS files), STGRPRIM (default general-purpose volumes), STGRIMS (for IMS volumes), STGRVIO (for data sets stored on paging storage simulating DASD volumes), STGRLARG (for allocation of large data sets, say in excess of 100 megabytes), STGRPAGE (for system paging data sets), STGRACCT (for accounting department application data sets), and so on. Storage groups could be assigned through data set naming conventions, or through other SMS constructs.

Note also that, under DFP V.3, the typical parameters used in IDCAMS coding on the DEF CLUSTER command are captured through the new JCL parameters, as shown in Figure 17-23. However, not all IDCAMS command parameters can be captured through the JCL, so that the programmer must either accept known defaults for other parameters, or use a non-JCL technique for more comprehensive control. This non-JCL technique can be any one of three alternatives: 1) standard IDCAMS DEF CLUSTER command coding; 2) a new set of extensions to the TSO ALLO-CATE command (which formerly could not be used to define VSAM clusters); or 3) a new DFP V.3 AMS command: ALLOCATE. But for many purposes the JCL technique may suffice and satisfy common requirements, and it has two major virtues: simplicity and control over powerful SMS constructs like storage class, for example, which provides a novel (even radical) way of specifying performance requirements and having them automatically assured (if at all possible, given the installation's I/O configuration).

To define a non-KSDS cluster, minor adjustments need be made to the JCL. For an ESDS, RECORG=ES is coded, and KEYLEN and KEYOFF are omitted, as an

ESDS has no (primary) key. (And the DATACLAS parameter, if used, would not specify FSPC, IMBED, REPLICATE, or other attributes associated only with a KSDS.) For an RRDS, RECORG=RR is coded, but otherwise the remaining coding is comparable to that of the ESDS. For a Linear Data Set, RECORG=LS is coded; an LDS has no key, so KEYLEN and KEYOFF are omitted, as well as any parameter associated with an index component (an LDS has none), or FSPC. Furthermore, the JCL coding for an LDS must omit LRECL specification, as an LDS has no record or CI/CA organization, all data being in a linear stream of 4K blocks, and this also entails that a CISZ specification is invalid for an LDS. (LDSs are discussed more fully in Chapter 18, on performance.)

Figure 17-23 gave the JCL for *creating* a VSAM cluster. On the other hand, *reference* to a cluster in the JCL continues as before, where a DSN and DISP parameter are all that need be coded, although we know at this point that DISP can now be any value, not just OLD or SHR. And this leads to a warning: do not, under DFP V.3, code (for an SMS-managed VSAM cluster) a DISP=(_____,DELETE); this may have been ignored before, when such data sets could only be deleted by an AMS DELETE command in an IDCAMS job, but SMS will honor the request as coded and delete the cluster upon normal termination, which may not—although it could—be what was intended.

Existing JCL for VSAM data sets converted to SMS-managed data sets must be carefully reviewed to assure no inadvertent use of the DELETE subparameter of the DISP parameter. Many production procedures ('procs') may have such coding for VSAM data sets, since it was viewed as wholly safe, but this is not true any longer (under DFP V.3).

In conclusion, it should be noted that the SMS facility under DFP V.3 is quite a radical change from standard techniques of defining and controlling VSAM data sets, and it will take considerable time for programmers to accustom themselves to it, but, as can be seen from the above discussion, there are some novel and very rich and powerful facilities available that can be exploited to considerable advantage. The use of STORCLAS to stipulate performance requirements to be assured by SMS will undoubtedly be one of the most important of all of these new facilities. (STORCLAS is revisited in Chapter 18, on performance.) The interested reader should consult the appropriate technical publications for further information on the new JCL techniques of DFP V.3.

18

HOW TO DESIGN AND OPTIMIZE A VSAM SYSTEM

18.1 INTRODUCTION TO PERFORMANCE AND DESIGN ISSUES IN VSAM

Extensive experience with VSAM-based applications has clearly demonstrated that optimal VSAM performance is attainable only through the careful design of the VSAM system and its data sets, coupled with precise fine-tuning of certain critical performance-related options and parameters. These two areas—performance and design—are intimately related: certain design choices may directly or indirectly affect performance, whether positively or adversely. Often, a well-designed VSAM data set brings more or less immediate benefits in terms of performance. However, this is not always the case.

To take an example, concerns about the security and integrity of the data stored in some VSAM data set may dictate certain well-defined restrictions concerning the sharing of the data set by multiple concurrent tasks. To gain the strongest degree of data integrity, it may be necessary to disallow concurrent changes to the data set altogether. Such a requirement can be communicated to VSAM directly through a particular parameter on the IDCAMS command DEFINE CLUSTER (this parameter is SHAREOPTIONS, which we will discuss in detail later in this chapter).

However, to provide the requisite level of data integrity, VSAM must 'police,' as it were, the processing activity against the data set in order to prohibit the relevant cases of concurrent access. Real program code implementing the needed restrictions must, therefore, be available in the execution environment, thus impacting adversely on program execution-time. We could, of course, avoid this performance overhead altogether, but only at the cost of losing the data set integrity assurance we wanted. More realistically, we may settle for a weaker form of integrity, which, although not complete, may be acceptable under certain circumstances, and this may have less of an adverse performance impact for the excellent reason that it shall require less comprehensive 'policing' by VSAM.

Most programmers are well acquainted with the classic *space versus time tradeoff*, where conserving space (DASD or virtual storage) is often at the cost of poorer execution-time performance, and vice versa. Here, in the case we are presently considering, we are confronted with a *design versus time tradeoff*. In other cases (as we shall see below), design considerations and performance may involve no tradeoff of this sort. Each case has to be considered separately. Although we will begin with performance considerations, therefore, we will necessarily be discussing design issues wherever relevant.

18.2   CHOOSING A VSAM FILE ORGANIZATION

Lets begin our discussion of VSAM performance and optimization with the topic of data set type (KSDS versus ESDS versus RRDS), primarily a design issue but, as we discussed above, one of several such issues with performance implications. We will then consider data set type, complicated by alternate index considerations.

The data set type most widely chosen in commercial environments is the KSDS. It is generally the most familiar type of VSAM data set to applications programmers, many of whom may never actually create an ESDS or an RRDS, or process against them, at all in their programming experience. Very few programmers are even aware of the existence of still another cluster type, the *LDS* (*Linear Data Set*), which we have briefly referred to earlier in the text, and which we shall take up in more detail later in this chapter.

However, there are advantages and disadvantages associated with each of the different possible data set types. Let us now examine some of the key considerations that must be weighed in determining optimal data set type (leaving the discussion of the LDS for later).

18.2.1.   Access Mode: KSDS versus ESDS with AIX Processing

1. KSDS + AIX Processing.   A KSDS supports both sequential and random processing; not widely appreciated is the fact that both of the other data set types do also. However, an ESDS supports random processing only if an alternate index is built over it; in addition, an ESDS supports the insertion of new records only at EOF (End-of-File), and prohibits record deletion. These restrictions may or may not be acceptable, under various circumstances. An example of a case in which the restrictions are acceptable *and* the performance benefits are exceptional is that of an online multi-key accessed inquiry file: that is, a file which is accessed wholly in read (browse) mode, and such access is over any of several fields (one of which, in a KSDS, may be the primary key, the others as alternate keys, or they may all be alternate keys). Such a file would support both sequential and random read access, but its common usage is for fast random read requests.

Now let's consider the issue of implementation. If implemented by a KSDS organization, such a file would require some number x of AIXes, while the equivalent ESDS may require x plus 1 AIXes if one of the keys of access is the primary key of the KSDS: this is so because with an ESDS—which lacks a primary key—access over this key must be effected by making the relevant field an alternate key in order to allow random access over the field.

It may seem remarkable that, for heavy random read (inquiry) activity, the simpler KSDS design—whose primary motivation was, after all, to provide fast sequential *and* random access—would be less efficient than an ESDS design, given that an ESDS was primarily implemented for sequential access only. But this is so, nevertheless, and part of understanding why hinges on appreciating that the KSDS design is actually more complex, even for random access activity. Let's see why this is so.

Let's begin by considering the structure of a KSDS + AIX (to simplify the discussion, only a single AIX need be considered). The base cluster (BC), being a KSDS, has both a data and index component. The index component consists of (compressed) primary keys in character form, along with associated pointers. As we learned in earlier chapters, the pointers are in the form of a CI-Number. Now, what of the AIX over this BC? It, too, is a KSDS: all AIXes over any BC are themselves separate data sets, always with KSDS organization.

Now, what of *this* file (the AIX itself as a KSDS)? Like any KSDS, this AIX consists of both a data and an index component, but with an internal structure specific to its function as an AIX. First, the internal structure of the AIX index component. This contains two fields: a *K-field* which is the *noncompressed* alternate key, in character form, representing the high-key of the CI in the data component with which this alternate key is associated. This K-field is simply a copy of the alternate key field.

More generally, therefore, the AIX index will consist of a set of index records, one for each unique alternate key of the BC file, and each containing our K-field as the representation of this key. Associated with this K-field—and found in the same index record—is a P-field, which is a CI-Number pointer into the data component of the AIX. These two fields of the AIX index component are the same in form and function as those in any KSDS index component—they jointly 'index' the data records in the data component, with two important differences.

First, the K-field of an AIX index component is a *full alternate key*, while the K-field of an index component of a standard KSDS is a *compressed primary key*. Second, the records being pointed to by the P-field in the case of an AIX index component, although found within the AIX data component, are not data records: they are control records which point into, and thereby locate, *the records of the base cluster associated with the AIX* (the cluster 'over' which the AIX is built). Thus, the AIX index points into the AIX data component which in turn points into the base cluster, to ultimately locate the actual data records of the base cluster's data component.

Now the hard part, critical to understanding the performance and design consequences of the two different structures: KSDS + AIX, versus ESDS + AIX. When the AIX is over a KSDS base cluster, the records of the AIX data component consist of two objects: one is another K-field containing the (full) alternate key; when an index 'lookup' occurs, it is a match between the two K-fields (one in the index, the other in the data component of the AIX) which is a 'hit'.

The other object in the AIX data component is what I will term the *Pointer-Set*, which does the work of locating the target data records. With a KSDS + AIX, the locating is indirect in the following sense. The Pointer-Set, which is associated with one and only one alternate key (in the form of the K-field), contains the value of all primary key *synonyms* of the alternate key. Primary key synonyms are all of the primary key values associated with the set of all data records which contain the specified alternate key.

For example, if social security number (SSN) is the primary key of the base cluster, and an AIX is built over the last name field as the—in this case, non-unique— alternate key, then the Pointer-Set will contain the SSNs of all, say 'Smith' records (or 'Jones' records, etc.). Thus, the set of all 'Smith' records are picked out and located, by primary key value (SSN). If there are 100 Smith records in the base cluster, there will be 100 different SSNs in the Pointer-Set associated with the alternate key (K-field) of Smith.

If we had, however, built a *unique* AIX over the base cluster (say, employee number), then the Pointer-Set would contain one and only one pointer, namely the single SSN associated with some one employee number value (remember, there is only one such base cluster record being picked out by a *unique* alternate key).

Now, to find the data records associated with some particular alternate key, VSAM uses the pointers of the Pointer-Set as search values *into the index component of the KSDS base cluster*. These (character) SSN values will be looked up in the index component of the KSDS base cluster in the same way that any index search is made within a KSDS (see the chapter on the index component of a KSDS, earlier): the index entries will point from the base cluster's index component into the base cluster's data component.

Hence, when dealing with a KSDS + AIX, a random read against any particular alternate key value involves following this chain of pointers: from the *index of the AIX* (using the P-field), into the *data component of the AIX*, and from there (using the Pointer-Set) into the *index component of the KSDS base cluster*, and finally from there into the *data component of the KSDS base cluster*. The entire process is represented diagrammatically in Figure 18-1a. This is a complex process, partly due

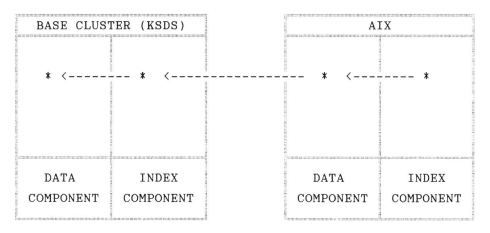

Figure 18-1a. AIX processing over KSDS + AIX.

to the fact that both data sets involved—the base cluster and the AIX data set—have KSDS organization: each has both an index and a data component.

2. ESDS + AIX Processing.   Now let's turn to the case of an AIX over an ESDS to see what's different and why the process of random retrieval is more efficient in this case. Starting at the index component of the AIX data set (where random retrieval by the alternate key must begin), the internal structure is identical to the KSDS + AIX case: the index records consist of K-fields and associated P-field pointers. And, just as before, the P-field pointers lead from this index component of the AIX into the data component of the AIX. Further, the data component of the AIX again consists of a K-field containing the alternate key values, along with a Pointer-Set.

Here, however, the cases begin to diverge. With an AIX over an ESDS, the Pointer-Set contains *RBA pointer synonyms*, rather than primary key synonyms. For any given alternate key value, the associated Pointer-Set now contains the relative byte address *within the data component of the base cluster* of all data records containing that alternate key; thus, for the alternate key of 'Smith,' the Pointer-Set contains the set of RBA's—offset from an arbitrary zero start point of the data component records—of all Smith data records.

There are several critical points to note at this time concerning the ESDS + AIX case:

1. The pointers of the Pointer-Set are RBA values, not primary key values; indeed, they could not be primary key values for the excellent reason that an ESDS, which is the base cluster, has no primary key at all.
2. These RBA-pointers point *directly from the data component of the AIX into the data component of the ESDS*; that is, they effect a direct hit in one step to the target data records, as there is no intervening index component within the base cluster.
3. The size of the Pointer-Set is the number of data records which contain the particular alternate key (the set of 'synonyms') times four, because each RBA-pointer, being an RBA, is exactly four bytes in length and there will be one such four-byte pointer for each data record containing any one specific alternate key. Thus, to use our earlier example, if the alternate key field is last name, say for an alternate key value of 'Smith,' the Pointer-Set will contain the RBA values of all of the Smith data records. If there are 100 such Smith records, then the Pointer-Set size will be 4 times 100 bytes in size, or 400 bytes.

Now, let's explore the performance consequences of all of this. To begin with, the data component of the AIX over an ESDS will generally be more compact than one over a KSDS. Consider the number of *synonyms* for any specific alternate key (the number of data records with that alternate key value), in each of the two cases we are examining. When the base cluster is a KSDS, then as we have already seen, the Pointer-Set will consist of *primary key synonyms*. Each such synonym, being a primary key value, is whatever is the *full* (uncompressed) keylength of the primary key field (the index of an AIX always contains full key pointers, unlike the index of a standard KSDS which always contains compressed key pointers).

In our example, where the primary key of the base cluster KSDS is social security number, then each primary-key synonym, say for an alternate key value of 'Smith,' is exactly 10 bytes long; if there are 100 synonyms (100 'Smith' records), then the size of the 'Smith' Pointer-Set within the data component of our AIX would be 10 times 100, or 1000, bytes.

In the parallel case of an ESDS + AIX, however, the data component of the AIX would be much more compact: the Pointer-Set in this case consists of RBA-pointers, one for each synonym of any particular alternate key value, and given that RBA-pointers are four bytes long, then for an alternate key value having 100 synonyms ('Smith' records), the total size of the Pointer-Set is only four times 100, or 400, bytes, considerably smaller than the comparable Pointer-Set when the AIX is over a KSDS.

Note also here that the primary key may be of any length up to 255 bytes, and large primary keys are quite common in commercial environments. If the primary key were just 20 bytes in length, then the 'Smith' Pointer-Set for an AIX over a KSDS would be 2000 bytes (the 20 byte length times 100 synonyms) over the example we are considering, while — and this is important to note — *the size of the Pointer-Set of an AIX over an ESDS does not change*, for any particular alternate key value, regardless of the length of the alternate key field; the Pointer-Set size is completely independent of the size of the alternate key (it's dependent only on the number of synonyms for that particular alternate key), since not the key itself, but rather an RBA pointing to the data record containing that key, is the pointer used when an AIX is built over an ESDS. Pushing this further, for a 50-byte primary key, the size of the 'Smith' Pointer-Set in the KSDS + AIX case would be 5000 bytes (assuming 100 synonyms), while for the ESDS + AIX case, the size is still just 400 bytes, quite a significant difference! (And we have considered space only for one alternate key Pointer Set.)

If the alternate key were unique (with, say, an employee number alternate key), then in both cases there would be only a single synonym, by definition, for each different alternate key value, and the pointer associated with this value would be the primary key of the single data record containing that (alternate) key value in the case of a KSDS + AIX, versus the RBA of the same single data record; in our example, the size of the Pointer-Sets would be 10 bytes and 4 bytes, respectively.

Indeed, the only case in which the Pointer-Set of an AIX over a KSDS would not be smaller than the corresponding set of an AIX over an ESDS, is one in which the primary key is four or less bytes in length, and this is almost never encountered in real commercial VSAM applications. Also note that a smaller AIX (due to a smaller data component within the AIX) will generally provide faster random retrieval by alternate key than a relatively larger AIX, as well as conserving more storage for the AIX data set itself.

But this is not the only performance advantage of an ESDS + AIX versus a KSDS + AIX. Recall from the above discussion the chain of pointers that had to be followed for random retrieval by alternate key when the base cluster was a KSDS: from the index of the AIX data set, into the data component of the AIX data set, from there into the index component of the base cluster KSDS, and finally from there into the data component of the base cluster KSDS.

In contrast, in the case of random retrieval against an ESDS + AIX, there is a shorter chain of pointers to follow: from the index of the AIX, into the data component of the AIX (no difference up to this point), but then from here directly into the target data component of the base cluster (necessarily, since the base cluster in this case is an ESDS which has no index component). That is, once the AIX is processed (the same in both cases), VSAM can make a direct hit to the target data records with no intervening (and complex) index search; see Figure 18-1b. This shorter chain of pointers has a profound effect on random retrieval performance, making the ESDS case considerably more efficient in terms of execution-time than the corresponding KSDS case.

Furthermore, VSAM can perform operations on RBA values far more efficiently than on character key values. Indeed, the higher optimization possible with an access method like VSAM, using RBA pointers rather than character strings key values (as with, for example, ISAM), was (as we have seen earlier in the text) one of the most central motivations for the introduction of VSAM itself.

The one case in which the ESDS + AIX implementation for random retrieval for inquiry may not afford higher optimization than the KSDS counterpart is the special case of access being needed only over the primary key field. In this case, the KSDS implementation does not require an alternate index at all for such retrieval, while the ESDS implementation—given that ESDSs have no index component to directly support standard random processing—would require one AIX to be built over the ESDS base cluster, using as the alternate key field whatever constitutes the primary key field in the KSDS case. Given that an AIX is an additional data set (generally part of the upgrade set), random retrieval in the ESDS implementation would entail

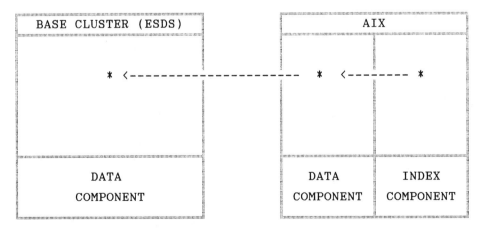

Figure 18-1b. AIX processing over ESDS + AIX.

additional OPEN/CLOSE processing of the AIX data set itself, not encountered with the one-data-set KSDS implementation.

But apart from this special case, multikey random inquiry would be consistently more optimal using an ESDS rather than a KSDS for the base cluster. Such read-only random retrieval inquiry files are quite common in on-line processing under CICS-type systems, and the discussion above makes clear that performance would be superior if the inquiry file were designed as an ESDS rather than a KSDS (this would still hold if the file were not strictly read-only, as long as the only write activity against the file were record addition to the end of file, assuming, in addition, no record deletion activity).

Thus, to summarize, if design considerations allow either a KSDS or ESDS implementation, where the restrictions associated with ESDS processing are acceptable or part of the design specifications, performance can be favored by the choice of an ESDS.

18.2.2   Access Mode: KSDS versus ESDS in Sequential Mode

More VSAM data sets are implemented as KSDSs than as ESDSs or RRDSs by far, and quite often this is precisely the right design choice if the essential features of a KSDS are really needed for the range of processing activity against the data set. However, far too often a KSDS implementation is used even if processing considerations would also support the choice of a different data set type, and where a different choice may, in certain cases, be more optimal (in terms of execution-time performance). A common case is that of a read-only inquiry file to be accessed solely in sequential mode (no writes or random retrievals against the file). Here, the most optimal choice would be that of an ESDS: strict sequential access of an ESDS is considerable faster than such access of the corresponding KSDS, for two related reasons.

Firstly, the ESDS implementation uses a less complex organization—just a single data component, and therefore just a single data set—than the KSDS counterpart, which adds an index component, treated by VSAM as a separate data set from the data component (indeed, the two components need not even be on the same DASD volume).

Secondly, a sequential read through the file (or through part of it) requires index processing in the case of the KSDS implementation, but not with an ESDS (necessarily, again, given that an ESDS lacks an index component). This may seem surprising—or even incorrect; most programmers have the (incorrect) intuition that sequential access of a KSDS, by virtue of being sequential, does not involve the index component at all.

Surely, it's reasoned, the index component is only used if random processing is involved. Not so. VSAM *always* uses the index component of a KSDS for sequential access: the *sequence set* of the index component is read by VSAM in order to fetch and return the records of the data component in their correct *logical* order of ascending keys, which after some VSAM processing (causing a CI- or CA-split) is not necessarily the same as the *physical* order of the records as encountered in the successive CIs of the data component.

Thus, the actual physical order of the data component CIs is not assured to be the same as their logical (ascending key) order for a KSDS except at create-time and after complete data set reorganization. But to honor the request of strict sequential retrieval, the records—and therefore the CIs—must be fetched and returned to the program in their logical (not physical) order, and the sequence set records of the index are precisely where the correct logical order is reflected and maintained by VSAM.

So reading a KSDS sequentially involves extra I/O operations during execution-time to read the sequence set records in addition to the I/O for fetching the associated data records. With an ESDS, the physical order of records and CIs is always the same as the logical order of records and CIs (no split activity occurs in ESDS processing), so that a sequential read through the data set involves the elementary process of reading the physically succesive (data) CIs, and this will invariably give higher preformance. Thus, if only sequential reads against a VSAM cluster are required, choose the ESDS implementation.

18.2.3   Random Access: KSDS versus an RRDS

Random access is supported by both a KSDS and an RRDS, without any AIX being needed if the access is over the primary key. An RRDS does not actually have a key field, but as we know from earlier discussions, access is by Relative Record Number (RRN) which is treated by VSAM as a key into the data set. Both record additions (internal and at EOF) and deletions are supported, although record length may not change. An RRDS is arguably the least familiar VSAM data set type, and also the one whose programming is not often encountered in many commercial environments, but it is an extremely simple and efficient data set organization and performance gains can be achieved if the restrictions of RRDS processing prove acceptable for the application.

In this connection, it is important to note that an RRDS is the VSAM counter-part to the OS BDAM file organization and access method; BDAM files are *direct* data sets, the most efficient OS files for random access. In COBOL BDAM files, and their VSAM RRDS equivalent, are known as *relative* files, in PL/I as *regional files* (there are three different types: regional (1), regional (2), and regional (3), reflecting different direct access programming techniques), and in Assembler as (simply) *direct* files.

The VSAM RRDS shares the high performance of such OS direct files, and achieves even greater optimization by an additional feature missing in the OS coun-terpart: an RRDS supports *blocking* of records (through VSAM CI organization), while direct files in OS are essentially unblocked, and record blocking speeds I/O operations considerably. Again, assuming that the processing restrictions of an RRDS organization are acceptable, an RRDS implementation is an excellent choice for random access on-line files (CICS) needing extremely fast data set access.

18.3   CONTROL INTERVAL SIZE (CISZ): THE DATA COMPONENT

The size of a VSAM data set's data component control interval—we will refer to this simply as *data CISZ*—is one of several critical determinants of VSAM processing performance for that data set. It is also a complex matter to determine what an optimal data CISZ might be under various circumstances. Let's look at several key issues that are involved.

18.3.1   Data CISZ and DASD Utilization

Different choices of CISZ make more or less effective use of DASD space. The Device Characteristics Chart (given in Appendix A) summarizes the percentage utilization of a DASD track that is obtained with different classes of CISZ (data or index CISZ yield the same results). We can see that the best DASD utilization is achieved by CISZs that are integral multiples of 4K, second best those that are integral multiples of 2K, etc., with the worst results associated with 512 (½K), 1536 (3 times 512), 2560 (5 times 512), etc., this last class yielding only 50 percent DASD utilization on the 3380 disk.

18.3.2   The Fuller Story: Unused Space

It would, however, be tempting (but incorrect) to quickly conclude that one should always choose a data CISZ of an integral multiple of 4K (4K, 8K, 12K, ...). This may optimize *DASD utilization*, but may not provide optimal overall performance, especially in terms of execution-time processing. Remember that there is often a time/space tradeoff involved in VSAM performance considerations. Let's look at a concrete case.

Assume a RECSZ of 460 bytes, and, as a first simplification, no freespace requested (that is, FSPC (0 0)). Against a data CISZ of 4096, 10 bytes would be consumed for VSAM CFs (control fields): four bytes for one CIDF plus an additional six bytes for two RDFs (assuming fixed-length records), leaving 4086 at most allocatable to store logical records. Now let's inquire what is the maximum number of LRs that can be packed into this available space within the CI; this number is known as *MAX-PACK* (maximum 'packing factor' for LRs within a data CI). MAX-PACK ignores FSPC, so the computation is very simple:

$$\text{MAX-PACK} = \frac{(\text{CISZ} - \text{CF})}{\text{RECSZ}} \quad [\text{floor}] \qquad [1]$$

where CF is the number of bytes per CI used for VSAM control fields, one CIDF and one or more RDFs (the reader is directed to review the discussion of Section 11.8, where the precise computation of CF was developed). For the case under consideration,

$$\begin{aligned}
\text{MAX-PACK} &= (4096 - 10)/460 = 4086/460 \\
&= 8.88 \,[\text{floor}] \\
&= 8
\end{aligned}$$

The 8.88 is 'floored,' that is, rounded down to the next *lower* integer (non-fraction) to 8. Now if the MAX-PACK equals 8, then the number of bytes of the CI used to actually hold records—known as *LR-AREA*—will be 8 times 460, which equals 3680 bytes. Now we may compute the amount of bytes per CI which are unused, which we shall term *UNUSED-SPC*:

$$\text{UNUSED-SPC} = \text{CISZ} - \text{CIFSPC-AMT} - \text{LR-AREA} - \text{CF} \qquad [2]$$

where CIFSPC-AMT represents the number of bytes out of each CI to be reserved by VSAM to honor our FSPC request at the CI level (ours is zero, since we are assuming FSPC (0 0)).

Before we compute UNUSED-SPC, however, it will be useful to clarify some terms we will be using here (and throughout the chapter). For any FSPC request of the form FSPC (CIFSPC% CAFSPC%), then the term *CIFSPC* is simply the decimal fraction equivalent of CIFSPC%, and the term *CAFSPC* is simply the decimal fraction equivalent of CAFSPC%. Say we have a specification of FSPC (32 25): CIFSPC% is 32 percent, so that CIFSPC is equal to .32, and CAFSPC is 25 percent, so CAFSPC equals .25. As we shall see, it will be easier for performance computations to use the decimal fractions CIFSPC and CAFSPC, rather than the percentage forms of CIFSPC% and CAFSPC%. To be really formal about it, CIFSPC and CAFSPC can be defined as:

$$\text{CIFSPC} = \frac{\text{CIFSPC\%}}{100}$$

and

$$\text{CAFSPC} = \frac{\text{CAFSPC\%}}{100}$$

Now, we return to our original consideration, namely, of computing CIFSPC-AMT, so that we can, in turn, compute UNUSED-SPC. CIFSPC-AMT is computed by:

$$\text{CIFSPC-AMT} = (\text{CISZ} \times \text{CIFSPC}) \, [\text{floor}] \qquad [3]$$

which, for the case under consideration, would yield zero bytes (we are assuming FSPC (0 0)). Then we have:

$$\text{UNUSED-SPC} = 4096 - 0 - 3680 - 10 = 406 \text{ bytes.}$$

These 406 bytes represent about 10 percent of the CI being wasted, as no record may be inserted into this remaining space, nor may it be used to lengthen records, for example, since that space must come from requested FSPC, and none was requested. Although we use the term UNUSED-SPC, it is really *unusable space*: it cannot be exploited by VSAM for any processing function. But 406 bytes of every CI, for even a relatively modestly sized data set, will amount to a very large quantity of wasted space which must be 'carried' along in the CI by VSAM, although it may never be used. Such unnecessary additional baggage will only degrade VSAM performance.

By way of comparison, consider a different choice of data CISZ, namely 6144 (6K).

$$\text{MAX-PACK} = (6144 - 10)/460 = 13.33\,[\text{floor}] = 13.$$

Then LR-AREA equals 13 times 460, which equals 5980 bytes. We can now compute UNUSED-SPC:

$$\text{UNUSED-SPC} = (6144 - 10 - 5980) = 154\text{ bytes}.$$

Using a CISZ of 6144 reclaims for VSAM use an additional 252 bytes per CI (the 406 bytes of UNUSED-SPC for CISZ equals 4096 less the 154 bytes of UNUSED-SPC for CISZ equal to 6144). Furthermore, 154 unused (and unusable) bytes represents only 2.5 percent of the CI being wasted (compared to 10 percent when CISZ was 4096).

18.3.3   CISZ, UNUSED SPACE, and FSPC

Now let's push these considerations further by adding in some constant request for FSPC. As we are only now considering utilization at the CI level, we will assume a request of, say, FSPC (10 0). Now we will develop a realistic measure of the 'packing factor' (number of LRs to the CI) which includes FSPC consideration. This new measure is termed *PACK*, and is computed as follows:

$$\text{PACK} = \frac{\text{CISZ} - (\text{CISZ} \times \text{CIFSPC})[\text{floor}] - \text{CF}}{\text{RECSZ}}\,[\text{floor}] \qquad [4]$$

Here the notation '(CISZ × CIFSPC)[floor]' is the same as our computation of CIFSPC-AMT in the previous section and indicates that we take 10 percent of the CISZ, equivalent to multiplying by the fraction .10, and then floor the result. This is 4096 times .10, which equals 409.6, floored to 409 bytes. This is the number of bytes VSAM will hold for FSPC out of every CI: that is, VSAM will load sufficient records into the CI to assure that 409 bytes are always reserved for FSPC (for record insertion and record lengthening operations).

The final '[floor]' indication means that, after the entire computation for PACK is carried out (including the division by RECSZ), the final result, if fractional, is to be floored. This is how VSAM itself handles these computations (verified by actual run-time experience).

In our CISZ equal to 4096 example,

$$PACK = (4096 - 409 - 10)/460 = 3677/460$$
$$= 7.99 \, [\text{floor}]$$
$$= 7$$

Now if only seven LRs are to be packed per CI, then LR-AREA, which is computed simply by:

$$LR\text{-}AREA = PACK \times RECSZ \qquad\qquad [5]$$

would be 7 times 460, equalling 3220. Now we can compute UNUSED-SPC:

$$UNUSED\text{-}SPC = (4096 - 409 - 3220 - 10) = 457 \text{ bytes}$$

per CI unusable, a very large amount given a CISZ of 4096. Since the size of any data buffer is equal to CISZ, then all I/O operations will be transferring 457 bytes of unusable space unnecessarily, and about 11 percent of each CI is being wholly wasted.

Now let's see how we fare with CISZ equal to 6144. The CIFSPC-AMT will be:

$$CIFSPC\text{-}AMT = (6144 \times .10) = 614.4 \, [\text{floor}] = 614$$

PACK, therefore, will be:

$$PACK = (6144 - 614 - 10)/460 = 5520/460 = 12$$

exactly. Since PACK equals 12, then LR-AREA is equal to 12 times 460, equalling 5520. This will yield the computation of UNUSED-SPC:

$$UNUSED\text{-}SPC = (6144 - 614 - 5520 - 10) = 0 \text{ bytes}$$

thus perfect utilization! Here, therefore, we can expect better performance than the CISZ equal to 4096 case, as the CI is utilized fully, with no unusable bytes, and so there is no extra I/O overhead to degrade performance. The reserved FSPC amount, furthermore, is sufficiently large to insert an additional record into any CI without causing a CI-split (remember RECSZ equals 460), and whatever space is left over after such an insertion (614 minus 460 equals 154 bytes) can be used for record lengthening operations, if any.

The point is that we have 614 bytes of *usable* space and *no unusable space*, while in the first case (CISZ equal to 4096), we had 409 bytes of usable space, and *457 bytes of unusable space*. But note that the 409 bytes reserved for FSPC are insufficient for inserting even a single additional record (requiring 460 bytes), so that any insertion will immediately cause a CI-split, the 409 bytes being usable only for record lengthening operations, not record insertions.

Here we have a lack of goodness of fit for LRs of 460 bytes against a CISZ of 4096, compared to a CISZ of 6144, assuming the same CI-level FSPC percentage in both cases. It demonstrates that the user must consider and balance together all of these five factors—and we shall shortly see still other factors to weigh—when dealing with CISZ choice:

1. CISZ itself
2. RECSZ
3. DASD utilization
4. FSPC
5. Unused space

and demonstrates further that choosing simply on the basis of DASD utilization may not yield the most optimal results for execution-time performance.

18.3.4   CISZ, PBSIZE, and I/O Operation Workload

It would now seem, from the above considerations, that for the case we have been discussing (LRs of 460 bytes, with CIFSPC equal to 10 percent) that a choice of 6144 bytes CISZ would be more optimal than one of 4096 bytes. However, there are additional considerations to be made. The number of I/O operations to accomplish some fixed input or output unit of work is its *I/O operation workload*, or more simply, its *I/O workload*. For this discussion of VSAM, the unit of work shall be the transfer of a CI across a data channel, either from DASD into a VSAM buffer in virtual storage, or from such a buffer back out to DASD.

It may be that different CISZs are associated with different I/O workloads, and—all other things being equal (which they almost never are)—the CISZ with a smaller I/O workload should be favored for run-time performance, since less work needs to be done to transfer the same CI-worth of records. I/O workload is determined by *physical block size* (*PBSIZE*), a virtual storage buffer storing precisely one physical block, and one I/O operation being required for the transfer of one physical block across the channel.

In enhanced VSAM, and even in DFP/VSAM Version 1 and Release 1.0 of Version 2, the I/O workload (determined by PBSIZE) was in turn determined by CISZ, through application of a rigorous principle we shall call the *CISZ/PBSIZE principle* (this is not true beginning with DFP/VSAM Version 2, Release 2.0, but we will return to this matter later below). Under this principle, only four PBSIZEs were permitted: 512, 1024, 2048, and 4096 bytes (½K, 1K, 2K, and 4K). For any choice of CISZ, the PBSIZE determined would be the largest of the allowable PBSIZEs to fit into the CISZ an integral number of times.

Let's see how this works with some examples. Consider a CISZ of 4K. All of the allowable PBSIZEs divide into 4K an integral number of times, but 4K is the largest to do so, so the PBSIZE is determined to be 4K. Thus, each CI will contain a single physical block. This entails that each CI of 4096 bytes can be transfered to or from virtual storage by a single I/O operation, the smallest I/O workload possible.

Now, consider a CISZ of 1536: 512 bytes is the largest PBSIZE to divide an integral number of times into 1536 (3 times), since 1K does not divide integrally (leaving a fraction), and 2K and 4K are too large altogether. Therefore, when a CISZ of 1536 is chosen, each CI will be constituted by three physical blocks, each with a PBSIZE of 512 bytes. This entails that each CI of 1536 requires three I/O operations for its transfer, since one I/O operation is required for the transfer of each physical block. This is clearly three times the I/O workload associated with a CISZ of 4K. Now what of a 6K CISZ. It will have exactly the same workload as that of a 1536 byte CISZ: the largest PBSIZE to divide an integral number of times into 6144 is 2048 (2K), so that each 6K CI consists of three 2K physical blocks, and such a CI requires three I/O operations to transfer.

But this now complicates the choice of CISZ. In the previous section we found, on the basis of UNUSED-SPC considerations, that a 6K CISZ would be more optimal than a 4K CISZ against the case of 460-byte LRs, with 10 percent as our CIFSPC. On the other hand, processing 6K CIs will entail an I/O workload three times greater than that needed for processing 4K CIs. We are confronted with a tradeoff between larger I/O workload but no UNUSED-SPC, against smaller I/O workload but 457 bytes of each CI as UNUSED-SPC, for the choice of 6K CISZ versus 4K CISZ, respectively. Which would provide more optimal performance would depend on many (complex) processing factors for any specific case, and the judgment would have to be made consequent to examining each case and measuring and comparing the performance associated with the two different choices.

We have deliberately made this a difficult choice. The dilemma is that in many cases, for specific RECSZs, a CISZ which is not an integral multiple of 4K (including 4K itself) may provide more optimal performance than one that is such a multiple, despite the fact that multiple of 4K CISZs yield the best DASD utilization (not in itself a decisive point when pursuing run-time optimization). In our example, the UNUSED-SPC of zero bytes obtained with a 6K CISZ is hard to beat, but ideally we would have preferred that the I/O workload compare more favorably with the 4K CISZ case.

Fortunately, this is no longer a dilemma! As of DFP/VSAM, Version 2, Release 2.0 (introduced in 1986), for ICF data sets as well as catalogs, the CISZ/PBSIZE principle we have been examining has been abandoned and replaced by the *enhanced CISZ/PBSIZE principle*. Under this principle, DFP/VSAM now supports the same PBSIZEs as CISZs: thus, PBSIZES of ½K to 8K, in increments of ½K, and of 8K to 32K in increments of 2K, are now supported and these are the same as the CISZs supported by VSAM.

So now our choice of a 6K CISZ will yield a 6K PBSIZE (not a 2K PBSIZE) and thus the most optimal I/O workload possible (a single I/O operation to transfer one CI), as well as (given our choice of a CIFSPC as 10 percent) perfect space utilization (no unusable space). Although the 4K CISZ gives somewhat (roughly 8 percent) better DASD utilization, this small advantage is easily defeated by the extremely poor CI utilization (457 unused bytes per CI). Until this enhanced CISZ/PBSIZE principle of DFP/VSAM was introduced, considerations of I/O workload favored certain CISZs over others, but now that is no longer the case. Note that this enhancement applies only to DFP/VSAM and not to Enhanced VSAM, which still follows the older, less efficient principle of CISZ/PBSIZE correlation. (There is an additional benefit to the enhanced CISZ/PBSIZE principle that affects index CISZ, but we will treat this later in our section on index CISZ selection.)

The reader should perhaps be cautioned at this point that the choice of a 6K CISZ yielded highly optimal performance characteristics solely for the specific case at hand. It does not follow that, against some other RECSZ and/or FSPC request, the same CISZ would yield comparably optimal results. Each case must be assessed individually, especially as to minimization of UNUSED-SPC. What the enhanced CISZ/PBSIZE principle has gained us is that at least I/O workload does not automatically favor ½K, 1K, 2K, and 4K CISZs over other CISZ choices.

18.3.5   Summary of Computations for UNUSED-SPC

From the discussion in the previous sections, we can summarize the steps that should be followed to calculate the amount of unused space (UNUSED-SPC) that results, given particular choices of CISZ and FSPC against some specific RECSZ for a VSAM KSDS.

Step 1:   Compute PACK   (See formula [4] earlier.)
Step 2:   Compute LR-AREA   (See formula [5] earlier.)
Step 3:   Compute UNUSED-SPC   (See formula [2] earlier.)

Ideally, the UNUSED-SPC should be kept as close to zero as possible, but as a general rough rule of thumb, this quantity should be kept well below 5 percent of the CISZ. In our discussion of the previous section, we found—keeping RECSZ and FSPC constant—that a CISZ choice of 4K yielded 457 bytes unusable space per CI (about 11 percent of the CI), and this is unacceptably high.

A CISZ of 6K, however, (using the same RECSZ and FSPC values) resulted in a (perfect) value of zero bytes for UNUSED-SPC. At this point, we would have to weigh in I/O workload considerations. Assuming the VSAM environment is, as is true of many installations, DFP/VSAM Version 2, Release 2.0, or any higher release, then the I/O workload for a CISZ of 4K and for a CISZ of 6K is identical: VSAM will select a PBSIZE equal to the CISZ, which entails that each CI is transferred with a single I/O operation. Therefore, the choice is clear: the 6K CISZ, for the values of RECSZ and FSPC considered, will provide decidedly better performance. (DASD utilization may be some 8 percent better with the 4K CISZ, but this degree of difference would not alter the higher performance of the 6K CISZ significantly, and we are primarily concerned with execution-time optimization rather than DASD conservation.)

18.3.6   CISZ and Processing Mode

Different processing modes—sequential, random, or mixed sequential/random—favor different *relative* CISZ choices. Two basic principles articulate the consequences of CISZ on processing mode performance.

CISZ Optimization.

1. Sequential processing performance is favored by relatively large CISZs, while random processing is favored by relatively small CISZs.
2. Mixed sequential/random processing mode may be favored by relatively small CISZs *associated with* a relatively large buffer allocation.

Sequential processing entails access to a relatively large proportion of the records of a data set, and access to one record is associated with a high likelihood that neighboring records will also be accessed. Therefore sequential processing performance can be favored by having as many records in virtual storage buffers as possible in order to minimize *DASD lookaside* (when VSAM, failing to find a record in existing buffers must cross the data channel, performing real I/O operations to fetch the record from external DASD). In addition, larger CISZs allow VSAM to transfer a larger number of records per I/O operation, thus optimizing I/O.

A caution is in order here concerning large CISZs on a 3380 device. The 3380 has a track capacity of 47,476 bytes. Forcing a physical block of one track capacity is not possible, as the largest PBSIZE and CISZ is 32K. The best utilization of the track capacity of a 3380 is to block at the half-track point, which would be 23,728 bytes, allowing two whole physical blocks to consume the track. At any point above a half-track, only one physical block could occupy the track, causing very appreciable wastage of the remaining track. A CISZ of 22K (equal to 22,528 bytes) is the largest CISZ not execeeding the half-track point, yielding at least 95 percent or better DASD utilization, so larger CISZs against a 3380 device should generally be avoided.

Random processing generally entails access to relatively few records of a data set, and given the typical scattered access pattern, access to one record is associated with a low likelihood that neighboring records will be accessed. Therefore, random processing performance can be favored by having relatively few records in virtual storage buffers, single record access being the norm in random retrieval. This will also minimize unnecessary I/O workload consequent to retrieving records unlikely to be accessed (other than the target record).

But what of a data set that is accessed sometimes in sequential mode and sometimes in random mode? For mixed sequential/random processing, the best strategy may be to keep the CISZ relatively small in order to favor random processing performance, but to concurrently favor sequential processing by providing a large number of buffers in virtual storage.

Notice that we can assure a large number of records in virtual storage either by large CIs and relatively few buffers, or by small CIs and relatively many buffers, and this latter approach serves us well for random performance too, since relatively few records other than the target record of a random retrieval will be fetched with each I/O operation (a smaller CISZ obviously entailing a smaller number of records per CI). We shall see later in our discussion of buffer allocation how to manipulate virtual storage buffers explicitly for processing performance.

Finally, as we shall see, as we proceed through this chapter, choosing a CISZ for optimal performance is a complex weighing of many factors: processing mode (sequential, random, or mixed), PBSIZE, I/O workload, FSPC, UNUSED-SPC, and still others that we shall be considering.

18.4 CONTROL AREA SIZE (CASZ)

As we have already noted (subsection 8.5.2), although we loosely refer to 'CASZ,' there is no IDCAMS parameter available to the programmer for setting or directly influencing the size of a control area. CASZ determination is made by VSAM, indirectly, from the space allocation parameter. If the allocation is in cylinder units, then VSAM sets CASZ to the maximum possible, namely one cylinder. If the allocation is in units of tracks or records, VSAM selects the smaller of the primary and secondary allocation quantities specified, converting (if necessary) the result into track units, subject to two principles: (1) that the CASZ may not be smaller than one track; and (2) that if the derived number of tracks is equal to or greater than one cylinder, for whatever DASD device being used, the CASZ is again set to the maximum of one cylinder. Thus, on a 3380, a space allocation of TRK (50, 2) yields a CASZ of two tracks, while one of TRK (200, 15) yields a CASZ of one cylinder, since 15 tracks on a 3380 is equal to one cylinder; for this latter case, a one cylinder CASZ would also result if the secondary allocation (typically the smaller) were 15 tracks or greater, since one cylinder is the maximum CASZ.

Finally, if the allocation (again on a 3380) were, say, RECORDS (1000, 200), using 80 byte records, then the CASZ would be set to one track: the secondary (smaller) allocation of 200 records requires a total byte capacity of 16,000 bytes (200 times 80), and since this is under one track (on a 3380, the track capacity is 47,476 bytes), VSAM selects the minimum CASZ of one track. (There is a special qualification on CASZ determination if the cluster is defined with an *imbedded sequence set* — IMBED parameter is chosen over NOIMBED — but we will defer discussion of this until our section on IMBED later in this chapter; our treatment of optimal CASZ in the present section is not affected by this in any way).

18.4.1 CASZ Optimization

From the point of view of VSAM optimization, performance is generally favored by a large CASZ. Indeed, except for small data sets (loosely, those under one cylinder in size), it is recommended that space allocation for a VSAM cluster be made in terms of cylinder units, as this will assure the largest CASZ available, one cylinder. There are four major reasons that justify this principle.

Reduction of CA-split Activity. With a larger CASZ, each CA can contain a relatively larger number of records than with a smaller CASZ, and this decreases the likelihood that a CA-split would be required after some fixed amount of processing activity. Furthermore, if a CA-split does occur, there is a smaller likelihood thereafter of additional splits, since the old and the new CAs involved contain more space for records. CA-splits, as noted earlier in the text, have considerably adverse consequences on processing performance, and so it is well advised to minimize their likelihood by choosing a large CASZ, optimally the maximum of one cylinder.

Avoidance of CA Cylinder-spanning. It is a principle of VSAM that when space allocation for a cluster is in units of TRK or REC *and* such allocation yields a CASZ of less than one cylinder, VSAM permits CA *cylinder-spanning*: a CA may cross a cylinder boundary, beginning on one cylinder and ending on another. CA cylinder-spanning can significantly increase *seek time*, the time required for the device read/write heads ('access arm') to be positioned to the target cylinder (containing the record to be accessed), that is, the time required to 'seek' out the correct cylinder on the device from an arbitrary point on the device.

For a standard model 3380 the minimum seek time, moving from one cylinder to the next contiguous one, is three milliseconds (ms), the maximium seek time is 30 ms (across the most distant cylinders), and the average seek time is 16 ms. However, if one uses—and this is strongly suggested—what are termed the *Enhanced Subsystem Models* (or more simply the '3380-Enhanced'), in particular the single capacity AJ4 BJ4 model, then these speeds improve to 2 ms, 21 ms, and 12 ms, respectively. But some seeks are what may be termed *empty seeks*: processing requires some target cylinder, and the access arm is already positioned at that cylinder, and this may occur an appreciable number of times during processing. Therefore, in our experience, average seek time, taking into account empty seeks, is more realistically between three to five ms (and as low as two ms on an Enhanced model).

However low the average seek time may be, it is nonetheless a significant component of overall I/O response time, so that performance is enhanced if seek time can be reduced, and having an entire CA not span a cylinder boundary does just that: all records of the CA can be accessed through a single seek, whereas if CA cylinder-spanning is allowed, two seeks (at least) are required. Whenever space allocation is in units of cylinders, VSAM sets the CASZ at the maximum value of one cylinder *and* prohibits any CA cylinder-spanning.

Minimization of Sequence Set Processing. With a larger CASZ, the CI-density (number of CIs per CA) increases (more CIs can fit into a larger CA), and since each CA then contains more CIs, there will be fewer total CAs to the dataset. Now recall that each sequence set record (SSR) indexes an entire CA full of CIs, that is, each SSR contains a pointer for each CI in the single CA that the SSR is indexing. It follows then that fewer SSRs are needed, given fewer CAs to the dataset. This, in turn means that there will be less sequence set processing (less 'reading' of SSRs), which benefits sequential performance considerably (and may indirectly, as will be seen below, also benefit direct processing).

Greater 'Compactness' of the Index.   It was seen from the above that a larger CASZ entails fewer CAs to the dataset, which in turn entails fewer SSRs. If the sequence set is smaller (contains fewer SSRs), then fewer index set records (ISRs), that is, index records above the sequence set level, are required (the larger the sequence set, the more ISRs required to index it). Fewer ISRs will generally entail fewer index *levels* (the more ISRs there are, the greater the likelihood of requiring more levels to index all lower levels).

An index with fewer index levels is said to be a more *compact* index. Since VSAM does a vertical search through all levels of the index when performing random processing, a more compact index distinctly favors random processing performance. Indeed, an increase in the number of levels of the index component rapidly degrades random performance and should be avoided if possible. Furthermore, a more compact index requires fewer index buffers and hence benefits space as well as time. A maximum CASZ of one cylinder, therefore, will generally yield the most compact index for improved random processing.

Although there are also some disadvantages to a larger CASZ, the benefits cited above more than compensate for this, so that the general recommendation of setting the CASZ to the maximum of one cylinder, wherever possible, will favor performance, and the most direct way of assuring this maximum CASZ is to allocate space for the cluster in cylinder units.

18.5   DISTRIBUTED FREESPACE

18.5.1 FSPC Performance Issues

VSAM allows the specification of (distributed) freespace (FSPC) at the CI and CA levels to support record insertion activity (as well as less common record lengthening operations). In designing a VSAM file for optimal performance, FSPC must be specified at levels sufficient to avoid significant split activity but not so excessively large as to both waste space and cause consequent increase in I/O operations for the file. We must address, therefore, two separate issues: (1) how to determine how much overall FSPC we need, and (2) how to apportion the total FSPC required between the CI and CA levels. The first determination is relatively straightforward, but the second is more complex, yet if done correctly will reward us with more optimal performance. Furthermore, the determination of optimal FSPC at the CI and CA levels must not cause an excessive amount of UNUSED-SPC, as that may compromise any performance gains made.

18.5.2   FSPC and the Growth Factor

As we discussed in detail in sections 10.3, 10.4, and 10.5, adequate FSPC is imperative for minimizing the performance-degrading effects of CI and CA split activity. As a first step in determining optimal values for the FSPC specification of a cluster, we must estimate what is termed the *growth factor (GRW)* of a VSAM file. This is most easily done on a record basis. First determine how many records will first be loaded into the file (this is generally known and is reflected in the REC-TOTAL field in the STATISTICS group of LISTCAT output).

Say we intend to load 40,000 records into a KSDS cluster. Now we ask ourselves what is the anticipated growth of the cluster over some *processing cycle*. The length of the processing cycle is highly dependent on the application, but we might reasonably take the cycle for a relatively active cluster to be some three to six months or so in typical commercial applications. At the end of the processing cycle, we may reevaluate the FSPC requirements of the cluster and can use the ALTER command to make appropriate adjustments, but we wish to allocate sufficient FSPC to suffice for the anticipated growth of one processing cycle.

Let's assume that we determine or estimate that, at the end of a three month processing cycle, our cluster of 40,000 records will grow by an additional 20,000 records to a total of 60,000 records. This translates into a growth factor (GRW) of 50 percent:

$$GRW = \frac{\text{NEW-FILESZ} - \text{CURRENT-FILESZ}}{\text{NEW-FILESZ}} \qquad [6]$$

where GRW is to be expressed as a percentage and where the NEW-FILESZ is the anticipated size of the file at the end of one processing cycle. In our example, we are anticipating that, over a three month processing cycle, the file will grow by 50 percent: GRW equal to $(60,000 - 40,000)/60,000$ which equals $20,000/40,000$, equalling .50, which, expressed as a percentage, is 50 percent.

18.5.3 Distributing FSPC

The question is, how do we allocate for 50 percent GRW for the entire file, when FSPC is expressed as percentages at the CI and CA level. A rash answer would be to specify FSPC (25 25): this will yield a little less than 44 percent total FSPC for the file, not 50 percent. The FSPC values are not (arithmetically) additive. Nor do we want to specify either FSPC (50 0) or FSPC (0 50), since either specification would force all the FSPC to be allocated at one level only (CI or CA level), and in general we want to distribute the total amount over both the CI and the CA level, to protect against CI and CA splits.

Indeed, from a given FSPC specification, we can determine the total amount of FSPC *to the entire file* that the specification represents (*TOTAL-FSPC*). Given a FSPC specification of the form FSPC (CIFSPC% CAFSPC%), then using CIFSPC and CAFSPC (the decimal fraction equivalents of the percentages), we can compute TOTAL-FSPC as:

$$\text{TOTAL-FSPC} = (\text{CIFSPC} + \text{CAFSPC}) - (\text{CIFSPC} \times \text{CAFSPC}) \qquad [7]$$

For example, FSPC (25 25) would yield TOTAL-FSPC equal to $(.25 + .25) - (.25 \times .25)$, equalling $(.50) - (.0625)$, which equals .4375 which, as a percentage (just multiply by 100), is 43.75 percent.

To return to our original question, therefore, we must determine how to *distribute* between the CI and CA levels the required total FSPC to support the growth factor, GRW, estimated for some VSAM file. The technique detailed below provides for a generally optimal distribution between these levels *and*, more critically, does so with built-in minimization of the resulting UNUSED-SPC (the formulas have been derived to yield an UNUSED-SPC value as close to zero as possible), within the boundaries of the specified GRW. Although the technique involves some ten steps, the factors it computes in many of these steps are key factors that need to be used elsewhere for other performance computations. We will use all of these factors repeatedly throughout this chapter, and so their calculation once will serve multiple duty.

For the example under consideration, we have computed a GRW of 50 percent. In addition to GRW, we must begin with specific choices of three other factors: CISZ, RECSZ, and CASZ. Let's take an example using the following:

```
CISZ   = 6144
RECSZ = 460
GRW    = 50% (.50)
CASZ   = 1 Cylinder
```

Step 1: CI-TRK.   We must first determine the number of CIs to the track for the specific DASD device type used; here we are assuming a 3380. The device chart of Appendix A gives the appropriate values; using a CISZ of 6K yields six CIs per track (CI-TRK = 6).

Step 2: TRK-CA.   Next we require the number of tracks to the CA (TRK-CA). Since our CASZ is one cylinder, then the number of tracks to the cylinder for our device type will give us an unadjusted TRK-CA. On a 3380, there are 15 tracks per cylinder (see Appendix A). However, for reasons that will become clear later in this chapter (when we discuss the index performance options of IMBED and REPLICATE), we will assume an imbedded index (the reader will understand what this means at that time), and with an imbedded index, one track of every data CA will *not* contain data records (rather it will contain index sequence set records). For the purpose of the present discussion, therefore, all we need really know is that, with an imbedded index, TRK-CA must be reduced by one, as it refers to strictly *data* tracks (containing data, not index, records). Thus, TRK-CA equals $15 - 1$, which equals 14 for our example.

Step 3: CIDEN.   From the above two factors, we must determine the *CI-density (CIDEN)*, the number of CIs per each CA. This is derived as follows:

$$\text{CIDEN} = \text{CI-TRK} \times \text{TRK-CA} \qquad |8|$$

and, for our example, this is CIDEN equal to 6 (from Step 1) times 14 (from Step 2), equalling 84. There are 84 data CIs (containing data records) in each CA.

Step 4: MAX-PACK. We have already encountered and learned how to compute MAX-PACK (see subsection 18.3.2), the maximum numbers of records that can be stored ('packed') into a CI, disregarding FSPC, but allowing for CF, the bytes VSAM uses for control fields in the CI (the CIDF and RDFs). We repeat the computation here:

$$\text{MAX-PACK} = \frac{(\text{CISZ} - \text{CF})}{\text{RECSZ}} \text{[floor]} \qquad [1]$$

Since we are assuming fixed-length records, CF equals ten (four bytes for one CIDF and six bytes for two RDFs, each three bytes), so that MAX-PACK is equal to (6144 − 10)/460, which equals 6134/460, equalling 13.33, which is floored to a MAX-PACK of 13. At most, 13 records (each 460 bytes) can be packed into a 6K CI.

Step 5: FREE-CI. We now need to determine the number of CIs of each CA that are to be kept free, due to the required GRW. We will assume that half of the anticipated file growth (reflected in the computed GRW) will be obtained at the CA level, thus equitably distributing file growth over CI and CA levels (this is not the only way to do the distribution, but it generally provides very good results in a wide range of cases). The computation is simply:

$$\text{FREE-CI} = \frac{\text{GRW} \times \text{CIDEN}}{2} \text{[ceil]} \qquad [9]$$

where 'ceil' indicates that the resulting number, if not an integer, will be rounded up to the next whole number (4.67 would, for example, be ceiled to 5). Here we would have FREE-CI equalling (.50 × 84)/2, which equals 42/2, equal to 21; that is, 21 of the 84 CIs of each CA will be kept free by VSAM.

Step 6: CAFSPC. We can now determine CAFSPC directly:

$$\text{CAFSPC} = \frac{\text{FREE-CI}}{\text{CIDEN}} \qquad [10]$$

and CAFSPC% is derived as follows:

$$\text{CAFSPC\%} = (\text{CAFSPC} \times 100) \text{ [ceil]} \qquad [10A]$$

This gives CAFSPC equal to 21/84 which equals .25. Therefore, CAFSPC% (the percentage equivalent of this decimal fraction) is 25 percent (CAFSPC% equal to 100 times CAFSPC, ceiled if necessary). We now know that the FSPC specification will be of the form (_____ 25). The remaining steps are dedicated to determining the other factor, CIFSPC (and its percentage counterpart, CIFSPC%).

Step 7: FREE-LR.   We next need to determine how many (logical) records slots of each CI are to be kept free, given our GRW requirement.

$$\text{FREE-LR} = (\text{GRW} - \text{CAFSPC}) \times \text{MAX-PACK [ceil]} \qquad [11]$$

Carrying this out, we get FREE-LR equal to (.50−.25) times 13, which equals .25 times 13, equalling 3.25, which is ceiled to 4. Thus, four records slots, of the 13 that are maximally possible in a CI (MAX-PACK for our example), will *not* be loaded with data records.

Step 8: DATA-LR.   It is now straightforward to determine the number of data records that *will* be loaded into each CI:

$$\text{DATA-LR} = \text{MAX-PACK} - \text{FREE-LR} \qquad [12]$$

giving DATA-LR = 13 minus 4 = 9. This makes sense: Step 7 determined that 4 record slots of a potential 13 in each CI would be kept free, so that leaves 9 records loaded by VSAM per CI.

Step 9: LR-AREA.   We had previously, in this chapter, computed LR-AREA, the number of *data* bytes in a CI (that is, total number of bytes used for stored data records), in a somewhat different fashion (see subsection 18.3.3, Formula [5]), but here we will determine it from the result of Step 8, DATA-LR, and the given RECSZ:

$$\text{LR-AREA} = \text{DATA-LR} \times \text{RECSZ} \qquad [13]$$

For our example, we have LR-AREA equalling 9 times 460, which is equal to 4140 data bytes per CI. We can now use this factor to directly compute (next step) CIFSPC.

Step 10: CIFSPC.   Finally, the amount of FSPC for the CI level can be computed as:

$$\text{CIFSPC} = \frac{\text{CISZ} - \text{LR-AREA} - \text{CF}}{\text{CISZ}} \qquad [14]$$

with CIFSPC% being derived as follows:

$$\text{CIFSPC\%} = (\text{CIFSPC} \times 100) \quad [\text{floor}] \qquad [14A]$$

This gives CIFSPC equal to $(6144 - 4140 - 10)/6144$, which equals $1944/6144$, equalling .322, so that CAFSPC% equals CAFSPC multiplied by 100, floored and this yields 32.2 percent, floored to 32 percent. This then completes the specification to be:

$$FSPC \ (32 \ 25).$$

18.5.4   Verification of FSPC Determination

Having used the technique of the previous section to determine a FSPC (32 25) specification for the example under discussion, let us verify two points: (1) that we do indeed obtain approximately 50 percent GRW, our original objective, and (2) that UNUSED-SPC is strongly minimized.

To verify the first point, we can use Formula [7] of subsection 18.5.3 against our computed FSPC (32 25): TOTAL-FSPC equals $(.32 + .25) - (.32 \times .25)$, which equals $.57 - .08$, equalling .49, expressed as a percentage into 49% (close enough to our 50% objective, and as will become clear shortly, the most optimal result for minimization of UNUSED-SPC).

Now what of the minimization of UNUSED-SPC? Here what we must do first is compute UNUSED-SPC by Formula [2] of subsection 18.3.2, using FSPC (32 25). The formula is repeated here for convenience:

$$UNUSED\text{-}SPC = CISZ - CIFSPC\text{-}AMT - LR\text{-}AREA - CF \qquad [2]$$

Note that the formula involves an intermediate factor, namely CIFSPC-AMT, so let us first compute this, through Formula [3] of that subsection (18.3.2), again repeated here for convenience:

$$CIFSPC\text{-}AMT = (CISZ \times CIFSPC) \ [floor] \qquad [3]$$

Since CISZ is equal to 6144 and CIFSPC equals .32 for the example under discussion, we obtain CIFSPC-AMT equal to $(6144 \times .32)$, equalling 1966.08, floored to 1966. Now, before we can use Formula [2] above, we must determine LR-AREA, but at this point a critical caution must be observed: *LR-AREA, for this verification process, must be computed from Formula [5] (subsection 18.3.3), not from Formula [13]* (of subsection 18.5.3). Formula [13] for LR-AREA is only used for the determination of FSPC, the ten-step technique of the previous subsection (18.5.3). The correct formula for the purposes of this verification, therefore, is repeated here:

$$LR\text{-}AREA = PACK \times RECSZ \qquad [5]$$

Note that this formula uses PACK, not MAX-PACK, so again (for the reader's convenience) we repeat the formula here:

$$PACK = \frac{CISZ - (CISZ \times CIFSPC)[floor] - CF}{RECSZ} [floor] \qquad [4]$$

which is the same as:

$$PACK = \frac{CISZ - CIFSPC\text{-}AMT - CF}{RECSZ} [floor] \qquad [4A]$$

For our example, we have already computed CIFSPC-AMT as 1966 and CF as 10 bytes. Therefore, using Formula [4A] we get PACK equalling (6144 − 1966 − 10)/460, which equals 4168/460, equal to 9.09, floored to 9. Substituting this in Formula [5] for LR-AREA, we have LR-AREA equal to 9 multiplied by 460, which equals 4140 bytes. Now we can finally compute UNUSED-SPC from Formula [2], which yields UNUSED-SPC equal to 6144 − 1966 − 4140 − 10, equalling 28 bytes of unusable space per CI, which is less than one half of one percent of the CISZ!

The reader might wonder at this point if, instead of flooring in the last step of the FSPC determination technique (Formula [14A] of the previous subsection), we might just as well have ceiled (after all, that's what we did for CAFSPC% in Formula [10A]): from 32.2, we then would have obtained 33 percent rather than 32 percent. Although this will actually yield a total FSPC a bit closer to our 50 percent growth objective, it would have tragic consequences for performance optimization, in that it would not be minimal in terms of UNUSED-SPC.

Indeed, if the verfication process we undertook in this section were repeated for a FSPC of (33 25) rather than (32 25), UNUSED-SPC would turn out to be 427 bytes, rather than 28 bytes (this can be verified by the reader through some painful arithmetic and a good calculator)! Similarly, if 31 percent were tried, some 90 bytes of UNUSED-SPC results. Given a GRW objective of 50 percent, the FSPC (32 25) specification, therefore, will yield only negligible UNUSED-SPC (28 bytes of 6144 bytes per CI).

Although it will not be apparent to the reader that the ten-step technique for FSPC determination presented in Subsection 18.5.3 is inherently optimal by forcing a minimization of UNUSED-SPC, while simultaneously yielding the correct FSPC quantities (CIFSPC% and CAFSPC%) at the CI and CA level to obtain our growth objective (GRW), that is in fact the case and we have designed the computations for just this goal of 'double' optimization. The technique both distributes the anticipated growth to obtain the requisite total FSPC, and assures that only a minimal amount of UNUSED-SPC results.

18.5.5   Summary of FSPC Optimization Technique

We summarize here for the reader's convenience the basic steps involved in the FSPC optimization technique presented in Subsection 18.5.3 above.

Step 1: Determine CI-TRK   Appendix A
Step 2: Determine TRK-CA   Appendix A
Step 3: Compute   CIDEN   Formula [8]
Step 4: Compute   MAX-PACK   Formula [1]
Step 5: Compute   FREE-CI   Formula [9]

Step 6:	Compute	CAFSPC%	Formulas [10] and [10A]
Step 7:	Compute	FREE-LR	Formula [11]
Step 8:	Compute	DATA-LR	Formula [12]
Step 9:	Compute	LR-AREA	Formula [13]
Step 10:	Compute	CIFSPC%	Formulas [14] and [14A]

18.5.6   Some Final Considerations in FSPC Optimization

In seeking to optimize FSPC distribution, the essential dual objectives are to support anticipated growth over some processing cycle, and to avoid performance-degrading split activity. The appropriate balance in FSPC allocation must be made to accomplish these primary goals, as both excessive FSPC and insufficient FSPC compromise performance. In addition to wasting DASD, excessive FSPC will (in general) require more I/O operations for sequential processing: the cluster contains a higher ratio of empty space to data space (occupied by actual records), and VSAM must 'carry' and transfer the excess space unnecessarily.

Furthermore, excess FSPC will typically increase the number of CIs and CAs required for the cluster, and this may often decrease the compactness of the index component, as more index levels may be needed to index the larger number of CIs and CAs. A less compact index, however, will cause performance degradation of random processing (the more compact the index, the fewer the number of index records VSAM need process when performing a vertical search of the index for random operations). The techniques we have presented in the previous subsections are designed to strike the appropriate balance of FSPC distribution to support anticipated growth.

18.6   CONTROL INTERVAL SIZE (CISZ): THE INDEX COMPONENT

Another critical determinant of VSAM performance for a KSDS cluster is the *index CISZ*, which is determined separately from the data CISZ. The index CISZ can be specified by the programmer explicitly on the DEF CLUSTER command:

```
DEF CLUSTER -
              .
              .
              .
     INDEX    -
              (NAME( ... ) -
              CISZ ( ... ))
```

However, programmers are often advised (especially, but not solely, by IBM technical publications on VSAM) to not code for index CISZ but rather allow it to be chosen by VSAM through built-in defaults. This is not good practice in terms of basic goals of VSAM optimization. Surprisingly enough, in a significant number of cases VSAM may not always make the best choice of index CISZ: VSAM uses a *fast approximation* for determining index CISZ from certain general assumptions about the KSDS cluster, especially assumptions concerning *key compression*. Before we look, however, at the specific concerns of optimal index CISZ, let's first briefly consider the performance issues relating to index CISZ in general form.

As a basic principle, the data CISZ and the index CISZ are inversely related: a relatively large data CISZ is associated with a relatively small index CISZ, and vice versa. Consider what happens as we increase the data CISZ. With increasingly larger data CIs, the CI-density becomes smaller: that is, the number of data CIs per fixed-size CA decreases with larger CIs (fewer can fit into a fixed-size CA). Now, the size of an index CI at the sequence set level (a sequence set record (SSR) CISZ) is dependent on the cluster's CI-density. This is so because each data CA is indexed by one SSR and an SSR must be large enough to hold a *CI-pointer* to every CI in one data CA. If there are fewer CIs to the CA (smaller CI-density), then fewer CI-pointers need be contained in a SSR. Since, as we have already noted, a larger data CI entails a smaller CI-density, then this in turn entails a smaller index CISZ. Conversely, a smaller data CISZ is associated with a larger index CISZ (the CI-density is larger, and therefore each SSR must contain more CI-pointers).

18.6.1   The Role of Key Compression

Index CISZ, therefore, is dependent on CI-density, and directly so: the larger the CI-density, the larger the associated index CISZ, since each SSR must contain more CI-pointers to data CIs. Now, the index CISZ is also dependent on the size of the index CI-pointer required to index one data CI. But on what does the size of this CI-pointer depend? With a KSDS, VSAM uses (as we noted in Chapter 11, especially Sections 11.4 and 11.5) a *compressed key*, not a full key, for a CI-pointer. Consequently, index CISZ is dependent on *compressed key size* (*CKSZ*). The degree of compression VSAM may be able to achieve depends on the structure of the key and on the relationship of the key to immediately adjacent (preceding and succeeding) keys.

Judging degree of key compression is extremely complex, but one key (no pun intended) generalization can be made. Poor key compression can be expected with multipart or multifield keys where change in key value occurs primarily on the key 'flanks', the high- and low-order parts, but rarely—if at all—in the middle portion of the key. Consider a three-part key made of the form 'XXXXXCCCYYYYYYYYY', where 'XXXXX' is a five digit employee identification number, 'CCC' is a department code, and 'YYYYYYYYY' is social security number; let's further assume that the installation differentiates only three departments: 'FIN' for financial department, 'CUS' for custody department, and 'TRU' for trust department. There will be numerous employees who are in the same department, so that the keys will have change in the high-order employee id part and in the low-order social security part, but will have a constant department designation. Clearly the least change is in the middle 'CCC' portion of this multipart key, and experience demonstrates that such a key will typically compress poorly: the full key size is 17 bytes, and VSAM may only be able to compress the key a byte or two, if at all.

Thus, compressed key size (CKSZ) will be little different from *full key size*

(*FKSZ*). The performance implication of this is that more space is required in the SSR for the compressed key used as a CI-pointer, and so each SSR may fit fewer such CI-pointers. If this is the case, then larger SSRs will be required, and possibly more of them, and this may in turn lead to a less compact index (more index levels). Performance of any operation requiring index processing may therefore degrade. It is well advised, then, to avoid multipart keys, especially those with rapidly changing 'flanks' and relatively constant middle portions. Either single part keys should be used wherever possible, or if a multipart key must be used, then it should be designed so that any middle portion is relatively rapidly changing with respect to relatively constant flanking portions. This will assure considerable redundancy in the front and rear portions of the key, and thus facilitate the front and rear compression operations VSAM undertakes as part of its key compression algorithm (discussed in Section 11.5), leading to a higher degree of key compression, which will favor index processing performance.

18.6.2 VSAM Fast Approximation for Index CISZ

Now to return to the matter of index CISZ selection, first looking at a *fast approximation* technique for such selection, and then (in the following section) examining a far more precise technique for index CISZ determination. If we make a very broad assumption that on an average all keys compress to approximately eight bytes, then allowing for a certain amount of control information in the index CI, we obtain a fast approximation of index CISZ based on CI-density, as shown in Table 18-1. As can be seen, if the CI-density is less than or equal to 58 (58 CIs per CA in the data component) then an index CISZ of 512 bytes can be selected. If CI-density is between 59 and 120, than a 1K CISZ can be selected, and so on, as specified in the table.

There are two problems with this fast approximation. First, it is exceptionally unsubtle, in that all keys of any allowable length (1 to 256 bytes) are assumed to be such that, regardless of structure, and therefore degree of compression, eight bytes

Table 18-1. Fast approximation of index CISZ.

CIDEN		INDEX CISZ
<=	58	512
>58	- 120	1024
>120	- 248	2048
>248	- 502	4096

(on an average) results from VSAM's key compression algorithm being applied. Real practical experience that this actually holds even *on an average* is lacking. Secondly, for all new VSAM later than an enhancement applied to DFP/VSAM Version 2, Release 2.0 (introduced approximately mid-1986), the CISZ of the index may take on any value that is a valid data CISZ, that is, ½K to 8K in multiples of ½K, and 8K to 32K in multiples of 2K. Thus, since that enhancement, the index CISZ is no longer restricted to ½K, 1K, 2K, and 4K only, and the fast approximation does not take this fact into account in any way. At the time of this writing, DFP/VSAM at V. 2, R. 3.0 and above is quite widespread, with many installations at Version 3 (especially when running under ESA), so that the applicability of the fast approximation is presently very minor.

18.6.3   Index CISZ Determination

To obtain a very accurate determination of index CISZ, the following formula may be applied:

$$\text{I-SIZE} = \text{CIDEN} \times (\text{CKSZ} + 2 + \text{P-LEN}) \\ + \{2 \times (\text{SQRT(CIDEN) [floor]}\} \\ + \text{HDR} + \text{CF} \tag{15}$$

This may appear quite intimidating, but once we unpack it, it will turn out to be fairly straightforward (as far as such performance computations get). The factors used in the computation are:

CIDEN	CI-density (CIs per CA)
CF	Bytes used for CI control fields
HDR	Size of the Header field in an index record
P-LEN	Length of the P-field of an index record
CKSZ	Compressed key size

The first three factors are quite simple. We are already familiar with computing CI-density (CIDEN) from Formula [8] in Step 3 of Subsection 18.5.3. The formula uses both CIDEN and the square root of CIDEN (given in the formula as 'SQRT(CIDEN)'), for which a handy calculator is invaluable. Note that, after the square root of the CIDEN is computed, it is floored to the next lowest integral number. (We will see a sample computation shortly). CF is the number of bytes used for the control fields of a CI, namely the CIDF and RDFs. In an index record, CF is always seven bytes, as there is a single CIDF and a single RDF (only one RDF is needed as there is only one (index) record per index CI). Finally, an index record always has a fixed-length Header field of 24 bytes (the reader may recall this from Chapter 11 on the structure of an index record, especially Section 11.4), so HDR is equal to 24.

Now let's discuss P-LEN. As we discussed earlier in the text, in Section 11.4, each SSR indexes one data CA, and consists of a set of index entries, one for each (data) CI of the CA being indexed. An index entry associated with a data CI contains a P-field which references the data CI with which the particular index entry is associated. That is, each index entry in an SSR points to a data CI by virtue of its P-field, which contains a binary number n (beginning by convention at zero) referring to the $n+1$th CI of the CA 'governed' by this SSR.

For example, the first SSR indexes the first data CA and within this SSR an index entry whose P-field contains a binary zero is pointing to (is indexing) the first data CI of that data CA, while an index entry with a P-field of one is pointing to the second CI, etc. (VSAM numbers data CIs within a data CA from zero.) P-LEN indicates the length of this P-field pointer, and this length may be either one, two, or three bytes, dependent on the CI-density. A one byte pointer in this P-field can handle a CI-density of up to 256 CIs per CA (two raised to the eighth power, that is, two times itself eight times).

A two byte pointer would then be needed only if CI-density were greater than 256, but less than 65,536 (this is 2 raised to the 16th power). Clearly, a three byte pointer would be needed only if the CI-density were in excess of 65,536! At present, given a 3380 disk, if we choose the largest CASZ possible, one cylinder, and the smallest CISZ possible, namely 512 bytes, the largest obtainable CI-density would be a mere 690 CIs per CA (with a CISZ of 512 bytes, 46 CIs may fit onto one 3380 track, and one 3380 cylinder contains 15 tracks, so CI-density is equal to 46 times 15, equalling 690). Therefore, given current DASD architecture P-LEN would not exceed two bytes. Therefore, we have:

$$P\text{-}LEN = 1 \qquad \text{if CIDEN} = 1 \text{ to } 256$$
$$P\text{-}LEN = 2 \qquad \text{if CIDEN} = \text{greater than } 256 \qquad\qquad [16]$$

(excluding, at this time, the need for a three byte field).

Finally, we need to consider the factor CKSZ (compressed key size). There is no direct and rigorous determination of the degree of key compression without an intimate examination of the actual pattern of key values throughout the data CIs of a cluster, and this is clearly unrealistic. We can, however, very roughly approximate CKSZ from FKSZ (full key size) on the basis of limited but nonetheles significant experience. Although the approximation is indeed rough, it will suffice, in that we will build in a certain 'cushion' above the value determined when we use I-SIZE (Formula [15]) to finally determine index CISZ. Still, the entire technique developed in this section is an approximation only, albeit as accurate as possible given the complexity of VSAM key compression algorithms.

Table 18-2 presents the expected (approximate) CKSZ given certain ranges of FKSZ (which is simply the primary key length for a KSDS cluster). As can be seen from the table, we are assuming that a FKSZ of less than three bytes does not compress (one and two byte keys remain so), and furthermore that for FKSZ of 88 to 256 bytes, we assume a fixed compression to 28 bytes; this is clearly not very accurate, but there was little experience to base a more precise figure on for this range of keys (most keys are smaller than this), and so the crude mapping to 28 compressed bytes was chosen, not wholly arbitrarily (it is based partly on an internal computation performed by AMS itself in certain circumstances).

There are two further matters we must dispense with before looking at a sample computation. The first is simply a variant of Formula [15] above, given that the HDR and CF factors are fixed at 24 and 7 bytes, respectively:

$$\begin{aligned} \text{I-SIZE} = {} & \text{CIDEN} \times (\text{CKSZ} + 2 + \text{P-LEN}) \\ & + \{2 \times (\text{SQRT}(\text{CIDEN})\ [\text{floor}]\} \\ & + 31 \end{aligned} \quad [15A]$$

The second matter concerns the determination of index CISZ: Formulas [15] or [15A] approximate I-SIZE, which is the number of bytes required in an index record in order to contain an index entry for every data CI in the CA governed by the index record (again, more precisely, an SSR). However, VSAM does not use any index CISZ, but only certain permitted CISZs. Formula 17 reflects the derivation of index CISZ from the I-SIZE computed by Formula [15] or [15A].

$$\begin{aligned} \text{I-CISZ} &= 512 & &\text{if I-SIZE less than or equal to 512} \\ \text{I-CISZ} &= 1024 & &\text{if I-SIZE greater than 512, but less} \\ & & &\text{than or equal to 1024} \qquad\qquad [17] \\ \text{I-CISZ} &= \text{next highest multiple of 2K,} \\ & & &\text{if I-SIZE greater than 1024} \end{aligned}$$

Table 18-2. Estimations of CKSZ based on keylength.

FKSZ			CKSZ
3	–	5	3
6	–	7	5
8	–	11	6
12	–	17	7
18	–	23	8
24	–	39	9
40	–	55	10
56	–	71	11
72	–	87	12
>87	–		28

Thus, the third part of this formula would, starting from a computed I-SIZE of, for example, 1800 bytes, yield an I-CISZ of 2K; an I-SIZE of 3100 bytes would yield an I-CISZ of 4K, and so on. This rounding up to either ½K, 1K, or a multiple of 2K, provides some cushion for the fact that CKSZ is a rough approximation at best.

Sample Computation.   We can best appreciate how to apply Formulas [15] (or [15A]), [16], and [17] to determine index CISZ (I-CISZ) by tracing through a sample computation. Let's use the example already discussed earlier in Subsection 18.5.3 of this chapter, where we have the following figures (some were given assumptions, some were computed by the techniques presented earlier):

CISZ   = 6144
KEYLEN = 9
CIDEN   = 84

Since we know CIDEN (= 84), let's first compute the factor SQRT(CIDEN): this is the square root of 84, which (using a handy calculator), is approximately 9.165, which floors to 9. Next, CKSZ can be approximated from Table 18-2: for a FKSZ (same as KEYLEN) of 9, CKSZ = 6. Finally, P-LEN can be determined from CIDEN: with a CIDEN = 84, P-LEN = 1 (according to Formula [16]). Thus our example we have:

CIDEN = 84
CF   = 7
HDR   = 24
P-LEN = 1
CKSZ   = 6

Applying Formula [15] we get:

$$
\begin{aligned}
\text{I-SIZE} &= 84 \times (6 + 2 + 1) \\
&\quad + \{2 \times (9)\} \\
&\quad + 24 + 7 \\
&= (84 \times 9) + 18 + 31 \\
&= 756 + 18 + 31 \\
&= 805
\end{aligned}
$$

Now, with an I-SIZE of 805 bytes we apply Formula [17] to obtain an I-CISZ of 1024. Thus, we have determined that the appropriate choice of index CISZ is 1K for the example under discussion. In this case—but just in this case—the VSAM fast approximation would also have chosen 1K for the index CISZ, and if we had allowed the index CISZ to default, by omitting its explicit specification from the DEF

CLUSTER command, VSAM also would have chosen 1K. There are cases, however, in which the three techniques:

(1) a VSAM applied default
(2) the fast approximation of Table 18-1
(3) the computation of I-CISZ presented in this section

would *not* yield the same choice, and in such cases extensive practical experience shows that the third technique would prove to be both the most reliable and the most optimal.

A Brief Technical Rationale for the I-CISZ Formula.   The curious reader may wonder about the basis of Formula [15], with its strange SQRT functions and other non-obvious factors. Without going into the detailed and highly technical discussion that would be needed to develop the formula, it is in fact based on sound knowledge of the internal structure of an index record. Briefly, the first line of the formula handles the fact that in each SSR there will be one index entry for each data CI of the CA being indexed by that one SSR, so that the number of entries is just CIDEN.

Then each entry may consist of four distinct fields, which we discussed earlier in the text in Section 11.4 (see Figure 11-4): (1) a K-field which contains the compressed key and whose size is approximated by CKSZ (through Table 18-2); (2) an F-field indicating the number of front-compressed bytes, whose length is always one byte; (3) an L-field which gives the length of the compressed key, this L-field always one byte in length; and (4) a P-field which contains the binary CI-pointer and whose length is our P-LEN factor (one, two, or three bytes, as discussed above). Therefore, the size of each index entry would be CKSZ + 2 (for the one byte each of F-field and L-field) + P-LEN, and there are CIDEN worth of such index entries in one SSR, so we have the expression:

$$\text{CIDEN} \times (\text{CKSZ} + 2 + \text{P-LEN})$$

Now a further fact of the structure of an SSR, not noted before, is that VSAM always partitions the SSR into *sections*, the number of sections being roughly the square root of the CIDEN (if CIDEN were 100, VSAM would have ten sections in each SSR). Thus, the index entries—one for each data CI—are organized into distinct sections, and these sections have between them a two byte *separator*. Therefore, the second line of Formula [15] gives the number of bytes in each SSR consumed by the separators, which is just:

$$\{2 \times (\text{SQRT(CIDEN) [floor]}\}$$

since there are SQRT(CIDEN) worth of sections in one SSR.

Finally, as already noted in Section 11.4, there is in each SSR a 24-byte system header, and a fixed seven bytes for control fields (a four byte CIDF and a 3 byte RDF), and this is reflected in the last line of the formula:

$$HDR + CF$$

These considerations about the internal structure of an index record, therefore, provide the technical basis for Formula [15]. Indeed, we could have made the formula more precise still by having it reflect the fact that there may be at least one wholly uncompressed key per index CI, given the operation of VSAM's key compression algorithm, but this complicates the formula and adds very little additional accuracy (and we cushion for this by rounding up to certain index CISZs through the application of Formula [17]). VSAM itself, when providing a default index CISZ (if none is explicitly coded by the programmer in the DEF CLUSTER command), uses an internal approximation technique that, although more precise than the fast approximation technique, is not as precise as the technique we have developed in this section. Therefore, the programmer is well-advised to use this technique to obtain an optimal index CISZ, which will in general be large enough to hold all the necessary pointers, but not excessively large, which may degrade index processing performance.

A Special Problem. The reader should always bear in mind the fact that our derivation is based on certain assumptions about key compression for keys of various lengths. It may turn out, however, in some cases, that the structure of the key is such that it compresses very poorly, if at all, so that any computation may underestimate the amount of space needed in the index for index entries. Indeed, it may be that a VSAM-chosen index CISZ (itself based on an approximation) may be insufficient to hold all of the necessary index entries: the index CISZ may be too small for the CIDEN involved (especially if that factor is very large), or the keys compress much more poorly than estimated, or do not compress at all.

Some discussions of VSAM give complex ways in which this possibility may be uncovered, typically involving very careful and fine examination and analysis of SSRs in dump format. We suggest a much simpler and more reliable way: for DFP/VSAM, the EXAMINE command (discussed in Appendix F) can detect such situations and provide a clear message indicating the problem. As discussed in that appendix, the EXAMINE command detects structural errors and inconsistencies within the data and index components of a KSDS, and *between* the data and index components of a KSDS. It should be run on a regular basis against both critical KSDS clusters, and VSAM and ICF (the BCS component) catalogs (catalogs are special KSDSs) to confirm the structural soundness of a KSDS. If a situation of the type we are considering were to arise, the following error is likely to be encountered in EXAMINE output:

```
IDC11706I MISSING SEQUENCE SET ENTRIES
```

indicating that some SSR does not contain pointers to *all* data CIs in the data CA being indexed by that SSR. This is the most likely error indication, but under certain circumstances the programmer might receive one or more of the following, also indicating the same type (or a very closely related type) of problem:

```
IDC11708I, IDC11711I, IDC11714I, IDC11719I, IDC11724I, or IDC11734I
```

(we omit the exact text of the message). The only remedy is to increase the index CISZ specification, which in current DFP/VSAM (post Version 2, Release 2) can take on the same range of values as the data CISZ. (It should not be necessary, as it sometimes was with earlier releases of VSAM, to change the structure of the data component, reducing the CIDEN: an index CISZ can be found to accommodate the features of any data component in the vast majority of cases). The index CISZ can be increased and EXAMINE rerun to determine if the problem has been corrected; if not, another increase in index CISZ followed by a confirmatory EXAMINE should be performed until the problem is resolved. The form of the EXAMINE would be simply:

```
EXAMINE -
          NAME (cluster name) -
          INDEXTEST -
          DATATEST
```

(See Appendix F for additional details on EXAMINE.)

18.7   INDEX OPTIONS: IMBED AND REPLICATE

There are two distinct but related options for index processing performance that may be specified on the DEF CLUSTER command (the valid abbreviations are given to the right of the options, and the defaults are also shown):

```
IMBED/NOIMBED                IMBD/NIMBD
REPLICATE/NOREPLICATE        REPL/NREPL

Defaults:        NOIMBED
                 NOREPLICATE
```

These options can be specified at the cluster or at the index level; however, as they really apply only to the index component, they may most accurately be coded at the index level as follows:

```
DEF CLUSTER -
             .
             .
             .
       INDEX    -
                (NAME(  ... ) -
                CISZ (  ... ) -
                IMBD/NIMBD -        [one is chosen]
                REPL/NREPL          [one is chosen]
```

Now let's examine each of these options in terms of their performance implications.

18.7.1 The IMBED Option

If the IMBED index option is chosen at DEF CLUSTER time for a KSDS (IMBED is meaningless for other than a KSDS, as only a KSDS has an index component), then VSAM performs two distinct actions, the benefits of each being discussed separately immediately below:

1. *SSR-Imbedding*
   Each sequence set record (SSR) is stored within the data component of the cluster, not the index component, and is written physically adjacent to the data CA that the SSR governs (that is, the data CA that the SSR indexes, or references), on the first track of the cylinder on which the data CA resides.
2. *SSR-Replication*
   In addition to imbedding each SSR with its associated data CA on the first track of that CA, the SSR is replicated (duplicated) on the track as many times as needed to fill the track.

Figure 18-2 represents the effect of the IMBED index option. Now let's discuss each of these in turn.

SSR-Imbedding.   To appreciate the benefit of this action of the IMBED index option, remember that each SSR governs one data CA and thus contains a

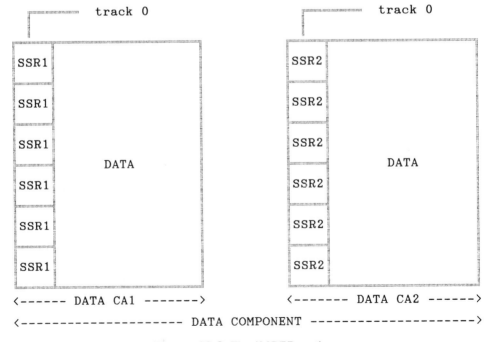

Figure 18-2. The IMBED option.

pointer to each CI of that data CA. VSAM locates a data CI within some data CA by using the CI-pointer in the SSR governing the data CA. Normally, without the IMBED option, a 'SEEK' operation (that is, one that positions the actuator (read/write access heads) to the target cylinder) is needed for fetching the SSR, and a separate SEEK is then required to fetch the correct data record. This is so because the index and data components are distinct and physically separate data sets, so that the SSRs reside on different cylinders from those on which the data records are stored.

SEEK time — the time consumed in order to position an actuator over the target cylinder — is a significant component of (DASD I/O) response time. If the number of SEEKs required for some I/O operation can be reduced, we may appreciably improve response time. This is one major objective of the IMBED index option: by forcing the index SSR and the data CA it governs to *coreside* on the same cylinder, a single SEEK positions the actuator over the correct cylinder for both some target SSR and the data record to be retrieved, and this can improve both sequential and direct processing; in essence, index (SSR) and data records may be retrieved in a single operation when an imbedded index is used.

There are two qualifications which must be made in connection with the SEEK time reduction effect of IMBED. First, it is possible, especially on a highly volatile volume (heavy I/O activity to the volume's data sets) that there occur a *mediate* (intervening) SEEK between the SEEK to the SSR and the subsequent SEEK to the target data record. A mediate SEEK against some other cylinder on the volume, after the SSR SEEK, could — even if it were an I/O operation to the same data set but to a different (cylinder) location of the data set — intervene between the two related SEEKs and thus require a second SEEK to complete access to the target data record, undoing the SEEK time reduction effect of the IMBED option. As many volumes containing VSAM KSDS clusters may be quite volatile, the SEEK time reduction may not always be realizable through the IMBED option; the benefit is more likely to be seen on volumes with relatively modest I/O activity. Nonetheless, the possible benefit of IMBED for volumes without heavy I/O contention can be very significant, so that unless there are reasons dictating otherwise, IMBED is a good index performance option choice.

The IBM product RMF (Resource Measurement Facility) may be used to determine which volumes are especially volatile in terms of contention activity; this will typically show up as high I/O queueing time (average time an application I/O operation waits on an I/O queue for other applications to complete their operations against the device), which in an RMF Direct Access Device Activity Report would be labelled *AVG IOSQ TIME*. AVG IOSQ TIME may be reduced by a *cached DASD storage controller* (more on this later) such as the 3880 Model 23, or the more recent and much more sophisticated 3990 (especially the Model 3), which yields some very exceptional I/O performance for large systems with high DASD I/O activity. But, for reasons to be discussed later, if a KSDS cluster resides on a device controlled by a cached DASD controller, IMBED should *not* be specified (specify, or allow to default, the NOIMBED option).

The second qualification concerns DASD utilization. Since the first track of each data CA is used for SSRs and thus cannot contain data records, as it otherwise would, effective DASD utilization in the data component is reduced by the IMBED option. However, if the CASZ is forced to be the maximum of one cylinder (as we recommended earlier in Section 18.4), then (on a 3380) the DASD utilization is reduced by a relatively modest amount of approximately 6.67 percent, not insignificant but neither overwhelming, given the possible performance benefit of IMBED.

SSR-Replication.   This aspect of the IMBED index option replicates the SSR governing a particular data CA as many times as it will fit on the first track of that data CA. The design objective of this SSR-replication is the reduction of another component of I/O response time, that of *latency* (also sometimes called *rotational delay*). Latency represents the time consumed for DASD to rotate until the target data on the target track is positioned under the actuator after a SEEK has positioned to the correct cylinder. This time may (on a 3380) be as little as (almost) zero milliseconds (ms) if the target data is encountered on the track virtually immediately, and as long as 16.6 ms, the time of a complete rotation of a 3380 track; the average latency is conventionally taken to be one-half of a DASD revolution, that is, 8.3 ms. Latency for an SSR is dramatically reduced by the SSR-replication aspect of IMBED, since the device may transfer whatever record is first encountered on the track (after all, any copy of the SSR will do, as they are all identical).

Thus, the combined performance benefits of IMBED are potential SEEK time reduction (due to SSR-imbedding) and latency reduction (due to SSR-replication), and as these are both significant components of I/O response time, VSAM processing performance for a KSDS cluster may be appreciably more optimal with IMBED (remembering the qualifications made above).

18.7.2   The REPLICATE Option

If the REPLICATE index option is chosen at DEF CLUSTER time for a KSDS (like IMBED, REPLICATE is meaningless for other than a KSDS, as only a KSDS has an index component), then VSAM performs the following action:

In-Place IR-Replication.   Each and every index record (IR)—both sequence set records (SSRs) and index set records (ISRs)—is segregated onto its own track (one IR per track) *and* replicated there as many times as needed to fill the track. This is done *in-place*, that is, in the index component of a KSDS cluster; the IRs are *not* stored within the data component (unlike IMBED which forces SSRs and data records to co-reside within the data component itself). See Figure 18-3. Since the IR-replication is done in-place, within the index component, there is no SEEK time reduction as there was with IMBED: index records must be retrieved by a SEEK separate from that which subsequently retrieves the target data record(s).

What REPLICATE does yield is a reduction in the latency component of I/O response time, in the same way that this was effected by the SSR-replication component of the IMBED option. Since every IR (SSRs and ISRs) is isolated onto its own

TRK	TRK	TRK	TRK	TRK	TRK	TRK	TRK	TRK	TRK	
ISR1	ISR2	ISR3	SSR1	SSR2	SSR3	SSR4	SSR5	SSR6	SSR7	
ISR1	ISR2	ISR3	SSR1	SSR2	SSR3	SSR4	SSR5	SSR6	SSR7	
ISR1	ISR2	ISR3	SSR1	SSR2	SSR3	SSR4	SSR5	SSR6	SSR7	. . . .
ISR1	ISR2	ISR3	SSR1	SSR2	SSR3	SSR4	SSR5	SSR6	SSR7	
ISR1	ISR2	ISR3	SSR1	SSR2	SSR3	SSR4	SSR5	SSR6	SSR7	
ISR1	ISR2	ISR3	SSR1	SSR2	SSR3	SSR4	SSR5	SSR6	SSR7	

<------------------- INDEX COMPONENT --------------------->

Figure 18-3. The REPLICATE option.

track and replicated to fill the track, whenever an IR is retrieved, the device may transfer whatever record is first encountered on the track (any copy of the IR will do). This improves response time by minimizing electromechanical device rotation needed to position the target record under the actuator. Although every IR requires its own track, and thus increases DASD utilization for the index overall, the total additional DASD space is generally modest, as an index component typically contains relatively few IRs (few index CIs, as only one index record is stored in one index CI), and the performance gain can be significant. However, it is important to bear in mind several qualifications.

First, newer and more advanced DASD devices themselves provide facilities (implemented in hardware and software) that directly or indirectly effect some reduction in latency, making the REPLICATE option less imperative for performance gains. Second, and related to the first point, is that use of cached DASD storage controllers, especially sophisticated models like the 3990 Model 3, can dramatically reduce I/O response time, especially the electromechanical (motion) components such as SEEK time and latency, far beyond whatever IMBED and RELICATE can achieve under the best of circumstances. Indeed, given the way caching is implemented, *it is imperative that neither IMBED nor REPLICATE be specified when using cached controllers*, as these options will waste, through index record replication, vital cache storage and may defeat the effectiveness of caching algorithms. Best results, therefore, with a cached controller are obtained with NOIMBED and NOREPLICATE.

Third, REPLICATE has no effect on latency if *optimal VSAM buffer allocation* (to be discussed later in this chapter) is assured. In such a case the options should be (assuming a noncached controller) IMBED and NOREPLICATE.

IMBED and REPLICATE. When both options are jointly on, it is important to note that the effect of IMBED is as described above, but the action of REPLICATE is modified to accommodate to the fact of an imbedded index. Rather than *every* IR, whether SSR or ISR, being replicated, in-place, on its own track within the index component, only the ISRs are affected, not the SSRs, as these are no longer in the index component at all, co-residing as they do, by the action of IMBED, with the data CAs they govern in the data component (and each being replicated on the first track of the governed data CA). Bearing in mind the qualifications cited above, IMBED + REPLICATE index options are generally good performance optimization features.

However, it will be recommended below that optimal VSAM buffer allocation should be effected for the very highest efficiency, so REPLICATE would offer no performance benefit in such a case, and such a case (of optimal buffer allocation) is strongly to be pursued. Furthermore, whenever possible the I/O response time performance benefits of cached DASD storage controllers should also be exploited, in which case neither IMBED nor REPLICATE should be specified. Finally, in terms of relative gains, optimal VSAM buffer allocation and use of cached controllers yield far higher VSAM performance optimization than the actions of IMBED and REPLICATE can provide.

18.8 LOAD-TIME OPTIONS: SPEED/RECOVERY

As we noted earlier in the text (Section 8.6), VSAM by default performs the loading of an empty cluster in what is called *recovery* mode, unless this is overridden by the programmer (the default is RECOVERY, overridden by coding SPEED at DEF CLUSTER time). What this means is that VSAM loads the cluster with a CA-full of records at a time, and just before each CA-full of records is loaded, the CA is *preformatted*: VSAM writes certain control information (the CIDF and RDFs) for each CI in the CA, and in addition writes a software-end-of-file (SEOF) indicator to keep track of the end of the content-portion of the cluster *up to that point of the load*. For a KSDS load, VSAM writes an SEOF to the first CI of the next CA following the last CA loaded with any data records, moving the SEOF forward in this fashion as each successive data CA is loaded. (For an ESDS and RRDS, the SEOF is handled somehat differently—as we noted in Subsection 8.8.1—but the basic concept of *forward-marking* the SEOF to indicate the 'load-point so far' is essentially the same.)

In terms of design objective, this is done to provide potential assistance in the recovery of part of the records loaded should the load operation be interrupted by a fatal error (one terminating the load prematurely). Recovery in such a case is done at the CA level: either one or more CA-full of records is recoverable or no part of any CA-full of records is recoverable. Here recoverable means the potential to continue the loading of records from the point of the last full CA loaded, without having to restart the load completely from the beginning.

But this is more of a theoretical benefit than a practical one in commercial programming environments. Rarely is it straightforward to determine the last record successfully loaded and to provide a *resume-load* routine that can continue the load with the next record through to the last, and moreover rarely would any installation trust that the resume-load operated perfectly, one might say 'seamlessly,' to yield a cluster with all records properly loaded. VSAM does not provide such a routine, and in the light of the fact that it must be user-coded, the suspicion of a possibly less-than-perfect resume-load routine is probably well-founded in most cases. Although, therefore, RECOVERY has the potential to avoid having to delete and then recreate the cluster from scratch, practical experience shows this is not a benefit often derived, most managers and programmers alike preferring the additional work of cluster deletion and recreation with a new reload, largely for the certainty this offers that all records are indeed properly loaded into the cluster.

For this reason, the programmer should always specify SPEED at DEF CLUS-TER time, thus overriding the default of RECOVERY. With SPEED, the record load occurs between the first OPEN and the final CLOSE without either (1) any CA preformatting, and (2) any forward-marking of SEOF; SEOF would in this case not be written CA-by-CA as these are loaded, but only when CLOSE is effected. Since SEOF is not forward-marked, resume-loading from some interrupt point in the load cycle is impossible and previously loaded records, not being recoverable, must be reloaded after the cluster is deleted and recreated. There is, however, a very significant gain in load-time performance, since the sizable overhead of preformatting and SEOF forward-marking is avoided. (Note that SPEED is strictly a load-time only option (although specified at DEF CLUSTER time): all post-load processing of a cluster is forced by VSAM to be effected in RECOVERY mode as the HURBA must be tracked throughout any significant processing activity and SEOF forward-marking makes HURBA tracking possible in a relatively simple way.)

18.9   KEYRANGE FACILITY

VSAM supports the distribution of a single KSDS across several volumes based on *keyranges*, that is on multiple separate ranges of keys. Say that, for some KSDS, keys are of the form 'FINxxxxxx' and we can identify four distinct keyranges with different processing activity characteristics:

```
FIN000000-FIN249999    very rare activity
                       ('archived records')
FIN250000-FIN499999    modest activity
FIN500000-FIN749999    high activity
FIN750000-FIN999999    very high activity
```

If we stored all of these records into a standard KSDS on a single volume, there would be considerable I/O contention between the the third and fourth keyrange portions of the cluster. Such a file exhibits high volatility, especially in its high keyrange portions, and we may be able to reduce contention considerably if we distributed the records by keyranges onto separate volumes; the physical segregation of the third and fourth keyranges is especially critical, for if these were accessed by distinct actuators on separate volumes, processing activity against both keyranges could be performed in parallel, allowing more concurrency and consequently improved I/O response time characteristics.

Figure 18-4 shows the IDCAMS coding for defining a *keyrange cluster* to exploit the performance benefits we discussed.

DISCUSSION

5. *KEYRANGES*: The KEYRANGES parameter is given in the form:

```
KEYRANGES ( (lowkey1 highkey1) -
             (lowkey2 highkey2) -
                    .
                    .
                    .
```

where each pair of *lowkey highkey* represents one keyrange. In the example under consideration, we have defined four distinct keyranges for this cluster, each to be stored on its own (distinct) volume. The keyrange facility has the following requirements:

1. Keyrange clusters cannot be reusable.
2. The multiple volumes for the keyranges of the data component must be of the same device type (all 3380s, for example); the index component may, however, be on a different device type.
3. The keyranges must be in strictly ascending order.
4. The keyranges may not overlap.
5. VSAM allows gaps between keyranges (one keyrange that may end at, say, 'FIN499999' while the next one begin at 'FIN600000'), but record insertion into the gaps is prohibited (no insertion of FIN555555 would be permitted, as this is within a keyrange gap of the example we just considered).
6. When defining a keyrange cluster, all volumes over which the keyrange cluster is distributed must be mounted.

6. *VOL(UMES)*: The multiple volumes to be used to store the individual keyranges are specified. This parameter is interpreted in conjunction with the ORDERED parameter, taken up immediately below.

7. *ORDERED*: This parameter instructs VSAM to allocate the individual keyranges onto the designated volumes in the order shown in the VOL paramater: thus, the first keyrange is allocated on FIN005, the second on FIN006, and so on. The default is UNORDERED (VSAM can assign the keyranges to volumes in any order), but it is recommended that ORDERED be coded for this facility.

```
 1.     DEF CLUSTER -
 2.          (NAME (FINCAT.ACCOUNTS.MSTR) -
 3.          RECSZ (460 460) -
 4.          KEYS (9 0) -
 5.          KEYRANGES ( (FIN000000    FIN249999) -
                         (FIN250000    FIN499999) -
                         (FIN500000    FIN749999) -
                         (FIN750000    FIN999999) ) -
 6.             VOL (FIN005 -
                    FIN006 -
                    FIN007 -
                    FIN008) -
 7.             ORDERED -
 8.             CYL (79 8) -
 9.             FSPC (32 25) -
10.             INDEXED -
11.             SPEED -
12.             NOREUSE) -
13.        DATA -
14.          (NAME (FINCAT.ACCOUNTS.MSTR.DATA) -
15.           CISZ (6144)) -
16.        INDEX -
17.          (NAME (FINCAT.ACCOUNTS.MSTR.INDEX) -
18.           IMBED)
```

Figure 18-4. IDCAMS keyrange cluster definition.

8. *Space allocation*: When defining a keyrange cluster, with the ORDERED parameter specified, the *primary* allocation must be available on *each* of the volumes on which a keyrange is to be stored. Here we have coded for a primary allocation of 79 CYL(INDERS) (cylinder allocation is recommended for performance optimization, as argued for earlier in this chapter), so 79 cylinders will (if possible) be allocated for each of the four keyranges on each of the four volumes specified (79 cylinders on FIN005, another 79 cylinders on FIN006, and so on). If this primary allocation quantity is not satisfiable on each keyrange volume, the DEFINE will fail. For technical performance reasons, the primary allocation should be generous enough to avoid secondary extenting as much as possible, so that the keyranges can grow strictly within the primary allocation. (The secondary extents allocated for any particular keyrange may not necessarily be on the same volume as the particular keyrange, and this may seriously degrade performance.)

18.10   SPACE ALLOCATION

We now turn to how to allocate space optimally to a VSAM cluster, given what we have learned about performance considerations up to this point. An optimal allocation is one in which we provide adequately for the primary allocation, plus some *primary (growth) cushion*, without excessive over-allocation, and with a reasonable amount of secondary allocation for additional cluster growth. To see how this may be accomplished systematically, we will use the same example as we used in Subsection 18.5.3, earlier in this chapter (and in this way may make use of many of the performance factors already computed there). We will first compute the primary allocation amount, without consideration for any cushion of growth other than that provided through the FSPC allocation amounts (Subsection 18.10.1, immediately following), and then consider the provision of a cushion of growth factor for the primary allocation, as well as a derivation of an appropriate secondary allocation quantity (Subsection 18.10.2). In our discussion, the relevant assumptions are:

```
CISZ    =  6144
RECSZ =  460
CASZ    =  1 Cylinder
FSPC       (32 25)
RECORDS 40,000
Device     3380
```

(The FSPC specification was computed in that subsection to yield an anticipated growth of approximately 50 percent.)

18.10.1 The Base Primary Allocation Computation

The first three steps for optimal space allocation are the same as the first three steps for the FSPC computation (Subsection 18.5.3).

Step 1: CI-TRK. We have already computed this in Step 1 of Subsection 18.5.3; CI-TRK is equal to 6.

Step 2: TRK-CA. This has been determined in Step 2 of Subsection 18.5.3: TRK-CA equals 14 (this allows one track being consumed for an imbedded index).

Step 3: CIDEN. This too has already been determined, in Step 3 of Subsection 18.5.3, with CIDEN equalling 84. For convenience, therefore, we can summarize our assumptions plus the factors derived in these first three steps:

```
CISZ    =  6144
RECSZ =  460
CASZ    =  1 Cylinder
FSPC       (32 25)
RECORDS 40,000
Device     3380
CI-TRK    6
TRK-CA   14
CIDEN     84
```

Step 4: PACK. This has also been computed for our example, in this case in Subsection 18.5.4: PACK equals 9.

Step 5: DATA-CI. This factor represents the number of *data-containing* CIs (not CIs held empty: 'data-less' CIs). This is derived by the following formula:

$$\text{DATA-CI} = \frac{\text{RECORDS}}{\text{PACK}} \, [\text{ceil}] \qquad [16]$$

which, for our example, would yield DATA-CI equal to 40,000/9, equalling 4444.4, ceiled to 4445 data-containing CIs.

Step 6: LOAD-CIDEN. This factor represents the number of data-containing CI *per CA*, which can be computed:

$$\text{LOAD-CIDEN} = \text{CIDEN} - (\,(\text{CIDEN} \times \text{CAFSPC})\,[\text{floor}]\,) \qquad [17]$$

which yields LOAD-CIDEN equal to $84 - (84 \times .25\,[\text{floor}])$, equalling $84 - 21$, which equals 63 CIs of each CA being data-containing. This means that $84 - 63$, equalling 21, of each CA are not loaded with data records, and this makes sense, since FSPC (32 25) means that at the CA level, one-fourth of the CIs contained in a CA are reserved for FSPC and thus held empty, and 84/4 equals 21.

Step 7: DATA-CA. This factor represents the number of CAs to the data set, and may be computed from the previous results as follows:

$$\text{DATA-CA} = \frac{\text{DATA-CI}}{\text{LOAD-CIDEN}} \, [\text{ceil}] \qquad [18]$$

which would yield DATA-CA equal to 4445/63, equalling 70.55, ceiled to 71. Now, since we have followed the practice of allocating in cylinder units, our CASZ is equal to one cylinder, so that a DATA-CA of 71 indicates 71 cylinders for the data component of the data set. We may refer to this allocation as the *base primary* allocation, one that is minimally sufficient to both satisfy storage of records loaded at data set load time, and to honor the FSPC allocations (CI- and CA-level) specified for the data set.

18.10.2 The Primary Cushion and the Secondary Allocation

It is important to realize that allowing a minimally sufficient base primary allocation may ultimately lead to a performance compromise, for two major reasons. One, if VSAM goes into secondary extenting (uses any part of the secondary allocation due to growth beyond the primary allocation amount), the secondary extents are generally noncontiguous with the primary extent(s), so that access to the entire data set involves additional SEEKs and rotational delays between the primary and secondary extents. Two, any one secondary extent allocation (there may be a maximum total allocation to the data set of 123 extents) is generally noncontiguous with respect to any other secondary extent. Thus, the primary and secondary extents typically are noncontiguous and the various secondary extents are typically noncontiguous to each other, making for a data set that is widely dispersed over the DASD volume. Wherever possible, therefore, it is better to provide an additional cushion of growth for the primary allocation to avoid early recourse to secondary extenting, which may compromise I/O activity performance.

Therefore, for optimal performance of VSAM data sets, the *base primary* allocation should be augmented with a factor for a growth cushion to yield what may be called a *buffered primary* allocation. This can be based on the *growth volatility* of the data set, broadly defined as either *light*, *medium*, or *high* volatility. A data set against which there is relatively light processing activity which extends the size of the data set (a balance of record additions) is usually easily recognized as such; LISTCAT output tracked over a significant processing cycle (say three months of activity) can be a valuable aid in confirming this classification. Similarly, for a data set sustaining a relatively high rate of processing activity that yields a large net file growth (critical on-line data sets often fall into this category), the appropriate classification is high volatility. Data sets whose growth pattern is neither exceptionally light nor exceptionally high can then be classed as having medium volatility; since these judgments are not rigorous and sometimes merely subjective, one can select the light or medium volatility category as a default one if no other impressions suggest otherwise. For very large data sets, roughly in excess of 100 cylinders of a 3380 device, however, it may be wise to categorize an otherwise medium volatility data set as light, to avoid excessive DASD over-allocation.

Now, assuming a judgment of growth volatility can be made broadly for any data set, or a satisfactory default accepted (medium for under 100-cylinder in size data sets, and light for larger data sets) when such a judgment cannot easily be made, then one can use the following as the appropriate cushion of primary growth (CUSH factor):

Light growth:	CUSH = .05	
Medium growth:	CUSH = .10	[19]
High growth	CUSH = .15	

We may therefore augment the base primary allocation (DATA-CA) derived in Step 7 by applying the following formula:

$$\text{PRM-ALLOC} = (\text{DATA-CA} \times \text{CUSH} \lceil \text{ceil} \rceil) + \text{DATA-CA} \qquad [20]$$

We will assume that, in the example we have been considering, the growth volatility is neither exceptionally light nor exceptionally high, so we will use .10 (that is, 10 percent) as our primary cushion factor. This means that, given that we computed the base primary allocation to be 71 cylinders, we would increase this ('cushion') by .10. So we would have PRM-ALLOC equalling $(71 \times .10 = 7.1$, ceiled to 8$) + 71$, equal to 8 + 71, which equals 79 cylinders, as the buffered primary allocation. (If the base primary allocation had been computed to be in excess of 100 cylinders, then we would have more conservatively selected a .05 primary cushion to avoid possible DASD overcommitment.) Therefore, we would specify CYL (79 __) for our space allocation at DEF CLUSTER time.

Now let's see how to approximate the secondary allocation quantity. Here I recommend that the secondary factor be derived as follows:

Light growth:	SEC = .05	
Medium growth:	SEC = .10	[21]
High growth	SEC = .10	

and the secondary allocation (SEC-ALLOC) would therefore be computed by:

$$\text{SEC-ALLOC} = \text{PRM-ALLOC} \times \text{SEC [ceil]} \qquad [22]$$

Thus [21] indicates the appropriate secondary factor (SEC) to be applied to the buffered primary allocation (PRM-ALLOC) already determined, and [22] carries through the actual computation of the secondary allocation quantity.

Notice that we use a .10 secondary factor (that is, 10 percent of the primary) for both medium and high growth volatility data sets (not .15 for high) to cap the secondary allocation to no more than .10 of the buffered primary allocation: remember that the secondary allocation allows for as many as 122 additional extents to the primary's one extent, for a maximum of 123 extents (the primary may, on occasion, require more than a single extent, in which case the secondary extents allowed are reduced correspondingly to still yield a primary plus secondary total extents of 123). This is different from OS non-VSAM secondary allocation where the maximum of the primary plus secondary extents is 16. VSAM's 123 is clearly much more generous and so more than 10 percent of the primary allocation would generally be an overcommitment of DASD.

For the example under consideration, assuming medium growth volatility would yield the computation SEC-ALLOC equal to $79 \times .10$, which equals 7.9, ceiled to 8 cylinders to be specified as our secondary allocation. Our space allocation coding at DEF CLUSTER time would therefore be CYL (79 8); if the primary allocation were satisfied by a single extent, then the secondary permits an additional 122 extents of 8 cylinders each, or 976 (equalling 8 times 122) cylinders *in addition* to our (buffered) primary allocation of 79 cylinders, for a total maximum growth of 1055 (equalling 976 plus 79) cylinders for the data set. More importantly, due to the primary cushion we built in, the 71 cylinders needed strictly to contain our 40000 records with 32 percent FSPC at the CI level and 25 percent at the CA level (since FSPC (32 25) was determined) could grow by an additional 8 cylinders before going into secondary extenting (and remember that the 71 cylinders of base primary space itself already allows for 50 percent file size growth from 40000 to 60000 records, by virtue of the FSPC specification of (32 25)).

18.10.3   A Brief Cross-Validation

Figure 18-5 shows LISTCAT output after the data set under discussion as our running example has been allocated as CYL (79 8) and loaded with 40000 records (as can be seen in the ALLOCATION group fields of SPACE-PRI and SPACE-SEC). The figure gives both HURBA and HARBA (labelled as HI-USED-RBA and HI-ALLOC-RBA, respectively, under the ALLOCATION group for the data component). We can use these two fields to cross-validate our space allocation computations, by either of two different approaches.

```
CLUSTER ------- VSAM.CK.MVS.OPTTEST1
    IN-CAT --- TESTCAT
    HISTORY
        OWNER-IDENT------STNKANT        CREATION----------88.248
        RELEASE----------------2        EXPIRATION--------00.000
        PROTECTION-PSWD-----(NULL)       RACF----------------(NO)
    ASSOCIATIONS
        DATA-----VSAM.CK.MVS.OPTTEST1.DATA
        INDEX----VSAM.CK.MVS.OPTTEST1.INDEX
DATA ------- VSAM.CK.MVS.OPTTEST1.DATA
    IN-CAT --- TESTCAT
    HISTORY
        OWNER-IDENT-------(NULL)         CREATION----------88.248
        RELEASE----------------2        EXPIRATION--------00.000
        PROTECTION-PSWD-----(NULL)       RACF----------------(NO)
    ASSOCIATIONS
        CLUSTER--VSAM.CK.MVS.OPTTEST1
    ATTRIBUTES
        KEYLEN----------------9          AVGLRECL-------------460      BUFSPACE----------13312     CISIZE--------------6144
        RKP-------------------0          MAXLRECL-------------460      EXCPEXIT----------(NULL)     CI/CA-----------------84
        SHROPTNS(1,3)    SPEED           UNIQUE         NOERASE        INDEXED      NOWRITECHK     IMBED        NOREPLICAT
        UNORDERED        NOREUSE         NONSPANNED
    STATISTICS
        REC-TOTAL----------40000         SPLITS-CI-------------0       EXCPS---------------4735
        REC-DELETED-----------0          SPLITS-CA-------------0       EXTENTS---------------1
        REC-INSERTED----------0          FREESPACE-%CI---------32      SYSTEM-TIMESTAMP:
        REC-UPDATED-----------0          FREESPACE-%CA---------25          X'9F1237059BEF9800'
        REC-RETRIEVED---------0          FREESPC-BYTES---13461504
    ALLOCATION
        SPACE-TYPE------CYLINDER         HI-ALLOC-RBA-----40771584
        SPACE-PRI------------79          HI-USED-RBA------36642816
        SPACE-SEC------------8
    VOLUME
        VOLSER-----------DSK003          PHYREC-SIZE--------2048       HI-ALLOC-RBA----40771584    EXTENT-NUMBER---------1
        DEVTYPE------X'3010200E'         PHYRECS/TRK----------18       HI-USED-RBA-----36642816    EXTENT-TYPE--------X'00'
        VOLFLAG----------PRIME           TRACKS/CA------------15
        EXTENTS:
        LOW-CCHH-----X'007C0000'         LOW-RBA---------------0       TRACKS-------------1185
        HIGH-CCHH----X'00CA000E'         HIGH-RBA--------40771583
INDEX ------ VSAM.CK.MVS.OPTTEST1.INDEX
    IN-CAT --- TESTCAT
    HISTORY
        OWNER-IDENT-------(NULL)         CREATION----------88.248
        RELEASE----------------2        EXPIRATION--------00.000
        PROTECTION-PSWD-----(NULL)       RACF----------------(NO)
    ASSOCIATIONS
        CLUSTER--VSAM.CK.MVS.OPTTEST1
    ATTRIBUTES
        KEYLEN----------------9          AVGLRECL---------------0      BUFSPACE---------------0    CISIZE--------------1024
        RKP-------------------0          MAXLRECL------------1017       EXCPEXIT----------(NULL)     CI/CA-----------------31
        SHROPTNS(1,3)  RECOVERY          UNIQUE         NOERASE        NOWRITECHK      IMBED        NOREPLICAT    UNORDERED
        NOREUSE
    STATISTICS
        REC-TOTAL-------------72         SPLITS-CI-------------0       EXCPS----------------495     INDEX:
        REC-DELETED-----------0          SPLITS-CA-------------0       EXTENTS---------------2       LEVELS----------------2
        REC-INSERTED----------0          FREESPACE-%CI----------0      SYSTEM-TIMESTAMP:            ENTRIES/SECT----------5
        REC-UPDATED-----------0          FREESPACE-%CA----------0          X'9F1237059BEF9800'      SEQ-SET-RBA-------31744
        REC-RETRIEVED---------0          FREESPC-BYTES-----38912                                    HI-LEVEL-RBA----------0
    ALLOCATION
        SPACE-TYPE---------TRACK         HI-ALLOC-RBA------112640
        SPACE-PRI-------------1          HI-USED-RBA-------104448
        SPACE-SEC-------------1
    VOLUME
        VOLSER-----------DSK003          PHYREC-SIZE--------1024       HI-ALLOC-RBA-------31744    EXTENT-NUMBER---------1
        DEVTYPE------X'3010200E'         PHYRECS/TRK----------31        HI-USED-RBA--------1024     EXTENT-TYPE--------X'00'
        VOLFLAG----------PRIME           TRACKS/CA-------------1
        EXTENTS:
        LOW-CCHH-----X'00020005'         LOW-RBA---------------0       TRACKS----------------1
        HIGH-CCHH----X'00020005'         HIGH-RBA----------31743
    VOLUME
        VOLSER-----------DSK003          PHYREC-SIZE--------1024       HI-ALLOC-RBA------112640    EXTENT-NUMBER---------1
        DEVTYPE------X'3010200E'         PHYRECS/TRK----------31        HI-USED-RBA-------104448    EXTENT-TYPE--------X'80'
        VOLFLAG----------PRIME           TRACKS/CA------------15
        EXTENTS:
        LOW-CCHH-----X'007C0000'         LOW-RBA------------31744      TRACKS-------------1185
        HIGH-CCHH----X'00CA000E'         HIGH-RBA---------112639
```

Figure 18-5. Sample LISTCAT output for cross-validation.

First, we can compute the total amount of space, expressed in CAs, that is allocated to the data set, this being derived from HARBA. As the reader may remember (Subsection 12.2.2), HARBA represents the last byte of the last *allocated* CA of the data set (whether or not any data is actually stored at this location). Thus, HARBA represents what we have called *maximal end-of-file (MAX-EOF)*. This is as opposed to *data end-of-file (DATA-EOF)*, where the actual data records end; VSAM uses HURBA to represent DATA-EOF. HARBA is computed by:

$$HARBA = ALLOC\text{-}CA \times CISZ \times CIDEN \qquad [23]$$

where *ALLOC-CA* represents the number of allocated CAs to the data set. ALLOC-CA may be either (1) the primary allocation quantity specified at DEF CLUSTER time, or (2) the last current extent of the data set if secondary extenting occurred (this can be determined from the EXTENTS field of the ALLOCATION group in LISTCAT output for the data set, by a procedure already discussed in Section 12.2). Since we wish to derive ALLOC-CA (we are given HARBA directly in LISTCAT output), we can rearrange Formula [23] into

$$ALLOC\text{-}CA = \frac{HARBA}{CISZ \times CIDEN} \qquad [24]$$

Thus, the first approach to cross-validation of our space allocation computations is to compute ALLOC-CA; for the example we have been using, and using the HARBA value given in the LISTCAT output of Figure 18-5 (shown to be 40,771,584), this yields:

$$ALLOC\text{-}CA = \frac{40,771,584}{6144 \times 84} = \frac{40,771,584}{516,096} = 79$$

and this is precisely right, as our primary allocation quantity was determined to be 79 cylinders or CAs. Now, under this first approach we next compute the DATA-EOF for the data set, which is just the factor DATA-CA (derived in Formula [18] of Step 7 of Subsection 18.10.1). HURBA itself is calculated as follows:

$$HURBA = DATA\text{-}CA \times CISZ \times CIDEN \qquad [25]$$

and DATA-CA can therefore be derived by:

$$DATA\text{-}CA = \frac{HURBA}{CISZ \times CIDEN} \qquad [26]$$

Given a value of HURBA = 36,642,816 (from the LISTCAT of Figure 18-5), Formula [26] yields:

$$\text{DATA-CA} = \frac{36,642,816}{6144 \times 84} = \frac{36,642,816}{516,096} = 71$$

which cross-validates precisely with our earlier computation of this factor in Subsection 18.10.1. In sum, the DATA-EOF (represented by HURBA) is 71 cylinders, while the MAX-EOF (represented by HARBA) is 79 cylinders, and this corresponds exactly with the facts as we know them about the sample data set.

The second approach is to compute the space allocated but not used (which we will call UNUSED-CA): in bytes, this is simply HURBA subtracted from HARBA, but we wish to express it in terms of CAs or cylinders, and this can be done through Formula [27]:

$$\text{UNUSED-CA} = \frac{\text{HARBA} - \text{HURBA}}{\text{CISZ} \times \text{CIDEN}} \qquad [27]$$

For our example, we would have:

$$\text{UNUSED-CA} = \frac{40,771,584 - 36,642,816}{6144 \times 84} = \frac{4,128,768}{516,096} = 8$$

and this cross-validates precisely, since we have already determined that MAX-EOF, in cylinders, is 79, while DATA-EOF, in cylinders again, is 71, the difference of 79 minus 71, equal to 8, being the UNUSED-CAs of the data set (corresponding to the primary cushion we determined for this data set). Both approaches, therefore, cross-validate our original space allocation computations of Subsections 18.10.1 and 18.10.2.

18.11   OPTIMAL BUFFER ALLOCATION

Of all performance factors, VSAM buffer allocation may often be the most critical determinant of processing performance, affecting the I/O workload of VSAM against any particular data set. At the most general level (we will be more specific, and more technically precise, very shortly) a relatively greater number of VSAM buffers allocated to a data set may allow more records, data and/or index, to be accessible in virtual storage; that is, more of the CIs of the data set are 'in core,' as it were, thus avoiding I/O operations across a channel for record retrieval. Typically, and very roughly, retrieval of a VSAM CI across an S/370 channel is measured in *milli*second (thousandths of a second) time, while access to a CI already read into a buffer in virtual storage is measured in *micro*second (millionths of a second) time (assuming a 4K CISZ and not folding in considerations of queueing delays, SEEK time, latency, and other components of an I/O operation, other than strict data transfer time). Clearly, the opportunity for significant, even dramatic, performance benefits is very high. But to properly understand principles of optimal VSAM buffer allocation we must first understand the basic principles of VSAM buffer management, taken up immediately following.

18.11.1   VSAM Buffer Management

First let us look at how buffer allocation may be controlled by the user. There are three facilities for buffer allocation available to the programmer:

1. *BUFSP Parameter at DEF CLUSTER Time.*
   The BUFSP (abbreviated from BUFFERSPACE) parameter on the DEF CLUSTER command may (it is optional) specify to VSAM the total amount of space, in bytes, to be used for program buffers. VSAM will determine how to partition this amount between data and any index buffers (for a KSDS only).
2. *BUFSP/BUFND/BUFNI Parameters of the ACB*
   For VSAM Assembler programs, the ACB (Access Method Control Block) macro for a specific data set permits three buffer allocation parameters to be specified: BUFSP (total bufferspace, as above), BUFND (number of data buffers), and BUFNI (number of index buffers).
3. *BUFSP/BUFND/BUFNI Parameters of AMP JCL Parameter*
   These parameters may be specified for a specific data set on the JCL DD statement referencing that data set, in the VSAM parameter *AMP*.

The technique recommended is the third, through the JCL DD statement AMP parameter, for several reasons. First, the specification here overrides any made at DEF CLUSTER time or in the ACB (but—and this is important to note—only if the AMP specification is largest amount specified). Second, BUFSP at DEF CLUSTER time is both unspecific—it does not allow for user-determined data and index buffers amounts separately—and too *global*: it applies to all programs accessing the data set, but it is unrealistic to assume identical buffer requirements for all applications against a data set. Finally, the AMP approach, unlike that in the ACB, requires no program-internal coding, so that different values for the parameters may be used as the situation dictates by simply changing or overriding the AMP parameter in the associated JCL. As we do not recommend using BUFSP, the coding would be of the form:

```
//ddname DD DSN= ...,DISP= ...,
           AMP=('BUFND=number,BUFNI=number')
```

In CICS, the same specification is made in the DFHFCT TYPE=DATASET macro:

```
DFHFCT TYPE=DATASET,
       ACCMETH=VSAM,
       DATASET= ...,
       BUFND=number,
       BUFNI=number,
       .
       .
```

If the programmer fails to specify an explicit VSAM buffer allocation, then VSAM uses an internal buffer management default, which is to allocate two data buffers (each equivalent in size to the data CISZ value), and—if the data set is a KSDS—one index buffer (equivalent in size to the index CISZ value). One of the two data buffers is used to hold the current CI (the target CI containing the target record for any operation), and the other is a *control buffer* used by VSAM for split activity, CA preformatting operations, and certain other control functions within VSAM buffer management. It may be surprising, but true, that these default buffer allocations are almost invariably (and woefully) inadequate for optimal VSAM processing performance.

To appreciate how to determine more optimal buffer allocations, we must next understand VSAM's buffer management determinations when more virtual storage is available for VSAM buffers than the minimal default amounts (two data and one index buffer). The strategy is different depending on processing mode.

18.11.2   Buffer Management: Direct Processing

Buffer Lookaside.   First, VSAM acquires two data buffers (one for the target CI and one as a control buffer). Then VSAM uses all remaining space (if any) for index buffers. The strategy here is to optimize for direct processing—which uses a vertical search of the index component—by allowing buffer space for as many index records (CIs) as can be accommodated; in this way, more index records will be buffered in virtual storage, enhancing index search operations, as these will not require a *DASD lookaside* (performing I/O operations across an S/370 channel) to be accessed. For index records that can be held in virtual storage buffers, VSAM can often perform a *virtual storage, or buffer, lookaside* (retrieval of the record from existing buffers in virtual storage without external I/O being performed) to access any individual index record after it has been transferred the first time from DASD into virtual storage.

We say VSAM can 'often' perform such a buffer lookaside when it has additional space for index buffers: if there is not sufficient space for maintaining in buffers the entire *index set* (all high-level index records, that is, above the sequence set), VSAM may have to reuse a specific buffer to accommodate the transferring in of some other needed index set record, if there is insufficient space for holding both index records, and this forces a DASD lookaside.

Note that, aside from the control buffer, VSAM does not require for direct processing any more *data* buffers than the minimum default, namely one: once a sequence set record (SSR) directs VSAM to the appropriate target CI containing the required data record, only that data CI is transferred in, so a single data buffer suffices for each access operation.

Buffer Readahead. Note further that, with direct processing, VSAM does *not* perform (data) buffer *readahead*: the prefetching of immediately successive data CIs (after the current data CI) into virtual storage buffers (given sufficient buffer space), prior to their being requested, in anticipation of access requests to these data CIs after the completion of processing activity against the current data CI held in buffer storage. It makes sense in sequential processing (for instance) for VSAM, while processing access requests against CIx, to read into buffer storage (prefetch) the next CI ($CIx+1$), since with sequential processing it is highly likely that the next CI may be subsequently accessed and so required in buffer storage; prefetching this next CI before an access request is actually issued against it avoids any delay that would otherwise be experienced by the subsequent request in order to bring the CI into buffer storage.

However, such readahead is inappropriate in direct processing, where there is little likelihood that an access to any one CI will be followed by an access to that CI's immediately successive neighbor CI, by virtue of the nature of random access patterns. Since, therefore, no readahead is called for in direct processing, VSAM requires only a single data buffer (in addition to the control buffer) and any remaining buffer space is best used to hold more index set records in virtual storage for improving the index search component of any direct operation.

18.11.3 Buffer Management: Sequential Processing

First, VSAM acquires two data buffers and one index buffer (the default minimums). Any remaining buffer space is allocated to additional data buffers, for performing buffer readahead for data CIs; this will (for reasons discussed immediately previously) improve sequential processing performance by minimizing waiting delays for I/O operations against CIs subsequent to the current CI being processed, as one or more of these subsequent CIs may already have been transferred into virtual storage by the buffer readahead strategy.

Note that in sequential processing, VSAM uses only one SSR per data CA processed, and therefore only a single index buffer is required to hold the currently accessed SSR (and remember that no index set records are used in sequential processing, only SSRs).

18.11.4 Buffer Management: Mixed (SEQ + DIR) Processing

When both sequential and direct access is being performed against the same data set (mixed mode: SEQ + DIR processing), VSAM first acquires two data buffers. VSAM then acquires *x* index buffers, where *x* equals the *STRNO (string number)* + 1. To understand this, we must develop the notion of a *string*.

Understanding Strings.   A string is an I/O request against a VSAM data set that requires *positioning*, that is tracking the current record position by using an internal VSAM control block called the *Placeholder*, or *PLH* (discussed briefly earlier in the text in Subsection 14.1.4) within the data set. A program may support multiple concurrent positioning requests, that is, multiple strings: for example, a program may issue two READ or WRITE requests *of different processing modes* against the same VSAM data set: one might be for sequential access, and another for direct access. VSAM would track the SEQ request, through a unique PLH control block, as one string, and the DIR request, through another PLH, as a second distinct string.

The most typical instances of what may be more tersely called *multistring* operation are encountered in the on-line environment: a VSAM file available to the on-line domain may be accessed concurrently by multiple programs, so that VSAM would have to maintain multiple concurrent positioning operations, tracking them separately by distinct PLHs, or strings. Each string forces a VSAM *control block build* (including a build of the individual PLHs required to track the distinct positioning requests of the multiple concurrent users). STRNO is simply, then, the number of concurrent requests to a data set from a single MVS Address Space (so-called 'region') and reflects the degree of concurrent operations from multiple users supported for that data set. In a multistring environment (on-line) like CICS, STRNO is generally set by a systems programmer in the DFHFCT TYPE=DATASET macro:

```
DFHFCT TYPE=DATASET,
       ACCMETH=VSAM,
       DATASET= ...,
       BUFND=number,
       BUFNI=number,
       STRNO=
       .
       .
```

where STRNO may be in the range of 1 (the default minimum) to 255. (Both the notions of string and STRNO are technically more complex than this discussion has suggested, but the understanding provided will suffice for our purposes.)

String-exclusive Buffers.   Now, a further point is that under multiple concurrent access to a data set, each string requires its own exclusive (nonshared) SSR buffer: we say that sequence set buffers (for holding SSRs) are *string-exclusive*, in that each SSR buffer has a specific string assignment which marks the buffer for exclusive use by that one string and no other. It is for this reason (to return to our original discussion) that, in mixed mode, VSAM (after acquiring two data buffers) seeks to acquire STRNO + 1 index buffers: one index buffer must be allocated to each string for its use to hold a SSR, and since SSR buffers are string-exclusive, each string's SSR buffer is distinct from any other, even if it may contain precisely the same SSR as some other buffer assigned to a different string.

In this sense, we say that there is no buffer lookaside across strings at the SSR buffer level; even if string2 requires the same SSR as string1, and this SSR has already been transferred into buffer storage, VSAM will perform a separate I/O retrieval from DASD of the same SSR for string2, into an SSR buffer assigned to string2, yielding two copies of the same SSR in virtual storage. It is in this sense that an SSR buffer is strictly string-exclusive.

But what of the additional buffer referred to in 'STRNO + 1'? VSAM attempts to acquire one more index buffer than is required by STRNO, and this would be used for the highest-level index set record (there is always only one index record or CI at the highest level of an index component). If available, this would enhance direct processing perfomance, since all strings must use the same highest-level index record given that direct operations require a vertical index search starting with this index record. If this index record could be held in buffer storage, it would therefore reduce time-consuming DASD I/O operations (DASD lookaside) significantly.

String-pooled Buffers.   Note here another key principle of VSAM buffer management. Unlike SSR buffers, which are string-exclusive, index set records (ISRs) are said to be *string-pooled*: any ISR in buffer storage may be used by any active string that may require that ISR; ISRs are pooled together for multistring sharing, and this fact will form the basis later in this chapter for a method of assuring certain high performance of direct processing through precise and optimal index buffer allocation.

Finally, in mixed mode, after VSAM acquires, first, two data buffers, and then, STRNO + 1 index buffers (given sufficient buffer storage), VSAM will allocate any remaining buffer space for data buffers: the acquisition of STRNO + 1 index buffers is for improving direct processing performance, and assignment of remaining buffers for data CIs improves sequential performance, thus balancing SEQ + DIR processing optimization.

A Generalization.   In a multi-string environment, given sufficient buffer space, VSAM will attempt to acquire a *minimum* of STRNO index buffers (the bare minimum needed to support an exclusive SSR buffer for each string—no index set records could then be buffered) and STRNO + 1 data buffers. The latter is motivated because, like SSR buffers, *data buffers are also string-exclusive*: each buffer holding a data CI is assigned exclusively to one specific string. The one additional buffer is for a single VSAM control buffer. We may, therefore, summarize the principles we have learned concerning buffer lookaside and buffer sharing as follows:

Data Buffers	String-exclusive
SSR Buffers	String-exclusive
ISR Buffers	String-pooled

374 VSAM: A COMPREHENSIVE GUIDE

and the *minumum* buffer allocations would be:

| Data Buffers | STRNO + 1 |
| Index Buffers | STRNO |

Note that these are minimal allocations, and do not represent *optimal* buffer allocations (we will determine these later).

Note also that only with index set buffers (again, provided sufficient buffer space exists), therefore, does VSAM permit sharing of the pool of all such buffers (if any) among all strings, so that any string may use any index set buffer if it contains the desired ISR (that is, if that ISR has already been transferred into virtual storage). This allows reuse of ISR buffers, yielding two performance benefits: (1) less buffer storage is required to support the multistring environment, as the ISR buffers are communally shared; had they been string-exclusive, each string would have required its own set of ISR buffers, and multiple identical copies of various ISRs could be concurrently in storage at the same time; and (2) I/O operations are reduced, since VSAM will first perform a buffer lookaside to the ISR buffer pool, and if the target ISR is already held in storage, no DASD lookaside is required.

String-specific Lookaside. Furthermore, there are actually two types of buffer lookaside which may be performed by VSAM. The first is *string-specific lookaside*: this occurs with data and SSR buffers which are, remember, string-exclusive. To understand this type of lookaside, consider a hypothetical case: String1 requires, for some specific VSAM data set, access to some particular data record or SSR, from data CIx or $SSRx$ (which is held in some index CIx, since there is one index record per index CI). Before incurring the cost of physical I/O operations for fetching the required data CIx or $SSRx$ across a channel from DASD, VSAM will first lookaside in virtual storage to determine if the required record is not already held (brought in by some previous operation) *in any of the data or SSR buffers assigned exclusively to string1*. The point here is that VSAM will *not* search any other data and SSR buffers associated with the data set but assigned to strings other than string1—no *cross-string lookaside* is permitted in this case (for data or SSR buffers). So even if the record required by string1 is already available in buffer storage but in, say, a data or SSR buffer assigned to string2, but not in any data or SSR buffer assigned to string1, this string2-owned copy may not be used to satisfy a string1 request, and VSAM would have to perform a DASD lookaside to read in another copy of the required record into an appropriate string1 buffer.

Cross-string Lookaside. The second type of lookaside performed by VSAM is *cross-string lookaside*, performed only with string-pooled ISR buffers. Here, we assume some specific VSAM data set, and string1 issuing a direct access request. This is satisfied by a vertical index search: the single highest-level index record is retrieved first, followed by the appropriate index record from the next lower level, etc. (we are assuming a sufficiently large data set with a multilevel index) until a

SSR is retrieved, which ultimately points to the target data CI, say CIx. Now before VSAM performs physical I/O across a channel for any index set record, say ISRx, VSAM will first lookaside to virtual storage buffers associated with this data set to see if a copy of IRSx is already held (by some previous operation) in *any* of the ISR buffers associated with the various mutiple strings accessing this data set. This is a cross-string lookaside, as VSAM is not restricted to string1 buffers: any copy of IRSx held for any string may be reused to satisfy from virtual storage the string1 request, thus avoiding DASD lookaside. Indeed, although some IRSx was originally fetched to satisfy a request from some specific string, say stringx, the ISR is held in string-pooled buffer storage, and is in no way assigned exclusively to stringx. All strings have equal access to the ISR buffer pool. DASD lookaside would, therefore, be required only if there were no copy of IRSx available in any buffer within the ISR buffer pool.

The above discussion of VSAM buffer management suffices to provide the necessary foundation for determining optimal (not minimal) VSAM buffer allocation strategies, to which we turn in the following section.

18.11.5 Optimal Data Buffer Allocation: SEQ Processing

There are two primary objectives for optimal data buffer allocation in sequential processing mode:

1. To provide sufficient buffer space to allow for *processing parallelism*: I/O operations to be performed in parallel with processing operations; such processing parallelism can significantly enhance total performance against the VSAM data set.
2. To provide sufficient buffer space to allow VSAM to process at least at the *full-track I/O level*: that is, to process at least one full track of data per each I/O operation (more precisely, per each EXCP instruction).

To accomplish the first objective, BUFND must be at least four: when four or more data buffers are available to VSAM, VSAM will use one for the control buffer, one for the target CI, and still have at least two buffers for buffer readahead, and at this level VSAM will overlap processing and I/O operations.

To accomplish the second objective, we must appreciate how VSAM *schedules* data buffers: half of the available data buffers are dedicated ('scheduled') as *processing buffers*, for VSAM processing (non-I/O) operations, while (the other) half are scheduled as *I/O buffers*, for VSAM I/O operations. Given this, if we allocate a full-track worth of data buffers, only half-track I/O level processing will occur, and our objective is to assure full-track I/O level processing. Therefore, we should set BUFND as follows to achieve this objective:

$$\text{BUFND} = (2 \times \text{CI-TRK}) + 1 \qquad \text{(SEQ)} \qquad [28]$$

where the factor CI-TRK (number of CIs per track) was introduced in Step 1 of Subsection 18.5.3 (and is derived from Appendix A). For the example we have been considering throughout this chapter, our CISZ equals 6144 and CI-TRK therefore is six (assuming a 3380 device). BUFND would hence be set to seven data buffers. The '+ 1' allocates for a single VSAM control buffer.

Although we can provide even more data buffers and allow VSAM to process multiple tracks per I/O operation (EXCP), increasing I/O efficiency still more, we risk the possibility that the increased virtual storage requirement *may* lead to increased paging rates (and buffers that are readahead too far in advance of being needed may indeed be paged out prior to being referenced, and thus may need to be paged back in again when required), and this may offset some of the performance benefit of the large data buffer allocation.

In terms of multitrack I/O level processing (that is, above a full-track), we can generalize Formula [28] to:

$$\text{BUFND} = (2n \times \text{CI-TRK}) + 1 \qquad [28A]$$

where $n = 1, 2, 3, \ldots$ in any instance; for example, if n is set at 2, then we will achieve 2 tracks of data being processed by VSAM per I/O operation (remember, only half of the data buffers are scheduled for I/O operations). In our example, we would have BUFND equal to $(4 \times 6) + 1$, which equals 25. Similarly, setting n equal to 3 yields 3 tracks processed per I/O operation; for our example, BUFND equal to $(6 \times 6) + 1$, equalling 37; and so on. Furthermore, in a multistring environment, the data buffer allocation can be pushed to even higher (maximal) values by using this (maximal) adaption of [28A]:

$$\text{BUFND} = (2n \times \text{CI-TRK}) + \text{STRNO} \qquad [28Mx]$$

There are several points to bear in mind in connection with [28A] and [28Mx], both of which are much less conservative than [28], with [28Mx] being the least conservative.

First, although [28] is the most conservative formula we have presented for BUFND, it is nonetheless not the *minimal* VSAM allocation for data buffers. The minimal allocation is:

$$\text{BUFND} = \text{STRNO} + 1 \qquad [28Mn]$$

which, in other than a multistring environment, simply becomes two data buffers (batch COBOL, for example). Generally, however, at least four data buffers should be allocated for strictly sequential processing. For on-line environments, however, one should begin with the minimum allocation dictated in [28Mn], increasing the allocation up to that derived from [28], monitoring performance statistics carefully for possible negative effects, using CICS statistics, LISTCAT output, and the more specific performance feedback from performance monitors like IBM's *RMF* (*Resource Measurement Facility*), IBM's *CICSPARS/MVS* (*CICS Performance Analysis Reporting System/MVS*), or an equivalent monitor (in terms of non-IBM products, Candle Corporation's *Omegamon* is very widely used).

In particular, the readahead function provided by [28Mx] may be wholly compromised in the on-line environment, where a product like CICS will allocate all of the buffers above the minimal allocation (two data buffers, one for data CIs and the other for the control buffer, for any one string) to the *first sequential request* (string), all subsequent strings obtaining only the minimal data buffer allocation, and hence obtaining no performance benefit from the additional buffers; in this case, the multiple strings are *not* given access to the extra buffers in any distributed (or pooled) fashion, and we say that CICS exhibits *first sequential string preference* in this regard. This is arguably a design defect, but one that must be remembered. (Note, however, that data buffers in excess of the minimal allocation can be used, even in an on-line environment, for example, to reduce the performance overhead of CA split activity.)

Second, although (as we have observed earlier) a large number of data records in virtual storage (a large data CISZ, or a large number of data buffers: see Subsection 18.3.6) generally favors sequential processing performance, performance studies (using a fixed CISZ of 4K) indicate that the increasing overhead of buffer lookaside on an ever-larger number of buffers begins to offset any performance gains obtained when more than approximately 50 to 60 data buffers are allocated. Given that data buffer allocation in excess of this cutoff range will frequently yield rapidly diminishing returns (in terms of EXCP operations), BUFND should generally be kept below these values.

Third, as we hinted at already, one must also consider the possibility that the increase in virtual storage used by a large number of data buffers may result in increased paging, which may offset some of the performance benefits in some cases. Here, the paging activity should be monitored directly (IBM's RMF, or an equivalent performance monitor, can be used), or the execution time of tasks against the data set can be tracked closely to determine when performance begins to fall off with increasing values of BUFND. In the on-line domain, the negative impact of higher paging I/O rates can be an especially critical concern: very roughly, *page-in* rates— CICS is not significantly adversely affected by page-out operations which are scheduled in parallel with CICS processing—should not exceed 5 to 10 page-ins per second, and optimally should be kept under one page-in/second if possible.

The Problem of Buffer Refresh.   Fourth, and finally, there is a special case to contend with when the data set is defined with SHAREOPTIONS (SHR) 4 (cross-region or cross-system) at DEF CLUSTER time. SHAREOPTIONS will be considered later in this chapter, but for now all we need to know is that for sequential retrieval operations under SHR 4, VSAM forces a *buffer refresh* upon completion of the retrieval of a data CI into buffer storage: that is, VSAM is prohibited from performing a buffer lookaside against the buffer if the same data CI is subsequently requested, and this forces VSAM to do a DASD lookaside to bring in a fresh copy of that data CI, thus 'refreshing' data buffers for each CI read. In addition to suppressing buffer lookaside, buffer refresh may nullify buffer readahead, as the data buffers will be refreshed in any case when a data CI is read, even though they may have been prefetched. BUFND, therefore, in excess of the minimum (STRNO + 1) may actually degrade, not improve, performance in sequential processing under SHR 4 (and there will be independent reasons, discussed later in this chapter, to avoid SHR 4 in all but very special cases).

All in all, therefore, it would be prudent to begin with the value dictated by [28], the most conservative formula, and increase upward slowly by application of [28A], to the maximum yielded by [28Mx], monitoring carefully for diminishing returns, and probably not exceeding 50−60 data buffers in any case. (Again, for CICS in particular it may be necessary to retreat to the VSAM minimum for sequential processing, which is [28Mn]: BUFND = STRNO + 1.) Hardware can also influence paging rates, and the *expanded storage* feature of IBM's 'Sierra' processors (3090 series) is designed to assist dramatically in reduction of paging/swapping I/O: without going into the technical details here, let us just note that the high-end model ES/3090S supports an impressive 2GB (2 gigabytes: appproximately 2 billion bytes) of expanded storage (and an additional ½G of central storage), and performance studies reported by installations through the SHARE IBM user's group have verified the strongly positive performance effects on response time, system throughput and−notably in our connection−on paging (and swapping) reduction.

18.11.6   Optimal Index Buffer Allocation: SEQ Processing

A fundamental point to appreciate in determining the optimal index buffer allocation for strictly sequential processing is that VSAM *always* uses, and *only* uses, the sequence set of the index component for any sequential processing request, from which it obtains a pointer to the data CI holding the target record; the index set (all levels of index above the sequence set) is not used by VSAM in such processing. Furthermore, when processing sequentially, no buffer readahead is performed on index records. Therefore, in a multistring environment, VSAM requires at any one time, for any specific processing request, one and only one SSR per string. BUFNI therefore is allocated as follows:

$$BUFNI = STRNO \qquad (SEQ) \qquad\qquad [29]$$

which in a batch single string environment yields the same as the VSAM default minimum of one index buffer. There is no performance benefit to exceeding the allocation dictated by [29].

18.11.7   Optimal Data Buffer Allocation: DIR Processing

For any one direct access request by a single string against a VSAM data set, VSAM generally uses only two data buffers: one to hold the target CI (only one data CI is read at a time for random retrieval), and the other to function as the VSAM control buffer (for such control functions as split activity, preformatting, etc.). We can therefore generalize to the multistring environment as follows:

$$BUFND = STRNO + 1 \qquad (DIR) \qquad\qquad [30]$$

Although in certain specialized cases VSAM may be able to use data buffers in excess of those delineated in Formula [30] (high CA split activity, or spanned records processing), in the vast majority of cases [30] provides both the proper minimum and maximum data buffer allocation for optimal direct processing performance.

18.11.8   Optimal Index Buffer Allocation: DIR Processing

For direct processing, VSAM performs a vertical (top-down) search of the index component, starting with the single highest level index set record and (assuming a typical multilevel index structure) following the vertical index pointers to ISRs at each successively lower level of the index set, until the sequence set is reached, at which point the appropriate SSR will point to the target data CI. This 'threading' through the index will require retrieval of one ISR from each level of the index set and one additional retrieval of an SSR, so that the total number of records retrieved from the index for any single direct request is the same as the number of levels of the index, and this is the factor LEVELS, which is given directly as a field within the STATIS-TICS group of LISTCAT output.

Now, if we allocated only as many index buffers as are threaded through for a single direct request, and this is equivalent to the factor LEVELS, then this would only assure that there is one *index buffer per index level*. Thus, for a three level index, three index records would be retrieved, two ISRs and one SSR. Generalizing to the multistring environment, the minimal allocation would be:

$$BUFNI = (LEVELS - 1) + STRNO \qquad (DIR) \qquad [31Mn]$$

In the single string environment (STRNO = 1), this would yield: BUFNI equal to LEVELS.

In the multistring environment, given that sequence set buffers are string-exclusive, one SSR would be required per string, and that is accounted for by the factor STRNO in [31Mn]; having thus accounted for the required sequence set buffers, 'LEVELS − 1' represents one index buffer per index set level (LEVELS includes the sequence set level and so we subtract this out, having already captured it in the factor STRNO). Note that 'LEVELS − 1' assures buffer storage for one ISR per index set level, and this buffer storage is shared communally by all strings: remember that ISR buffers are string-pooled, not string-exclusive.

Since there is one and only one index record at the highest level, the minimal specification of [31Mn] assures that this index record is always found in virtual storage, and hence buffer lookaside will avoid any physical I/O (DASD lookaside) for the one index record that must always be retrieved for any direct request (all vertical index searches, being strictly top-down, must fetch this highest level record) and this is obviously a performance advantage. But, as we shall soon see, we can do even better.

To understand how we may improve upon [31Mn], we must recognize the one absolutely critical objective for optimal, rather than minimal, index buffer allocation in direct processing:

Optimal Index Buffer Allocation.
To maximize direct processing performance, allocate index buffers sufficient to maintain the entire *index set* (all ISRs) of a data set's index component in virtual storage, along with one SSR per string.

This can be accomplished by:

$$BUFNI = ISRNO + STRNO \qquad [31Mx]$$

where the factor ISRNO represents the number of records in just the index set (that is, excluding the sequence set). Using [31Mx] would yield an index buffer *for each ISR* (not just an index buffer for each index *level*, as provided for by [31Mn]), so that the entire index set is in virtual storage, along with one SSR per string. This is most optimal in that it avoids any *intralevel contention* among ISRs. To appreciate what this means, assume we have a three-level index, so that there are two levels above the sequence set; there is one ISR at the highest index level, which we shall refer to as ISR1. Further assume that there are two ISRs at the next level (just above the sequence set), which we shall refer to as ISR2x and ISR2y:

level 1:		ISR1
level 2:	ISR2x	ISR2y

In a multistring environment, all direct requests by any string must retrieve ISR1. Now what of the index records at level 2? If we allocated according to [31Mn], rather than [31Mx], then there would be one ISR buffered in storage *per index level*; therefore, either ISR2x *or* ISR2y, *but not both*, would be resident in virtual storage. It may be that two different direct requests by two distinct strings have the following pattern of usage: string1, by virtue of the key value of the target record, requires (in addition to ISR1, which everyone requires) ISR2x, but string2 requires ISR2y (the other second level ISR).

Now if we have allocated according to [31Mn], then there would be only two buffers for ISRs, one buffer for the highest level ISR (ISR1), and the other for storing *one* of the multiple records at level 2 (the rest of the buffers, represented by STRNO, are all sequence set buffers). Say that VSAM begins by maintaining ISR2x in buffer storage, in the single level 2 buffer. String1 benefits immediately, as buffer lookaside will locate ISR2x, and thus avoid physical I/O associated with DASD lookaside. But the single level 2 buffer, being an ISR buffer, is string-pooled (as are all ISR buffers), so that if string2 requires, by virtue of the key value of its target record, ISR2y, then the level 2 buffer must be cleared of ISR2x in order to accommodate the transferring into virtual storage of ISR2y; since ISR2y was not resident, a DASD lookaside is required, entailing physical I/O overhead for string2's direct request.

This, then, is intralevel contention among index records for the limited resource of an ISR buffer, forced on us by [31Mn], which allocates only one index set buffer per index level above the sequence set. A simple solution for the example under discussion suggests itself. We can avoid the intralevel contention, and the consequent performance loss due to forced DASD lookaside, by allocating as many ISR buffers for each index level (above the sequence set) as there are ISRs at that level. For level 1, there is always a single index record; for level 2 of our example, there are two ISRs (this is not necessarily so), and so we should allocate a total of three ISR buffers, one to hold ISR1, and the other two to hold concurrently in buffer storage all (in this case, both) ISRs at the second and last level of the index set. This would maintain ISR1,

ISR2x, and ISR2y concurrently in virtual storage, so that no physical I/O would need to be performed for any ISR. Then, since SSR buffers are string-exclusive, we add to this allocation one sequence set buffer per string (the factor STRNO assures this), so that for the index component the only physical I/O operation that would be required would be for SSRs. This is the logic behind [31Mx] for optimal direct processing index buffer allocation.

It might seem that the factor STRNO in [31Mx] would assure that no physical I/O need be performed even at the sequence set level, but this is not the case. Consider our example a bit further and assume that there are only two active strings concurrently processing against the data set. Since ISRNO is equal to three (we are assuming a three level index with ISR1 at the top, and ISR2x and ISR2y at the second level) and STRNO equal to two, then BUFNI would be five. Thus, three buffers hold (all) three ISRs, while two will hold string-specific SSRs.

Now consider a direct request by string1 that requires some SSRi and another direct request by string2 that requires SSRj. Neither string will incur any DASD lookaside overhead when threading, top-down, through the index set, as all ISRs are resident (the factor ISRNO in [31Mx] provides for this). Then string1's single SSR buffer contains SSRi and string2's single SSR buffer contains SSRj. If VSAM receives another direct string1 request, which by virtue of the target key value, requires some SSR other than SSRi, say SSRk, then DASD lookaside must be performed to transfer that SSRk into virtual storage, where it will overwrite SSRi: each string only has a single buffer for holding SSRs, serially (one at a time).

Such physical I/O would be required even if the SSR required by this second string1 request is SSRj, currently being held in string2's SSR buffer: as noted earlier (Subsection 18.11.4), for SSR (and data CI) buffers, VSAM will perform only string-specific lookaside in virtual storage. SSRj is held exclusively for string2 in string2's SSR buffer and can not be reused by any other string, even though some other string may require precisely that SSR. For the string1 request, VSAM will do a string-specific lookaside into string1's SSR buffer to see if the required SSRj is already resident, but as it is not (SSRi occupies the single SSR buffer associated with string1), another copy of SSRj must be brought into buffer storage to satisfy string1's request, even though a copy of SSRj—inaccessible to string1—exists in string2's SSR buffer.

Generalizing, there are typically relatively many SSRs (one per data CA of the data set), compared to relatively few ISRs. In the example we used in earlier sections of this chapter, where we computed 71 data-containing CAs to the data set being discussed there, there would be 71 SSRs, and one ISR, as the LISTCAT output of Figure 18-5 confirms: the REC-TOTAL field under the STATISTICS group for the index component is given as 72, and we know from computation of Step 7 of Subsection 18.10.1 that DATA-CA is equal to 71; furthermore in the STATISTICS group LEVELS field, LEVELS is reported as two, and since there is always one index record at the highest level of an index, we know there are 71 SSRs, and one ISR, so that ISRNO here equals one.

With a two level index, the derivation of the factor ISRNO in [31Mx] was relatively straightforward, but what of an index with three or more levels, where we do not know directly how many records there are at the intermediate (not highest, and not lowest) levels. There are two approaches to this. The first is to compute the factor DATA-CA, the number of data-containing CAs to the data set, which can be done through the seven-step procedure presented in Subsection 18.10.1, where Formula [18] (in the seventh step) finally computes DATA-CA. Since there is one SSR per data CA, DATA-CA also represents the number of SSR in the index. LISTCAT output (the REC-TOTAL field for the index component) then gives us the total number of index records (those in the index set plus those in the sequence set). ISRNO can then be computed as follows:

$$\text{ISRNO} = \text{REC-TOTAL [for index]} - \text{DATA-CA} \qquad [32]$$

and for our example, this gives ISRNO equal to $72 - 71$, equalling 1 ISR.

A second approach derives DATA-CA from the factors HURBA, CISZ, and CIDEN, all given in LISTCAT output (and all also computable by the computations of this chapter), using Formula [26] of Subsection 18.10.3, and then applies [31] above. *Note in particular* that this approach uses the *data HURBA* value (HURBA for the data component), *not* the index HURBA. (Although a derivation of ISRNO, and more directly, BUFNI, is possible using the index HURBA, we do not recommend it, as it requires subtle adjustments for imbedded and/or replicated indexes.)

By way of an example, consider a very large KSDS of 800 cylinders as the primary allocation, all data-containing, and with a CASZ of one cylinder. (We are making some extensive simplifying assumptions for the sake of discussion.) This large a data set would typically require a three-level index: there would be 800 data CAs to the data set, which means 800 sequence set records. Assuming an index CISZ of even 4K, the index would typically require two index set records at the level (level 2) just above the sequence set (very roughly, each 4K sequence set record could contain sufficient pointers to index up to 502 CAs (see the VSAM fast approximation of Table 18-1, so two level 2 index set records would be required to contain pointers to 800 SSRs), so a third level (level 1) would be required, as the highest level of the index must contain only one index record. In this case, therefore, ISRNO equals three. It is relatively rare to obtain an index of more than three levels, and exceedingly rare to have any case in which the number of index set records (ISRNO) exceeds 10 to 20. Thus, the virtual storage commitment to accommodate the factor ISRNO in formula [31Mx] is relatively modest, while the performance benefit can be extremely dramatic in terms of direct processing improvement (over more conservative index buffer allocations, and certainly over the generally woefully inadequate minimal VSAM default).

18.11.9 Optimal Buffer Allocation: Mixed Processing

Since index buffers in sequential processing and data buffers in direct processing are not critical performance determinants, then when dealing with mixed mode processing (sequential and direct), where neither type of processing activity clearly dominates the other, it is best to optimize data buffers for sequential and index buffers for direct processing. Therefore, the key formulas for optimal buffer allocation in such cases would be:

$$BUFND = (2n \times CI\text{-}TRK) + STRNO \qquad\qquad [28Mx]$$

and

$$BUFNI = ISRNO + STRNO \qquad\qquad [31Mx]$$

Again, it would be wise to monitor performance statistics closely to avoid any performance degradation that may occur from excess allocation.

18.11.10   Optimal Buffer Allocation: A Summary

Table 18-3 summarizes the guidelines we have developed and discussed above for optimization of VSAM buffer allocation. For SEQ processing, BUFND should generally be determined by [28Mx], with $n = 1$; this can be increased by setting $n = 2$, then $n = 3$, etc., monitoring performance for any diminishing returns, in no case allowing

Table 18-3. Summary of optimal buffer allocation.

```
                 OPTIMAL BUFFER ALLOCATION


  OPTIMAL DATA BUFFER ALLOCATION: SEQ PROCESSING


     [28Mn]     BUFND  =  STRNO  +  1
     [28Mx]     BUFND  =  (2n  x  CI-TRK)  +  STRNO


  OPTIMAL INDEX BUFFER ALLOCATION: SEQ PROCESSING


     [29]       BUFNI  =  STRNO


  OPTIMAL DATA BUFFER ALLOCATION: DIR PROCESSING


     [30]       BUFND  =  STRNO  +  1


  OPTIMAL INDEX BUFFER ALLOCATION: DIR PROCESSING


     [31Mn]     BUFNI  =  (LEVELS  -  1)  +  STRNO
     [31Mx]     BUFNI  =  ISRNO  +  STRNO


  OPTIMAL BUFFER ALLOCATION:  MIXED PROCESSING


     [28Mx]     BUFND  =  (2n  x  CI-TRK)  +  STRNO
     [31Mx]     BUFNI  =  ISRNO  +  STRNO
```

BUFND to exceed 50 to 60 buffers. Typically, however, [28Mx] should provide quite high optimization in standard processing environments. In the on-line environment, it may be prudent to begin with the more conservative [28Mn], bearing in mind the considerations discussed earlier in this connection. BUFNI is determined simply by [29] for sequential processing.

For direct processing, [30] should be used to determine BUFND. For the highest VSAM optimization in direct processing, including in the on-line environment, BUFNI should be determined by [31Mx]. (Only if virtual storage is under severe constraints in an environment should retreat to [31Mn] be considered, and this should happen rarely, given typically systems environments with MVS/XA or ESA.)

Finally, for mixed (SEQ + DIR) processing, BUFND and BUFNI should be determined by [28Mx] and [31Mx], respectively.

18.11.11 Optimal Buffer Allocation: Some Final Points

Optimal data and index buffer allocation for VSAM data sets, following the guidelines presented above, can yield exceptionally high VSAM performance optimization in both batch and on-line environments. As we have seen, the VSAM default allocations are not optimal and the programmer should always specify BUFND and BUFNI explicitly to override the defaults. Of all tuning techniques, optimal VSAM buffer allocation often provides the most impressive processing performance benefits, and is well worth the effort of following the computations and guidelines given in this section.

There are two special cases that need be noted. First, in dealing with ESDSs and RRDSs, only the data buffer allocation guidelines need be attended to, as these clusters have no index component. Bear in mind that an ESDS is accessed typically in sequential mode, although it can be accessed in direct mode if one or more AIXes are built over it, while RRDSs support both sequential and direct processing, but random access activity is the more common against an RRDS.

Second, the newest cluster type, an LDS (Linear Data Set), does not follow the tuning guidelines of this section: for although an LDS must be *defined* to DFP/VSAM and must have its catalog entry in an ICF (not Enhanced VSAM) catalog, it is typically not *processed* by VSAM as an access method (how it is processed, and by whom, is the subject of a later section of this chapter) and standard VSAM performance tuning methodology is largely (almost wholly, but not completely) inappropriate for an LDS.

Finally, throughout this section we having been assuming, but have not made explicit, what is known as the VSAM *Non-Shared Resources* (*NSR*) environment. This does not entail that a VSAM data set is not shareable: it is, in terms of concurrent access to it by multiple strings. This is *data set sharing*. But, more specifically, I/O resources—which includes buffers, I/O-related control blocks, and *channel program areas* (*CPAs*, the storage for the channel programs themselves which actually perform the I/O operations)—can be shared *among multiple VSAM data sets*, and this is *I/O resource sharing*. We will look at I/O resource sharing later in this chapter, but note that the discussion so far has assumed that I/O resources of the sort just enumerated were always *data set-exclusive*, that is, assigned exclusively for the use of one specific VSAM data set (and thus for the possibly multiple string users of only that data set), and this is what is meant by the NSR environment.

18.12   VSAM DATA SET SHARING

VSAM provides extensive support for *sharing* facilities: allowing concurrent access to VSAM resources by multiple tasks. We will begin by discussing the VSAM facility known as *Non-Shared Resources* (*NSR*). Observe that this is unfortunate nomenclature: this facility fully supports *data set sharing* among multiple concurrent tasks, but *I/O buffers and I/O-related control blocks* are *not* pooled for *multiple* VSAM data sets; that is, NSR permits a *single* VSAM data set to support multiple concurrent access. A different facility, known as the *Shared Resources Facility* (*SRF*), handles the case of multiple VSAM data sets sharing a common set of I/O resources (buffers and certain control blocks). Thus, NSR deals with *multiple tasks* sharing a single VSAM data set, while SRF deals with *multiple VSAM data sets* sharing certain common I/O resources. (SRF comes in two distinct forms: *Local Shared Resources* (*LSR*) and *Global Shared Resources* (*GSR*); we take up LSR and GSR later in this chapter.)

18.12.1   Sharing Objectives

The primary objective of the sharing facilities of NSR is optimization of resource usage by allowing concurrent access by multiple tasks to the data set, avoiding the time delays that would be consequent to serializing (queueing up) tasks one at a time for access to a VSAM data set; it is this objective that allows for *multistring operation*, typical of an on-line (CICS, for example) environment (the reader may wish to briefly review here the discussion under 'Understanding Strings' earlier in this chapter, in Subsection 18.11.4). SRF adds an additional primary objective, that of conserving virtual storage by pooling certain I/O resources among multiple data sets, avoiding the overhead of assigning distinct I/O resources to each VSAM data set. Both NSR and SRF seek to optimize execution time by allowing a high degree of concurrency of access to resources.

18.12.2   The Issue of Read and/or Write Integrity

The issue of *data* (or resource) *integrity* always arises in any environment supporting shared facilities, where a fundamental goal under multiple concurrent access to a resource is to preserve as high a degree of integrity as possible or feasible under the known processing circumstances. We can best appreciate what is captured by the concept of integrity by considering the two distinct types of integrity possible, that of *write integrity* and *read integrity*.

A resource is said to have write integrity if and only if it is not possible for more than one user to engage the resource in an output operation (write operation, including update as a special case) at one time; that is, only one *write-user* (*W-user*) at a time is permitted against the resource. If multiple concurrent W-users were permitted to the same resource at the same time, then a set of write operations representing updates to the resource by one user may be interrupted before completion by the write operations of one or more other users, which may leave the resource in a *corrupted state*, not accurately reflecting the final state the resource would have had if the sets of changes to the resource by each user had been strictly serialized. Loss of data integrity of this sort—write integrity loss—is always a possible hazard with multiple concurrent W-users, and it is often the case that such loss must be guarded against, especially for certain critical/sensitive data sets.

Note that, in discussing issues of integrity, as above, we must address the question of what will be the *granularity of the integrity*, that is, at what level is the integrity to operate: at the (full) data set level, or the CI level, or the record level, or possibly even at the field (within a record) level. When the resource is a VSAM data set, the granularity of integrity is typically (but not always) at the CI level. Data set level integrity is generally too broad, as it would lock out W-users from updating a data set already engaged in update mode by an earlier, but still in progress, W-user, when in actual fact the multiple users may require access to wholly different CIs from one another, in which case there is no possible loss of integrity. Since VSAM fetches one CI at a time for any processing request, the CI is the most appropriate level for integrity operation. Since VSAM cannot, in general, anticipate which, and how many, records of a CI may be accessed in any batch of output/update operations, record level granularity is too fine, and field level granularity is typically available only when using a database management system, not just an access method like VSAM (although many DB2 files, for example, are implemented as specialized VSAM files). Thus, in the ensuing discussion, unless we say otherwise, we will assume CI-level granularity.

A resource is said to have read integrity if and only if it is not possible for one or more *read-users* (*R-users*)—that is, users not attempting any output operation against the resource—to be accessing the resource concurrently with any W-user. If at least one R-user were to access the resource concurrently with a W-user, then if the set of changes being applied by the W-users were not wholly complete ('update-in-progress') at the time the R-user issues a retrieval request (we are assuming, remember, that the same CI is being accessed), then we have a loss of read integrity, in that the R-user may obtain what is termed *backlevel* information: information that does not reflect the most current and/or most accurate state of the resource. In such a case, the R-user may obtain, when retrieval is concurrent with an update-in-progress operation, information different from what would have been returned after completion of the entire update operation, and so read integrity is lost.

A mechanism to assure read integrity would be to allow multiple R-users concurrent access to the resource (R-users are not changing the resource so no integrity is lost by multiple concurrent read operations) *or* a single W-user access to the resource, thus prohibiting *concurrent* read and write operations to the same resource. Note that this mechanism would also assure write integrity by virtue of the fact that only one W-user is supported at any one time against the resource.

Thus, we can distinguish different degrees of data integrity, from strongest to weakest, as follows:

1. Full read and write integrity (R/W-integrity).
2. Write-only integrity (W-integrity).
3. No read or write integrity.

Each application must decide what degree of integrity against a VSAM resource is required. For some applications against especially critical and/or sensitive resources, full R/W-integrity may be required; some applications against less critical/sensitive resources may be satisfied with W-integrity only, or in certain cases with no integrity at all. Furthermore, there may be any division of labor between the user and VSAM in providing integrity: VSAM can provide any of the degrees of integrity distinguished above (there are special problems in a cross-system (multiple processor) environment, which we will consider later), or the user may take on the quite serious and demanding responsibility of providing the integrity mechanism, shared, either wholly or in part, with VSAM-provided mechanisms. Our discussion will be essentially restricted to VSAM-provided mechanisms, possibly supplemented by MVS mechanisms in certain cases; user-provided coding for various integrity schemes is beyond the scope of this text.

18.12.3   The SHAREOPTIONS Parameter

At DEFINE-time for a VSAM cluster, a user may specify to VSAM the degree of integrity to be assured for that data set, through the *SHAREOPTIONS* (abbreviation: *SHR*) parameter on the DEFINE command for a CLUSTER, an AIX, or a UCAT (the SHR parameter is also ALTERable, that is, specifiable on the ALTER command). The form of this parameter is:

SHR (xregion xsystem)

where the first subparameter, *xregion*, defines the degree of integrity for *cross-region* sharing of a VSAM data set, while the second subparameter, *xsystem*, defines the degree of integrity for *cross-system* sharing of a VSAM data set. The meaning, and coding, of each of these types of sharing—cross-region and cross-system—is taken up in separate sections below, along with some performance considerations.

18.12.4   Cross-Region Sharing

Cross-region sharing refers to the sharing of a VSAM resource across multiple *address spaces* (this is the correct term in MVS systems; the SHR parameter still uses the older term 'region,' a holdover from non-MVS systems). In MVS, one address space represents the block of virtual storage dedicated to a single MVS user, where the user may be a batch or logged-on interactive (TSO or TSO/E, typically) user, or what is termed a *system-type* user. A system-type user in MVS includes an application subsystem of MVS like CICS, with a single CICS system running in one MVS address space (in the subarea of an address space known as the *Private Area*), or a system component such as JES (either JES2 or JES3), which is, in current MVS systems, resident in its own dedicated address space. The size of this block of virtual storage varies with the three major versions of MVS presently supported: MVS/SP Version 1 (pre-XA, sometimes referred to as 'MVS/370'), MVS/SP Version 2 (alias MVS/XA), and MVS/SP Version 3 (alias MVS/ESA: Enterprise Systems Architecture), the supported address space sizes being:

MVS/SP V. 1:	16M
MVS/SP V. 2 (MVS/XA):	2G
MVS/SP V. 3 (MVS/ESA):	2G

where 16M equals 16 Megabytes (million-bytes) and 2G is equal to 2 Gigabytes (billion-bytes)

(the exact numbers do not concern us here). With ESA, the size of an individual address space is still, like MVS/XA, 2G (both systems use 31-bit addressing schemes), but ESA permits *multiple address spaces per user* (unlike MVS/SP V.1 and V.2, each having the restriction of *one address space per user*, or two at most under Cross Memory Services), the theoretical limit being 8000 address spaces per user, yielding — since each address space is still, at most, 2G in size — a virtual storage capacity per user of (potentially) 16,000G (16 thousand billion-bytes) or, expressed equivalently *16T*, that is, 16 *Terabytes* ('tera' for a thousand billion (formerly often called a 'trillion')).

Now, it is critical to note that all tasks within a single CICS system (really, address space) collectively are part of one address space, considered by MVS to be a single (system-type) user: it is *not* the case that each on-line (CICS) task is associated with a distinct address space; CICS tasks (within one CICS system) are *intra-address space* units of work. MVS sees a CICS system as a (large and complex) set of problem programs, typically as VTAM application programs, running within the Private Area of an address space. A single MVS system, running on a single processor complex (3084Q, or a Sierra like the 3090-600, etc.) may support multiple distinct CICS systems, each running in a distinct address space: this is the CICS *MRO (Multi-region operation)* facility. Each such CICS 'region' constitutes one system-type user to MVS.

Now let's return to cross-region sharing of VSAM data sets and connect it to the above discussion of MVS users. A VSAM data set may be shared cross-region, that is, among the multiple users of a single MVS system, where such users are represented by individual address spaces. Any number of batch and interactive (TSO) users (within one MVS system) can share a VSAM data set configured to that system. Furthermore, these users can share the data set with any of the CICS tasks in one or more CICS 'regions' within the same system (and therefore on the same processor complex), since the CICS tasks running in any CICS address space are considered collectively to constitute one user.

There are two important points to take especial note of here. First, the xregion subparameter of the SHR parameter affects only the sharing of a VSAM data set in a cross-region (that is, *interregion*) environment: it has nothing to do with *intraregion* access, that is, access to the data set by multiple tasks *within one address space*. In particular, if any CICS task within one CICS region has access to the data set, then all have concurrent access to the data set (unless a CICS-specific mechanisms imposes some restriction on concurrent access), and this is unaffected by the coding of the SHR parameter for that VSAM data set. Second, xregion pertains strictly to a single operating system on a single processor complex: it has nothing to do with sharing that is cross-system (xsystem), that is, between users on different systems and processor complexes; that is determined by the second subparameter of SHR, namely xsystem, which will be discussed in the next subsection.

There are four possible values of the xregion subparameter:

SHR (1/2/3/4 xsystem)

which we take up, in turn, immediately below.

SHR (1 xsystem).   This cross-region specification (on a DEF CLUSTER command) indicates to VSAM to provide full read *and* write integrity for the data set being defined. VSAM implements this by allowing multiple R-users (read-users) concurrent access to the resource (R-users, by definition, do not change the resource, so no integrity is lost by multiple concurrent read operations) *or* allowing a single W-user (write-user) access to the resource, thus prohibiting *concurrent* read and write operations to the same resource. And as observed in Subsection 18.12.2 above, this mechanism would also assure write integrity by virtue of the fact that only one W-user is supported at any one time against the resource. This is the strongest degree of data integrity that can be provided by VSAM for a data set within one system, and requires the most restrictive mechanisms for its implementation.

SHR (2 xsystem).   This cross-region specification indicates to VSAM to provide write integrity only for the data set being defined. No read integrity whatever is provided, the result being that an R-user might obtain backlevel information. VSAM implements this second strongest degree of integrity by permitting only one write-user (W-user) at a time against the resource *and* any number of concurrent R-users (concurrent to each other and possibly concurrent with the single permissible W-user). Although any R-user might obtain backlevel information (read integrity loss), there is no problem with write integrity since multiple concurrent update access is prohibited.

SHR (3 xsystem).   This specification of the cross-region SHR parameter results in VSAM providing *no read or write integrity* whatsoever: no concurrent access restrictions are implemented by VSAM. There is therefore strict user responsibility for data integrity (if any is implemented by the user at all). However, VSAM does provide some *limited integrity assistance*; the nature and implications of this will be discussed in the next subsection (18.12.5) in connection with the comparable cross-system specification (SHR (xregion 3)).

SHR (4 xsystem). Like the SHR (3 xsystem) specification, this coding of the SHR parameter assures *no read or write integrity* whatsoever, and any type of multiple concurrent access (read and/or write access, including update) to the data set is permitted. Again, it is the user's sole responsibility to provide any data integrity that might be required. Here too, as in SHR (3 xsystem), VSAM does provide some limited integrity assistance, but in both cases such assistance is not, on its own, sufficient to assure read or write integrity; we will discuss this further in Subsection 18.12.5 when examining the comparable cross-system specification (SHR (xregion 4)).

18.12.5 Cross-System Sharing

In the cross-system environment—multiple distinct operating systems on distinct processor complexes (often, more loosely referred to as the cross-processor or cross-cpu environment)—VSAM permits only two SHR parameter specifications:

SHR (xregion 3)
SHR (xregion 4)

which, like the cross-region specifications of SHR (3 xsystem) and SHR (4 xsystem), do not provide any read or write integrity whatever for a VSAM data set being shared among the multiple systems (the VSAM data set must reside on *shared DASD* configured to each of the multiple systems).

SHR (xregion 3). This specification places no concurrent access restrictions on the VSAM data set being shared cross-system; given this, concurrent update against the same resource by two (or more) different tasks in two (or more) systems (on different processor complexes) may cause a data integrity exposure. The sole responsibility for integrity assurance resides with the user. VSAM provides limited integrity assistance, but on its own such assistance is insufficient for read or write integrity assurance. Whenever an xsystem=3 option is specified in a *no-integrity* condition, which holds whenever neither SHR (1 xsystem) or SHR (2 xsystem) has been specified, these being the only specifications providing any integrity assurance at all (that is, we have a SHR (3 3) or SHR (4 3) specification), then VSAM, as part of its limited integrity assistance, implements the *CBUF (Control Block Update Facility)*, described immediately below. The SHR (xregion 4) case will be considered below.

CBUF (Control Block Update Facility).   VSAM implements CBUF in two cases only:

SHR (3 3)
SHR (4 3)

Under this facility, certain critical VSAM control blocks for a shared VSAM data set are maintained by VSAM Record Management routines in an area of the MVS address space known as the *CSA (Common Service Area)*; the CSA, which contains control blocks, queues, and other control storage (but contains no executable routines) is itself part of the MVS *Common Area* portion of an address space, where the Common Area, and everything in it (which includes the CSA) is common to all MVS address spaces within a single MVS system, that is, it is shared by all MVS users. MVS 'maps' the Common Area and the *System Area* (which contains the MVS nucleus) into every user's address space; only the third (and last) area of an MVS address space, namely the Private Area, is truly 'private,' each user having a dedicated and distinct Private Area, separate from the Private Area of any other user. The critical VSAM control blocks for a shared VSAM data set are stored into the CSA by VSAM under CBUF, and are therefore accessible to each address space sharing the data set.

What this entails is that accurate VSAM control block information for a shared VSAM data set is available to all MVS users sharing access to that data set, *but if and only if* a strict user-provided serialization protocol is implemented by each such user (serialization protocols are most commonly and directly implemented by ENQ, DEQ, and possibly RESERVE macros, which can serialize access to a resource in order to control and restrict concurrent access by multiple users). The maintenance of correct critical VSAM control blocks in the CSA, under CBUF, therefore assists the user in providing some integrity through user-implemented serialization protocols. Nonetheless, this VSAM integrity assistance through CBUF should not be misconstrued as itself assuring any degree of integrity: data integrity of any form, if any, must be assured by user-provided mechanisms, so that the responsibility for integrity assurance still, and once again, rests with the user, not VSAM. Furthermore, no cross-system integrity of any form is provided.

We earlier said that both SHR (3 3) and SHR (4 3) specifications cause VSAM to automatically provide CBUF as partial integrity assistance. The two cases are distinguished by the fact that, with SHR (3 3), absolutely no further VSAM integrity assistance whatever (other than CBUF) is provided, while with SHR (4 3) VSAM provides additional VSAM integrity assistance of a type different from CBUF: this additional integrity assistance comes in two forms: (1) *special VSAM buffer management strategies*, and (2) *VSAM processing restrictions*. These strategies for VSAM limited-integrity assistance are an artifact of the xregion=4 or xsystem=4 SHR specification, so they are more appropriately discussed in the subsection immediately below.

(SHR (xregion 4).   This specification also implements no concurrent access restrictions on cross-system shared VSAM data sets, so that neither read nor write integrity is assured by VSAM. The sole responsibility for integrity assurance again resides with the user. Although VSAM provides limited integrity assistance of the types referred to above, namely buffer strategy assistance, and VSAM processing restrictions, these too, on their own, are not sufficient for read or write integrity assurance without a user-provided serialization protocol.

VSAM Buffer Strategy Assistance.   One type of integrity assistance VSAM provides to xsystem=4 VSAM data sets (whether xregion=3 or xregion=4) is in the form of special buffer management strategies. There are two key strategies provided by VSAM in this connection; which will be discussed immediately following.

1. *Forced DASD write*. All *direct* WRITEs are snapped out, that is, immediately written out to DASD rather than being *deferred* (which is the normal strategy for output buffers when xsystem=4 is not in effect).

2. *Buffer invalidation and buffer refresh*. All data and *sequence set* (not index set) buffers are marked by VSAM as *invalid* immediately after a *direct access* (not sequential access) DASD I/O operation. This *buffer invalidation* by VSAM signifies that the buffer in virtual storage so marked *cannot* be used to satisfy any subsequent direct access I/O request for the CI that the buffer contains. This forces VSAM to obtain a fresh (new) copy of the requested CI from DASD, rather than reusing the old, and possibly backlevel, copy of the CI available in the virtual storage buffer. This operation, which is forced consequent to buffer invalidation, is (appropriately) known as *buffer refresh*. Any buffer marked invalid must be refreshed from DASD and not reused to satisfy other direct requests. This disables virtual storage lookaside and forces DASD lookaside for direct processing requests.

Forced DASD write, and buffer invalidation and refresh, are VSAM buffer management strategies intended to minimize the possibility of a CI in storage remaining ('aging') in virtual storage long enough for it to become out-of-date (backlevel) and, further, to minimize the opportunity for a write integrity exposure from multiple concurrent update users. However, although this is stronger VSAM integrity assistance than CBUF, it is still insufficient, on its own, for full read or write integrity assurance.

VSAM Processing Restrictions.   For the xsystem=4 specification (whether with xregion=3 or xregion=4), VSAM—in addition to the buffer management strategies discussed above—provides further limited integrity assistance in the form of special VSAM processing restrictions. The restrictions stem from an imposed VSAM prohibition against change to HURBA, HARBA, or HKRBA (HURBA and HARBA were discussed in detail earlier in the text, in Subsection 12.2.2, and HKRBA was discussed (along with HURBA and HARBA again) in Subsection 15.2.1). The implications of disallowing HURBA or HARBA to change under xsystem=4 are:

1. *No CA-splits* (KSDS).
2. *No new CAs can be added to (physical) EOF* (KSDS). This restriction essentially disallows new extents to be added to the data set (secondary extenting is thus prohibited). The restriction is consequent to the fact that, under xsystem=4, VSAM will not permit change to two critical control blocks which track data set extents and the range of RBAs associated with each such extent. (These control blocks are the EDB (Extent Definition Block) and the DEB (Data Extent Block), often collectively referred to as VSAM *extent descriptors*).
3. *No new CIs can be added at EOF* (ESDS and RRDS). This prohibits the data set from being extended past the current EOF (for ESDS and RRDS clusters only).

In addition, the prohibition of change to HKRBA entails:

4. *No split of the High-Key-CI (HKCI)* (KSDS). The CI which contains the highest key of a KSDS (the *High-key CI*, or *HKCI*) may not be split, as this is a split which, if allowed, would require an update of index entries (VSAM is disallowing splits that entail index entry update).
5. *No new CIs at logical EOF* (KSDS). A new CI may not be added after the CI which contains the cluster's highest key, as this would change the RBA of the highest key (the HKRBA, which VSAM will not permit to be changed under xsystem=4 restriction).

Again, severe as all of these processing restrictions are, and coupled with the buffer strategies discussed above, they are still insufficient for full read or write integrity unless supplemented by user-provided serialization protocol.

There is one additional case of SHR we must consider, the special case of SHR (4 3).

SHR (4 3): A Special Case.   Like any case of xsystem=3, whether xregion=3 or xregion=4, VSAM provides for the data set with SHR (4 3) specification the limited VSAM integrity assistance of CBUF, which we have already described above. In addition, VSAM also provides for buffer invalidation and buffer refresh (see discussion above) for all data and *all index buffers* (both sequence set and index set) buffers), rather than just for data and *sequence set* buffers, as provided under xsystem=4 (that is, for SHR (3 4) and SHR (4 4)). The combination of CBUF plus buffer invalidation and refresh for *all* buffers (data, sequence set, and index set) yields a very significant benefit: *for SHR (4 3), the VSAM processing restrictions* (discussed above for any xsystem=4 specification) *are removed*—CA-splits are permitted, as are CI-splits of the HKCI (High-key CI), but *only for DFP/VSAM* (not for Enhanced

VSAM) data sets (that is, those cataloged in an ICF catalog). But although processing is not restricted by VSAM in its attempt to provide limited integrity assistance (as it is in any case of an xsystem=4 specification), nonetheless SHR (4 3), like any xregion and xsystem specification of 3 or 4, is insufficient (without a user-implemented serialization protocol) to assure either full read or write integrity.

18.12.6 Summary of VSAM Limited Integrity Assistance

SHR specifications for a VSAM data set with:

```
xregion   =   3 or 4
xsystem   =   3 or 4
```

provide, as we have seen, no full read or write integrity: only a specification of xregion = 1 or 2 provides integrity:

```
SHR (1 xsystem):    Full read and write integrity
SHR (2 xsystem):    Write integrity only.
```

We have also seen that, despite the absence of integrity assurance, xregion = 3/4 and xsystem = 3/4 SHR specifications yield various forms of VSAM limited integrity *assistance* (not *assurance*). The form such limited VSAM integrity assistance takes is summarized below:

```
SHR (3 3):    CBUF
SHR (3 4):    1. VSAM buffer strategies
              2. VSAM processing restrictions
SHR (4 3):    1. VSAM buffer strategies
              2. CBUF
SHR (4 4):    1. VSAM buffer strategies
              2. VSAM processing restrictions
```

With this understood, we can now draw out the performance implications of VSAM SHAREOPTIONS.

18.12.7 Performance and VSAM SHAREOPTIONS

In terms of overhead required to provide VSAM's limited integrity assistance, performance is most compromised in the xsystem=4 case—that is, for SHR (3 4) and SHR (4 4)—as VSAM implements buffer strategies (invalidation and refresh) which entail increased DASD I/O by virtue of forcing DASD lookaside, as well as enforces special VSAM processing restrictions. Although these actions are taken to enhance integrity assistance to users attempting to implement serialization protocols, the overall effect on performance is typically negative, and it is still up to the user to assure any and all integrity that may be required in any processing circumstance; and the coding mechanisms for implementation of a user-provided serialization protocol may themselves add additional processing overhead.

Somewhat less performance degradation than the xsystem=4 case may be encountered with SHR (4 3), for although VSAM buffer strategies are still provided, the enforcement of processing restrictions is avoided; CBUF, a more efficient mechanism, is substituted. Still, the overhead of buffer invalidation and buffer refresh is not avoided. The most efficient of the cases supporting limited integrity assistance is that of SHR (3 3), as no buffer strategies are implemented and only CBUF is deployed. This admittedly provides better processing performance at the expense of less integrity assistance. However, it is important to bear in mind that none of the xregion=3/4 or xsystem=3/4 specifications assure full read or write integrity, which must still be user-provided through serialization protocol, so SHR (3 3) at least has the virtue of causing the least performance degradation.

Finally, what of SHR (1 xsystem) and SHR (2 xsystem), the only SHR specifications providing integrity? Maximal integrity is obtained through SHR (1 xsystem), as this assures both full read and write integrity; SHR (2 xsystem) obtains only write integrity. However, SHR (1 xsystem) may have a more adverse impact on performance than SHR (2 xsystem): the degree of concurrency against the VSAM resource is reduced significantly since multiple output/update operations are prohibited (to ensure write integrity), and all read-users *and* write-users are locked out if a single write-user has already engaged the resource in output/update mode (to ensure read integrity in addition to write integrity). This is a severe requirement and, for a highly volatile file, it may compromise performance dramatically in order to achieve its full data integrity objectives.

SHR (2 xsystem) will sacrifice read integrity but consequently allow a higher degree of processing concurrency against the resource, as only concurrent output/update operations are disallowed: an arbitrary number of read-users may engage the resource, concurrently with each other and/or concurrently with a single write-user. What has to be accepted is the possible integrity exposure that may result when R-users retrieve a copy of a CI that is in the process of being updated by a W-user, passing backlevel information to the R-users, since the W-user may write out to DASD the changes it has made to the CI while the R-users obtain noncurrent information from an 'aged' copy of the CI in virtual storage; each user, being a distinct string, will have a separate copy of the same CI, since under NSR data CIs are string-exclusive, not pooled. (If the application requires read integrity but wishes to avoid the system-wide restrictions of SHR (1 xsystem), then a serialization protocol may be implemented by the user for this purpose, quite typical in an on-line environment such as CICS.)

18.12.8   The Problem of Cross-System Integrity

The astute reader may have noted throughout these discussions that no SHR specification provided the slightest degree of cross-system integrity: the xsystem subparameter of SHR can only be 3 or 4, neither of which yields any integrity assurance (in the cross-region environment, read and/or write integrity is easily obtainable with a SHR (1/2 xsystem) specification). This is often not appreciated by programmers, especially in working within an on-line environment: neither the VSAM SHAREOPTIONS parameter, nor a supplementary user-provided ENQ/DEQ protocol provides protection against an integrity exposure when cross-system users engage the same resource concurrently.

Many programmers believe that, for instance, issuing a CICS ENQ for exclusive control of a resource immediately prior to update processing preserves full integrity during update until a DEQ releases the resource; although it is true that other write-users *within the same system (on the same processor complex)* are locked out during the 'ENQ/DEQ bracket,' write-users from a different system are not restricted in any way and may gain concurrent update access to the same resource, effecting an integrity exposure. Furthermore, it is often believed, again incorrectly, that disallowing both xregion and xsystem sharing by coding for exclusive control through the JCL DD statement DISP=OLD specification—note that VSAM SHAREOPTIONS have no effect unless DISP=SHR is coded by all users of the VSAM resource—will lock out other concurrent users; this is true in a single system environment, but even exclusive control through DISP=OLD has no effect whatever on blocking concurrent access to the resource by users from another system (we are assuming the resource resides on shared DASD configured to both systems).

The only protection from an integrity exposure in the cross-system environment is, without special facilities, a RESERVE macro being issued against the resource; however, this is a hardware device locking mechanism on the volume, not merely on the data set, and would lock out all cross-system users from access to any data set on the volume, not just the one for which integrity protection was required. (The RESERVE macro would have to be issued by an Assembler program, as COBOL in the batch and on-line environments does not support any serialization control directly.) Given the typical capacity of DASD volumes (3380s in general), this is often impractical in any real-time environment.

The question is, if cross-system integrity at the data set level is not available through VSAM SHAREOPTIONS or serialization macros, how can integrity exposures be avoided in such cross-systems environments, given how typical these environments are? The answer is, through implementation of the MVS facility known as *Global Resource Serialization (GRS)*.

Global Resource Serialization (GRS). This advanced MVS facility was first introduced with MVS/SP 1.3, and subsequently refined in MVS/XA and MVS/ESA and constitutes, when implemented, a functional extension of the ENQ/DEQ/RESERVE macro facility for resource serialization. Among the many resource control features of GRS, it provides for full data integrity in a cross-system environment at the *data set level* without requiring a hardware device lock against the entire volume on which the resource to be protected resides. This is said to be *fine granularity of the data integrity mechansim.* An extension to the standard ENQ/DEQ macros permits these same mechanisms to—for the first time—provide cross-system integrity for cross-system configured data sets.

The basic operation of GRS is, in its barest form, to first establish dedicated intersystem communication links between all systems which are to participate in GRS-based resource serialization. The dedicated *ISC link* (this should not be confused with the IMS and CICS intersystem communication (ISC) facility which employs advanced SNA (LU6.x) protocols under VTAM) may be one of two types of links: the older (and weaker) *integrated channel-to-channel (CTC) adapter*, or preferably, for better performance, flexibility, and reliability, the newer IBM *3088 Multisystem Channel Communication Unit* (*MCCU*). The multiple participating systems and their dedicated ISC links make up a *GRS complex* with various shared DASD resources. The systems active at any time and participating in cross-system resource serialization constitute the *GRS ring*.

GRS implements a conceptually simple ring-processing protocol for cross-system communication using a *Ring System Authority* (*RSA*) message which is 'spun' around the GRS ring and carries notification of requests for *global resources* (resources to be shared cross-system) to each system on the ring. The RSA message allows for one system on the ring to communicate its intent to access a cross-system shared resource to all systems on the ring so that access to the resource can be strictly serialized among the systems, disallowing concurrent cross-system access that might otherwise cause an integrity exposure. (The RSA message can be viewed as an 'in-flight' resource serialization mechanism.) The precise details of GRS are not of concern here. Suffice it to observe that, if a set of interconnected systems are configured into a GRS complex and implement the ring-processing protocol using the RSA message for cross-system communication, then data sets on shared DASD can be provided with full data integrity as an extension of the available ENQ/DEQ protocol for resource serialization. (GRS can even provide data integrity through resource serialization to non-data set resources, not residing on shared DASD, but this is not directly relevant to our concerns here.)

In such a case, VSAM SHAREOPTIONS plus an active GRS mechanism can provide any degree of data integrity, cross-region and cross-system. GRS is therefore highly recommended for any multisystem environment having high data integrity requirements for critical VSAM data sets that must be shared cross-system. A recent enhancement, available only if all of the systems of a GRS complex are running MVS/ESA, known as *ring acceleration*, provides a dramatic reduction in task wait time for access to a global resource. Thus it is possible to achieve high performance/high integrity assurance for shared resources in the cross-system environment, especially VSAM data sets. (GRS is available within MVS systems but must be activated and configured by the installation; it is optional but should be considered essential to any comprehensive data integrity scheme in complex cross-systems environments).

18.13   THE SHARED RESOURCE FACILITY (SRF): LSR AND GSR

As we noted earlier, VSAM provides extensive support for *sharing* facilities that allow concurrent access to VSAM resources by multiple tasks. Non-Shared Resources (NSR), described earlier, fully supports *data set sharing* among multiple concurrent tasks, but, again as noted, I/O buffers and I/O-related control blocks are *not* pooled for multiple VSAM data sets. NSR permits a *single* VSAM data set to support multiple concurrent access. A different facility, known as the *Shared Resources Facility (SRF)*, handles the case of multiple VSAM data sets sharing a common set of I/O resources (buffers and certain control blocks). Thus, NSR deals with *multiple tasks* (strings) sharing a single VSAM data set, while SRF deals with *multiple VSAM data sets* sharing *certain common I/O resources*, these including I/O buffers, I/O-related control blocks, and *channel program areas* (*CPAs*, the storage for the channel programs themselves which actually perform the I/O operations). I/O resources of the sort just enumerated were, under NSR, always *data set-exclusive*, that is, assigned exclusively for the use of one specific VSAM data set (and thus for the one or more users of only that data set).

The control blocks that can be shared by multiple VSAM data sets under SRF are two VSAM control blocks, the *PLH* (with which we are already acquainted) and the *IOMB* (Input Output Management Block), which is used as a 'gateway' to accessing certain MVS I/O control blocks, and four such MVS I/O control blocks themselves, namely the *IOSB* (Input Output Supervisor Block), the *IQE* (Interruption Queue Element), the *IRB* (Interrupt Response Block), and the *SRB* (Service Request Block). The many other I/O-related control blocks associated with VSAM data sets are *not* shared, as they provide unique data set-specific information needed for distinguishing distinct files from one another.

SRF's primary objective is that of conserving virtual storage by pooling certain I/O resources among multiple data sets, avoiding the overhead of assigning distinct I/O resources to each VSAM data set. (Remember, both NSR and SRF seek to optimize execution-time by allowing a high degree of concurrent access to VSAM and VSAM-related resources.) A reduction in virtual storage requirements may in turn reduce paging I/O (it yields a smaller *working set*, or pages required to be active) and thus real storage requirements; furthermore, the operation of SRF, as we will see shortly, is designed to minimize DASD I/O (and hence, additionally, channel utilization and contention). Properly used and controlled, SRF may provide highly optimal VSAM performance, especially for an on-line (CICS) environment. VSAM's SRF consists of two distinct forms: *Local Shared Resources (LSR)* and *Global Shared Resources (GSR)*. We turn to LSR immediately below, and then briefly discuss GSR.

18.13.1 Local Shared Resources (LSR)

Under LSR the I/O-related resources we identified above (basically, VSAM I/O buffers and certain I/O-related control blocks) are pooled among multiple VSAM data sets for shared access by requests (strings) *within one address space* ('region') *only*. Given that requests only from a single address space may concurrently access the shared resources, it is for that reason that we speak of *local* shared resources. Note further that there are two types of sharing going on: the resources are shared by multiple VSAM data sets, rather than being data set-exclusive, as under NSR; and the resources are shared by multiple concurrent user requests against these VSAM data sets within the same address space. This breaks with the convention that an I/O buffer, for example, is some one data set's resource, different data sets having wholly distinct sets of buffers associated with each of the different data sets. Now such a resource—a buffer—is *communal*, not data set-exclusive, and can hold in virtual storage a CI belonging to any one of several (pooled) data sets. If some buffer, BUFx, at one time holds a CI, CI1 from data set1, it may subsequently be cleared to hold some other CI2 from either the same data set, data set1, or some other data set, data set2, whichever is needed to satisfy the next retrieval request. Now let's discuss the how LSR effects its pooling of I/O resources among multiple data sets.

18.13.2   Basic Operation of LSR Pools

LSR provides its I/O resource sharing through the creation of one or more *VSAM Resource Pools* (*VRPs*) within an address space; we say that the user *builds* these VSAM Resource Pools, where for any one address space as many as 16 such pools can be built exclusively as *data VRPs* and another 16 exclusively as *index VRPs*; when we do not need to differentiate data from index resource pools, we will simply speak of an *LSR pool*. An LSR pool is simply the virtual storage allocated to hold the shared I/O resources (buffers and control blocks) for multiple VSAM data sets which are said to be *assigned* to the pool. Under LSR, the sharing of the I/O-related control blocks in one LSR pool among the multiple data sets assigned to that pool is always automatic, requiring no user implementation; I/O buffers, however, are not automatically shared and hence require explicit user implementation.

Building an LSR Pool.   Each LSR pool may have mutiple *subpools*: a subpool is simply a set of buffers of one size. Let's take an example to see how all of this is implemented. An LSR pool is built by issuing the *BLDVRP* (Build VSAM Resource Pool) macro (this is an Assembler VSAM macro, but certain subsystems, like CICS, cause the macro to be issued, rather than requiring user coding of the macro). For example, this partial coding:

```
BLDVRP      TYPE=(LSR,DATA),
            SHRPOOL=1,
            STRNO=n,
            RMODE31=ALL,
            BUFFERS=(1024(4),4096(3)),
               .
               .
```

builds a *VRP* to be shared by multiple *data* components of VSAM data sets. The LSR pool built is assigned an identification number (the SHRPOOL 'ID') of 1 (the SHRPOOL ID may be any of the 16 numbers, 0 through 15, but CICS currently uses only a maximum of 8 LSR pools, with IDs of 1 through 8) which permits explicit reference to precisely this LSR pool and no other. The STRNO parameter represents the anticipated degree of concurrent access (number of concurrent requests) against all data sets assigned to this pool; VSAM will allocate an equivalent number of PLHs to represent these concurrent requests. Note, however, that the PLHs are not assigned permanently—as would occur under NSR—to individual strings, or to individual data sets; they are a shared resource, shared among the strings (and *transiently* allocated as needed) accessing the multiple data sets assigned to the LSR pool. The value *n* of STRNO may be 1 through 255. The RMODE31=ALL specification instructs VSAM to allocate both the shared control blocks and the shared buffers of the pool in the extended virtual storage available under MVS/XA and ESA above the 16M boundary (a good choice in general).

Finally, the BUFFERS parameter indicates the number of subpools to be organized and allocated within the LSR pool, and how each subpool is to be constituted. Two subpools are to be allocated, the first subpool—let's call this SUBPL(1K)—to contain four buffers each 1K in size (this is the BUFSIZE), and the second subpool— SUBPL(4K)—to contain three 4K buffers. The operation of *LSR pool assigment*— how the LSR facility associates a data set assigned to the LSR pool with a particular subpool—occurs at OPEN time; the VSAM component's (whether data or index) CISZ determines subpool assignment, if any assignment is possible, and we say that LSR pool assignment is *CISZ-based*. The principle of LSR pool assignment is that a component with CISZx is assigned either (1) to the subpool whose BUFSIZE is equal to CISZx, if any such subpool exists, or (2) to the subpool with the next larger BUFSIZE (larger than CISZx). Thus, for our example, a data component assigned to the LSR pool whose SHRPOOL ID=1 and having a CISZ of 2K would be assigned to SUBPL(4K). A data component with a CISZ larger than the largest BUFSIZE of any subpool in the LSR pool (this would occur in our example for a data component with, for example, a CISZ=6K) would not be processible at all.

If the LSR facility is being used for VSAM resources under CICS, then starting with CICS 1.7, and higher releases (CICS/MVS 2.1, ...) the LSR facility is the default; previously, NSR was the default and had to be overridden if LSR was desired. We therefore restrict our attention to CICS 1.7 and higher releases. The CICS counterpart to the BLDVRP macro above would be the *DFHFCT TYPE*=SHRCTL macro:

```
DFHFCT     TYPE=SHRCTL,
           LSRPOOL=1,
           STRNO=n,
           BUFFERS=(1024(4),4096(3)),
             .
             .
```

The TYPE=SHRCTL on the above DFHFCT macro serves the same function as the TYPE=(LSR,...) parameter on the BLDVRP macro; note that the BLDVRP macro gives an additional explicit degree of control by allowing the specification of DATA or INDEX in order to segregate data from index buffers within the same LSR pool. The DFHFCT LSRPOOL=1 is the equivalent of the BLDVRP SHRPOOL=1 coding, and the STRNO and BUFFERS parameters are identical for both codings. Note that the DFHFCT macro has no counterpart to the BLDVRP RMODE31=ALL parameter: CICS releases 1.6.1 and higher all default LSR pools to above the 16M boundary, yielding the same results as the RMODE31=ALL coding.

Assigning Data Sets to LSR Pools.   The question now arises as to how a data set, or more specifically, a data set component, is assigned—not to a subpool but to a specific LSR pool—in the first place. The way VSAM handles this natively (that is, ultimately in Assembler programming using VSAM macros) is through the *ACB* (Access Method Control Block) macro; partial coding for this purpose is shown below:

```
ACB       AM=VSAM,
          MACRF=(LSR,...),
          SHRPOOL=1,
             .
             .
```

Thus the data set component associated with this ACB is assigned to the LSR pool whose ID=1. The equivalent coding in CICS is effected through the DFHFCT TYPE=DATASET macro:

```
DFHFCT    TYPE=DATASET,
          ACCMETH=VSAM,
          LSRPOOL=1,
             .
             .
```

Finally, in native VSAM (using Assembler VSAM macros), we can explicitly build an index VRP (at the time of this writing, CICS does not support such explicit index pool allocation):

```
BLDVRP    TYPE=(LSR,INDEX),
          SHRPOOL=1,
          BUFFERS=(512(16),1024(10),2048(6)),
             .
             .
```

This sets up an index LSR pool with three subpools (as coded on the BUFFERS parameter). STRNO and RMODE31 are taken from the previous BLDVRP TYPE=(DATA,...) macro coding for the pool with the same ID (SHRPOOL=1). Note that, although this builds an index LSR pool with the same SHRPOOL ID as the associated data LSR pool, these are *two* physically separate pools, but they are logically connected (by virtue of identical SHRPOOL=1 parameters): this index LSR pool is the LSR pool for the index components of the data sets whose data components are assigned to the data LSR pool with the same ID.

   As we noted earlier, such data and index component resource segregation into different LSR pools was not supported prior to DFP/VSAM 2.3. It is a high-optimization feature of the LSR facility, in that previously data and index buffers contended against each other, often to the detriment of performance: a highly volatile data set's data CIs may replace index records, especially index set records, in the pool's shared buffers; remember, buffers are neither data set-exclusive nor string-exclusive under LSR, and hence are reused by VSAM as necessary. VSAM, whenever it requires a buffer for CI storage under LSR, will follow an *LRU—least recently used—*algorithm for buffer reuse, and more active data CIs may 'chase out' less active index CIs from the pooled buffers. However, a subsystem may not support the building of separate data and index LSR pools; this is the case, at least at present, with CICS. The user must arrange for non-contention between data and index CIs for shared buffers; this is typically done by assuring that within any LSR pool, data component CISZs are different from index CISZs, thus forcing the data and index components to be assigned to different subpools within the LSR pool—remember, subpool assignment is strictly CISZ-based, so there is no direct buffer contention among components with different CISZs. (However, this is certainly an ad hoc solution and one not always easy to implement in complex cases.)

18.13.3   Performance Considerations with LSR

We now examine a number of performance issues to be considered in the LSR versus NSR environment, which should help the reader both to appreciate LSR at a deeper level, and to weigh the performance benefits of these two different types of sharing when pursuing high VSAM optimization.

Virtual Storage Optimization.   We have already noted (Section 18.13) LSR's primary objective of optimizing the use of virtual storage by sharing I/O resources among multiple data sets (and multiple strings against those data sets), with the consequent possibility that such virtual storage conservation will reduce paging I/O, and hence real storage requirements for the VSAM data sets participating in LSR. Note that another form of virtual storage optimization is effected under LSR: only one copy of any CI is held in an LSR pool; under NSR, there may be, and typically are, multiple copies of a CI in virtual storage, as each string concurrently accessing the data set is assigned its own (string-exclusive) copies of data and SSR CIs. Buffers (data, ISR or SSR) are not string-exclusive—and are not even data set-exclusive—under LSR, and so are used and reused for data and index CIs as needed (with buffer replacement, as noted above, occuring on an LRU basis). This is clearly more virtual storage-conservative than NSR. (Note also that the fact of a single copy of any CI in storage under LSR enhances read integrity.)

It should be remembered, however, that in an MVS/XA or ESA environment, virtual storage conservation is not as critical an objective as in non-XA systems, especially given the fact that LSR pools may (and typically are, as in CICS) allocated in extended storage (virtual storage in the 2G address space located above the 16M boundary).

Exhaustive Lookaside.   Under NSR, buffer lookaside *at the cross-string level* (see our previous discussion of string-specific versus cross-string lookaside in Subsection 18.11.4) occurs against index set records (ISRs) only: data and sequence set record (SSR) buffers are string-exclusive, so that even if VSAM requires the retrieval of a data or SSR CI to satisfy a request from some particular string, and that CI is already held in virtual storage in a buffer reserved for a different string, no buffer lookaside will occur (cross-string lookaside for data and SSR CIs being prohibited), and VSAM is forced to perform DASD I/O to retrieve another copy of the requested CI.

Under LSR, VSAM performs *exhaustive lookaside*: prior to retrieving *any* CI (data or index, that is, SSR or ISR), VSAM will perform buffer lookaside to determine whether the target CI is already held in some virtual storage buffer within the LSR subpool being used for the data set, regardless of for what string it may have been fetched; if there is a *lookaside hit* (the lookaside successfully locates a copy of the target CI in some subpool buffer), then VSAM reassigns (all assignments are transient, not permanent) the buffer holding the copy to the current request, and this   ids DASD I/O for retrieval. Thus lookaside occurs for data and SSR CIs as well as for (as under NSR) index set CIs, and given such extensive lookaside operations under LSR, reduction in DASD I/O can be quite dramatic, compared to that possible under the more restrictive lookaside of NSR.

Against this, however, bear in mind that if we implement optimal buffer allocation techniques (as detailed in Section 18.11), then we can avoid any DASD I/O for ISR CIs, and can, by selecting IMBED, retrieve with one DASD I/O operation both the SSR and the target data CI to which the SSR points; furthermore, with optimal buffer allocation for sequential processing, we enhance sequential retrieval performance by allowing buffer readahead. Under LSR, it is not possible by optimal buffer allocation to directly assure that all ISRs for a data set are held in virtual storage buffers (all I/O buffers are a shared, not an exclusive (string or data set) resource), and readahead is not performed by VSAM in any SRF (LSR or GSR) environment.

In addition, the exhaustive lookaside strategy of LSR encounters diminishing success with larger data sets and/or more volatile random activity against data sets: there is diminished likelihood of CIs already being held in buffer storage coincident with some specific retrieval request. And it may also be the case that the lookaside operation itself can potentially consume more processor cycles in such cases. This was a very serious concern with LSR until recently: more processor resources were typically needed for buffer management of a shared pool of resources, as opposed to such resources being pre-allocated to data sets at OPEN time under NSR, given less buffer search and reaccessing operations. However, the performance of buffer lookaside under LSR was optimized dramatically under DFP/VSAM Ver. 2 Rel. 3 and later releases: the exhaustive sequential search of buffers in an LSR pool has been replaced by a *hash buffer search* algorithm, a hash search being *nonexhaustive*, using some effective transformation to derive ('best-guess') buffer addresses from target key values (or equivalent representation of the to-be-retrieved record or CI). Without entering into the complex details, suffice it to say that a hash buffer search will require inspection of only a fraction of the total of all buffers in a pool in order to determine if the target CI is already held in storage, and this minimizes the processor cycle-cost of buffer lookaside, a lookaside hit being possible much faster than with the full sequential buffer search previously used by VSAM (where on an average half of the pooled buffers were inspected for a lookaside hit).

Given that buffer lookaside is, under LSR, attempted for all CIs, data and index, it is especially valuable to have a more optimal lookaside strategy, especially as LSR (not NSR) is now the default under a CICS 1.7 or higher environment. (This on its own does not assure that LSR will yield consistently better performance than NSR, but does serve to enhance LSR whenever it is enabled. The user should undertake a careful performance comparison of LSR versus NSR in the cases seen to be problematic for LSR: large data sets and/or highly volatile ones in terms of random activity; other problematic cases are further discussed below.) All in all, however, it is now no longer necessarily true—given the new hash buffer search strategy being employed with LSR—that LSR will consume more processor cycles for its basic operation, especially as it involves buffer lookaside, than would be needed under NSR; specifc cases would have to be determined by careful individual analysis. It is, however, still true by and large that it is harder to tune LSR for higher optimization than to tune NSR, as NSR allows very precise data set-specific tuning techniques which are not directly implementable in an LSR environment where I/O resources are shared among multiple data sets, and this should always be born in mind. (Certain performance options, however, benefit NSR and LSR: IMBED and REPLICATE are cases in point.)

Use-driven Buffer Management: the LRU Algorithm. As we noted earlier (Subsection 18.13.2), VSAM uses an LRU algorithm for buffer replacement under LSR: if a buffer needs to be reused, that buffer which contains the least recently referenced ('used') CI will be selected; this will favor more volatile files to acquire more buffers and also tend to retain high-reference index CIs in virtual storage. In this sense, LSR is frequently said to be 'self-tuning.' Against this, however, one must weigh the possibility that highly volatile files will dominate a subpool, possibly degrading performance for less active files assigned to the same subpool. Furthermore, there may be considerable counterproductive contention among many volatile files if these are assigned to the same subpool. Careful segregation and balancing of files either into different subpools by virtue of (forced) different CISZs, or into different LSR pools altogether, may alleviate this problem to some extent, under certain carefully controlled and tuned LSR environments. Given the choice, it is better to exploit distinct LSR pools, rather than different subpools within one LSR pool: CISZ choice is not a casual matter, as we have demonstrated earlier in this chapter, and should be made on the basis of the performance considerations we have already articulated, rather than chosen to simply effect subpool segregation of files by CISZ; this latter approach may, in seeking to avoid file contention within subpools, force a choice of CISZs (for purposes of segregation of files into different subpools) which are not optimal and may cause their own performance degradation.

Deferred DASD WRITE.   Under sequential processing, VSAM typically defers the writing out (to DASD) of an output buffer (contents generated by WRITEs) as long as possible in order to minimize I/O, but under direct processing, a *forced DASD WRITE* occurs after each direct WRITE request. This is effected through the ACB macro:

```
ACB   AM=VSAM,
      MACRF=(LSR,DFR),
      .
      .
```

No Readahead or Chained I/O Operations.   LSR does not support buffer readahead or the chaining of certain I/O buffer operations for enhanced sequential processing performance. High sequential activity against a file may, therefore, encounter a performance compromise under LSR (extra data buffers favor sequential browse and mass insertion operations in particular). Furthermore, the availability of extra data buffers under NSR can reduce the overhead of CA-split activity; without extra buffers, CA-split activity under LSR may incur higher performance degradation than under NSR (although, optimally, CA-split activity should be minimized by FSPC tuning for both NSR and LSR). Finally, sequential performance may be compromised by the shared nature of the PLH control block under LSR: since PLHs are not data set-exclusive, VSAM does not effect automatic *SOF (Start-of-File) positioning* with sequential operations against LSR files.

LSR Buffers in Hiperspace.   A recent performance enhancement to LSR is the option (on a BLDVRP macro) of building (allocating) the LSR buffers within any subpool in an ESA *hiperspace* (we will discuss hiperspaces later in this chapter); this *hiperspace buffering* serves to reduce DASD I/O operations through the use of *expanded storage* (see later in this chapter) as a very high speed cache; more on this later. Suffice it to say at this point that this facility may, along with the new hash buffer search (discussed earlier), provide dramatic improvement to LSR performance.

The Problem of Over-Serialization.   LSR serializes at the CI level to a much stricter degree than under NSR: (1) a READ forces potentially concurrent update requests to be enqueued until the READ completes (although multiple read-users are permitted), and (2) an update acquires the CI exclusively and locks out *both* other updates *and* read-users until the update completes; that is, LSR attempts to assure read *and* write integrity. In CICS, this may result in (1) higher WAITs against data sets in LSR pools when read and update activities are high, (2) deadlock under certain cases of concurrent browse and update activity by one transaction against the same file in an LSR pool (the browse should be explicitly ended before initiating the update in order to minimize the chance of deadlock in such cases), and (3) heavy browse activity against an LSR file may dominate an LSR pool (the browse will acquire more and more data buffers on an LRU basis), to the detriment of other data sets (and possibly of index components, if data and index component buffers have not been segregated into either separate subpools or separate LSR pools). The adverse effects under LSR of this *over-serialization* is independent of what SHAREOPTIONS are chosen (this having no effect on the multiple tasks *within* a CICS region).

Monitoring LSR Performance.   The complex details of fine-tuning LSR performance are beyond this discussion, but the user is strongly enjoined to monitor LSR performance statistics regularly and very carefully to assure that anticipated positive performance benefits which are possible under LSR are indeed being realized. Under CICS, the CICS shutdown statistics are especially valuable in this connection. (Best results in this environment are often seen for programs that engage a large number of data sets concurrently in their processing, especially if the files are not very large.) These statistics report the critical statistic: the number of lookaside hits (successful lookasides), a number which is expected to be high if LSR is really offering performance benefits over NSR in this area, as well as the total number of buffer READs, giving the user a direct measure of the proportion of buffer operations which avoided DASD I/O. The interested reader should consult the CICS *Performance Guide* for further performance issues specific to LSR under CICS.

18.13.4   Global Shared Resources (GSR)

GSR, as noted briefly earlier, supports the sharing of I/O-related resources among ('across') multiple MVS address spaces (it is 'global' in this sense), rather than solely within a single address space, as with LSR. The degree of sharing is seen to be much more extensive with GSR. GSR builds its shared resource pools (as well as certain other VSAM control blocks) in the Common Area of the address space (specifically within the subarea known as the CSA (Common Service Area)), as this is shared across all MVS address spaces and is thus accessible to all MVS users. However, this also entails a special privilege: to build and manipulate GSR pools, a program must be in supervisor state (not easy to come by) and have a privileged *storage protection key* (*SPK*) of 0 through 7 (16 SPKs are used in MVS, and 8 through F (hex) are all problem state modes for unauthorized programs). Given these very restrictive requirements, we do not discuss GSR further here. (The *VSAM Administration Guide* contains additional material on GSR.)

18.14   CACHE STORAGE CONTROLS

Cache is high-speed randomly accessible electronic storage for retaining frequently accessed instructions and/or data; it functions as a high-speed buffer into which information is pre-fetched, in order to severely reduce normal access time to the information. A CPU cache is typically used for pre-fetching instructions. We are concerned here not with a CPU cache but with a *storage control cache*, hereafter simply cache, which is configured within *storage control*: storage control is the DASD subsystem component connecting DASD and the (host) processor channels, managing the DASD devices and executing the channel commands. Cache of this sort, within storage control, functions to retain frequently referenced *data* for I/O response time reduction: high-reference data will often not need to be transferred from the channel to DASD or from DASD to the channel, as it can be much more rapidly retrieved from the cache internal to storage control (remember that cache within the storage control is intermediate between DASD and the processor channel(s)).

IBM presently implements cache storage control units in the form of the 3880 Model 21 (the cache is available only for paging, not application data), the 3880 Model 23 (for system and application data), and the most advanced such unit, the 3990 Model 3 (hereafter, 3990-3). As the latter is the most sophisticated cache storage control and offers enhanced performance benefits not available elsewhere, we will restrict our attention to the 3990-3. This unit supports cache sizes from a low (!) of 32M (mega—million—bytes) to a high of 256M.

The basic objective of cache is to minimize the mechanical motion components of I/O response time: SEEK, latency (both discussed earlier in this chapter, Section 18.7), and RPS (Rotational Position Sensing) reconnect time (time required, after the target record arrives under the actuator (read/write-head) to reconnect to any eligible path after finding none available; this entails a wait of one disk rotation before path retry). This is accomplished by maintaining a working set of high-reference data in the cache within storage control; continued reference to the data retains the data in cache so that subsequent reference to the cached data is satisfied at electronic storage speed without the SEEK, latency, and RPS reconnect time *mechanical delays*. (A 4K block of data may be transferred in as little as two milliseconds (or better) using cache storage controls.)

18.14.1   Basic Cache Operation

With the 3990-3, the storage control contains three components of interest to our discussion: (1) a directory which maintains entries for the data and its whereabouts within storage control, (2) cache, and (3) *NVS* (Nonvolatile Storage), which is high-speed randomly accessible electronic storage, like cache, but which is *battery-backed*, that is, with a battery power source to retain data during a power failure, for as long as 48 hours; upon restoration of power, storage control automatically 'destages' (retrieves and transfers) the data in NVS to DASD. NVS ensures a high degree of data integrity, as data lost from volatile memory by an adverse event can typically be retrieved from NVS during its 'retain period' (48 hours after power failure). This is shown in Figure 18-6.

A READ (a retrieve from DASD, transfer-to-channel, request) when using a cache storage control like the 3990-3, initiates a directory scan of storage control to determine if the target data is already being held in cache; if it is—a *read hit*—then

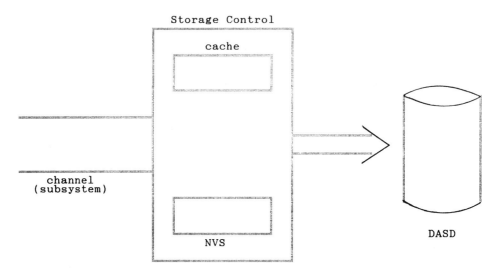

Figure 18-6. The 3990 Storage Control.

storage control forwards the data from the cache to the channel, this transfer being necessarily faster than retrieval (all the way) from DASD. A *read miss* (data not found in cache) forces storage control to *concurrently* (1) transfer the data from DASD to the channel, and (2) load the data (and data physically after it but on the same track) into cache (anticipating later access to this sequence of data), so that subsequent retrieval is optimized, as it will occur at cache transfer rates (faster than standard DASD-to-channel, or channel-to-DASD speeds). A WRITE effects the process in reverse: if the to-be-updated data is already cache-resident (a *write hit*), the data is transferred concurrently to both DASD and cache (to update the data in cache), allowing subsequent retrieval to be satisfied from cache, avoiding a DASD transfer; in a *write miss*, the data is simply written to DASD, and cache is not involved at all. Clearly, a READ with a cache storage control yields performance advantages over non-cached retrieval, as does a write hit; but a write miss (unlike a read miss) does not load the data into cache, so that no performance is gained in this case. The 3990-3 improves the WRITE situation to provide the same high performance of READ by offering two optimal WRITE operations different than normal WRITE (described above); these are *DASD fast write* and *cache fast write*.

DASD Fast Write and Cache Fast Write. DASD fast write is similar to the WRITE operation described above, with the difference that, under a write hit, the data is transferred concurrently to *both* cache and NVS, but only thereafter to DASD. This is a high performance strategy, as storage control will signal operation end when the cache/NVS transfer completes (at very high speed), so that the application may immediately continue to other work without, as traditionally would occur, having to wait for the slower DASD transfer to complete. (Also, future retrievals against the cached data benefit from the avoidance of going out to DASD for the data.) The data 'destaging' to DASD is deferred until storage constraints in cache or NVS demand freeing the space for other data.

Cache fast write functions like a DASD fast write, but omits transfer of the data to NVS; the operation is signalled complete when the cache transfer finishes, and transfer to DASD is again deferred. Both cache and DASD fast write load data and the rest of the track into cache upon a write miss. Both have equivalent performance advantages (and comparable to a cached READ operation). However, data integrity is not assured with cache fast write, since the data may be cache-resident for some time and this is without a backup copy in NVS, so that a power failure occurring prior to destaging to DASD results in data loss. Therefore, cache fast writes are generally exploited for temporary, noncritical data (DFSORT work files presently use cache fast write, for example).

Dual Copy. The 3990-3 also offers a high availability feature called *dual copy*, maintaining two copies of critical data on two physically distinct devices, which are accessed and synchronized automatically (and transparently), these being known as the *duplex pair*. Data is automatically accessed on the 'secondary device' (the backup) whenever the primary device (the original) proves unavailable. Dual copy, established by a system command, uses the same concept of backup and recovery through *duplexing* I/O as we saw being used in Enhanced VSAM with Catalog Recovery Areas (CRAs), although the latter facility was restricted to catalog data sets, not any data sets, as under dual copy. Dual copy can—and this is highly recommended—be combined with DASD fast write to yield high optimization of I/O performance, data availability/integrity, and reliability. This excellent feature is known as *fast dual copy*.

VSAM and the 3990-3 Cache Storage Control. Establishment and management of cache storage controls is effected (1) through the IDCAMS AMS commands SETCACHE, BINDDATA, and LISTDATA (see the *Cache Device Administration* manual), or (2) through the new SETCACHE function (technically known as the 'SETCACHE line operator') available under ISMF in a DFP/SMS environment (see Section 17.8 for an introduction to DFP/SMS).

Two final points to note concerning cache storage control. First, as noted earlier, the index options IMBED and REPLICATE may defeat cache strategies and should, therefore, never be specified for a VSAM data set on a device under the control of cache storage controls, such as the 3880 Model 23 or the newer 3990 Model 3. Second, for data sets whose activity patterns are such as to make good candidates for caching, the performance improvements can be dramatic, and can far exceed whatever benefits may have otherwise been available through IMBED and REPLICATE. (Note that batch and on-line VSAM data sets may benefit from caching, as may non-VSAM data sets (caching is not restricted to VSAM)). The publication referred to above gives guidelines for determining good candidates for caching.

18.15   LINEAR DATA SETS

As we noted briefly earlier in the text, DFP/VSAM Version 2, Release 3 introduced the fourth VSAM cluster type, the *Linear Data Set* (*LDS*). The LDS is supported by an MVS/XA facility known as *Data-In-Virtual* (*DIV*), itself introduced with Release 2 of MVS/XA (this is more formerly known as MVS/SP Version 2, Release 2). The LDS is commonly referred to as a *(linear) data object*, or occasionally, a *DIV object* given that the MVS/XA DIV facility is used to process an LDS, in a fashion we will discuss shortly. Since the introduction of the LDS, newer and more advanced facilities of MVS/ESA can also be used against an LDS. But let's see precisely what an LDS is.

An LDS consists of a linear byte stream, or string of data, organized solely into 4K blocks; it has no record structure and the stream of 4K blocks that make it up on a permanent DASD device are seen by VSAM as *unstructured CIs*, with CISZ=4K. We say unstructured, in that there is no CI-internal structure: no CIDF or RDF control fields exist in the CIs of an LDS, and there is no segmentation of the CI into logical records; the entire 4K CI is pure data. Given this unstructured linear data stream, applications process LDSs without the overhead of I/O record or buffer management and blocking facilities that traditionally make up an access method. Indeed, it is deceptive to speak of the LDS as a VSAM cluster: it is *defined* through VSAM, but it is not *processed* by VSAM macros at all. Directly, or indirectly, the new Assembler macro DIV is used for LDS access and processing (although it is possible to treat the LDS as a specialized ESDS and process it through control interval processing (CNV) using standard Assembler instructions, this is not the typical manipulation of LDSs). Part of the design objective of LDSs is, indeed, to bypass the execution-time overhead of an access method and provide a more efficient form of I/O against the LDS, the I/O used being simply an extension of the basic MVS paging mechanism.

18.15.1   Creating/Defining an LDS

To begin to appreciate LDSs and the DIV facility of MVS/XA, let's first see how an LDS is created. The DEFINE CLUSTER command is used to create an LDS cluster, as it is to create any VSAM cluster. A typical definition would be:

```
DEFINE CLUSTER -
            (NAME (LDS.TEST) -
            VOL (volser) -
            ⟨space⟩ -
            SHR (xregion 3) -
            LINEAR
```

Not being record-structured, there is no key field, no index component, no FSPC, etc., but space is allocated as for any data set. The CISZ is implicitly 4096, and this is signalled by the LINEAR parameter (as opposed to INDEXED, NONINDEXED, and

NUMBERED for KSDSs, ESDSs, and RRDSs, respectively). The cross-system SHR specification must be 3 (no cross-system read or write integrity), but the cross-region specification is unrestricted (1 through 4, interpreted as for any VSAM data set); although shared access to an LDS is now supported with weaker degrees of integrity than both read and write integrity (xregion=1), there are special complications that must be explicitly controlled for by the user if other than SHR (1 3) is coded, so this is the most common specification (earlier releases of DFP/VSAM and MVS/XA did not even allow for other than SHR (1 3), although this is now no longer the case).

18.15.2 Basic Operation of an LDS

Applications process an LDS by viewing any part of the data contained in an LDS through a virtual storage *window* into the LDS; the window is simply some part of the user's virtual space, that is, a portion of user-controlled virtual storage which will be used to process parts of the LDS in (the user's address space is the most familiar type of virtual space, but, as we shall see below, there are now (under ESA) other types of virtual spaces). MVS system services collectively known as Data-In-Virtual (DIV) facilities handle mapping (making 'visible,' and therefore manipulable, to the user) whatever part of the LDS the user chooses to process at any one time, as if that part of the LDS were read into the user's window. In fact, the data that appears in—is mapped into—the window is simply an image of whatever part of the LDS the user selects for processing; the selection is communicated to DIV systems services through the specification of an *offset* into the LDS and a *span* (width of the window) from that offset. This yields some set of 4K blocks within the LDS, starting at some specified starting point and this set of blocks to be processed we may call the *object target area* (the part of the LDS being mapped at any one time, to be available to the user for processing 'in the window'); since the DIV facility treats the LDS as a 'seamless' byte-addressable string, any part of the LDS—that is, any object target area—can be mapped in this manner into the user's address space as long as an explicit indication of offset and span is provided for every operation the user undertakes against the LDS.

Since the system, through DIV services, will make any object target area available for processing by the user, in the user's window, we may say that the user is given a *sliding window* facility: just by changing the offset and span specifications, the user can 'slide' the window over any part of the LDS object, changing the object target area thereby (it is typically not necessary to view the entire LDS object, although this can be done by moving the window through the object in either 4K increments, or multiples of 4K increments, from the start of the LDS to the end of the LDS).

The DIV facility makes available to the user a set of services (all parameters on the new DIV Assembler macro instruction) for processing an LDS. The IDENTIFY service does just that: identifies the LDS object to be processed (through a DDNAME reference to a JCL DD statement that gives DSNAME and DISP information concerning the LDS), priorly created by the DEF CLUSTER ... LINEAR command coding we presented above. UNIDENTIFY terminates the identification. The ACCESS and UNACCESS services effect the opening and closing of the identified LDS object; an LDS may be opened in READ or UPDATE mode on the DIV ACCESS instruction. The MAP service specifies the object target area to be mapped for processing into the user's predefined window (the window typically defined as a page-aligned storage area in the user's address space, often retrieved from MVS by a GETMAIN macro); UNMAP frees the window, allowing a subsequent MAP to access another (usually different) target area on the LDS object, mapped again into the user's window for processing.

Note that none of these services effects any actual transfer whatever of any data on the LDS (sitting on permanent DASD) into the user's address space. Real data transfer occurs only upon first reference in the user's program to data in the window; the transfer is transparent to the user who has the (false) sense that the data from the object target area has been moved into the window by the MAP service (similar to a READ, without necessarily any data transfer at the time of the MAP service being issued). The DIV facility minimizes real I/O by performing actual data transfer only when an explicit program reference requires it. No readahead or anticipatory buffering is done, as would be the case when using a true access method; paging I/O is used instead of an access method for effecting the data transfer, and this is considerably more efficient than standard record-oriented I/O services (although care must be taken to avoid adverse system-wide performance effects, possible with any paging operations). Thus we say that the processing of an LDS using DIV services is through *user-driven paging* (rather than system-driven paging, typically not directly manipulable by the user). The goal is to replace the considerable overhead of access method techniques by a 'background' high performance system service (paging), natively implemented for MVS components and subsystems, paring it down to the bare essentials of data transfer (more on this in a moment). Note that until recently (with ESA), this meant that LDS objects had to be processed in Assembler; the DIV facility provided system services to *support* the processing of LDSs, but the user provided the actual processing instructions in the form of Assembler coding. (As we will see, this has now changed.)

The two remaining DIV (facility) services are SAVE and RESET. The SAVE service posts any changes made to the data in the user window (that is, made through user processing instructions) out to the LDS object. Note that update of the LDS is *not* performed when the user makes the changes (in the user's processing program), but only when explicitly requested by SAVE; this too is for performance optimization, minimizing I/O operations by posting updates only at various explicit 'syncpoints', rather than as they occur. Any pages in the user window at the time of SAVE that have not been changed *are not written out to the LDS*—as they would be by a standard access method—but rather are simply thrown away (a 'system discard'), still another advantage over standard access method techniques. Furthermore, any pages mapped into the user window, but never referenced by the time of SAVE, have in actual fact *never been fetched from DASD* at all; pages are retrieved only upon explicit reference, even though they may be part of the object target area (and hence mapped to the window), thus automatically bypassing all unnecessary I/O operations. If a page (a 4K block) was explicitly referenced by the user's processing program, then that page would really have been fetched; but it is still the case that, although retrieved, if the page is not changed, it is discarded by SAVE, as it entails no change to the corresponding object target area. Indeed, the user may use the RESET service at any time to remove any and all changes made to the data in the window; this 'refreshes' the window with the image of the (unchanged) pages on the LDS (an 'update-cancel').

As can be seen, the various DIV services are primitive system services which avoid access method techniques in favor of the techniques the system is otherwise using for basic operation (namely, paging services). It thus turns out that LDSs are most suitable for large data structures (performance is favored by increasing size) which have primitive access requirements: random access of scattered (noncontiguous) portions of a structure seen as a linear byte stream; arrays (tables) fall into this class, as do the primitive structures of OS BDAM files and VSAM RRDSs (directly accessible 'flat' structures), as well as the flat structures of DB2 tables.

18.15.3   Data Window Services (DWS)

Although the performance benefits of LDSs were considerable from the start, a serious limitation was the inaccessibility of LDSs to other than Assembler programs (the DIV facility is obtained through the DIV Assembler macro instruction). DFP Version 3, part of ESA, has recently addressed this limitation by providing the facility known as *data window services* (*DWS*). DWS (1) extends the mechanism of virtual storage windows to allow processing of additional objects other than just LDSs, and (2) provides direct support for application program access to such data windowing services—including LDS processing—without Assembler programming, through a consistent and easy-to-use set of high level language (HLL) interfaces known as *Callable Services* (*CSR*). DWS provides advanced facilities for windowing to both HLLs and 'native' Assembler; CSR provides a 'CALL' interface to windowing services for HLLs only; at present COBOL, FORTRAN, PL/I, and PASCAL are supported under CSR, but other HLLs are soon to be added (and may have been when this text appears).

The services of CSR are provided through a simple CALL statement; five interfaces are presently supported (as callable service routines). A call to the CSR service *CSRIDAC* effects the equivalent of the DIV IDENTIFY/UNIDENTIFY and ACCESS/UNACCESS services together. To perform MAP/UNMAP services, a call is made to CSRVIEW (effecting an association between a user window and some object to be processed). CSRSAVE is called to post updates to the object from changes made to data in the window (parallel to the DIV SAVE service), while CSRREFR refreshes the window's pages from the unchanged pages of the object (parallel to the DIV RESET service). Finally, there is a CSRSCOT ('scroll out') interface called when the current view in the user window is to be posted, not to the object itself, but to a temporary *scroll area* (in ESA, this is a *hiperspace* (see below)); this service has no counterpart in DIV facilities, and represents a hint of the 'value-added' aspect of CSR, providing more advanced services than DIV. The precise coding of these calls varies somewhat, depending on the HLL used (the details are beyond this discussion; see the *MVS/ESA Callable Services for High Level Languages* publication), but the critical point is that a simple interface is now available for advanced windowing services without any Assembler coding being needed at all. Since DWS, and its CSR component, supports windowing access to (among other objects) an LDS object, the new VSAM cluster (it must be a DFP/VSAM data set) can now be used directly by HLL programmers. This should lead to greater exploitation of the benefits of LDSs by programmers coding in the languages supported by CSR; LDS use prior to the introduction of CSR has been relatively modest, given the coding complexities (and the unfamiliarity of the LDS in general).

18.15.4   Data Spaces and Hiperspaces

Data Spaces.   ESA introduced two new virtual storage objects, over and above the traditional MVS address space: *data spaces* and *hiperspaces;* we now speak of *virtual spaces* to refer to any of the three types of objects: address spaces, data spaces, and hiperspaces. A data space is a block of virtual storage (up to 2G in size, like an address space) which, unlike an address space, may hold only data, not programs: in a sense, a 'data-only' address space. A data space contains no system-related areas (the System Area and Common Area of an address space) and thus requires less systems overhead for its creation, manipulation, and deletion. A set of new system services under ESA provide program management (including creation and deletion) of, and access to, data spaces; these services are accessed though the *DSPSERV* (data space service) macro instruction, handled through the *Real Storage Manager* (*RSM*) component of MVS. *DSPSERV CREATE, TYPE=BASIC* is used to create a data space. A data space is byte-addressable virtual storage, and multiple data spaces may be accessible to an ('owning') address space. A data space, like an address space, may reside anywhere in central (formerly 'main memory') storage, expanded storage (ES), or auxiliary storage. ES, provided on Sierra processors, is 'electronic block storage': processor-accessible memory like real storage, but slightly slower in terms of access rates by the processor, and—unlike central storage—not byte-addressable, only addressable in 4K blocks/pages. Now, the term *real storage* refers to central storage (main memory) *plus* expanded storage. Note that pages of ES to be accessed by the processor must be transferred first into central storage (ES pages are thus not as directly accessible as central storage frames).

Hiperspaces.   Extending the concept of data space further, ESA introduced *high performance data spaces, *hiperspaces*. Hiperspaces are, unlike data spaces, not byte-addressable; they may be accessed only in 4K block units (hiperspace pages). Furthermore, although they are a special form of data space, they may never reside in central storage; they typically reside in expanded storage. There are two types of hiperspaces: (1) *standard hiperspaces*, which may be backed by either expanded storage, when available, or auxiliary storage; and (2) *ESO* (expanded storage only) *hiperspaces* which, as the name suggests, reside only in expanded storage and are never backed by auxiliary storage. A standard hiperspace is sometimes referred to as a *scroll-type* hiperspace, while an ESO hiperspace is sometimes referred to as a *cache-type* hiperspace. The DSPSERV macro is used to create hiperspaces (as well as data spaces): *DSPSERV CREATE, TYPE=HIPERSPACE, HSTYPE=SCROLL* creates a standard hiperspace, while the *DSPSERV CREATE, TYPE=HIPERSPACE, HSTYPE=CACHE* form is used to create an ESO hiperspace. Only an authorized program may create an ESO hiperspace, while a standard hiperspace may be created by unauthorized programs. Hiperspaces provide higher performance access to data than that typically provided by data spaces, especially to the extent that they remain largely resident in ES. Data spaces and hiperspaces are further distinguished by the fact that data in a data space is processable there (in the data space), while data in a hiperspace is not directly processable, but must be transferred for access into an address space. As noted earlier, ESA permits a maximum of 8000 2G 'spaces': address spaces, data spaces, and hiperspaces together, yielding a virtual storage capacity of 16,000G (16 *terabytes*, that is, 16 thousand billion bytes), far in excess (at this time) of the paging capability of any current system.

18.15.5   Recent Enhancements Under DFP/VSAM

One important recent enhancement related to the above discussion is that now, under ESA, DWS provide an extension to the DIV facility, where the object to be processed—the *DIV object*—may be either (as before) an LDS (on permanent DASD), a data space, or a hiperspace (a 'temporary LDS'); in addition, a hiperspace (standard type only) may be used as a high-speed temporary buffer between the user's address space and the LDS on DASD, that is, a 'scroll area,' which we briefly referred to in connection with the CALL CSRSCOT interface (this is complex, advanced processing and should not be attempted without extensive internals knowledge). Callable Services can be used to facilitate program access to such hiperspaces. However, VSAM services do not, at present, directly support all of these possibilities. Let's see some of what is available under recent releases of DFP/VSAM.

DFP/VSAM Version 3 (under ESA) supports a facility known as *Catalog in Data Space*. Catalog in Data Space allows ICF user catalogs to reside in ESA data spaces, providing a high-performance 'caching' of catalog records in order to avoid DASD I/O for many catalog record retrievals (most should—given available expanded and central storage—be found by a 'data space lookaside,' which entails no real I/O unless the records have been paged out to auxiliary storage due to storage constraints). This facility uses a new ESA component: *Virtual Lookaside Facility (VLF);* VLF uses data spaces for store and retrieve operations of frequently accessed objects (ICF catalog data, load modules, TSO lists).

Even prior to ESA (starting with DFP/VSAM Version 2, Release 1), another performance enhancement to DFP/VSAM catalog processing had been made, in the form of the *Catalog Address Space (CAS)*. This facility promotes most DFP/VSAM ICF catalog management routines (along with most of their control blocks) to their own dedicated address space, the Catalog Address Space. Priorly, the routines were resident in the Link Pack Area (LPA) of the Common Area within an MVS address space, while the control blocks were resident in the Common Service Area (CSA), also within the Common Area; since the Common Area is mapped into all address spaces, the virtual storage overhead impacted on all MVS users. CAS thus provides *virtual storage constraint relief (VSCR)*, possibly 1M or more, depending on the specific catalog configuration. In addition, CAS provides enhanced catalog integrity and catalog availability, since the catalog routines are segregated into their own address space and less subject to corruption or integrity exposures. (An MVS operator has direct communication—through the MODIFY command—with CAS, facilitating catalog operating and catalog monitoring procedures, especially recovery, problem diagnosis, and some performance functions.)

Furthermore, a *catalog locking* facility is available to prohibit access to ICF catalogs during backup and recovery operations; this requires use of a new locking authorization facility, *IGG.CATLOCK*. Along with this, ICF catalog recovery is enhanced still further by an *automatic reorientation* after the recovery process is complete and the catalog is unlocked (LOCK/UNLOCK parameters on certain catalog-related AMS commands enable and disable the locking mechanism): the system does not need to be quiesced (or IPLed) during the recovery process, and VSAM applications may often continue to run without interruption, with no special intervention subsequent to recovery to reestablish user access to ICF catalogs. (This is a considerable simplification, but satisfactory for our purposes; the *Catalog Administration Guide* provides further detail, although most of these considerations are not directly relevant to VSAM application users.)

In addition, in connection with new DFP/VSAM catalog-related enhancements, there should be noted the new *Multilevel Alias (MLA)* facility: MLA enhances the catalog selection process by allowing up to four qualifiers (not just the single high level qualifier (HQL) previously) to constitute the name or alias of an ICF catalog (note that, under DFP/VSAM with SMS, JOBCAT and STEPCAT DD statements are no longer valid for ICF catalog identification when SMS-managed data sets are involved, so identification through an MLA may become quite common); this allows considerably greater naming convention flexibility in the VSAM environment. Furthermore, DFP/VSAM under SMS takes another step in integrating the entire data set environment, through a new VVDS entry called a *Non-VSAM Volume Record (NVR)* for SMS-managed non-VSAM data sets (this includes (Q)SAM data sets, PDSs, temporary data sets, and VIO data sets), which previously had no entry in the VVDS, only a BCS entry (if they were cataloged in an ICF catalog). Finally, the restriction of 36 ICF catalogs per volume has been removed.

Independent of the above catalog-related enhancements, some of which were available under DFP/VSAM before ESA, there is an important facility (briefly alluded to in our earlier discussion of LSR) which *is* strictly ESA-only, that of *LSR hiperspace pools*. The BLDVRP macro (on the BUFFERS parameter) has been extended to allow the specification of any subpool buffers to reside in hiperspaces (so-called 'hiperspace buffers'); this, as previously remarked, can dramatically reduce

DASD I/O by, in effect, caching in expanded storage, the total effect being still higher performance for VSAM data sets assigned to LSR pools containing hiperspace buffers. However, as even our brief earlier discussion of ESA objects might have suggested, this may prove problematic, since a hiperspace is not guaranteed to remain constantly resident in expanded storage: whatever MVS address space is providing the LSR facility may be swapped out to DASD, and under this circumstance all expanded storage used ('owned') by the address space is cleared, effectively discarding all of the LSR hiperspace buffers that the address space was controlling, not a very appealing possibility. Either the user must countenance such a loss and have provided some form of recovery and/or journaling to reconstruct lost data (an intimidating task, given the complexity of LSR processing and hiperspace buffering) or, through authorized facilities, the address space within which the LSR pools are built must be marked nonswappable. If this can be assured, then LSR hiperspace pools for an especially critical address space may, thereby, be both safe and highly optimal. Just as of this writing, an enhancement to CICS/MVS 2.1 (March, 1989) provides CICS support for such LSR hiperspace buffers (DFP/VSAM files only), and this should prove an important optimization feature of CICS/MVS 2.1 running under an MVS/ESA system (required for this support).

Finally, again just at the time of this writing (March, 1989), an additional CICS/MVS 2.1 facility under ESA has been released: the *Data Table Feature*. This allows the loading of VSAM KSDS, called the *source data set*, records into CICS-controlled extended virtual storage (above 16M boundary), thereby building what is called a (CICS) *Data Table*; access to the Data Table so built, when this table is the type known as a *CICS-maintained Data Table* (*CMDT*), appears to be direct access to the original KSDS source, with updates to the Data Table being automatically posted by CICS to the original KSDS file. Since the Data Table KSDS data can be accessed by a virtual storage lookaside, DASD I/O can be considerably reduced. There are also User-Maintained Data Tables (UMDT), which are high-performance but for which CICS does *not*, as with CMDT, provide for updates to the table to be performed in synchrony with changes to the source data set (the source data set and the UMDT are wholly distinct objects in this case). Data tables are created by two new options on the DFHFCT macro: *TYPE=CICSTABLE/USERTABLE* and *SIZE=n*, where *n* is the maximum number of table entries to be used for the data table.

The Data Table Feature will enhance CICS performance by sharply reducing CICS DSA (Dynamic Storage Area) utilization (since the data table is loaded into the extended private area of the CICS address space), and by reducing the number of physical I/O operations for record access (many records would be retrieved from the data table in virtual storage rather than from the source data set on DASD). In addition, retrieval operations from the data table have a *shorter path length* (fewer instructions used by MVS to implement the operation) than retrieval operations from VSAM LSR pools; this is because data table processing uses a hashing technique (transparent to the application) to improve execution-time performance of table accesses (CICS implements a *hash table* through which records are accessed using special fast random access ('hash') techniques).

Initial performance studies suggest that very high transaction rates can be supported with the Data Table Feature, even as compared to file processing with all VSAM data and index buffers rigged to be in virtual storage. It will be interesting to see if the Data Table Feature might be extended not just to use extended virtual storage within an MVS address space, but within data spaces and hiperspaces (at the time of this writing, IBM's precise implementation of the Data Table Feature is not wholly clear in all its internals); this is certainly a possibility to be explored for further performance optimization of VSAM processing in the on-line domain under ESA. The near future should bring additional advanced, complex, but exciting high-performance technologies for VSAM processing, exploiting some of the most sophisticated of ESA facilities being made available.

As can be seen clearly from the discussion above, the VSAM product has proven exceptionally capable of evolving smoothly to accommodate the highest level technical advances—especially high optimization features—that future software and systems developments will bring.

APPENDIX A:
DEVICE CHARACTERISTICS CHART

COMMON CISZs	PBSIZE*	CIs PER TRACK			% TRACK UTILIZED**		
		3330	3350	3380	3330	3350	3380
512	512	20	27	46	79	72–74	50
1024	1024	11	15	31	86–88	81–85	67
2048	2048	6	8	18	94	86	78–80
6144		2	2	6			
10,240		1	1	3			
14,336		—	1	2			
18,432		—	1	2			
22,528		—	—	1			
26,624		—	—	1			
30,720	↓	—	—	1	↓	↓	↓
4096	4096	3	4	10	94-97	96-98	85-88
8192		1	2	5			
12,288		—	1	3			
16,384		—	1	2			
20,480		—	—	2			
24,576		—	—	1			
28,672		—	—	1			
32,768	↓	—	—	1	↓	↓	↓

Note:

	BYTES/TRK	TRK/CYL
3330	13,030	19
3350	19,069	30
3380	47,476	15

*For *Pre*-DFP/VSAM Ver. 2, Rel. 2 (thereafter PBSIZE=CISZ)
**Approximate* percentage utilization (computations differ)

APPENDIX B:
ALLOWABLE CHARACTERS

SUBPARAMETER	ALLOWABLE CHARACTERS
entryname aliasname	• 1 to 44 alphanumeric (A thru Z, 0 thru 9) or national ($@$, $\$$, $\#$) characters or special character '-' (hyphen) • names in excess of 8 characters must be segmented by periods into groups (qualifiers) of 1 to 8 characters • first character of any name or qualifier must be either alphabetic (A-Z) or national character (see above)
code password	• 1 to 8 alphameric or special characters (see Table 6-1 in Chapter 6 of text)

APPENDIX C:
THE EXAMINE COMMAND

BASIC FORM:

```
EXAMINE      NAME (clustername) —
             INDEXTEST/NOINDEXTEST —
             DATATEST/NODATATEST —
             ERRORLIMIT (number)
```

DEFAULTS:

```
EXAMINE      NAME (clustername) —
             INDEXTEST —
             NODATATEST —
             ERRORLIMIT (2147483647)
```

BASIC OPERATION:

1. EXAMINE analyzes the *structural integrity* (errors in the internal structure (makeup) of a component) and *structural consistency* (errors in the internal relationships *within* a component and *between* components) of a KSDS data and/or index component. A comprehensive check is made of the correctness of the makeup of any KSDS cluster, and any internal errors and inconsistencies are reported.
2. EXAMINE can be issued against KSDSs only; this includes (Enhanced) VSAM catalogs and the BCS of an ICF catalog (both of these are KSDSs).
3. The data and index components can be tested separately or jointly.
4. Structural testing of VSAM catalogs and BCS components of ICF catalogs through EXAMINE should typically be undertaken by system, not application, programmers (and master level access to catalogs is required in such cases).
5. Further detail on EXAMINE is available in the *Access Method Services Reference* manual.
6. EXAMINE error messages (all beginning with IDC) may be looked up in the *System Messages* manual.

NAME (clustername)

Note that a component name is invalid here, even if the test is restricted to one component.

INDEXTEST

VSAM checks the cross-validation of internal pointers (vertical and horizontal) within all index records.

DATATEST

VSAM reads both sequence set records from the index component, and all data CIs, checking the integrity of records, CIs, and internal pointers, as well as checking the status of any freespace within the data component. DATATEST consumes many more processor cycles than INDEXTEST, so will entail longer operation time.

ERRORLIMIT (number)

Limits the number of structural error messages written out by the EXAMINE facility. The default (over 2 billion), which is also the maximum value of ERRORLIMIT, is absurdly large and should always be overridden with a more reasonable number. Often detailed error messages are not required and ERRORLIMIT (0) may suffice (EXAMINE will still report on the basic structural integrity and consistency of the cluster).

```
Sample EXAMINE Output


     IDCAMS  SYSTEM SERVICES   TIME: 19:39:28   03/11/89   PAGE  1

        EXAMINE -
                 NAME (VSAM.CK.MVS.VSTESTEX) -
                 INDEXTEST -
                 DATATEST -
                 ERRORLIMIT (100)
     IDC01700I INDEXTEST BEGINS
     IDC01724I INDEXTEST COMPLETE - NO ERRORS DETECTED
     IDC01701I DATATEST BEGINS
     IDC01709I DATATEST COMPLETE - NO ERRORS DETECTED
     IDC01708I 4445 CONTROL INTERVALS ENCOUNTERED
     IDC01710I DATA COMPONENT CONTAINS 40000 RECORDS
     IDC01711I DATA COMPONENT CONTAINS 0 DELETED CONTROL INTERVALS
     IDC01712I MAXIMUM LENGTH DATA RECORD CONTAINS 460 BYTES
     IDC01722I 54 PERCENT FREE SPACE
     IDC00001I FUNCTION COMPLETED, HIGHEST CONDITION CODE WAS 0
```

APPENDIX D: REFERENCES

(MVS/ESA) VSAM Administration Guide Version 3 Release 1 (SC26-4518)
(MVS/ESA) VSAM Administration: Macro Instruction Reference (SC26-4517)
(MVS/ESA) VSAM Catalog Administration: Access Method Services Reference (SC26-4501)
(MVS/ESA) Integrated Catalog Administration: Access Method Services Reference (SC26-4500)
(MVS/ESA) Catalog Administration Guide (SC26-4502)

(MVS/ESA) Data Facility Product Version 3: General Information (GC26-4507)
(MVS/ESA) Data Facility Product Version 3: Planning Guide (SC26-4513)
(MVS/ESA) Data Facility Product Version 3: Master Index (GC26-4512)
Cache Device Administration (GC35-0101)
(MVS/ESA) Interactive Storage Management Facility User's Guide (SC26-4508)
(MVS/ESA) Storage Administration Reference (SC26-4514)
IBM 3990 Storage Control Introduction (GA32-0098)
IBM 3380 Direct Access Storage Introduction (GC26-4491)
IBM 3990 Storage Control Planning, Installation, and Storage Administration Guide (GA32-0100)
Using the IBM 3380 Direct Access Storage in an MVS Environment (GC26-4492)

(MVS/ESA) General Information for System Product Version 3 (GC28-1359)
(MVS/ESA) Library Guide for System Product Version 3 (GC28-1563)
(MVS/ESA) Application Development Guide (GC28-1821)
(MVS/ESA) Message Library: System Messages, Volumes 1 and 2 (GC28-1812 and GC28-1813)
(MVS/ESA) Planning: Global Resource Serialization (GC28-1818)
(MVS/ESA) Callable Services for High Level Languages (GC28-1843)

CICS/MVS Version 2.1 Performance Guide (SC33-0521)
CICS/MVS Version 2.1 Data Tables General Information (GC33-0684)
CICS/MVS Version 2.1 Data Tables Guide (SC33-0632)

APPENDIX E: ACRONYMS

ACB	Access Method Control Block
AIX	Alternate Index
AMDSB	Access Method Data Statistics Block
AMS	Access Method Services
APF	Authorized Program Facility
ARDB	Address Range Definition Block
ARDHRDA	Address Range Definition Block HURBA Field
AS	Addressed Sequential
BCS	Basic Catalog Structure
BDAM	Basic Direct Access Method
BPAM	Basic Partitioned Access Method
CA	Control Area
CAFSPC	CA-internal FSPC
CA-HPK	CA-Highest-Possible-Key
CAS	Catalog Address Space
CASZ	Control Area Size
CBIC	Control Blocks in Common Option
CBUF	Control Block Update Facility
CCHH	Cylinder-Head
CF	Control Field
CI	Control Interval
CICS	Customer Information Control System
CICSPARS/MVS	CICS Performance Analysis Reporting System/MVS
CIDEN	CI Density
CIDF	Control Interval Definition Field
CIFSPC	CI-internal FSPC
CISZ	Control Interval Size
CKSZ	Compressed Key Size
CL-Subfield	Common Length Subfield
CMDT	CICS-maintained Data Table
CNV	Control Interval Processing
CPA	Channel Program Area
CRA	Catalog Recovery Area
CRP	Current Record Pointer
CSA	Common Service Area
CSR	Callable Services
C-Subfield	Control Subfield
CTC	Channel-to-Channel Adapter

CTLPW	Control Password
CUSF	Cryptographic Unit Support Facility
CVOL	Control Volume
CV-Timestamp	Catalog Volume Timestamp
DADSM	Direct Access Device Space Manager
DASD	Direct Access Storage Device
DB2	DATABASE 2
DC	Data Component
DCB	Data Control Block
DEB	Data Extent Block
DES	Data Encryption Standard
DFDSS	Data Facility Data Set Services
DF/EF	Data Facility/Extended Function
DFHSM	Data Facility Hierarchical Storage Manager
DFP	Data Facility Product
DFSMS	(Data Facility) Storage Management Subsystem
DFSORT	Data Facility Sort
DIS	Direct Insert Strategy
DIV	Data-in-Virtual
DFP	Data Facility Product
DFP/SMS	Data Facility Product/Storage Management Subsystem
DFP/VSAM	Data Facility Product/VSAM
DSCB	Data Set Control Block
DWS	Data Window Services
EDB	Extent Definition Block
ECC	Error Correction Code
EHK	Effective High Key
EOD	End-of-Data-Set
EOF	End-of-File
EOV	End-of-Volume
ES	Expanded Storage
ESA	Enterprise Systems Architecture
ESDS	Entry Sequenced Data Set
ESO	Expanded Storage Only
EXCP	Execute Channel Program
FAO	FSPC-Area Offset
FAL	FSPC-Area Length
FDBK	Feedback field
FKSZ	Full Key Size
FPI	File Position Indicator
FSPC	(Distributed) Freespace
FS1	File Status 1
FS2	File Status 2
GDG	Generation Data Group
GRS	Global Resource Serialization
GRW	Growth Factor
GSR	Global Shared Resources
HARBA	Highest Allocated Relative Byte Address

HK	CI-High-Key
HKCI	High-Key-CI
HKRBA	High-Key Relative Byte Address
HLL	High-Level Language
HLQ	High Level Qualifier
HLRBA	High-Level Relative Byte Address
HOS	Head of String
HPK	CI-Highest-Possible-Key
HSM	(Data Facility) Hierarchical Storage Manager
HURBA	High Used Relative Byte Address
IC	Index Component
ICF	Integrated Catalog Facility
ICI	Improved Control Interval Access
IDCAMS	Access Method Services (Command Processor)
IIP	ISAM Interface Program
IOMB	Input Output Management Block
IOS	I/O Supervisor
IOSB	Input Output Supervisor Block
IQE	Interruption Queue Element
IR	Index Record
IRB	Interrupt Response Block
IS	Index Set
ISAM	Indexed Sequential Access Method
ISC	Inter-System Communication
ISMF	Interactive Storage Management Facility
ISR	Index Set Record
JCL	Job Control Language
JES	Job Entry Subsystem
KOR	Key of Reference
KSDS	Key Sequenced Data Set
LC-Subfield	Length/Count Field
LDS	Linear Data Set
LPA	Link Pack Area
LR	Logical Record
LRA	Logical Record Area
LRU	Least Recently Used
LSR	Local Shared Resources
MAX-PACK	Maximum 'Packing Factor'
MCAT	Master Catalog
MCCU	(3088) Multisystem Channel Communication Unit
MLA	Multilevel Alias Facility
MRO	Multi-Region Operation (CICS)
MSI	Mass Sequential Insertion
MVS	Multiple Virtual Storage
MVS/ESA	Multiple Virtual Storage/Enterprise Systems Architecture
MVS/SP	Multiple Virtual Storage/System Product
MVS/XA	Multiple Virtual Storage/Extended Architecture
NIL	Number-of-Index-Levels

NSR	Non-Shared Resources
NVR	Non-VSAM Volume Record
NVS	Nonvolatile Storage
OS	Operating System
PBSIZE	Physical Block Size
PCF	Programmed Cryptographic Facility
PDS	Partitioned Data Set
PLH	Place Holder
PLPA	Pageable Link Pack Area
QSAM	Queued Sequential Access Method
RACF	Resource Access Control Facility
RBA	Relative Byte Address
RDF	Record Definition Field
RKP	Relative Key Position
RMF	Resource Measurement Facility
RPL	Request Parameter List
RPLCMPON	(RPL) Component Code Field
RPS	Rotational Position Sensing
RRDS	Relative Record Data Set
RRN	Relative Record Number
RSA	Ring System Authority
R-user	Read User
SAA	Systems application Architecture
SAM	Sequential Access Method
SAM/E	Sequential Access Method/Extended
SD-VVR	Self-Describing VSAM Volume Record
SEOF	Software-End-of-File
SIS	Sequential Insert Strategy
SKP	Skip-Sequential Processing
SMF	System Measurement Facilities (also: System Management Facilities)
SMS	Storage Management Subsystem
SOF	Start-of-File
SPK	Storage Protection Key
SRB	Service Request Block
SRF	Shared Resources Facility
SRM	System Resources Manager
SS	Sequence Set
SSN	Social Security Number
SSR	Sequence Set Record
STRNO	String Number
SVC	Supervisor Call (Instruction)
TOD	Time-of-Day
TSO	Time Sharing Option
TSO/E	Time Sharing Option/Extensions
UBF	User Buffering Facility
UCAT	User Catalog
UCB	Unit Control Block
UMDT	User-maintained Data Table

VRP	VSAM Resource Pool
US	Unused Space
USAR	User Security Authorization Record
USVR	User-Security-Verification Routine
VSAM	Virtual Storage Access Method
VSCR	Virtual Storage Constraint Relief
VSP	VSAM Space Pool
VTOC	Volume Table of Contents
VVCR	VSAM Volume Control Record
VVDS	VSAM Volume Data Set
VVR	VSAM Volume Record
W-user	Write User
XA	Extended Architecture
XRF	Extended Recovery Facility

INDEX

429